Introduction to Technical Services

Library and Information Science Text Series

The Academic Library: Its Context, Its Purpose, and Its Operation. By John M. Budd.

Information Sources in Science and Technology. 3d ed. By C. D. Hurt.

The School Library Media Center. 5th ed. By Emanuel T. Prostano and Joyce S. Prostano.

The School Library Media Manager. 2d ed. By Blanche Woolls.

Introduction to Library Public Services. 6th ed. By G. Edward Evans, Anthony J. Amodeo, and Thomas L. Carter.

A Guide to the Library of Congress Classification. 5th ed. By Lois Mai Chan.

The Organization of Information. By Arlene G. Taylor.

Developing Library and Information Center Collections. 4th ed. By G. Edward Evans, with the assistance of Margaret R. Zarnosky.

The Humanities: A Selective Guide to Information Sources. 5th ed. By Ron Blazek and Elizabeth Aversa.

Wynar's Introduction to Cataloging and Classification. 9th ed. By Arlene G. Taylor.

Systems Analysis for Librarians and Information Professionals. 2d ed. By Larry N. Osborne and Margaret Nakamura.

The Economics of Information: A Guide to Economic and Cost-Benefit Analysis for Information Professionals. 2d ed. By Bruce R. Kingma.

Reference and Information Services: An Introduction. 3d ed. Richard E. Bopp and Linda C. Smith, General Editors.

The Collection Program in Schools: Concepts, Practices, and Information Sources. 3d ed. By Phyllis Van Orden and Kay Bishop, with the assistance of Patricia Pawelak-Kort.

Libraries in the Information Age: An Introduction and Career Exploration. By Denise K. Fourie and David R. Dowell.

The Social Sciences: A Cross-Disciplinary Guide to Selected Sources. 3d ed. Nancy L. Herron, General Editor.

Introduction to Technical Services. 7th ed. By G. Edward Evans, Sheila S. Intner, and Jean Weihs.

Library Information Systems: From Library Automation to Distributed Information Access Solutions. By Thomas R. Kochtanek and Joseph R. Matthews.

United States Government Information: Policies and Sources. By Peter Hernon, Harold C. Relyea, Robert E. Dugan, and Joan F. Cheverie.

Library and Information Center Management. 6th ed. By Robert D. Stueart and Barbara B. Moran.

Introduction to Technical Services

SEVENTH EDITION

G. Edward Evans
Sheila S. Intner
Jean Weihs

2002
LIBRARIES UNLIMITED
A Division of Greenwood Publishing Group, Inc.
Greenwood Village, Colorado

LIBRARIES UNLIMITED
7730 East Belleview Avenue, Suite A200
Greenwood Village, CO 80111
1-800-225-5800
www.lu.com

Library of Congress Cataloging-in-Publication Data

Evans, G. Edward, 1937-
Introduction to technical services / G. Edward Evans, Sheila S. Intner, Jean Weihs. -- 7th ed.
p. cm. -- (Library and information science text series)
Includes bibliographical references and index.
ISBN 1-56308-918-1 -- ISBN 1-56308-922-X (pbk.)
1. Technical services (Libraries)--United States. 2. Technical services (Libraries)--Canada. I. Intner, Sheila S. II. Weihs, Jean Riddle. III. Title. IV. Series.
Z688.6.U6 E84 2002
025'.02--dc21

2002008904

Contents

Part Two
Acquisitions and Serials

Part Three
Cataloging and Processing

17—DESCRIPTION AND ACCESS (*continued*)

Preface to the Seventh Edition

It was more than thirty years ago when my co-author, Marty Bloomberg, and I submitted the manuscript for what became the first edition of this book. I bet Bloomberg a dinner at the best restaurant in Los Angeles that the book would never sell more than 500 copies. Needless to say, I was wrong. Looking back over the past thirty years and the previous six editions, it is clear how much technical services have changed through the intervening years. Readers familiar with earlier editions will quickly see that this seventh edition includes changes that go far beyond new co-authors joining me in this work.

The evolution of technical services during the past thirty years has been dramatic. With all of the public and professional press hype about the Internet, electronic services, and the "Virtual Library," people tend to forget that it was in technical services that the technology "revolution" got its start in libraries. The paper-based type of catalogers and public catalogs led the way into the computer world for most libraries. Representing a library's holdings, the bibliographic database is still the heart of integrated library systems. That "database," manifested first in book form and then on card stock, and available today electronically, is the key that end-users need to unlock information resources of a library. And, it is technical services that provide both the key and the resources.

This seventh edition has changed so much as to almost call for a new title. All of the chapters have been rewritten. Sheila Intner and Jean Weihs, the new co-authors, bring an outstanding background and publication record in the fields of cataloging and classification. In addition, Jean provides the Canadian perspective to all aspects of the book, which is a first for this title. There are three broad sections to this edition: Part One provides an overview of technical services and current issues; Part Two explores the issues of the acquisition of materials for collections; and Part Three covers the work of preparing materials for the end-users.

Part One, General Background, consists of four chapters. The first is an overview of technical services and the changing environment. Chapter 2 examines the various types of staffing that libraries use, particularly technical service units, with a special focus on library technicians and other support staff. Administrative issues in technical service units is the subject of Chapter 3, and the impact of cooperation and consortia on technical services constitutes Chapter 4.

Part Two, Acquisitions and Serials, examines the acquisitions functions of technical services, covering all types of formats—both print-based and digital. Chapters 5 through 14 in Part Two cover the activities and processes of the unit, as well as the issues associated with the acquisition of each major type of material.

Part Three, Cataloging and Processing, comprises eight chapters beginning with an overview in Chapter 15. The decisions that one must make in cataloging are discussed in Chapter 16. How one goes about describing items in the collection is fundamental to end-users being able to locate desired materials, which is covered in Chapter 17. Issues related to providing subject access are explored in Chapter 18, while the formal headings used for subjects appear in Chapter 19. The common classification systems used in the United States and Canada are described in Chapter 20. Cooperation among technical services units within a country and across national boundaries is dependent upon a variety of standards, the most important of which is the MARC format. This topic is covered in Chapter 21. The final chapter, 22, looks at the special management issues in cataloging units.

I welcome my new co-authors and look forward to years of collaboration on yet future editions.

G. Edward Evans
Los Angeles, California
2002

Part One

General Background

Introduction and Overview

WHAT ARE TECHNICAL SERVICES?

Until recently, the vast majority of libraries divided their services and activities into two broad categories, technical services and public services. Technical services traditionally handled those tasks associated with bringing materials into the library and making them ready for the general public or service population to use. Public services managed those activities that directly assisted the end-user in gaining access to information in the library's collection as well as from other collections. As discussed elsewhere in this chapter, that pattern is changing. However, although the administrative structure is evolving, libraries still need to acquire materials in some manner for the end-user and process the items, be they paper or electronic-based.

All libraries, regardless of type, perform nine basic functions to carry out their information transfer activities:

Identification: Locating potentially worthwhile items to add to the collection(s).

Selection: Deciding which of the identified items to add to the collection(s).

Acquisitions: Securing the items selected for the collection(s).

Organization: Indexing and cataloging the items acquired in a manner that will aid the end-user in locating materials in the collection(s).

Preparation: Labeling and otherwise making the items ready for storage in a manner that allows for easy retrieval.

Storage: Housing the prepared items in units that take into consideration the long-term preservation of the items while allowing staff and end-users easy access to the material.

Interpretation: Assisting end-users in locating appropriate materials that meet the users' needs.

Utilization: Providing equipment and space to allow staff and end-users to make effective use of the items in the collection(s).

Dissemination: Establishing a system that allows for the use of items away from the library.

This book focuses on the first five activities; for information on the four remaining activities, please see *Introduction to Library Public Services.*[1]

TECHNICAL SERVICE UNITS

The two broad traditional divisions within technical services are acquisitions and cataloging. Within those two divisions larger libraries often have sub-units such as serials, bindery/repair, copy cataloging, original cataloging, and gifts and exchange. (No matter the size of the library, all of the items listed, with the possible exception of original cataloging, do take place to some degree.) The acquisitions section always handles securing materials. In many libraries, it's also responsible for some of the identification of potentially useful materials, if only by directing publishers' catalogs and flyers to the appropriate decision-maker. Selection activity takes a variety of forms and depends on the type of library and its size. In some cases the acquisition unit is the primary collection development unit for the library. The cataloging section handles the other two functional activities: organization and preparation.

Acquisition activities also focus on securing items desired for the library's end-users and handling the financial transactions associated with the purchase or leasing of the item(s). Today most libraries acquire materials in a variety of formats: print, electronic, and audiovisual. Those broad categories include a number of types of material such as books, journals, videocassettes, CD-ROMs, electronic journals, and online databases. We explore the broad types of material in subsequent chapters.

Cataloging units provide the basic material upon which a library's service program is built. They determine the appropriate form for identifying authorship of works in the collection, describe the item as a physical item (or, increasingly, a "virtual source"), and assign subject access points. They also add a classification and author number to the physical items acquired; this "call number" allows the public service staff to group materials on the same topic together in storage units. Without cataloging it would be difficult at best for anyone to know what was in the collection, much less how many items dealt with, say, geology. What one sees in the public catalog is the result of the efforts of the cataloging staff. (Although cataloging activities are essential for operating a successful library/media center, this does not necessarily mean that there is a cataloging unit in the library. For example, in 1993 Arnold Hirshon announced that the Wright State University Library was closing its cataloging department and outsourcing all of its cataloging work to OCLC. He has since published a book on the subject.[2])

TECHNICAL SERVICE BACKGROUND AND PHILOSOPHY

Over the past fifty years there has been a steady shift in the philosophy underlying technical services. Emphasis is increasingly being placed on the end-user. Cataloging activities, which are the core element in providing access to collections, are dependent on rules and codes that are complex and difficult for non-catalogers to fully comprehend or use when seeking information. The codes and rules are essential in providing consistency when organizing the collection(s). Acquisitions financial transactions are also dependent on a set of codes and rules that are almost incomprehensible to anyone without a background in accounting or bookkeeping. The previous approach was that these activities did not require, need, or want much involvement with end-users. As late as the 1960s and early 1970s a general opinion prevailed that the public catalog, the means for determining the collections' content, was a tool created by librarians for librarians.

Over time, and with a growing focus on attempting to understand end-users' information-seeking behavior and adjusting processes and procedures to reflect that understanding, there were efforts to make technical services outputs more "user-friendly." An example of the shift in thinking is illustrated in an article by Karen Drabenstott, Schelle Simcox, and Eileen Fenton[3] reporting the results of a study of end-user understanding of public catalog subject headings. In their conclusion, they noted, "It is time for the library community to grapple with the difficult questions about its subject access system and make informed decisions about solving the problem of low levels of end-user subject heading understanding."[4]

Libraries have tried a number of structures in the hope of breaking the "front room/back room" view that prevailed in the past and that one may still encounter in some libraries. As early as 1948, Ray Swank argued that catalogers and bibliographers were the key staff to create a collection that end-users would find valuable.[5] However, for a variety of reasons, he was ahead of existing practice and it was almost ten years before anyone attempted to implement some of his ideas. In the late 1950s the University of Nebraska experimented with a subject approach to the provision of information. What this meant at Nebraska was that librarians had a subject area responsibility for all the functions listed previously except preparation and storage.[6] The idea that a person working directly with the public is best able to understand the needs and behavior of users and thus create collections and access tools tailored to local conditions is probably correct.

From a practical point of view, there are problems in applying the concept in the real world. Individual librarians are neither all equally skilled nor interested in all the functional areas. In those cases functions of interest receive a greater share of the person's time and effort, and less attention is given to those areas of least interest. Too great a variance causes substantial unevenness between subject collections and the quality of access to those collections. As Laura Harper stated in a presentation at the 1998 midwinter meeting of the Academic Technical Services Discussion Group (American Library Association) dealing with the idea of blending public and technical service responsibilities, one cannot force people to do what they cannot or do not want to do.[7]

One of the most common methods for achieving some of the benefits of Swank's and others' ideas about blending the two traditionally distinct areas is to have technical service librarians work some hours at the reference desk. Libraries employ different approaches to that idea, ranging from voluntary to required desk hours. At the University of Texas–Pan American campus, technical service librarians were asked to work some desk hours.[8] Such requests may, in fact, be a directive; in other instances compliance is truly up to the individual. However, when that request is generated by a library-wide reorganization plan and/or staff reductions, it is likely that some of those receiving the request may believe it would be impolitic not to "volunteer." At the Loyola Marymount University (Los Angeles) Library two newly graduated catalog librarians asked if they could have some reference desk hours at the time they were hired. Both believed working at the reference desk would help maintain their reference skills and enhance their career options. Ten years later, they are still working at the reference desk and have not tested the career development idea; however, if one or both were to leave, the head of public services probably would want to make desk hours a part of the required duties for their successors.

There can be significant advantages in terms of making better informed decisions about access tools and for collection development from having technical service librarians work in public services. However, there are some disadvantages to consider before implementing such a plan. One is loss of productivity. For example, for technical services personnel an hour spent on the reference desk is an hour not spent on the "real job." When there is a processing backlog, the sense of what is "real work" becomes even stronger. Reference staff also lose some productivity because they must train or update the reference skills of the technical service librarians. When reference work drew solely on printed materials this was not a major concern; today, with ever-increasing dependence on constantly changing electronic resources, it can be a significant issue.

Another issue is the quality of service that part-timers are able to provide, especially if desk hours are required. The Loyola Marymount University (LMU) Library recently conducted several faculty and student surveys regarding all aspects of library service as part of an assessment program in preparation for an institution-wide accreditation visit. One of the surprise findings was that while the reference staff service overall was very highly regarded by both students and faculty, there were numerous written comments about those librarians who only worked a few hours a week (none of the "part-timers" works more than four hours). Comments indicated that although those individuals tried to help and sometimes succeeded, the time required was high and the degree of confidence in the results of the assistance was low. Essentially the users reported that they would wait, if they could, for one of the "regular librarians." The library staff is attempting to develop a system that will give the part-timers a better opportunity to stay current with the changing menu of online services the library provides to it users.

A third issue is staff perception. When only technical service librarians are asked to cross over (that is, reference staff are not asked to assist in technical services), this sends a message about values—that of devaluing technical service activities. With some administrative effort one can reduce the sense of devaluation but seldom eliminate it.

Another method for blending the two areas, not often used, is a modified version of the subject approach. Sometimes this is referred to as "matrix teams," in which several people share a set of duties but allocate their time according to their interest and skill levels. An example might be four persons who share acquisitions, cataloging, reference, and collection development responsibilities for the humanities. They might allocate their work time as illustrated in Table 1.1; notice that both the rows and columns add up to 100 percent.

Table 1.1 Matrix Team

	Person A	Person B	Person C	Person D	
Acquisitions	30%	20%	25%	25%	100%
Cataloging	40%	20%	25%	15%	100%
Reference	15%	15%	25%	45%	100%
Collection Development	15%	45%	25%	15%	100%

Clearly, the benefit of this approach is a better use of skills, knowledge, and interests of each team member. At the same time, team members gain a holistic view of the library's activities and service programs, which in turn should result in improved decision making, at least in terms of end-user needs. It is also clear that a matrix team needs individuals who are not only committed to the concept but also reasonably skilled in all the areas. That type of person is not always available, and developing in-house interest and skills or seeking such breadth during the hiring process takes time. Thus, this is not currently a model one sees often.

TRENDS AFFECTING TECHNICAL SERVICES

Three of the most prominent trends affecting technical services are technology, budgetary issues, and outsourcing. We begin by discussing technology.

Technology

As mentioned in the opening section of this chapter, it was cataloging that brought computers and networking into libraries on a large scale more than thirty years ago. The integrated library systems (ILS)—computer systems and programs that automate various library operations and link them together in an almost seamless manner—that most libraries have today in one form or another grew out of libraries' efforts to provide cost-effective handling of acquisitions and cataloging activities. During the 1960s, U.S. librarians engaged in a variety of efforts to create cooperative or centralized technical service centers. Some projects focused on a type of library, such as academic or public. Later efforts focused on multi-type regional or statewide programs. Today we see the results of those efforts in the Online Computer Library Center (OCLC) and state and regional "networks" that go well beyond technical service activities. We sometimes forget that the roots of these programs were in technical services. Few of us who began our careers in technical services at the time fully understood where these efforts would lead.

Today's ILS handle all of the traditional technical service functions. That use of technology has both accelerated activities and improved consistency throughout the library; perhaps the area where this is most evident is technical services. For example, at the LMU library in 1987 there were four OCLC terminals in the cataloging department and no other computers anywhere. There was an acquisitions budget of just under $400,000, and the library processed (cataloged) between 3,500 and 4,000 items. By 1990 there was an ILS and computers or terminals on about two-thirds of the staff desks. The acquisition budget was just over $2 million, and processing exceeded 15,000 items per year in fiscal year 2000/2001. Although the dollar amount and processing increases may not be impressive by themselves, what is impressive is that a staff that had *declined* by one full-time equivalent (FTE) handled the larger workload in its entirety. It is also noteworthy that the library did not employ outsourcing to handle the increased processing. This was possible only by using technology, primarily the ILS.

Productivity gains from an ILS come about in several ways. One of the most significant arises from the ability to share files at the desktop throughout the library. One of the great challenges for architects designing a new library facility in pre-ILS days was that almost every staff member wanted to be adjacent to the card catalog to make the workday easier. Exacerbating those demands was the fact that the end-users had to have access to the catalog. Obviously satisfying all of them was physically impossible, but the online public access catalog (OPAC), a key element in an ILS, now makes it possible.

Sharing files electronically reduces the amount of time staff have to spend walking to and from their desks to shared physical files. Some of the shared files for technical services include on-order, in-processing, serials check-in, shelflist, and of course the public catalog. Both technical and public service staff require access to information contained in such files; in pre-computer times, a substantial amount of staff time was spent walking. Another problem was that some of these files contained basically the same information, but arranged differently. Creating and maintaining such files also required staff time, especially when there were hundreds, and often in large libraries, thousands of slips of paper. (A traditional format in U.S. libraries was, and still is to some degree, a 3-by-5-inch [ca 8-by-13-cm] card or paper slip.) Maintaining paper-based files was a challenge for every technical services unit. Misfiled slips were a constant issue and could cost the library money. For example, if a book was already on order but the order slip was in an incorrect location, a second unwanted copy might be ordered.

An ILS generally provides keyword searching of a variety of "fields" in the electronic bibliographic record. (There is more information about fields and bibliographic records in Chapters 15, 16, and 21.) Keyword searches provide a more complete view of collection holdings on a subject than does a straight subject search. This is because such a search scans multiple fields such as title, subtitle, and notes. When LMU first installed its ILS, many faculty members commented that the number of titles they found when using a keyword approach to a search surprised them. Such information is clearly something end-users like, and for collection development staff it is also very useful.

Many of the automation systems offer staff and end-users the opportunity to "browse" the collection electronically. That is, they can see the bibliographic record of each physical item in the collection in the order in which the material is stored (the equivalent of the traditional shelflist). The advantage of electronic browsing is that all items appear on the screen even if the item is checked out.

One of the attractions of journals and newspapers is the currency of the information they contain. A frequently asked question in public service is, "Has the latest issue of XX arrived yet?" In pre-ILS days such queries required either a telephone call or a trip to the serials check-in file, usually located in technical services, to provide the answer. Today most ILS will quickly provide the answer at the location where the question is asked, and in some cases the end-user can determine the answer directly from the OPAC. Even "on-order" information is available to end-users in some systems, which is particularly useful in academic institutions where faculty requests are important in building the collections.

Another reason for increased productivity is that a single electronic record can serve many purposes. With paper-based systems, technical services staff often had to re-create the same information in a slightly different arrangement or attempt to use multiple carbon copies of a form and then arrange files in the desired order. Anyone who has worked with the multiple-copy order forms can recall how faint the images were on the fourth, fifth, or sixth copy. Not having to re-create records and having the computer rearrange information has freed up a considerable amount of staff time. There is also greater consistency and accuracy in the files, assuming the original entry was correct.

Overall, the ILS has given libraries a strong incentive to review what, how, and who does what. Technical services units have taken advantage of the opportunities and made numerous adjustments in their workflows and staffing patterns (see Chapter 2, "Staffing," and Chapter 5, "Acquisitions—Overview"). There is every reason to believe that the ILS will continue to evolve and provide further opportunities for improvements in productivity.

Certainly the impact of technology now goes far beyond the ILS. The Internet and the World Wide Web (the Web) have a substantial impact on library activities. Vendors, especially those handling books or journals, are providing more of their services through the Web. Following are two examples of ways in which vendor Web services influence technical services. First, importing (downloading) OCLC bibliographic data has been a staple activity in libraries for many years. What has changed and is changing is that it is becoming easier to download files from vendors into the ILS and then modify the files to meet local needs. In the not too distant past, the best one could expect was to make modifications of files in the bibliographic utilities' or vendor's database and then import the file. The supplier also determined the amount of modification or manipulation that could be made. In general, they allowed limited modification. Another change is the ability to order materials and pay invoices electronically, which makes for faster service and, assuming the electronic data are correct, fewer errors. These and other electronic influences on technical services are covered in Chapters 3 and 4.

An important element in the area of electronic influences is *metadata,* which is the generic term for cataloging and indexing for electronic documents. Internet/Web sites are a mixed bag of information ranging from the worthless, or even dangerous, to the authoritative. Libraries have been engaging in "electronic collection development" for a number of years by attempting to sort out the good from the bad and the ugly. Essentially, the idea is to identify worthwhile and reliable electronic resource sites and provide end-users with access to those sites. A serious issue for libraries is how to go about describing such locations in the library's OPAC or on its Web page. Metadata (information about information) is a term used to identify this concern. The Dublin Core is an example of an effort to reach agreement on a standardized method for describing Internet/Web resources.[9] In July 2000 OCLC and hundreds of cooperating libraries launched the Cooperative Online Resource Catalog (CORC) project, a service that allows libraries around the world to retrieve and describe outstanding Internet resources.

Electronic issues will be an ever-increasing factor for technical services. Linda Bills provides an accurate assessment of some of the directions that libraries will follow in this area:

> (1) Cooperation among vendors, often instigated by libraries,
>
> (2) Standards, either *de facto* or *de jure* for the exchange of various types of data, and
>
> (3) Re-allocation of responsibilities for various processes both within libraries and between libraries and vendors.[10]

Budgetary Issues

Budget considerations have played a significant role in determining all aspects of library services, not just technical services, over the past thirty years. All of the usual economic and financial suspects appear on the following list of influences:

- Overall economic conditions,
- Reluctance of taxpayers to raise taxes (and in some cases rolling them back),
- Shifting allocation priorities by funding authorities,
- Increasing collection material prices, far beyond that of overall inflation rates, and
- Rapidly changing technology and the constant need to upgrade systems.

From the mid-1970s until the early 1990s, the economic conditions in different regions of the country varied, but overall it was a time of little real economic growth. Phrases such as "small is beautiful," "less is more," "downsizing," and "reengineering" were commonplace and reflected the idea that people and organizations could be more effective, often with fewer staff. For libraries, the approaches represented by these expressions resulted in major changes in services, staffing, and collections.

Related to the overall economic conditions were taxpayers' "revolts" against tax increases in the United States. The notion that taxpayers could have a major say in determining tax levels, both new and existing, started in California and quickly spread across the country. These efforts had an impact on government revenues, especially at the community and county levels. Libraries were not very successful in securing voter support for bond issues that might provide funds for new or remodeled buildings or increases in the level of base support. In a few extreme cases, the lack of support led to the closure of the library. An example is the closing of the Shasta County (California) operated libraries in 1987.[11] (Citations to other examples of library misfortunes appear in the Suggested Reading section of this chapter.) Libraries in other countries do not raise money through bond issues but rather are funded directly by governments. Taxpayers everywhere in the United States are reluctant to have increased taxation, and politicians are anxious not to alienate voters, with the result that libraries in many jurisdictions are not generously supported.

Government officials understood that voters wanted certain services maintained. Police, fire, sanitation, and road maintenance services were high priorities. Services such as schools, libraries, museums, and parks had to struggle for a share of the small amount of funding that remained after top priority services were almost fully funded. Often the best a library could hope for was funding at the same level as the previous year. With inflation, at times even the Consumer Price Index (CPI) was in the double-digit range, and "last year's funding" did not go as far in each succeeding year.

During those years, and to some extent continuing up to the time we prepared this chapter, the cost of materials for the library's collection increased at rates that were even higher than the CPI. Journal prices in particular escalated rapidly. The magnitude of the problem is illustrated by some late 1990s data about serial prices for libraries. For public libraries in 1995 the average price of a journal was U.S. $52.59; by 1999 the average was U.S. $62.98 (a 19.45 percent increase in five years), and these were considered by many librarians to be the "good times." In the case of academic libraries, the situation was grim: The 1995 average price was U.S. $282.51, and by 1999 it was U.S. $419.22 (a jump of 48.39 percent).[12] (Journal prices vary in large measure by the size of the potential market for a given title. Popular titles, with millions of potential subscribers, have relatively low prices, whereas low-interest titles, with a few thousand subscribers, have high prices. This is discussed in more detail in Chapter 10). Book and media prices were also increasing faster than the CPI throughout much of this period.

While addressing these challenges, libraries also faced the need to first install a variety of technologies and then maintain them at an appropriate level, if the library was to remain a viable player in the new "Information Society." Technology changes rapidly, and it is often impossible not to move forward with those changes if one hopes to receive support for the technology. Upgrading always seems to cost more than expected, which puts an additional strain on the budget.

All of these factors, and others, created an environment in which libraries faced difficult financial and service choices. Initially, some libraries thought reducing service hours might generate a demand from end-users to funding authorities for increased funding to restore service levels. This seldom was the outcome, and circumstances did not improve. Another approach that almost every library tried was to change or reduce its collection-building activities. One change was to reduce one-time purchases—books and media formats—to maintain current journal subscriptions. However, year after year of double-digit price increases for serials forced many libraries to engage in serial cancellation projects and also try to increase book purchases as those collections began showing serious signs of aging.

One of the other frequently seen outcomes of the overall reduction or minimal growth in the library budget was changes in staffing patterns. Sometimes this took the form of hiring "freezes" (not being allowed to fill a staff vacancy) for long periods of time. At other times it involved losing a position when a staff member resigned (staff attrition). Occasionally, it was outright staff reductions through voluntary or involuntary terminations (called "reductions in force," "riffing," or "redundancy" depending on location). Not surprisingly, having fewer one-time purchases to make and fewer serial titles to process, as well as seeing an overall drop in the number of materials to catalog, meant technical services had staffing and workload issues to face and greater pressure to reduce its staff. It also meant that there was pressure to look at alternative methods for handling the workload. One such method is outsourcing.

Outsourcing

Outsourcing means having some service or activity performed by persons or organizations ("third parties") that are not part of a library or library system. When looking at the professional literature of the past ten years for discussions about the concept, a newcomer to the field might believe that outsourcing is a new phenomenon in libraries. That impression is only partially correct. Technical services units have been outsourcing activities for a great many years: using jobbers for ordering books rather than purchasing directly from the publisher;

using serial vendors to place the bulk of subscriptions rather than going directly to the publishers; and using outside companies to bind and repair materials for the collection. Somewhat new are efforts to use outside agencies for collection building and even overall library operations. In the case of overall operations, U.S. government agencies have used such services for their library programs for many years, just as have some corporations.

The current emphasis on outsourcing started in the for-profit sector at the same time that topics such as reengineering and downsizing were popular. Like libraries, businesses had employed the concept for many years without media attention. The difference in coverage was that the idea was often linked with staff reductions. Another term that came into play at the time was *contingent workforce*. Anne Polivka and Thomas Nardone defined this concept as

> a wide range of employment practices, including part-time work, temporary work, employee leasing, self-employment, contracting out, and home-based work. As a result, the operational definition of a contingent job has become an arrangement that differs from full-time, permanent, wage, and salary employment.[13]

"Contracting out" is a synonym for outsourcing. Karen Jette and Clay-Edward Dixon discussed contingent work in libraries in an article in *Library Administration & Management*, noting that libraries have also employed that concept for many years.[14] Their article has a sound section on the pros and cons of such work, including outsourcing.

In an excellent article addressing some of the management issues related to outsourcing, James Marcum reviewed both management and library literature on the subject; this article is a good starting place for those considering outsourcing.[15] One of his points is especially noteworthy: "To the extent that outsourcing is a stand-in for downsizing, it is an act of a desperate management seeking short-term survival and not a strategy of implementing a transformation for the future."[16] Although Marcum's focus is on the general concept rather than its application to technical services, the issues he raises apply to any aspect of library outsourcing.

As a cost-reduction tactic, outsourcing may be correct and effective in the short run but may have unexpected long-term consequences. No matter what one does, certain coordination costs will always be present. Reducing those coordination and monitoring costs results in long-term quality control issues. Expertise that will be needed later may also be lost, and the cost of re-securing that expertise can be high. There may also be unexpected salary implications, if the activity outsourced involves staffing changes. What happened in the Hawaii State Library system is a good example of the unexpected outcomes of outsourcing when the focus is on cost reduction.[17] The director/state librarian outsourced selection to Baker & Taylor, a vendor. Resulting collections were not satisfactory and the public outcry caused the contract to be rescinded. Lawsuits were filed by both the state against the vendor and the vendor against the state.

Despite these drawbacks, there is substantial potential for using outsourcing as another tool for helping to control costs or supplement and expand services. This is how libraries have effectively employed the concept in the past without labeling it "outsourcing." Two examples from acquisitions and one from cataloging illustrate the point that outsourcing has a long tradition in libraries. As mentioned previously, using either, or in most instances both, a book or a serials jobber is not absolutely essential for libraries. A library could place all its orders for books or journals directly with the publishers. For very small libraries that may be a reasonable option. However, as the volume of orders increases the work involved in maintaining address files, credit terms, discount information, and so forth from hundreds or even thousands of publishers becomes prohibitive. Years ago, acquisitions librarians saw the value of placing a single order with a jobber or wholesaler for the items needed from various publishers. (Placing one order for 100 books from thirty-five different publishers instead of thirty-five orders with the individual publishers saves staff time in order preparation alone.) The idea was not to reduce staff or cut costs; it was to make the most effective use of existing staff and keep costs from increasing.

Another example, and one that is not often mentioned as outsourcing, is the use of approval plans in academic libraries. In these plans, the vendor identifies items that match a list of subject areas that the library wants to collect and ships various materials that fall into the category to the library for review. Thus, the library outsources the identification function, one of the basic functions discussed previously in this chapter.

Cataloging departments have an equally long, if not longer, history of using outsourcing. For example, until widespread implementation of the ILS took place most libraries made extensive use of catalog cards produced by commercial companies and the Library of Congress. (LC started selling its cards around 1901.) Certainly there was even greater use of the *National Union Catalog* (NUC) and *Canadiana* in creating cards for public catalogs. (One of this book's authors well remembers his days as a cataloger with the responsibility of overseeing the duplication of LC/NUC and local copy for use in the library's public catalog and shelflist.) No one thought of this as outsourcing; at best it may have been regarded as resource sharing (although libraries were depending on "third parties" to provide the product and did pay for the services and cards).

By the 1960s there were efforts to create shared processing centers. As noted previously, these efforts resulted in bibliographic utilities such as OCLC (Online Computer Library Center). This form of outsourcing is an accepted and very valuable service.

A common first response to suggestions of using outsourcing for a library activity, especially cataloging, is the lack of quality control on the part of third parties. Local catalogers are known to "correct mistakes" made by the Library of Congress, and many have grave doubts that bibliographic records from other libraries can possibly be as accurate as ones produced in-house. Obviously doubts about a third-party source (another library or one that is for-profit) are even greater. As Sheila Intner has noted, the goal of the perfect catalog record and perfect public catalog is akin to seeking the Holy Grail—a worthy idea but, at least in the case of cataloging, highly unrealistic and costly in many ways for the library.[18] Certainly there are quality concerns, but they exist no matter where the work is done or by whom, and the reality is that perfection is highly unlikely to exist anywhere at reasonable cost to the library and end-users. Quality of third-party work therefore should not be a limiting factor in deciding to move ahead with an outsourcing project; it should just be one of many issues that must be addressed.

Perhaps the most ambitious effort at outsourcing technical services is that taking place at Florida Gulf Coast University (FGCU). FGCU is the newest university in the Florida university system; it opened in late 1997. FGCU's outsourcing project consists of five major technical service activities:

- The retrospective conversion and reclassification of a collection of 65,000 volumes purchased from a college that had closed. This also included the physical processing of the volumes.
- The selection and processing of 35,000 volumes from a collection of 160,000 volumes that were part of the library collections at two Florida academic institutions.
- The merging and de-duplication of the two retrospective collections and the creation of a retrospective purchasing list for the balance of an "opening day" collection.
- The creation of an opening day collection consisting of 130,000 volumes, fully processed and shelf ready, with bibliographic records for all items in both OCLC and the Florida Center for Library Automation database.
- The creation of a fund accounting system for the collection.

The primary vendors of the services were OCLC and Academic Book Center (now part of Blackwell North America). At press time it was still too early to predict the outcome of the efforts at handling essentially all of the library's technical services by third parties. However, it does seem to be more successful than the aforementioned Hawaiian efforts, perhaps because this is a start-up situation and there were no vested interests in "how we did it better." Another factor that has made this effort less controversial than the Hawaiian project is that the selection activities are based on collections from previously established academic libraries. Thus there is a sense that the titles were vetted by librarians at an earlier time.

SUMMARY

Technical services provide both information resources that end-users need and the means of gaining effective and efficient access to those materials. Technology has played an ever-greater role in changing the way in which technical services operate but has not changed their basic functions. In addition to technology, general economic conditions also have had a significant impact on the activities performed. One of the most notable of those effects is a growing emphasis on outsourcing.

NOTES

1. G. Edward Evans, Anthony J. Amodeo, and Thomas L. Carter, *Introduction to Library Public Services,* 6th ed. (Englewood, CO: Libraries Unlimited, 1999).

2. Arnold Hirshon and Barbara Winters, *Outsourcing Library Technical Services* (New York: Neal-Schuman, 1996).

3. Karen M. Drabenstott, Schelle Simcox, and Eileen Fenton, "End-User Understanding of Subject Headings in Library Catalogs," *Library Resources & Technical Services,* 43 (July 1999):140-160.

4. Ibid., 60.

5. Raymond C. Swank, "The Catalog Department in the Library Organization," *Library Quarterly* 18 (1948): 24-32.

6. Frank A. Lundy, "The Divisional Plan Library," *College & Research Libraries* 17 (1956): 143-148.

7. "Blurring the Lines: Mingling Technical and Public Service Responsibilities," *Technical Services Quarterly* 15, no. 4 (1998): 69.

8. Ibid., 68.

9. "The State of the Dublin Core Metadata Initiative," *Bulletin of the American Society for Information Science* 25 (June/July 1999): 18-22.

10. Linda Bills, "Technical Services and Integrated Library Systems," *Library High Tech* 18, no. 2 (2000): 147.

11. Kathy Malady, "Shasta Closing All Its Libraries," *The Unabashed Librarian* 64 (1987): 1+.

12. EBSCO, *Serials Prices 1995–1999 with Projections for 2000* (Birmingham, AL: EBSCO, 1999).

13. Anne Polivka and Thomas Nardone, "The Definition of 'Contingent Work,' " *Monthly Labor Review* 112 (December 1989): 10.

14. Karen Jette and Clay-Edward Dixon, "The Outsourced/Contingent Workforce: Abuse, Threat, or Blessing?" *Library Administration & Management* 12 (Fall 1998): 220-225.

15. James Marcum, "Outsourcing in Libraries: Tactic, Strategy, or 'Meta-Strategy'?" *Library Administration & Management* 12 (Winter 1998): 15-25.

16. Ibid., 17.

17. Carol Reid, "Down and Outsourced in Hawaii," *American Libraries* 28 (June/July 1997): 56-57.

18. Sheila S. Intner, "Copy Cataloging and the Perfect Record Mentality," in *Interfaces: Relationships Between Library Technical and Public Services* (Englewood, CO: Libraries Unlimited, 1993), 154-159.

SUGGESTED READING

Ahronheim, Judith. "Technical Services Management Issues in the Metadata Environment." *Technicalities* 19 (June/July 1999): 4-6.

Anemaet, Jos. "Merger, Reorganization and Technology Meet Technical Services." *Serials Librarian* 34, nos. 3/4 (1998): 397-384.

Arnold, Stephen. "Library Integration Trends." *Electronic Library* 17 (July 1999): 161-163.

Baker, Barry. "Resource Sharing: Outsourcing and Technical Services." *Technical Services Quarterly* 16, no. 2 (1998): 35-45.

"Branch Closures: 'Fewer but Better' Strategy Slated." *Library Association Record* 101 (May 1999): 259.

Chu, Felix Tse-Hsiu. "Assessing the Infrastructure: Technical Support for Library Services." *Illinois Library Association* 19 (August 2001): 9-11.

Clark, Kim. "Technical Services: The Other Reader Service." *Library Collections, Acquisitions, and Technical Services* 24 (Winter 2000): 501-502.

Crosby, Ellen. "Technical Services in the Twenty-first Century Special Collections." *Cataloging & Classification Quarterly* 30, nos. 2/3 (2000): 167-176.

Diedrichs, Carol. "Using Automation in Technical Services to Foster Innovation." *Journal of Academic Librarianship* 24 (March 1998): 113-120.

Fetch, Deborah. "The Human Side of Outsourcing." *Library Collections, Acquisitions and Technical Services* 23 (Spring 1999): 110-113.

Fietzer, William. "Technical Services Librarians and Metadata: Reining in the New Frontier." *Technicalities* 18 (July/August 1998): 7-10.

Foster, Constance. "Color Us Bold: The Spectrum of Library Technical Services." *Serials Review* 24, nos. 3/4 (1998): 142-144.

Gilliland-Swetland, Anne, Ysmin Kafai, and William Landis. "Application of the Dublin Core Metadata in the Description of Digital Primary Sources in Elementary Classrooms." *Journal of the American Society for Information Science* 51 (January 2000): 193-201.

Glick, Andrea. "One Library Closes, Another Opens." *School Library Journal* 45 (December 1999): 20.

Gordon, Mary Jane. "Creating a Library Technical Services Outsourcing Operation." *Serials Librarian* 32, nos. 1/2 (1997): 53-76.

Gorman, Michael. *Technical Services: Today and Tomorrow.* 2nd ed. Englewood, CO: Libraries Unlimited, 1998.

Hirshon, Arnold, and Barbara Winters. *Outsourcing Library Technical Services: A How-to-Do-It Manual for Librarians.* New York: Neal-Schuman, 1996.

Intner, Sheila S. "An Editor's Musings About the Differing Opinions on the Outsourcing Controversy." *Technicalities* 17 (September 1997): 2-3+.

———. "Putting the Service in Technical Services." *ALCTS Newsletter* 9, nos. 4-6 (1998): 38-39.

Koh, Gertrude Soonja. "Knowledge Access Management: The Redefinition and Renaming of Technical Services." *Libri* 50 (September 2000): 163-173.

Kristl, Carol. "Wichita Schools Consider Closing Library Center." *American Libraries* 28 (April 1997): 19+.

Leonhardt, Thomas W. "Technical Services in the 21st Century." *Technicalities* 20 (September/October 2000): 1, 12-13.

Makinen, Ruth. "Scheduling Technical Services Staff at the Reference Desk." *The Reference Librarian* 59 (1997): 139-146.

Myers, Marilyn. "Blurring the Lines: Mingling Technical and Public Service Responsibilities." *Technical Services Quarterly* 15, no. 4 (1998): 67-70.

Ouderkirk, Jane Padham. "Staff Assignments and Workflow Distribution at the End of the 20th Century." *Cataloging & Classification Quarterly* 30, nos. 2/3 (2000): 343-355.

Platten, Bessie. "The Case Against Outsourcing." *Library Collections, Acquisitions & Technical Services* 23, no. 2 (Summer 1999): 210-212.

Proctor, Richard, and Sylvia Simmons. "Public Library Closures: The Management of Hard Decisions." *Library Management* 21, no. 1 (2000): 25-34.

"Public Library Closures: Friends Groups Vary Legal Attacks." *Library Association Record* 101 (July 1999): 384.

Ray, Ron. "Outsourcing Technical Services: The Selection Process." *Library Acquisitions* 21 (Winter 1997): 490-493.

Thornton, Glenda. "Renovation of Technical Services: Physical and Philosophical Considerations." *Technical Services Quarterly* 15, no. 3 (1998): 49-61.

Webster, Keith. "Technical Services: Serving the Customer." *New Review of Academic Librarianship* 4 (1998): 123-132.

Younger, Jennifer. "Technical Services Organization." In *Technical Services: Today and Tomorrow,* 2nd ed., edited by Michael Gorman. Englewood, CO: Libraries Unlimited, 1998.

Zuidema, Karen. "Reengineering Technical Services Process." *Library Resources & Technical Services* 43 (January 1999): 37-52.

REVIEW QUESTIONS

1. Describe the five basic functions that are normally part of technical services.
2. Discuss the changing philosophy of technical service work.
3. Discuss the ways in which integrated library systems (ILS) have had an impact on technical service activities and organization.
4. What are some of the other ways technology affects technical services?
5. Discuss how the economy has influenced technical services.
6. Discuss what is new and not new about the concept of outsourcing technical services.

Chapter 2 Staffing

Clearly a library without staff would indeed be "virtual"; however, more often than not its end-users would be unable to locate the precise information they need. Even the so-called virtual organizations require people power. Anyone who has used an online service, no matter how intuitive it supposedly is, knows there are always a few questions that need answering, preferably by a knowledgeable human being. In terms of technical services, there will always be a need for individuals who understand and can handle the basic technical service functions discussed in Chapter 1. Outsourcing of technical service activities may mean that a person does not work for an individual library but rather works for an organization that supplies technical services to a number of libraries. Whether someone works for a library or for a technical service outsourcing organization, the skills and knowledge required are the same. This chapter explores a number of staffing and personnel issues as they affect technical service activities.

LIBRARY PERSONNEL CATEGORIES

End-users of libraries generally view anyone working in the library as a "librarian." Actually libraries, like most other organizations, utilize several categories of employees. The labels for the categories vary from library to library; however, there are three basic groups:

- Full-time individuals who have a master's degree in library and information science and/or a subject graduate degree (librarians/professionals/subject specialists),
- Full-time individuals with degrees ranging from high school to post-graduate (paraprofessional, nonprofessional, support staff, library assistant, technical assistant, library media technical assistant, and clerical staff are some of the more common titles), and

- Part-time individuals with or without a degree (pages, shelvers, interns, student assistants, volunteers).

Large research and academic libraries often have full-time staff who have graduate degrees in subject areas that are of primary interest to the library; often these are doctoral degrees. Other professionals who do not have library degrees also work in large libraries (for example, personnel officers and networking specialists). Although the end-user seldom recognizes, and may not understand or care about, these variations, such differences do matter to library staff.

Starting in the 1960s, an ever-increasing volume of literature examined the question of library staffing categories, job titles, job duties, and related issues. Two of this book's authors have been writing about these issues for a much longer period. The interest in the topic has grown substantially since the 1970s. Part of the reason for the increasing coverage arises from the factors discussed in Chapter 1 relating to the changing nature of library activities. To a large degree what has been taking place is summed up in a statement by Michael Gorman: "No librarian should do a job a paraprofessional can do, no paraprofessional should do a job that a clerical staff member can do, and no human being should do a job a machine can do."[1] Budget reductions, downsizing, technology, and changing staffing patterns all create an environment of uncertainty, tension, and often fear. Add to that mix variable beliefs or understandings about the types of work and who should do what, when, and how, and there are bound to be concerns about employment security and what jobs will exist in the future as well as the labels associated with those positions. Liz Lane and Barbara Stewart have correctly noted that "many staff members are being assigned higher-level work which then require an upward reclassification of jobs in the automated technical services environment. Work previously done at lower levels has either become automated, outsourced to a library vendor, or is not done anymore."[2]

As Paula Kaufman wrote some years ago, the categories used to classify library employees "can create problems, tensions, and conflicts between library nonprofessional and professional staffs."[3] (These tensions, at least in technical services, go back to at least the mid-1960s and the movement to create computerized processing centers.) Brian Nettleford addressed some of the key issues when he looked at the relationship between staff performing "professional" activities and those performing other library activities.[4] Nettleford defined librarians as individuals who act "as planners, administrators, or practitioners of librarianship, and have the ability to analyze information in depth and with perspective, based on an appreciation of the role of the library as a service organization."[5] He defined paraprofessionals as individuals who have "the knowledge, use, and understanding of a range of specific techniques, procedures, and services that can be undertaken according to a set of predetermined rules, without the need to exercise professional judgment in decision-making."[6]

Labels carry different meanings to different people and can have implications for overall organizational morale. Using the term *nonprofessional* is likely to cause some tension, especially among those who are part of that group. Terms such as *support staff, library assistant,* and *technical assistant* cause less tension but are not universally appreciated by those so labeled. The term used in this book is *paraprofessional* because it is widely used in other fields as well.

Five broad categories of library employees are covered in this chapter: the three mentioned previously as well as clerical staff (for positions that call for basic office skills, such as keyboarding and filing abilities) and volunteers. The terms *professional, paraprofessional, clerical, part-time staff*, and *volunteer* are used for these categories. Because the issues of professional background and skills are widely discussed in library literature, little space is devoted to it here. The primary focus is on the other categories; however, all five categories of employee play important roles in technical service programs.

Professional Staff

When the first edition of this textbook appeared (1970), graduates of library schools had at least a basic understanding of cataloging, classification, and collection development. Library schools of the time had a "core curriculum" that included at least one course in each of these subjects. That type of background permitted libraries to experiment with organizational structures cutting across technical and public services, such as those mentioned in Chapter 1.

During the intervening years library schools, like libraries, have encountered a changing social environment that required significant responses. Like some libraries, a few schools closed; others reduced their size or focused on one or two types of libraries. Some of the schools shifted their focus to a generic "information" curriculum in an attempt to broaden employment opportunities for their graduates as well as reflecting an external environment that emphasizes information and technology. Several have gone so far as to drop the word "library" from the school's name. Name changes and changing curriculum needs led to revised "core requirements," as few schools in the United States were willing to expand their programs beyond one year in length. The result has been that fewer and fewer graduates have a background in cataloging, classification, and collection development at a level that was once typical. Most schools still offer course work in these areas, but as electives rather than as requirements.

It is therefore not surprising to see articles such as Janet Hill's "Why Are There So Few of Us? Educating Librarians for Technical Services,"[7] in which she stated that

> Another wrong message is sent by the curriculum itself. Once cataloging and technical services topics occupied about half of the curriculum . . . no librarian got out of library school without knowing how to catalog at least at some level. As other subjects have needed to be accommodated, however, bibliographic control and technical services have been pinched and squeezed and shaved so that they now represent only a small portion of the course offerings . . . [which] carries the message that the technical services functions are of little importance.[8]

We believe that there is a message in the new curricula. However, perhaps that message is less that technical services are unimportant and more that employers are, or should be, able to provide training in these functions. Essentially this boils down to the long-standing debate about library education: Should it be theory- or practice-based, for "day one skills" or "career skills," and can everything fit into the existing time frame for the course of study? There is an ever-growing tendency for the employers of new graduates to provide more and more of the training needed for success in beginning positions. This adds yet another task to the load on staff members who are usually stretched almost to their limit.

Historically, acquisitions departments have employed a limited number of librarians unless the department has collection development responsibilities. Today, a single professional usually fills the department head position in most small, medium-sized, and even a few large libraries. The balance of the departmental staff usually consists of a combination of paraprofessionals, clerical, and some part-time personnel. Traditionally, if there was a separate serials department, the department head was a professional. Today that is also changing, at least in medium-sized academic libraries, and the position, if it exists at all, is held by a paraprofessional.

Another aspect of the challenge of professional staffing in technical services, particularly for acquisitions and serials work, is that in the past individuals developed an interest in these areas as a result of working under the direction of an experienced librarian. With fewer professionals working in these departments, where will libraries be able to find librarians with the necessary background to head up the departments? (Ed Evans wonders and worries about what will happen when the LMU library's head of acquisitions and serials decides to retire. Both joke about making a written pact that they will retire at the same time to prevent either of them having "to break-in a new person." This is only partly a joking matter, at least for the director, as finding a new professional to fill the department head position would in all likelihood mean attracting an experienced person from another library. Doing that will become increasingly difficult and costly as the pool of suitably experienced candidates shrinks.) Why the issue is more significant for acquisitions and serials work is that even in the past these topics were often only a subset within a course on collection development in library schools. Very few schools had full courses on acquisitions work; more had or have a full course on serials, but enrollment in such courses apparently is small. Becoming a professional in acquisitions or serials work is a matter of on-the-job training and self-teaching.

Lisa German and Karen Schmidt summed up the current education situation for librarians in the area of acquisitions, and their comments are applicable to serials work:

> At present there are sporadic instances of library schools in the United States offering acquisitions courses, but it is more commonplace for acquisitions to be included in technical services courses that may or may not include the administrative details

> that make for successful acquisition procedures. . . . The detailed and more clerical aspects of acquisitions are being codified by computer systems, but the framework of theory and knowledge upon which these skills hang is lost."[9]

In the area of cataloging the challenges are only slightly less daunting. Although almost every library school offers full courses on cataloging and classification, they may be electives rather than requirements. Yes, most of the schools have a required course that covers the theories and concepts related to organizing knowledge, and certainly cataloging and classification is a subset of that field of study, but such courses seldom focus on the real world aspects of how libraries currently organize their collections. For students to learn about these issues they must take one or more electives covering such topics. Not many students make that choice. One of the factors contributing to the lack of interest in the field is that schools are placing little emphasis on the topics as central to a career choice.

Paraprofessional Staff

Paraprofessional and clerical staffs are often difficult to differentiate in some libraries. Unionized libraries have clearer staff divisions that everyone on the staff understands, even if those divisions are not readily apparent to end-users. There is also what some people perceive as overlap between paraprofessional and professional staff. During the first half of the twentieth century, libraries had three very clear categories of staff: librarians, clerks, and pages. Starting shortly after the end of World War II, a steady blurring of those categories has taken place, and the number of categories has increased. Several factors combined to initiate this process.

The post–World War II period was a time of expansion in North American society, in communities, institutions, and education. Home ownership grew as developers built housing tracts or even created entirely new communities near large urban centers to meet the housing needs of returning veterans and war workers. With the development of "suburbia," urban-area public libraries built new branches to serve these communities. Some new communities created their own public library systems when they incorporated as independent political entities. Higher education also went through a "boom" period from the 1950s to the early 1970s as a result of government actions. National legislation allowed veterans to go to college at government expense. The number of students exceeded the capacity of existing institutions despite the construction of new classrooms and student housing. This resulted in the establishment of new colleges and universities and, of course, new libraries to support these institutions. There was an expansion of primary and secondary schools and growth in school library/media centers. The new and expanding libraries needed more librarians than existing library schools could supply, and people began to look at librarians' activities and ask who else could do the work.

This was also a period of very large budgets for collection building, which in turn resulted in a huge increase in acquisitions and cataloging work. At the time the "standard" methods for handling the workflow resulted in acquisitions departments ordering and receiving much higher levels of new materials than catalog departments could process. The outcome was a "cataloging backlog," at least in most academic institutions. Ed Evans's experience as a cataloger took place just as the peak funding was drawing to a close. When he started, the shelves surrounding his workplace held books awaiting cataloging arranged by the *year* of purchase. The oldest section was four years old. The seven other catalogers in the department had similar collections in their work areas. Departmental policy was for librarians to prepare all cataloging copy and edit card sets, including those from the Library of Congress (LC), and pass the material on to a clerical assistant for typing. Other clerical staff handled the physical preparation of the items and filed the cards in the public catalog and shelflist under close supervision of librarians.

It was clear that short of hiring four or five more librarians as well as additional support staff, there was no way to reduce the backlog and still use the existing procedures. Two catalogers received permission to survey other state university libraries to see what they were doing. The data suggested that everyone was struggling with the same issue, and one or two departments were trying to have clerks work on materials with LC copy. Soon that approach became commonplace, and, in time, as duties changed, the backlogs, at least in small- and medium-sized academic libraries, began to disappear.

Use of paraprofessional staff and their education is much more organized in countries other than the United States. A number of European countries have formal education programs for paraprofessionals. Examples of non–North American guidelines are the Library Association of Australia, Working Party on Work Level Standards, *Work Level Guidelines for Librarians and Library Technicians* (Canberra: Library Association of Australia, 1985) and D. Baker's *Training Library Assistants, Guidelines for Training in Libraries,* 6 (London: Library Association, 1985).

Both Canada and Australia have highly developed programs. All of the programs for technicians and paraprofessionals, including those in the United States, are two years in length in post-secondary institutions. Australian programs are part of Technical and Further Education (TAFE) colleges, whereas Canadian programs are found in community colleges, institutes of technology, and some universities. Nordic country programs are part of each country's two-year college system. A good article on non–U.S. programs with in-depth coverage of the Canadian system is "Library Technician Programs."[10] As of 2001, there was no national system in the United States, and many states have no formal education programs for paraprofessionals. ALA's Support Staff Interests Round Table is moving toward a national program or a model for state programs; see their report, issued in May 2000, at http://www.ala.org/ssirt/contedu.pdf.

The first Canadian program was started at the Manitoba Institute of Technology in 1962.[11] Since that time, programs have been developed in eight of the ten provinces. The Canadian Library Association (CLA) played an active role in monitoring the quality of these programs in three ways. First, they were instrumental in the development of guidelines for the training of library technicians.[12] Second, CLA several times funded the visits of John Marshall, a professor at the University of Toronto Faculty of Library Science, to each program. Third, for many years CLA published surveys documenting how well these programs conformed to the guidelines.[13] Several programs did not follow CLA's guidelines; most closed because their graduates had difficulty obtaining jobs as library technicians.

Tracing the history of U.S. paraprofessionals is beyond the scope of this book; however, we do want to provide a thumbnail outline to illustrate the relatively long and slow development of the field. Los Angeles City College (a two-year college) offered what was the first course for "library assistants" in 1937. The first full program for paraprofessionals we are aware of was the one started in 1947 by the U.S. Department of Agriculture Graduate School. Two years later, the Special Libraries Association instituted course work in clerical and assistant practices as a joint effort with the New York City YWCA's Ballard School. The American Library Association's reaction to such efforts was mixed at best and discouraged such programs on the basis that they created "cheap librarians."[14] However, by 1967 ALA was following the lead of the Canadian Library Association in affirming the need for technicians and paraprofessionals and programs to educate them. Today the Council on Library Technology (COLT) is the leading U.S. association representing the interests of paraprofessionals. COLT has been affiliated with ALA since 1976, the same year that Australia adopted national guidelines for educating paraprofessionals.

Although the concern about librarians (professionals) losing their positions because of the existence of technicians and paraprofessionals has abated, some issues remain. The flavor of library technicians' early struggles for recognition can be found in Jean Riddle's [Weihs] "Professionalism for Library Technicians."[15] Perhaps the most problematic issue is that of a "career ladder." ALA issued a "Library Education and Manpower" statement in 1970, with a proposed revision in 1999 (still pending approval). This statement and various articles about the statement put forward the concept of a career ladder for library personnel. Unfortunately, we have to agree with Anthony Wilson and Robert Hermanson that "library rhetoric has included the notion of a career ladder since the 'Library Education and Manpower' statement.... But the ladder has not been implemented to a degree that has been satisfactory in terms of 'growing our own' and promoting people in libraries in a way that taps their potential or their ambition."[16]

In 1973 the U.S. Office of Education published a comprehensive study on the role and training of technicians and paraprofessionals. The study detailed the types of positions (and their related activities) in a library in which technicians and paraprofessionals could expect to work. Although the document is dated, it does provide a sense of where and how far the field has come in terms of technicians and paraprofessionals as key personnel in library operations:

> Graduates ... can expect to find employment in many types and sizes of libraries requiring a variety of responsibilities. Most graduates will further develop their abilities by continued study on a part-time basis to keep pace with new developments in their fields. The following listing shows a sampling of only a few of the job opportunities for library technical assistants, as

described by employers. Some are beginning positions; others are attained through work experience or further study, or both.

1. *Library Technical Assistant I*—May perform one or more of the following: assist readers in locating books and using the public catalog; supervise shelving and other tasks performed by student assistants and clerks; supervise the maintenance and distribution of special collections and equipment; assist in the cataloging department; and, may be responsible for the reproduction of media materials.

2. *Library Technical Assistant II*—May perform all of the duties of the Library Technical Assistant I, as well as one or more of the following: supervise the work of Library Technical Assistant I; assist in the preparation of bibliographies; develop displays; supervise multiple book stack areas; and, be responsible for the production of media materials.

3. *Library Technical Assistant III*—May perform all duties of the Library Technical Assistant II, as well as one or more of the following: be responsible for supervision of all other library technical assistants and clerical staff; prepare special bibliographies; do basic uncomplicated cataloging; provide reference services on information desks and answer reference questions of an uncomplicated nature; supervise circulation, interlibrary loan or periodical services; and, assist with special community projects and services. The classifications and degrees of responsibility may vary somewhat depending on the objectives and size of the particular library, and the clientele it serves. Library technical assistants work in a great variety of libraries. These include public and private school libraries, academic libraries, public libraries, and special libraries such as medical, business, and government.[17]

As noted previously, many of these activities were performed by librarians at one time, and today many are markedly changed as a result of technology.

The importance of technicians and paraprofessionals in U.S. academic libraries is clear from data collected in 1990. A research team conducted a comprehensive survey on the role, status, and working conditions of paraprofessionals.[18] They reported that there were 9,466 paraprofessionals working in the reporting libraries and 7,644 librarians. Some of the data of interest to readers of this book follow:

- More than 90 percent of the responding Association of Research Libraries reported using paraprofessionals for copy cataloging work.
- More than 50 percent reported having paraprofessionals engage in some original descriptive cataloging.

- A somewhat surprising 20 percent reported assigning book selection duties to paraprofessionals.

A good case study article that covers the changes and developments in the role of technical services is "Blurring the Boundaries Between Professional and Paraprofessional Catalogers at California State University, Northridge."[19]

In recent years, many of the major library journals have contained articles or notices about matters of concern to library technicians. This increase in articles and announcements is an indication that the role and importance of the technician are steadily increasing. An excellent source of current information is the *COLT Newsletter*. COLT also publishes a directory of LMTA programs. Additional information on COLT activities is available at http://library.ucr.edu/COLT. Another good publication is *Library Mosaics*. A list of Canadian library technician programs can be found at www.nlc_bnc.ca/services/elic.htm#5.

Susan Chapman has made an interesting observation about differences between technicians and paraprofessionals and clerical staff:

> Library technicians also have an outlook distinct from clerical staff members with whom they may share some tasks. Preparation of library technicians results in workers who possess complex skills coupled with a dedication to library service. Clerical workers' specific knowledge of particular institutions does not necessarily indicate commitment to the profession which may be transferred to other libraries.[20]

Library technicians very often supervise clerical and part-time staff as well as volunteers.

Clerical Staff

Clerical staff perform essential activities such as typing, data entry, filing, answering telephones, and sorting and delivering the mail. The educational level required ranges from fewer than twelve years of schooling to specialized office training to several years of college. Most library positions require a high school degree. Although their work is essential, clerks are usually the lowest paid full-time library staff members.

Clerical positions often have a high turnover rate, not only because of the low salary level, but because some of the work is highly repetitive. There is still a fair amount of what some people label "donkey work" in the library. If, occasionally, all library staff do some of the "donkey work," for example helping out with unusually heavy mail or book deliveries, the staff members who perform this work full-time will see that their efforts are important to the success of the library. (Ed Evans, the longtime author of this book, recalls the words of the library director at his first professional job: "I expect everyone to get their hands dirty whenever necessary. When it comes to the work, there are only library staff—no librarians and clerks." Those have proven to be words worth remembering and implementing throughout Ed's career.) Using part-time staff for these duties can help reduce turnover. Another method is to provide cross-training for staff in several areas. This not only gives the staff some variety but also enables the library to provide coverage of areas during vacations and sick leave or when a staff member resigns.

Part-Time Nonprofessional Staff

Part-time employees are often students or retired persons who work just a few hours per week. There are many library duties suitable for people working fewer than twenty hours per week, such as sorting and delivering mail, bibliographic checking, attaching spine labels, attaching plastic book jackets, and affixing and recording bar code labels. Like clerical work, this work is often very routine but nevertheless requires accuracy. Part-time staff often require more supervisory time and attention than do full-time personnel. This is true even when the number of total working hours is the same for full- and part-time staff. Two half-time people often require double the supervision of one full-time person.

It is possible to keep clerical turnover down by using a variety of management techniques, but it is almost impossible to control part-time turnover. Low pay, routine work, and better full-time employment opportunities inevitably cause a constant cycle of recruitment, selection, training, supervision, and termination.

When the part-timers are full-time students, there is yet another dimension to the situation. For most full-time students, their schooling is paramount, as it should be. However, test schedules, vacation periods, term paper deadlines, and a host of other crises create a workforce that is not always dependable. Normally, full-time staff must cover for absent part-timers, which of course means that their regular tasks go undone.

There are challenges in having part-time staff, especially students, but there are some basic steps to make their employment worthwhile for all concerned. The key is to use the same selection, orientation, and training for all staff whether they are full- or part-time. All too often part-timers do not get the same orientation or depth of training. This is the result of a self-fulfilling prophecy: "They won't stay long so there is no point in spending time orienting and training them." Not surprisingly, more often than not they do leave.

Giving the new part-timer an orientation and training on both the job *and* how that work is an essential element in the library's service program provides the person with a sense that his or her efforts are important and worth doing well. Knowing the library's mission as well as how the various departments interact to achieve it also helps part-timers understand the context of their tasks. Orienting them only to the department does little to show the ultimate worth of the work.

When working with students there are several issues that do not come up with other part-timers. First, there is the annual cycle of the academic term. There are the challenges of a changing workforce as terms start and end, scheduled holidays occur, term paper "crunch time" comes, and examinations take place. This cycle also means there are training challenges: large numbers of students to orient and train in a very short period of time. It is difficult to train a large number of students without careful planning. The planning is relatively easy compared to how to train them in using equipment and systems in spaces where only one or two actually work at the same time.

A second issue is the narrow time window between selection, training, and having to do the work. Students rarely return more than a day or two before the term starts, so there is little opportunity for spreading the training out and giving individuals time to practice. This usually means either a superficial orientation to a host of situations that may arise or a highly selective set of skills that the immediate supervisor is concerned about at the time.

Trainers who must also carry out their "normal duties" during the training period also have a time crunch: how to perform their other duties while conducting the training. If the training is not considered a major duty, the person may not give the part-timers the attention they deserve and need to become effective employees. One way to make the importance of the training clear to all concerned, including senior management, is to have the work be a significant part of the person's annual performance review.

Another useful step, especially for student workers, is to have both a job description and a set of performance expectations for *all* part-time positions. The material does not have to be complex but should outline key activities, results, behavior, and skills needed, as well as two or three performance expectations.

A final step, more often an issue with student employees, is follow-up training. There is seldom time to cover everything that may come up for the students in a single session; in fact, it is not always a good idea to try to do so. Single-session training for students is rather common. Saving the infrequent situations for later follow-up sessions, after the individuals have had time to practice the basic or key activities, also permits the trainer to address any problems in those areas.

Nonprofessional Volunteers

Volunteers are important in staffing many libraries; however, they are a mixed blessing. The initial thought is, "Of course we can use some free help." Certainly in school media centers and small public libraries volunteers play a critical role. From the budget point of view, one can easily see the pros and cons of using volunteers. Limited funds for staffing make using volunteers appealing, especially if one has tried and failed to get a new staff position approved. But if a volunteer "helps out for a while" and the work gets done, all too often the budget officers see no reason to approve additional staff. A comprehensive study of library volunteers that includes useful information for public libraries in any country is *The Use of Volunteers in Public Libraries.*[21]

Libraries have had volunteer programs for years. However, since the mid-1970s, when budget constraints led to at least hiring freezes, if not staff reductions, securing an additional full-time equivalent (FTE) position for a library has been and remains a rare event. There has been a growing use of volunteers, who are more and more called upon to perform necessary work rather than work that is nice to have done if there is extra time. That change carries with it important implications for the salaried staff. One result of the budget crunch is that small libraries, especially those in schools and small towns, are all too often completely dependent on volunteers to provide any level of service. Many libraries outside the corporate environment have some volunteers working on their behalf even if they do not have a formal volunteer program.

A few years ago there was a national publicity effort to promote the importance and value of volunteerism. At the beginning of 2002, there was little evidence that the publicity has done much to increase the number of volunteers. Some press coverage focused on building volunteerism and service into educational curricula in high schools and colleges. This is not a new concept; John Dewey pushed it in the 1930s. There are, and long have been, many successful educational programs of that type, including in libraries. One such example is a joint project of the St. Paul (Minnesota) Public Library and public school system. They created a library youth volunteer corps, a mentoring program that involves teaching others how to use library technology such as online catalogs and CD-ROM products.

Another factor that may increase the use of "volunteers" in publicly funded libraries is government initiatives in some jurisdictions, commonly known as "welfare reform." One component of the "from welfare to work" concept is some community service. Because many libraries are public institutions, there will be an expectation that libraries *will* take on their share of former welfare recipients, who must perform as much as forty hours of community service work per week. The "community service" component now appears to be an established element in such programs. This will probably result in increasing pressure on public and school libraries to take on more and more "volunteers," especially in communities where the libraries say they are in need of staff. Two additional "volunteer" programs that present both opportunities and challenges are court-ordered community service and work placement programs.

There will be a number of challenges for existing full- and part-time paid staff in a situation where the library takes on some of the participants in such a program. One expectation is that the "host site" will provide the volunteers with opportunities that both help establish an appropriate work behavior pattern—such as on-time, regularly scheduled attendance—and develop work skills to prepare them to be more competitive in the labor market. The first goal will not be too much of a challenge because an existing volunteer program has the same expectations for all its participants: Often work schedules are an area of flexibility in existing programs to retain the volunteer help.

However, the second goal, developing marketable job skills, may present a challenge in at least two ways. First, many of the tasks that libraries have for volunteers are specific to the library environment, especially given the high degree of automation in libraries. Thus the tasks that are available do not translate well into the general labor market. (Perhaps if libraries can count on the community service component lasting for a number of years, it would be possible to create the equivalent of several FTEs for participants. These FTEs could be incorporated in the regular operating procedures, performing necessary rather than desirable activities.)

A second factor is the amount of staff time necessary to train and supervise program participants. Anyone who has been a supervisor of an intern—someone who is taking course work and wants a career in the field—knows how much time that activity takes. Further complicating the issue is the level of motivation of the participants, which may not be high. Library trainers need to learn how to increase or maintain a high level of motivation. Motivation of volunteers is always a factor in any program and becomes more important with welfare-to-work participants. One hopes that some of the groups identified in Georgean Johnson-Coffey's article[22] as currently involved in working with welfare reform participants will publish their experiences to assist other libraries starting a program.

Volunteers have become an important element in operating many types of libraries and are likely to increase in number as a result of welfare reform initiatives. A review of literature on volunteerism suggests "that effective management of volunteer activities in public organizations requires a management style that is less technically rational and bureaucratic than the traditional model . . . at a very minimum, a public organization using volunteers as well as paid staff must be flexible to accommodate two work forces with very different expectations and backgrounds."[23]

Depending on the amount of background a volunteer brings to the job, training and supervisory time can far exceed that needed to train and supervise a person the library would hire. No matter how much knowledge and skill they bring with them, volunteers usually require more supervisory time than do paid staff. Supervisors, or "volunteer coordinators," must devote time to working and interacting with the volunteers. Volunteers' "salaries" come in the form of satisfaction in knowing the library fully appreciates their efforts, so the coordinators should spend time providing positive feedback to maintain volunteer interest and willingness to contribute their time. Providing corrective feedback that does not cause the volunteer to quit is also a challenge for the coordinator. Normally the library has fewer corrective options with volunteer staff than with paid personnel, and the coordinator needs excellent "people skills" to bring about the desired change while retaining the volunteer.

If the volunteer works alongside permanent staff, different treatment for the volunteer can cause serious staff morale problems. An excellent guide to using volunteers is Carla Campbell's *Volunteer Involvement in California Libraries: Best Practices.*[24] This publication addresses all aspects of volunteer work, including full-time staff reactions and relations. It also contains a number of forms and materials used in libraries across the state. Richard Sundeen has been researching the topic for more than ten years. One of his articles, published in 2000, addressed the value of and obstacles to teenagers becoming volunteers;[25] another, "Differences in Personal Goals and Attitudes Among Volunteers," appeared in 1992.[26]

STAFF DEVELOPMENT AND TRAINING

One key to having a successful customer service–oriented library is making certain *all* staff have adequate and appropriate training and development opportunities. (Training funds are sometimes the most difficult to secure from funding authorities.) There are several types of needs and opportunities. Needs are related to a person's specific job duties; opportunities may or may not be directly job related. Those libraries that provide opportunities for and encourage all staff to continue their education generally have high morale.

There is no question that staff needs continuous updated training as libraries add to or upgrade existing technology. (Because securing training funds is difficult, it is sometimes helpful to have a vendor include the cost for training the staff in the price of the hardware or software rather than attempting to secure separate training funds.) One "downside" of technology is that it changes constantly and there is a never-ending need for staff and customers to adjust to the changes and receive frequent training.

Chapter 1 noted the impact technology has had on technical services. There are probably few, if any, large or medium-sized libraries that are not virtually closed when their computer systems go down. With "integrated" library systems handling most of basic library functions and local networks providing "productivity software," such as word processing and spreadsheet applications, library staff members often spend a substantial part, if not all, of their workday at a PC or terminal. When one adds an ever-increasing variety of electronic services, there is almost no full-time staff member who would not benefit from some training on a software package or system upgrade. (There is a need for ergonomic training for staff who spend several hours a day "online." There is also a management responsibility to ensure that workstations are ergonomically correct.) Libraries must think about three types of technology training needs: existing staff, new hires, and customers. Where does the library turn for such training?

Vendors are one option; especially those who handle integrated library systems and those selling electronic products. Unfortunately, most of the system vendors charge for their training, which usually means newly hired staff must receive their training from existing staff. This works well if the existing staff fully understand the system. Marketing needs may force vendors of electronic products to offer free training; this is a "service" the library should take advantage of, especially because it is built into the cost of the product.

The least desirable approach is to try to do in-house (self) training based on vendor documentation; however, it may be the only immediately available option. When necessary, the most cost-effective approach is having the most experienced person work through the material and then teach other staff members. If the product affects most of the departments in the library, using a "mentor" approach often is effective. That is, one person in each department becomes the "teacher or expert" and works with colleagues as a trainer.

Another option is to seek workshops offered by various library groups. For example, almost every vendor of integrated library systems has a "users' group"—customers using the product who have some voice in how the product changes. Users' groups often have regional "chapters" that have occasional meetings at which experiences are exchanged, as well as holding workshops on a new "module" or upgrade. Sometimes library consortia acquire an electronic product or service and then arrange one or more workshops for staff members in the use of the item. State, provincial, regional, and national library association meetings are other sources for workshops that are job related; many now offer programs designed for librarians and paraprofessionals. The major drawback to all these sources is that a particular type of training may not be available when a library most needs it.

Productivity software training is another matter. If the library's parent organization does not provide training, the library must either handle it in-house or use a commercial training organization. Commercial training is usually available in larger communities for most of the widely used word processing, database management, graphics presentation, and spreadsheet applications. Companies often offer several levels of training—beginning, intermediate, and advanced—so there is some hope of getting the training at the level needed. Expect to pay a price for such availability, often $300 to $400 per person for six hours of training. Another option is to use video or CD-ROM training packages that cost about the same as the fee for a single person at a commercial program. The obvious advantage of this approach is that many staff members can benefit from the expenditure, and they can select the best time for them to take the training. One such source (and there are others; this is not an endorsement) of productivity and network training programs is Learn Key, a company that the LMU library uses.

Organizations such as OCLC (http://www.oclc.org/support/training) and the National Library of Canada are major resources for technical service training. Also, universities with library schools frequently offer continuing education programs; two examples are the University of Toronto and the University of California, Los Angeles. The LMU library's cataloging department sends all new staff to OCLC training as soon as possible and makes extensive use of the advanced training offerings. Other training opportunities are frequently offered by regional OCLC organizations such as CAPCON or SOLINET, with a substantial discount for system members.

All staff should have opportunities to develop personal skills and knowledge that may or may not be directly job related. Encouraging staff to secure an academic degree, whether library related or not, is good for overall staff morale. In fact, the better educated the staff is, the better service the library is likely to provide. When staff members know there is support for self-development they generally view the library as more than the place they have to spend time to get a paycheck. Such an attitude often translates into high-quality performance and customer service.

Staff training is essential and costs money as well as time away from "normal duties." One public library director estimated that he spends about 1 percent of the total operating budget on staff training (in this case just over U.S. $150,000 in 1995) and wondered if that was even enough.[27] Loyola Marymount Libraries plan for just under 1 percent but know that by year's end they will exceed that amount and still not have addressed all the year's training needs. We agree with the following statement by Glen Holt:

> One thing is certain, however, no library can create a customer-oriented information-and-knowledge institution without considerable staff training. A solid staff training program is an operational imperative for an effective bottom line in the twenty-first-century library, and library budgets need to reflect the library training effort.[28]

SUMMARY

The function of the paraprofessional, regardless of the type of library, is to assume clerical and paraprofessional duties so librarians can perform professional-level work. In the Suggested Reading section of this chapter are listed older items related to paraprofessional issues; they contain information that is still useful and valid.

NOTES

1. Michael Gorman, "Innocent Pleasures," In *The Future Is Now: The Changing Face of Technical Services,* proceedings of the OCLC symposium, ALA Midwinter Conference, Los Angeles, February 4, 1994 (Dublin, OH: OCLC, 1994), 40.

2. Liz Lane and Barbara Stewart, "The Evolution of Technical Services to Serve the Digital Academic Library," in *Recreating the Academic Library: Breaking Virtual Ground,* edited by Cheryl LaGuardia (New York: Neal-Schuman, 1998), 156.

3. Paula Kaufman, "Professional Diversity in Libraries," *Library Trends* 41 (Fall 1992): 214.

4. Brian Nettleford, "Paraprofessionalism in Librarianship," *International Library Review* 21 (1989): 519-531.

5. Nettleford, "Paraprofessionalism in Librarianship," 522.

6. Ibid., 523.

7. Janet S. Hill, "Why Are There So Few of Us? Educating Librarians for Technical Services," *Colorado Libraries* 26 (Spring 2000): 411-414.

8. Ibid., 43.

9. Lisa German and Karen Schmidt, "Acquisitions," in *Advances in Librarianship* vol. 24, edited by Elizabeth Chapman and Frederick Lynden (New York: Academic Press, 2000), 141.

10. Frances Davidson-Arnott and Deborah Kay, "Library Technician Programs: Skills-Oriented Paraprofessional Education," *Library Trends* 46 (Winter 1998):444-467.

11. Jean Riddle Weihs, "The Library Technician," in *Canadian Libraries in Their Changing Environment*, edited by Lorraine Spencer Garry and Carl Garry (Toronto: York University Centre for Continuing Education, 1977), 420-442.

12. Guidelines have been amended through the years. Some still worth considering are Canadian Library Association, Task Force on Roles and Responsibilities of Librarians and Library Technicians, *Roles and Responsibilities of Librarians and Library Technicians* (Ottawa: Canadian Library Association, 1989); Canadian School Library Association, Committee on the Role of the Library Technician in Respect to School Libraries, *The Qualifications for Library Technicians Working in School Systems* (Ottawa: Canadian Library Association, 1985); and Canadian Library Association, Task Force on the Professional Review Process for Library Technician Programs in Canada, *Guidelines for the Education of Library Technicians* (Ottawa: Canadian Library Association, 1991). A view of Canadian programs in the mid-1990s can be found in Jean Weihs, "Technical Services Education for Library Technicians in the 1990s," *Technical Services Quarterly* 15, nos. 1/2 (1997): 43-50.

13. By 1973 five surveys had been done by John Marshall. These annual surveys were continued by Jean Weihs until mid-1980 and then by Ann Galler.

14. Anthony Wilson and Robert Hermanson, "Educating and Training Library Practitioners," *Library Trends* 46 (Winter 1998): 467-504.

15. Jean Riddle, "Professionalism for Library Technicians," *Ontario Library Review* 55 (March 1971): 17-18.

16. Wilson and Hermanson, "Educating and Training Library Practitioners," 491.

17. United States Department of Education, No. 8 from 6th edition. Manpower Development and Training Program. *A Suggested Two-Year Post High School Curriculum: Library Technical Assistant* (Washington, D.C.: U.S. Government Printing Office, 1973), 5–6.

18. Larry Oberg, Mark Mentges, P. N. McDermott, and Vitoon Harusadangkul, "The Role, Status, and Working Conditions of Paraprofessionals," *College & Research Libraries* 53, no. 3 (1992): 215-238.

19. Jina Choi Wakimoto and Gina Hsiung, "Blurring the Boundaries Between Professional and Paraprofessional Catalogers at California State University, Northridge," *Library Collections, Acquisitions & Technical Services* 24, no. 2 (2000): 171-188.

20. Susan Chapman, "Paraprofessionals in a Cataloguing Unit," *Canadian Library Journal* 41 (August 1984): 190.

21. Noeleen Cookman, David Haynes, and David Streatfield, *The Use of Volunteers in Public Libraries* (London: Library Association, 2000).

22. Georgean Johnson-Coffey, "Trends in Volunteerism," *Bottom Line* 10, no. 2 (1997): 60–64.

23. Virginia Walters, "For All the Wrong Reasons? Implementing Volunteer Programs in Public Organizations," *Public Productivity & Management Review* 16 (Spring 1993): 271-287.

24. Carla Campbell, *Volunteer Involvement in California Libraries: Best Practices* (Sacramento: California State Library, 1999).

25. Richard Sundeen and Sally Raskoff, "Ports of Entry and Obstacles: Teenagers Access to Volunteer Activities," *Nonprofit Management & Leadership* 11 (Winter 2000): 179-197.

26. Richard Sundeen, "Differences in Personal Goals and Attitudes Among Volunteers," *Nonprofit and Voluntary Sector Quarterly* 21, no. 3 (1992): 271-291.

27. Glen Holt, "Staff Training: How Much Is Enough?" *Bottom Line* 9, no. 1 (1996): 43.

28. Ibid., 44.

SUGGESTED READING

American Association of School Librarians. Certification of School Media Specialist Committee. *Paraprofessional Support Staff for School Library Media Programs—A Competency Statement.* Chicago: American Library Association, 1978.

American Library Association. Library Education Division. "Criteria for Programs to Prepare Library/Media Technical Assistants." *American Libraries* 2, no. 10 (November 1971): 1059-1063.

Bakke, Celia. *Training of Technical Services Staff in the Automated Environment.* Washington, DC: Association of Research Libraries, Office of Management Services, 1991.

Bazirjian, Rosann, and Nancy Markle Stanley. "Assessing the Effectiveness of Team-based Structures in Libraries." *Library Collections, Acquisitions, and Technical Services* 25 (Summer 2001): 131-157.

Beales, Karen. "Non-professional Information and Training." *Education for Information* 7 (March 1989): 29-41.

Bednar, Marie. "Hiring Tests for Technical Services Support Staff." *Technical Services Quarterly* 11, no. 1 (1993): 3-19.

Boelke, Joanne. *Library Technicians: A Survey of Current Developments.* Review Series, no. 1. Minneapolis, MN: ERIC Clearinghouse for Library and Information Sciences, 1968.

Bucknall, Tim. "Techno Teamwork." *North Carolina Libraries* 54 (Winter 1996): 161-164.

Campbell, Allen, and Irene Dawson, eds. *The Library Technician at Work: Theory and Practice: Proceedings of the Workshop Held at Lakehead University, Thunder Bay, Ontario, May 8-9, 1970.* Ottawa: Canadian Library Association, 1970.

"Career Development: Defining the Issues of the Nineties: A Paraprofessional Movement." *Library Journal* 114 (July 1989): 52-55.

Cervera, Barbara. "There Is Life After Technical Services." *Technicalities* 21 (May/June 2001): 10-11.

Chirgwin, F. John, and Phyllis Oldfield. *The Library Assistant's Manual.* 3rd ed. London: Clive Bingley, 1988.

Cohen, Lucy R. "Creating a New Classification System for Technical and Supervisory Library Support Staff." *Journal of Library Administration* 10, no. 4 (1989): 59-85.

Cookman, Noeleen, David Haynes, and David Streatfield. *The Use of Volunteers in Public Libraries.* London: Library Association, 2000.

Duda, Andrea L. "Staff Empowerment: Effective Training for Greater Responsibilities." *Technical Services Quarterly* 16, no. 4 (1999): 11-33.

El-Sherbini, Magda. "Changes in Technical Services and Their Effect on the Role of Catalogers and Staff Education." *Cataloging & Classification Quarterly* 24, nos. 1/2 (1997): 23-33.

Folsom, Sandy L. "Out of the Nest: The Cataloger in a Public Service Role." *Library Collections, Acquisitions, and Technical Services* 24 (Spring 2001): 65-71.

Fuller, F. Jay. "Employing Library Student Assistants as Student Supervisors." *College & Research Library News* (October 1990): 855-857.

Gill, Suzanne. "Comparing Two Criteria." *COLT Newsletter* 12, no. 11 (December 1979): 1-20.

Halstead, Deborah D., and Dana M. Neely. "The Importance of the Library Technician." *Library Journal* 115 (March 1, 1990): 62-63.

Howarth, Lynne. "The Role of the Paraprofessional in Technical Services in Libraries." *Library Trends* 46 (Winter 1998): 526-539.

Jasper, Richard. "Reorganizing Collections and Technical Services: Staffing Is Key." *Library Acquisitions* 16 (Winter 1992): 361-366.

Johnson, Judy. "Coping with Personnel Issues Due to Reorganization." *Technical Services Quarterly* 16, no. 2 (1998): 60-62.

Jones, Dorothy E. "Library Support Staff and Technology: Perceptions and Opinions." *Library Trends* 37 (Spring 1989): 432-456.

Kenreich, Mary Ellen. "Physical Settings and Organizational Success." *Library Collections, Acquisitions, and Technical Services* 25 (Spring 2001): 67-79.

Kew, Dorothy. "Library Technicians in Ontario: They've Come a Long Way." *Ontario Library Review* 64, no. 1 (March 1980): 38-43.

Lehn, Carla. *Volunteer Involvement in California Libraries: Best Practices.* Sacramento: California State Library, 1999.

Library Technology in California Junior Colleges: Papers Presented at a Conference on the Training of Library Technical Assistants. Washington, DC: Communication Service Corporation, 1968.

McGrath, Marsha, and Jana Fine. "Teen Volunteers in the Library." *Public Libraries* 29 (January 1990): 24-28.

Mohr, Deborah A., and Anita Schuneman. "Changing Roles: Original Cataloging by Paraprofessionals in ARL Libraries." *Library Resources & Technical Services* 41, no. 3 (July 1997): 205-218.

Moriarity, Wendy. "The New Breed: Library Technicians in Canada." *Canadian Library Journal* 39, no. 4 (August 1982): 237-239.

Morris, Dilys E., Collin B. Hobert, and Lori Lynn Osmus. "Cataloging Staff Costs Revisited." *Library Resources & Technical Services* 44 (April 2000): 70-83.

Pantazis, Fotoula. "Library Technicians in Ontario Academic Libraries." *Canadian Library Journal* 35, no. 2 (April 1978): 77-91.

Rakovszky, Ingeborg, comp. *Bibliography of Library Technology.* Thunder Bay, ON: OALT/ABO Thunder Bay Regional Branch, 1976.

Riddle, Jean. "Professionalism for Library Technicians." *Ontario Library Review* 55, no. 1 (March 1971): 17-18. Reprinted in *Reader in Library Technology*, edited by Shirley Gray Adamovich, 94-95. Englewood, CO: Microcard Editions Books, 1975.

Roy, Loriene. "Use of Volunteers in Public Libraries." *Public Library Quarterly* 8, nos. 1/2 (1987/1988): 127-145.

Silverman, Scott. "Is Technical Services Being De-Professionalized?" *Library Collections, Acquisitions and Technical Services* 23 (Spring 1999): 107-108.

Smith, Glenda "Aiming for Continuous Improvement: Performance Measurement in a Re-engineered Technical Services." *Library Collections, Acquisitions, and Technical Services* 25 (Spring 2001): 81-92.

Strasner, Teresa. "Continuing Education Needs for Technical Services Paraprofessionals in Academic Libraries." *Colorado Libraries* 26 (Spring 2000): 2-4.

Tijerino, Cathy. "Implementing Teams for Technical Services Functions." *Serials Librarian* 28, nos. 3/4 (1996): 361-365.

Weihs, Jean, with Warren Grabinsky. "Library Technicians in School Systems: The Story Behind the Document: The Ad Hoc Committee on the Role of the Library Technician in Respect to School Libraries." *School Libraries in Canada* 4, no. 4 (Summer 1984): 17-21.

Weihs, Jean. *Library Technician*. 4th ed. Guidance Centre Occupational Information. Toronto: Guidance Centre Faculty of Education, University of Toronto, 1981.

———. "Library Technician Training in Canada." *COLT Newsletter* 14, no. 11 (November/December 1981): 2-3.

Weihs, Jean Riddle. "The College-Trained Library Technician (The New Non-Mechanical Miracle Ingredient)." *APLA Bulletin* 38, no. 2 (Summer 1974): 44-45.

———. "Library Technicians, a Personal View." *Emergency Librarian* 4, no. 1 (September/October 1976): 24-26. Reprinted in *LTBC* 9, no. 3 (February 1983): 3-4.

Wilson, Anthony, and Robert Hermanson. "Educating and Training Library Practitioners." *Library Trends* 46 (Winter 1998): 467-504.

Wilson, Pauline. *Stereotype and Status: Librarians in the United States*. Westport, CT: Greenwood Press, 1982.

Wright, Alice E. *Library Clerical Workers and Pages (Including Student Assistants)*. Hamden, CT: Linnet Books, 1973.

REVIEW QUESTIONS

1. What are the usual categories of library employees?
2. Discuss the issues related to education of professionals for technical services work.
3. What are the differences between professional and paraprofessional duties, especially in the area of cataloging?
4. What are the differences between paraprofessional, clerical, and part-time staff duties?
5. What are the advantages and disadvantages of using volunteers?
6. Discuss the major issues related to staff training and development.

Technical Services Administration

In "Technical Services Organization," Cecily Johns wrote that the motto for cataloging and technical services is and will be "more, better, cheaper, faster."[1] These are shorthand labels for what today's administrators of technical services units must constantly address. This chapter covers how unit heads in technical services try to respond to those needs. The first sections of this chapter are organized around those labels, in a slightly different order: more, faster/better, cheaper.

Supervising or administering a unit in technical services calls upon all of the same basic management skills and knowledge as does any other unit in the library. However, some of those "basic" skills are being called upon with ever-increasing frequency as libraries try to adjust to a changing external environment. Some of the skills that need to come into play more often are managing change, fostering innovation and creativity, cost containment, team building, and staff motivation.

THE "MORE" FACTOR

For most libraries in the 1980s and early 1990s, "more" did not mean higher volumes of books and serials to acquire, catalog, and process. The "more" was and is the expanding range of material formats that have to be dealt with on a regular basis. A seemingly constantly changing "information industry" that creates, and occasionally drops, new formats for delivering material has generated pressures on technical service units. Electronic materials quickly demonstrated that libraries had to "gear up" to handle not only constant change but also very rapid shifts in direction. In addition, as economic conditions improved, there has been some increase in library budgets that allows for increasing the volume of print materials acquired; however, in many instances that increase falls upon a significantly reduced technical services staff.

As both a library school educator and library administrator for many years, Ed Evans has experienced those events from both the classroom/conceptual point of view and the "how are we going to deal with this development" practical perspective. The factors noted in Chapter 1 as leading to the changing shape of technical services—economic, technological, and financial—make it difficult for practitioners to keep abreast of the shifting landscape of information resources and still get today's work done.

For practitioners a major problem is finding time to carry out necessary duties and attempt to learn about the most critical new developments in their area(s) of responsibility. Time management is one of the skills that technical services supervisors and administrators increasingly must call upon. To learn about new formats, who handles them, pricing/discount models, how to represent the format in a MARC record or OPAC, and so forth takes more time than outsiders realize, and the day's ongoing work does not stop. Most of the time, the new formats do not replace an existing format; rather each is just one *more* for the unit to handle.

Whereas public, school, and community college libraries have a long history of acquiring and building collections of audiovisual and nonbook formats, the same is not true of large academic libraries. Today, with the proliferation of electronic databases, even the largest research libraries are adding formats that fifteen to twenty years ago were considered inappropriate for their collections.

An example of the problems encountered when adding a new format to a library's collecting profile is what took place at Harvard University when Edward Evans was head of the anthropology library. Interviews with the full-time faculty and graduate teaching assistants revealed a strong demand for adding ethnographic and archaeological videocassettes to the collection for both teaching and research purposes. At that time, Harvard College Libraries collected only print materials. When the first invoices for videos arrived in the central accounting office, the result was a telephone call stating that this type of purchase was not allowed. After considerable discussion, a decision was reached that, if the anthropology library could secure grant money for such purchases, they would be acceptable. It was relatively easy to find some "seed funds" to establish a collection, but securing ongoing funding from granting agencies was next to impossible. The budget committee asked for an in-person presentation as well as a written document explaining why operating funds should be allocated for nonprint acquisitions. (It was notable there were no such requests to justify the 30 percent increase in book funds and a 42 percent increase in the serials budgets—both were granted without comment.) Finding the funds was the easy part of the process; learning about sources, establishing business relationships, determining how to handle the cataloging in a system not set up for anything but print materials, and so forth, required significant amounts of technical service staff time. Most of the staff were longtime employees who had no prior experience with video and felt this was a major increase in their workload, yet they were happy about the very substantial budget increases for print materials. With effort the staff made the transition to handling a new format.

This example highlights two facets of the current technical services environment: time allocation/availability and staff morale. Although the underlying steps for handling the new format or material may be the same as for other materials, there are special characteristics that make each one a separate process, thus requiring remembering many more details. Some formats carry with them issues that require new steps or procedures. One example is legal issues associated with electronic resources, such as licensing agreements and contracts (covered in more detail in Chapters 7 and 11).

Extra steps or procedures, even having to think "what do I need to do differently with this format," take a little more time. Unfortunately, time is finite. While there is always a chance, however remote, of acquiring additional money, people, or other resources, there is no chance of expanding the time available. All one can do is use time as effectively as possible or find new ways of doing things that are more efficient.

TIPS FOR EFFECTIVE TIME MANAGEMENT

Being a good manager of time can assist in more ways than just "getting more work done." It can help reduce work stress for one's own benefit (and sometimes for one's colleagues as well). For some individuals, it may also assist in delegation of activities or reduce the tendency to "put off until tomorrow whatever one can do today" behavior.

These tips are relatively easy to implement; what is more difficult is to follow them long enough to make them habits rather than special activities. Perhaps the least complicated but hardest to follow is avoiding the "paper shuffle" game. In most work situations, there is a steady flow of paper across the desk or into the in-basket. Some of it is informational in nature and should be the easiest to read and dispose of. Too often there is a tendency to quickly look at such items and think, "I'll get to this later when I have more time" and set it aside in what becomes an ever-growing pile of "when I have time reading." For many people that growing pile (mountain) becomes a source of stress because "when I have time" never seems to come. Reading the material when it arrives and taking the appropriate action—file it for future reference, pass it on, or recycle the paper—will resolve the problem.

Some material may call for a response by a given date. Again, responding right away will save time in the long run. There is a tendency to think, "Oh, this is due in two weeks (or whenever), I'll do this later." If nothing more, handling the matter immediately saves the review time involved in rereading the material at the time the response is due. In addition, given that many issues arise unexpectedly, having completed an "expected" project ahead of time allows for more flexibility in responding to "rush" projects that suddenly appear. Waiting until later may lead to the item getting mislaid until after the date due, and that can cause an even greater expenditure of time and effort by various people. There are items that require some searching for information or just straightforward time to think about before taking the appropriate action; a useful method for handling such items is to have a filing system based on action time requirements—start tomorrow, the day after, in three days, and so forth. (This approach also helps organize time, as discussed later.)

A few items are complex or difficult "projects" that may seem overwhelming. One way to handle those items is to establish a "finish date" that is slightly earlier than the required date and break the activity into small, daily actions to maintain a sense of progress and a measure of success.

Perhaps the second most common suggestion for managing time is to create "to-do" lists. Using a file folder system is a sound variation of the to-do list. Set up a file for each day of the week, one for next week, two weeks, and three weeks, thus covering a month. The files can hold some of the papers mentioned previously that require some time to address. Each day just before leaving work go into the next day's folder and set up the priorities for the items in the folder (the next day's to-do list). This establishes for the next day the items to attend to and their priorities. It is a good idea to make the first item something of high interest and relatively easy to accomplish; this creates a positive sense of achievement that may carry over into less interesting but necessary activities. At the end of each work week, again at the end of the day, go through the next week's folder and sort the material into the appropriate folders by the day each item should be handled. Certainly setting up such a system takes some time, and the daily review does so as well; however, as one of the authors can attest, it saves a surprising amount of time in the long run.

Interruptions are one of the most common reasons given for not having enough time. "If it weren't for all the interruptions I'd be fine," is a lament of many staff members. Interruptions cost time, even when they are warranted, because they fragment one's activities. It always takes a few minutes to get back to where one left off in a task or thinking after the interruption. The two most frequent sources of interruptions are the telephone and colleagues "dropping by." Managing the telephone is easier to handle than workmates, but both can be done without offending people.

With telephone calls, batch the necessary ones and spend a few minutes planning each: "What do I need to convey or learn." Make a list for each call and stick to it. Use a large writing pad to keep all the notes and lists together. (Looking for the lunch napkin, business card, or empty envelope with the needed information is a great time waster.) Time management consultants often suggest that a business call should not require more than three minutes.[2] If the matter is too complex or detailed to handle in that time, consider some form of written communication. This is a useful guideline for the majority of calls, but there are exceptions, especially when developing or maintaining a working relationship with someone in another organization, such as a library vendor or bindery firm. It is also good, if not always possible, to batch return calls. A useful approach to handling incoming calls, at least from other library staff members and those with whom one works closely on a regular basis, is to tell people "the best time to call me is between x and y." Although this does not and should not stop calls from coming in at other times, it does in time lead to batching of many, if not most, incoming calls. During that calling time frame, engage in activities that take less concentration, making the interruptions less of a problem.

In today's technology environment, e-mail can become almost as big a time waster as the telephone. Use the same approach to e-mail as to the telephone. Batch the reading of and responses to these messages. Don't fall into the pattern of leaving your e-mail active all day or frequently checking to see whether there is mail if you want to make the most effective use of your time.

With colleagues, if at all possible, try to establish time frames when "dropping by" is welcome and times when dropping by is not welcome. For supervisors, it is a little easier to establish times when staff can just come by with questions as well as some time during the day when "the door is closed," even if there is no physical door to close. In smoothly running units, establishing such times for everyone is relatively easy. In times of change or uncertainty creating such time is problematic, but even in those circumstances having some private work time can be beneficial. However, supervisors need to make it clear that a "closed door time" does not mean they are unavailable for unusual or emergency situations.

Sometimes a person likes to engage in "small talk" before and after getting to the purpose of the visit. Frequently these are also individuals who, if allowed, will spend more time on the informal and social aspects of the "visit" than on the issue in question. Setting time limits and sticking to them—"I can give you xx minutes"—is a sound method for any interruption, unless of course the person in question is a supervisor. However, a supervisor should be as concerned about effective time usage as the person interrupted and take no more time than necessary. Finally, there is nothing wrong with asking people what it is they want to discuss, in a polite way, if they are having trouble getting to the point.

There are many other time management techniques; several books on this topic are listed in the Suggested Reading section of this chapter.

THE "FASTER/BETTER/CHEAPER" FACTORS

Certainly the Internet has contributed significantly to the "more" factor. On the plus side, it has helped with the faster/better factors. Think of the Internet as just another tool rather like the MARC format that facilitates more effective use of time and effort.

For example, in the not-so-distant past libraries often compared working practices and policies by conducting a field trip or site visit to neighboring libraries. Although such trips still occur, they are becoming rare. In their place, staff use the Internet through e-mail systems and discussion lists to post questions such as, "How do you handle x?" In addition to saving travel time and expenses, responses can come in from around the world in some cases and staff can draw on a much wider range of experience. Furthermore, discussion lists help keep the staff informed about new developments and issues. Technical service librarians and senior paraprofessional staff usually subscribe to several such lists.

Each of the topics covered in this book has a number of Web sites devoted to it. There are URLs throughout the book, but these addresses were last verified during the final proofreading and may well have changed. A good starting point, no matter what library topic is of interest, is the *Internet Library for Librarians* (http://www.itcompany.com/inforetriever).

Although collection development is only of passing interest for this book, a number of Web sites are useful to both collection development staff and acquisitions personnel. These range from information producer home pages (an example is the Association of American University Presses—AAUP—http://aaup.princeton.edu) to general online vendors such as Amazon (http://www.amazon.com). Looking for an out-of-print (OP) title? Try Bibliofind at http://www.bibliofind.com. Sites like the last two provide links to reviews and other information as well as providing the ordering capability. A few offer Boolean searching in addition to the expected author, title, publisher, and ISBN (International Standard Book Number) searches.

Acquisition Web sites are covered in more detail in Chapters 7 and 8, but a few general points are worthy of mention here, given that the capabilities they provide can be considered management tools. Almost all library vendors now have a Web presence and at least a limited search capability of their databases in conjunction with online ordering. Some offer electronic invoicing and downloading, at least with some ILS systems. A library's ability to take advantage of these electronic services is, in part, dependent on the relationship between the library's ILS vendor and other library vendors. The interface between the ILS and vendor systems is something these firms must resolve. All the library can do is press both firms to create, maintain, and improve the interface. Carol Pitts (now Carol Diedricks) outlined the problem of technology and vendors in "Using Automation in Technical Services to Foster Innovation":

> For example, the Ohio State University Libraries (OSUL) was an early test site for OCLC's PromptCat. The library tested the product in early 1994 and made the decision at that time that it was an innovation that would be adopted to free staff for more complex cataloging. However, OSUL had to first wait for Innovative Interfaces, Inc. (III) to write the necessary programming to incorporate the new product. Once the programming was available, the Libraries' approval plan vendor, Baker &Taylor, was in the midst of a system change which precluded them from completing their implementation of the product. Finally, in 1997, the Libraries are in the actual implementation stage of a product which was tested and adopted in 1994.[3]

A specific example of how technology assists in the "faster/better" side of acquisitions work is in the area of letting end-users know what new titles are ready for use. Years ago many libraries—academic, public, and special, in particular—issued some type of "Recent Additions" or "New Titles" lists. Producing such lists was labor intensive: collecting the slips for recently processed titles, typing the list, verifying the information was correct, maintaining a mailing list for interested recipients, and producing and distributing the information. By the mid-1980s such lists were disappearing from the workload as libraries struggled with budget and staff reductions. End-users voiced concerns about the loss and questioned the factors that led to dropping the lists.

Today such lists are making a comeback thanks to technology. Many systems make it possible to run a management report that lists all the titles added to the database between x and y dates. Most allow downloading of the information into a word processing program where a staff member can quickly format the data for "publication." The end product is often both a paper list and an electronic version for posting on the library's home page. Another step can be to e-mail specific information such as the "item is ready for use" to the requestor and others who have an interest in the topic. This is a return to what was part of a service called selective dissemination of information (SDI) back when there was staffing available for such activities.

Serials have always been a challenge for library staff due to their changing nature. (Years ago they were thought to be THE challenge; today technology has assumed that mantle.) New titles, changing titles, variations in numbering systems, special issues, delays in publications, suspension of publication, and ceasing to exist are but a few of the variations serials present to libraries. Keeping up to date in a print-only environment was almost impossible; today the Internet makes it *almost* possible. Anyone with an interest in serials should subscribe to SERIALST (http://www.uvm.edu/~bmaclenn/serialst.htm), an open forum for discussing the perplexing world of serials. Because subscribers are from around the world—more than forty countries are represented—one quickly learns that many, if not most, of the concerns about serials are global rather than local in character. Electronic journals and/or paper-based titles with electronic editions represent another challenge for technical services. Some vendors have records that can be downloaded, assuming that the ILS allows for that and can make the necessary links. For many libraries, if the process depended solely on manual inputting, there would be many fewer records for electronic resources.

Cataloging departments and catalogers have been "online" for longer than most others in the library world. A popular discussion list for catalogers is AUTOCAT, initiated many years ago by list owner Judith Hopkins of the State University of New York, Buffalo. Cataloging questions often elicit dozens of responses, sometimes within hours of being posted. Opinions and answers come from all over the world, sometimes with documentation. Some of the most prolific participants work at national libraries, research institutions, or specialized information centers. Subscriptions can be entered by sending a message to LISTSERV@LISTSERV.ACSU.BUFFALO.EDU with a blank subject line and the message SUBSCRIBE [YOUR NAME]. The Canadian counterpart to AUTOCAT is the Canadian Library Association Technical Services Interest Group Forum, TSIG-L. It can be located via the Canadian Library Association Web page at www.cla.ca.

Catalogers frequently are able to obtain authoritative information, free cataloging advice, selected tools, and other assistance from Web sites maintained by national libraries and bibliographic networks as well as by commercial vendors of cataloging systems, publishers, and other companies. Some of the most useful government and nonprofit organization Web sites are the Library of Congress Cataloging Directorate, available at www.loc.gov/catdir; the National Library of Canada, available at www.nlc-bnc.ca; OCLC, available at www.oclc.org; and the Research Libraries Group, parent organization of the RLIN bibliographic network, available at www.rlg.org. Offerings at these Web sites vary from organization to organization and change over time. Features include descriptions of the organization's latest activities and projects, lists of publications and online order forms, and e-mail access to persons responsible for answering inquiries or providing additional information. Occasionally, full text of some documents or methods of downloading them free of charge are posted. Early in 2001, OCLC began giving an online course for a fee on the cataloging of Internet resources. A description of the course, fees, and subscription process are posted on OCLC's Web site.

The Internet and the Web are great tools, but they can also be a problem in that the staff can spend a little too much time "surfing" with or without realizing it. Some control and self-monitoring is necessary to maintain unit productivity. However, supervisors should keep in mind the comments of Patricia McCoy: "Is any of this [Internet/Web browsing] related to the work piled up on my desk? Sometimes. Is it related to my position in the library as whole? Again, sometimes. Is it related to my personal job satisfaction and career goal? Most defintely."[4] Allowing some level of "surfing" may help reduce some of the workplace stress that is so commonplace in today's changing technical services environment. Also, staff need to become comfortable with the electronic databases the library purchases to provide proper service.

RESTRUCTURING TO PROVIDE "FASTER AND BETTER"

Pressure for "more, better, faster, cheaper," combined with budget woes and all too frequently with staff reductions, have led to restructuring of technical service units. A recent buzzword for what is taking place is "reengineering." Close inspection of what the "gurus" of reengineering suggest reveals that the concept has much in common with what was once labeled "operations analysis" and "scientific management." Essentially, good management practice calls for ongoing assessment and evaluation of policies, procedures, workflow, and so forth. Unfortunately, in most situations daily demands seem to keep people from doing this on a regular basis. What follows is a description of one library's rethinking of technical services. It is not presented as a "best practice" but rather as one example with the process from Ed Evans's work experience. The Suggested Reading section in this chapter provides references to a number of articles that describe similar experiences.

Like most academic libraries during the late 1980s and 1990s, the technical services units at Loyola Marymount University (LMU) have undergone several changes. The first change, in large measure triggered by the purchase of an ILS, was to merge the serials and acquisition units. This was both a supervisory and a physical merger as well as one that led to an overall reduction in staff by one FTE. Although it was not thought of as reengineering (the term was not yet popular in 1988), it did draw on some of the standard work analysis and scientific management techniques that are now part of the reengineering consultant's toolkit.

As the first step, senior staff in both units formed a working team, with the head of the serials unit acting as team leader. (The head of acquisitions was retiring and the university was in the process of tightening its budget. As a result the vacancy was "frozen" for almost three years.) Members developed flow and decision charts for the existing processes. Senior library managers worked with the ILS staff and several local libraries using that system to develop similar charts for several variations for the post-ILS system.

Reengineering consultants disagree about the effectiveness of charting existing practices. For example, Michael Hammer and James Champy believe that it is best to completely ignore what exists and think in terms of what could be best.[5] Others, such as Raymond Manganelli and Mark Klein, think it essential to take into account the existing environment or work culture while designing the new system.[6] In retrospect, the LMU staff might have decided some things differently had they tried to ignore existing processes. However, overall their planning took into account existing skills and knowledge as well as limitations imposed by the available physical space, and created a highly workable plan. Ignoring those factors probably would have created more problems than it would have solved.

The second phase was to ask the standard work analysis questions—easy to ask but sometimes painful for staff to answer. For each point in the flow and decision charts they attempted to answer the following:

- What is done?
- Why is it done?
- Where is it done?
- When is it done?
- Who does it?
- How is it done?

At various times the team met with the senior library managers for what became known as "hot seat sessions." The goal and atmosphere were not confrontational, but the sessions were intended to ensure that the team was giving serious thought to each of the questions. The first two sessions generated responses that were some variation of "because that is the way I/we have *always* done it." Later sessions made it clear that the team gave careful thought to each question and took into account limiting factors such as skill and knowledge sets.

One of the most difficult aspects of the project for the team was to keep in mind the "system concept." That is, they had to remember that the merged units were part of a larger system of interacting units. Changes they were considering might have consequences far beyond the new unit. Therefore, there were several team presentations to other unit heads to gain feedback about possible impact(s) on other units. An early presentation focused on several alternatives under consideration and a last session presented what the team hoped was the final plan, subject to unforeseen concerns from other units.

Was the project a success? The staff believes it was, as does senior management. (The reader may recall that in the Chapter 1 we noted how the workload has increased for the merged unit over the intervening years.) Was the process painful? Yes, but because the staff members made the decisions, they worked hard to make it a successful operation. Is the system the same today as they designed it in 1989? No, because developments in the field required additional changes. Perhaps the best outcome of the project was that the staff saw the value of asking the "why" and "how" questions and continue to do so. They see the process as one that can make their work easier and somewhat less stressful. From senior management's point of view, the best news is that the entire planning team is still at the library.

Other developments that required units to rethink work patterns included electronic ordering and invoicing, especially because the new method was to be "paperless." The change had an unexpected outcome. The university's internal auditor requires a paper copy of all orders and invoices in addition to the invoice copies that go to the business office. Although not a significant issue, it did mean that some steps staff expected to eliminate are still in place.

Another planning example can be seen in the implementation of PromptCat, which called for a new planning team of catalogers and acquisition staff. The process was not as complicated as the merger but was more contentious because it demonstrated that neither unit really understood what the other did. While the early implementation stages were just taking place at the time of writing, it appears likely the team will recommend substantial cross-training for staff in both units.

STANDARDS

One of the reasons the LMU library was a latecomer to PromptCat was the catalog department's concern about database quality. Currently the catalog department is solely responsible for quality control of the bibliographic and item records in the OPAC database. (Everything in the collections, with the exception of Special Collection items, is part of the database. Print materials in Special Collections are slowly being added. However, because the unit serves as something like the university's attic—including items ranging from furniture to paintings to "gold records" to postcards—it will be some time until everything will be in the OPAC, if it ever is.) Because of that responsibility, the catalogers spent considerable effort making it "perfect." Concerns about PromptCat records led to a rejection of that product in early 1997.

OPACs are the end-user's key to unlocking the library's resources and in some cases the resources of other libraries. They play a more prominent role for users than did the public card catalogs of years gone by, if for no other reason than that they generally offer more modes of access and are considered quicker and easier to use than their forerunners. Given their importance to quality customer service, it is a good practice to have just one unit responsible for OPAC maintenance.

One long-standing management technique for assigning responsibility for a task is to give it to the unit or person who most frequently performs the task or works with the equipment or system. Although all units in a library access the OPAC database on a regular basis, it is the catalog department that creates the initial bibliographic record for each new title and item records for additional copies or volumes in a set that ultimately constitutes the core of the database.

Thus it is rather common that the cataloging unit is responsible for maintaining the database content and its quality.

If it was just a matter of initial inputting of data, the task would be of less concern; however, it goes far beyond that. There are ongoing adjustments that must be, should be, or are desirable to make in the existing records. On the "must" side is making changes in the location information when that changes, say from "open stacks" to "storage." Another "must" is to delete records for withdrawn items or those declared "lost." A "should be" issue is making cross-links when it is discovered that several records are for works by a single author, who has several name variations, for which there are none. One of the most desired adjustments, but not implemented as often as staff would like, is updating subject headings, which seem to change on a regular basis. Handling the changes manually eats up limited staff time. If the ILS does not provide updating capability, some libraries have found it cost-effective to outsource the work.

Having "perfect" records and databases is no longer a realistic goal for most libraries. In the case of the LMU library catalog department, it was the "more factors" that finally triggered the decision to address the question, "What is an error in the bibliographic record?" (The question for the database is just beginning to be thought about, but everyone knows it is "less than perfect" as it stands and will be more so over time.) The "more factor" took several forms:

- A variety of new nonbook formats requested by the School of Education,
- An ongoing gift of screenplays and music scores from two television/motion picture production companies (the College of Communication Arts wants these added to the database),
- The desire to incorporate Web sites into the OPAC (a Reference Department request),
- New electronic journals,
- Paper-based serials that include a "free" electronic subscription, and
- The Faculty Library Committee's insistence that the paper-based journal collection be classified.

All these concerns made it clear that something(s) had to give because there was to be no additional staffing. One of the "somethings" that gave was perfection in the bibliographic records.

In many ways, the process of deciding what was not an error was more difficult and painful than the merger of serials and acquisitions. Several of the cataloging staff took pride in their perfect records, and the idea that it would be acceptable to allow less accurate records into the OPAC was a serious personal issue. It required almost six months of discussion before the department came to a reluctant agreement on items that could be less than perfect and still go into the OPAC. That agreement allowed the library to move forward in setting up a PromptCat program.

One important factor in moving the group's discussions forward was the Internet/Web, where they could post questions and receive responses within a few days, if not hours. Among the responses was a referral to a University of California, Berkeley Library site dealing with performance and quality standards in technical services. Performance standards and benchmarking have become a part of technical service operations over the past ten years. Essentially reflecting the world of technical services in the 1990s, the UC Berkeley Library Technical Services document begins by stating:

> Since the early 1990s, the Library had experienced the loss of many skilled, veteran staff through UC early retirement programs and through normal attrition, without the financial means of replacing those staff and the critical expertise they once provided. At the same time the Library began a series of reorganizations in order to increase efficiency and reduce expenses. . . . In addition, all staff including the Library's most experienced, was finding it more and more difficult to keep up with rapidly changing technology and the new policies and procedures that come with them. . . . The *Technical Services Performance Standards* serve as a basic measurement for determining the quality of technical service in central and branch units. . . . The standards are meant to be applied to the performance of the unit as whole."[7]

The standards are a good starting point for anyone thinking about the need for something similar. They also contain some very useful outlines for staff training.

An example of a standard created by a technical service unit is illustrated in Table 3.1, page 52. The LMU library uses the chart for handling incoming PromptCat items. The basic concept underlying the chart is that it should have standards that are clear enough so individuals who have no cataloging background can quickly review incoming materials and decide if they are acceptable or require the attention of the cataloging staff. (See chapter 21 for a discussion of MARC tags.)

An article by Theresa Bomford and Sue Howley discusses how British libraries have addressed the issue of standards and comparisons.[8] The Centre for Interfirm Comparisons handles the data collection, which focuses on the issues of costs and outputs. Although not perfect, the data do allow for comparing costs and outputs in public and academic libraries. Bomford and Howley conclude: "In Britain, costing activities and comparisons are very much back in fashion. . . . There are also, of course, fewer libraries in Britain than in the United States to persuade. Whether standard costing methods will soon prevail depends perhaps not so much on those powers of persuasion as on the ability of current research to overcome some of the technical and separate problems which have bedeviled the interlibrary comparison program."[9]

Table 3.1 Minimal Cataloging with Library of Congress Records

MARC tag	REQUIREMENT	ACTION IF RECORD NOT AS REQUIRED
FF: ELvl	ELvl is blank, 1 or 4. There is no need to check ELvl for PromptCat books—only when cataloging on OCLC.	Refer to cataloger. Record is incomplete.
050	050 call number is present. Second indicator is zero.	Refer to cataloger. Needs verification.
	No explicit |a is visible in the 050.	Refer to cataloger. Need to choose/complete call number.
	Call number does not begin with PZ or Z5000+	Refer to cataloger. Usually needs different call number.
245	245 field matches title on title-page exactly, except for punctuation.	Refer to cataloger. Needs adjustment or different record.
	245 |c (if present) matches form of author's name on title-page exactly, omitting titles like "Dr." or "The Reverend."	Refer to cataloger. Needs adjustment.
	Title does not begin with an initial article in a foreign language (e.g. La, El, Los, Le, Das, Der, Eine, Une, etc.)	Refer to cataloger. Needs added title to index initial article. If in doubt, refer foreign language titles to cataloger.
	Different title on spine, or prominent embedded portion of title on title-page, is recorded in a 246 field.	Refer to cataloger. Needs added title field.
250	Edition statement (if any) on the cover, title-page, page before t-p or back of t-p, is shown in 250 field.	Refer to cataloger. Needs adjustment or different record.
260	Publisher named in 260 |b appears on the cover, title-page, page before t-p or back of t-p.	Refer to cataloger. Needs adjustment or different record.
300	Height of book in 300 |c is less than 29 cm.	Measure book, rounding to next full cm. Adjust 300 |c to match. If 29 cm. or more, make bib loc and item loc "lmlo." If book is labeled for Main Stacks, relabel for Oversize.
440/490	Series title (if any) appearing on the cover, title-page, page before t-p or back of t-p is shown in 440 or 490 field.	Refer to cataloger. Needs adjustment or different record.
Screenplays	Item is not a screenplay (TV or movie script).	Refer to cataloger. Needs additional title information and subject headings.

Revised 11/07/2000

BENCHMARKING

Benchmarking, at least in U.S. libraries, is a recent phenomenon as jurisdictions and organizations have become increasingly concerned about operating costs. Benchmarking is basically a tool for either internal or external comparisons. The National Association of College and University Business Officers (NACUBO) conducted a number of benchmarking studies of various areas in academic institutions during the 1990s. These were large-scale efforts involving more than 400 institutions in the United States and Canada. LMU's library took part in three of the projects between 1992 and 1997. Following is some background on the benchmarking process.

The goal of benchmarking is to provide data that can help managers answer the following questions:

- How well are we doing compared to others?
- How good do we want to be?
- Who is doing the best?
- How do they do it?
- How can we adapt what they do to our organization?
- How can we be better than the best?

There are four basic types of benchmarking—internal, competitive, industry, and best in class—but the first two are most commonly used in libraries. As the label suggests, *internal benchmarking* looks at internal practices within an organization. An example is what it costs to create a purchase order in various departments across a campus. A *competitive benchmarking* project might collect data on the cost of creating purchase orders in various departments in a number of institutions. *Industry benchmarking* would collect data from all or a representative sample of all organizations within an "industry." (The NACUBO studies mentioned previously were essentially an industry effort.) *Best in class benchmarking* collects information across industries, essentially seeking the most effective practices.

Internal benchmarking may also vary between vertical and horizontal projects. A *vertical project* seeks to quantify the costs, workloads, and productivity of a defined functional area; for example, handling accounts payable. A *horizontal study* analyzes the cost and productivity of a single process that crosses two or more functional areas; an example is database searching in acquisitions, cataloging, and interlibrary loan departments.

The NACUBO studies had several objectives:

- To assist participating institutions to identify best practices,
- To provide data that might allow participants to identify areas for improvement,

- To provide data to assess relationships between inputs (primarily resource costs) and outputs (generally the quantity and quality of products and services), and
- To introduce the concepts of "process improvement" and awareness of the value of benchmarking.

When developing a benchmarking project a key issue is establishing for each benchmark a clear understanding, by all the participants, of what it will measure and what to include in the data collected for that benchmark. Understanding what will and will not be included—time, staff salaries, equipment costs, staff benefits—is essential if the data are to be useful. (A common problem in first-time projects is not making it clear what to include in staff costs: just salary, salary and directed benefits such as health insurance, or all of those plus vacation and sick leave costs.) If several approaches are used, the data will be essentially useless for comparative purposes.

One of the problems for the first NACUBO library project was the failure to establish clear guidelines for handling multiple campuses and libraries where the entities have separate operating budgets. For the LMU library there were two problems. The first was the fact that Loyola Law School has a separate campus, as well as name, but shares the same governing board as LMU. Rarely does the institution issue data combining the LMU library with the Law School library; however, for many institutions such reporting is common. The second issue was the fact that the LMU library also functions as the university's official archives and records management unit. Although the holdings are not included in the library's statistics, the staffing costs and other operating costs are part of the overall operating budget.

Table 3.2 shows the results for two of the 1995 benchmarks for the LMU library and some of the assessment undertaken based on the tabulated results. Data supplied after the completion of the study included the individual institutional results, the total average results (also the high and low amounts), and "cohorts" based on the Carnegie Classification System for academic institutions. The system also differentiates between public and privately funded institutions. Loyola Marymount University falls into the "Comprehensive University" category, thus making that cohort the primary area of concern for the library (although the staff did look at other categories as well). Column A in Table 3.2 shows the "cost per library holding"—essentially the total library operating budget divided by total library holdings. Column B represents the total materials acquisition cost as a percentage of library cost. In the first instance, the assumption was that the lower the number the more efficient, if not necessarily effective, the library's collection building program was. For the second set of data, a high number was assumed to be desirable; that is, more of the operating budget went toward building the collections. Had LMU either included the archives and records collections as part of its holdings or pulled out those programs' operating costs, the number for LMU in Column A would have been near the bottom of the Private Comprehensive semi-quartile range, rather than near the top. For the last NACUBO study, the issues of what to include or not include were much clearer, and the expectation is that when the data become available they will be much more useful.

Table 3.2 Benchmarking Analysis

	A	B
LMU's data	7.51 low number desirable	38.19 high number desirable
All participants mean Semi-quartile range Assessment	5.62 4.10 to 6.51 Significantly above the mean but near midpoint of range. Two-year colleges a factor in range.	33.68 27.06 to 39.47 Higher percent than average. Public institutions had lower percent.
Private Comprehensive mean Semi-quartile range Assessment	6.33 4.25 to 8.72 Above primary cohort and near top of range. Need to check with other libraries about their data/practices.	34.39 31.66 to 39.09 Significantly higher than cohort average. We have increased percent each year for past 9 years.
Public Comprehensive mean Semi-quartile range Assessment	5.10 4.10 to 5.65 Even greater difference. It is function of public universities' budget problems over the past ten years.	32.39 25.51 to 38.86 Well above cohort average. Usage of LMU library by local state university students reflects a stronger acquisitions program.

The benchmarking project discussed here indicated some of the problems that occur when attempting to compare cost data with other institutions. Although there are potential pitfalls, there is also a value in looking at an institution's operations in comparison to peer libraries. At the least, if the comparisons are favorable, there can be a political value in terms of funding authorities

COST ANALYSIS

Conducting internal cost studies provides useful data and occasionally reveals unexpected insights. Three of the most common reasons for engaging in such projects are to identify possible cost reduction areas and tasks, to provide data for cost recovery programs, and to evaluate alternatives for carrying out a task or activity. Such studies can, and in most cases should, take a pragmatic approach to data collecting. That is, one should not worry too much about using complex models or statistical analysis; "rules of thumb" are generally satisfactory and basic statistics work well for local projects. A good starting point for engaging in such a project is *Cost Effective Technical Services: How to Track, Manage, and Justify Internal Operations*.[10] Not everyone believes in the value of such studies, in part because they apparently associate the projects with some of the worst aspects of "scientific management" of the early twentieth century. A balanced discussion touching on the pros and cons of cost studies (although it is essentially "pro") is Joe Hewitt's "Using Cost Data Judiciously."[11] Hewitt makes a point that the authors of this book strongly agree with:

> Cost studies are a useful, at times necessary, tool of management in libraries. They tend to be used selectively for specific purposes. In decision making, they are used with sensitivity as data illuminating a single (albeit important) factor involved in complex decisions. . . . On the whole, libraries using cost studies are aware of their limitations and dangers and are attempting to make use of cost studies as tools of rational, humane management.[12]

One example of the "complex decisions" is whether a library should use an outsourcing service such as PromptCat. Although the decision involves much more than fiscal considerations, one strong factor in the decision is whether doing so would provide some form of savings (time or money) or have some other significant benefit. An article by Mary Rider and Marsha Hamilton discusses fitting cost analysis into a PromptCat decision.[13] It includes a long section on cost/benefit analysis work that was part of a decision-making process. The article concludes by stating:

> When considering the PromptCat service, the library should ideally study local costs and work flow implications. The service provides an excellent impetus to review expensive and time-consuming local practices. . . . Psychological and staffing

implications should be considered. Many staff and librarians are concerned about job security and satisfaction in the face of increasingly sophisticated vendor-supplied services and the specter of outsourcing. Finally, the increased speed with which materials can be made available to patrons should be considered, especially if changes in workflow and local systems can be adopted to maximize the benefits that PromptCat can provide.[14]

TIPS ON STAFF MOTIVATION

As the previous discussion suggests, cost studies, restructuring, outsourcing, and so forth can and do have an impact on all staff members. Addressing their concerns requires some understanding of the psychological aspects of the situation at hand. Restructuring, or even undertaking studies of the existing structure, normally creates four stages, in which the staff experience

- Disbelief and denial,
- Anger, rage, and resentment,
- Emotional bargaining—anger to depression, and finally,
- Acceptance.[15]

During the first stage, there is often shock that changes might or will take place. There is also a belief that the changes cannot or will not work, and some staff may actively work against the changes. Having the staff involved and allowing them maximum input will help, as will providing honest and forthright explanations about what is involved in the study or proposed change(s). Indicating the benefits is also helpful. If there will be staff reductions, that should be made clear to the staff. Trying to hide such facts until later will damage credibility with the staff.

Stage two involves denial and shock usually shifting to anger, especially if there are to be staff reductions that require layoffs rather than "normal attrition." That anger is normally focused on the immediate supervisor rather than the actual factor making the changes necessary. During the third stage, staff members likely to be affected by the change begin to start thinking about their options. Occasionally, some resign before there is any final decision. Often, these are the most qualified individuals who are less likely to lose their positions. Others become depressed, and their work quality and quantity begins to fall. Eventually there is an acceptance that what seemed unthinkable will in fact take place.

Susan Cartwright and Cary Cooper identified twelve of the most common workplace "stressors." Today's technical services environment appears to have the potential for the appearance of all twelve factors from time to time. The stressors are

- Loss of identity as organizational size changes;

- Lack of information, poor/inconsistent communication;
- Fear of job loss or demotion;
- Possible transfer/relocation;
- Loss of or reduced power, status, and prestige;
- Disrupted/uncertain career path;
- Change in rules, regulations, procedures, and reporting structure;
- Change in colleagues, supervisors, and subordinates;
- Ambiguous reporting systems, roles, and procedures;
- Devaluation of old skills and expertise;
- Personality/workplace culture clashes; and
- Increased workload.[16]

Some of the factors are more controllable than others; for example, workload increases are often difficult to control at least in the short term. Some of the steps to take to reduce the stress were discussed previously. Providing more information can be very helpful; "the word" does not always get out as much as one might assume. Keep the communication process open to feedback; make it clear that questions and expressions of concern are welcome. Be as specific as possible about the "what's, why's, when's, and wherefore's" of events or projects that may be stressful situations. Involving staff in the process as much as possible helps them have a sense of control over their destiny. Work at developing a team approach, if not actual work teams.

TEAM BUILDING

Team is a word with several meanings in the management area; *empowered*, *project,* and *working* are three of the most common delineations. *Empowered* teams have a high degree of autonomy in some activity and are more or less permanent in character. Such a group might be a retrospective cataloging team, if they have great latitude to determine their work activities. *Project* teams are assembled to carry out a specific task usually with a target completion date. Such a team might be a PromptCat implementation team. *Working* teams are developed by supervisors to improve the cooperation or coordination of work activities within the areas of responsibility and to involve the staff in more of the unit's planning and decision-making activities. In the first two types of teams, there is often a selection process in terms of personnel to be on the team that is designed to bring to the team all the skills needed to handle the assigned task. Working teams seldom start with a selection process, but over time the supervisor might adjust job descriptions to bring in new or missing skill sets to improve the team's performance. No matter what type of team is being considered, most of the elements of good team building apply.

Good team building starts with creating two types of matrices: *skills* and *responsibilities*. Even when someone is not in a position to select team members, it is useful to develop a skills matrix to identify the ideal skill sets. That way, if there is an opportunity to select a new person, one can quickly rewrite the appropriate job description. Such a matrix also helps one think about skill sets that exist in the work unit for meeting the existing responsibilities. It may even lead to reassigning duties among the existing staff. Table 3.3, pages 60–61, illustrates a simplified responsibility matrix for handling PromptCat.

COMMUNICATION ISSUES

Given today's work environment, team-based technical service activities that cut across traditional activity lines are more likely to produce good results. This is true in part because, to be effective, team-based work groups require emphasizing some of the basics of good management practice. Good teams should have a broad range of skills and be cross-trained; have strong senior management support; have a greater than traditional latitude in determining work activities; and, perhaps most essential, be well-informed. Communication with and among team members is at the heart of good team performance. Therefore, having a team communication plan that addresses the who, when, what, and how of the process, based on team input, goes a long way toward building both good performance and team spirit.

Everyone can benefit to some degree from occasionally recalling the fundamentals of the communication process—beyond the need for team building. People often slip into the habit of thinking of communication as a one-way process based on oral and written messages sent and received. To be truly effective, communication must be based on a two-way feedback process to prevent misunderstandings and to clarify points. (Clearly these issues become even more important when working in a team environment.) Even when remembering that communication is two-way in nature, people frequently forget the importance of *listening* as well as thinking *before* providing feedback.

Listening is an art that many of us need to practice more than we do and one that some individuals never seem to develop. One reason is that we tend to forget that we can hear at least four times faster than most people normally speak. The difference between speaking and listening speeds allows ample time for the listener's mind to "wander" away from the speaker's message. If in doubt about this difference, take a few minutes to think carefully about the last lecture or speech you attended. Did you really only think about the presentation? No thoughts about the quality of the presentation? No thoughts about what you needed to do after "this is over"? No doodles on the page(s) if you were taking notes? No thoughts about the room, the people, or what the weather was like outside? The list could go on and on; the point is that any such thoughts take one's attention away from the message and illustrate that listening speed was not taxed to any great extent by the presentation.

Table 3.3 Responsibility Matrix

	Head Cataloger	Head of Acquisitions	Cataloging Assistant	Receiving Assistant	Invoice Assistant	Physical Processing
Establish PromptCat profiles and processing requirements with OCLC and vendors.	P	S				
Define cataloging review process, including definition and handling of errors and exceptions.	P		S			
Load PromptCat files into local system.	S	S		P		
Compare books to PromptCat records and approve payment.	S		S	P		

Route errors and exceptions to appropriate staff.	S		S	P		
Pay invoices.		S			P	
Correct errors and exceptions.	S		P			
Relabel books as necessary.			S			P
Provide feedback to OCLC and vendors.	P	P				

P = primary responsibility
S = supporting responsibility

Improving listening skills is necessary for effective team performance. Tips for improving listening include (1) thinking about questions the presentation brings to mind that need to be raised for clarification; (2) asking for examples or providing paraphrased feedback during the presentation; (3) concentrating on what is new, different, or questionable; (4) planning on summarizing points after the presentation, which is a way of concentrating attention on message and not allowing one's mind to wander off to other matters.

There is a passive side to the communication process as well as the active side just discussed. Nonverbal behavior can be almost as important, if not the most significant part, of the communication process. Speakers and listeners both "pick up" on the nonverbal behaviors and may have very different reactions to those behaviors. Libraries are becoming more and more diverse both in staff and the end-users served. Communication is a process highly influenced by cultural and societal factors. Although we are more likely to think about the importance of our word choice in a diverse environment, we sometimes overlook the nonverbal issues.

Three examples illustrate our point about cultural differences and nonverbal behavior. Generally in Western European societies, direct eye contact during a conversation is considered a sign of a listening, open, straightforward, honest person. Lack of such eye contact suggests just the opposite. However, in other cultures such eye contact is insulting, disrespectful, and even threatening. Likewise, European-based patterns expect some nonverbal signals that the person is listening, such as nodding in agreement. In some cultures, such behavior is not expected or is even viewed as presumptuous on the listener's part. Physical space during a conversation is also a factor. Some societies expect individuals to be "up close and personal," while in others such behavior is viewed as pushy and rude. Knowing something about the expected communication behavior of the various cultures represented in the team or workplace can be beneficial for both overall working relationships and productivity. (A note about diversity: The LMU PromptCat team consisted of members of the cataloging and acquisitions departments, with a total of eleven people. In terms of cultural diversity there are two people from the Philippines, one from India, one from Taiwan, one from Japan, one Chinese-American, and one Latino, with the balance from Western European backgrounds. Clearly, to work effectively the team had to address different communication styles.)

Effective leaders not only must communicate and build team spirit, they also must exercise influence and possess negotiating skills if they are to consistently inspire high performance. Authority and coercion will only work for a short while in most of today's work environments. There are several key elements in exercising influence in general and specifically in teams:

- Be consistent in what you ask for and what you do.
- Be certain to follow through on commitments.
- Be clear about how decisions are made and follow that process.

- Be flexible in your interpersonal style to adjust to the person you are with, especially your tone of voice and nonverbal behavior when working with a culturally diverse group.

Following these guidelines will not resolve every team-based communication problem, but it will go a long way toward building a work group that has confidence in its leader as well in its other members.

There are times when influence is not enough, and negotiating will be necessary to achieve the desired results. Negotiating should be, both within the group and with other units, a process of give and take. Before starting negotiations it is advisable to have a clear understanding of what the various "bottom lines" are for all the parties involved, that is, what cannot be modified. In the workplace setting, there are usually at least three "bottom lines." First is the institutional goal of what *must* take place—for example, implementing PromptCat in a cost-effective manner. Second is a goal the staff desires—for example, that any new process *must* not result in added workload but rather be a replacement. A third bottom line is that of the leader or supervisor: The outcome *must* be something he or she can be comfortable with implementing. Some tips on negotiating follow:

- Differentiate between wants, needs, and musts for all sides.
- Asking high and giving low is expected, but don't be ridiculous about either end.
- Conceding something, which is necessary if there is to be negotiation, is also expected, but when doing so don't "give in."
- Winning something and losing something is the goal of negotiations; no side should leave believing it has been "taken" or lost on every issue.

SUMMARY

The management issues in today's technical services environment are essentially the same as for other areas of the library: too much to do, too few people to do what must be done, and constant pressure to "do more with less." Basic management practices are key elements in making the "more, faster, better, cheaper" pressures somewhat more manageable. There are a host of management resources available for technical services staffs to consult. We were only able to cover a few of the topics in this chapter; management of organizations in times of change and stress is the subject of a great many full-length books.

It does not appear likely that the library work environment is going to change much from the present circumstances in the very near future. Concepts of time and stress management are helpful for all staff. Developing ways of sorting out what is essential, desirable, and "nice to have" with all staff members is also worthwhile. Creating even an informal sense of team membership prevents members from feeling as if they are alone. Working on communication and negotiating skills promotes a work environment that is effective and somewhat, if not completely, comfortable for everyone.

NOTES

1. Cecily Johns, "Technical Services Organization," in *Technical Services Today and Tomorrow,* edited by Michael Gorman (Englewood, CO: Libraries Unlimited, 1998), 174.

2. Susan Cartwright and Cary Cooper, *Managing Workplace Stress* (Thousand Oaks, CA: Sage Publications, 1997), 116-117.

3. Carol Pitts, "Using Automation in Technical Services to Foster Innovation," *Journal of Academic Librarianship* 24 (March 1998): 113.

4. Patricia McCoy, "Technical Services and Internet," *Wilson Library Bulletin* 69 (March 1995): 40.

5. Michael Hammer and James Champy, *Reengineering the Corporation* (New York: Harper Business, 1993).

6. Raymond Manganelli and Mark Klein, "Should You Start from Scratch?" *Management Review* 83, no. 7 (1994): 45-47.

7. University of California, Berkeley, Library Technical Services Performance Standards Steering Committee, *Technical Services Performance Standards,* March 1997 www.library.berkeley.edu/AboutLibrary/staff/stanrds/, 1.

8. Theresa Bomford and Sue Howley, "Standardization: The British Approach," in *Cost-Effective Technical Services,* edited by Gary Pitkin (New York: Neal-Schuman, 1989).

9. Ibid., 171-172.

10. *Cost Effective Technical Services: How to Track, Manage, and Justify Internal Operations*, edited by Gary Pitkin (New York: Neal-Schuman, 1989).

11. Joe Hewitt, "Using Cost Data Judiciously," in *Cost Effective Technical Services,* edited by Gary Pitkin (New York: Neal-Schuman, 1989).

12. Ibid., 50-51.

13. Mary Rider and Marsha Hamilton, "PromptCat Issues for Acquisitions: Quality Review, Cost Analysis, and Workflow Implications," *Library Acquisitions* 20, no. 1 (1996): 9-21.

14. Ibid., 21.

15. P. H. Mirvis, "Negotiation After the Sale," *Journal of Occupational Behavior* 6, no. 1 (1985): 67.

16. Cartwright and Cooper, *Managing Workplace Stress*, 34.

SUGGESTED READING

Ahronheim, Judith. "Technical Services Management Issues in the Metadata Environment." *Technicalities* 19 (June/July 1999): 4-6.

Cohen, Laura. "Librarians on the Internet: The Search for Quality Begins." *Choice* 34 (September 1997): 5-17.

Cook, Eleanor. "Reorganization Revisited; or, Is Acquisitions an Endangered Species?" *Library Acquisitions* 20, no. 1 (1996): 77-84.

De Jager, Martha. "The KMAT: Benchmarking Knowledge Management." *Library Management* 20, no. 7 (1999): 367-372.

Diedrichs, Carol Pitts. "Rethinking and Transforming Acquisitions." *Library Resources & Technical Services* 42 (April 1998): 113-125.

———. "Using Automation in Technical Services to Foster Innovation." *Journal of Academic Librarianship* 24 (March 1998): 113-120.

Eustis, Joanne, and Donald Kenney. *Library Reorganization and Restructuring.* ARL SPEC Kit 215, May 1999. Washington, DC: Association of Research Libraries, 1999.

Gammon, Julia. "Partnering with Vendors for Increased Productivity in Technical Services: Or, Bleeding Edge Technology." *Library Acquisitions* 21, no. 20 (1997): 231-232.

Garick, Marina. "Public Libraries Benchmarking Database." *Australasian Public Libraries and Information Services* 10 (March 1997): 19-20.

Garrod, Penny. "Performance Measurement, Benchmarking and the UK Library and Information Sector." *Libri* 46 (September 1996): 141-148.

Martinez, Rebecca. "Role Reversal: How People Cope with Job Changes." *Library Collections, Acquisitions, and Technical Services* 24 (Fall 2001): 407-410.

McCoy, Patricia. "Technical Services and the Internet." *Wilson Library Bulletin* 69 (March 1995): 37-40.

Olaison, John, Hugo Lovhoiden, and Olva Djuovik. "The Innovative Library: Innovation Theory Applied to Library Services." *Libri* 45 (June 1995): 81-89.

Olsgaard, Jane K. "Relocation, Reorganization, Retrenchment." *Library Collections, Acquisitions, and Technical Services* 24 (Fall 2000): 426-428.

Ouderkirk, Jane. "Technical Services Task Assignment: From Macros to Collection Management Intelligent Agents." *Journal of Academic Librarianship* 25 (September 1999): 397-401.

Pritchard, Sarah. "Library Benchmarking: Old Wine in New Bottles?" *Journal of Academic Librarianship* 21 (November 1995): 491-495.

Propas, Sharon. "Ongoing Changes in Stanford University Libraries Technical Services." *Library Acquisitions Practice and Theory* 19, no. 4 (1995): 431-433.

Raugust, Karen. "A Wired World for Old Books." *Publishers Weekly* 248 (April 28, 2001): 22-24.

Ren, Wen-Hua. "To Merge or Not To Merge—What Are the Questions?" *DttP* 28 (Winter 2000): 23.

Robertson, Margret, et al. "Benchmarking Academic Libraries: An Australian Case Study." *Australian Academic & Research Libraries* 28 (June 1997): 126-141.

Slight-Gibney, Nancy. "How Far Have We Come? Benchmarking Time and Costs for Monograph Purchasing." *Library Collections, Acquisitions and Technical Services* 23 (Spring 1999): 47-59.

Stanley, Nancy. "Reorganizing Acquisitions at the Pennsylvania State University Libraries: From Work Units to Teams." *Library Acquisitions* 19, no. 4 (1995): 417-425.

Williams, Pauline C., and Kathleen Barone. "Impact of Outsourcing Technical Service Operations in a Small Academic Library." *College & Undergraduate Libraries* 7 (Spring 2001): 1-9.

Zuidema, Karen. "Reengineering Technical Services Process." *Library Resources & Technical Services* 43 (January 1999): 37-52.

REVIEW QUESTIONS

1. Discuss the issues that contribute to the pressure on technical services units to do "more."
2. Discuss the issues that contribute to pressures to do things "faster, better, and cheaper."
3. What steps have technical services taken to address the need to do things faster, better, and cheaper?
4. What are some of the steps that can lead to serious staff concerns regarding their jobs? What can be done to help staff members handle such concerns?
5. What are three steps to take to help manage work time more effectively?
6. Teamwork or projects call for some changes in the way individuals do their work. What are some of those changes?

Chapter

4 Cooperation/Consortia and Technical Services

Over the years, a great deal of printer's ink has been expended on books and articles addressing some aspect of library cooperation or consortia activities. If there were a direct correlation between the volume of literature and actual cooperative activities, there would be little left in the way of independent library activities. Such is not the case, although libraries do have an admirable record of both trying grand cooperative programs and succeeding in cooperative ventures. This chapter provides a brief history of the major cooperative ventures, as well as looking at current programs that have an impact on technical services.

BACKGROUND AND HISTORY

A great many efforts at cooperative activities have taken place at the local, regional, national, and even international levels. This chapter briefly covers three of the major efforts; two successful and one unsuccessful. Without doubt, the most successful has been the interlibrary loan program, which is international in scope. Another highly successful cooperative project is OCLC. The unsuccessful effort is the Farmington Plan and its European counterpart, the SCANDIA Plan. Why cover worthy efforts if they didn't succeed? Primarily because of *why* they failed and how the basic concept underlying the plan is now returning in a new form. The new form may affect acquisitions activities in the future.

Before going into the history and background of cooperative/consortia programs we should briefly address what we mean by cooperation and describe typical models for library cooperation. Library cooperative initiatives of interest in this book fall into one of two categories; sharing staff workloads or expanding library resources (resource sharing). *Webster's Third New International Dictionary* defines *cooperative* as "given to or marked by working together or by joint effort toward a common end"; it defines *coordinate* as "to bring into a common action, movement, or condition; regulate and combine in harmonious action."[1] Cooperative resource sharing programs are likely to continue to grow in scope and size. There may even be a future for true coordinated collection development. Some years ago, John N. Berry III editorialized in *Library Journal* about how the then-current tight funding situation was causing cooperative ventures to cease:

> The pressure is reported by public, academic, and school librarians from across the United States. One state's fine multitype systems are near collapse. Cooperative county systems in another have been reduced to bickering disarray from years of no-growth funding. Consortia members are scrapping over slices of a shrinking pie. New, harsh limitations on interlibrary loan crop up. Stiff nonresident fees and interlibrary charges proliferate. Old battles between small and large libraries in shared jurisdictions flare anew. State agency and cooperative system operating budgets are openly attacked by constituent librarians. . . . Librarians, torn between professional commitment to library cooperation and local pressure to provide service with deeply diminished resources, have to make the choice to cut service to outsiders.[2]

Unfortunately, the situation has not improved much since Berry wrote those words.

Today, what seems to be the most likely outcome of e-resources and cooperative efforts is best described as *resource sharing*. ALA's *Glossary* defines *resource sharing* as "activities engaged in jointly by a group of libraries for the purposes of improving services and/or cutting costs. Resource sharing may be established by informal or formal agreement or by contract and may operate locally, nationally, or internationally. The resources shared may be collections, bibliographic data, personnel, planning activities, etc."[3] That definition is broad enough to allow for almost any activity.

There are four general models for library cooperative projects. Model 1 is a bilateral *exchange model,* in which two or more participating libraries exchange materials or services. In practice, libraries calculate the exchange rate according to some agreed-upon value (for example, one for one, two for one); frequently, there is an annual review of the actual results as part of the formal exchange agreement. All of Loyola Marymount University's reciprocal borrowing agreements with other libraries contain an annual review clause. A number of regional resource sharing plans exist that employ this model; OHIOLink, and California's LINK+ are examples, as is the traditional interlibrary loan program.

Model 2, a multilateral development of Model 1, is the *pooling model.* In this model, two or more libraries contribute to and draw from a common pool of materials. Many of the early cooperative library systems were of this type; in a sense, OCLC started as a pool.

In Model 3, the *dual service model,* two or more participating libraries take advantage of the facilities of one of the participants to produce a common output—for instance, a shared online public access catalog (OPAC). The term *dual service* distinguishes this model from the next and emphasizes the fact that *all* participants, including the facilitator, contribute to the common output. Many of the early library systems evolved into this type; frequently, they refer to the facilitator as the flagship library.

In Model 4, the *service center model,* a number of libraries employ the services of a facilitating organization to input and process materials for the individual libraries, rather than for common output. Today's OCLC/WLN is this type.

These four types are adequate to cover all existing systems; however, new systems under consideration may not fit this classification system. For information about Canadian cooperatives, see http://novanet.ns.ca/consort.

Library cooperative systems operate on a series of assumptions. Perhaps the most important, although the one least often stated, is that all of the participants in the system are or will be equally efficient in their operations involving the cooperative activities. Another assumption is that every member will achieve somewhat different benefits or contribute materials that are of greater or lesser value to the overall project. A third assumption is that each library is somewhat unusual, if not unique (that is, each library has different clientele, collections, and service programs). If the last point is valid, why then assume that each participant is equally efficient? It is clear that one cannot legitimately make such an assumption about efficient operations. However, if libraries do not make that assumption, it is difficult to believe that every library will gain something, or, at least, receive a value equal to its contribution. Each library hopes that it will receive more than it puts into the system. If a library enters into a cooperative program with the "something for nothing" goal in mind, there is little hope of success. During periods of low funding from outside sources, libraries have a tendency not to cooperate. According to Boyd Rayward, "Networks (cooperatives) are a phenomenon of relative affluence. They cannot be created unless each member at the local level has sufficient resources of time, staff, materials, and basic equipment and supplies to participate."[4] It is worth remembering that OCLC started and became established during a high point in library funding in the United States.

The following sections examine some of the efforts libraries have made in the past to address the end-user's insatiable desire for more information, beginning with how libraries have changed as technology has opened up new techniques for satisfying the user's need for more and faster service.

ATTEMPTING TO COLLECT THE WORLD

For many years academic and research libraries around the world attempted to achieve an impossible goal: complete self-sufficiency. Users still clamor for more and more local resources—print and electronic—no matter how large the existing collections may be. The authors have worked in a variety of libraries, from the newly established to the "Harvards" of the library world. In almost every case, end-users, if asked, would say "there are serious gaps in the collection that ought to be filled" or "we need more journals." Services such as interlibrary loan (ILL) have been viewed as unsatisfactory solutions to the problem, most often on the grounds that they are too slow.

During the post–World War II period in the United States, academic libraries made a major effort to make the country, if not the local collections, self-sufficient. The Farmington Plan was a valiant but unsuccessful effort to have at least one copy of any currently published research work available somewhere in the United States, regardless of where in the world it was published. After years of effort the plan was abandoned in the 1970s. It originally assigned acquisition responsibility on the basis of institutional interests. In twenty years, those interests changed, but the goal of having one copy remained. Another problem was that some topics were not a major area of interest to any institution. Sufficient national interest existed to warrant coverage, but deciding which institution should have the responsibility for buying such materials was a constant problem.

A careful study of why the Farmington Plan failed provides invaluable data for future cooperative ventures. Technical services units were often flooded with materials of low interest and low priority for processing. Near the end of the program libraries unboxed Farmington Plan shipments, checked the packing slip against the invoice, assigned a special number to each box, and repacked the material, shipping it off to a storage facility. In the final analysis, the plan failed due to ever-changing institutional interests as well as lack of staff to process the materials acquired so researchers would know the material was available. Another problem at the time was knowing where one might find the material, because there were only the traditional card catalog and a few book catalogs for a some of the largest academic libraries and the Library of Congress.

A European example of a similar effort was the SCANDIA Plan, implemented in the Scandinavian countries, which experienced similar problems. This plan never achieved the same level of activity as the Farmington Plan, primarily because of problems of changing needs and the assignment of responsibilities.

Some years ago Bendik Rugaas, the national librarian of Norway, presented a paper titled "The End of All and Forever" at a meeting of national librarians.[5] In that paper, Rugaas outlined the reasons why no national library could hope to collect and preserve all the information materials created within its country's boundaries. All the participating librarians agreed that this was an impossible task. Evidence that national libraries are starting to act on that knowledge appeared in the lead article of the September 19, 1994, *Library Hotline*. The article stated that the British Library was giving up the goal of collecting every edition of every book, magazine, and journal printed in Great Britain.

If the giants of the library world are giving up local self-sufficiency, what can other libraries of more modest means hope to accomplish? Librarians know there always will be items a client will someday need but the library does not have the funds to buy. Librarians know that self-sufficiency is an unattainable goal, along with the goal of the "perfect catalog." However, user pressure keeps libraries seeking new means of coming closer to the impossible just as they continue to improve the public catalog. Almost all the efforts are some form of interlibrary loan or document delivery system to fill most of the gaps.

INTERLIBRARY LOAN AND DOCUMENT DELIVERY

Interlibrary loan (ILL) exemplifies both the problems and success of cooperative efforts. It is the process by which a borrower in one library obtains the use of books, periodical articles, or other library materials from another, sometimes distant, library. In ILL's simplest form, one branch of a large public library might borrow a book from the central library for the benefit of a requesting borrower. A more complex transaction might be a researcher requesting a filmed or paper copy of a medieval manuscript from an overseas library. In either case, aside from the number of steps in each procedure and the needed expertise of the parties involved, the goal and overall activities are basically the same.

Document delivery is a growing service that supplements the traditional interlibrary loan program. Document delivery involves purchasing information sources (especially periodical articles) from commercial document suppliers when access from other libraries is either unavailable or too slow. Document delivery is sometimes preferred over traditional interlibrary loan because of its timeliness; some commercial suppliers deliver most requested items within twenty-four hours or less; more rapidly than interlibrary loan can accommodate. However, a number of studies have shown that turnaround time for most document suppliers is no faster than the average interlibrary loan turnaround time. In addition, document suppliers often charge between U.S. $10 and $15 per item plus copyright fees of U.S. $3 to $7, making the service too expensive for many libraries.[6] Some libraries use document delivery to stretch their materials budgets by supplying information to their customers in lieu of subscribing to low-use or expensive periodicals. In many libraries document delivery became part of the interlibrary loan department, which in many cases led to a name change for the unit that is some variation of "document delivery services."

According to the annals of U.S. library history, ILL began in the early 1900s and was first codified in 1917. Cooperative loaning of materials from library to library in Western Europe, however, goes back at least as far as early medieval times, if not to the Middle Ages. Monasteries often loaned their books for copying to the scriptoria of other monasteries, sometimes hundreds of miles distant. These libraries sometimes never recovered the loaned materials, due to the exigencies of medieval travel, warfare, fire, barbarian raids, and the occasional thief. On the whole, libraries fare much better today regarding materials loaned to other libraries, although problems occur and materials do not get returned.

An active ILL program is a significant commitment of library resources. A 1997 study of ILL costs in the United States revealed average borrowing costs of $18.35 per item for research libraries and $12.08 for college libraries, as well as lending costs of $9.48 for research and $7.25 for college libraries. Approximately two-thirds of the cost of ILL is staff time.[7] Each library must make decisions about which services to emphasize based on its mission and priorities. There are some libraries that do little ILL work because it might cripple their basic services. A few get around the problem by borrowing from others but limiting the amount of their lending. Because good faith cooperation between libraries is the basis of interlibrary loan, this is acceptable only in the case of true financial distress. Interlibrary loan requires staff time for patron contact, verification, searching, communicating, record keeping forms, shipping, computer or telecommunications, packaging, furniture and space, and billing costs.

At the same time, ILL saves some money. Libraries can borrow (just in time) rarely used items rather than having to purchase them (just in case). Many libraries belong to networks formed for the purpose of facilitating interlibrary borrowing. Access to information becomes a matter of not only what one library can purchase but what subject strengths all participating libraries can provide. Libraries in a region can divide subject specializations within the group. Instead of each library collecting thinly in all areas, a solid basic collection can be built in each library, while those with particular subject strengths or needs can build an in-depth or special collection in one or two areas. Rarely used expensive volumes, sets, or specialized periodical subscriptions will be bought only by the most appropriate library, but access is maintained for the users of all participants. There are specific institutions that have as their mission the lending of materials to other libraries, as others have as their mission the preservation of last or only copies. Examples of these are the British Lending Library and the Center for Research Libraries, respectively.

Such schemes might lead one to believe that large university research libraries or large public libraries would be drained by many smaller libraries nibbling away at their substance. In fact, when the number of loans both ways is tallied, many of the smaller college and public libraries wind up being net lenders to, rather than borrowers from, larger libraries. Smaller libraries often have local materials and collections that are desired by customers of larger institutions, and smaller institutions often have a faster turnaround time, making them preferred lenders.

Interlibrary loan can remove the limitations of borrower location and is thus inherently democratic. Should rural borrowers be denied access to knowledge because of their physical distance from research centers? Should scholars have to drive or fly hundreds of miles to see a particular book? Should foreign-born or non-English-speaking customers be denied access to library books in their native language because they do not live in the right part of town? Should immobilized citizens be unable to read where their interests lead them because they cannot travel across town? Interlibrary loan solves many more problems than it creates, removing barriers to information and knowledge across all levels.

Herein lies the reason for covering ILL in a book on technical services. The services are only as good as the public catalogs. Participants must know which library has a copy of the desired material. Knowing if the item in question is available assists in speeding up the process by directing the request to a library that has a copy available for loan, which implies that the catalog reflects the status of the item. Part of the "slowness" of ILL in the past was the fact that borrowing libraries did not know the availability and might have to send the request to several institutions before locating a copy they could borrow. Today OPACs can provide such information almost instantaneously.

An interesting outcome of more and more libraries having OPACs and being part of regional or statewide networks is that the large libraries are actually borrowing more material from smaller institutions than they are lending. This suggests that in the past it was lack of information rather than weak collections that led to the imbalance in ILL activity. In 1993, the library directors at U.S. Jesuit colleges and universities completed an agreement after three years of discussion about concerns that the large libraries would be overused by their smaller colleagues. As of early 2001, the amount of borrowing was not a burden for any institution. In fact, some of the smaller libraries say their small document delivery staff face an increasing workload from the "big" schools.

At the international level is the ambitious UNESCO program, Universal Availability of Publications (UAP). Although it is not actually a cooperative collection development plan or ILL, it must be mentioned. In concept, UAP is grand. It proposes that all published knowledge, in whatever form it is produced, should be available to anyone whenever he or she wants it. Every information professional knows there is a long way to go in achieving that goal, and it is probably not attainable, even in countries with strong library systems and economies, let alone in developing countries. As Maurice Line has stated:

> One of the main reasons why the situation with regard to UAP is so unsatisfactory is that availability has been approached piecemeal; particular aspects such as acquisitions and interlending have been tackled by individual libraries or groups of libraries, but uncoordinated piecemeal approaches can actually make things worse. . . . UAP must ultimately depend on action with individual countries.[8]

If the concept is to succeed, it will be necessary to develop coordinated collection development plans in all countries and effective delivery systems, because everyone cannot buy, process, and store everything everywhere.

Groups, associations, and networks bring us to another aspect of cooperation. The linking of libraries through electronic networks and how such programs also help in sharing the ever-increasing workload of technical services is another story.

EARLY PROGRAMS, DATABASES, AND NETWORKS

By the mid-1960s in the United States, with the availability of federal funds, libraries had established a variety of local cooperative programs. Some of these projects explored the possibilities of "centralized processing." An old but still valid definition of centralized processing is "those steps whereby library materials for several independent libraries, either by contract or informal agreement, are ordered, cataloged, and physically prepared for use by library patrons." [9] (Clearly the concept of outsourcing technical services has a long history, as this statement appeared in 1964.)

Many states had one or more such centers by the end of the 1960s. When the Ohio College Association hired Wyman Parker to develop a cooperative center in 1963, no one imagined this would lead to the world's largest bibliographic database by the twenty-first century. Like many such projects, it started with the premise that the association needed a union catalog.

Certainly government funding was a key element in the move toward cooperative technical processing; however, computer technology was equally critical in making the projects succeed. Cooperatives seemed to appear overnight in the 1960s at all levels, from local to national. As OCLC began to take on a national service character with its online bibliographic database, it started offering a variety of technical services to members. There was less need to maintain union catalogs for current titles, at least for libraries using OCLC. However, in most cases libraries only added current cataloging and holdings information to the database, so there was still a strong need for union lists for older titles.

National databases such as OCLC serve a number of functions. Catalog departments can use data in the system to assist in cataloging activities or, if the item matches the data, simply add the library's identification code to the database record. By adding the code to the record (creating a holdings statement), member libraries know who owns what. Selection officers and interlibrary loan staff can use the holdings information in their work. As mentioned in Chapter 2, acquisitions departments can download bibliographic records into their automated order systems and save staff time by not having to rekey the information.

During the 1960s and 1970s, large libraries contributed their original cataloging to the database, which was largely dependent on the Library of Congress's cataloging in the form of MARC tapes. Increasingly the term used for this activity was *shared cataloging*, reflecting the fact that many libraries contributed data to the database.

Larger libraries also were actively developing computer-based systems for most of their basic activities. By the 1980s, national database services (also known as bibliographic utilities), commercial vendors, and some large libraries were offering automation packages to libraries. One frequent requirement was to provide linkages to national databases while allowing the library to fully catalog items just using the local system. Today there is a move back toward local processing. Many libraries download data from the network to their systems but do not always add to the national database. Jo Ann Segal has noted in her article on library networking that "another area of consensus was that the greatest threat to networks is the defection of members that come to rely on local systems and optically stored databases, rather than contribute shared cataloging."[10] An article by Sheila Intner outlines the issues in the trend toward less-shared cataloging.[11]

The relationship between national and local or regional networks can be confusing. If a library uses OCLC, for example, why does it also have to have some connection with a regional group such as SOLINET or PACNET (Southeastern Library Network, and the OCLC Pacific Network, respectively)?

MAJOR ONLINE BIBLIOGRAPHIC SERVICES

Currently there are two national nonprofit online bibliographic networks in the United States: OCLC (Online Computer Library Center) and RLG (Research Libraries Group). Each system started as an online cataloging project but over time added other services. Both provide an ILL component. However, cataloging is still one of the most important aspects of their programs. (Additional discussion of online cataloging is in Chapter 21.)

A-G Canada Ltd.

A-G Canada Ltd. and AMICUS are the two primary suppliers of bibliographic data in Canada. The roots of A-G Canada Ltd. began in 1965 when the University of Toronto Library became involved in an internal effort to automate its cataloging operations. This work resulted in the establishment of UTLAS (University of Toronto Library Automation Systems). UTLAS eventually separated from the university and was acquired by Thomson Canada Ltd., a multinational communications corporation, which changed its name to Utlas International Canada. In 1992 Utlas was purchased by ISM Information Systems Management Corporation, which changed its name, once again, to ISM Library Information Services. It is presently owned by Auto-Graphics of Pomona, California, and now operates as A-G Canada Ltd.

A-G Canada offers resource sharing, cataloging services, and proprietary database management with access to and from the database through Z39.50 search and retrieval protocol and World Wide Web facilities. A-G Canada's database design differs from OCLC's. Customers have a choice of maintaining a separate file of their own holdings or attaching their holdings to an existing file. Libraries and media centers do not join A-G Canada as members with a voice in its governance but purchase products and services from it as would the customers of any other commercial company.

A-G Canada is programmed to support English and French bilingual databases containing Canadian and Université de Laval French-language subject headings as well as LCSH (Library of Congress Subject Headings). Its database includes catalog records from many sources, such as the National Library of Canada, the Library of Congress, and the U.S. National Library of Medicine, as well as the REMARC file containing 4 million records from the pre-1968 Library of Congress shelflist. The National Library of Canada has designated A-G Canada as a node on the NLC-sponsored Virtual Canadian Union Catalogue (vCuc). As of July 2001, A-G Canada had a database of over 50 million bibliographic and authority records representing the collections of more than 600 libraries.

One of the differences between A-G Canada and OCLC is that A-G Canada's authority control system links bibliographic records with records in LC's name and subject authority files, the National Library of Medicine's MeSH (Medical Subject Headings) file, the National Library of Canada's name file, and *Répertoire de vedettes-matière*, permitting a local library's own authority files to be maintained and used in conjunction with all these authority files.

AMICUS

It is essential that the National Library of Canada (NLC) provide access in both of Canada's official languages, English and French. AMICUS, a free Web-based service that replaced DOBIS in 1995, provides bilingual access to the holdings of the National Library and more than 500 Canadian libraries. As of April 1, 2001, there were over 1,100 institutions subscribing to the service.

AMICUS is considered the premier collection of Canadiana in the world. The relational database contained 22 million bibliographic records as of April 1, 2001, and it is growing at an annual rate of nearly 1 million records. Because customized products are produced only for a small number of clients, AMICUS calls itself a resource sharing database rather than a bibliographic utility. In addition to bibliographic records created by NLC and the Library of Congress, there are holdings from more than 500 Canadian libraries that contribute to NLC's Canadian union catalog. Subscribers can download records free of charge, create bibliographies, and order items from other AMICUS contributors via an ILL feature.

AMICUS also contains NLC's name authority file, subject authorities for *Canadian Subject Headings*, and authorities created online. The authorities, which are MARC 21 compatible, can be searched by name, title, subject, and control number. The data include scope notes for subject headings and information and history notes for name headings as well as cross-references.

AMICUS records are used to produce many widely distributed products, such as Canada's national bibliography, *Canadiana, Canadiana Authorities*, several union lists, and catalogs. NLC also offers a MARC Records Distribution Service (MRDS). Records selected by local libraries are available on a twenty-four-hour turnaround batch basis via file transfer and other methods. In addition, NLC can supply acquisition lists, bibliographies, and related items.

OCLC

As noted previously, OCLC's origins go back to the 1960s when a group of Ohio academic libraries wanted to investigate the possibility of establishing a cooperative processing center. The project quickly developed from a "simple union catalog" concept into a total service center. Frederick G. Kilgour began work on transforming the concept into a working reality in 1967. Since its inception, the acronym OCLC has served as the shorthand label for a variety of official organizational names. Initially the name was Ohio College Library Center; today the name is OCLC: Online Computer Library Center, Inc. There was even a brief period when the name was just OCLC, Inc.

Online access to OCLC's database began in 1971, and shared online cataloging was initiated. The process of participating in OCLC is relatively simple. A member library either adds new bibliographic material to the database (original cataloging) or adds its three-letter OCLC code to an existing bibliographic record. This three-letter code lets other OCLC member libraries know which other libraries own or hold that item; this is called *holdings information* or the *holdings symbol*. (The codes for two of the authors' libraries are LML [Loyola Marymount University] and SCL [Simmons College].) During OCLC's first decade of operation as a bibliographic utility, most members used it to acquire catalog cards. By the 1980s, more members had local online public access catalogs (OPACs), which meant they no longer needed to buy cards. This resulted in a decline in income for OCLC, which affected the pricing structure of OCLC services. Furthermore, as noted previously, some members no longer contribute bibliographic records or holdings information.

OCLC's database grew quickly and continues to grow at an impressive rate. It took about three years for the database to reach the 1 million-record level; by its tenth anniversary it had reached over 8 million. Sometime in 1993 it surpassed the 28 million mark. By mid-2001, there were more than 48 million records. Annual growth is between 1.6 million and 1.9 million records.

The database contains records for audiovisual materials, books, computer files, government documents, manuscripts, maps, microforms, music scores, serials, sound recordings, and videorecordings. More than 30 percent of the records are for non-English-language materials. Such a rich bibliographic database is valuable not only for cataloging purposes but also for collection development and ILL activities.

Several times during its history OCLC offered members packages for automating acquisitions and serials control work. Today, commercial vendors offer more complete packages for automating library activities at lower overall operating costs. OCLC now focuses on its database as a source for supporting and enhancing cataloging, ILL activities, and other types of access services. One such enhancement was the development of a workstation that can handle Chinese, Japanese, and Korean characters. Another change was the move to using microcomputers rather than dumb terminals connected to a mainframe computer to access the system. This change allows libraries greater flexibility and frees them from the need to acquire and use expensive equipment. In the area of public services, there is FirstSearch, which is a collection of online reference databases, as well as a number of CD-ROM products.

Although OCLC is a nonprofit organization, it still must recover its full operating expenses. This means there are substantial usage fees that each member incurs for most services. There are several exceptions to the use charges. OCLC gives a credit for each original cataloging record contributed to the system by a library and for filling an ILL request. The other exception is a credit for deleting a holdings symbol. This occurs when a library withdraws an item from its collections and deletes its holdings symbol from the bibliographic record in OCLC. Access to the network is either dial-up using a public data network or, for high-volume usage, via a private telecommunications network (a "dedicated line") as well as Internet connectivity. In either case there are telecommunication charges in addition to the various service usage costs. A medium-sized library can easily spend between U.S. $30,000 and $40,000 per year on OCLC services, the bulk of which will be the result of technical services activities. All of the online databases generate similar costs; they are not unique to OCLC. Having the staff become proficient in using the bibliographic utility the library belongs to is clearly important to the financial well-being of the library.

At the time it started operating, OCLC's name reflected the academic library composition of the founding group. Soon, membership became open to any type of library. In 2001 there were more than 38,000 participating libraries of all types located in many countries around the world. An example of the international character of OCLC is the successful effort started in 1988 between the National Library of Canada and OCLC to develop an electronic ILL system drawing on the resources of both organizations. Another project is with the British Library (BL), which announced that libraries in Great Britain and Northern Ireland would have access to OCLC through an interface with BL's BLAISE service. During 1989, OCLC established an international office to handle its operations in twenty-six countries. Eleven years later more than sixty countries were participating.

Over the years a number of articles have appeared outlining various weaknesses of OCLC. However, so far OCLC has stood the test of time and is a good example of successful library cooperation. Nonetheless, there are problems with OCLC that may affect daily work. One is that sometimes more than one record for a particular item exists in the database, and these records may contain significantly different information. Another issue is that the quality of some contributed cataloging is poor, so poor that some libraries only accept cataloging contributed by the Library of Congress and major libraries known for their quality cataloging. These problems arose because OCLC is a shared cataloging database. Any member may input a new cataloging record at any time. Although there are guidelines and standards for inputting new records, quality control is difficult to maintain. OCLC makes a conscious effort at quality control, however, and corrects master records whenever errors are reported. With the implementation of PRISM, improvements were made to the software that make it easier to find and update records globally, such as when a subject heading changes. For most libraries the high "hit rate" (number of items found) and the overall quality of the database counterbalance its weaknesses.

One aspect of OCLC that is difficult for newcomers to the field to understand is its management operating procedure. Why does one sometimes call a regional service center rather than OCLC when there is a problem with the system? Early in its development as a national network, OCLC and most of the existing regional networks developed an operating agreement related to marketing their system. In very simple terms, OCLC sets overall directions for the system and develops products and services. The regional networks serve as the distributors of the products and services as well as providing the training needed to use the system effectively. Currently there are twenty such networks; the list can be viewed online at http://www.oclc.org/contacts/regional.

Part of the problem in understanding OCLC's arrangement is that there are three types of regional network distributors affiliated with it. One type is the pre-OCLC cooperative such as BCR, located in Colorado, which was a local and regional program that existed when OCLC began to go national with its system. Such networks are administratively independent of OCLC. The second type is a network created by a group of libraries specifically to distribute OCLC services; an example is OHIONET. These networks are independent organizations, but their original purpose ties them more closely to OCLC than is the case with the first type. The third type, represented by PACNET, is an OCLC-created and controlled regional network. OCLC set up PACNET because the West Coast did not create its own network.

Although the OCLC distribution system is similar to the retail model of manufacturer, distributors, and customers, there is one exception: There is a high degree of shared governance in OCLC. There is a Regional OCLC Network

Directors Advisory Committee (RONDAC) as well as a users' council. RONDAC looks after the interests and concerns of the networks; the users' council is where member libraries' voices are heard. The council must ratify all amendments to OCLC's Articles of Incorporation and Code of Regulations. This body also elects six of its members to serve on the OCLC board of trustees. All of this means that the users have a strong voice in what OCLC does and does not do as well as in how it operates. This brief description only highlights major aspects of OCLC governance and operations. Irene Hoadley's article, "The Future of Networks and OCLC," provides a good starting point for anyone wishing to learn more about this topic.[12]

Research Libraries Group/ Research Libraries Information Network (RLIN®)

The twenty-first-century RLG/RLIN® is very different from what is was in its early days. It is not completely clear where the process will end. It is unlikely that it will cease offering cataloging services to its members, but it may not actively market the services to libraries in general. The majority of its development activities will probably focus on databases of interest to scholars. In short, RLG has realized that the library technical services market cannot support RLIN® as a direct general competitor of OCLC.

Like other networks, the original purpose of RLG was to establish a joint program to improve access to scholarly material. The founding group consisted of Columbia, Harvard, New York Public Library, and Yale. After several years of looking at alternatives for developing a computer-based bibliographic database, the group signed a contract with Stanford University to use its BALLOTS system in 1978. (BALLOTS is an acronym for Bibliographic Automation of Large Library Operations using a Time Sharing System.) BALLOTS then became RLIN®. Ten years later, there were thirty-six governing members and almost 200 associate, special, or affiliated members. All the members were research libraries or libraries with specialized areas of interest, such as the Getty Center for the History of Art and the Humanities in Los Angeles. As in other cooperative networks, there is a sharing of governance among member libraries.

In all of the RLIN® technical processing services there is a strong emphasis on quality control and the needs of researchers. Libraries have greater control over their data than is the case with OCLC. Each library develops its own profile for cataloging activities. Because of a desire to help control the costs of building large research collections, the in-process file control system is an important element in RLIN®. One of the strong points of the system is the name authority file. RLIN® divides its bibliographic database into eight files: archives/manuscript control, books, films, maps, recordings, scores, serials, and visual materials.

Like OCLC, RLG has realized that it must move in the direction of becoming an information provider rather than just a technical services tool and has placed more emphasis on specialized services and information. It has developed Eureka®, which provides direct access to all the union catalog databases that RLG provides, and CitaDel®, a citation database. Another database from RLG is AMICO™ Library (Art Museum Image Consortium) database, a multimedia resource of more than 78,000 digitized and cataloged works of art from leading museums. RLG clearly focuses on the needs of the large or highly specialized research library.

THE ELECTRONIC WORLD AND COOPERATION TODAY

One of the benefits that can arise from any library cooperative effort is the potential for improving access for end users—improving in the sense of making available a greater range of materials or better depth in a subject area. We noted previously that lack of information about holdings was a problem in the past for ILL "resource sharing." This has become less of a problem as libraries automate their catalogs, join various networks, and move to Web-based distribution. Some resource sharing networks are statewide, such as OHIOLINK and LINK+ in California, which include both public and private institutions.

Loyola Marymount University library joined LINK+ in 1999, with the result that its service population went from having access to a collection of just over 400,000 volumes to having online access to a collection of more than 4 million titles and 6 million copies. Although the LMU collection was the smallest added to the database up to that time, over 37 percent of the items were unique additions to the system. (Each new member contributes between 30 percent and 40 percent unique titles, according to the firm that handles both OHIOLINK and LINK+. This suggests that to some degree the claim that each library is "special" is true, at least in terms of its collections.)

In today's electronic world there are ways to address some of the classic concerns about ILL service. Projects like OHIOLINK and LINK+ provide quick delivery of materials; in both cases member libraries have a courier service that picks up and delivers items every day. David Kohl has listed five key factors that need to be in place for successful resource sharing:

- Libraries belong to a consortium,
- Libraries have both their catalogs and circulation components integrated and available online,
- Libraries provide prompt physical delivery of print materials,

- Libraries have online delivery of electronic resources, and
- Libraries develop a coordinated/integrated collection development program.[13]

The list is more or less in order of priority: joint collection building after libraries demonstrate they can quickly satisfy users' demands for materials not held locally. Two of the key issues are of concern to technical services staff. These issues are becoming increasingly important in the electronic information world.

Based on LMU's experience, the promise of delivery of an item within twenty-four hours is kept by the courier service whether it is from a library in San Diego or one in Sacramento. The process begins by a person looking up an item in the local OPAC. If that library does not own the item the person may, with a single keystroke, search the LINK+ database. If a copy of the item is available in a member library, the person can fill out an online request form, and the system verifies that the individual is a valid user. The holding library immediately receives the electronic request information. There the staff locates the item, checks it out to the requester in his or her home system, and places the item in a pouch for the courier to pick up. Essentially this is a self-service ILL process with a twenty-four- to thirty-six-hour turnaround time. Given the system's performance to date, many of the traditional issues about local self-sufficiency are no longer major factors. Perhaps by the time the next edition of this book is published LINK+ libraries will have started some true cooperative collection development activities.

Tom Ballard published a provocative article in 1982 titled "Public Library Networking: Neat, Plausible, Wrong."[14] He raised a number of points regarding the primary service population, making a strong case, with data supporting his arguments, that for public libraries and others in a multi-type library system, the idea of cooperative collection development with an eye toward resource sharing (ILL, generally) is fine, but it does not work. Drawing on data from a number of systems across the United States, Ballard showed that interlibrary lending accounts for very little of the total circulation, almost always representing less than 2 percent of the total. He cited studies indicating that people tend to select from what is available at the time they come in, even if it is a second or third choice, rather than seek and wait for the desired material. It would be interesting to see what the results would be if such a study were done today, when many more libraries have their holdings readily available online. Again, by the time the next edition of this book comes out we may have some interesting data on these issues, as four large public library systems have joined the academic libraries that made up LINK+'s original membership.

Although Ballard emphasized public libraries and provided examples relating to them, his statements hold some truth for anyone who works in a school media center or an academic library serving undergraduates. Undoubtedly, part of the explanation for low use is that many people are not aware of the possibility of getting needed items somewhere else, so more active marketing by the library may be necessary. A more important factor is that people tend to wait until the last minute to seek out needed information and cannot wait even a few days to get a specific item. Perhaps a third factor is that most people do not really need or want the material enough to pay the price for its delivery. If it is immediately available (LMU is finding that twenty-four-hour availability is acceptable), fine; if not, forget it. These considerations make a strong case for maintaining a greater degree of local self-sufficiency.

Another form of consortial efforts in an electronic world is group purchasing of electronic databases, products, and services. Although these are rarely true shared purchases, libraries are finding that they can sometimes achieve some cash savings by negotiating a group rate on a product. Many of the regional networks discussed previously are entering into this arena as a means of gaining additional income. A library that belongs to several cooperative groups may have to sort out its "best price" from three or four possibilities, including what it would cost going alone. Pricing of electronic databases, as discussed in Chapter 11, can be very confusing and the licenses even more bewildering.

Acquiring Web-based databases alone is more complex than acquiring other formats, especially if there is a full-text component to the product. There are technical issues to address: a possible trial of the product just for the library staff or staff and end-users, IP (Internet Protocol) addresses to supply for those being given access, if and how to provide remote access, the means of controlling access if that is required, and so forth. There are issues of how the library will provide access; for example, if the product has full-text from journals, will there be links to the individual journal titles in the OPAC in addition to the links provided in the database? Additional linking means additional work for the cataloging department, which may well be stretched close to its limit.

When the acquisition of an electronic resource is made through one or more consortia the complexity increases. There is a need to carefully calculate the cost of the product under each option. Just looking at the "bottom line" figure is not adequate. Pricing of electronic information services and products is unpredictable at best. There are no standards at present, so each group negotiating with a vendor may end up with very different prices for what may at first appear to be the same product, at least based on the product's name. Because the product is electronic, the vendor has great latitude in packaging it. Vendors can and do add one feature, drop another, or provide this or that "extra" for no cost. Thus there may be two or three possible packages to examine to determine which one is appropriate and affordable. Clearly this becomes a coordination issue within the library. It is also a coordination issue for the consortia involved, both individually and as a group. Very often the price offered is based on how many libraries sign up for a given package. If fewer are interested, the price always increases per library; if more decide something is interesting, the price *may* go down.

Based on several years of firsthand experience as "president/chair" of a large California consortium, Edward Evans can say that this is probably the most difficult aspect of group purchasing. It is rather like the concept of which came first, the chicken or the egg. Libraries say, "We are interested in knowing what the price will be and what we'll get for that price." Vendors say, "That will depend on how many libraries actually sign up. So we cannot really give a solid cost figure at this time." Eventually one is able to work out something resembling the final price; however, when there is more than one group purchase option on the table, the individual library has to be certain that the offers are in fact identical. This issue is explored further in Chapter 11.

Recently, yet another issue for group purchasing or pricing and collections has emerged: the e-book. E-books are discussed in more detail in Chapter 11; here, we address only the cooperative issues. The problem is really twofold. When a consortium purchases a set of e-books for the group, who actually "owns" the titles? Does each library own some small percentage, or does the consortium own them, even if there is no physical location for the consortium? The question of ownership would not matter, and does not seem to matter to member libraries, but it does matter to organizations such as OCLC. These organizations assert that member libraries have a contractual obligation to add their holdings information for such titles as if the title belonged to each library. This would be a non-issue if it were not for cost considerations. There is a charge for adding holdings data to the OCLC database. Although the charge is not that much for single titles (U.S. $.28 in 2001), when several thousand titles are involved as well as a large number of libraries, the amount becomes significant. There is also a question of the increased workload for the cataloging department. At the time we prepared this text, Edward Evans and the LINK consortium were attempting to resolve these issues with OCLC. The consortium members were disinclined to pay the fee individually; their position was that none of them *owned* the material. OCLC offered a single consortium load cost plus a fee for each library taking part in the purchase, including a fee for libraries that were not OCLC members. The matter has not yet been resolved.

Without question, technology offers more opportunities than barriers to cooperation. The major concern is what the ultimate costs will be. Adjustments to changing needs in a network of more than two members become complex. It is much easier to respond to changing local needs when one does not have to worry about the impact the adjustments will have on other libraries. Of course, any proposed change may require modification of the original agreement. Although most changes would be minor, each requires discussion with other member libraries and may have unexpected impacts on workloads.

SUMMARY

Cooperation has a very long history in libraries, and technical services have led the way in many respects. It is difficult to imagine what librarianship would be like if cataloging had not so quickly embraced computers and then the idea of cooperative networking and work sharing. End-user needs and desires for ever-greater access to information materials were an underlying driving force in this movement.

The electronic world is bringing added pressure for increased cooperative activities that often have unexpected consequences for technical service units. What the future holds is impossible to predict with any degree of accuracy; however, it is likely to be filled with change and challenges.

NOTES

1. *Webster's Third New International Dictionary* (Springfield, MA: G & C Merriam, 1976).

2. John N. Berry III, "Killing Library Cooperation: Don't Let Professional Principles Become the Economy's Next Victim," *Library Journal* 117 (August 1992): 100.

3. *ALA Glossary of Library and Information Science* (Chicago: American Library Association, 1983), 194.

4. Boyd Rayward, "Local Node," in *Multiple Library Cooperation*, edited by B. Hamilton and W. B. Ernst (New York: R. R. Bowker, 1977), 66.

5. Bendik Rugaas, "The End of All and Forever," paper presented at IFLA Conference, Sydney, Australia, 1988.

6. Mary E. Jackson, "Loan Stars: ILL Comes of Age," *Library Journal* 123 (1 February 1998): 46.

7. Mary E. Jackson, *Measuring the Performance of Interlibrary Loan and Document Delivery Services* (1997). Available: http//www.arl.org/newsltr/195/illdds.html. (Accessed 15 April 2001).

8. Maurice Line, "Universal Availability of Publications: An Introduction," *Scandinavian Public Library Quarterly* 15 (1982): 48.

9. James R. Hunt, "Historical Development of Processing Centers in the United States," *Library Resources & Technical Services* 8 (Winter 1964): 54.

10. Jo Ann Segal, "Library Networking in 1988," in *Bowker Annual—1989/90* (New York: R. R. Bowker, 1990), 27.

11. Sheila S. Intner, "Bibliographic Triage Revisited," *Technicalities* 8 (October 1988): 3-4.

12. Irene Hoadley, "The Future of Networks and OCLC," *Journal of Library Administration* 8 (Fall-Winter 1987): 85-91.

13. David Kohl, "Resource Sharing in the Changing Ohio Environment," *Library Trends* 45 (Winter 1997): 445.

14. Tom Ballard, "Public Library Networking: Neat, Plausible, Wrong," *Library Journal* 107 (1 April 1982): 679-683.

SUGGESTED READING

General

Cary, Karen, and Joyce Ogburn. "Developing a Consortial Approach to Cataloging and Intellectual Access." *Library Collections, Acquisitions and Technical Services* 24 (Spring 2000): 45-51.

Charnes, Alan. "Regional and Global Library Networks: Why Bother?" *Technical Services Quarterly* 17 no. 4 (2000): 33-41.

Colvin, Gloria. "Both a Borrower and a Lender Be." *Florida Libraries* 43 (Spring 2000): 8-11.

Hawkins, Margaret. "All for One and One for All." *Library Association Record* 101 (June 1999): 350-351.

Helmer, John. "Library Consortia Around the World." *Information Technology and Libraries* 18 (September 1999): 119-168.

———. "Library Consortia Around the World—Part Two." *Information Technology and Libraries* 19 (June 2000): 59-102.

Lindh, Agneta. "Planning for Wider User Involvement in Document Delivery and Interlending in the Nordic Countries." *Resource Sharing & Information Networks* 13, no. 2 (1998): 39-46.

Williams, Delmus. "Living in a Cooperative World: Meeting Local Expectations Through OhioLINK." *Technical Services Quarterly* 17, no. 4 (2000): 13-32.

Academic

Martin, Murray S. *Budgeting for Access.* Chicago: American Library Association, 1998.

Public

Brown, Carolyn, and Carol Walker. "Does Cooperation Really Work?" *Nebraska Library Association Quarterly* 32 (Spring 2001): 4-5.

Poustie, Kay. "The Bertlsmann International Network for Public Libraries: A Model of Public Library Cooperation on an International Scale." *Asian Libraries* 8 (1999): 305-313.

Sharpe, Dave. "Pooled Expertise Lights the Way in Sunderland." *Public Library Quarterly* 15 (Summer 2000): 48-49.

Shier, Cathy. "Resource Sharing: A Case Study of a Joint Use Library in South Australia." *Australasian Public Libraries and Information Services* 12 (September 1999): 123-127.

School

Ragsdale, Allan. "North Florida Area Students Gain from Partnerships," *Florida Media Quarterly* 24, no. 3 (1999): 8-9.

Special

Johnson, William. "Resource Sharing Among West Texas Special Libraries: Initial Steps & Future Prospects." *Texas Library Journal* 74 (Spring 1998): 28-30+.

Simon, Elisabeth. "Business Libraries: Means and Forms of International Cooperation." *INSPEL* 31, no. 1 (1997): 181-194.

REVIEW QUESTIONS

1. What are the four models of library cooperative activities, and how do they differ?
2. The desire of end-users to have most of their needed information materials locally available (self-sufficiency) led to what cooperative activity?
3. Traditional ILL services have never been very popular. Many of the problems were a function of what aspect of technical services? How have they been resolved?
4. Discuss the role of OCLC in creating effective end-user services.
5. Resource sharing has been a long-term goal for libraries. What developments have taken place recently to make that goal appear to be attainable?
6. In what ways do consortial purchases make technical services more complicated?

Part Two

Acquisitions and Serials

Chapter

5 Acquisitions—Overview

The acquisitions department's contribution to the process of providing service to end-users consists primarily of handling business matters of ordering and receiving the materials selected for inclusion in the collection. (Note: Not all items added to the collection are the result of purchases; some are gifts or exchanges.) The department is usually responsible for handling all such materials. Occasionally the department is also responsible for bindery preparation work.

Because of the standardized nature of much of acquisitions work, there is little need for more than one or two librarians in the department. Most of the work requires knowledge of bibliographic tools and searching skills. Support staff does a large portion of the work in this department because very little of it requires graduate-level education. In some libraries, the unit does not have even one librarian staff member.

Library acquisitions work covers the procedures used in buying or otherwise acquiring materials for the collection: books, serials, audiovisual materials, and other items. Acquiring office supplies and library equipment such as computers, desks, or book trucks is seldom part of the acquisitions department's duties. Most acquisitions work involves a high degree of repetition and lends itself to the development of a series of standard routines. More and more, libraries are receiving funding to support the development and operation of various automated routines, thus reducing the amount of tedious work.

COLLECTION DEVELOPMENT AND ACQUISITIONS

A common misconception of individuals who do not work in a library is that acquisitions units determine what materials are in the library's collections. Decisions regarding what to add to a collection are rarely made in this unit. The usual practice is that some other group (usually the collection development staff) makes such decisions and passes the "request" on to the acquisition staff, who attempt to secure the item.

A library's basic objective is to serve the information needs of its end-users. The purpose of collection development is to select materials that serve the information, educational, and/or recreational needs of its primary service community. However, broad objectives such as these are difficult to interpret because one person's recreation may be another's education.

Each type of library—academic, public, school, or special—has a set of specific objectives for its service programs that support the community's activities. Selection officers must know the community and its needs. Thus, they spend time getting to know the community or institution they serve and learning what materials are available to satisfy a given need. Because few libraries have adequate funds to buy all the materials needed, selection officers also decide which needs and materials will receive the highest priority.

Selection policies help reduce some of the problems of making such decisions. In all but the smallest libraries, several individuals normally share the responsibility for selecting materials. Naturally, the involvement of several people in the selection process increases the need for coordination and understanding of selection procedures. Policies usually include all of the following:

1. A statement regarding who has the authority to select materials. Often the director has this authority, but delegates it to staff members. In such cases, this must be clearly stated.
2. A statement concerning who has the responsibility for selecting materials.
3. A statement of the library's goals and objectives for its collections.
4. A list of the criteria for selecting materials.
5. A list of review sources used in selecting materials.
6. An outline of the procedures for handling problems (complaints about having or not having certain items).
7. Guidelines for allocating available funds for the collections.

SELECTION RESPONSIBILITY

Written policies or program guidelines must be specific, but not so detailed that selection officers cannot effectively handle changing circumstances. More often than not, library selection officers are librarians. However, in some situations, such as school and public libraries, committees are the favored method of making selection decisions. Frequently, in small- and medium-sized academic libraries, teaching faculty are responsible for selecting materials.

Public Library Selection

Public libraries seldom encounter a problem about selection responsibility: Librarians have the authority and responsibility for this work. If only one library building serves a community, few problems of coordination arise that require any length of time to resolve. Often in such situations, one librarian has the responsibility for a specific area of the collection: children's books, reference books, fiction, nonfiction, and so forth.

When the library grows, and branches or bookmobiles become part of the system, problems in coordinating selection increase. It is at this point that selection committees come into existence. Selection committees usually consist of two or three people from the main library and the head of each branch or bookmobile. In large systems (ten or more branches), the committee becomes representational of the branch units. Normally some type of rotating committee assignment ensures that all branches eventually have a voice in the process. A primary purpose of committee work is to coordinate orders for multiple copies of a single item. Submitting a single order for ten copies rather than ten orders for one copy each saves acquisitions staff time. Multiple-copy orders frequently qualify for a higher discount from the supplier and thus help stretch limited acquisitions budgets.

School and Academic Library Selection

School and academic libraries share a dilemma in the selection process: To what extent should teaching faculty share responsibility for collection development? In an elementary and a secondary school situation, frequently there is a districtwide committee that functions as a general selection body. A committee of librarians and teachers creates lists of recommended items from which individual schools make their selections. The purpose of the list is to facilitate ordering multiple titles at the same time, so that the district's acquisitions unit can save the time and effort of ordering single copies several times.

Academic libraries cannot handle the problem so easily. In small institutions or institutions with limited acquisitions budgets, each teaching department wants its subject area adequately covered. That fact usually means that each department receives an allocation, a portion of the total acquisitions budget, which it may then spend on materials of interest. Whenever a library allocates funds to departments, to branch libraries (public or academic), or to divisions within a library, the work of the acquisitions department becomes more complex. In an academic departmental fund allocation situation, departments usually designate one faculty member as the library liaison person. However, if there are twenty departments on the campus, the acquisitions department could be dealing with at least twenty selectors, each of whom has his or her own idiosyncrasies.

If an academic library has enough money to honor almost any request for current materials, then responsibility for collection development often resides in the library. Often public service librarians take on the selection duties as well as reviewing faculty requests. A major disadvantage is that librarians usually lack the subject expertise of the faculty members. Most of the major research libraries employ full-time subject specialists who do the collection development work.

Special Library Selection

Defining collection development goals is easier for special libraries than for any other kind of library. Most special libraries serve a clearly defined set of needs, such as the research and development needs of a business or industry. A special library may serve as the repository for rare books or may collect all available items on some specific topic or geographical area. This does not mean that the work is simple, but clearly defined goals do limit the range of problems. In a non-business, non-industrial special library, the librarian(s) usually has full responsibility for developing the collection. Industrial and business librarians usually share selection duties with the group of individuals served. In some cases, all selections are the result of user requests.

Approval of Selections

If selection responsibility lies with individuals not on the library staff, the requests usually require the approval of someone with final budget responsibility. For example, in an academic situation, any faculty member may request an item, but the departmental library liaison, who supervises the department's library expenditures, must approve the request. Most request forms provide space for the required signature. When sorting book request forms, the acquisitions staff must check for the required approval. This is very important because money will be drawn from various allocated funds on the basis of the approving signature.

Acquisitions departments normally return forms lacking the requisite signature. The entire matter of approval signatures and departmental unit allocation of funds creates many challenges and makes public relations complicated for the acquisitions department. Therefore, everybody in the department—librarians, support staff, and part-time help—should be aware of the difficulties and do all they can to keep problems to a minimum.

Other Sources of Requests

Although libraries assign collection development responsibility to just a few individuals, most libraries accept suggestions for additions to the collection from anyone. These requests usually take longer to process, however, because they must fit into the overall collection plan, and naturally there must be money enough to buy the items. In most cases, the individual responsible for the subject area within which the suggestion falls must give final approval to buy the item.

Because the requests come from so many different sources, the individuals filling out the request (or order) cards are often unaware of all the information the acquisition unit needs to quickly order the desired item. Staff members should view all the information on the request cards with a certain amount of skepticism. In time, though, one learns which individuals take the time to supply accurate information.

This discussion only summarizes how various types of libraries handle selection and collection development work. Each library has its unique way of handling the process. All staff assigned to the acquisitions unit should be aware of how the selection process operates in their library.

Departmental Functions

Collection development and acquisitions have always been closely coordinated, if not integrated, in libraries and information centers with successful programs. In today's increasingly electronic environment, that coordination is vital. Joyce Ogburn once noted that managing an acquisitions program calls for a special set of skills and activities: assessment, prediction, control, choice, validation, and quantification. Libraries

> assess the risk and feasibility of acquisition, the availability of the resources, and the chances of success, control the system and methods needed, the choice of the source, the supporting services, and the resources themselves; and quantify the resources, work, and costs involved to conduct the business of acquisitions and measures of success.[1]

These skills and activities are a constant, but today libraries may need to draw upon the expertise of a number of staff members to acquire the desired electronic resources. We fully agree with Ron Ray's comment that, "Library administrators cannot afford to leave acquisitions expertise out of their considerations as libraries navigate into new technology environments and unconventional patterns of information distribution. But neither should they feel constrained to continue organizing acquisitions expertise as it historically developed in libraries."[2]

To be fully effective, selection and acquisitions personnel must have a close, cooperative work relationship. Poor coordination will result in wasted effort, slow response time, and high unit costs. Achieving coordination requires that all parties understand the work processes, problems, and value of each other's work. Beyond the obvious purpose of supporting overall library objectives, the acquisitions department has both library-wide goals and departmental goals. Library-wide goals can be grouped into five broad areas of purpose:

- Assist in developing a knowledge of the book, media, and electronic resources trade;
- Assist in the selection and collection development process;
- Assist in processing requests for items to be added to the collection;
- Assist in monitoring the expenditure of collection development funds; and
- Assist in maintaining all of the required records, and produce reports regarding the expenditure of funds.

By disseminating materials from the various information producers and vendors, the acquisitions department aids in the selection process, even if there is duplication. (Most information producers are uncertain who in the library makes purchasing decisions. With electronic materials, the process is generally more complex, with two or more persons involved in the decision making. Thus, it is not surprising that producers buy a number of mailing lists to use when promoting a new or revised product, resulting in several copies of the promotional literature being received. However, never assume that the item in hand is a duplicate unless you are the only person to decide on the item in question.)

Traditionally, acquisitions departments have maintained collections of publishers' catalogs, prepublication announcements, and vendors' catalogs. It is reasonable to expect to have *a* location where such items are kept. Such a location, when properly maintained, can help assure that selectors have the opportunity to review all the appropriate items regardless of whose name appeared on the mailing label. Acquisitions units also collect information regarding changes in publishing schedules, new publishers, and new services. Many departments serve as clearinghouses for this type of information for the entire library. Indeed, in larger libraries, the department sometimes operates a limited selective dissemination of information (SDI) system by routing information to selectors based on each individual's subject or area of responsibility. Despite the changing environment, there is no particular reason to change the location of such activities unless there is a major reorganization, and even then the activities ought to be retained in some form somewhere.

Processing requests for materials involves several activities to ensure that the library acquires the needed items as quickly and inexpensively as possible. Libraries would waste time and money if they simply forwarded requests to the appropriate publisher or vendor. Inaccurate information, duplicate requests, unavailable material, and similar problems would generate unacceptable costs for both the library and the supplier (and would probably cause considerable ill will). Each acquisitions department develops its own set of procedures to reduce such problems. Although there are hundreds of variations, the basic process is the same: preorder searching, ordering, receiving, fiscal managing, and record keeping.

Acquisitions departments also have internal goals. Four common goals are:

1. To acquire materials as quickly as possible.
2. To maintain a high level of accuracy in all work procedures.
3. To keep work processes simple to achieve the lowest possible unit cost.
4. To develop close, friendly working relationships with other library units and with vendors.

Internal goals are important to the achievement of the broader, library-wide goals, because all of the department's decisions regarding internal goals will have some impact on other operating units in the library.

Speed is a significant factor in meeting user demands and determining their satisfaction. An acquisitions system that requires three or four months to secure items available in local bookstores will create a serious public relations problem. A system that is very fast but has a high error rate will increase operating costs and will waste time and energy of both departmental staff and suppliers. Studies have shown that, in many medium-sized and large libraries, the costs of acquiring and processing an item are equal to or greater than the price of the item. By keeping procedures simple and by periodically reviewing workflow, the department can help the library provide better service. Speed, accuracy, and thrift should be the watchwords of acquisitions departments. Certainly online ordering, electronic invoicing, and credit card payments greatly enhance the speed with which the department can handle much of the traditional paperwork. What has not changed much is the speed with which items actually arrive. The label "snail mail" is still all too often appropriate for the shipping speed, unless one is willing to pay a premium price for faster service.

STAFFING

The rapidly changing electronic environment also has an impact on staff. New technologies and applications put pressure on the staff to quickly learn new skills because the workload seldom will decrease and there is a need to maintain a steady flow of materials into the library. Acquisitions is but the first step in the technical services process of making the materials ready for the users. Keeping a flow of materials as even as possible allows other units, such as cataloging, to plan their work more effectively.

One popular label for the technology pressure on staff is "technostress." Technology pressures exist for all the library staff, not just in acquisitions. Sally Kalin and Katie Clark have suggested that, "The rapid change of technology necessitates a different approach to training. . . . Staff also have to make a commitment to learn new skills. Training must become an integral part of their work life, not an adjunct."[3] Given the need for training as well as time to become reasonably comfortable in using the new skill(s), and that such activities become integral to daily work activities, there is a need to rethink duties. Many of the new technologies and applications make the process of acquisitions less paper-based and in some ways more efficient. Funding sources are more willing to spend money on technology than they are to commit resources to additional positions. What this means is that the library must not just move the traditional paper-based methods over to a computer system. Staff must rethink activities and duties, which, more often than not, leads to still more change for them to handle. In addition, libraries must also factor in time for the staff to receive training and develop new skills. This is a challenge for all concerned.

Efficient staffing involves using four classes of employees: professionals, paraprofessionals, other support staff, and part-time help. Persons in each category supply certain skills and knowledge required for the optimum operation of the department.

Librarians provide in-depth knowledge of library operations and the information trade, in all its various guises. They set departmental objectives and goals, prepare operating plans, develop policies, and supervise departmental operations. They also carry out tasks requiring special skills or knowledge, such as negotiating license agreements, monitoring/forecasting possible price increases for budget requests, and working with vendors to secure discounts. If the acquisitions department does not have any selection responsibility (and few do), only the largest departments need to have many professionals. With properly planned procedures, support staff can handle most of the department's activities.

Several surveys indicate that this staffing pattern is typical of U.S. libraries. One of the more comprehensive studies was done by Karen Schmidt. Her data showed that support staff perform at least 75 percent of each of the major acquisitions activities (preorder searching, ordering, claiming, and receiving).[4] Another study by James Coffey reviewed personnel costs of library acquisitions. His message was that there is a need to carefully consider staffing patterns when trying to control the cost of acquisitions work.[5] Similar studies done today would have much the same results despite the changes brought about by technology.

An interesting aspect of the Schmidt article is her data showing the continuing division of acquisitions and serials work in the majority of the responding libraries.[6] (We did not identify any similar later study, but we believe that more merged units exist today.) A somewhat dated, but still sound, review of technical service reorganization efforts, including merging acquisitions and serials departments, is an article by Joni Gomez and Jeanne Harrell.[7] As noted in Chapter 3, there is a trend to merge the departments, as Loyola Marymount University did, when a library installs an integrated automation system. After eleven years, we can say with confidence that the merger at LMU works well. (A reflection of the ease of securing funds for collections and technology but not people is found in the LMU acquisitions/serials department. In the time since the merger, collection development funds went from just under $400,000 to $2.4 million, and the library went through two generations of automation systems, all without the benefit of a single new staff member.)

As noted previously, few acquisitions departments have any selection responsibility. Most libraries divide selection responsibility among all librarians and, in some instances, users. Many large public and research libraries employ full-time subject specialists for collection development work. Even in such libraries, the individuals involved in the process must cover broad subject areas or select materials published in many countries. Beyond those basic selection functions, excluding acquisitions, selectors perform ongoing liaison activities with their primary user groups:

- Review gift and exchange materials;
- Review acquisition programs, such as approval plans and standing orders;
- Take part in fund allocation discussions;
- Conduct various user and circulation studies;
- Be involved in deselection decisions;
- Plan and implement collection evaluation studies; and
- Identify needed retrospective materials.

Adding these duties to other full-time activities, as is typical in most libraries, results in not all the duties being performed as often as everyone wishes. Some activities receive little attention; deselection and user studies are two areas commonly given less time and effort than is desirable. Figure 5.1 illustrates the basic functions of an acquisitions unit.

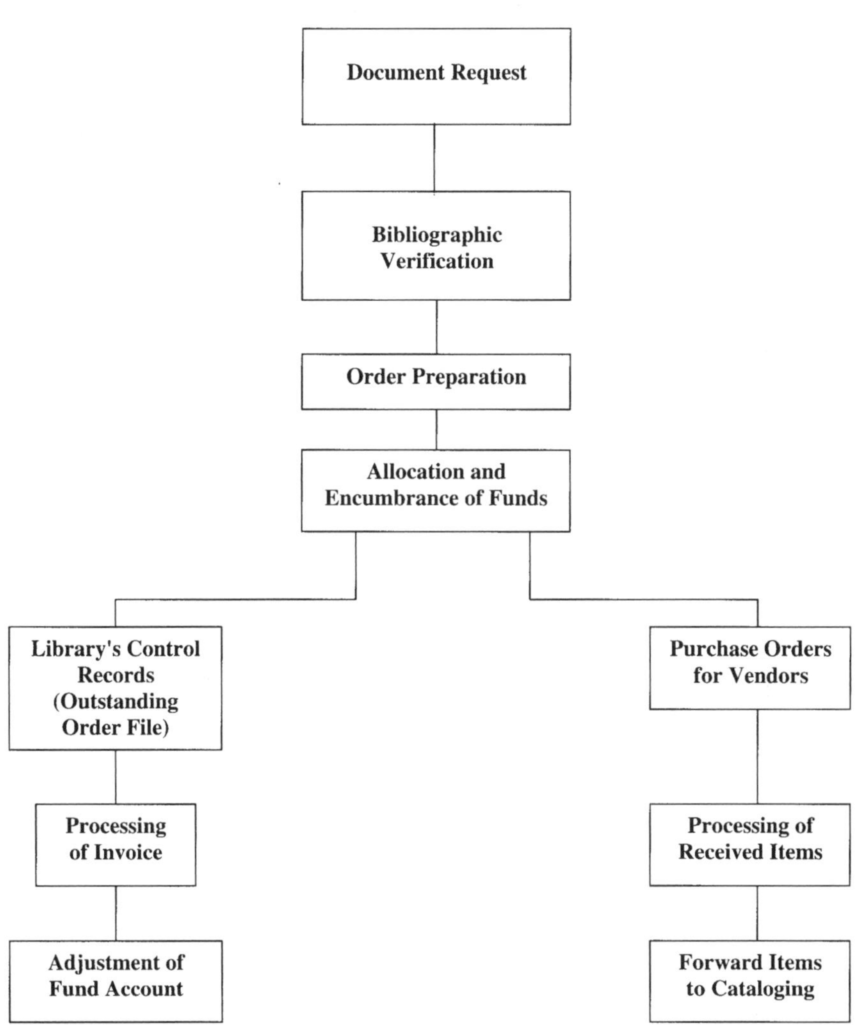

Figure 5.1. Acquisition process.

A few comments about outsourcing are applicable in the acquisitions context. If one only read the 1998/1999 literature about library outsourcing, one might think this was a radical departure for libraries. To the degree that it is being done to reduce staff ("downsizing" in current management jargon), it is relatively new. However, libraries have outsourced a variety of activities for many years—using jobbers/vendors to consolidate order placement for books and/or serials, for example. When used for what Arnold Hirshon and Barbara Winters labeled "strategic reasons,"[8] that is, to supplement existing staff efforts or to handle ever-increasing workloads without benefit of additional staff, outsourcing can be a useful tool in the acquisitions department.

TYPES OF MATERIALS ACQUIRED

Acquisitions departments, whether merged with serials or not, acquire materials using several methods, each involving different processing. Essentially there are seven standard methods of acquisition: firm order, standing order, approval plans, blanket order subscriptions (for serials departments), leases (increasing in use), gifts, and exchange programs. Each of the order types is discussed in Chapter 8.

A library's collection exists to achieve certain objectives: education, information, aesthetic appreciation, recreation, and research. Each objective requires a different mix of formats. Aesthetic appreciation often requires recorded music, dramatic readings, and visual and graphic materials of various types. Research objectives often require acquiring report literature, conference papers, and proceedings. The acquisition of these materials requires in-depth knowledge about the materials and suitable sources of supply.

Printed Materials

Books and printed materials represent the bulk of library purchases. Publishers in the United States produce more than 30,000 new titles each year and more than 10,000 new editions. Even if they devoted all their acquisitions money to buying books, most libraries could (and would want to) buy only a fraction of the total output. Some larger jobbers dealing only in English-language books have well over 100,000 titles available. Out-of-print materials range from 20 million to 50 million titles just for Western Europe and North America. Any of these titles could be of interest to a library.

In addition to books, thousands of periodical and serial titles appear every year. Government documents—national, state, local, and international—are another category of printed material acquired by libraries of all sizes (see Chapter 12). There are also scholarly publications, dissertations, theses, and publications of learned societies. Atlases, sheet maps (topographic maps; county highway maps; maps of national parks, forests, and recreation areas; aviation charts; and navigational charts), folded maps (highway maps), raised relief maps, and globes are staples in many library collections.

Printed music is still another category of material that should be familiar to acquisitions department personnel. Piano-vocal scores, miniature scores, and monumental sets are in larger library collections. Pamphlets and ephemera of all types (broadsides, house organs, personal papers, and documents) are also part of material the acquisitions department orders and receives. Chapters 6 and 10 provide a discussion of publishers and producers of print and other formats as well as of print-based journals.

Nonbook Materials

Microfilm and microfiche are two different aspects of the nonbook medium called microforms: films that carry copies of printed matter. Many out-of-print books are now available only in microform because the cost of reprinting is very high for the small number of copies that might sell. Making a microfilm or electronic copy and reproducing it is much less expensive. Also, it is possible to reproduce all or parts of a book on demand from a master negative at a reasonable price. To order microforms, the selector must know something about the proposed use of the material and what methods of reproduction are available. This is especially true when the purpose is to have a preservation copy. Sometimes, when a microform is not satisfactory, a hard copy is reproduced in the same size as the original. The order department must be aware of such factors before placing the order.

Other popular nonbook materials are audiotapes, CD recordings, videocassettes, and DVDs. Most libraries (medium-sized or larger) have at least a small audio collection. Public and school libraries tend to have larger nonbook collections than do academic libraries. Videocassettes and DVDs are increasingly becoming part of the circulating collection. Some libraries, generally public libraries, have been circulating software packages for home computers. Libraries face a number of challenges in acquiring these items, but many of the steps used to order a book apply to these other media as well. (See Chapter 13 for more information about media formats.)

Electronic Resources

Electronic resources also come in a variety of forms: CDs, tape loads, Web resources, and Web-based products. Many of the products are variations of print-based materials such as encyclopedias, indexes, and abstracting services. Others are the full text of print-based publications such as books and journals. Still others are original publications in an electronic format. More and more products are appearing that are multimedia in character, including text, sound, and graphics. Each variation has some special features that must be taken into account at the time of acquisition. There are also special legal issues that do not arise with print-based items. These points are explored in Chapter 11.

SUMMARY

Knowing something about why the library is acquiring the materials helps the acquisitions staff understand the whys and wherefores of the department's procedures and responsibilities. Also, knowing something about the operations of the companies from whom they buy the materials helps in maintaining good library-vendor relations. It is important that all staff in the department have opportunities to expand and update their knowledge about these topics to have the department operate as effectively as possible.

NOTES

1. Joyce L. Ogburn, "T2: Theory in Acquisition Revisited," *Library Acquisitions* 21 (Summer 1997): 168.

2. Ron Ray, "Where Is the Future of Acquisitions Expertise?" *Journal of Academic Librarianship* 24 (January 1998): 82.

3. Sally Kalin and Katie Clark, "Technostressed Out?" *Library Journal* 121 (August, 1996): 32.

4. Karen Schmidt, "Acquisition Process in Research Libraries," *Library Acquisitions* 11, no. 1 (1987): 35-44.

5. James Coffey, "Identifying Personnel Costs in Acquisitions," in *Operational Costs in Acquisitions*, edited by J. Coffey (New York: Haworth Press, 1990), 55–74.

6. Schmidt, "Acquisition Process in Research Libraries."

7. Joni Gomez and Jeanne Harrell, "Technical Services Reorganization: Realities and Reactions," *Technical Services Quarterly* 10, no. 2 (1992): 1-15.

8. Arnold Hirshon and Barbara Winters, *Outsourcing Library Services: A How-to-Do-It Manual for Librarians* (New York: Neal-Schuman, 1996).

SUGGESTED READING

General

Alvin, Glenda M., Jennifer D. Ware, and Tamara Frost Trujillo. "Charge It: Going Plastic in Acquisitions." *Library Collections, Acquisitions, and Technical Services* 24 (Summer 2000): 305-307.

Anderson, Rick. "Acquisitions in a Wired World." *Against the Grain* 13 (February 2001): 26-28.

Cargille, D. "Acquisitions and Collection Development." *Library Acquisitions* 20 (Spring 1996): 41-47.

Case, Beau David. "Approval Plan Evaluation Studies." *Against the Grain* 8, no. 4 (1996): 18-21, 24.

Cledenning, Lynda Fuller. "Crossing the Great Divide Between Acquisitions and Collections: Selectors Order Online." *Against the Grain* 12 (December 2000/January 2001): 85-88.

Conant, Roy B. "Libraries Are Businesses: Not! A Citizen's Response." *Library Acquisitions* 21, no. 2 (1997): 158-159.

Dickinson, Dennis W. "Free Books: Are They Worth What They Cost?" *Library Issues: Briefings for Faculty and Administrators* 17 (May 1997): 1-4.

Dilys, E. Morris, et al., "Monographs Acquisitions: Staffing Costs and the Impact of Automation." *Library Resources & Technical Services* 40 (October 1996): 301-318.

Dugger, L. J. "Fundamentals of Acquisitions." *Serials Review* 23, no. 3 (1997): 85-87.

Eaglen, Audrey. *Buying Books: A How-to-Do-It Manual for Librarians.* 2nd ed. New York: Neal-Schuman. 2000.

Fisher, William H. "Core Competencies for the Acquisitions Librarian." *Library Collections, Acquisitions, and Technical Services* 25 (Summer 2001): 179-190.

———. "Libraries Are Businesses." *Library Acquisitions* 21, no. 2 (1997): 151-155.

Forsyth, J. H. "Monitoring a Business Approval Plan for Balance and Numbers." *Library Acquisitions* 22, no. 3 (Fall 1998): 335-340.

Miller, H. S. "Monographic Series Approval Plan: An Attempt to Refine Purchasing of Books in Series." *Library Resources & Technical Services* 42 (April 1998): 133-139.

Saunders, L. M. "Transforming Acquisitions to Support Virtual Libraries." *Information Technology and Libraries* 14, no. 1 (March 1995): 41-46.

Schmidt, K. A., ed. *Business of Library Acquisitions.* 2nd ed. Chicago: American Library Association, 1999.

Vickery, J. E. "Library Acquisitions 1986–1995: A Select Bibliography." *Collection Management* 22, nos. 1/2 (1997): 101-186.

Academic

Association of Research Libraries. *Gifts and Exchange Function in ARL Libraries.* Washington, DC: Association of Research Libraries, 1997.

Ladizesky, K., and R. Hogg. "To Buy or Not to Buy—Questions About the Exchange of Publications Between the Former Soviet Bloc Countries and the West in the 1990s." *Journal of Librarianship and Information Science* 30 (September 1998): 185-193.

Walpole, M. G. "The Meta-Exchange Pilot Project: A New Way to Organize Book Exchanges with Russia." *Library of Congress Information Bulletin* 58 (February 1999): 21+.

Public

Montgomery, J. G. "Issues in Public Library Acquisitions." *Library Acquisitions* 22, no. 2 (1998): 206-207.

Strand, Benita. "How to Look a Gift Horse in the Mouth, or How to Tell People You Can't Use Their Old Junk." *Collection Management* 14, no. 2 (1995): 29-30.

REVIEW QUESTIONS

1. Identify the major purpose(s) of library collections.
2. Discuss the basic elements and purposes of book selection policies.
3. How is materials selection handled in public libraries? How does this differ from selection in educational institution libraries?
4. In what ways does selection for special libraries differ from that of other types of libraries?
5. What is final approval of selection? Why is it important?
6. Discuss the factors that require close cooperation between selectors and acquisitions units.
7. Identify five of the most commonly acquired nonprint formats.
8. Discuss the way in which electronic acquisition differs from that of other formats.

Chapter 6 Information Producers

Collections in today's libraries and information centers contain a wide variety of information formats. In the not too distant past, the vast majority of the collections were print-based. Acquisitions departments probably could function without knowing very much about the producers of the product they purchase. However, the departments will be both more effective and efficient when the staff understands something about the production side of the information cycle: creation, production, distribution, access/storage, and usage. (The distribution process is covered in Chapter 7. Issues of access are covered in Chapter 11. The topics of creation and usage are beyond the scope of this book.) Understanding the factors that enter into the costs and discounts of the products a library purchases assists in the business activities it undertakes (better vendor relations) as well as end-user interaction (better public relations).

Production of information materials underwent a series of changes during the last half of the twentieth century, and the pace of change is accelerating. Print-based publishing began to change in the 1950s when most publishing firms were private partnerships. Company control was in the hands of only one family (or perhaps two or three families) throughout a firm's history. Family pride and a feeling of personal involvement with each title published was a characteristic of such companies. Although they did not set out deliberately to lose money, many such firms passed up manuscripts they knew would make a profit simply because they felt that the material did not merit carrying their company's name.

Expanding educational programs in the post–World War II era translated into an explosive growth in demand for print materials. (See Chapter 1.) Private publishing firms lacked the capital to expand fast enough to meet the growing market. One method of securing the necessary money was to "go public," that is, to sell company stock. Selling stock changes the nature of a firm's business because the firm takes on a commitment to attempt to return the maximum profit to the investor. As a result, the primary concern for many firms became profit rather than maximum quality.

As publishing grew more and more profitable, larger nonpublishing businesses decided that the field was a worthwhile investment arena. Major electronic, computer, and other communication media companies bought publishing firms; in a sense this was the start of the blending of print and nonbook production activities within a single firm. Some companies of this type controlled seven or eight publishing firms, each firm operating under its old name but actually controlled by nonpublishing interests. If individual investors caused a change in the nature of publishing, it is not difficult to imagine the long-term effects of corporate investment. Profitability and corporate well-being became the primary factors in selecting materials for publication.

Beginning in the 1980s, the movement began toward electronic publishing. "Electronic publishing" has taken on several meanings; however, initially it meant producing a publication solely in a digital format and frequently selling it to individual users on demand. Today the term has taken on broader and less precise meanings, ranging from the original concept to producing some combination of print and digital material.

In the past, information producers could be categorized by their products: (1) those who produced printed matter (books, periodicals, newspapers, and the like), and (2) those who produced nonbook materials. Seldom did a producer work in both areas. Today the situation is different. Although some companies are solely devoted to the production of print or audiovisual materials, most trade book publishers also have one or more electronic and audiovisual lines. University presses and other scholarly publishers are also moving into electronic publishing, including the "publication" of materials solely on CDs or other digital formats. One such example is the University of North Carolina Press's *Excavating Occaneechi Town* (R. P. S. Davis, P. C. Livingood, H. T. Ward, and V. P. Steponaitis. University of North Carolina Press, 1998).

Some time in the future we may see the "paperless" world often predicted in both the popular and scholarly press. (F. W. Lancaster has written extensively about this topic; see *Libraries and Librarians in an Age of Electronics.*[1]) Despite such predictions, printed materials are still very much with us and probably will be for some time. Print materials still make up the largest percentage of items available through most libraries and information centers.

A sense of the staying power of print is found in sources such as *Books in Print* (*BIP*). The 1988 edition of *BIP* listed 781,292 titles; by 1998 that number had more than doubled to over 1.6 million. (Note: These numbers are based on unique ISBNs; titles are double counted if there were both hardcover and paper editions in print. Some popular titles might even be triple counted, if there were also an audio edition available.) Electronic products are being produced in increasing numbers, but as of 2001 they had not noticeably slowed the production of print materials.

A major reason for the staying power of books is that paper copies still provide the least expensive means of distributing large quantities of timely information to a large number of people. A long document (300 or more pages) can be mounted on the Internet, and many people do so. Obviously any number of individuals can simultaneously read that document. However, very few individuals using that material attempt to read it on the computer screen. Rather, they print some portion (or the entire file) and read the material in a printed form. (Anyone with experience in a reference department is well aware of the volume of printing being done of electronic data, mostly relatively short files.) Also, some people are uncomfortable with technology-based information sources. There is always some question, with electronic files, about the integrity of the material: Is what one sees on the screen what the author originally input? Finally, many people still like to read in bed, on the subway, at the beach, and other places where technology-based systems are inconvenient, if not impossible, to use. (Try reading a CRT screen in full sunlight at the beach.)

Albert Greco has summed up the present day situation in U.S. publishing as follows:

> Many industry analysts believe that publishing is in disarray, dangerously weakened by steep returns, stark sales figures, fickle and price sensitive customer base, the "rise" of chains and superstores and price clubs and the concomitant "decline" of independent book stores, a population more interested in watching television than in reading books, paper-thin profit margins, staggering technological challenges, and author advances that dumbfound even seasoned industry veterans. . . . Its best days are indeed ahead, a fact that excites tens of thousands of people every day about this wonderful, funny, and, at times, hard business.[2]

WHAT IS PUBLISHING?

What is publishing? That question has been with us, at least in North America, for almost 300 years. Publishers and others have debated whether publishing's purpose is cultural or commercial.

In the abstract, and to some degree in the real world, "The Book" is a cultural artifact as well as an essential means of recording and preserving the culture of a society. Certainly libraries of all types have to a greater or lesser degree some role to play in preserving and passing on their society's cultural values and heritage. Thus, books have taken on a special aura of importance, some might even say sacredness, that is very different than that of, say, clothes, cars, or cameras. Discarding worn-out items like the latter may bring some scowls from a few people, but there is widespread disapproval of doing the same with a book. From early childhood one hears, "Don't bend the pages," "Wash your hands before using your books," "Treat your books with respect," and being labeled a "book burner" is something most people would consider an insult.

HOW PUBLISHING WORKS

Publishers supply the capital and editorial assistance required to transform an author's manuscript into a book and electronic product. (Two exceptions to this are vanity and subsidy presses, discussed later in this section.) Generally, publishers in Western countries perform six basic functions:

1. Tap sources of materials (manuscripts).
2. Raise and supply the capital to produce books or e-products.
3. Aid in the development of the manuscript.
4. Contract for the manufacturing (printing, binding, formatting) of the materials for sale.
5. Distribute the materials as well as promoting and advertising the titles.
6. Maintain records of sales, contracts, and correspondence relating to the production and sale of materials.

A thumbnail sketch of the basic publishing development pattern is pertinent. This pattern seems to be worldwide, and it does have an impact on the acquisitions process. In the history of publishing, there appear to be three stages of development. These stages have occurred around the world as publishing has developed in a particular country.

In stage one, the publishing, printing, and selling of the product were all combined into one firm. The early giants of the "industry" in Europe acted as publisher, printer, and retail bookseller. These publishers included Froben, Schoffer, Manutius, and Caxton. When one examines North American publishing history, the same pattern appears on the eastern seaboard, moving west with the frontier; names like Franklin, Green, and Harris in the United States and Gilmore & Brown and Thomson in Canada fall into this period. Elsewhere in the world, publishing exhibits a similar evolutionary pattern, which is largely a function of how societies organize economic, educational, and human resources. In countries with limited resources, technical skills, and small markets, it is unfeasible, and in many cases impossible, to have specialty firms handling the several functions required to produce books, journals, and today, electronic resources.

From an acquisitions point of view, stage one development presents many interesting challenges. Research libraries buy materials from around the world, but countries with weak economies and low literacy rates seldom have anything resembling a national bibliography or trade bibliography (mainstays in identifying important titles). As if this were not enough of a challenge, most publishers operating at this level produce a limited number of copies of each item. In many cases, they take orders before going into production. When they do this, they produce just a few more copies than the number ordered. Many acquisitions departments have experienced the frustration of having an order returned with the comment "unavailable, only xxx copies printed." Some items are, in fact, out of print on the date of publication; this frequently occurs in areas where publishing is at the stage one level.

In stage two, specialization begins, with firms emphasizing publishing or printing. New firms, many with a single emphasis, appear. The factors creating this situation relate to available economic, educational, and human resources. Better education creates a greater market for books among both individual and institutional buyers. The retail trade develops at the same time, because the reading public exists countrywide and a single outlet in the country's major population center is no longer adequate.

Often, when bookstores begin to develop, a company will decide to create a listing or publication through which publishers inform bookstores about new and existing titles. Acquisitions librarians expend time and energy trying to track down such systems in countries where the book trade is in stage two. The usual procedure is to establish a good working relationship with a large bookstore, with that shop functioning as a purchasing agent. This may entail signing an agreement to spend a certain amount of money each year with the store, but it normally results in much better coverage, and usually better service, than trying to buy directly from the publishing houses.

The third stage is the complete separation of the three basic functions, as publishers discontinue printing activities. For example, John and James Harper started as printers in 1817. Today, HarperCollins is one of the leading publishers in the United States. It ceased printing years ago. When publishing reaches stage three, all the trappings we see in contemporary U.S. publishing are evident: specialty publishers, literary agents, trade journals, sales personnel, jobbers and wholesalers, and so forth. Normally, there is something resembling a national bibliography as well as a trade bibliography, both of which are essential for collection development work.

A fourth stage—electronic publishing—is developing quickly. Some publishers offer information in two or more formats, for example, print and electronic, and others offer some information only in an electronic format. Digitization is especially useful in the production process; submission of electronic manuscripts containing digitized images also speeds editorial work. The implications of electronic publishing for the bottom line are clear to most publishers, as suggested by Gayle Feldman: "Whether it be CD-ROM opportunities for scholarly presses, document delivery revenue for journal publishers, or multimedia packages for the reference crowd . . . the coffee breaks buzzed with conviction that publishers who ignore new technology do so at their peril."[3] As the next millennium begins, few publishers are risking being left behind in a print-only world.

Insight into the impact of technology on the publishing bottom line appeared in a *Publishers Weekly* (*PW*) report showing that a completely digital publisher spends an average of $13.60 per page to prepare material for printing. A traditional approach costs slightly over $43 per page.[4]

TYPES OF PUBLISHERS

The publication *Book Industry Trends* employs a ten-category system for grouping the book publishing industry in the United States:

Trade

Mass market

Book clubs

Mail order (including e-mail)

Religious

Professional

University presses

El-Hi (elementary and high school textbooks)

College textbook

Publisher/distributor

Because *Book Industry Trends* is primarily interested in economic and statistical data and publishers can and do have several "lines," this grouping is slightly different from the one used in this book. (Note: Publishers often have several "lines" or divisions that handle a specific type of publishing such as trade books, college textbooks, and mass-market paperbacks.) The following discussion provides an overview of these and two additional types of publishing firms, some of which mirror the categories used by *Book Industry Trends*, and some more specific to the library world. Some are identified by different names.

Trade publishers produce a wide range of titles, both fiction and nonfiction, that have wide sales potential. HarperCollins; Alfred A. Knopf; Doubleday; Macmillan; Little, Brown; Thames & Hudson; Random House; and McClelland & Stewart are typical trade publishers. Many trade publishers have divisions that produce specialty titles, such as children's, college textbooks, paperback, and reference. Trade publishers have three markets: bookstores, libraries, and wholesalers. To sell their products, publishers often send sales representatives to visit buyers in businesses or institutions in each of the markets. Discounts for trade titles tend to be higher than for many other types of publications.

Specialty publishers restrict output to a few areas or subjects. Facts on File is an example of a specialty publisher in the field of reference titles. Specialty publishers' audiences are smaller and more critical of the material than are trade publishers' audiences. The categories of specialty publishers include reference, paperback, children's, microform, music, cartographic, and subject area. Discounts tend to be low for titles in this category.

Textbook publishers, especially those that target the primary and secondary schools (El-Hi), occupy one of the highest risk areas of publishing. Most publishers in this area develop a line of textbooks for several grades, for example, a social studies series. Preparation of such texts requires large amounts of time, energy, and money. Printing costs are high because most school texts feature expensive color plates and other specialized presswork. Such projects require large, up-front investments that must be recouped before a profit can be realized. If enough school districts adopt a text, profits can be substantial, but failure to secure adoption can mean tremendous loss. Larger textbook firms, such as Ginn or Scott, Foresman & Company, produce several series to help ensure a profit or to cushion against loss. Given the extreme volatility of this venue, the question remains, "Why would a company take this risk?" During the 1990s U.S. El-Hi publishers faced increased pressure to change the content of their publications from a variety of special interest groups.[5] This pressure adds yet another element of risk to textbook publishing. Discounts are rare for El-Hi titles, except in very large quantities, and low for college-level materials.

Subject specialty publishers share some of the characteristics of textbook houses. Many have narrow markets that are easy to identify. Focusing marketing efforts on a limited number of potential buyers allows specialty publishers to achieve a reasonable return with less risk than a trade publisher takes on a nonfiction title. Specialty houses exist for a variety of fields; examples include art (e.g., Harry N. Abrams), music (e.g., Schirmer), science (e.g., Academic Press), technical (e.g., American Technical Publishers), law (e.g., West Publishing), and medical (e.g., W. B. Saunders). Many specialty books require expensive graphic preparation or presswork. Such presswork increases production costs, which is one of the reasons art, music, and science, medical, and technology (SMT) titles are so costly. Another factor in their cost is their smaller market compared to the market for a trade title. A smaller market means the publisher must recover production costs from fewer books. Although the risk level is greater for specialty publishing than for trade publishing, it is much lower than that for El-Hi publishers. Discounts for such items are low to nonexistent.

Vanity presses differ from other publishing houses in that they receive most of their operating funds from the authors whose works they publish. An example is Exposition Press. Vanity presses always show a profit and never lack material to produce. They offer editing assistance for a fee, and they arrange to print as many copies of the book as the author can afford. Distribution is the author's chore. Although providing some of the same functions as other publishers, they do not share the same risks. Many authors who use vanity presses donate copies of their books to local libraries, but such items frequently arrive with no indication that they are gifts. Books arriving in the acquisitions department without packing slips or invoices create extra work for the staff as they attempt to determine why the item arrived. By knowing vanity publishers, acquisitions department staff can make their work easier.

Private presses are not business operations in the sense that the owners do not always expect to make money. Most private presses are an avocation rather than a vocation for the owners. Examples are Henry Morris, Bird, and Poull Press. In many instances, the owners do not sell their products but give them away. Most private presses are owned by individuals who enjoy fine printing and experimenting with type fonts and design. When an owner gives away the end product (often produced on a hand press), only a few copies are printed. In the past, many developments in type and book design originated with private presses. Some of the most beautiful examples of typographic and book design originated at private presses. Large research libraries often attempt to secure copies of items produced by private presses.

Scholarly publishers, as part of a not-for-profit organization, receive subsidies. Most are part of an academic institution (University of California Press), museum (Museum of the American Indian Heye Foundation), research institution (Battelle Memorial Institute), or learned society (American Philosophical Society). Scholars established these presses to produce scholarly books that would not be acceptable to most for-profit publishers. Most scholarly books have limited sales appeal. A commercial, or for-profit, publisher considering a scholarly manuscript has three choices: (1) publish it and try to sell it at a price to ensure costs are recovered; (2) publish it, sell it at a price comparable to commercial titles, and lose money; or (3) do not publish the item. Because of economic factors and a need to disseminate scholarly information regardless of cost (that is, even if it will lose money), the subsidized (by tax exemption, if nothing else), not-for-profit press exists. As publishing costs have skyrocketed, it has been necessary to fully subsidize some scholarly books, almost in the manner of a vanity press.

The role of the scholarly press in the economical and open dissemination of knowledge is critical. Every country needs some form of this type of press. Without scholarly presses, important works with limited appeal do not get published. Certainly there are times when a commercial house is willing to publish a book that will not show a profit because the publisher thinks the book is important, but relying on that type of willingness will, in the long run, mean that many important works will never appear in print. Discounts for scholarly press titles are normally modest at best.

Like their for-profit counterparts, scholarly presses are making ever-greater use of electronic publishing techniques. Two good survey articles about how electronics are changing scholarly publishing are William Arms's "Scholarly Publishing on the National Networks"[6] and Ann Okerson's "Publishing Through the Network: The 1990s Debutante."[7] Although the networks hold promise, they also hold the possibility of higher information costs. As Lisa Freeman notes:

> If profit rather than commitment to scholarly communication becomes the primary goal of those controlling access to the Internet, university presses would find themselves unable to afford to publish the scholarly works that are the core of their activities. Thus the public nature of the Internet must be carefully guarded if we want to realize the true benefits of a democratic networked environment: broad access to scholarly research and information not driven by financial concerns. A diverse range of independent, nonprofit publishers is critical to that goal.[8]

Government presses are the world's largest publishers. The combined annual output of government publications—international (UNESCO); national (U.S. Government Printing Office and Canadian Government Publishing); and state, provincial, regional, and local (Los Angeles or State of California)—dwarfs commercial output. In the past, many people thought of government publications as being characterized by poor physical quality or as uninteresting items that governments gave away. Today, some government publications rival the best offerings of commercial publishers and cost much less. (The government price does not fully recover production costs, so the price can be lower.) Most government publishing activity goes well beyond the printing of legislative hearings or actions and occasional executive materials. Often national governments publish essential and inexpensive (frequently free) materials on nutrition, farming, building trades, travel, and many other topics. (See Chapter 12 for more detailed information about government publications.)

Paperback publishers produce two types of work: quality trade paperbacks and mass-market paperbacks. A trade publisher may have a quality paperback division or may issue the paperbound version of a book through the same division that issued the hardcover edition. The publisher may publish original paperbacks, that is, a first edition in paperback. Distribution of quality paperbacks is the same as for hardcover books. Mass-market paperback publishers issue only reprints, or publications that first appeared in hardcover. Their distribution differs from that of other books. Their low price is based, in part, on the concept of mass sales. Therefore, they sell anywhere the publisher can get someone to handle them. The paperback books on sale in train and bus stations, airline terminals, corner stores, and kiosks are mass-market paperbacks. These books have a short shelf life compared to hardcovers.

Books with paper covers are not new. In some countries all books come out with paper covers, and buyers must bind the books they wish to keep. The major difference is that most people think of only the mass-market paperback as a "paperback." The emphasis on popular, previously published titles issued in new and colorful covers and sold at a low price is apparent. Those are the elements of the paperback revolution, not the paper cover or even the relatively compact form. Nor has the paperback created a whole new group of readers, as some over-enthusiastic writers claim. It has merely tapped an existing market for low-cost, popular books.

Contrary to popular belief, using a paper cover rather than a hard cover does not reduce the unit cost of a book by any significant amount. Original paperbacks incur the same costs, except for the cover material, as a hardcover title, which is why their cost is so much higher than that of reprint paperbacks. The reason the price of paperbacks is so much lower than hardcovers is that most first appeared as hardcovers. The title already sold well in hardcover, or there would be no reason to bring out a paper version, so the book probably has already shown a profit. This means the publisher has already recovered almost all of the major production costs, thus making it possible to reduce the price. In addition, releasing a paperback version of a hardcover title allows the publisher to benefit from marketing efforts expended on the hardcover version. Marketing efforts for the hardcover carry over to the paperback, which further reduces publishing costs. Economies of scale, or high sales volume and low per-unit profits, also reduce the price. Discounts for original titles in paperback are similar to those for hardbacks, while mass-market discounts tend to be higher.

Small presses are important for some libraries. Small presses are thought of as literary presses by some people, including librarians. Anyone reading the annual "Small Press Round-Up" in *Library Journal* could reasonably reach the same conclusion. The reality is that small presses are as diverse as the international publishing conglomerates. Size is the only real difference; in functions and interests small presses are no different than large trade publishers.

Small Press Record of Books in Print (*SPRBIP*) annually lists between 15,000 and 17,000 titles from about 1,800 small publishers.[9] Many of these presses are one-person operations, a sideline from the publisher's home. Such presses seldom publish more than four titles per year. The listings in *SPRBIP* show the broad range of subject interests of small presses and that there are both book and periodical presses in this category. Some people assume that the content of small-press publications is poor. This is incorrect, for small presses do not produce, proportionally, any more poor quality titles than do the large publishers. Often, it is only through the small press that one can find information on less popular topics.

Another factor that sets small presses apart from their larger counterparts is economics. Large publishers have high costs and need substantial sales to recover their costs, but small presses can produce a book for a limited market at a reasonable cost and still expect some profit. Small presses also can produce books more quickly than their larger counterparts.

From an acquisitions point of view, small presses represent a challenge. Tracking down new releases can present a variety of problems. Locating a correct current address is one common problem. Another is learning about the title before it goes out of print. *SPRBIP* tries to provide current information. However, waiting for the annual *SPRBIP* may take too long, because small presses frequently move about and their press runs are small, that is, only a limited quantity of books are printed.

Acquisitions departments interested in small presses have had some commercial help. Quality Books of Oregon (a vendor that in the past was known primarily as a source of remainder books) has become active in the distribution of small press publications. Although it stocks books from only a small percentage of the presses listed in *SPRBIP* (about one-fifth), the fact that it does stock the items is a major feature. Like other distributors it has a "Web presence" (www.quality–books.com).

Serial (newspaper and periodical) *publishers* are a different class of publisher. Usually, book publishers depend on persons outside their organization to prepare the material that they publish. Newspaper and periodical publishers have staff reporters or writers. Of course, there are exceptions to the exception. For instance, some popular (and most scholarly) periodicals consist of articles written by persons not employed by the organization that publishes the journal. In general, in newspaper or periodical publishing, one finds the same range of activities found in book publishing. In other words, there are commercial publishers of popular materials, specialty publishers, children's publishers, scholarly or academic publishers, and government publishers. All subcategories share the characteristics of their book publishing counterparts; some are divisions of book publishing organizations. Chapters 10 and 11 cover serial publishers in more detail.

Publisher/distributors are an important part of the publishing industry in Canada. Because Canada's small population is stretched over a very large country, distribution costs are higher and production runs are lower than in the United States. Many Canadian publishers, such as Thomas Allen and Fitzhenry & Whiteside, also function as distributors or agents of foreign publishers to supplement their publishing activities. A list of Canadian publishers is found in Quill & Quire's *Canadian Publishers Directory,* published semi-annually.

FUNCTIONS OF PUBLISHING

Publishing consists of five basic functions, which apply equally to print and nonprint materials: administration, editorial work, production, marketing, and fulfillment. A publisher must be successful in all five areas if the organization is to survive for any length of time. Just because the organization is a nonprofit does not mean it has any less need for success in each of these areas. Administration deals with ensuring that there is coordination among the functional departments, as well as making certain there are adequate funds available to cover the costs of doing business.

It is in the editorial area that publishers decide what to produce and when to release it for sale. Acquisitions and managing editors discuss and review ideas for books or articles. Publishers develop trade lists (a combination of prior publications, manuscripts in production, and titles under contract) that they hope will achieve a profit while avoiding unnecessary competition with other publishers.

Securing and reviewing manuscripts is a time-consuming activity for most editors. An educated guess is that editors reject approximately nine-tenths of all unsolicited manuscripts after the first examination. After the first complete reading still more manuscripts are rejected. Even after a careful review by several people, all of whom have favorable reactions, the editor may not accept the manuscript. Three common reasons for nonselection are that (1) the title will not fit into the new list, (2) the sales potential (market) is too low, and (3) the cost of production would be too high.

Librarians and readers often complain that commercial publishers are exclusively, or at least overly, concerned with profit and have little concern for quality. What these people forget is that publishing houses are businesses and must show a profit if they are to continue to operate.

In 1998, the *New York Times* published an article about rising book production costs, loss of editors, and the increase in errors in books. This article noted that there was a 16 percent decrease in the publishing workforce in New York City between 1990 and 1998, primarily in the editorial category. It also speculated about the role mergers played in the situation. One editor was quoted as saying, "It's all become a big, fat, screaming, mean, vicious, greedy, rude, and crude feast. . . . So little of your time is spent doing creative work that I'm seriously considering leaving."[10] One hopes that the critical situation in New York City does not reflect the field as a whole.

Production and marketing join with the editorial team to make the final decisions regarding production details. Most publishers can package and price publications in a variety of ways. Some years ago, the Association of University

Publishers released an interesting book, *One Book Five Ways*.[11] The book provides a fascinating picture of how five different university presses would handle the same project. In all five functional areas, the presses would have proceeded differently, from contract agreement (administration), copyediting (editorial), physical format (production), pricing and advertising (marketing), to distribution (fulfillment).

Production staff consider issues such as page size, typeface, number and type of illustrative materials, and cover design, as well as typesetting, printing, and binding. Their input and the decision made regarding the physical form of the item play a major role in how much the title will cost. Although electronic and desktop publishing are changing how and who performs some production activities, the basic issues of design, layout, use of illustrations, and use of color remain unchanged.

Marketing departments are responsible for promoting and selling the product. They provide input about the sales potential of the title. Further, this unit often decides how many review copies to distribute and to what review sources. Where, when, or whether to place an ad is the responsibility of the marketing department. All of these decisions influence the cost of the items produced. Many small publishers use direct mail (catalogs and brochures) to market their books. Publishers' sales representatives visit stores, wholesalers, schools, and libraries. When salespeople visit the library or information center, they keep the visits short and to the point. Each visit represents a cost to the publisher, and the company recovers the cost in some manner, most often in the price of the material.

One activity for which most marketing units are responsible is exhibits. For library personnel, conventions are one of the best places to meet publishers' representatives and have some input into the decision-making process. From the publishers' point of view, if the conferees go to the exhibits, conventions can be a cost-effective way of reaching a large number of potential customers in a brief time. Library staff members should also remember that the fees exhibitors pay help underwrite the cost of the convention.

Fulfillment activities are those needed to process an order as well as those connected with the warehousing of the materials produced. In many ways, fulfillment is the least controllable cost factor for a publisher. Libraries and information centers sometimes add to the cost of their purchases by requiring special handling of their orders. Keeping special needs to a minimum can help keep prices in check. Speeding up payments to publishers and vendors will also help slow price increases, because the longer a publisher has to carry an outstanding account, the more interest has to be paid. Ultimately, most increases in the cost of doing business result in a higher price for the buyer, so whatever libraries can do to help publishers control their fulfillment costs will also help acquisitions budgets.

For various reasons, despite strong marketing efforts, some publications do not sell as well as expected. When this happens, sooner or later the publisher has to dispose of the material; often these become remaindered items. A decision by the U.S. Internal Revenue Service (*Thor Power Tool Co. vs. Commissioner of Internal Revenue,* 439 U.S. 522 [1979]) has influenced press runs in the United States and the speed with which publishers remainder slow-moving warehouse stock. Remaindered items sell for a small fraction of their actual production costs. Prior to the *Thor* decision, businesses would write down the value of their inventories, or warehouse stock, to a nominal level at the end of the tax year. The resulting loss in the value of the inventory (which was, by and large, only a paper loss) then became a tax deduction for the company, thereby increasing the profit margin. Since *Thor,* publishers can only take such a deduction if the material is defective or offered for sale below actual production costs. Under the previous method, publishers could find it profitable to keep slow-selling titles in their warehouses for years. Thus far, efforts to get an exemption from the ruling for publishers have been unsuccessful. At first, the ruling increased the number of remaindered books, but now most publishers have cut back on the size of their print runs in an attempt to match inventories to expected sales volume. More often than not, this means higher unit costs and retail prices. Despite all the problems for the field, U.S. total net sales income for book publishing has increased steadily, from $14.1 billion in 1989 to an estimated $24.02 billion in 1999.[12]

What is a "typical" return for a 250-page trade book selling for U.S. $25.00? Following are costs for a hypothetical first press run:

Suggested Retail Price	$25.00
Printing/binding	–2.00
	23.00
Warehouse/distribution	–2.00
	21.00
Discount to retailer	–12.50
	8.50
Overhead (including editorial)	–2.00
	6.50
Marketing	–1.50
	5.00
Author royalty (10–15%)	–1.25*
Profit	3.75

*Most royalties are based on the net sales income, not the list price.

Werner Rebsamen published some percentages of costs provided by a major New York publisher to use at his presentation at the Book Manufacturing Institute in 1997:

24.1% Royalties and guarantees

5.7% Editorial production

16.4% Marketing

24.2% Manufacturing

9.2% Returns

8.4% Fulfillment

9.3% General administration[13]

Annual sales data are available in a variety of sources: *PW, The Bowker Annual of Library & Book Trade Almanac,* Standard and Poor's *Industry Surveys,* and so forth. Anyone concerned with acquisitions budgets must make use of statistical data about publishing to develop intelligent budget requests and work plans. Statistical data about the number of new titles available as paperbacks, reprints, and so forth can be useful in planning the workload for the next fiscal year. For example, perhaps the library will need to hire some temporary staff or redirect efforts of existing staff, if the volume of acquisitions increases. Knowing the pricing patterns over a period of years and the expected acquisitions budget allows libraries to project workload. The two most accessible sources of publishing statistics for the United States are *PW* and *The Bowker Annual.* Data in both sources, and almost all other printed statistical data about publishing, come from the American Book Producers Association (ABPA), and not all publishers belong to the group. In fact, a great many small and regional publishers are not members.

Publishers use a variety of distribution outlets, selling directly to individuals, institutions, retailers, and wholesalers. Distribution is a major problem for both publishers and libraries because of the number of channels and the implications for acquiring a specific publication. Each channel has a different discount, and they are accessed through different sources. Figure 6.1 illustrates in a general way the complexity of the system. Production and distribution of information materials, whether print or nonprint, consist of several elements, all interacting with one another. Writers and creators of the material can and do distribute their output in several ways: directly to the community or public, to agents who in turn pass it on to producers, or directly to the producers. Producers seeking writers often approach agents with publication ideas. Figure 6.1 illustrates the variety of channels publishers use to distribute their publications to the consumer.

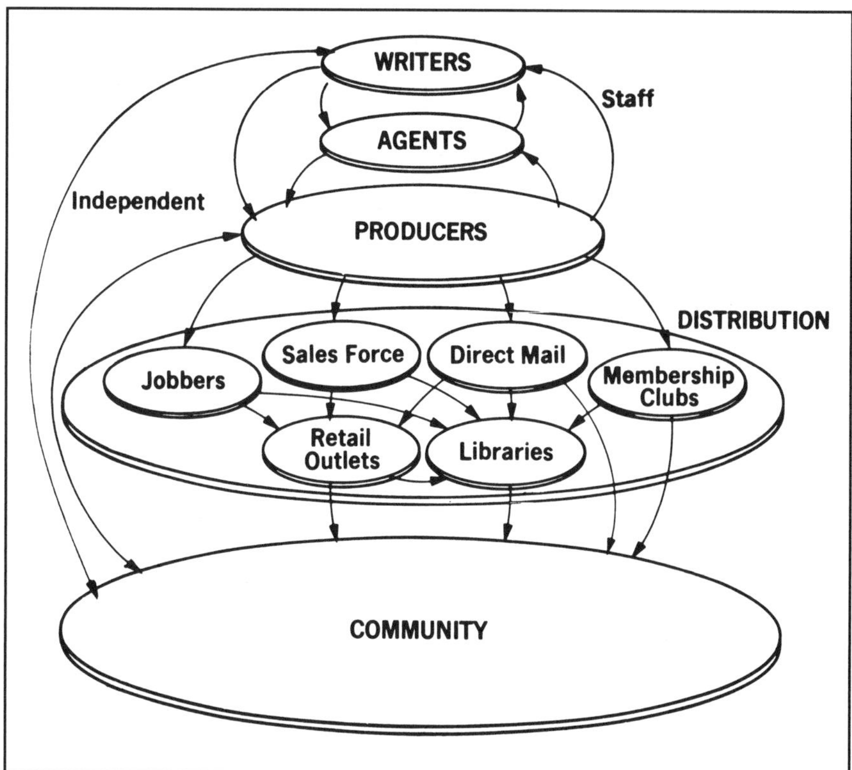

Figure. 6.1. Distribution system.

Most publishers use all these sales channels. Wholesalers, direct mail companies, and retail store operators act as middlemen; a retailer may buy from the jobber or directly from the publisher. Each seller will have different discounts for different categories of buyers, ranging from no discount to more than 50 percent. Not only are there a great many choices available to the buyer, but the sources compete with one another. These factors combine to push up the cost of distributing a publication, which in turn increases its list price. With multiple outlets, different discounts, and different credit conditions, the publishing industry has created a cumbersome, uneconomical distribution system.

This brief overview outlines the most basic elements of publishing. Its purpose is to start a technical services novice thinking about the trade. The next section discusses nonbook producers. Unfortunately, because of their diversity, it is not possible in a limited space to parallel the discussion of print publishing.

PRODUCERS OF NONBOOK MATERIALS

Nonbook media producers are a diverse group working in a variety of formats (sound recordings, film, video, models, and so on), making it difficult to generalize about their operations. The following discussion is an attempt to cover all of these nonbook formats, but it would require a full-length book to describe all the individual variations and exceptions.

Media producers enjoy substantial annual sales to schools and libraries. In fact, this market is almost the sole sales outlet for the majority of educational media producers. Two major exceptions are audio and videorecordings. The audio and videorecording industries are major sources of "other media" for most libraries. Recorded music, as part of a growing sound collection that includes talking books, is a common feature of libraries, reflecting the fact that a large segment of the general population buys or listens to music. In terms of sales, however, libraries and other institutions represent only a fraction of the music industry's income.

Considering average circulations per title, videorecordings are often the top circulation format, especially in public libraries. Video collections in libraries contain both educational and theatrical film recordings. The sales of motion picture videocassettes are far larger to the general public than to libraries, but libraries (including school media centers) are the largest market for educational video.

One important fact to remember about most media, with the exception of books, is that they require the user to follow the material at a fixed pace—the pace of the machine involved. The equipment allows for rewinding and reviewing a section of special importance, and video players can freeze a frame, but aside from DVDs most formats make it difficult to skip around as one can do in a book. Interactive video and hypermedia allow for easy random access, and these technologies are most likely to replace many of the traditional media formats libraries have made available. What newer formats and technology will replace interactive systems is impossible to guess. To many people who follow developments in the field, "virtual reality" is an enhancement of interactive systems and not really a new "system."

Most media producers design products for the average ability or level of knowledge of the target audience. In the case of educational media, the producer assumes the item is for group presentations, with a teacher adding comments and creating a context for the material. Although individuals working alone can benefit from the material, many will gain less from the use of the item without some interaction with an instructor. More teachers in schools and higher education are assigning media use outside the classroom in the same way they have employed print material to supplement the instructional program. This translates into libraries and media centers receiving requests for bigger and more diverse media collections, part of the "more factor" discussed in Chapter 3. It also means more money is needed to acquire materials, often with the added cost of securing "performance rights" (see Chapter 13).

The primary difference between book publishers and media producers is that media producers market a product designed primarily for group use, and book publishers market a product designed primarily for individual use. This difference has an influence on how media producers market and distribute their products. Media producers place heavy emphasis on direct institutional sales. Also, there is less use of wholesalers. Although some book jobbers do handle audio and videorecordings, a large percentage of media acquisitions are made directly from the producer.

One characteristic of media production that is frequently overlooked is authorship. Most books are the result of the intellectual effort of one or two persons. Textbook publishers frequently commission books. (Perhaps in the age of mergers, this approach will become more common for trade publications as well.) For media, the process is opposite. Normally, the producer generates the ideas and seeks the necessary persons to carry out the project if the company's staff cannot handle the project. *This means that in most cases the producers have almost total control over the final product.*

Despite the producers' control, people often think of the media field as one of independence and freedom. One reason for this view, at least in the past, is the relatively low cost of entering it. One hears stories about the individual who started off with a few thousand dollars and some equipment and is now a major producer. One does not hear about the thousands of others who tried and failed. Mediocre equipment and a low advertising budget usually mean a mediocre product and few, if any, sales. The opportunity is there, but the chances of success are only slightly better than for any other business venture. High-quality professional media production equipment is exceedingly expensive; however, many of the so-called producers do not invest in quality equipment.

Another characteristic of media producers is that their products have a fairly high cost per unit of information conveyed. Many media items are single-concept materials. Books, on the other hand, have a low cost per unit of information. For example, no single film, videotape, audiotape, or set of 35mm slides can convey the same amount of information about Native Americans as one 300-page book. This fact has budget implications for the library, as most media cost more than do books. Today, educational videocassettes range from U.S. $200 to $300 for educational videos to theatrical cassettes under U.S. $20. Sets of 35mm slides range from U.S. $5 to $500. In general, the kit combinations of media are high-profit items. Prices on such combinations run from U.S. $20 to more than U.S. $100.

Although book publishers use a multitude of outlets to sell their products, media producers use few outlets. With the exception of audio and video stores and a few map shops, there are no retail outlets for "other media." There are no media-of-the-month clubs (except for music recordings and videos), few mail-order houses, and no remainder houses (except for recordings and some videos). Even wholesalers dealing with all media are few and far between. The main source, and in some cases the *only* source, is the producer. Because the producers are the basic source, acquisitions department personnel must spend large amounts of time and energy maintaining lists of producers' addresses. Without such records, schools and libraries would almost have to halt their acquisition of "other media." Because many producers are small and move frequently, updating addresses is a constant problem for the library. Directories more than twelve months old are likely to be out of date.

The one advantage to this situation is that the market for media is clearly identifiable: schools and libraries. Like the specialty publisher, the media producer is better able to focus advertising and sales activities on a small area with a high probability of success. Trade book publishers use a broad spectrum of advertising sources, newspapers, periodicals, flyers, radio, and television. In general, the trade publisher must take a "shotgun" approach, but specialty publishers and media producers should have a much better idea of their market.

The majority of media producers are small-business owners without a large capital reserve. For the small media producer, cash flow is a real problem. Anything that the library can do to help the small media firm control its costs will help to control the unit cost of products as well, such as using cooperative previewing and keeping order and billing procedures simple.

One other important characteristic of the media field is the speed with which its technology changes. This characteristic is a central problem for everyone concerned, both producers and consumers. Improvements in equipment constantly make existing equipment almost obsolete; occasionally, a new format may, in fact, make equipment obsolete. Given the volatile nature of the field, many users, with good reason, are reluctant to invest heavily in equipment. For the producer, the problem is greater; it means deciding quickly whether to go with the new or stay with the old. Staying with the old too long may cut the producer out of the field because of licensing and franchising considerations, or simply not keeping up to date. On the other hand, moving too soon may expend precious capital on a change that does not last. Chapter 13 provides more information about media formats and their acquisition.

Table 6.1 provides an overview of the basic differences between book publishers and media producers, differences that have an impact on acquisitions work. It presents broad generalizations to which there are many exceptions.

Table 6.1. Differences Between Media Producers and Book Publishers

	Media Producers	Book Publishers
Audience	Individual as part of a group	Individual
Idea authorship	Company generated	Agent generated
Use	Group and sequential; equipment paced	Single and nonsequential; self-paced
Cost per concept	High	Low
Library selection process	Usually group	Individual
Cost to enter field	Relatively low, except for interactive formats	Moderately high; desktop publishing low
Inventory	Low	High
Market	Clearly defined	Highly variable
Potential sales	Low (except for audio and video recordings)	Medium
Cost per copy to buy	Moderate	Relatively low
Ease of copying	Easy to copy; high sales price	Easy to copy; low sales price
Distribution	Mostly single source	Multiple source
Changes in format and equipment	Very rapid; high rate of obsolescence	Relatively slow

SUMMARY

This chapter briefly outlines the history and development of organizations that produce the materials that libraries acquire, catalog, and process to create the collections for their user communities, touching on how these businesses function as well as some of the major types of material they produce. It also notes how the various types of businesses differ and what impact those differences have on the cost of the materials acquired.

NOTES

1. F. W. Lancaster, *Libraries and Librarians in the Age of Electronics* (Arlington, VA: Information Resources Press, 1982).

2. Albert N. Greco, *The Book Publishing Industry* (Boston: Allyn & Bacon, 1997), x-xi.

3. Gayle Feldman, "Professional Publishing Goes Electronic," *Publishers Weekly* 239 (May 11, 1992): 31.

4. Sally Taylor, "The Joys of Electronic Togetherness," *Publishers Weekly* 240 (March 29, 1993): 24.

5. "State Board of Education Approves New Texts Despite Groups' Protests," *San Fernando Valley Daily News,* October 13, 1990, 1, 23.

6. William Arms, "Scholarly Publishing on the National Networks," *Scholarly Publishing* 23 (April 1992): 158-169.

7. Ann Okerson, "Publishing Through the Network: The 1990s Debutante," *Scholarly Publishing* 23 (April 1992): 170-177.

8. Lisa Freeman, "Big Challenges Face University Presses in the Electronic Age," *Chronicle of Higher Education* (April 28, 1993): A44.

9. *Small Press Record of Books in Print* (Paradise, CA: Dustbooks, 1975-).

10. Doreen Carvajal, "The More Books, the Fewer the Editors," *New York Times,* June 29, 1998, B1, B3.

11. *One Book Five Ways* (Los Altos, CA: William Kaufmann, 1977).

12. *Bowker Annual—2000* (New York: R. R. Bowker, 2000), 515.

13. Werner Rebsamen, "Trends in Publishing, New Technologies and Opportunities," *The New Library Scene* 16 (December 1997): 10-12.

SUGGESTED READING

Arbolleda, Amadio Antonio. "The Gutenberg Syndrome: An Illusion of International Research." *Journal of Scholarly Publishing* 32 (April 2001): 155-163.

"Audiobook Producers & Distributors." *School Libraries in Canada* 19, no. 3 (1999): 26.

Baker, J. F. "Canada: It Can Only Get Better." *Publishers Weekly* 248 (May 14, 2001): S2-S3.

Baldwin, James A. "Why Do We Still Buy Books." *Library Collections, Acquisitions, and Technical Services* 24 (Spring 2000): 403-404.

"Canadian Publishing: Weathering the Storm." *Publishers Weekly* 248 (May 14, 2001): S1-S24.

Greco, A. N. *The Book Publishing Industry*. Boston: Allyn & Bacon, 1997.

Hilts, Paul. "21st Century Publishing." *Publishers Weekly* 248 (May 21, 2001): 44-45.

Holzenberg, Eric J. "Second-hand and Antiquarian Books on the Internet." *RBM* 2, no. 1 (2001): 35-46.

Lawal, Ibironke. "Scholarly Communication at the Turn of the Millennium: A Bibliographic Essay." *Journal of Scholarly Publishing* 32 (April 2001): 136-154.

Maughan, Shannon. "Checking Up on Children's Audio." *Publishers Weekly* 248 (June 11, 2001): 46-48.

Missek, Marla. "Universities Cut Their Teeth on DVD." *Emedia* 14 (April 2001): 37-39.

Parang, E. "The Convergence of User Needs, Collection Building and the Electronic Publishing Marketplace." *Serials Librarian* 38, nos. 3/ 4 (2000): 333-339.

Quill & Quire: Canada's Magazine of Book News & Reviews. Markham, ON: Key Media. This is the periodical that deals with English-language publishing in Canada. For information about French-language publishing see the Web site of L'Association nationale des éditeurs de livres at http://www.anel.com.

Rosenblum, Trudi. "Audiobooks: Soaring Upward." *Publishers Weekly* 248 (June 11, 2001): 38-41.

Scales, Pat R. "Natural Born Editor." *School Library Journal* 47 (May 2001): 50-53.

Waldrep, Mark. "Surround from the Ground Up: The Making of a DVD-Audio Title." *Emedia* 14 (April 2001): 30-36.

Winter, K. "From Pulp to the Web: The Online Evolution." *American Libraries* 31 (May 2000): 70-74.

REVIEW QUESTIONS

1. What are the typical stages of publishing in a country, and how do those stages affect the work of acquisitions departments?
2. What are the six basic functions performed by a company producing information materials (books, media, e-products)?
3. Discuss the types of publishing organizations and note the factors about their primary markets that affect the cost of products to libraries.
4. What are the basic functions in the production process? Which one appears to add the greatest cost to the end product?
5. Discuss how nonbook media producers differ from print producers. In what ways do those differences affect the cost of the materials?

Chapter

Acquisition Process

Figure 5.1 (p. 99) provides an overview of the acquisition process. The steps can be divided into three broad categories: preorder, order, and postorder activities. This chapter touches on all the steps; however, the primary focus is on preorder activities. Chapter 8 focuses on the means of acquiring materials by purchase or gift and exchange and postordering activities.

TYPES OF MATERIALS PURCHASED

A library's collection exists to achieve certain objectives: education, information, aesthetic appreciation, recreation, and research. Each objective requires a different mix of formats. Aesthetic appreciation often requires recorded music, dramatic readings, and visual and graphic materials of various types. Research objectives often require acquiring report literature and conference papers and proceedings. The acquisition of these materials requires in-depth knowledge about the materials and suitable sources of supply. These formats are discussed in Chapter 5 but are briefly reviewed here.

Printed Materials

Books and printed materials still represent the bulk of library purchases. As noted previously, U.S. publishers produce over 30,000 new titles each year and more than 10,000 new editions. Most libraries only purchase a small percentage of the total output. In addition to books, thousands of periodical and serial titles are available in both print and electronic formats. Government documents of national, state, local, and international scope are additional considerations for libraries of all sizes. Scholarly publications, dissertations, theses, and publications of learned societies as well as atlases, maps, and globes are staples in many library collections. Printed music, pamphlets, and ephemera of all types are also material the acquisitions department orders and receives.

Nonbook Materials

As demonstrated in Chapter 13, microfilm and microfiche are two frequently ordered microformats. Other popular nonbook materials are audiobooks, CD recordings, videocassettes, and DVDs. Libraries face a number of challenges in acquiring these items, but many of the steps used to order a book apply to these other media as well.

Electronic Resources

Over the past ten-plus years, electronic products have moved from being a relatively rare acquisition to forming part of a triad of format categories that technical services must handle on a regular basis. Within the electronic group there are two primary types of products: databases of what are usually thought of as reference materials (indexes and abstracting services) and full-text products of journal articles. Increasingly the material is Web-based, but there are still a significant number of CD-ROM products available, many of which are digitized versions of reference materials (for example, encyclopedias and dictionaries) or large seldom-used sets (such as *American National Bibliography*). Some of these products are digitized version of titles that also exist in print and others are original electronic titles. Chapter 11 provides more information about electronic products as well as information about acquiring them.

GENERAL ORGANIZATION AND PROCEDURES

Staffing patterns vary in acquisitions departments, but a librarian is almost always the unit's immediate supervisor. As the workload increases, the library may divide the work into several sub-units. Generally, support staff members have the supervisory responsibility for the sub-units. A very large library might have separate units for verification, ordering, bookkeeping, receiving, bindery preparation, and gifts and exchange.

Most verification activities are the responsibility of library support staff or part-time help. The librarians usually only work on items the support staff could not verify or with foreign-language materials. As staff size increases, library assistants are very likely to gain supervisory responsibility in this area.

Request Processing

The first step in the acquisitions process is to organize the incoming requests. The format of the request can range from oral requests or a scrawled note on a napkin to a completed formal request card. Eventually, the staff organizes all requests so they can carry out an efficient checking process. Each library will have its own request form, typically a card produced by a library supply firm, such as Gaylord or Brodart. To make it easier to conduct the necessary searches, requests arriving in other forms are transferred to a request card. Sometimes, when selectors use a trade bibliography (such as *Publishers Weekly*) or national one (such as *Canadiana* or the National Library of Canada's *Forthcoming Books*), they simply check desired items in the publication, and the searchers work with the entire publication rather than transferring everything to request cards. (Despite the electronic aspects of acquisitions work, there is a rather large dependence on paper-based forms, especially for international titles. It may be some time before that dependence disappears.)

Commercially produced request cards cover all the categories of information called for in the *Guidelines for Handling Library Orders for In-Print Monographic Publications*[1]: author, title, publisher, date of publication, edition, ISBN or ISSN, Standard Address Number (SAN), price, and number of copies. Many provide space for other information that is of interest only to libraries, such as requester's name, series, vendor, funding source, and approval signature. For any person not familiar with library or book trade practice, the most confusing item on the request card is the space labeled "date/year." Many nonlibrary requesters often assume the library wants the date they filled out the form, rather than the items' copyright or publication date. Anyone with acquisitions department experience knows how often this confusion takes place. If the form specifically calls for the date of publication, there will be no problem.

Many patrons request items already in the collection because they do not know how to use the public catalog effectively. People occasionally combine or confuse authors' names, titles, publishers, and so forth. Therefore, bibliographic searching is the next step in acquisitions work. (Sample request forms are illustrated in Figures 7.1, page 132, and 7.2, page 133.)

Liz Chapman has provided a good six-point checklist for designing or selecting a request form:[2]

1. Is it easy for users to fill in?
2. Does it provide a logical checking route for library staff?
3. Does the checked form reflect the order in which data will be input to the order system or put onto an order form?
4. Does it provide an accessible format for checking during the stage *after* the book has been ordered but *before* it has arrived?
5. Does it provide an efficient format for checking that the book you receive is the one you ordered?
6. Will it be able to move with the book from acquisitions through cataloging and processing?

Order No.	Author:	L.C. No.
Dealer	Title	
Requested by:	Publisher: Year: Edition: Vols:	
Fund Chgd.	No. Copies:	List Price

Figure 7.1. Book request card.

Preorder Work—Verification

Bibliographic verification or searching consists of two steps: searching to establish the existence of a particular item and searching to determine whether the library needs to order the item. In the first case, the concern is with identifying the correct author, title, publisher, and other necessary ordering data. In the second case, the process determines whether the library already owns the item (perhaps received, but not yet represented in the public catalog), whether there is a need for a second copy or multiple copies, and whether the item has been ordered but not received. Integrated automated library systems make this latter step quick and easy, except for determining the need for additional copies. Many systems show ordered and received status in the online public catalog, which tends to reduce the number of requests that duplicate existing orders. (Some vendors are now offering this type of service, for a fee, of course. A few vendors may be able to actually Telnet, or otherwise gain access, to the library's OPAC and determine if the item already exists in the system. A potential problem with this is that the library may want a second copy or the item is to be a replacement copy. When using a vendor for this activity, there must be a system in place to handle such cases.)

Where does the process begin? The answer depends on the collection development system employed by the library. Although it is true that all requests require searching, it also is true that not all request cards have sufficient correct information to search accurately. If the majority of information comes from bibliographies, dealers' catalogs, publishers' flyers, or forms filled out by experienced selection personnel, then determining the need is generally the most efficient way to start.

SERIAL/PERIODICAL REQUEST CARD

TITLE ______________________________

______________________ ISSN NO.______________

VOL./YEAR REQUESTED ______________ BACKSET ______________

PUBLISHER ______________PLACE ______________PRICE ______________

PRIORITY: ______________CORE ______________RELATED ______________ RESEARCH

COURSES IT WOULD SUPPORT (COURSE NO.): ______________

REQUESTED BY ______________DATE ______________

APPROVED BY ______________

PLEASE JUSTIFY THE SUBSCRIPTION TO THIS TITLE IN THE LIGHT OF OUR VERY LIMITED BUDGET FOR NEW SERIALS.

ACA/SER/12/90 rev.

LIBRARY USE ONLY FUND ______________

TITLE ______________________________

______________________FREQUENCY ______________

BEGINNING DATE OF PUBL. ______________ BEGINNING DATE OF SUBS. ______________

RECOMMENDATION AS TO DISPOSITION: ______________BIND: ______________

RETAIN ONE YEAR ONLY ______________ RETAIN TWO/MORE YEARS ______________TO BE DECIDED

REVIEWED IN ______________ INDEXED IN ______________

ORDER NO.______________ ORDER FROM: ______________PUB. ______________AGENT

DATE ORDERED ______________DATE RECEIVED ______________COST ______________

VERIFICATION:	CHECK	FOUND		CHECK	FOUND
SR	______	______	SPD	______	______
NST	______	______	SD	______	______
ULRICH'S	______	______	SS	______	______
LINUS	______	______	EBSCO	______	______
MFL	______	______	OCLC	______	______

ACQ/SER/12/90 rev.

Figure 7.2. Serials/periodicals request form.

A survey by Karen Schmidt of preorder searching indicates that between 30 and 40 percent of nonlibrarian requests are incorrect or for items already in the collection.[3] When a large percentage of the requests are from nonlibrarians, it is advisable to start with determining the existence of the title as requested.

One of the major activities for preorder searchers is establishing the correct author (main entry). Some requestors, usually nonlibrarians, know little about cataloging rules of entry. Even bibliographers may not keep up-to-date on rule changes. Knowing something about main entry rules, as well as how the standard bibliographic sources list titles, will save search time.

Corporate authors (see Chapter 17), conference papers, proceedings, or transactions are the most troublesome to search. If the department maintains its paper-based order files by title rather than main entry order, it may be possible to reduce bibliographic training to a minimum while improving accuracy. Titles do not change after publication and are easier to search. On the other hand, catalogers' decisions about the proper main entry may change several times between the time of the request and the time the item is on the shelf. Main entry searching requires a greater knowledge of cataloging rules, which, in turn, requires more time for training searchers and more time spent searching.

There are some common problems to be aware of when checking bibliographies. One obvious problem is variant spellings of an author's name, both first and last, such as the last names Smith, Smythe, Johnson, or Johnsen or a first name such as Gail, Gale, or Gayle. Another problem is variations of the author's name, for example, Ed Evans, Edward Evans, Edward G. Evans, G. Edward Evans, Gayle Edward Evans, or Gayle E. Evans. Each of these variations has appeared on at least one of Evans's publications. Corporate author entries provide even bigger challenges to the searcher's imagination and ingenuity. Collected works and joint authors also present challenges for the searcher. Searchers must understand bibliographic rules of entry. They must also use their imagination when working with problem requests. Some libraries maintain a name-authority file, especially libraries with online catalogs, which can be of great assistance with variant forms of a name.

If the author main entry search procedure does not verify 60 percent to 90 percent of the items, the staff should review the procedure. It is probable that either the requests lack adequate information (requiring additional education or training for the requesters), or the staff is searching the wrong verification tools. A title search should verify most, if not all, the requests that cannot be verified by author main entry. Occasionally, it is impossible to verify an item using the submitted information. At that point, all the department can do is contact the requester to try to acquire additional information. If the requester cannot provide additional information, a subject search may produce a verification.

The success rate of subject searches is low for several reasons. First, some bibliographies do not provide subject access, making it impossible to search all the commonly used bibliographies. A more critical reason is that the assignment of subjects is somewhat arbitrary. Even with a work in hand, two individuals may well provide two different subject categories for the same title. Searchers must look under as many subjects as seem likely and still can never be certain they have examined all the appropriate headings. Because of its low success rate, subject verification is a last resort for urgently needed items.

Occasionally, it is necessary to examine three or four sources to establish all of the required order information. One may quickly find the author, title, publisher, date of publication, and price, but it may be difficult to find information determining whether the item is in a series. Failure to identify series information may lead to unwanted duplication. For example, one copy may be received on a series standing order and another copy from a direct order. *Books in Series* was helpful but is no longer published. The 1991 edition covered only the United States and contained 37,619 series with more than 326,688 titles.[4] There is no good single source for this information today, and the problem has only increased with libraries receiving unwanted duplicates. If caught early enough in the receiving process, it "only" costs library staff time to resolve the issue and return the unwanted material. Not catching the duplication before items are property marked or stamped results in the library having two copies, needed or not.

There are several files to check when establishing the library's need for an item; this is true whether the file is paper or electronic. The most obvious starting point is the OPAC. A searcher should look first under the assumed main entry; if the results are negative and there is some doubt as to validity of the main entry, then a title search is appropriate. Many librarians suggest that checkers begin with the title because there tends to be less variation and doubt. In some libraries, even if there is an online public catalog, there may be several other paper-based public catalogs to search, for example, special collections or a media catalog, and all should be part of the checking process, if appropriate. Audiovisual materials, government documents, serials, and collections in special locations often are not fully represented in the OPAC or main card catalog. Other public service files that searchers need to examine are those for lost, missing, or damaged items (replacement files). The searcher would not examine all of these files for all items, but merely for those popular items not marked "added copy" or "replacement."

There are files that are unavailable to the public that searchers may have to examine to determine whether the item is already somewhere in the acquisitions or cataloging process. If the library has a manual system, there are usually three files to consult: the in-process file, the verified requests file (items awaiting typing on order forms), and the standing order file. The in-process file represents books on order, books received but not yet sent to cataloging, and books in the cataloging department. The standing order file represents items that will arrive automatically from a supplier and that may end the search.

Online systems are available in many libraries to speed preorder checking. *Books in Print* is available in both online and CD-ROM formats, as well as in the traditional print version. Other commercial bibliographic selection aids are also available in electronic formats. Bibliographic utilities such as OCLC and RLIN provide large bibliographic databases that are useful in verification and searching. Integrated automation systems have eased the workload on some aspects of acquisitions. For example, it is possible to download bibliographic data from a bibliographic utility. With some systems, the staff can use the downloaded data to prepare a computer-generated order form, provide an online status report, and create the basis for local cataloging work. In some libraries, a person responsible for preorder activities may be able to do 90 percent or more of the work at one terminal merely by logging on and off the integrated system and the bibliographic utility.

Bibliographic verification, the first step in the acquisitions procedure, is perhaps the most interesting and challenging duty in this department. The attempt to establish an item's existence when there is very little information is similar to detective work.

Searching Sources

Today one can carry out searching activities relatively quickly, if the library has an OPAC and has access to the Internet as well as the appropriate databases. In the not so distant past, the searching process was very labor intensive using a variety of print-based resources. Obviously, libraries lacking an OPAC or Internet access must still depend on the print sources. We devote only a small amount of space to the print materials here because they play an ever-decreasing role in preorder work in most libraries.

This section begins by describing some of the most frequently used bibliographies for printed materials. A bibliography is a publication that lists and describes information materials of any type. The term generally applies to lists of books, but in its broadest sense, it includes all materials (print or nonprint).

The types of bibliographies most frequently used in verification work are national, trade, and general bibliographies. A national bibliography (e.g., *Canadiana*) has four functions, to list all works (1) about the country, (2) produced in the country, (3) written by citizens, and (4) written while citizens of a foreign country were resident in the country. A trade bibliography lists current in-print books judged to be of interest to the general book-buying public (e.g., *American Book Publishing Record*). A general bibliography lists all books or items that exist in the collection of a particular library or on a particular subject (e.g., *Library of Congress Catalog*).

Other types of bibliographies are retrospective, current, and comprehensive. A retrospective bibliography lists older items not generally available (e.g., *Books Relating to America from Its Discovery to the Present Time*). Never assume, however, that items that are several hundred years old are not available. The activity of reprint publishers has brought many older works back into print. In practice, the terms retrospective bibliography, out-of-print bibliography, and out-of-print catalog are almost synonymous, although the latter two imply that the items listed are not generally available. A current bibliography lists items that are presently available or forthcoming (e.g., *Subject Guide to Children's Books in Print*). This is the type most frequently used in bibliographic verification work. The final type is the comprehensive bibliography, which is useful today for retrospective items (e.g., *National Union Catalog*).

Actually, many bibliographies are a combination of several of these types. For example, one commonly used source in the past was the series of Library of Congress (LC) catalogs. These are general bibliographies in that they include only the books acquired and cataloged by LC. Nevertheless, they also serve as a major segment of the U.S. national bibliography series because they include a very high percentage of all the books published in the United States.

Yet in another sense, LC's catalogs are general comprehensive bibliographies because they contain current and retrospective materials. The *British Museum Catalog of Printed Books* would be another example of a general comprehensive catalog. Therefore, keep in mind that the inclusion of the name of a country or a library in its title does not necessarily mean that a bibliography is solely national in scope. The catalogs of both the British Library and LC represent national bibliographies, but they also are more than that. They are general and national bibliographies. A strictly national bibliography that is also a trade and current bibliography is *Books in Print* (*BIP*), which lists books currently available from a number of U.S. publishers and from other countries that have publishing activities in the United States. A national retrospective bibliography that a searcher may encounter is Joseph Sabin's aforementioned *Dictionary of Books Relating to America from Its Discovery to the Present Time*, published in 1892.

U.S. Sources

The Bowker Company is the mainstay in publishing current U.S. trade bibliographies. They are also taking on an ever-increasing role in the bibliographic control of English-language publishing around the world in conjunction with the UK firm of Whitaker. Their publications make acquisitions work less complicated and time-consuming. Bowker publishes a series of bibliographies that list new titles from a U.S. publisher's first announcement of a new title until the publisher declares it out-of-print. Although acquisitions departments use all of the Bowker publications, either in print or electronic versions, a few receive very heavy use. We focus here on those high-use titles. The following are major Bowker bibliographic publications for books; the company has other publications that are useful in the acquisition of other formats:

Forthcoming Books

American Book Publishing Record

Books in Print

Books Out-of-Print

Subject Guide to Books in Print

Forthcoming Books (*FB*) and its subject guide is a useful bimonthly publication for acquisitions departments to check on the status of announced titles. Publishers submit information to Bowker about titles they expect to publish in the near future, anywhere from two to five months out. Occasionally, publishers submit information before receiving the book's manuscript. Once in a while the manuscript never does come in, so the title announced in *FB* never appears. A more frequent problem occurs when the title changes, which means that the published work will not appear under its originally announced title. *FB* also provides information about postponements and price changes. Changes in main entry between the announcement and the publication of the book also create verification headaches. Because of these limitations, searchers use *FB* primarily for problem verification work. That is, it is useful to check on requests that cannot be verified elsewhere or on vendor reports that an ordered title is "NYP" (not yet published). *FB* arranges works by author and title; an asterisk next to an entry indicates an item is appearing for the first time. Entries in *FB* have publisher-generated annotations that can be helpful in selecting items, as long as one keeps in mind that a publisher is not going to say this item is not very good or has limited appeal. Users must keep in mind that the publication is based on information publishers submit to the Bowker staff. They do not attempt to verify the information for accuracy, nor do they engage in follow-up activities on such issues as postponements or price changes.

American Book Publishing Record (*ABPR*) currently is the starting point for U.S. trade bibliographies. ABPR is a monthly listing of books published in the previous month. The author and title indexes are the primary points of access for verification and order purposes, although a subject search is also possible. *ABPR* is the one source that allows a good chance of finding an item when the searcher must attempt to verify something using the subject approach.

The *ABPR* does an excellent job and is as comprehensive as the Bowker staff can make it; however, it does have some major limitations. The most important are that (1) it lists only books of forty-nine or more pages, (2) publishers must submit title information for inclusion (Bowker does not seek out this information), and (3) it does not include serial publications. Changes in coverage do occur, so it is wise to check introductory statements periodically. However, despite these limitations, several factors make *ABPR* an essential tool in larger technical services departments. As indicated, it is the first and the most comprehensive listing of a book's availability in the United States. Another important factor is that each entry usually provides full cataloging information. The *ABPR* gets most of its cataloging information from the LCMARC records and a limited amount from cataloging done by Bowker's staff.

Verification through *ABPR* will yield information complete enough for order work. Nevertheless, using *ABPR* for verification work is time consuming because, with very few exceptions, a book only appears once. *ABPR* is a monthly, so the searcher may have to search many issues unless he or she knows the book's publication date. There is the option of using the annual volume, if the library is willing to accept a gap in current publications. Very often acquisitions departments receive a copy of *ABPR* with the desired items marked by a selection officer. In that case, all the searcher needs to do is make certain the item is not already on order. The annual cumulation volumes are a separate subscription, not part of the basic monthly service.

For retrospective searching, the *American Book Publishing Record* cumulative sets are very useful. There are three sets covering 1970–1974, 1975–1979, and 1980–1984. The volumes have information on more than 490,000 titles published in the United States during the time covered and that have gone out-of-print in most cases. Entries are arranged by Dewey class number and each set has author, title, and subject indexes.

Books in Print (*BIP*) is an annual publication with a mid-year supplement. Thus, in theory, the searcher should only need to consult *Forthcoming Books* and *American Book Publishing Record* for the latest books. But as noted, this is not always the case. Occasionally, books disappear for a few months and then reappear in the listings. Because *BIP* has become so valuable to booksellers and libraries, all major U.S. publishers submit information about their current lists of books (in print). (Note: Many small specialty and regional publishers do not submit information.) *BIP* is a multiple-volume author-title set in which the searcher can find the most complete information under the author entry. There is also a subject guide, so the searcher can gain access to information in a variety of ways. Both *FB* and *BIP* subject guides use the *Library of Congress Subject Headings* (see Chapter 19 for a description of LCSH).

Books in Print comes in a variety of electronic versions as well as print. There is an Internet edition available from Bowker (www.booksinprint.com/bip) as well as from some book jobbers or through a database such as *FirstSearch*. As of July 2001, the online version contained 3.5 million book titles, 300,000 videos, and 120,000 audiocassettes. It also included 1.3 million out-of-print titles (mirroring the print format, *Books Out-of-Print*) as well as book reviews from a dozen sources and fourteen media sources. *BIP On DISC*™ comes in either DOS, Mac, or Windows versions. The electronic versions provide faster access as well as more ways to search for information that are almost impossible in the print edition. For example, search by type or genre of book, limited edition, or technical monographs. Another plus is that one can order electronically from more than twenty-five jobbers and publishers.

Bowker puts out a print set that allows searchers to do some subject searching, if the library does not have access to an electronic version of *BIP*. *Subject Guide to Books in Print* only covers nonfiction titles. Works to which the Library of Congress does not assign subject headings (fiction, poetry, drama, and bibles) do not appear in *Subject Guide to Books in Print*. However, an exception is made for collections and criticism of fiction and poetry and for individual works of fiction whose subject background seems "extensive enough to warrant mention." Entries are in alphabetical order under LCSH and include the same bibliographic information provided by *BIP*. Juvenile books usually appear separately under subject headings designed for this purpose; however, sometimes they are listed with adult books. No matter where they are the user can always determine their grade level.

Books in Print and its companion, *Subject Guide to Books in Print*, are the basic tools for determining both availability and price of a book published in the United States. Keep in mind that information supplied by publishers comes in during the spring and early summer and that the new edition of *BIP* does not come out until the fall (usually in October). A time lag of that length is particularly significant when using *BIP* to determine prices. No printed bibliographic tool can be completely accurate and up-to-date, because publishers can and do change prices and reschedule publishing dates whenever necessary. The online version addresses some of these issues. The CD-ROM product is slower but is updated monthly. *Forthcoming Books* supplements *BIP*, serving as a bimonthly cumulative index to books published after the summer closing date for the current *BIP* and to forthcoming books.

Another of the *BIP* spin-off products is a CD-ROM entitled *Books in Print Plus with Book Reviews On Disc*™, available in Windows only. Updated bimonthly, this service is particularly useful in libraries that have a policy of not ordering items that lack a published review. (Most often it is public libraries and school media centers that have such requirements.) The CD includes the full-text reviews from publications such as *Library Journal*, *Publishers Weekly*, *School Library Journal*, *Choice*, *Booklist*, *Reference and Research Book News*, *Sci-Tech Book News*, *University Press Book News*, and *BIOSIS*.

Books Out-of-Print CD-ROM covers 1979–2001 and is a source for verifying items vendors report as out-of-print, out-of-stock indefinitely, or back-ordered. It can help cut the cost of continued searching and the unproductive holding of funds (encumbered) for items that never will arrive. The data are collected directly from the 6,000 participating publishers. The quarterly updates add to the growing number of OP titles in the database.

Other Bowker publications include such specialized bibliographies as *Medical and Health Care Books and Serials in Print*, *Children's Books in Print*, *The Complete Directory of Large Print Books and Serials*, and *El-Hi Textbooks* and *Serials in Print*. In addition, Bowker offers a range of titles to assist in the acquisition of books from around the world. Starting with the co-produced *Bowker/Whitaker Global Books on DISC*™, there are several products of great value to acquisitions departments that actively collect outside their national boundaries. *Global Books* covers titles from Australia, Canada, New Zealand, the United Kingdom, and the United States. Bowker and Whitaker staff also try to identify English-language publications no matter where they are published. This product is also available online through www.globalbooksinprint.com. Other titles in the Bowker line include *Italian Books in Print* and *African Books in Print*.

Canadian Sources

Canadiana (National Library of Canada) is a comprehensive bibliography of post-1950 Canadian materials, including book and nonbook materials, periodicals, and electronic documents. The printed edition ceased publication in 1991 and the microfiche edition at the end of 2000. *Canadiana* is now available on CD-ROM, magnetic tape, and as an online service. *Forthcoming Books*, a free publication of the National Library, is also an excellent acquisitions tool. All National Library publications are bilingual and include English- and French-language publications. *Canadiana* provides full cataloging records and *Forthcoming Books*, Canadian Cataloguing-in-Publication (CCIP) data.

Canadian Books in Print (University of Toronto Press, 1975-) publishes two volumes per year, an author/title index and a subject index. The 2001 edition has 48,148 entries, including 4,512 with a 2000 imprint. This is a listing of predominantly English-language publications based on information supplied by publishers and includes French-language titles published by Canadian publishers outside Quebec. The hardcover annual edition is followed by complete microfiche editions in April, July, and October.

The Canadian Book Review Annual is a print publication that provides 200- to 400-word reviews of English-language trade, scholarly, and reference books that are published in Canada and written by Canadians or those residing in Canada. Each review provides CCIPs. The same company also publishes *Children's Literature*.

Books in Print, Canadian Edition (Bowker) covers the books and audio titles available from all Canadian publishers and distributors, with Canadian prices. This listing includes books published in the United States and elsewhere that are distributed through Canadian agencies. The 2001 edition has information on over 100,000 titles only available in Canada.

Books in Canada (Canadian Review of Books Ltd.) is a periodical that is published nine times a year. It is selective, with some long reviews and feature articles.

There are several additional review sources for materials for children and young adults. These are not comprehensive because they rely on the willingness of publishers to submit their books for review. The following two sources are examples. *Resource Links*, a print periodical published five times a year (resourcelinks@nfld.com), reviews book and nonbook English- and French-language materials. *CM: Canadian Review of Materials* (www.umanitoba.ca/cm) is a free online service that provides reviews of English- and French-language books, CD-ROMs, sound and videorecordings, as well as foreign books sold in Canada by Canadian distributors. It is published by the Manitoba Library Association and updated biweekly from September to June. A print version was published by the Canadian Library Association from 1971 to 1994 under the title *Canadian Materials*. Back issues of this journal are available in the CM online archive.

In addition to the comprehensive list in *Canadiana*, those seeking only books published in Quebec can consult *Bibliographie du Québec* (Bibliothèque nationale du Québec), which provides bibliographic records (with subject headings in French) for books, microforms, printed music, maps, serials, sound recordings, and electronic resources published in Quebec.

Biblio-Data has a complete list of all titles available in French, including a selection of government publications of interest to the public and generally available through bookstores. It does not include maps, sheet music, newspapers, periodicals, and microfiches, or annuals not considered to be of general interest.

Because of Canada's small population, small Canadian publishers print limited runs of works that deal with Canadian topics. To be certain of obtaining these works, some libraries place prepublication orders selected from their trade catalogs.

UK Sources

Bookseller (Whitaker, formerly J. Whitaker & Sons) provides a weekly listing of trade books in an author, title, subject arrangement. Several distinctions exist between *Bookseller* and the weekly *British National Bibliography* (*BNB*), published by the British Library. First, *Bookseller* lists only trade books, and *BNB* lists everything received for copyright. Second, *Bookseller* lists British and U.S. titles, whereas *BNB* covers only British books. Note also that *Bookseller* lists new issues and cheap editions that are sometimes omitted from U.S. bibliographies. Whitaker also provides an online version of *Bookseller*.

Whitaker's Books in Print (*WBIP*) (Whitaker) is the equivalent of *BIP* in the United States. An annual publication, its information is "the definitive source of bibliographic data . . . of English language titles published in the UK, Ireland, and in Europe."[5] Whitaker's staff updates information such as price before issuing *WBIP*. A monthly microfiche service helps maintain its currency. Its author, title, and subject approach makes it a very useful searching tool. Entries also provide series information, which can be most valuable. Note that the only complete bibliographic entry is under the author, or under the title if there is no author. The data in *WBIP* are also available online through Whitaker's *BookBank*.

British National Bibliography (*BNB*) (British Library) is an annual publication that lists new British books received by "The Agent for the Copyright Libraries." It allows for an author, title, or series search. Libraries can also subscribe to this publication in a microfiche format or gain online access. The online version is UK MARC and contains post-1950 materials.

British Museum General Catalog (British Museum) is similar to the *Library of Congress Catalog*. Because of the great size of the British Museum collections, however, it is not up-to-date. In 1979, the museum announced a project intended to generate a new complete, up-to-date catalog. In the older volumes, the amount of information available varies depending on when the library cataloged the item. There is minimal information for most early works and full cataloging information for contemporary titles. A subject index exists for the set, but volumes are slow in appearing. The greatest difficulty in using this catalog stems from the fact that the rules of entry varied over time. This is particularly true of works that require a corporate author entry.

The British Library also publishes *Books in English*. Whereas *BNB* is for British imprints only (items received for UK copyright), *Books in English* (*BIE*) is worldwide in coverage. The bimonthly issues are cumulated annually. Full bibliographic data appear only under the main entry. *BIE* is available in microfiche; one set covers 1971 to 1980. At this writing, the other issues were available only as annual sets. Because the set includes data from the Library of Congress, it can be a very useful source.

Whitaker also produces *BookBank OP*, which lists over 1.4 million UK titles that have gone out-of-print since 1970. There are quarterly updates.

There are many other national equivalents to *BIP* and *WBIP*: *Australian Books in Print* (D. W. Thorpe), *New Zealand Books in Print* (D. W. Thorpe), *Italian Books in Print* (K. G. Saur), and *German Books in Print* (K. G. Saur).

Serials Sources

The ordering and verification procedures for serials are very similar to those for books. There are, however, several important differences. It is essential that the verification process establish an accurate price and the title and frequency of publication. Price is an issue because serials represent an ongoing expense for the library, and recently, the annual rate of increase in subscription prices has far exceeded the general inflation rate. Knowing the precise current price will assist the selection officer in making the final decision whether to subscribe.

A number of specialized jobbers deal exclusively or extensively with libraries' periodicals and serials needs. Among these are Faxon Company, EBSCO, and Blackwell's. Most of the jobbers supply catalogs listing the serials they handle on a regular basis and prices for various delivery options. For example, a library may want to receive its foreign serials by air rather than by surface mail. Naturally, there are different costs associated with each option. Another example is newspapers that may be available in different editions. (For more information about these variations, see Chapter 10.) The only way to accurately determine the current price is to call the jobber. Printed prices are likely to be too low, especially those in bibliographies or guides.

It is extremely important to establish the correct title because most libraries arrange their check-in files by title. If the cover title and the title used to place the subscription are different, the staff will spend unnecessary time and effort in determining the status when the first issue arrives. A related concern is the frequency of publication. This is especially true when the library has an automated serials control system, because there is a need to record the expected interval time between issues. Normally the basic information for the new subscription is input when the library places the order.

Serials order work varies from library to library. Usually, a library orders only a few new titles each year. Nevertheless, there are annual payment activities associated with serials. Most orders are on a "til forbidden" basis. That is, the jobber renews the subscription for the library automatically until notified to the contrary. This approach eliminates the need for typing renewal orders each year, thus saving valuable staff time.

Several commercial guides and bibliographies for serials exist that both selectors and acquisition staff need to be familiar with. The sources are of little value for pricing information, but they are invaluable for locating information about publishers' addresses, editorial policy, which indexing or abstracting services include the title, and what titles are available on a given subject.

Ulrich's Periodicals Directory™ *2001* (Bowker), is an annual one-source approach that helps speed up the verification work by providing information about the publication frequency. The 39th edition covers 164,000 serials worldwide as well as information about 7,550 titles that ceased publication since the last edition. It also provides information on more than 20,000 Internet, online, and CD-ROM serials. Its coverage of U.S. newspapers is sound for dailies and weeklies (6,700) but is not as strong for non-U.S. titles. Like *BIP*, it is available in several formats: book, CD-ROM, and online.

Although *The Serials Directory* (EBSCO Information Services) is an irregular jobber's publication, its broad international coverage—over 150,000 titles—makes it useful in any library, even if it does not use EBSCO's services. Searchers can identify online and CD-ROM serials, peer review journals, controlled circulation titles, which publications accept advertising, and, very important, which journals are registered with the Copyright Clearance Center through various indexes and the main entry. As are many of the Bowker products, *The Serials Directory* is available on CD-ROM and online.

One of the strengths of *The Standard Periodical Directory* (Oxbridge Communications, irregular) is its in-depth coverage of North American serials, more than 75,000 titles. It has strong newspaper coverage and is a very useful source for those collecting newsletters.

The *Gale Directory of Publications and Broadcast Media* (Gale Group) was formerly *Ayer Directory of Publications.* An annual, it covers newspapers, magazines, and journals as well as radio and television stations and cable systems. It is particularly useful for verifying newspapers.

New Serial Titles (Library of Congress, irregular) covers new serials received by the Library of Congress and more than 700 cooperating libraries. There are annual, five-year, and twenty-year cumulations. This is a good source to use when trying to determine if the title you are searching for ever did exist. Unfortunately, LC stopped printing the section that listed title changes and titles known to have ceased.

Media Sources

The most reliable source for establishing the required information for media products is producers' catalogs. Any library buying media must maintain an extensive file of producers' catalogs. Book publishers' catalogs are not as critical because *BIP* and *WBIP* list most of the commercial publications. Unfortunately, there are no equally comprehensive equivalents for media materials. Bibliographic control of this field is improving, but records are still rather chaotic. Therefore, the producer's catalog is a most important verification tool. Because there are thousands of producers' catalogs, we discuss only selected general commercial tools here. In Canada producers' catalogs are particularly important because many producers will not deal with wholesalers.

AV Market Place™ 2001 (Bowker) is one of the most useful general media directories. It covers producers and distributors of AV software; equipment manufacturers; companies that provide cataloging, film processing, or media service; media associations; reference books; and review journals (more than 7,500 firms). Each major section is an alphabetical listing by company name, followed by indexes classified by media subject or product type. Coverage is good but not comprehensive. This book is not an evaluation tool but a directory.

The Software Encyclopedia™ 2001 (Bowker) provides information about almost 33,000 computer programs. *Words on Cassette™ 2001* (Bowker) lists over 90,000 audiocassettes. Both provide adequate information for ordering. In *Words*, only the title entries provide adequate ordering data; however, the user can search by author, reader, or performer. *Bowker's Audio & Video Database™*

2001 is a CD-ROM combination of *Words* and its *Video* (see below) publications and available in either Windows or MS-DOS with quarterly updates.

Another general resource is from the National Information Center for Educational Media (NICEM). Its databases have succeeded *Educational Media Index.* This is without doubt the most comprehensive source for information about educational nonbook materials produced in North America and the United Kingdom. It also contains materials in Spanish, French, German, and 130 other languages. If the library does not have online access or a PC with a CD-ROM drive, it will be unable to take advantage of this service. All the print publications, with the exception of the *NICEM Thesaurus,* have been discontinued.

As of August 2001, the NICEM database contained over 465,000 bibliographic records for more than 650,000 nonprint items. The database is searchable by title, date of production, age/grade level, subject area, and media type. MARC records are available for printing or downloading into an OPAC. It operates on Macintosh or Windows PCs with any Web browser. Although it is available directly from NICEM, as of August 2001 three vendors also offer the product: SilverPlatter (*A-V Online*), EBSCOhost (*NICEM AV*), and The Library Corporation (*A-V MARC*). SilverPlatter and The Library Corporation also have CD versions.

There are many nonbook media formats (see Chapter 13). NICEM uses fifteen "major media types"; however, most of the major types have several sub-types and a few have a large number (the audiotapes/cassettes category has twenty-two sub-types). Reviewing the NICEM types and sub-types makes it clear why searching for media requires careful attention to detail as well as full understanding of the types of media equipment the library owns.

The *Video Source Book* (Gale Group) is a sound guide to both educational and entertainment videos. There were almost 160,000 programs in the 2001 edition. Arranged in alphabetical title order, the entries provide brief annotations as well as running time, format, recommended use (e.g., home, institutional, and CCTV), audience, producer, distributor, and how to acquire the item (rent, lease, purchase, or off-air recording). A subject index provides access to the educational content; for the entertainment videos there are genre listings (e.g., fantasy, mystery, science fiction, westerns). Despite the large number of titles covered, the searcher will have to consult other sources if there is a need to comprehensively cover educational materials.

Another source is *Bowker's Complete Video Directory*™ *2001.* It is a four-volume set that covers both entertainment videos and educational materials; each volume contains its own index. The 2001 edition listed 250,000 titles. There are several features that make this set especially useful. Entries include citations to published reviews and, for educational items, indicate previewing information. A Spanish-language index, series index, and laser disc/DVD index all provide useful access points. It is also probably the best general starting point when the library needs to acquire non-U.S. entertainment films. Like most of the other Bowker citation publications, this is also available on CD-ROM.

Film Index International (British Film Institute) is an annual that covers more than 90,000 entertainment films produced worldwide in its latest edition (2000). It is available on CD-ROM from Chadwyck-Healey, Inc.

The British Library produces *The British Film & Video Guide* on a quarterly basis. This is a listing of films and videotapes available for rent (noncommercial use) or purchase in the United Kingdom. Coverage includes educational and training films, independent productions, and documentaries as well as broadcast television programming and feature films.

A semiannual publication is the *Library of Congress Catalog—Music, Books on Music and Sound Recordings* (Library of Congress 1973- , current semiannual issue and annual cumulation). This catalog covers music scores, disk recordings, and (since 1963) librettos and books about music. The main entry is under the name of the composer or author. The catalog includes subject entries as well as added entries. All entries are from LC's cataloging program. The catalog includes records from all producers, but emphasis is on commercial rather than educational recordings. Classical music, pop and contemporary vocal instrumental music, dramatic readings, motion picture soundtracks, children's records, and sacred music are all included.

The Library of Congress also publishes a catalog titled *National Union Catalog: Audiovisual Materials,* with quarterly updates. This is a compilation of bibliographic records for motion pictures, videorecordings, filmstrips, sets of transparences, slide sets, and kits cataloged by LC. In addition, there is an attempt being made to catalog materials released in the United States or Canada that have educational or instructional value. At present, LC catalogs kits only if it adds them to its collections. *NUC Audiovisual Materials* is a quarterly microfiche publication distributed by LC. Data needed for the catalog entries come from producers, manufacturers, film libraries, or distributing agencies. The National Audiovisual Center provides information for U.S. government materials. In most cases cataloging is done from the information thus provided without actual viewing of the material itself.

LC also provides information about maps (*National Union Catalog—Cartographic Materials*). This source is good; however, map cataloging tends to be very slow. It is a quarterly publication issued since 1983 in microfiche. LC catalogs single-sheet maps, map sets, and atlases.

The *National Register of Microform Masters* (Library of Congress, 1965–1983) had two basic purposes. One was to provide a complete national register of microform masters from which libraries could acquire prints. The other was to help libraries ensure the preservation of our intellectual heritage. The *Register* covered both monographs and serials, but not newspapers. It included the holdings of U.S. libraries, associations, and microform publishers. It is now available as a retrospective MARC record database (www.lcweb.loc.gov/cds/mds.html). Microformat information is now part of *NUC Books* or in *New Serial Titles.*

Guide to Microforms in Print (K. G. Saur) is a two-volume guide to currently available microforms worldwide. This guide covers all microformat materials: reel microfilm, micro-opaque cards, microfiche, and ultramicrofiche. The *Guide* distinguishes fifteen types of microforms (see Chapter 12 for a discussion of the importance of these categories). The arrangement is alphabetical; books appear under the author's name, and journals under the title. Entries give author and/or title, date of publication in original format, publisher of the microfilm, and price. A directory of pub lishers gives addresses and phone numbers.

Electronic Searching and OCLC

As noted previously, searching electronically is faster and almost always provides more realistic options for verifying an item than is possible through print sources. Because OCLC has become a, if not *the,* major worldwide source for bibliographic data, we focus here on OCLC searching methods. OCLC's *Quick Reference: Searching for Bibliographic Records* provides an overview of the various searching methods (see Figures 7.3 through 7.6, pages 148–51).

Users can employ numeric, derived, title phrase, keyword, and qualifying searches in *WorldCat*™. Numeric searches are possible for ISBNs and ISSNs. Also possible are searches by Library of Congress catalog number, music publisher number, U.S. Superintendent of Documents number, CODEN, and OCLC control number.

Derived searches can be by title, personal name (author), corporate name, or author/title. Title phrase searching allows the searcher to input up to sixty letters, numbers, spaces, or special characters (such as & or %) from a title. Keyword searching permits up to eight keywords, if the searcher is using the *WorldCat*™ or Harvard databases, and up to eleven words for searches of the *Books in Print, EUR-OP,* or *NetFirst* databases.

Searching OCLC databases is fast and offers a variety of search options. However, searchers must remember that each search generates a charge to the library's account with OCLC. Thus, it is *very* important to be certain the elements are correct *before* striking the "send" key. A miskeyed entry costs the library just as much as one that is correct. It is also important to select the search method most likely to provide a "hit" (correctly verify the item) on the first attempt. The fewer searches performed to correctly verify the item, the less it costs the library.

Following is an example that could be encountered in many types of libraries. The goal is to accurately identify information about the following item:

<u>Information provided by the requester:</u>

Author: D. Champagne

Title: *American Indian Almanac*

Publisher: unknown

Publication date: 1994?

<u>Actual item desired by the requester:</u>

Editor: Duane Champagne

Title: *The Native North American Almanac: A Reference Work on Native Americans in the United States and Canada*

Publisher: Gale Research

Publication date: 1994

SEARCHING WORLDCAT™

Title Phrase and Keyword Searching

Basic Searching Procedure

1 Press <Home>.
2 Type *cho ol* and press <F11>.
3 Type *[your search]* and press <F11>.

Title Phrase Searching

- Choose WorldCat *(cho ol)*.
- Exclude articles (*a, an, the,* and non-English articles) when they are the first word of a title. Include articles found within titles.
- Include up to 60 letters, numbers, spaces, and these characters: ( ) # & ♭
- Omit punctuation, diacritics, and other characters.
- Include hyphens or omit hyphens and leave a space.

Title Phrase Access Point (Index Label: ti)	Example
Megatrends	*sca ti megatrends*

Keyword Searching

- Choose WorldCat *(cho ol)*.
- Include up to 18 letters, numbers, ampersands, and hyphens.
- Combine up to 8 keywords in WorldCat.
- Use the question mark (?) to mask more than 1 character.
- Use the number sign (#) to mask 0 or 1 character.
- **Stopword list:** Do **not** use the following words in Keyword searches:

a	as	by	have	in	of	the	with
an	at	for	he	is	on	this	which
and	be	from	her	it	or	to	you
are	but	had	his	not	that	was	

Keyword Access Point (Index Label)	Example
Author (**au**) Elsa Kircher Cole	*fin au cole and au kircher and au elsa*
Frequency (**fq**) Monthly publications from Random House	*fin fq monthly and pb random and pb house*
Language (**la**) Spanish and Quixote	*fin la spanish and ti quixote*
Notes (**nt**) Lizard	*fin nt lizard*
Publication location (**pl**) Copenhagen	*fin pl copenhagen/1997*
Publisher (**pb**) Cornmarket	*fin pb cornmarket*
Report number (**rn**) EPA 530 SW 90060 E	*fin rn epa530sw90060e*
Series (**se**) Olive	*fin se olive*
Subject/Title/Contents (**st**) Designing	*fin st designing/1997*
Subject (**su**) Scotland	*fin su scotland/map*
Title (**ti**) *Carmen*	*fin ti carmen/vis*
Uniform title (**ut**) Beowulf	*fin ut beowulf*
Vendor information (**vn**) Puvill for Gredos Publications in 1996	*fin vn puvill and pb gredos/1996*

Figure 7.3. Searching WorldCat™: Title Phrase and Keyword Searching. ©OCLC. Reprinted by permission of OCLC. WorldCat® is a registered trademark of OCLC Online Computer Library Center, Inc.

Numeric and Derived Searching

Searching WorldCat

Numeric Searching

- Choose WorldCat (*cho ol*).
- Numeric searching is the most efficient method to find 1 record.
- Enter numeric searches with or without the Find (fin) command and index label.
- Include prefixes: **cd:** for CODEN **mn:** for music publisher number and **gn:** for government document number searches.
- Omit hyphens from ISBN searches.
- Include the hyphen in ISSN and LCCN searches.

Numeric Access Point (Index Label)	Example
CODEN (**cd**)	**cd:** all characters
BASICR	***cd:basicr***
AISJB6	***cd:aisjb6***
Government document no. (**gn**)	**gn:** 1–2 letters, 1–10 numbers
A 1.2:R31/14/984	***gn:a123114984***
NAS 1.2:SP1/46	***gn:na12146***
ISBN (**bn**)	Number, no hyphens
0-8247-7142-7	***0824771427***
0-85109-130-x	***085109130x***
ISSN (**sn**)	Number with hyphen
0098-3527	***0098-3527***
0018-165x	***0018-165x***
LCCN (**ln**)	Number with hyphen
78-52051	***78-52051***
Music publisher no. (**mn**)	**mn:** 1–2 letters,1–10 numbers
CO 1979-AB5-1	***mn:co197951***
OCLC control no. (**an**)	# or * followed by number
10998406	***#10998406*** or ****10998406***

Derived Searching

- Choose WorldCat (*cho ol*).
- Enter derived searches with or without the Find (fin) command.
- Omit articles (*a, an, the,* and non-English articles) when they are the first word of a title. Include articles found within titles.
- Include letters, numerals, and these characters: & $ * % @ £ ♭
- Exclude punctuation, diacritics, and these characters: - # / + = ±
- Use a circumflex (^) to make the search precise. For a name with only 2 words, type a circumflex in the third segment. **Example:** To search for *Harvey, Henry,* type ***harv,hen,^***
- If a personal name begins with *Mc* or *Mac* followed by an uppercase letter, type the *m* and omit the *c* or *ac*. **Example:** To search for *MacDonald, Marion B.,* type ***mdon,mar,b***

Derived Access Point (Index Label)	Example
Derived title (**dt**)	3,2,2,1
***Realism** in **Mod**ern **L**iterature*	***rea,in,mo,l***
*The **Com**plete **Ci**rcuit **Tr**aining **G**uide*	***com,ci,tr,g***
***I Be**lieve **in U**nicorns*	***i,be,in,u***
***Hot**el*	***hot,,,***
***Mir**acle **on 34**th **S**treet*	***mir,on,34,s***
Derived personal name (**dp**)	4,3,1
Becker, **Geo**rge **J**oseph	***beck,geo,j***
Sobey, **Edw**in **J**. C.	***sobe,edw,j***
cummings, **e. e.**	***cumm,e,e***
De Groot, **Adr**iaan	***degr,adr,***
Kübler-Ross, **Eli**sabeth	***kubl,eli,***
Derived corporate name (**dc**)	=4,3,1
Hershey **Foo**ds **C**orporation	***=hers,foo,c***
American **Rock Gar**den **S**ociety	***=rock,gar,s***
Adrian **Col**lege	***=adri,col,***
Symposium on a **New Int**ernational **O**rder	***=new,int,o***
Derived name/title (**da**)	4,4
Hailey ***Hote**l*	***hail,hote***
Clarke ***2001**: a space odyssey*	***clar,2001***

Stopword list

Begin corporate name searches with the first word **not** on the list. Include stoplist words thereafter. All United States state names are also stopwords.

a	Colloquium	East	Institute	Seminar	U. N.
A.	Commission	for	Institution	Senate	U.N.
American	Committee	France	International	Society	United Nations
an	Conference	Great Britain	Joint	South	United States
Association	Congress	Gt. Brit.	National	State	University
Australia	Council	Gt.Brit.	North	Subcommittee	U. S.
Bureau	Department	House	of	Symposium	U.S.
Canada	Dept.	India	on	the	West

Figure 7.4. Searching WorldCat™: Numeric and Derived Searching. ©OCLC. Reprinted by permission of OCLC. WorldCat® is a registered trademark of OCLC Online Computer Library Center, Inc.

Qualifiers, Combined Searches, and Search Results

Searching WorldCat

Qualifiers

Qualification By (Qualifier Label)	Example
Type of material, format (**ft**)	
Books	*bks*
Computer Files	*com*
Maps	*map*
Mixed Material	*mix*
Serials	*ser*
Scores	*sco*
Sound Recordings	*rec*
Visual Materials	*vis*
Years of publication (**yr**) (**m**=millennium, **c**=century, **d**=decade, **y**=year)	
Single year *[mcdy]*	*1994*
Decade *[mcd?]*	*199?*
Century *[mc??]*	*19??*
Single year and all later years *[mcdy-]*	*1995-*
Single year and all earlier years *[-mcdy]*	*-1995*
Range of years	
[mcdy-y]	*1880-3*
[mcdy-dy]	*1880-91*
[mcdy-cdy]	*1880-920*
[mcdy-mcdy]	*1880-1920*
No date (derived and numeric only)	*????*
Microform or not microform (**mi**) (derived and numeric only)	
Microform	*mf*
Not microform	*nm*
Cataloging Source (**so**) (derived and numeric only)	
Library of Congress	*dlc*

Default Qualifiers

Type commands at the Home position and press <F11>.

Command	Result
set qual	Select Qualifiers screen
set act	Default qualifiers active
set inact	Default qualifiers inactive

Derived Qualified and Combined

Derived	Example
Qualified	*chi,ma,of,s/1956-* *gon,wi,th,w/bks/1956* *cat,of,th,m/1990/mf* *gon,wi,th,w/bks/19??/mf/dlc*
Combined	*fin dp mich,jam,a and dt tal,of,th,s*
Qualified and Combined	*fin dp mich,jam,a and dt tal,of,th,s/bks/1974*

Keyword Qualified and Combined

Keyword	Example
Qualified	*fin su scotland/map* *fin pl copenhagen/1947* *fin au michener and ft bks* *fin au michener and yr 1996*
Combined	*fin ti gone and ti wind* *fin au bizet and ti carmen* *fin la spanish and ti centennial* *fin la french and au camus*
Qualified and Combined	*fin au roget and ti thesaurus/bks/1977* *fin au bizet and ti carmen/rec* *fin au bizet and ti carmen/rec/1947* *fin su arco and su venice and ft bks* *fin su basket? and su navajo and yr 1980-*

Title Phrase Results

Title phrase searches result in a Title phrase index. To view the records in the list, type commands at the Home position and press <F11>.

Command	Result
pup	Move 1 screen back.
pdn	Move 1 screen forward.
[item number]	View the selected item on the list. **Example:** *8* **Note:** If you chose an item that has more than **1** listed in the **Hits** column, the system displays a Truncated or Brief list from which you choose a record.
gob bi	Return to the Title phrase index from a record. **Note:** If you view no other lists (Group, Truncated, Brief) after selecting a record from the Title phrase index, the **bi** is optional.

Numeric, Derived, Keyword Results

Numeric, derived, and keyword searches result in one of the following default displays:

No. of Records	Default Display
100–1,500	**Group list.** Lists groups of records by type of material and year.
6–99	**Truncated list.** Lists truncated entries containing a 1-line description.
2–5	**Brief list.** Lists brief entries, 2 to 6 lines for each record, containing descriptive fields and other information.
1	**Full record.** Full bibliographic records.

Figure 7.5. Searching WorldCat™: Qualifiers, Combined Searches, and Search Results. ©OCLC. Reprinted by permission of OCLC. WorldCat® is a registered trademark of OCLC Online Computer Library Center, Inc.

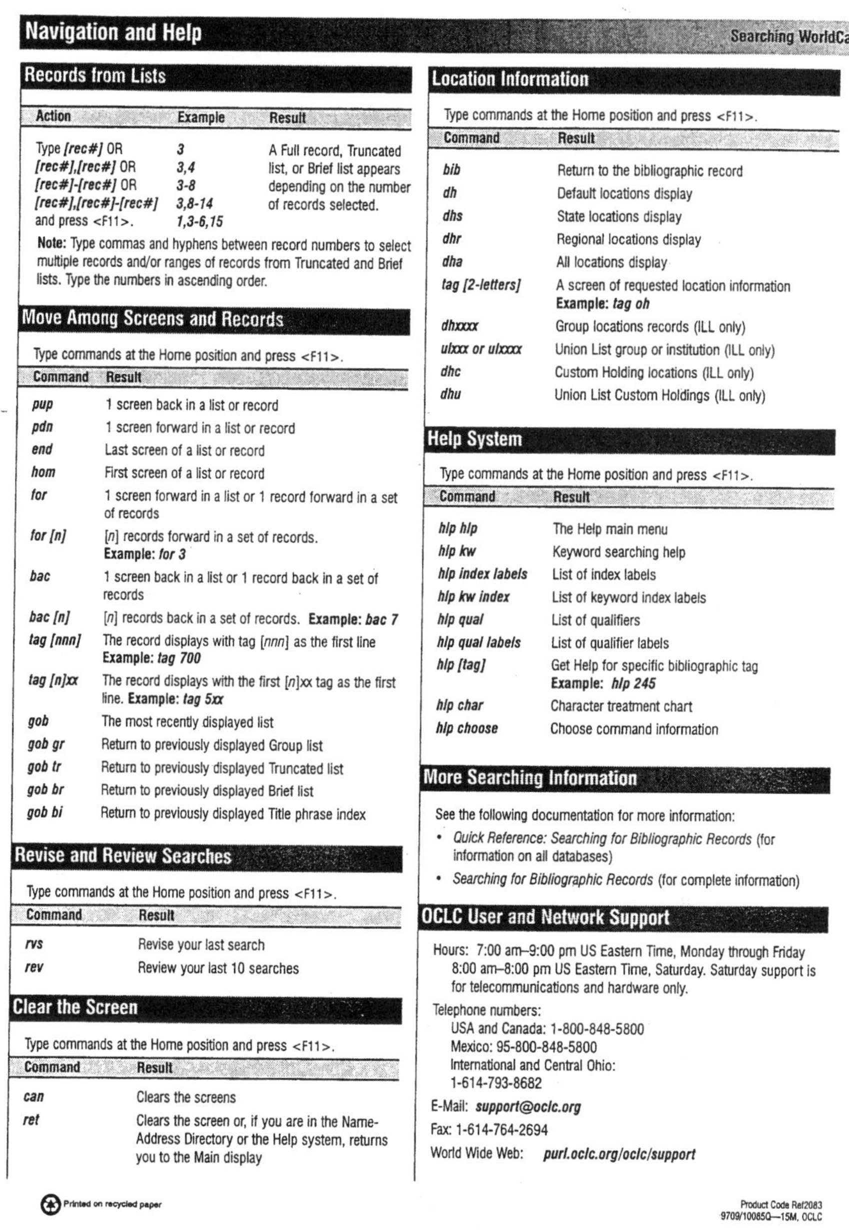

Navigation and Help

Searching WorldCat

Records from Lists

Action	Example	Result
Type *[rec#]* OR *[rec#],[rec#]* OR *[rec#]-[rec#]* OR *[rec#],[rec#]-[rec#]* and press <F11>.	*3* *3,4* *3-8* *3,8-14* *1,3-6,15*	A Full record, Truncated list, or Brief list appears depending on the number of records selected.

Note: Type commas and hyphens between record numbers to select multiple records and/or ranges of records from Truncated and Brief lists. Type the numbers in ascending order.

Move Among Screens and Records

Type commands at the Home position and press <F11>.

Command	Result
pup	1 screen back in a list or record
pdn	1 screen forward in a list or record
end	Last screen of a list or record
hom	First screen of a list or record
for	1 screen forward in a list or 1 record forward in a set of records
for [n]	[*n*] records forward in a set of records. **Example:** ***for 3***
bac	1 screen back in a list or 1 record back in a set of records
bac [n]	[*n*] records back in a set of records. **Example:** ***bac 7***
tag [nnn]	The record displays with tag [*nnn*] as the first line **Example:** ***tag 700***
tag [n]xx	The record displays with the first [*n*]xx tag as the first line. **Example:** ***tag 5xx***
gob	The most recently displayed list
gob gr	Return to previously displayed Group list
gob tr	Return to previously displayed Truncated list
gob br	Return to previously displayed Brief list
gob bi	Return to previously displayed Title phrase index

Revise and Review Searches

Type commands at the Home position and press <F11>.

Command	Result
rvs	Revise your last search
rev	Review your last 10 searches

Clear the Screen

Type commands at the Home position and press <F11>.

Command	Result
can	Clears the screens
ret	Clears the screen or, if you are in the Name-Address Directory or the Help system, returns you to the Main display

Location Information

Type commands at the Home position and press <F11>.

Command	Result
bib	Return to the bibliographic record
dh	Default locations display
dhs	State locations display
dhr	Regional locations display
dha	All locations display
tag [2-letters]	A screen of requested location information **Example:** ***tag oh***
dhxxxx	Group locations records (ILL only)
ulxxx or ulxxxx	Union List group or institution (ILL only)
dhc	Custom Holding locations (ILL only)
dhu	Union List Custom Holdings (ILL only)

Help System

Type commands at the Home position and press <F11>.

Command	Result
hlp hlp	The Help main menu
hlp kw	Keyword searching help
hlp index labels	List of index labels
hlp kw index	List of keyword index labels
hlp qual	List of qualifiers
hlp qual labels	List of qualifier labels
hlp [tag]	Get Help for specific bibliographic tag **Example:** ***hlp 245***
hlp char	Character treatment chart
hlp choose	Choose command information

More Searching Information

See the following documentation for more information:

- *Quick Reference: Searching for Bibliographic Records* (for information on all databases)
- *Searching for Bibliographic Records* (for complete information)

OCLC User and Network Support

Hours: 7:00 am–9:00 pm US Eastern Time, Monday through Friday
8:00 am–8:00 pm US Eastern Time, Saturday. Saturday support is for telecommunications and hardware only.

Telephone numbers:
USA and Canada: 1-800-848-5800
Mexico: 95-800-848-5800
International and Central Ohio:
1-614-793-8682

E-Mail: ***support@oclc.org***

Fax: 1-614-764-2694

World Wide Web: ***purl.oclc.org/oclc/support***

Printed on recycled paper

Product Code Ref2083
9709/10085Q—15M, OCLC

Figure 7.6. Searching WorldCat™: Navigation and Help. ©OCLC. Reprinted by permission of OCLC. WorldCat® is a registered trademark of OCLC Online Computer Library Center, Inc.

One reasonable starting approach would be a title search because the request appears to have a complete, valid title. The results of such a search are illustrated in Figures 7.7a and 7.7b. The problem with the results is clear: There is a title and publication match but the author does not match. What should the searcher do? If the requester works in the library or is easy to contact, it would be wise to check with the person to determine if the search has identified the correct item before searching further. Doing an author (derived) search for D. Champagne produced no useful results.

```
                              ¶ ILL              SID: 02598        OL


OLUC  ti american indian almanac
      Phrase Index                                                Hits
▶  1¶ AMERICAN INDIAN ALASKA NATIVE WOMEN                            1
▶  2¶ AMERICAN INDIAN ALASKA NATIVE WOMEN BUSINESS OWNERS            1
▶  3¶ AMERICAN INDIAN ALASKA NATIVE WOMEN WITH HIV INFECTION         1
▶  4¶ AMERICAN INDIAN ALASKAN NATIVE DROPOUT STUDY 1991              1
▶  5¶ AMERICAN INDIAN ALASKAN NATIVE LEARNING STYLES RESEARCH AND    2
▶  6¶ AMERICAN INDIAN ALASKAN NATIVE WOMEN AND THE ECONOMY STRATEG   1
▶  7¶ AMERICAN INDIAN ALCOHOLISM EVALUATION MONITORING DESIGN PROJ   1
▶  8¶ AMERICAN INDIAN ALCOHOLISM IN ST PAUL A NEEDS ASSESSMENT       1
▶  9¶ AMERICAN INDIAN ALMANAC                                        7
▶ 10¶ AMERICAN INDIAN ALUMNI NEWS                                    1
▶ 11¶ AMERICAN INDIAN AN ANNOTATED BIBLIOGRAPHY                      1
▶ 12¶ AMERICAN INDIAN AN EXHIBITION OF PAINTINGS BY GEORGE CATLIN    1
▶ 13¶ AMERICAN INDIAN AN EXHIBITION OF PAINTINGS DRAWINGS BOOKS MA   1
▶ 14¶ AMERICAN INDIAN AN EXPERIMENT WITH A TEACHING UNIT IN THE TH   1
▶ 15¶ AMERICAN INDIAN AN ILLUSTRATED MAGAZINE SPECIAL SYMBOL NUMBE   1
▶ 16¶ AMERICAN INDIAN AN INTROD TO THE ANTHROPOLOGY OF THE NEW WOR   1
▶ 17¶ AMERICAN INDIAN AN INTRODUCTION TO THE ANTHROPOLOGY OF THE N  10
▶ 18¶ AMERICAN INDIAN AN INTRODUCTION TO THE CULTURE AND LIFE ACTI   3
▶ 19¶ AMERICAN INDIAN AN OVERVIEW OF THE ISSUES                      1
```

Figure 7.7a. Title Search. ©OCLC. Reprinted by permission of OCLC. WorldCat® is a registered trademark of OCLC Online Computer Library Center, Inc.

```
                              ¶ ILL              SID: 02598        OL
Entire list displayed.

OLUC  ti "AMERICAN INDIAN ALMANAC"                  Records: 7
 Rec#  Title                      Name or 245          Publisher       Date L
▶  1¶  An American Indian almanac /  Terrell, John Upton World Pub. Co. 1971
▶  2¶  American Indian almanac /     Terrell, John Upton T. Y. Crowell, 1971
▶  3¶  American Indian almanac.      Terrell, John Upton World Pub. Co. 1971 D
▶  4¶  American Indian almanac /     Terrell, John Upton World Pub. Co. 1973
▶  5¶  American Indian almanac.      Terrell, John Upton T. Y. Crowell  1974
▶  6¶  American Indian almanac /     Terrell, John Upton Barnes & Noble 1994
▶  7¶  American Indian almanac /     Terrell, John Upton Barnes & Noble 1998
```

Figure 7.7b. Title Search. ©OCLC. Reprinted by permission of OCLC. WorldCat® is a registered trademark of OCLC Online Computer Library Center, Inc.

A title phrase search (see Figures 7.8a and 7.8b) produces some interesting results that might make one question which item the requester really wanted. There is one "hit" that matches the two title words and the publication date. Also, all three deal with the same subject matter.

```
                                        ¶ ILL                 SID: 02598       OL
Beginning of list displayed.

OLUC  ti indian and ti almanac                                Records: 28
 Rec#    Main Entry          Title                          Publisher        Date L
 ▶   1¶                      Ayer's British Indian almanac  Dr. J.C. Ayer    18uu
 ▶   2¶                      Dr. Morse's Indian root pills  W.H. Comstock    1800
 ▶   3¶                      Dr. Morse's Indian root pills  W.H. Comstock    18uu
 ▶   4¶                      The Indian almanac.            Bharati Resear   1977
 ▶   5¶                      Indian almanac : Kikinawa den  s.n.,            1834
 ▶   6¶                      Indian economic almanac.       Delhi Research   1980 D
 ▶   7¶                      The Indian ephemeris and anut  Manager of Pub   1966
 ▶   8¶                      Indian ephemeris and nautical  Manager of Pub   1958 D
 ▶   9¶                      Indian motion picture almanac  Shot Publicati   19uu D
 ▶  10¶                      Indian motion picture almanac  Film Federatio   1953
 ▶  11¶                      Indian motion picture almanac  Film Federatio   1953
 ▶  12¶                      Kickapoo Indian almanac.       Healy and Bige   18uu
 ▶  13¶                      Kickapoo Indian almanac 1892.  Kickapoo Medic   1891
 ▶  14¶                      Morse's Indian root pill ...   W.H. Comstock]   18uu
 ▶  15¶                      Morse's Indian root pills alm  s.n.]            18uu
 ▶  16¶                      Post office almanac, and East  H. Hooper,       18uu
 ▶  17¶                      The South Indian English and   Printed for th   1853
 ▶  18¶                      Year-book and almanac of Brit  Lowe & Chamber   1866
 ▶  19¶  Swamikannu Pillai,  An Indian ephemeris, A.D. 700  Agam,            1982 D
```

Figure 7.8a. Title Phrase Search. ©OCLC. Reprinted by permission of OCLC. WorldCat® is a registered trademark of OCLC Online Computer Library Center, Inc.

```
                                        ¶ ILL                 SID: 02598       OL
End of list displayed.

OLUC  ti indian and ti almanac                                Records: 28
 Rec#    Main Entry          Title                          Publisher        Date L
 ▶  20¶  Swamikannu Pillai,  An Indian ephemeris, A.D. 700  Agam Prakashan   1982
 ▶  21¶  Taylor, Alexander S Outline map of Upper and Lowe                   1864
 ▶  22¶  Terrell, John Upton An American Indian almanac /   World Pub. Co.   1971
 ▶  23¶  Terrell, John Upton American Indian almanac /      T. Y. Crowell,   1971
 ▶  24¶  Terrell, John Upton American Indian almanac.       World Pub. Co.   1971 D
 ▶  25¶  Terrell, John Upton American Indian almanac /      World Pub. Co.   1973
 ▶  26¶  Terrell, John Upton American Indian almanac.       T. Y. Crowell    1974
 ▶  27¶  Terrell, John Upton American Indian almanac /      Barnes & Noble   1994
 ▶  28¶  Terrell, John Upton American Indian almanac /      Barnes & Noble   1998
```

Figure 7.8b. Title Phrase Search. ©OCLC. Reprinted by permission of OCLC. WorldCat® is a registered trademark of OCLC Online Computer Library Center, Inc.

An author/title search based on using the least common words produced the results in Figure 7.9. (The person who performed the search for us is a highly experienced searcher and used this approach first. He did have a clue there might be something missing in the "request" when he was told "it may be a bit of challenge." However, the example does illustrate what an experienced, thoughtful searcher can accomplish while saving the library time and money.)

```
                                  ¶  ILL                SID: 02598        OL
Entire list displayed.

OLUC  au champagne and ti almanac                       Records: 3
 Rec#  Description
 ▶  1¶  Native North American almanac / Cynthia Rose and Duane Champagne,
        editors.  [Detroit, Mich.] : UXL, c1994.  DLC  OCLC: 31370227

 ▶  2¶  The Native North American almanac / Duane Champagne, editor.  [S.l.] :
        Multiculture in Print, c1994, 1997 printing.  OCLC: 37218496

 ▶  3¶  The Native North American almanac : a reference work on native North
        Americans in the United States and Canada / Duane Champagne, editor.
        Detroit, Mich. : Gale Research, c1994.  OCLC: 29456357  In LML
```

Figure 7.9. Author/Title Search. ©OCLC. Reprinted by permission of OCLC. WorldCat® is a registered trademark of OCLC Online Computer Library Center, Inc.

SUMMARY

Although preorder work is often repetitive and perhaps usually easy, it is in fact critical to the overall performance of the acquisitions department. Staff need careful training in the methods of searching, the basics of cataloging rules of entry, and which verification sources are most likely to produce the requisite information in a timely and accurate manner. Poor preorder searching is costly for the library and staff in terms of time and money wasted. Verification sources are constantly changing. New ones appear and old familiar ones (like the *Weekly Record)* disappear. They change coverage and arrangement. This means that searchers must regularly check the front matter of the verification sources to determine what, if any, changes occurred. With online sources, the log-on screen often provides this type of information. As any experienced searcher knows, when there is both a print and an electronic version of a verification source, searching both formats is essential before deciding an item is not listed.

NOTES

1. *Guidelines for Handling Library Orders for In-Print Monographic Publications*, 2nd ed. (Chicago: American Library Association, 1984).

2. Liz Chapman, *Buying Books for Libraries* (London: Clive Bingley, 1989), 3-4.

3. Karen Schmidt, "Cost of Pre-order Searching," in *Operational Costs in Acquisitions*, edited by J. Coffey. (New York: Haworth Press, 1990), 5-20.

4. *Books in Series* (New York: R. R. Bowker, 1991).

5. "Whitaker's Book In Print 2000" (16 September 2001). Available: http://www.whitaker.co.uk/wpublish.html.

SUGGESTED READING

Hamilton, Marsha. "ALCTS Pre-order/Precataloging Search Discussion Group." *Library Acquisitions* 19 (Fall 1995): 343-344.

Su, Julie Tao. "Highlights of the ALCTS Pre-order/Precatloging Search Discussion Group." *Library Collections, Acquisitions, and Technical Services* 24 (Winter 2000): 487-490.

REVIEW QUESTIONS

1. What are the typical kinds of materials a library acquires?
2. Discuss the three broad categories of acquisitions work.
3. What are the steps in preorder work? Discuss each.
4. What are some of the major challenges in conducting preorder searching?

5. What is a bibliography?
6. Name the types of bibliographies and give one title of each type.
7. What is the main advantage of using *ABPR*?
8. What are the differences between *Bookseller* and *BNB*?
9. What are the major differences in the verification of books and nonprint materials?
10. In what ways do nonprint verification sources differ from book verification sources?

Order Processes

As noted in Chapter 7, libraries employ several acquisitions methods. Each has a useful role to play in developing collections for end-users in an efficient, cost-effective manner. Today, a majority of libraries use computer-generated orders and store the data electronically, thus reducing the volume of paper associated with ordering activities. For a few libraries, there is no paper order form for current trade books, because the libraries handle the entire order process electronically, storing the transaction in both the library's and the supplier's computers. In the future, this may be the way all libraries place their orders; however, for thousands of libraries, the paperless order is not yet a reality.

A key publication for acquisitions departments is *Guidelines for Handling Library Orders for In-Print Monographic Publications.* Prepared by the Book Dealer–Library Relations Committee of the Resources and Technical Services Division of the American Library Association (now called Association for Library Collections & Technical Services), it reflects the needs of both groups. It also contains recommendations for establishing and maintaining good working relationships between vendors and libraries. One suggestion is that libraries use the American National Standards Institute (ANSI) Committee Z39 single title order form, which measures 3 by 5 inches (ca. 8 by 13 cm.), a size that has been common for years in technical service units.

Regardless of the method used to order material, the vendor must receive enough information to ensure shipment of the correct materials: author, title, publisher, date of publication, price, edition (if there are various editions), number of copies, order number, and any special instructions regarding invoicing or methods of payment. Also, more suppliers are asking for the International Standard Book Number (ISBN) or International Standard Serial Number (ISSN). In time, International Standard Numbers (ISNs) may be all the library needs to send, because ISNs are unique numbers representing a specific journal or a specific edition of a specific title. Other uses of these numbers are in cataloging, data processing, and public service activities, so it is important to understand ISBNs and how they work.

One important characteristic of ISBNs is that each edition of a book has a unique ISBN, as do the paper and hardbound versions. For example, the number for the first edition of this book was 0-87287-029-4; the second edition was 0-87287-125-8. The number for the hardbound version of the fourth edition was 0-87287-228-9 and for the paperbound, 0-87287-248-3. The number(s) before the first hyphen represents the country of origin; the next set of numbers is for the individual publisher; the next set represents the title, edition, and format; and the last number is the "check digit." The last number serves as a way of verifying the rest of the ISBN.

From the point of view of some acquisitions departments, the ISBN is the *only* information needed to order a book from a jobber because it identifies the specific edition and binding. Ordering by ISBN could be a major time-saver: no more keying in of author, title, publisher, place, date, or price. However, mistakes might arise from just using the ISBN (e.g., transposed numbers, errors in copying). If the library provides author, title, and publisher, for example, the jobber may be able to provide the desired item despite a typographic error. Nevertheless, we think serious consideration should be given to using only the ISBN.

The ISBN is one of several ways to search for bibliographic data in an electronic environment, for example, in the OCLC database. Vendor systems such as Baker & Taylor's ACQUIRE system use it as *the* search technique. When one is searching hundreds of titles a day, saving ten to twenty seconds per search is important.

However, acquisitions department staff need to realize that because the ISBN *is* unique, it should only be used in conjunction with other search techniques to verify information about a title, not to determine if the library already has a copy of a particular book. A reprint of a particular title will have a different ISBN than the original; perhaps the requester does not know that the library already has the originally published edition. Further, if a book is published simultaneously in the United States and in Europe, each edition will have its own ISBN. Acquisitions department staff should be very careful that one person isn't ordering a particular book using the U.S. ISBN when another has just ordered the same title using the British or Canadian ISBN.

An article by Audrey Eaglen outlines several additional issues related to using ISBNs.[1] First, she notes that publishers sometimes use the number for inventory control, getting a new number for each reprinting of the title and using the number to track the number of copies sold from that print run. Second, publishers only give part of the ISBN, usually the third element (title/edition) in their ads and promotional literature. A third problem she noted is that review media, when they include ISBNs, often do not list the correct number. She states that, "Approximately ten percent of the ISBNs given in its (*PW*) 'Forecasts' reviews are simply incorrect." These problems, combined with the fact that a book published in both cloth and paperback formats by different publishers in the United States and the United Kingdom can have four different ISBNs, illustrate the limitations of the system.

The Library of Congress is investigating the problems and advantages of replacing LC control numbers with ISBNs. The British Library has already made this switch, and BNB catalog cards are now ordered using the ISBN. Using the ISBN in accounting activities could reduce typing required because invoices could use only the ISBN even if the order form provides additional information. This would save some effort for both suppliers and libraries.

The International Standard Serial Number (ISSN) is an eight-digit number that identifies the publisher and title for periodicals. As with the ISBN, the last digit serves as the control. ISBNs and ISSNs were both developed in the expectation of extensive computer use in book distribution.

At present, there is no equivalent standard for electronic order transmission; however, ANSI Committee Z39 is working on such a standard, "Computerized Book Ordering Standard." As of June 2001, the standard was still under development.

Another standard of ANSI Committee Z39 is the Standard Address Number (SAN). Like the ISBN, the SAN is a unique number (of seven digits) that identifies each address or organization doing business in the U.S. and Canadian book trade. For example, the SAN of the Charles Von der Ahe Library at Loyola Marymount University is 332-9135, Brodart is 159-9984, Libraries Unlimited is 202-6767, and Thomas Allen & Son is 115-1762. Perhaps eventually all that will be necessary to order a title electronically will be three sets of unique numbers: the ISBN or ISSN and the SANs for the supplier and the buyer. Again, such simplified ordering is some time in the future, if it ever becomes a reality. Nevertheless, these unique numbers are useful as a cross-check for accuracy. Keys to SANs appear in a variety of sources, such as the *American Library Directory*, which includes library SANs in its entries.

With a manual system, libraries commonly use a multiple-copy order form for placing orders. (Almost any computer-based acquisition system handles all of the following tasks with little or no paper.) These forms are available in a number of formats and contain from four to as many as twelve copies. The 3-by-5-inch (ca 8-by-13-cm.) size is standard in North America. Normally, each copy is a different color for easy identification. There is no standard dictating a specific color for a particular purpose. A minimum of four copies is typical: (1) outstanding order copy, (2) dealer's copy, (3) claiming copy, and (4) accounting copy. Only the staff's imagination limits the number of potential uses of additional copies. A few libraries still use all twelve copies. Some libraries mail two copies to the dealer and keep three or four in the in-process file. In some larger systems, where selectors are not in close contact with the acquisitions department (as in research libraries, where faculty members do much of the selecting), an information copy goes to the selector. (Figure 8.1, page 160, and Figure 8.2, page 161, illustrate order forms.)

PURCHASE ORDER #

DATE

CITE P.O. # ON INVOICE, BILL IN TRIPLICATE

ACQ/SER DEPT • CHARLES VON DER AHE LIBRARY • LOYOLA MARYMOUNT UNIVERSITY
LOYOLA BOULEVARD AT WEST 80TH STREET • LOS ANGELES, CA 90045 • (310) 338-2792

ISBN/ISSN PRICE FUND VENDOR RL

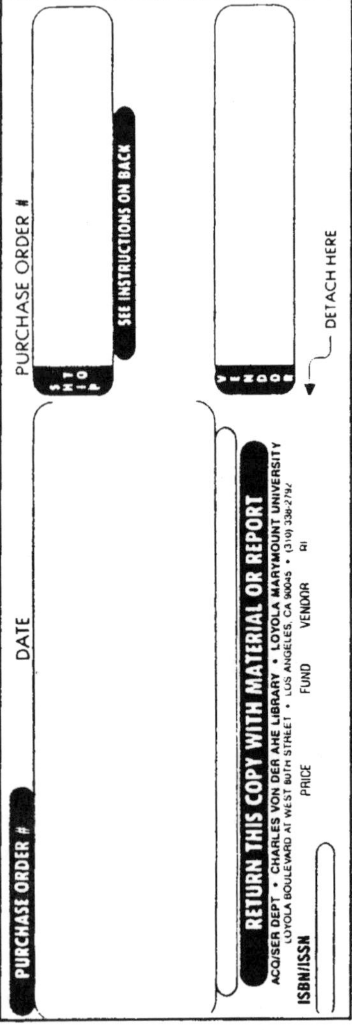

PURCHASE ORDER #

DATE

RETURN THIS COPY WITH MATERIAL OR REPORT

ACQ/SER DEPT • CHARLES VON DER AHE LIBRARY • LOYOLA MARYMOUNT UNIVERSITY
LOYOLA BOULEVARD AT WEST 80TH STREET • LOS ANGELES, CA 90045 • (310) 338-2792

ISBN/ISSN PRICE FUND VENDOR RL

PURCHASE ORDER #

SHIP TO

SEE INSTRUCTIONS ON BACK

VENDOR

DETACH HERE

Figure 8.1. Multiple-order form prepared by the library.

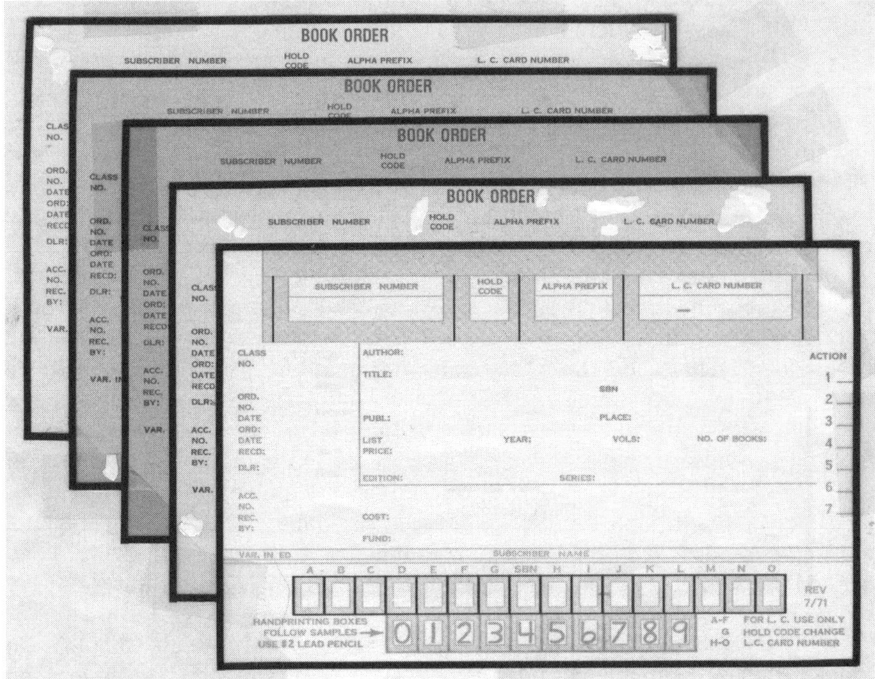

Figure 8.2. Multiple-copy order form prepared by the wholesaler.

The in-process file may contain several copies of the order form. For example, after sending the order, the staff might place five copies in the in-process file. One copy represents on-order status; two are available for use for possible claims; one is forwarded to cataloging with the item when it arrives; and the final one remains in the file, indicating that the item is being processed but is not yet ready for public use. Upon receipt, a staff member pulls all slips except the in-process slip. When the item is ready for circulation, the cataloging department returns a slip to acquisitions to prompt the removal of the in-process slip. Presumably at this point a set of entries is in the public catalog indicating that the item is available for use.

Claiming and handling supplier reports is one of the more time-consuming and frustrating aspects of the order function. Most multiple-copy order forms have slips for these purposes. Purchasers have every reason to expect U.S. commercial publishers, or vendors supplying titles from such publishers, to deliver or report on the status of the order within 90 days, if there is some delay in filling the order. For American noncommercial publishers (for example, university presses or professional associations), an additional 30 days (120 days total) is common for delivery or a report. Western European titles delivered to the United States normally require 180 days, and a year or more is not uncommon for items from countries with a developing book trade. This estimate of delivery times is similar for Canada, with the added note that shipments of books from the United States must cross a border. This always takes more time than shipments within Canada. When there is an active collecting program from developing countries, libraries must expect a certain percentage of nonresponses. Learning how long to wait for delivery or a status report comes with experience with various dealers and countries.

When dealing with U.S. publishers, allowing for the normal two-way "snail mail" time, it is reasonable to send a second claim in 60 days after the first claim, if there has been no status report. Many order forms have a printed note stating "cancel after *x* days." Although such statements are legally binding, most libraries send a separate cancellation notice. (Note: The order slip is in fact a legal contract committing the library to pay for the item upon delivery.) Cancellation should not take place until after the normal response time passes, unless there are unusual circumstances, such as an unexpected budget reduction. Unfortunately, over the past twenty years many such cuts have taken place, and most vendors have been cooperative about making the adjustments. By establishing a regular cancellation date, libraries that must expend funds within a period of time (usually twelve months) can avoid or reduce the last-minute scramble of canceling outstanding orders and ordering materials that the vendor can deliver in time to expend the funds. (Budgets, timeframes, accounting, and expenditures are explored in greater detail in Chapter 14.)

Vendors should respond with a meaningful report when they cannot fill an order within a reasonable period. One less-than-helpful report that vendors did and occasionally still do use is "temporarily out of stock" (TOS). How long is "temporarily?" What has the vendor done to secure the item? Poor or inaccurate reporting costs the library money, as Audrey Eaglen pointed out in "Trouble in Kiddyland: The Hidden Costs of O.P. and O.S."[2] In periods of rapid inflation, each day the funds remain committed but unexpended erodes buying power because producers and suppliers raise prices without notice. Recommended vendor reports are "not yet received from publisher" (NYR); "out-of-stock, ordering" (OS, ordering); "claiming"; "canceled"; "not yet published" (NYP); "out-of-stock, publisher" (OS, publisher); "out-of-print" (OP); "publication canceled"; "out-of-stock indefinitely" (treat this one as a cancellation); "not our publication" (NOP); "wrong title supplied"; "defective copy"; and "wrong quantity supplied." After staff members learn how long a vendor takes to supply items first reported in the recommended manner, it is possible to make an informed decision regarding when to cancel and when to wait for delivery.

Before placing an order, the staff must make three important decisions:

1. Which acquisition method to use.
2. What vendor to use.
3. What funding source to use.

The remainder of this chapter explores the methods of acquiring materials. Chapter 9 discusses vendors: when and how to use them and what to expect from them. Chapter 14 covers the fiscal side of acquisitions work.

ACQUISITION METHODS

Acquisitions departments, whether merged with serials or not, acquire materials using several methods, each having somewhat different processing. Essentially there are eight standard methods of acquisition—firm order, standing order, approval plans, blanket order, subscriptions (for serials departments), leases (increasing in use), gifts, and exchange programs. A *firm order* (for example, orders in which desired items are individually named) is the usual method for acquiring many titles that the library *knows* it wants. For most current items, the firm order is the only logical method to use. It is often the best method for the first volume in a series, even if the selectors are thinking about ordering all the items in the series. Ordering directly from the individual producers takes substantially more time than placing an order for a number of titles, from different producers, with a jobber/wholesaler. The major drawback of this method is the time it takes to prepare the individual orders.

Standing orders (for example, open orders for all titles fitting a particular category) work best for items that are somewhat serial in nature. That is, they appear on an irregular basis or as an annual or other predictable time frame. Some examples are a numbered or unnumbered series from a publisher that deal with a single subject area. The library places the order for the series/items rather like it places a journal subscription. The supplier (vendor or producer) automatically sends the items as they appear along with an invoice. There is a distinction between "thinking about" and "planning on" when considering series items. When the selector knows that the reputation of the publisher or editor of the series is sound, it is probably best to place a standing order. *If* the library knows it wants all the items, then a standing order will save staff time and effort due to the automatic shipments. However, especially in academic libraries, standing orders are often the result of one person's request, and if the library does not periodically review its standing orders it may find that the requester left the institution years before or no longer has an interest in the series subject. The result is money spent on less useful items. If there is some question about suitability or content of the series, a firm order or approval copy order for the first volume is the better choice. Not all "publishers series" are in fact quality titles and in some cases they are almost, if not in fact, fraudulent. For example, in 1993 there were a number of e-mail messages on one of the collection development discussion lists regarding an article in *Lingua Franca* about a publisher that appears to be a vanity house but markets books as part of a series.[3] (Remember that vanity publishers simply publish any person's book as the individual pays for the work.) Getting to know publishers and editors is an important activity for acquisitions department staff.

The greatest drawback to standing orders is their unpredictable nature in terms of both number and cost. Certainly there is no problem about numbers for the regular series, but their cost per item may vary. When it comes to publishers' series or irregular series, a library may go several years without receiving a title, then receive several in one year. This is one of the areas where Joyce Ogburn's prediction skills come into play,[4] as one must "guesstimate" how much money to set aside at the start of the budget year to cover standing order expenses. Looking at past experience and using an average amount is a safe approach; however, the library is seldom able to set aside exactly the right amount. Committing (encumbering) too much money for too long may result in lost opportunities to acquire other useful items. Committing too little can result in having invoices arrive and not having the funds available to pay them. Standing orders are a valuable acquisition method, but one that requires careful monitoring throughout the year.

Approval plans are, in a sense, a variation of the standing order concept. They involve automatic shipment of items to the library from a vendor along with automatic invoicing, after the library accepts the item. The differences are that the approval plan normally covers a number of subject areas and the library has the right to return items it does not want. Approval plans are usually available from book jobbers such as Yankee Book Peddler, Academic Book Center, and Coutts. Saving staff time and effort is one of the major advantages of such plans. Another advantage is the right to return unwanted items; the underlying assumption is that collection development staff can make better decisions about an item's appropriateness by looking at the item before committing to its purchase. However, there is research evidence that indicates the approval plan can result in a substantially higher number of very low or no-use items being added to the collection.[5]

The key element in making the approval plan a cost-effective acquisition method is in developing a sound "profile" with the plan vendor. A profile outlines the parameters of the plan and covers issues such as subjects wanted, levels of treatment (undergraduate, graduate, etc.), countries covered, no reprints, no collections of reprinted articles, and so forth. The greater the time spent in preparing the profile, as well as monitoring the actual operation of the plan and making adjustments, the greater the value of an approval plan to the library and the acquisitions unit. The monitoring of operations and actually reviewing the item is also an obvious key to success. Given today's staffing situation in most libraries, there is a real danger that the plan will shift from approval to blanket order, simply because the staff has to attend to more pressing duties.

A *blanket order* is a combination of a firm order and an approval plan. It is a commitment on the library's part to purchase all of something, usually the output of a publisher, or a limited subject area, or from a country. In the case of a subject area or country, there is a profile developed between the library and the blanket order vendor. The materials arrive automatically along with the invoice, thus saving staff time. Another advantage, for country blanket order plans, is that they ensure the library acquires a copy of a limited print run title. (It is not uncommon to have very limited print runs of scholarly items in most countries. Waiting for an announcement or a listing in a national bibliography may mean that there are no copies available to purchase.) Like the standing order, the major drawback of blanket order plans is predicting how much money the library will need to reserve to cover the invoices. There is even less predictability with blanket order plans because there are more variables.

Subscriptions, for journals, newspapers, and many other serials, are a combination of standing and blanket orders. A library may enter a subscription for a given time frame just as an individual does for personal magazines. However, rather than going through an annual renewal process, many libraries enter into an agreement with a serials vendor to automatically renew subscriptions until the library requests a cancellation (" 'til forbidden"). Doing this saves both the library and vendor staff time and paperwork. This is a cost-effective system for those titles the library is *certain* are of long-term interest to end-users.

Leases are now commonplace for handling electronic resources, especially those that are Web-based. Even many of the reference CD-ROM products that are frequently updated are essentially leased—the library is supposed to return or destroy the disc when an updated disc arrives or when it cancels the subscription. The decision to lease is almost always in the hands of the supplier rather than the library, although sometimes a library can "buy" the product, usually at a substantially higher price. The difference between buying and leasing has significant implications for the library and its users. Essentially the library pays for *access* to the information for as long as it pays the annual fee. At the end of a lease the library generally loses all access to the material it was paying for, although some suppliers will provide long-term access to the material that was available during the time the lease was in force. Chapter 11 provides more information about this and other issues related to electronic resources.

Usually, acquisitions departments are the ultimate recipients of unsolicited *gifts* of books, serials, and other materials (sometimes accompanied by a variety of molds and insects) that well-meaning people give to the library. Both solicited and unsolicited gifts can be a source of out-of-print materials for replacement, extra copies, and the filling of gaps in the collection. The collection development policy statement on gifts will help acquisitions personnel process the material quickly. A good article outlining all aspects of handling gifts is Mary Bostic's "Gifts to Libraries: Coping Effectively."[6] Another excellent survey of both gift and exchange programs is by Steven Carrico[7]; it covers all management aspects of the work.

Reviewing gifts is important, as a library cannot afford to discard valuable or needed items that arrive as gifts. However, the library must keep in mind the fact that it should not add unnecessary items just because they were "free." Processing and storage costs are the same for a gift as for a purchased item. Older books require careful checking, as variations in printings and editions may determine whether an item is valuable or worthless. (Usually, a second or third printing is less valuable than the first printing of a work.) Persons with extensive training and experience in bibliographic checking must do the searching.

Steven Carrico provides an excellent summary of the advantages and disadvantages of gift programs:

Positive Points of Gifts

1. Gifts can replace worn and missing items in a library.

2. Out-of-print desiderata often surface from gift donations.

3. Gifts can foster communication and goodwill in a library community.

4. Gifts may become heavily used or important research additions to a collection.

5. Some titles that are not available by purchase are available as gifts.

6. Worthwhile gift material not selected for a library collection can be put in a book sale, sold to dealers, or given away to underfunded libraries and institutions.

Negative Points

1. Gifts require staff time and are costly to process.

2. Dealing with even well meaning gift donors is frequently an aggravation to staff.

3. Gifts take up precious space in a library.

4. Many collection managers give gifts low priority, so they may sit on review shelves for a long time.

5. A large percentage of most gifts are not added to a collection, which creates disposal problems.

6. Overall, since most gift books added to a collection are older editions, they will be less frequently used by library patrons.[8]

There are some legal aspects about gifts, at least in the United States, that staff must understand. One IRS regulation relevant to libraries has to do with gifts and donations to a library or not-for-profit information center. Any library, or its parent institution, that receives a gift in-kind (books, journals, manuscripts, and so forth) with an appraised value of $5,000 or more must report the gift to the IRS. A second regulation forbids the receiving party (in this case the library) from providing an estimated value for the gift in-kind. A disinterested party or organization must make the valuation. The latter requirement grew out of concern that recipients were placing unrealistically high values on gifts. The donor received a larger tax deduction than was warranted, and it did not cost the receiving organization anything to place a high value on the gift. Normally, an appraiser charges a fee for valuing gifts, and the donor is supposed to pay the fee. Most often, the appraisers are antiquarian dealers who charge a flat fee for the service unless the collection is large or complex. If the appraisal is complex, the appraiser either charges a percentage of the appraised value or an hourly fee.

Typically, with gifts thought to be worth less than $4,999, the library may write a letter of acknowledgment indicating the number and type of items received. For gifts of less than $250, the IRS does not require a letter. The donor can set a value on the gift for tax purposes. (The best practice is to provide a letter for any accepted gift.) If asked, the library can provide dealer catalogs for the donors to see retail prices for items similar to their donation. However, the final value of the gift is established by the donor and his or her tax accountant.

Just because the gift is small in number of items does not mean that the fair market value is below $5,000. Recently, Loyola Marymount University (LMU) received a gift of 483 books about Japanese art, architecture, and landscape design; its appraised value was $39,743. The donor might well have accepted a letter simply stating the number of books given and thus have lost a substantial tax deduction.

To meet IRS requirements, a letter must contain the library's name, the date of the contribution, the location/place of the gift (even if it is the library), and a description of the gift. At a minimum that description should provide number and kind of gift (for example, 100 mass-market paperbacks, 40 hardcover books, six complete and unbound volumes of *National Geographic*). More information regarding these regulations can be found in the IRS publications *Charitable Contributions* (IRS Publication #526) and *Charitable Contributions—Substantiation and Disclosure* (IRS Publication #1771). Both are available online at http://www.irs.gov/prod/forms_pubs/pubs.html.

Deciding to use the gift or deposit method of acquisition will almost always result in a long delay in receiving the desired item. Verification may establish that the item is a government publication that may be part of the library's depository program, or it may be a new government series that should become part of the program. In either case, the acquisitions staff would not issue a firm order but would notify the requester so that he or she can decide what to do.

Donations and gifts also present an acquisitions option that can be appropriate at times. Sometimes a library user or board member donates certain materials on a regular basis, making it unnecessary to order the item if there is no immediate demand for the material. Occasionally, an appropriate series or set costs so much a library cannot buy it with regular funding sources. Seeking out a donor to assist with funding or to pay for the purchase is not unheard of, but again, there may be substantial delays in acquiring the item. Most often, this takes place with rare books and special collections items. An active (and well-to-do) Friends of the Library group may be the answer to a special purchase situation. Friends groups, used judiciously, can significantly expand the collection and stretch funds.

One final acquisition category is the *exchange* method. There are two basic types of exchange activity: the exchange of unwanted duplicate or gift materials and the exchange of new materials between libraries. Usually, only large research libraries engage in exchange of new materials. In essence, cooperating institutions trade institutional publications. Tozzer Library (Harvard University's anthropology library) has exchange agreements with several hundred organizations. These organizations send their publications to Tozzer, which, in turn, sends them Peabody Museum publications. Often, this method is the only way a library can acquire an organization's publications, especially from countries with a developing book trade.

Occasionally, libraries use this system to acquire materials from countries in which there are commercial trade restrictions. Where government trade restrictions make buying and selling of publications from certain countries difficult or impossible, the cooperating libraries acquire (buy) their local publications for exchange. Exchanges of this type are complex and difficult to manage, and this is a method of last resort. Libraries can exercise better quality control when they trade for known organizational series or titles than when the choice of publications from the organization is more or less left to chance. Exchanges of this type exist on the basis of formal agreements between the cooperating organizations. They play an important role in developing comprehensive subject collections.

The Canadian Book Exchange Centre (CBEC), a service operated by the National Library of Canada, is a redistribution center and a clearinghouse for the exchange of materials in all formats between libraries. The service is free; participating libraries must pay shipping charges. Individuals can donate items to the Centre but cannot receive items in exchange. Details about CBEC's activities can be found at www.nlc-bnc.ca/6/10/index-e.html.

Libraries normally add only a small percentage of unsolicited gifts to the collection. This means the library must dispose of many unwanted items. In some libraries, a separate unit handles unneeded material; this unit usually is called the exchange unit. In most cases, it is the gift unit that handles the disposal work.

Disposition of unwanted gift materials is an activity that almost every library engages in at some time. One method is to list the unwanted items and mail the list to exchange units in other libraries, and the first library to request an item gets it for the shipping cost (usually book rate postage). This method is time-consuming as well as taking up scarce shelf space in many libraries. Another method is to arrange with an out-of-print dealer to take the items, usually as a lot rather than for a per-item price. It is unusual to receive cash; instead, the dealer gives the library a line of credit. The library uses the credit to acquire materials from the dealer. This system works well when the library has specialized materials the dealer wants and when the dealer stocks enough useful material so that the library can use its credit within a reasonable time (eighteen to twenty-four months). Holding a book sale is yet another method of disposing of unwanted material, one that is gaining in popularity as dealers resist the credit memo system. However, this is not a "free" venture, as staff must select the items for sale, establish a fair price, find a suitable location, and monitor the sale. Depending on the volume of gifts, annual, semiannual, or monthly sales are appropriate. Sales can be an excellent Friends of the Library project that can save some staff time. A few libraries use an ongoing sale tactic, especially when they have limited staff and space and a high volume of unwanted gifts. There is a Web site devoted to listing book sales (http://www.book-sales-in-america.com).

ORDER PLACEMENT AND RECEIVING

After selecting an acquisition method, the next step in the order process is to select a vendor. Chapter 9 addresses issues of dealer and vendor selection as well as what they can and cannot do for a library. Once a vendor has been selected, order placement may begin. In this step, a staff member assigns an order number and determines which fund to use for payment. Order numbers are essential for the staff to track orders after they are placed. The assignment process is simply a matter of checking the last order number and using the next number in the sequence. As soon as the department head signs the orders, they are ready for mailing.

Receiving orders, although not difficult, requires careful planning. If not handled properly, receiving can be more costly and time-consuming than ordering. As strange as it may seem, proper unpacking of shipments will save everyone in the department a great deal of time, energy, and frustration. Finding the packing slip or invoice is the key first step in the process. A packing slip lists, at least in most cases, all the items in a particular shipment. An invoice is an itemized bill, which business offices require before they will issue a voucher or check. For receiving convenience, most vendors attach a clearly marked envelope containing the packing slip to the outside of one of the boxes. Unfortunately, a few vendors seem to delight in hiding the slip in strange places. One technique is to enclose the slip inside one of the items, and another favorite hiding place is under a cardboard liner on the bottom of the box. If no packing slip is found, it is essential to keep the items separated from other materials in the receiving area. Mixing shipments can create endless problems.

A second important step is to check each item against the packing slip as it comes out of the box. This serves as a check on what the shippers think they sent against what the library actually received. After all, boxes go astray in shipment, shipping room clerks overlook items or add something not on the order, and sometimes items disappear from the library before processing.

Checking the physical condition of each item is another step in the receiving process. Defective materials may be returned for credit or replacement without prior approval from the vendor. Imperfections can be of many kinds. With books, typical problems are missing or blank pages or improperly collated texts. Staff members need to check audiotapes and videotapes for gaps, blank or fogged sections, and proper recording speed. Microforms need to be examined to assure the producer processed them properly; sometimes they have fogged, streaked, or spotted areas, and occasionally there is chemical residue that can ruin the film. The following list highlights some common receipt problems:

- The wrong edition sent. (Note that the checker must be aware of the difference between an edition and a printing. A new *edition* means there are substantial changes—material added or deleted; a new *printing* merely indicates the publisher sold out the previous printing and reprinted more copies with no changes in the text.)
- Items ordered but not received.
- Items received that were not ordered.

- Too many or not enough copies sent.
- Imperfect copies received.

Vendors are usually good about accepting returns of unwanted items, even when it turns out to have been the fault of the library—as long as the library has not put its property mark in them.

After determining that the shipment is complete, property marking (such as stamping or embossing) takes place. As noted above, sometimes items disappear, so the sooner property marking takes place the more difficult it will be for materials to vanish without a trace. Property marking takes many forms. Stamping the fore edge and the title page of books is a common practice. (Rare books are handled differently.) Another method is to accession items, that is, to give each item a unique number. A staff member records the number and title of the item in an accessions book. Today, linking the bar code in an item to its item record in a database accomplishes the same type of inventory control with much less effort.

Special leaders attached to films and microforms provide both "eye legible" information about the content and an indication of library ownership. Microfilm and film reels may be large enough to take a bar code label, but microfiches seldom carry ownership markings. Sound discs, which are disappearing from collections as audiocassettes and CDs replace them, usually have a stamp on the record label as well as on the record jacket. Cassette items often have bar code labels attached or the library's name and the accession number engraved on the cassette.

SERIALS PROCESSING

Previously we mentioned the importance and complex nature of serials. Control of incoming serials is a key factor in the library's realizing the maximum value for its investment in subscriptions.

End-users and librarians often want to know the library's exact holdings for a single title. Are some items missing? What is the latest issue? When did the library pay for the subscription? How often does the library bind the issues? What is the publication's format? Where can the library subscribe to a particular periodical? Most libraries maintain files that answer all these questions and many more. But without careful attention to the number of files being generated and maintained, the paperwork can become overwhelming. Even an automated system requires that someone input the appropriate data. Too often, files contain needless duplication, which means wasting staff time in updating files.

Most librarians agree that serials control constitutes one of the major record-keeping headaches in technical services. The basic controlling method is to maintain a unit control record for each title. This can be a page in a notebook, a 3-by-5-inch (ca 8-by-13-cm) card file, a card in a visible file (see Figures 8.3 through 8.5, pages 171–72), or a computer record (see Figure 8.6, page 173). A single record should contain all information for a given title, such as when the subscription began, its acquisition source, renewal frequency, and binding information. As files grow, it becomes exceedingly difficult to extract the desired information quickly. With a centralized manual record system for each title, the library can only arrange the records by one element of information, normally alphabetically by title. The alternative is to set up several files to counteract the limited access of a central file. However, then the library faces all the disadvantages of a decentralized record system, such as a growing number of files to maintain, duplication of information, and increased searching time for users and library staff.

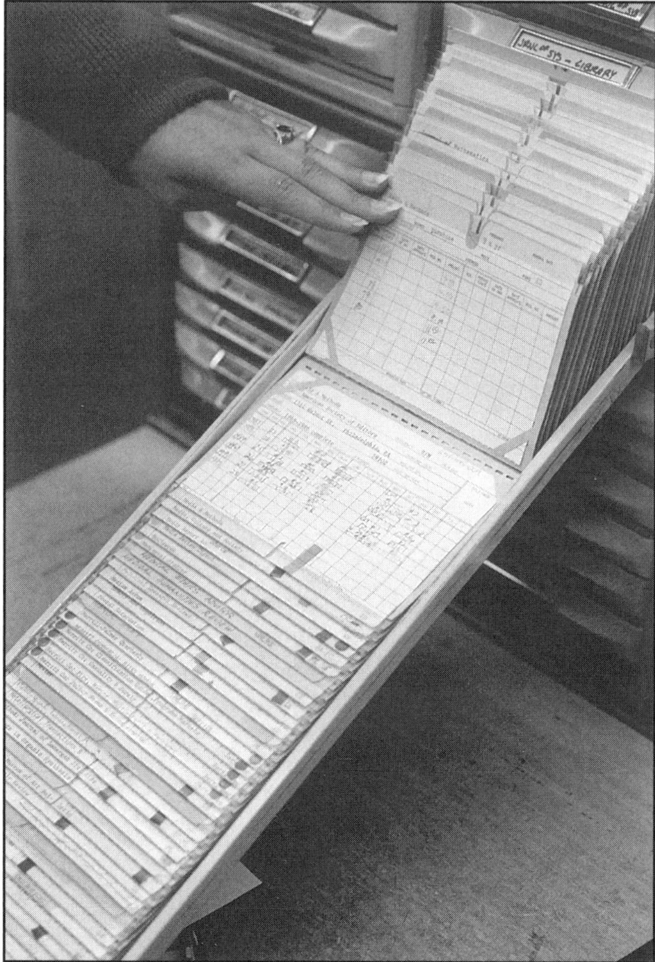

Figure 8.3. Visible file check-in system.

PUBLISHERS ADDRESS

ORDER NO.

DATE

FUND

BIND

SOURCE

YEAR & VOL.	INVOICE NO.	COST	CLAIM RECORD	YEAR & VOL.	INVOICE NO.	COST	CLAIM RECORD

ACME VISIBLE CROZET VIRGINIA #88055-6

Figure 8.4. Check-in card for serials.

TITLE. CALL=

HOLDINGS.

ROUTE.

LOCATION–	Bound			
	Unbd.			
BIND	in bindery	frequency	marking	cost
	ind. and t.p.		color	
FREQUENCY		price	nos. per vol.	vols per Year

RENEWAL DATE

TITLE CHANGES

CAT. ENTRY.

PUBLISHER.

VENDOR.

NOTES.

FUND CHARGED.

BACK FILE LANGUAGE SUBJECT REQUESTED BY

Figure 8.5. Central record card.

```
 C1041435              Last updated: 09-27-01 Created: 09-29-94 Revision: 488
TITLE            Time
LOCATIONS        1mlp             CALL #        AP2 .T37
NOTE             Library keeps both formats (mfm & print)

Boxes 1 to 84 of 84
|      Jul 3|     Jul 10|     Jul 17|     Jul 24|     Jul 31|      Aug 7|     Aug 14|
| BOUND     | BOUND     | BOUND     | BOUND     | BOUND     | BOUND     | BOUND     |
| 05-18-01  | 05-18-01  | 05-18-01  | 05-18-01  | 05-18-01  | 05-18-01  | 05-18-01  |
|156:1     1|156:2     1|156:3     1|156:4     1|156:5     1|156:6     1|156:7     1|
|     Aug 21|     Aug 28|      Sep 4|     Sep 11|     Sep 18|     Sep 25|      Oct 2|
| BOUND     | BOUND     | BOUND     | BOUND     | BOUND     | BOUND     | BOUND     |
| 05-18-01  | 05-18-01  | 05-18-01  | 05-18-01  | 05-18-01  | 05-18-01  | 06-26-01  |
|156:8     1|156:9     1|156:10    1|156:11    1|156:12    1|156:13    1|156:14    1|
|      Oct 9|     Oct 16|     Oct 23|     Oct 30|      Nov 6|     Nov 13|     Nov 20|
| BOUND     | BOUND     | BOUND     | BOUND     | BOUND     | BOUND     | BOUND     |
| 06-26-01  | 06-26-01  | 06-26-01  | 06-26-01  | 06-26-01  | 06-26-01  | 06-26-01  |
|156:15    1|156:16    1|156:17    1|156:18    1|156:19    1|156:20    1|156:21    1|
|     Nov 27|      Dec 4|     Dec 11|     Dec 18|           |     Win 01|      Jan 8|
| BOUND     | BOUND     | BOUND     | BOUND     | BOUND     | BOUND     | BOUND     |
| 06-26-01  | 06-26-01  | 06-26-01  | 06-26-01  |Dec25/Jan1 |Life issue | 09-27-01  |
|156:22    1|156:23    1|156:24    1|156:25    1|156:26    1|156:27    1|157:1     1|
|     Jan 15|     Jan 22|     Jan 29|      Feb 5|     Feb 12|     Feb 19|     Feb 26|
| BOUND     | BOUND     | BOUND     | BOUND     | BOUND     | BOUND     | BOUND     |
| 09-27-01  | 09-27-01  | 09-27-01  | 09-27-01  | 09-27-01  | 09-27-01  | 09-27-01  |
|157:2     1|157:3     1|157:4     1|157:5     1|157:6     1|157:7     1|157:8     1|
|      Mar 5|     Mar 12|     Mar 19|     Mar 26|      Apr 2|      Apr 9|     Apr 16|
| BOUND     | BOUND     | BOUND     | BOUND     | BOUND     | BOUND     | BOUND     |
| 09-27-01  | 09-27-01  | 09-27-01  | 09-27-01  | 09-27-01  | 09-27-01  | 09-27-01  |
|157:9     1|157:10    1|157:11    1|157:12    1|157:13    1|157:14    1|157:15    1|
|     Apr 23|     Apr 30|      May 7|     May 14|     May 21|     May 28|      Jun 4|
| BOUND     | BOUND     | BOUND     | BOUND     | BOUND     | BOUND     | BOUND     |
| 09-27-01  | 09-27-01  | 09-27-01  | 09-27-01  | 09-27-01  | 09-27-01  | 09-27-01  |
|157:16    1|157:17    1|157:18    1|157:19    1|157:20    1|157:21    1|157:22    1|
|     Jun 11|     Jun 18|     Jun 25|      Jul 2|      Jul 9|     Jul 16|     Jul 23|
| BOUND     | BOUND     | BOUND     | BOUND     | ARRIVED   | ARRIVED   | ARRIVED   |
| 09-27-01  | 09-27-01  | 09-27-01  | 09-27-01  | 07-03-01  | 07-10-01  | 07-18-01  |
|157:23    1|157:24    1|157:25    1|157:26    1|158:1     1|158:2     1|158:3     1|
|     Jul 30|      Aug 6|     Aug 13|     Aug 20|     Aug 27|      Sep 3|     Sep 10|
| ARRIVED   | ARRIVED   | ARRIVED   | ARRIVED   | ARRIVED   | ARRIVED   | ARRIVED   |
| 07-24-01  | 08-07-01  | 08-06-01  | 08-14-01  | 08-22-01  | 08-30-01  | 09-07-01  |
|158:4     1|158:5     1|158:6     1|158:7     1|158:8     1|158:9     1|158:10    1|
|     Sep 17|     Sep 11|     Sep 24|     Fal 01|      Oct 1|      Oct 8|     Oct 15|
| ARRIVED   | ARRIVED   | ARRIVED   | ARRIVED   | ARRIVED   | EXPECTED  | E         |
| 09-11-01  |Special is |Special is |Special is | 09-24-01  | 10-10-01  | 10-17-01  |
|158:11    1|158:12    1|158:13    1|158:14    1|158:15    1|158:16     |158:17     |
|     Oct 22|     Oct 29|      Nov 5|     Nov 12|     Nov 19|     Nov 26|      Dec 3|
| E         | E         | E         | E         | E         | E         | E         |
| 10-24-01  | 10-31-01  | 11-07-01  | 11-14-01  | 11-21-01  | 11-28-01  | 12-05-01  |
|158:18     |158:19     |158:20     |158:21     |158:22     |158:23     |158:24     |
|     Dec 10|     Dec 17|     Dec 24|     Dec 31|      Jan 7|     Jan 14|     Jan 21|
| E         | E         | E         | E         | E         | E         | E         |
| 12-12-01  | 12-19-01  | 12-26-01  | 01-02-02  | 01-09-02  | 01-16-02  | 01-23-02  |
|158:25     |158:26     |159:1      |159:2      |159:3      |159:4      |159:5      |
```

Figure 8.6. Staff mode serials check-in screen. Reprinted by permission of Innovative Interfaces, Inc.

Electronic Serials Processing

E-serials are an example of how technology changes the process of acquisitions. An excellent article by Ellen Duranceau spells out the differences between print and electronic serials acquisitions.[9] Her major points are that more teamwork is required, more higher level personnel are involved, it takes more time because it is not a linear process (in most cases), and it requires input from legal and technical staff that may not be part of the library staff. Further, she noted that the concept of " 'til forbidden" does not work well for e-serials as producers and aggregators change the "product" all the time—even during a subscription period.

Check-In Routines

The most critical aspect of serials work is the daily checking in of periodicals, serials, and newspapers. This is the point at which the system can succeed or fail. The staff must rigorously follow the established routines. When a library loses a single issue of a serial, it may have to spend four or five times the cover price to secure a replacement copy, delay binding a volume, or risk creating a gap in the collection.

Each library must make a decision on how to set up the check-in file. With manual files there are two basic arrangement choices: by the official catalog (main) entry or by the title as it appears on the issue's cover. When the library's subscription list consists of popular commercial magazines such as *Time* or *Good Housekeeping,* either approach is fine. However, as the list grows, cover titles and catalog entry forms will diverge. The problem, of course, is that the person at the check-in file has only the particular issue in hand. Even for a fully trained and capable cataloger, examining the issue to determine the main entry in order to locate the check-in record is very time consuming. Publications that have cover titles such as *Journal of*. . . or *Bulletin of*. . . are likely to have a corporate entry; when one adds journals in other languages, the problem is compounded. A library is fortunate if it has check-in staff who are capable of reading more than one or two languages.

Another problem is how to set up the record for a new subscription. With the cover-title method the check-in person can set up the record when the first issue arrives. The main-entry approach requires that the catalog department provide full cataloging information before establishing the check-in record. Depending on publication frequency and the catalog department's workload, additional issues may arrive before the check-in record exists. This may cause some confusion and perhaps lead to issues being lost.

Because of these problems, most libraries with manual files use the cover-title approach in a visible file system. This approach is advantageous because less time is needed to train checkers, and they make fewer errors. Certainly one advantage of automated serials control (check-in) modules is the ability to use a variety of approaches to bring up the proper check-in record. Figure 8.7, page 175, and Figure 8.8, page 176, illustrate an OPAC public serials screen and one type of manual system for public access. Note the difference in detail provided in the staff records and those for the public.

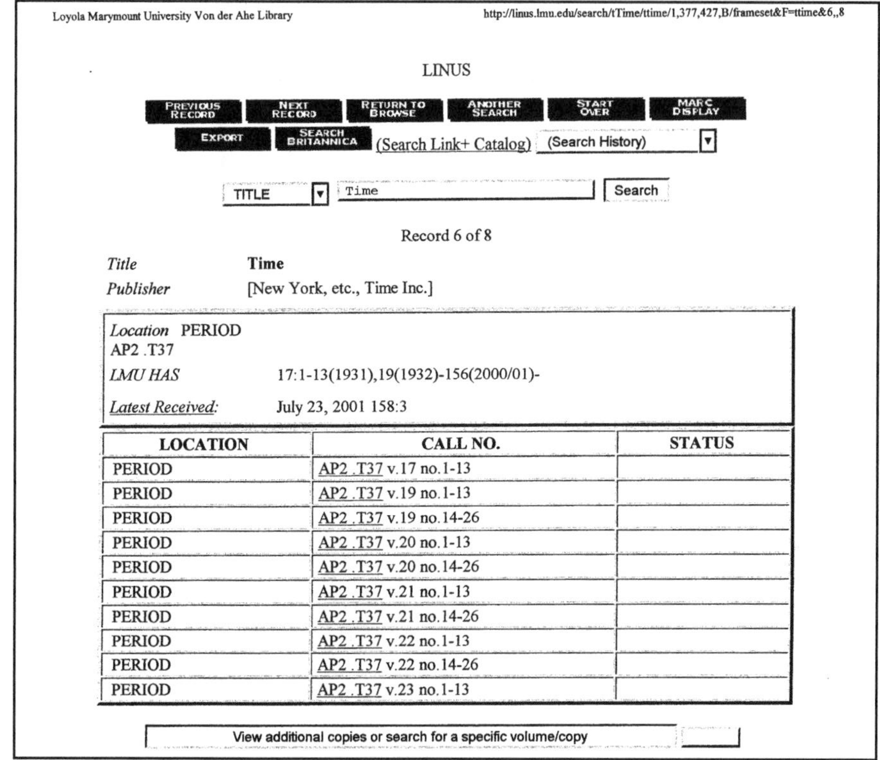
Loyola Marymount University Von der Ahe Library http://linus.lmu.edu/search/tTime/ttime/1,377,427,B/frameset&F=ttime&6,,8

LINUS

PREVIOUS RECORD | NEXT RECORD | RETURN TO BROWSE | ANOTHER SEARCH | START OVER | MARC DISPLAY
EXPORT | SEARCH BRITANNICA | (Search Link+ Catalog) | (Search History)

TITLE | Time | Search

Record 6 of 8

Title **Time**
Publisher [New York, etc., Time Inc.]

Location PERIOD
AP2 .T37
LMU HAS 17:1-13(1931),19(1932)-156(2000/01)-
Latest Received: July 23, 2001 158:3

LOCATION	CALL NO.	STATUS
PERIOD	AP2 .T37 v.17 no.1-13	
PERIOD	AP2 .T37 v.19 no.1-13	
PERIOD	AP2 .T37 v.19 no.14-26	
PERIOD	AP2 .T37 v.20 no.1-13	
PERIOD	AP2 .T37 v.20 no.14-26	
PERIOD	AP2 .T37 v.21 no.1-13	
PERIOD	AP2 .T37 v.21 no.14-26	
PERIOD	AP2 .T37 v.22 no.1-13	
PERIOD	AP2 .T37 v.22 no.14-26	
PERIOD	AP2 .T37 v.23 no.1-13	

View additional copies or search for a specific volume/copy

Figure 8.7. OPAC public serials screen.

Upon receipt of the daily mail, the staff arranges the items in alphabetical order by title. A checker *cannot* assume that the issue in hand is the next issue due to arrive. The staff member checks the table of contents or legal notice to determine the volume number, issue number, and date of the particular issue in hand. If there is a gap in the receipts, the claiming process should begin immediately. Because serials publishers seldom print many copies of an issue beyond the number of active subscriptions, the claim for a missing issue should go out quickly if the library hopes to receive a replacement copy.

The last step in processing is approving the invoice for payment. Normally, this requires the signature of the head of the department or that person's representative. Usually, only a completely filled order may be approved for payment. The library bookkeeper passes on the approved invoice to the agency that actually issues the check. Rarely does a library itself write such checks; it is done by the governing agency.

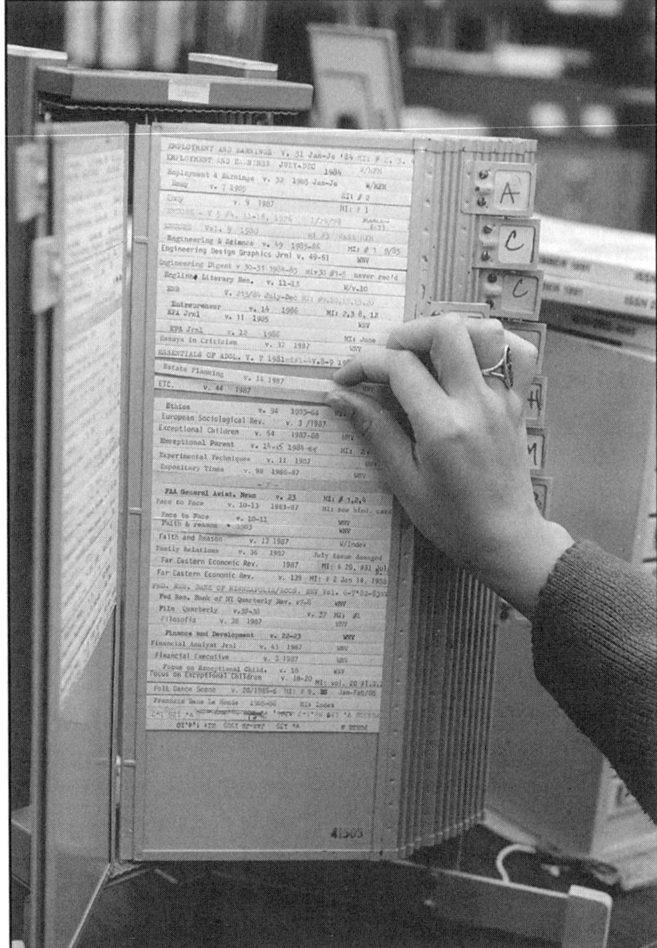

Figure 8.8. Manual system for public access to serials.

Before books and other individually ordered items leave the acquisitions department, the on-order file records need updating or pulling. The follow-up work on receipt procedures—for example, preparing letters regarding items not received, duplicate copies, or errors in invoicing and checking on vendors' responses to inquiries—accounts for much of the acquisitions department's time.

SUMMARY

This chapter covers the basics of ordering and receiving materials, highlighting the fact that not all acquisitions activities relate to buying materials. Although the different formats have their special characteristics, the underlying steps are the same regardless of format—print, electronic, or nonbook media. There are also a surprising number of legal issues involved in acquisitions work. For example, a firm order slip is a contract, electronic products come with contracts and lease forms, and even gifts may have legal implications. Technology is helping acquisitions staff keep up with an ever-increasing volume of work; however, at the end of the day it is still the individuals who take the time to really understand the information trade that make the process work as well as it does.

NOTES

1. Audrey B. Eaglen, "The ISBN: A Good Tool Sorely Misused," *Collection Building* 10, no. 1 (1989): 76.

2. Audrey Eaglen, "Trouble in Kiddyland: The Hidden Costs of O.P. and O.S.," *Collection Building* 6 (Summer 1984): 26-28.

3. Warren St. John, "Vanity's Fare: The Peripatetic Professor and His Peculiarly Profitable Press," *Lingua Franca* 3 (September/October 1993): 1, 22-25, 62.

4. Joyce L. Ogburn, "T2: Theory in Acquisition Revisited," *Library Acquisitions* 21 (Summer 1997): 168.

5. G. Edward Evans, "Book Selection and Book Collection Usage in Academic Libraries," *Library Quarterly* 40 (July 1970): 297-308; G. Edward Evans, "Approval Plans and Collection Development in Academic Libraries," *Library Resources & Technical Services* 18 (Winter 1974): 35-50.

6. Mary Bostic, "Gifts to Libraries: Coping Effectively," *Collection Management* 14, nos. 3/4 (1991): 175-184.

7. Steven Carrico, "Gifts and Exchanges," in *Business of Acquisitions,* 2nd ed., edited by K. Schmidt (Chicago: American Library Association, 1999).

8. Ibid., 210.

9. Ellen F. Duranceau, "Beyond Print: Revisioning Serials Acquisitions for the Digital Age," *Serials Librarian* 33, nos. 1/2 (1998): 83-106.

SELECTED WEB SITES AND DISCUSSION LISTS

025.2 Acquisitions (AcqLink), http://link.bubl.ac.uk/acqlink/

Welcome to AcqWeb, sister publication of ACQNET, http://acqweb.library.vanderbilt.edu/
ACQNET is a managed or edited listserv, which aims to provide a medium for acquisitions librarians. http://acqweb.library.vanderbilt.edu/acqweb/acqnet.html

ALCTS Publications Acquisitions Bibliography, http://www.ala.org/alcts/publications/acqbib.html

Backmed—Informal exchange of medical serial back issues and books, http://lists.swetsblackwell.com/mailman/listinfo/backmed

Backserv—Informal exchange of serial back issues and books among libraries, http://lists.swetsblackwell.com/mailman/listinfo/backserv

SERIALST WELCOME, http://www.uvm.edu/%7ebmaclenn/serialst.html

Developing Library and Information Center Collections Fourth Edition, http://lib.lmu.edu/dlc4/dlc4web.htm

SUGGESTED READING

Anderson, Byron. "Print and Electronic Books." *Behavioral & Social Sciences Librarian* 18, no. 2 (2000): 69-72.

Association of Research Libraries. *Gifts and Exchange Function in ARL Libraries*. Washington, DC: Association of Research Libraries, 1997.

Brown, Linda. "The Evolving Approval Plan." *Library Collections, Acquisitions, and Technical Services* 23 (Fall 1999): 231-277.

Byerly, Greg. "Special Orders! Specialized Search Engines." *School Library Media Activities Monthly* 16 (October 1999): 35, 37.

Case, Beau David. "Approval Plan Evaluation Studies," *Against the Grain* 8 no. 4 (1996): 18-21, 24.

———. "Cutting-Edge Articles on Cutting-Edge Approval Plans," *Against the Grain* 12 no. 3 (2000): 16-34.

Chen, Chiou-sen Dora. *Serials Management: A Practical Guide*. Chicago: ALA, 1998.

Dickinson, Dennis W. "Free Books: Are They Worth What They Cost?" *Library Issues: Briefings for Faculty and Administrators* 17 (May 1997): 1-4.

Dilys, E. Morris, et al. "Monographs Acquisitions: Staffing Costs and the Impact of Automation." *Library Resources & Technical Services* 40 (October 1996): 301-318.

Dugger, L. J. "Fundamentals of Acquisitions." *Serials Review* 23, no. 3 (1997): 85-87.

Dwyer, Rob. "Thou Shalt Look a Gift Horse in the Mouth." *Technicalities* 21 (January-February 2001): 9.

Eaglen, Audrey B. *Buying Books.* 2nd ed. New York: Neal-Schuman, 2000.

Forsyth, J. H. "Monitoring a Business Approval Plan for Balance and Numbers." *Library Acquisitions* 22, no. 3 (Fall 1998): 335-340.

Haar, John. "Paperbacks on Approval." *Against the Grain* 7 (June 1995): 16.

Hale, Marylou. "How Title Source II Changed the Way North Las Vegas Library District Does Acquisitions." *Against the Grain* 13 (April 2001): 72-75.

Heller, Anne. "Online Ordering: Making Its Mark." *Library Journal* 124 (September 1, 1999): 153-158.

Kairis, Rob. "Comparing Gifts to Purchased Materials: A Usage Study." *Library Collections, Acquisitions, and Technical Services* 24 (Fall 2000): 351-359.

Kay, Mary H. "Biz of Acq.—Web-based Ordering for Libraries." *Against the Grain* 12 (April 2000): 75-76.

Ladizesky, K., and R. Hogg. "To Buy or Not to Buy—Questions About the Exchange of Publications Between the Former Soviet Bloc Countries and the West in the 1990s." *Journal of Librarianship and Information Science* 30 (September 1998): 185-193.

Miller, H. S. "Monographic Series Approval Plan: An Attempt to Refine Purchasing of Books in Series." *Library Resources & Technical Services* 42 (April 1998): 133-139.

Rouzuer, Steven. "Acquiring Monographic Series by Approval Plan: Is the Standing Order Obsolescent?" *Library Acquisitions* 19 (Winter 1995): 395-401.

Schmidt, K. A., ed. *Business of Library Acquisitions.* 2nd ed. Chicago: American Library Association, 1999.

Sennyey, Pongracz. "Assessing Blanket Order Effectiveness." *Library Acquisitions* 21 (Winter 1997): 445-454.

Shendenheim, Laura. "Book Vendor Records in OCLC Database: Boon or Bane?" *Library Resources & Technical Services* 45 (January 2001): 10-19.

Stadler, Peter, Ernest Mernke, and Martin Thomas. "Introduction of Electronic Book Ordering With EDIFACT in a Special Library." *The Electronic Library* 17 (February 1999): 23-26.

Strand, Benita. "How to Look a Gift Horse in the Mouth, or How to Tell People You Can't Use Their Old Junk." *Collection Management* 14, no. 2 (1995): 29-30.

Tenopir, Carol. "Should We Cancel Print?" *Library Journal* 124 (September 1, 1999): 138.

Walpole, M. G. "The Meta-Exchange Pilot Project: A New Way to Organize Book Exchanges with Russia." *Library of Congress Information Bulletin* 58 (February 1999): 21+.

REVIEW QUESTIONS

1. What are the three special "numbers" associated with the book trade and acquisitions work that save time?
2. Discuss the various vendor reports that libraries receive regarding the orders they place.
3. What are the three key decisions that the acquisitions department makes about acquiring an item?
4. List and discuss each of the methods of acquisitions. What are the advantages and disadvantages of each?
5. Discuss the legal issues associated with gifts to U.S. libraries.
6. Discuss the steps in the receiving process.
7. What challenges do e-serials present in terms of receipt?

Chapter 9 Distributors and Vendors

The rather simple statement in the previous chapter, "select the vendor," does not do justice to the importance and complexities of the issues associated with making that selection. This chapter explores the issues involved in making the decision to go with a specific vendor. Acquisitions departments have two basic means of purchasing materials, directly from the publisher or producer or through an intermediary such as a wholesaler or jobber or a retail outlet. The publishers and producers in some cases require direct purchases and in other cases require the use of an intermediary source. Often direct purchases will provide the highest discount, which is good for the collection budget *as long as the acquisitions department has staff enough to handle hundreds of individual orders and invoices.* The more typical source is the intermediary (jobber or wholesaler or retail outlet, for example). Although the discount will be lower than that offered by a publisher or producer directly, the advantage of placing one order with an intermediary for titles from hundreds of publishers or producers and reducing the library's paperwork more than compensates for the lower discount. Because publishers and producers were discussed in detail in Chapter 6, space is devoted here to discussing two types of intermediary suppliers.

JOBBERS

The most commonly used intermediary source is the jobber or wholesaler. These organizations carry large inventories of titles from thousands of publishers and producers. Three of the larger U.S. library book jobbers are Baker & Taylor, Blackwell North America, and Brodart. Two of the larger Canadian book wholesalers are National Book Service and United Library Supply. Two of the largest U.S. serials jobbers are EBSCO and Faxon. In addition, there are smaller firms that provide good-quality service to libraries and information centers. However, as discussed below, their numbers are decreasing. Most countries with an active book trade have similar organizations. Libraries often use a jobber in countries where they buy large quantities of materials. As a general rule a jobber in the country of origin has a better chance of locating a desired item than does a jobber from another country.

Like all other organizations involved in the information business, library vendors and distributors are facing a changing environment, in large measure due to technology. Another factor is what has and is happening to the majority of libraries. That is, the past twenty years or so have not been the best of times for library funding and support in general. As a result of wanting to continue to do business with libraries as well as taking advantage of new business opportunities, many vendors and suppliers are offering a wider range of services to libraries. This is one of the sources for libraries to consider outsourcing some of their traditional in-house activities.

Chapter 6 identified two major problems for materials producers: economics and distribution. Having knowledge of the information product distribution system is essential for developing the most cost-effective collection of information materials. Wholesalers, retailers, and remainder houses are major sources of material for the library collection. Often, several different sources can supply the same item. Is there an important difference between these sources? What services does each provide? For example, if a library is looking for a book published last year, it is possible to acquire a copy from various sources. Would it matter which source is used? How likely is it that all would have the book? For that matter, what function does each source perform?

Jobber or Wholesaler?

Librarians in the United States refer to *jobbers* or *vendors* rather than wholesalers, whereas many Canadian firms are known as *wholesalers.* There is a technical difference between a wholesaler and a jobber,[1] but for libraries that difference is insignificant. Jobbers purchase quantities of books from various publishers, then sell the copies to bookstores and libraries. Because they buy in volume, they receive a substantial discount from publishers. When the jobber sells a book, the purchaser receives a discount off the producer's list price, but it is much lower than the discount that the jobber received. For example, if the jobber received a 40 percent discount from the producer, the discount given the library will be 15 to 20 percent. If the library or bookstore orders the book directly from the publisher, the discount may be just as high as the jobber received or even higher.

Discounting is a complex issue in any commercial activity, and it is highly complex in the book trade. Every producer has a discount schedule that is slightly different, if not unique. Some items are *net* (no discount); usually these are textbooks, STM titles, or items of limited sales appeal. *Short discounts* are normally 20 percent; these are items the producers expect will have limited appeal but that have more potential than the net titles. *Trade discounts* range from 30 to 60 percent or more; items in this category are high-demand items or high-risk popular fiction. Publishers believe that by giving a high discount for fiction, bookstores will stock more copies and thus help promote the title. Jobbers normally receive 40 to 50 percent discounts, primarily because of their high-volume orders (hundreds of copies per title rather than the tens that most libraries and independent bookstore owners order).

Recently, jobbers have encountered financial problems in the form of rising costs and declining sales. A number of publishers are requiring prepayment or have placed jobbers on a *pro forma* status. Pro forma status requires prepayment, and suppliers extend credit on the basis of the current performance in payment of bills. Much of the credit and order fulfillment extended by publishers depends on an almost personal relationship with a jobber. This means that libraries must select a jobber(s) with care. It is not inappropriate to check a prospective jobber's financial status (through a rating service, such as Dun and Bradstreet).

One question for the library to answer is how many vendors to use. There are pros and cons for consolidating business with only one or two vendors just as there are for using a number of vendors for the same type of product. Consolidation usually means the vendor gains a better sense of the library's requirements, perhaps provides a better discount, and may even offer some "free" services. The primary danger is the vendor's viability. Today's environment requires regular, substantial investments in technology, which combined with libraries' budget woes, means smaller firms may not be able to survive or at least not keep up with technological developments in the field. Having several vendors for a type of product may provide a higher discount, at least when there is a degree of competition for the library's business. One drawback is that the service may not be as good and perhaps the vendors will not have the resources to invest in newer technology. The primary concern should be service followed by financial strength—it is not unheard of for major vendors to have serious financial problems.

What Can Jobbers Do?

Why buy from an indirect source that charges the same or a higher price than the direct source would? Service! Jobbers provide an important service in that they can save a library a significant amount of time and money. Although jobbers do not give high discounts, the time saved by placing a single order for ten different titles from ten different publishers (instead of ten different orders) more than pays for the slightly higher price. Other savings can result from the "batch effect" of unpacking fewer boxes and authorizing fewer payments. Most jobbers also promise to provide fast, accurate service. It is true that a few publishers, if they accept single-copy orders (and most do), handle these orders more slowly than they do large orders. But it is also true that jobbers do not always have a specific title when the library wants it, which means that the library must allow additional time to secure the desired item.

Many jobbers promise twenty-four-hour shipment of items in stock. Do they make good on such claims? Generally, yes; however, the key phrase is *in stock*. Frequently, there can be delays of three to four months in receiving a complete order because some titles are not in stock. When talking with jobbers, do not become impressed by numbers quoted in their advertising, such as, "more than 2 million books in stock." What is important is how many titles and which publishers they stock. For various reasons, from economic to personal, some publishers will refuse to deal with a particular jobber. Four important questions to ask any jobber before a library contracts for that firm's services are

1. Will you give me a list of all the publishers that you do not handle?
2. How does your firm handle a request for a title not in stock?
3. Will you give me a list of series that your firm does not handle?
4. Do you have any service charges on any category of material? (If so, ask if the charge is indicated on the invoice as a separate cost.)

Often, the answer to the first question is difficult to obtain. Sales representatives want to say they can supply *any* title from *any* publisher, with only minor exceptions. However, libraries in the same system may simultaneously receive different lists from various representatives of the same firm. The issue is important, and the acquisitions department must resolve the question if it is to operate effectively. Sending an order for a title from a publisher that the jobber cannot handle only delays matters. In some cases, the jobber will report that it is trying to secure the item; this often leads to a later report of failure, making the acquisition process even slower. Buying directly from the publisher is the best approach to this problem, if the library knows which publishers the jobber cannot handle.

The second question relates to the speed of service. Some jobbers order a single title from a publisher when it is not in stock. Others say they will do this and they do; however, they frequently wait until they have received multiple requests before placing the order. By placing a multiple-copy order, the jobber receives a better discount. For the library, the delay may be one to several months, because it will take that long for the jobber to accumulate enough individual requests for the title to make up an order of sufficient size. The impact of this practice may or may not be serious depending on where the library is in its budget cycle, and inflation rates. (More about these issues appears later in this chapter.) Usually, jobbers that place single-copy orders for a customer offer a lower discount on such items or impose a service charge. Again, the acquisitions staff must weigh service and speed against discount. Occasionally, a jobber will have a title in stock after the publisher has listed the item as out-of-print (OP). On occasion, a jobber can supply out-of-print material, and a few jobbers will even try to find out-of-print items for their best customers. This is a special service that is never advertised and is offered only to favored customers.

Beyond fast, accurate service, jobbers should provide personal service. A smooth working relationship is based on mutual understanding and respect. When those are present, it is much easier to solve problems, even the difficult ones. The jobber, because of the smaller base of customers, normally can provide answers more quickly than a publisher's customer service department can. Even the small account customer receives a jobber's careful attention (to hold the account), something that seldom happens with publishers.

No single jobber can stock all of the in-print items that a library will need. However, most large firms do carry the high-demand current and backlist items. Book trade folklore says that 20 percent of the current and backlist titles represent 80 percent of total sales. All of the good jobbers try to stock the right 20 percent of titles. Some are more successful at this than others. The approach works well for bookstores; however, for libraries the need to acquire a broad range of titles, including less popular ones, makes this practice less useful.

One problem with a jobber that has limited stock is invoicing and billing procedures. A small jobber may ship and bill for those items that are in stock, then backorder the remainder of the titles. In this case, the jobber expects to receive payment for the partial fulfillment of the order. However, some funding authorities allow payment only for complete orders. That is, the library must receive or cancel every item on an order before the business office will issue a check. This procedure can cause problems for small jobbers and libraries alike. Few small vendors are able or willing to wait for payment until a particular order is complete. For small libraries with small materials budgets, the challenge is to find a jobber that will accept complicated procedures and delays despite low volume. It is becoming harder to find such firms, and libraries are attempting to persuade their funding authorities to simplify ordering and payment procedures.

Status reports are an area of concern for both the acquisitions and collection development staff. Almost everyone in the field has been frustrated by these reports. Does a report stating a book is out of print mean the book is *really* out of print? It should, but occasionally, by contacting the publisher, the library may have the item in hand in less than thirty days. This happens often enough to keep doubts alive about the quality of jobber reports. An article in a 1989 issue of *School Library Journal* reported that 10 percent of all school library orders and 7 percent of public library orders are unavailable for some reason.[2] These figures have not changed significantly since then.

Does it really matter how accurate the reports are? Yes, it does matter, and the result can have an impact on collection development. An item on order encumbers (sets aside) the necessary funds for payment. The acquisitions staff cannot determine the precise cost of the item until the invoice arrives; the price may change, the exact discount is unknown, and shipping and handling charges vary. Libraries hope to set aside slightly more than the total cost. Most libraries and information centers have annual budgets and operate in systems where any unexpended monies at the end of the fiscal year revert to the general fund (that is, the funds do not carry forward into the next fiscal year). In essence, the library loses the unspent money. Having large sums of money tied up (encumbered) in outstanding orders that are undeliverable before the end of the fiscal year can result in a real loss for the collection. In a sense, the library loses twice: wanted items go unreceived, and the library loses funds.

Finally, as previously mentioned, the library does lose some buying power as funds remain encumbered. Unlike money in a savings account, which earns a small amount of interest each day, encumbered funds lose a small amount of purchasing power each day. If inflation is rapid or if a library is buying foreign books and the currency's value is fluctuating widely, losses can be large. Producers raise prices without notice, and in times of inflation, libraries can count on regular price increases. The less time funds remain encumbered, the more purchasing power the library has. Thus, the accuracy of vendors' reports is important. If the vendor cannot supply an item (OP, OS, or TOS) in time, and so informs the library, the library can cancel the order and use the funds for something that is available for delivery. Monitoring of vendor performance in report accuracy and speed of delivery can help control the problem.

Where does a library learn about vendors and services? Beyond attending library association conferences and "word of mouth" suggestions from peers, there are several guides available. General publications such as *Literary Market Place, International Literary Market Place, International Subscription Agent,* Quill & Quire's *Canadian Publishers Directory,* or specialized lists by format, region of the world, and subject matter will provide a long list of possibilities. One can also post questions about vendor experiences on acquisitions discussion lists, such as ACQNET (ACQNET-L@listproc.appstate.edu).

A number of jobbers offer their services to U.S. libraries. Some of the larger and more active firms in marketing their programs are Brodart, Baker & Taylor, Ingram, Yankee Book Peddler, Ballen, Coutts, and Blackwell North America, as well as National Book Service in Canada. There also are specialized jobbers, such as Majors, a leading firm for medical, science, and technical books, and French Language Resources, a Canadian firm that provides French-language books for schools and classrooms. Serials jobbers include EBSCO, Faxon, and Readmore.

When selecting a vendor, keep the following factors in mind:

- Service—a representative, toll free numbers, Web sites, and so forth.
- Quality of service—ask for and check references, ease of handling "problems"
- Speed of fulfillment—including accuracy
- Discount/pricing
- Vendor's financial viability
- Vendor ability to work with the library's automation system
- Special services available—free or at a cost

Needless to say, these are the same factors to use to evaluate the vendor(s) *after* selection.

Vendor-Added Services

Today, most vendors offer services beyond the basics of supplying books, serials, media, and electronic resources at "wholesale prices." Some of the more common services are

- Acquisition assistance—e.g., searching and verification
- Automated selection assistance programs (some including book reviews)
- Book rental plans
- Cataloging and shelf-ready processing

- Customized management data
- Electronic financial transactions beyond the basics
- More than one information format
- Provision of electronic tables of contents or machine readable data
- Library furniture
- Library supplies

As this list suggests, vendors are entering the outsourcing market and some are attempting to offer most of the supplies and services necessary for library operations.

One jobber, Brodart, offers a rather unusual service, the McNaughton Plan, to help solve the problem of providing an adequate number of high-demand titles for both books and audio books. Most libraries have suffered the problem of high demand for a popular book, with the demand lasting only a few months. Should the library buy many copies and discard all but one or two after the demand subsides, or buy only a few copies and take reservations? The McNaughton Plan offers another alternative: rent multiple copies for the duration of the title's popularity. Brodart describes the plan as a *leasing* program. The plan offers high-demand items that Brodart's staff selects. A library cannot order just any book; it must be on Brodart's list of high-demand titles. Savings occur in several areas. There are no processing costs because the books come ready for the shelf, and the leasing fee is considerably lower than the item's purchase price. End-users are happy because of shorter waiting times for the latest bestseller. All in all, anyone involved in meeting recreational reading needs will find the program worth investigating. College and university libraries may use it to stock a variety of materials for recreational reading without taking too much money out of the book fund. Libraries also avoid filling their valuable shelf space with large numbers of duplicates of once-popular titles.

Two additional services many vendors offer are electronic ordering and, especially useful for serials, electronic invoicing. Access to an electronic version of *Books in Print* is often part of the service as well. With electronic ordering, acquisitions staff have online access to the vendor's inventory database. This allows them to learn the availability of a title, place an order, receive confirmation of receipt of the order, and receive the invoice electronically, in a matter of a few seconds. One problem with electronic ordering is that most acquisitions departments use many different vendors, and each vendor offering this type of service seems to develop a number of variations in its system. This is an area where standards could be beneficial to everyone. Learning and remembering, or consulting vendor manuals, or calling help desk numbers for several different electronic ordering systems, cuts into the potential time savings from using such systems.

Some vendors offer useful management reports based on their electronic systems. Figure 9.1, page 188–89, represents a sample report from a serials vendor. An example from a book vendor is illustrated in Figure 9.2, page 190. Such reports assist the library in making budget requests and estimating encumbrances for standing orders and blanket orders.

Office	Acct	Title Number	Title Name	ISSN	LCC
LA	xxxx	000792002	AB Bookmans Yearbook	00650005	Z990
LA	xxxx	009259003	ACTA Musicologica	00016241	ML5
LA	xxxx	019928829	Aerospace America	0740722X	TL501.A68
LA	xxxx	043255009	American Journal of Botany	00029122	QK1
LA	xxxx	479766693	Journal of Forecasting	02776693	H61.4
LA	xxxx	586273005	Modern Language Journal	00267902	PB1
LA	xxxx	969344001	Writers Market	00842729	PN161
LA	xxxx	969539659	Writing on the Edge	10646051	PE1404

Figure 9.1. Charles Von der Ahe Library EBSCO data.

What Should Jobbers and Acquisitions Departments Expect from Each Other?

Departmental staff have a responsibility for helping to maintain good working relationships with vendors. Simply stated, a vendor's profits are the difference between the price it pays producers and the resale price. Is this any different than for any other type of business? Not in the fundamentals, but there are some special aspects to the book trade and library market. One such variation is that anyone can buy directly from the materials producer. This is seldom true in other fields. Another difference is that, to a large degree, libraries can determine what is the maximum price of any item by checking in-print lists, such as *Books in Print,* or by consulting the producer. When every buyer knows the maximum price as well as any producer discount, vendors must at least match the maximum price and provide superior service to retain customers.

As explained previously, volume buying and selling is the only way a jobber can make a profit. Efficient plant operations and low overhead can help, but no matter how efficient the operation, it will fail without high volume. One order for fifteen or twenty titles in quantities will yield a high discount for the jobber, perhaps as high as 60 percent. Even after giving a 20 percent to 25 percent discount to the library, the jobber has a comfortable margin with which to work. In the library market, such orders are usually the exception rather than the rule. More often, the jobber's discount is 50 percent. A smaller margin is still acceptable

DDC	Retail Year 4	Retail Year 3	Retail Year 2	Retail Year 1	Retail Curr	Subscriber	Country of Origin
015	2500	2500	2500	2500	2500	AA	US
781	11000	0	0	0	0	AA	GE
625	8500	9500	13000	13000	13000	AA	US
585	15500	16500	16500	16500	19500	AA	US
005	35500	41500	49500	57500	69500	AA	EN
805	4500	4700	5200	5900	5900	AA	US
825	2995	3099	3149	3149	3149	AA	US
825	1500	1500	1500	1500	1500	AA	US

if all the items sell. But all of them do not! Many publishers have a return policy (in which a publisher buys back unsold books). However, many producers are changing or dropping the return policy, thus increasing the risk for the vendor. Returns normally result in credits against the current account or future purchases. They seldom result in a cash refund for book jobbers.

To get the maximum discount, some librarians dump their "problem" orders on vendors and order easy items directly from the publishers. Nothing could be more shortsighted. Without the income from easy, high-volume items, no jobber can stay in business. Someone has to handle the problem orders, and most vendors will try to track down the difficult items, especially for good customers. However, libraries should give jobbers easy orders as well. Many of the problems facing jobbers involve cash flow. Lack of cash has been the downfall of many businesses, and it becomes critical for jobbers when they handle only problem orders; staff expenses go up, but income does not. Failure of jobbers would lead to higher labor costs for most acquisitions departments as a result of having to place all orders directly with publishers.

Whenever possible, the library should use the order format preferred by the vendor (this is almost always the outlines in the *Guidelines* mentioned previously) and not plead legal or system requirements for a particular method of ordering, unless it is impossible to change the requirement. Most vendors and publishers go out of their way to accommodate the legal requirements of library ordering procedures. The fewer variations libraries ask for, the better service vendors can provide because they do not have to keep track of hundreds of variations.

REPORT DATE 5/3/99
MIDWEST LIBRARY SERVICE
UNIVERSITY PRESS PUBLICATIONS ANALYSIS BY SUBJECT
FOR THE PERIOD 5/1/98 TO 4/30/99

LC Classification #	Description	Number of Titles	Total Price	Average Price
AC 1-195	Collections of monograph	2	54.95	27.48**
AG 1-90	Dictionaries. Minor encyc	2	38.90	19.45**
AM 10-101	Museography. Individual	1	32.50	32.50**
AM 111-160	Museology. Museum methods	1	25.00	25.00**
AS	Academies & learned soc.	4	322.00	80.50**
AZ	History of scholarship	2	55.00	27.50**
	A'S SUBTOTALS	12	528.35	44.03**
B	Philosophy (General)	7	409.90	58.56**
B 69-5739	History & systems	13	679.70	52.28**
B 108-708	Ancient	25	1,361.10	54.44**
B 720-765	Medieval	2	119.90	59.50**
B 770-785	Renaissance	1	54.95	54.95
B 790-5739	Modern	24	1,197.20	49.88**
B 850-5739	By region or country	40	2,042.25	51.06
B 1801-2430	France	23	1,319.70	57.38**
B 2521-3396	Germany. Austria(German)	48	2,382.25	49.63**
BC	Logic	12	809.25	67.44**
BD	Speculative philosophy	1	35.00	35.00**
BD 10-41	Gen'l philosophical wks.	2	122.00	61.00**
BD 95-131	Metaphysics	2	129.95	64.98**
BD 143-236	Epistemology	14	705.30	50.38**
BD 300-450	Ontology	20	849.18	42.46**
BD 493-701	Cosmology	2	124.90	62.45**
BF	Psychology	17	704.65	41.45**
BF 173-175	Psychoanalysts	17	684.25	40.25**
BF 180-210	Experimental psychology	2	97.00	48.50**

Figure 9.2. Vendor book price report.

Finally, libraries should process invoices promptly; the acquisitions department should not hold them longer than necessary. Most library systems require at least two approvals before issuing a payment voucher: the library's approval and the business office's approval. Some systems have three or more offices involved in the approval process. The acquisitions department should fully understand the payment process for its parent organization (e.g., school district, city, or university)—from department approval to final payment. If payment takes longer than six weeks, the library should inform any new jobber of that fact so the firm can decide whether it can do business with the library. It is also necessary to inform jobbers of any changes in the system that may have an impact on the speed of payment. Most jobbers would like to receive payment within thirty days because they are on a thirty-day payment cycle with publishers.

Jobbers provide a valuable service to libraries. Given a good working relationship, both parties benefit. Following is a summary of the basic factors at work in establishing such a relationship.

What Do Libraries Expect from Jobbers?

Acquisition departments have a right to expect that a jobber will provide

- A large inventory of titles in appropriate formats,
- Prompt and accurate order fulfillment,
- Prompt and accurate reporting on items not in stock, and
- Personal service at a reasonable price.

What Do Jobbers Expect from Libraries?

Jobbers have a right to expect

- Time to get to know what the library needs,
- Cooperation in placing orders,
- Keeping paperwork to a minimum, and
- Prompt payment for services.

VENDOR EVALUATION

In the 1990s, many libraries entered into formal contracts with vendors. The contract is the result of either a formal bidding process or responding to a "Request for Proposal" (RFP). If a library has a choice (often public and academic libraries have to employ a bidding process), the RFP is the better option. Often the bid process is out of the library's hands and conducted by business officers who do not fully understand that information materials are *not* the same as pencils, paper, or even computers. With the RFP there should be at least some library input as to the requirements, if the library is not solely responsible for creating the document. An RFP will (or should) contain all the elements that the library will use to evaluate the vendor's performance as well as specifying performance perimeters. The Suggested Reading section in this chapter provides references to resources that will assist in preparing an acquisitions RFP.

Even without a formal contract, acquisitions departments should monitor vendor performance. In the past, monitoring vendors was time-consuming and difficult, and it still is if a library is working with a manual acquisitions system. However, today's automated acquisitions systems can produce a variety of useful management and vendor reports very quickly and in various formats. Knowing what to do with the quantity of data the systems can produce is another matter. (Note: There are two types of evaluation acquisitions staff undertake. One is more a monitoring of vendor performance with an eye to identifying small concerns that left unnoticed could become a major issue. The other is a formal assessment of the vendor with an eye toward changing vendors or renewing a contract.)

One obvious issue that arises in the evaluation process is which vendor performs best on a given type of order (examples are conference proceedings, music scores, or videorecordings). The first thing to do is to decide what *best* means. Highest discount? Fastest delivery? Most accurate reports? Highest percentage of the order filled with the first shipment? All of the above? The answer varies from library to library depending on local needs and conditions. Once the library defines *best*, it knows what data to get from the system. This is a situation in which the RFP process is of assistance; the answers to these questions should be in that document. Other evaluation issues are

- Who handles rush orders most efficiently?
- Who handles international orders most effectively—a dealer in the country of origin or a general international dealer?
- Are specialty dealers more effective in handling their specialties than are general dealers?

Figure 9.3, pages 193–95, is a sample of system reports illustrating several years' performance of some of Loyola Marymount University Library's book vendors. It shows quantities of titles ordered, total expended, average delivery time, percentage of the order received, average cost of each order, what, if any, shipping/handling charges there were, and the discount for each of the vendors.

Vendor Performance Statistics - Delivery Time
Processed Record # : 1583591 to 1984433
Count orders Placed in period 06-01-96 to 04-20-99

	Ave Del Time	# orders received in 02 wks	04 wks	08 wks	12 wks	16 wks	17+ wks
1 a&e	7.7	0	2	5	0	0	1
2 abc	10.3	21	323	3020	1506	369	622
3 abca	0.0	5208	1	3	1	0	1
4 abcc	3.1	115	3	11	0	1	7
5 aber	6.2	1	8	10	3	1	1
6 aip	3.0	0	1	0	0	0	0
7 ala	0.6	54	1	1	1	1	0
8 alss	6.7	1	1	5	2	0	0
9 ama	0.0	1	0	0	0	0	0
10 amazc	3.4	10	3	5	1	0	0
11 amb	13.5	9	31	1194	831	252	370

Vendor Performance Statistics - Percentages
Processed Record # : 1583591 to 1984433
Count orders Placed in period 06-01-96 to 04-20-99

Total Claims	# Orders	Ave Est Price/ Order	Ave Est Price Recd Order	Ave Amt Paid/ Order	% Orders Recd	% Orders Cancld	% Orders Claimed	
1 a&e	11	$27.68	$33.70	$32.63	72.72	9.09	0.00	0
2 abc	6687	$45.96	$46.81	$41.75	87.64	1.85	0.00	0
3 abca	5226	$162.50	$47.78	$139.94	99.77	0.09	0.00	0
4 abcc	144	$57.74	$59.59	$104.72	95.13	0.69	0.00	0
5 abcr	24	$43.52	$43.52	$48.57	100.00	0.00	0.00	0
6 aip	2	$0.00	$0.00	$259.06	50.00	0.00	0.00	0
7 ala	58	$32.48	$32.48	$42.66	100.00	0.00	0.00	0
8 alss	10	$249.50	$253.88	$295.88	90.00	0.00	0.00	0
9 ama	1	$0.00	$0.00	$0.00	100.00	0.00	0.00	0
10 amazc	21	$25.44	$27.59	$26.71	90.47	4.76	0.00	0
11 amb	3399	$41.32	$41.56	$40.74	79.05	1.26	0.20	7

Figure 9.3. Vendor performance statistics.

Figure 9.3—*Continued*

Vendor Performance Statistics - Amounts
Processed Record # : 1583591 to 1984433
Count orders Placed in period 06-01-96 to 04-20-99

	Est Price Orders	Est Price Recpts	Est Price Cancls	Est Price O.ords	Amt Paid
1 a&e	$304.50	$269.60	$0.00	$34.90	$261.04
2 abc	$307,399.34	$274,411.86	$80.00	$32,907.48	$244,698.59
3 abca	$849,246.70	$249,134.80	$150,000.00	$450,111.90	$729,696.37
4 abcc	$8,315.96	$8,165.01	$0.00	$150.95	$14,347.08
5 abcr	$1,044.66	$1,044.66	$0.00	$0.00	$1,165.90
6 aip	$0.00	$0.00	$0.00	$0.00	$259.06
7 ala	$1,883.91	$1,883.91	$0.00	$0.00	$2,474.81
8 alss	$2,495.00	$2,285.00	$0.00	$210.00	$2,662.97
9 ama	$0.00	$0.00	$0.00	$0.00	$0.00
10 amazc	$534.31	$524.31	$0.00	$10.00	$507.54
11 amb	$140,458.35	$111,693.47	$0.00	$28,764.88	$109,479.45

(Figure 9.3 continues on page 195.)

Vendor Performance Statistics - Quantities
Processed Record # : 1583591 to 1984433
Count orders Placed in period 06-01-96 to 04-20-99

# Orders Claimed	# Order Records	# Copies Ordered	# Orders Recd	# Copies Recd	# Orders Cancld	# Outstd Orders	# Claims	
1 a&e	11	11	8	8	1	2	0	0
2 abc	6687	6689	5861	5863	124	702	0	0
3 abca	5226	5226	5214	5214	5	7	0	0
4 abcc	144	144	137	137	1	6	0	0
5 abcr	24	27	24	27	0	0	0	0
6 aip	2	2	1	1	0	1	0	0
7 ala	58	58	58	58	0	0	0	0
8 alss	10	10	9	9	0	1	0	0
9 ama	1	1	1	1	0	0	0	0
10 amazc	21	22	19	20	1	1	0	0
11 amb	3399	3405	2687	2692	43	669	7	7

Vendor Performance Statistics - TOTAL
Processed Record # : 1583591 to 1984433
Count orders Placed in period 06-01-96 to 04-20-99

Average Estimated Price per Order :	$2,517,010.67 / 39060 = $64.43
Average Paid Amount of Receipts :	$2,235,412.84 / 35270 = $63.38
Average Estimated Price for Received Orders :	$1,682,515.20 / 35270 = 47.70
Average Delivery Time :	219988034 / 35270 = 6237
% Orders Received in 2 weeks :	2663 / 35270 = 35.90 %
% Orders Received in 4 weeks :	3839 / 35270 = 10.88 %
% Orders Received in 8 weeks :	10920 / 35270 = 30.96 %
% Orders Received in 12 weeks :	4700 / 35270 = 13.32 %
% Orders Received in 16 weeks :	1341 / 35270 = 3.80 %
% Orders Received in 17+ weeks :	1807 / 35270 = 5.12 %
% Cancelled :	577 / 39060 = 1.47 %
% Claimed :	9 / 39060 = 0.02 %
Average Claims per Claimed Order :	9 / 9 = 1.00
Average Claims per Order :	9 / 39060 = 0.00

In addition to generating system reports based on normal operating procedures, a library can conduct some experiments by placing a random sample of a type of order with several vendors to assess their performance. When doing a test or experiment be certain that each vendor receives approximately the same mix of titles, that no vendor receives more or fewer easy or hard-to-handle items. Often, the normal procedure data reflect the use of a particular vendor for only one type of order. This makes comparing vendor performance rather meaningless because one is not comparing like groups. The library can use the test method to select a vendor for a particular type of order and use the operating data approach to monitor ongoing performance.

Checking on the performance of serials vendors is more difficult. Most libraries use only one domestic serials vendor and perhaps a second firm that specializes in journals from other countries. A library that is just establishing a current subscription list, or starting a large number of new subscriptions, might consider splitting the list between two or more vendors for several years to determine which would be the best sole source for the long term.

A limited amount of checking is possible through comparisons with other libraries. Often, this type of checking is done in a casual manner, that is, by merely asking a colleague in another library, "Do you use vendor *X*? How do you like them?" or "How much is your service charge?" To make valid and useful comparisons, a library needs to know the other library's title mix. Recent developments of union catalogs based on OPAC data suggest that collections, even in apparently similar libraries, have surprisingly different holdings. A comparison was made of the monograph holdings of Loyola Marymount University, Santa Clara University, University of San Francisco, and the University of San Diego libraries for a ten-year period using the AMIGOS CD-ROM collection analysis software (Note: Does not contain serials titles). The university librarians thought the collections would have a large percentage of overlap because the institutions are similar in size, programs, and general emphasis on the liberal arts. All were surprised to learn that more than 80,000 titles of the 159,000 titles in the database were unique; that is, only one of the four schools held the title. Although the results were not as striking for serials holdings, the number of titles held by just one library was a surprise. These discoveries served to reinforce the idea that casual impressionistic assessments are suspect.

One way to compare serials vendors is to investigate a sample of commonly held titles. Factors to examine include the service charges on those titles, the effectiveness of claims processing, and other issues like vendor follow-up and handling of credit memos.

In any vendor evaluation, keep in mind some of the problems vendors have with producers:

- Changes in title, or not publishing the title;
- Not being informed when publishing schedules change or when publishers suspend or cease publication;
- Incorrect ISBNs or ISSNs;
- Producers refusing to take returns;

- Producers refusing to sell through vendors;
- Producers reducing discounts or charging for freight and handling, when those were free in the past;
- Poor fulfillment on the producer's part;
- Constantly changing policies on the producer's part; and
- Producer price increases without prior notice.

References to several "models" for conducting vendor evaluation studies are included in the Suggested Reading section of this chapter.

Several years ago, a student in one of Ed Evans's courses asked during a discussion of vendors, "Why are you so pro-vendor? They are our enemies, with all their high prices and low discounts." Perhaps Ed Evans's work experience in bookstores, publishing, and libraries is a factor in his not being highly negative about vendors. However, it is not a matter of being "so pro-vendor" but rather recognizing that there are at least two sides to most stories. Libraries depend on vendors; they offer services that save libraries time, effort, and staffing. Libraries need vendors and need to understand their problems.

That said, libraries must monitor their performance, question charges, and challenge charges that seem inappropriate. Maintaining good relations is everyone's business. If librarians, vendors, and producers take time to learn about one another's business, working relationships will be better.

Some years ago a new regional manager of the serials vendor used by LMU who had no prior experience in the library marketing sector asked if he could spend a week in the library learning how LMU library handled journals and how library customers use journals. He spent three days in technical services with the serials acquisition staff and two days in public services. Even if LMU operations are not completely typical, his experience made him more aware of the problems libraries face in handling serials. Another outcome was that several of the LMU staff spent two days observing the vendor's operations. Increased understanding of one another's problems solidified an already good working relationship. It is not necessary to go to such lengths, but reading about developments in each other's field and asking informed questions builds mutual understanding and respect. Having realistic expectations is key, just as it is in personal relationships. Be professional and ethical in working with vendors and publishers; expect and demand the same from them.

RETAIL OUTLETS

The book distribution system in the United States is cumbersome and frequently adds to the cost of books. A simplified system would benefit everyone. Perhaps the best illustration of the complexity of the system is in the area of discounts, returns, billings, and so forth. Each year the American Booksellers Association (ABA) publishes a 500-page guide, *ABA Book Buyer's Handbook* (New York: American Booksellers Association, 1947-). Pity the poor bookseller, confronted with all of the other problems of a bookstore, that also must work through a mass of legal forms and sales conditions for purchasing from various publishers. This process does create extra work for the bookseller and publisher, and they undoubtedly pass their costs on to the buyer.

In general, bookstores can be a valuable means of acquiring new books. Carrying out visual inspection of local stores and discussing the library's needs with their owners can forge an important link in the selection and acquisition program. Libraries in large metropolitan areas generally have good bookstores nearby, but many libraries are lucky if there is one bookstore in the community. Although most libraries will spend only a small portion of the materials budget in such stores, the possibility is worth exploring. Most bookstores have limited potential as a major source of supply for acquisitions departments, but when a general bookstore exists nearby, the library ought to talk to the owner to determine what, if any, business relationship might be possible. It may take time for the relationship to fully develop, but it can prove mutually beneficial. (Note: The large U. S. national chains, such as Borders and Barnes & Noble, operate very differently from local stores and are not likely to be able to accommodate library needs beyond occasionally allowing a "corporate" or "educational" discount on some of the titles they carry.)

Quebec libraries must purchase their books from at least three accredited bookstores. Such bookstores must be based in Quebec and owned by a Quebecer. Some libraries, however, are able to buy books directly from distributors because they have private funding also.

A reasonable question to pose at this point is "what about Internet bookstores?" Is, in fact, Amazon.com considered a retailer or a wholesaler? An early 2001 check of Yahoo's "Books" page had links to more than 490 online stores (both new and out-of-print sources). Certainly these stores are popular, but not always the quickest means of getting a book in hand, at least during holiday periods.

Loyola Marymount University library has been using Amazon.com for several years for the purchase of some popular items. (We should note that it did take some effort to develop a workable means of payment.) Monica Fusich wrote a brief article on the use of Amazon.com and other e-stores that appeared in *C&RL News*.[3] She outlined several services she found useful as a collection development officer who has other duties as well. (Being a reference librarian or some other "full-time" assignment as well as having selection responsibilities is very common in today's library environment.) The features she mentioned were

- Cumulated book reviews (one must remember some of the reviews are from the general public),
- Search and browsing capability,
- Size of the database(s),
- Coverage of both in- and out-of-print titles as well as nonbook media, and
- Notification services (a rather limited SDI service as of mid-1999).

Although e-stores are not *the* answer to the challenges facing busy acquisition departments, they can be of assistance and should not be dismissed out-of-hand.

OUT-OF-PRINT, ANTIQUARIAN, AND RARE BOOK DEALERS

Retrospective collection building is one of the most interesting and challenging areas of acquisitions work. It was also one of the last to experience the impact of technology and the Internet. Libraries buy retrospectively for two reasons: to fill in gaps in the collection and to replace worn out or lost copies of titles. There has been a steady decline in retrospective buying on the part of libraries over the past twenty years due to limited budgets, as well as the need to increase purchases of nonprint and electronic resources. Another factor in the decline has been the proliferation of bibliographic databases such as OCLC, which make locating a copy of an out-of-print title to borrow through ILL much easier. As a result, acquisitions staff and selectors have decreasing experience to draw upon when they need to work in this field. (Dealers in this field are a "special breed" unlike other vendors with which the library has more experience.) One outcome of the decline is that the field, which has always been very dependent on collectors, is even more driven today by collector interests than by library needs.

Allowing for overlap, there are two broad categories of out-of-print (OP) dealers. (It should be noted that most of these individuals dislike the label "secondhand dealer.") One category focuses primarily on general OP books, that is, on buying and selling relatively recent OP books. Often, these books sell at prices that are the same as, or only slightly higher than, their publication price. The other category of dealer focuses on rare, antiquarian, and special (for example, fore-edged painted, miniature, or private press) books. Prices for this type of book can range from around U.S.$10 to several thousand dollars per item.

The face of this field is changing. Margaret Landesman provides an excellent, detailed outline of the current types of dealers:

- *Book scouts*, working part-time or full-time, searching out desirable books and selling them to dealers and collectors.
- *Neighborhood stores* that operate part- or full-time from low-cost facilities and depend primarily on walk-in trade and a few very loyal customers. They seldom issue catalogs or engage in searching except for their best customers.
- *Specialized dealers* that often issue catalogs and do searching in their specialty but more and more often operate only by mail or electronically (via e-mail or an Internet Web site).
- *General out-of-print dealers* who have a rather large stock in varied areas; many have specialties as well. Some offer search services; some issue catalogs.
- *Mixed in- and out-of-print stores*—often a store that is an independent new bookshop trying to survive the competition from the "superstores" by diversifying.
- *Academic library book vendors* that also offer out-of-print search services.

- *Rare book dealers* specializing in rare and expensive titles. Most established rare book dealers do not handle the more ordinary scholarly out-of-print titles, but many general out-of-print dealers also handle some rare books.[4]

The vast majority of such dealers have small shops in low-rent areas or operate out of their homes. Because of this diversity, it is difficult to make many generalizations about this group. Sol Malkin paints a cheery picture of at least part of the out-of-print trade:

> Imagine a separate book world within the world of books where dealers set up their businesses where they please (store or office, home or barn); where the minimum markup is 100 percent; where they can call upon 5,000 fellow dealers throughout the world and a stock of over 200 million volumes, practically from the beginning of the printed word; where books are safely packed and mailed with no extra charge for postage; where there is no competition from the publishers and discount houses; where colleagues help one another in time of need to provide fellow dealers with a unique service that makes customers happy all the time—an ideal imaginary book world that never was nor ever will be? Perhaps . . . but the above is 99 percent true in the antiquarian book trade.[5]

Most libraries will have occasion to use the services of these dealers. Acquisitions departments that handle purchases for large research collections tend to spend much of their time (or at least they did in the past) engaged in retrospective purchasing activities. Changes in organizational goals and programs may result in developing whole new areas of collecting both current and retrospective materials. Public libraries also buy from OP dealers, especially for replacement copies and occasionally for retrospective collection building. School libraries make limited use of this distribution system. When they do it is for replacement copies. Scientific and technical libraries rarely need to worry about acquiring retrospective materials.

Several directories to antiquarian or rare book dealers (for example, *American Book Trade Directory* from R. R. Bowker) provide information about specialties, and anyone concerned with acquisitions work should become familiar with these directories. Some major metropolitan areas have local directories or guides to special bookstores. An acquisitions department will find it worthwhile to develop a listing of local shops. Such a list can provide quick information about search services, hours, and true specialties. Although a buyer can go to a shop that advertises itself as a "Western Americana" store only to find the specialty stock very limited or overpriced, one should still examine the shop's stock to identify its true specialties and assess its general pricing polices. Maintaining this private directory can prove well worth the time required to keep it up-to-date. This is not to say that the published sources are worthless. However, owners do change their emphasis, and their stock turns over and is subject to local economic conditions that often change faster than published sources can monitor.

Many acquisitions librarians and book dealers classify OP book distribution services into three general types: (1) a complete book service, (2) a complete sales service, and (3) a complete bookstore. The first two may operate in a manner that does not allow, or at least require, customers to come to the seller's location. All contact is by mail, e-mail, and telephone. The owner may maintain only a small stock of choice items in a garage or basement. In a *complete book service*, a dealer actively searches for items for a customer even if the items are not in stock, by placing an ad in a publication like *AB Bookman's Weekly* (Antiquarian Bookman).

A *sales service* is just what the name implies: A dealer reads the "wanted" sections of book trade publications and sends off quotes on items in his or her stock. Such services seldom place ads or conduct searches for a customer. The *complete bookstore* is a store operation that depends on in-person trade. Stores of this type often engage in book service and sales service activities as well. Given the unpredictable nature of the OP trade, it is an unusual store that does not need to exploit every possible sales outlet.

AB Bookman's Weekly (*AB*) is a weekly publication devoted solely to advertisements from dealers offering or searching for particular titles. Publications of this type are an essential ingredient in the OP book trade, because they serve as a finding and selling tool. Without services like this, the cost of acquiring an OP item would be much higher (assuming the library could locate a copy without the service).

Other useful publications for both dealers and libraries are *AB*'s *Yearbook, Bookman's Price Index* (Gale), Bowker's *Books Out-of-Print*, Ruth Robinson and Daryush Farudi's *Buy Books Where—Sell Books Where* (Robinson Books), *American Book Prices Current* (Bancroft Parkman), and *Library Bookseller* (Antiquarian Bookman). Some of the more useful Web sites are listed near the end of this chapter; one such site is Bibliofind (http://www.bibliofind.com).

Prices OP dealers set are based on a number of interrelated factors:

1. How much it costs to acquire the item.
2. The amount of current interest in collecting a particular subject or author.
3. The number of copies printed and the number of copies still in existence.
4. The physical condition of the copy.
5. Any special features of the particular copy (autographed by the author or signed or owned by a famous person, for example).
6. What other dealers are asking for copies of the same edition in the same condition.

Without question, the current asking price is the major determining factor—given equal conditions in the other five areas—thus making sales catalogs and *AB* major pricing tools.

A few additional facts about the condition of OP books are important for beginning librarians to know because they bear directly on price. The condition of the book will affect its price. A library may assume that most OP dealers sell their stock as described or "as is." If there is no statement about the item's condition, it should be in good or better condition. A common statement in catalogs is "terms—all books in original binding and in good or better condition unless otherwise stated."

Working in this area can be fun and frustrating at the same time. Clearly there is a need for experience with dealers to know if their descriptions of their offerings are good enough for the library. There is also the nagging question of "fair market price" for what is often a one-of-a-kind offering, at least at that moment. There are commercial guides that can help with evaluating the asking/quoted price such as *Bookman's Price Index* (Detroit: Gale Research, 1964-), *American Book Prices Current* (New York: Bancroft-Parkman, 1930- , annual), and *Book-Auction Records* (London: W. Dawson, 1902- , annual).

OTHER MEDIA RETAIL OUTLETS

Because of the variety of their formats and purposes, it is not possible to generalize about retail outlets for other media. In most cases, libraries acquire most of the formats directly from their producers or from an educational media jobber.

Other than music and video stores, for music recordings two of the frequently used are Rose's in Chicago, and Berkshire Record Outlet in Lee, Massachusetts. There are some others, too, but these have huge inventories and give significant discounts to libraries. Acquisitions staff should keep in mind that for media there are a few map shops in larger cities. Most metropolitan areas have at least one sheet music store, and there are museums that sell slides and art reproductions. Sometimes needed educational models and games can be found at a teacher supply store.

SELECTING VENDORS

By this point it should be clear that the process of selecting a vendor is rather complex. When selecting the source from which to secure materials (vendor assignment), the staff should consider speed of delivery, discounts given, and service. *Speed of order fulfillment* is significant because users may be waiting to use the material. The longer the wait for the material, the more unhappy the requesters become. In essence, speed is a public relations consideration as well as a service issue. Public relations is an especially important aspect in a tax-supported institution. Speed of order fulfillment may also come into play at the end of the fiscal year. In addition, in educational and special libraries, occasionally there is a need to place a "rush order" for urgently needed material. Sometimes the need is so urgent that the library places the order electronically or by fax and pays for next-day delivery.

Obviously, the greater the *discount* a library receives, the more money will be available to buy additional materials. Because very few libraries have enough money to buy everything they could use, stretching funds can contribute to an improved library collection. The question of discounts can occupy a major segment of the department head's time. Library materials—whether books, films, or phonograph records—are unique in that each item appeals to different groups of users. The producers of the items are aware of this differing appeal, and they vary their discounts accordingly (the wider the appeal, the greater the discount). For this reason, very few sources of library materials will promise a blanket discount on all items purchased on a single purchase order. Because of variable discounts, shipping and handling charges, and taxes, no one in the department knows exactly how much money is available, except on the first and last day of a fiscal year.

Service is the most important factor to consider in selecting a supplier. Questions to consider when evaluating a firm's service policy include the following:

- Does the firm correct mistakes quickly with minimal paperwork?
- Does it offer extra services in addition to the basic service (such as full processing for a small added fee)?
- Does it provide free shipping or forgo handling charges on orders over a certain amount?
- Can it handle the library's invoicing and payment requirements?

Ease in dealing with a source is the most important service factor. A great deal of time and energy goes into handling problems with orders. Finding a supplier who reduces such problems and frees staff members for more productive work is the goal in vendor assignment. Figure 9.4, page 204, provides an overview of some of the factors involved.

Most libraries maintain a file of current vendors. In most automated acquisitions systems, the file is available online. Coding allows the system to print the full address of the vendor selected to receive the order. It is fairly common for a system to have several codes for the same vendor (note the four codes for Baker & Taylor in Figure 9.5, page 205). The reason for that is that the library may have two or more programs operating with the vendor and may want to track each one separately. In that case the library needs a code for each program. In the example, the code "bakea" is for an approval plan, "bakec" is for items from the notification slip program, "baker" is for direct orders (nonapproval or slip), and "bakev" is for video and other media orders. Large libraries frequently have hundreds of vendors on their list. Most automated acquisitions systems provide a vendor-coding arrangement that allows a keystroke or two to generate the vendor's full name and mailing address. The coding also allows the department to more easily evaluate vendor performance because the staff can quickly sort the orders by vendor.

	Wholesaler			Retailer			Publisher		
	Speed	Discount	Service	Speed	Discount	Service	Speed	Discount	Service
Current Trade Publications	excellent	medium	excellent	good	low	excellent	excellent	high-medium	good
Society Publications	slow	low	fair	slow	low	fair	good	low	good
Government Publications	seldom handle			seldom handle			good	none	good
Technical Publications	slow	low	fair	slow	low	fair	good	low	good
Out-of-Print Items	seldom handle			medium to slow	none	good	(Reprint houses) medium to slow	low	fair
Foreign Items	good	low	good	good	low	good	fair	low	fair
Serials and Periodicals	good	low	good to excellent	seldom handles subscrip-tions			excellent	low	good

Figure 9.4. Chart of suppliers.

CODE	: abc	NAME : Academic Book Center
CODE	: aclio	NAME : ABC-CLIO
CODE	: ajcu	NAME : Association of Jesuit Colleges & Universities
CODE	: ala	NAME : American Library Association
CODE	: amb	NAME : Ambassador Book Service, Inc.
CODE	: bakea	NAME : Baker & Taylor Books
CODE	: bakec	NAME : Baker & Taylor
CODE	: baker	NAME : Baker & Taylor

Figure 9.5. Vendor Codes.

Because so many variables enter the picture, the choice of sources is complex and important. In some states (for example, New York and Minnesota), publicly supported libraries must select vendors from an approved list of suppliers. Even in those circumstances the list of approved companies can be long and the same selection factors come into play.

Following are the only generalizations that can be made regarding how libraries tend to operate in this area:

1. For current trade items, libraries use jobbers.
2. For other current materials, libraries use the publisher or jobbers.
3. For very popular current materials with an immediate need, libraries may try retailers.
4. For out-of-print items, libraries rely on retailers.
5. For items and serials from other countries, most libraries use jobbers.

SUMMARY

The distribution system for books and other library materials is varied and complex and must be understood and appreciated by acquisitions staff. This chapter provides highlights of what the library needs to know; and it portrays just the beginning of a long, challenging, but enjoyable learning process. Jobbers, book dealers, and media vendors are more than willing to explain how they modify their operations to accommodate library requirements, when they know that a librarian has taken time to learn something about their operations. Figure 9.4 summarizes some of the key points involved in selecting a vendor.

NOTES

1. A *jobber* buys merchandise from manufacturers and sells it to retailers. A *wholesaler* sells large quantities of goods to a retailer. (In Canadian libraries, the publishing terms *jobber* and *wholesaler* are synonymous.) A *drop shipper* orders materials from manufacturers after receiving an order from a retailer (or library). Unlike jobbers and wholesalers, a drop shipper does not have a stock of materials, just a telephone.

2. Lotz Wendall, "Here Today, Here Tomorrow: Coping with the OP 'Crisis'," *School Library Journal* 35 (July 1989): 25-28.

3. Monica Fusich, "Collectiondevelopment.com: Using Amazon.com and Other Online Bookstores for Collection Development" *C&RL News* 59 (October 1998): 659-661.

4. Margaret Landesman. "Out-of-Print and Secondhand Market," in T*he Business of Library Acquisitions*, edited by K. A. Schmidt (Chicago: American Library Association, 1990).

5. Sol Malkin, "Rare and Out-of-Print and Secondhand Market," in *The Business of Library Acquisitions,* edited by K. A. Schmidt (Chicago: American Library Association, 1990).

SELECTED WEB SITES

Advanced Book Exchange, http://www. abebooks.com

ALIBRIS, http://www.alibris.com/cgi-bin/texis/bookstore

Antiquarian Booksellers Association of America, http:/www.abaa.org

Biblio Magazine, http://www.bibliomag.com

Book Finder.Com, http://www.bookfinder.com

Books.COM, http://www.books.com

International League of Antiquarian Booksellers, http://www.ilab-lila.com

Internet Bookshop, http://www.bookshop.co.uk/

UMI Book Vault, http://www.UMI.com/ph/Support/BOD/bkvault.htm

Yahoo: Books: Booksellers, http//www.yahoo.com/Business_and_Economy/Companies/Books/Booksellers/

SUGGESTED READING

Anderson, R. "How to Make Your Book Vendor Love You." *Against the Grain* 10 (1998): 68-70.

Brown, Linda A. "Approval Vendor Selection—What's the Best Practice?" *Library Acquisitions* 22, no. 3 (Fall 1998): 341-351.

Brown, Lynne C. "Vendor Evaluation." *Collection Management* 19 (1995): 47-46.

Gammon, J. A. "Partnering with Vendors for Increased Productivity." *Library Acquisitions* 21, no. 4 (1997): 229-235.

Hirshon, Arnold, and Barbara Winters. *Outsourcing Library Technical Services: A How-to-Do-It Manual for Librarians*. New York: Neal-Schuman, 1996.

Hubbard, W. J., and J. Welch. "An Empirical Test of Two Vendors' Trade Discounts." *Library Acquisitions* 22, no. 2 (1998): 131-137.

Kuo, Hui-Min. "Comparing Vendor Discounts for Firm Orders: Fixed vs. Sliding." *Technical Services Quarterly* 18, no. 4 (2001): 1-10.

———. "Flat or Float? A Study of Vendor Discount Rates Applied to Firm Orders in a College Library." *Library Acquisitions* 22, no. 4 (1998): 409-14.

Nardini, Robert F. "Issues in Vendor/Library Relations—The Sales Call." *Against the Grain* 13 (June 2001): 88-89.

National Acquisitions Group. *The Value to Libraries of Special Services Provided by Library Suppliers: Developing a Costing Model.* Leeds, England: National Acquisitions Group, 1996.

Rendell, Kenneth. "The Future of the Manuscript and Rare Book Business." *RBM* 2, no. 1 (2001): 13-33.

Rosenstein, Linda L. "What Does Vendor Consolidation Mean to You?" *Library Collections, Acquisitions, and Technical Services* 24 (Winter 2000): 503-504.

Stankus, T. "Death of a Salesman: The Decline in Library Visits from Serial Marketers." *Technicalities* 17 (July/August 1997): 11-13.

Steinhoff, Cynthia K. "The Coming Restructuring of the Library Book Vendor." *Library Collections, Acquisitions, and Technical Services* 24 (Fall 2000): 439-440.

Swords, David A. "Issues in Vendor/Library Relations—Report on the OhioLINK—YBP Relationship." *Against the Grain* 13 (June 2001): 75-77.

"Vendor Connections: Relations with School Media Specialists." *School Librarian's Workshop* 17 (May 1997): 1-2.

Walther, James. "Assessing Library Vendor Relations: A Focus on Evaluation and Communication." *Bottom Line* 11, no. 4 (1998): 149-157.

Wilmering, Bill. "Using the RFP Process to Select a Serials Vendor." *Serials Librarian* 28, nos. 3/4 (1996): 325-329.

REVIEW QUESTIONS

1. What are the typical discounts on books and to which category of books do they *normally* apply?
2. List four important questions to ask any book jobber/wholesaler.
3. Identify seven key factors to consider when selecting a jobber/wholesaler.
4. What do jobbers/wholesalers expect from libraries?
5. Identify some important factors to examine when assessing jobber/wholesaler performance.
6. List the seven types of out-of-print sources and describe what is special about each one.
7. Pricing OP materials is complex. What are the factors dealers take into account when pricing these materials?

Chapter 10 Print-Based Serials

Serials, regardless of their format, are important sources of current information for the public. Libraries attempt to maintain as large a collection of serials as their budgets will allow, but costs and space considerations have significantly modified the "all and forever" retention philosophy that many serials departments employed in the past.

Serial work is interesting, challenging, and frustrating. The following poem sums up the work nicely:

> The Publisher is my Tormentor. I shall not smile:
> He maketh me to work all day at my desk.
> He leadeth me astray with misnumbered issues:
> His Roman numerals confound me:
> He changeth titles over and over for His own sake.
> Yea, when I walk through the shadow of missing or irregular issues, I can find no respite, for He has moved.
> He answereth not my letters, nor useth the correct mailing label;
> He starteth not when I ask and quitteth before it is time;
> My work never endeth.
> Rising prices and duplicate issues shall follow me all the days of my life; and
> I shall moan and groan in the library forever.[1]

In the past ten to fifteen years paper-based serials have begun to change in character. Once started, the move toward electronic and Web-based serials publication gained significant momentum. Chapter 11 explores the new dimension of electronic serials management. Here it is important just to note that the issue exists and is rapidly becoming another major cost concern for libraries and a major consideration for acquisitions staff.

WHAT IS A SERIAL?

Individuals (customers and librarians alike) frequently use the words *journals, magazines, periodicals*, and *serials* interchangeably, with no great misunderstanding resulting from the imprecise usage. Thomas Nisonger, in his fine book on serials management,[2] devoted over six pages to how different groups have attempted to define the material that is covered in this and the next chapter.

The *ALA Glossary of Library and Information Science* provides the following definitions of two key terms, which are adequate for the purposes of this chapter:

> *Serial*—"a publication issued in successive parts, usually at regular intervals, and, as a rule, intended to be continued indefinitely. Serials include periodicals, annuals (reports, yearbooks, etc.) and memoirs, proceedings, and transactions of societies."
>
> *Periodical*—"a publication with a distinctive title intended to appear in successive (usually unbound) numbers of parts at stated or regular intervals and, as a rule, for an indefinite time. Each part generally contains articles by several contributors. Newspapers, whose chief function it is to disseminate news, and the memoirs, proceedings, journals, etc. of societies are not considered periodicals."[3]

Definitions in general dictionaries have more overlap:

> *Journal*—"a periodical publication especially dealing with matters of current interest—often used for official or semi-official publications of special groups."
>
> *Magazine*—"a periodical that usually contains a miscellaneous collection of articles, stories, poems, and pictures and is directed at the general reading public."
>
> *Periodical*—"a magazine or other publication of which the issues appear at stated or regular intervals—usually for a publication appearing more frequently than annually but infrequently used for a newspaper."
>
> *Serial*—"a publication (as a newspaper, journal, yearbook, or bulletin) issued as one of a consecutively numbered and indefinitely continued series."[4]

The term *serials* is used here because it represents the broadest spectrum of materials.

Some years ago, Fritz Machlup and others developed an eighteen-part classification system for serials.[5] The following discussion follows their classification system because it covers all types of serials, including serials "not elsewhere classified." We have yet to encounter a serial that does not fit into one of the other seventeen categories. Each of the major categories described in this chapter has some special features that have implications for the acquisitions staff.

Institutional Reports

The first major category is "annual, semiannual, quarterly or occasional reports of corporations, financial institutions, and organizations serving business and finance." Academic libraries serving business and management programs frequently need to acquire this type of serial. Some corporate libraries also actively collect this category. Most of the reports available to libraries and information centers are free for the asking. Some organizations will add a library to their distribution list, but others will respond only to requests for the current edition. Collecting in this area is labor-intensive, because it requires maintaining address and correspondence files, especially if a library collects much beyond the large national corporations. Without question, having a computer system that has both word processing and e-mail capabilities will make collecting less tedious, but it will not reduce the need to constantly monitor the program. Corporate annual reports are issued every month. Many companies issue their annual reports for the annual meeting of the management board, owners, or stockholders, which normally occurs in the month the organization was established. It had been difficult to find a satisfactory vendor for this serials category, except for 10-K reports to the Securities and Exchange Commission, which had previously been available on microfiche from Disclosure, Inc. Thanks to the advent of electronic full-text resources, EDGARÒ (SEC) filings are now available from a number of sources including *Dow Jones Interactive* and *Moody's Company Data Direct*. (A good discussion of the vendors that offer annual report assistance appears in Judith Bernstein's "Corporate Annual Reports: The Commercial Vendors.")[6]

Yearbooks and Proceedings

A related category is "annuals, biennials, occasional publications, bound or stapled, including yearbooks, almanacs, proceedings, transactions, memoirs, directories and reports of societies and associations." Many libraries collect serials in this class, especially academic, special, and large public libraries. The more libraries that collect a particular society's or association's publications, the more likely it is that a commercial vendor will handle a standing order for the material. Although it is possible to secure some of these serials through a vendor, there are a significant number that must be obtained directly from the society or association. Again, this category normally requires setting up and maintaining address and correspondence files, which is only slightly less labor intensive than doing the same for annual reports of organizations.

Superseding Serials

Two other labor-intensive collecting categories are (1) "superseding serial services (each new issue superseding previous ones, which are usually discarded) including telephone directories, airplane schedules, catalogs, loose-leaf data sheets, etc.," and (2) "nonsuperseding serial services bound, sewn, stapled, or loose-leaf, including bibliographic and statistical data." A library must acquire most of the materials in these classes directly from the publisher. Superseding serials are important but problematic: important because people need the correct or current information, problematic because they can be difficult to track and sometimes to obtain. Airline schedules, current hotel guides, and other travel-related serial sources have been something of a problem for libraries to acquire. In the past, the publishers would sell the material only to qualified travel agencies. As more and more corporations handle staff travel on their own, it has become easier for libraries to subscribe to such services. In many corporations, the library or information center maintains current travel information. In the United States since the break-up of AT&T, libraries have found it more difficult and expensive to get telephone directories outside their immediate area. Finding a reasonably priced and reliable source for these materials can be both frustrating and time consuming. Free online access to some of these items may reduce the acquisitions department's workload, if another unit handles Web-based services that do not involve payment for access.

Loose-leaf services are particularly important in U.S. and Canadian law libraries and accounting firms (examples are *Labor Relations Reporter* from the Bureau of National Affairs, *Standard Federal Tax Reporter* from Commerce Clearing House, and *Ontario Annotated Law Reporter* from Butterworths). Proper filing and discarding of the material is of critical importance because incorrect information can be very costly to a firm as well as to its customers. With a loose-leaf service, the library must make certain that all sections released are received. Another critical issue involves removing the superseded papers and making certain the new ones are filed properly. Many publishers of loose-leaf services make their services available through the Internet/Web, and some also offer CD-ROM versions. Naturally there is a substantial cost for the electronic versions; however, the library must consider the value of reducing staff labor in filing the service as well as the greater assurance that what is available is in fact correct.

Nonsuperseding serials are less of a problem, and some are available from serial jobbers. However, the materials in this class tend to be expensive, and many must be ordered directly from the publisher. Indexing and abstracting services fall into one of these two classes. All types of libraries need a few of these reference serials. As the serial collection grows, there is an increasing demand from users for more indexing and abstracting services.

Newspapers

All types of libraries, with the exception of elementary school media centers, collect newspapers, another serial category. Almost every small public library receives the local newspaper and one or two newspapers from nearby communities. Large public and academic libraries try to have some level of national and international newspaper coverage. Serial jobbers handle subscriptions to major newspapers for libraries. Thus, it would be possible to place one order with a jobber, such as Faxon or EBSCO, for almost all the major newspapers from around the world. At the time the order is placed, collection development officers must establish the value of the newspapers' content, in the sense of the demand or need to have the latest issue in the shortest time. Acquisitions staff need to know this so as to be able to place the proper order. For example, *The London Times* can be ordered in a variety of packages, each with a different cost: daily airmail edition by air freight, daily airmail edition by airmail (the most expensive option), daily regular edition by air freight, daily regular edition in weekly packets (the least expensive option), or microfilm edition. *The New York Times* offers an even wider variety of editions: city edition, late city edition, national edition, New York edition, large-type weekly, same day, next day, two day, weekly packets, microfilm, and others. Clearly, each variation has cost as well as workload implications.

A number of the major newspapers are now available online, some from online vendors (for example Lexis-Nexis) and some only through the publisher. According to Wallys Conhaim, 600 daily newspapers (about one-third of the U.S. total) were operating some level of online service in early 1998.[7] Online versions work well for many readers because the articles are not very long and people are more willing to read short articles on the computer without wanting to print a hard copy. Often, however, people demand good quality printing capability for electronic journal articles because of their length or choose to e-mail copies to their home computers. If a library subscribes to a sizable number of regional or local newspapers that are available electronically through a service such as *Newsbank*, it may be more economical to choose this option. In any event, choosing the electronic version would lessen the "housekeeping" (such as checking-in issues and claiming missing issues) costs for the print versions held. These costs can be difficult to track, thus making it difficult to know just how much staff time the library will save.

Newsletters

Newsletters, leaflets, news releases, and similar materials represent yet another serial category of major importance for some libraries. Special libraries are the most likely to become involved in the ongoing collection of this class of serial. Many of the items in this class are very inexpensive or free. Others, especially newsletters containing economic or "trade" data, can be exceedingly expensive. (There are a number of U.S. services that cost in excess of $20,000 for quarterly newsletters of ten to fifteen pages. It is at that point that the difference between the cost of the information and the cost of the package it comes in becomes evident.) Whether a service is free or subscription-based, someone must put in the time and effort to identify the sources and get on the appropriate mailing lists or enter the subscription. Libraries in marketing and public relations firms are likely to be active collectors of this type of material

Magazines

Without question, magazines are the most common serials and the category that most often comes to mind when one thinks of this material type. According to Machlup's definition, magazines are "mass-market serials." These are the titles that almost any serial jobber will handle for a library. Machlup's magazine categories include

- Mass market serials, weekly or monthly news magazines (such as *Newsweek* or *Macleans*);
- Popular magazines dealing with fiction, pictures, sports, travel, fashion, sex, humor, and comics (such as *Sports Illustrated* or *Toronto Fashion*);
- Magazines that popularize science and social, political, and cultural affairs (*Smithsonian* or *Canadian Geographic*);
- Magazines focusing on opinion and criticism—social, political, literary, artistic, aesthetic, or religious (an example is *Foreign Affairs* or *This Magazine*); and
- "Other magazines not elsewhere classified." An example of an item in this category is an organization publication (governmental or private) that is really a public relations vehicle, sometimes called a "house organ." These publications often contain general interest material, but there is usually some clearly stated or implied relationship between the subject covered and the issuing organization (e.g., *Plain Truth*). Another type of publication in the "other" category is the magazine found in the pocket of airline seats. The publication contains interesting short articles about people, places, and things. Many contain advertising, so the magazine not only helps distract the nervous traveler but also provides an additional source of revenue for the airline. Libraries may receive a substantial number of house organs since their publishers give them away. Vendors seldom handle this type of magazine.

Journals

Machlup similarly divided journals into four subcategories, with one category divided into two smaller units:

- Nonspecialized journals for the intelligentsia well-informed on literature, art, social affairs, politics, etc. (*Science* and *Equinox* are examples);

- Learned journals for specialists—primary research journals and secondary research journals (*American Indian Culture and Research Journal* and *The Canadian Historical Review,* for example);
- Practical professional journals in applied fields, including technology, medicine, law, agriculture, management, library and information science, business, and trades (*RQ* or *Canadian Journal of Emergency Medicine*); and
- Parochial journals of any type but addressed chiefly to a parochial audience—local or regional—(*Kiva* or *Toronto Life*).

Most titles in these categories are available through vendors, although the library must place direct orders for some of the more specialized learned journals. Most parochial journals must be purchased directly from the publisher; local history and regional archaeological publications are examples of this class of serial. Sometimes a library must join an association to obtain its publications.

The final serial category identified by Machlup is "government publications, reports, bulletins, statistical series, releases, etc. by public agencies, executive, legislative and judiciary, local, state, national, foreign and international." Because this group is covered in Chapter 12, no discussion is included here.

With these variations in serials in mind, it is clear why there is confusion about terms and challenges in collecting and preserving them. Each type fills a niche in the information dissemination system. Although they do create special handling procedures and problems, they are a necessary part of any library's collection, and the public service staff must deal with them.

Unlike a monograph, a serial normally implies a long-term commitment. Subscriptions require renewals, but with most vendor plans, the renewal process is automatic, requiring no action on the part of the acquisitions department staff. When the subscription renewal requires a positive decision by the library staff, the serial holdings are more likely to reflect the current interests of the library's customers. With automatic renewal, there is a substantial chance that the library will continue to collect inappropriate serials long after they cease to meet community needs.

A long-term commitment to a serial results in subscription costs becoming a fixed feature of the budget. With rapidly rising prices and small budget increases, each year serials take up an increasing proportion of the total materials budget. Chapter 14 (on fiscal management) provides more information about this problem, but in general, serial prices have been increasing at a much faster rate than general inflation. Thus, each year the amount of money required to maintain the present serials subscriptions increases at a rate greater than many libraries are able to sustain.

Another fixed cost is processing. When ordering and receiving a monograph, the library incurs a one-time cost. Serials have ongoing receiving and renewal costs, in addition to the cost of placing the initial order. Claiming missing issues is a normal part of maintaining a serials collection. A staff member records each issue when it arrives in the library. When the person notes an issue is missing or a number skipped, the library contacts the publisher or agent to attempt to secure the missing material. (This is called *placing a claim.*) Acting promptly on claims is important because serial publishers print only slightly more copies than the number of subscribers. Serial publishers know a certain percentage of issues sent do go astray in the mail, and they print extra copies to cover the expected claims. However, at times the number of claims is greater than the number of available copies. When that happens, a number of unlucky libraries receive out-of-print notices. The closer the claim is made to the publication date, the greater the chances are of receiving the missing issue. (The consequences of small print runs appear again when it is time to bind the volume and the library discovers one of the issues is missing. Locating a copy can be time consuming if not impossible.) Daily serial check-in is a must to avoid missing issues. Automated serial systems help speed routine serials work, including providing automatic claiming, but in a library with a large serials list, one or more full-time staff members may work exclusively on processing serials. Clearly, each new serial adds to the workload on an ongoing basis.

By their nature, serials arrive in successive issues, normally as paperbacks. If the library maintains serials for long periods of time or the titles receive relatively heavy use, the library must repackage the serial for more convenient handling. One method is to store the loose issues in a cardboard or metal container (sometimes referred to as a Princeton File) that keeps a limited number of issues together in a vertical position. This makes it easier to shelve the loose issues alongside bound materials. The container must have room on its outfacing side to record the title and issue or volume number of the items in the box. The most common long-term storage treatment is binding, representing yet another cost for the library. Bindery operations are usually part of technical services and associated with serials activities. (Bindery activities are addressed later in this chapter.) A third alternative, microformat storage, represents an additional cost. Whatever choice is made, there is an ongoing cost to package each serial year after year.

An important consideration in serials selection is how end-users gain access to the information each issue contains. Going through each issue is not efficient, and few individuals are willing to do this. Many serials produce an annual index, but this is of no help with current issues. An entire industry has developed around providing access to serials. A variety of indexing and abstracting services now provide services that assist in locating information in serials. Naturally, most of these services are expensive and yet another cost of building a serials collection. Although Harvard's Tozzer Library (an anthropology library) is atypical, it illustrates the nature of the problem. That library receives more than 1,200 anthropology serials each year. If it did not do its own indexing, the library would have to spend more than $60,000 per year for indexing and abstracting services to achieve only 83 percent coverage of its serial holdings. Tozzer's solution to the indexing problem is to index all the serials it receives. It publishes the index as *Anthropological Literature*, which helps offset the indexing costs.

When a library does not start a subscription with volume 1, number 1, the librarian must decide whether and to what extent to acquire back issues or volumes. Are backfiles needed? Some serial publishers have full runs available, but most do not. Titles widely held by libraries may be available from reprint houses. Backfiles are expensive, they may be difficult to find, they may require binding, they certainly take up valuable shelf space, and many receive little use. Libraries also cannot assume that vendors handling online full text serials will maintain backfiles or make them available for all titles.

Serials can and do change over time. New editors, governing boards, or owners make major and minor shifts in the content and orientation. A major shift in emphasis usually is well publicized. As selectors become aware of such shifts, they can reassess serials. A title change is something librarians frequently complain about, primarily because of internal concerns (see articles by Foggin[8] and Nelson[9]). From the acquisitions department point of view, a title change is yet another workload issue. It is very important for cataloging and the OPAC that there be a clear "trail" from former to current title. For some journals there is a long history of title changes, which can be confusing for end-users who may not know of the changes over time and may think the library has fewer holdings than it actually does. We revisit this issue later in this chapter.

IDENTIFYING SERIALS

Serials employ a different bibliographic network than that used by monographs. Few of the verification aids used for books cover serials. However, there are several general and specialized guides to serial publications. Reviews of serials are few and far between. Michael Colford's column in *Library Journal* is one regular source of serial reviews. In the past, when publishers would supply several free sample copies of a title for the library to examine, the lack of reviews was not a problem. Every few years, Bill Katz and Linda Sternberg Katz compile *Magazines for Libraries*.[10] Today, many publishers charge for sample issues, and although it depletes the funds for subscribing to serials and adds to the time it takes to acquire them, it is useful to get sample issues before committing the library to a new serial.

Four useful general guides to serials are *Ulrich's International Periodicals Directory* (R. R. Bowker), available in print, online as UlrichsOnline at http://www.ulrichsweb.com, or on CD-ROM as *Ulrich's On Disc*; *Irregular Serials & Annuals* (R. R. Bowker); *Serials Directory* (EBSCO), also available as EBSCO Online at http://www.ebsco.com; and *Standard Periodical Directory* (Oxbridge Communications), also available electronically as a CD or online at http://www.oxbridge.com. All employ a subject arrangement, and entries provide all necessary ordering information. Bowker updates the annual *Ulrich's* with *Ulrich's Update. Standard Periodical Directory,* which covers U.S. and Canadian titles, has a reputation for providing the best coverage of publications with small circulations, lesser-known organizations, and processed materials.

Newspapers, newsletters, and serials published at least five times a year are identifiable in guides like *Gale Directory of Publications and Broadcast Media* (Gale Research), available online as the Gale Database of Publications and Broadcast Media at http://www.galegroup.com and *Willings' Press Guide* (Thomas Skinner Directories). For literary publications, consult *International Directory of Little Magazines and Small Presses* (Dustbooks), *MLA International Bibliography*

(Modern Language Association), and *L'Annee Philologique* (Societe International de Bibliographie Classique).

All of these guides, with the exception of the electronic versions, have limited value in identifying new titles because they are annuals, which means the information is at least several months old upon receipt. (As noted previously, serials change in a variety of ways—titles, frequency, editorial policy, and so forth—and keeping up with existing titles is enough of a problem without adding the need to identify newly created serials.) The best source of information about serials acquired by both U.S. and Canadian libraries is the Library of Congress's *New Serial Titles (NST),* which reflects data in OCLC. The data in *NST* are the result of a cooperative effort called Cooperative Online Serial Program (CONSER). As an illustration of the number of existing serial titles, in 1981 there were 339,000 CONSER records in OCLC; by the fall of 2001 there were over 2 million records for serials in WorldCat. If the library can justify the cost, online systems provide the most current information. OCLC, BRS, and DIALOG are major sources. The latter two contain information from *Ulrich's.* Such services are current, but costly, so acquisitions personnel must be certain that the speed and currency are essential. Some serial vendors also supply directories.

SERIAL VENDORS

For most libraries, it is not cost-effective to place serial subscriptions directly with the publisher. The amount of work required to monitor expiration dates, place renewals, and approve payments repeatedly for each title is too great. In any sizable serials collection, a few titles will be direct orders to the publisher; however, if a library uses a serials vendor for most orders, there will be more time for other problem-solving activities related to serials.

Serials jobbers tend not to handle monographs, just as book jobbers tend not to handle serials. *Tend* is the key word here, given the variety of serials; in the area of annuals and numbered monograph series, lines become blurred and jobbers overlap. Given the nature of serial publications, a library is better served by an experienced serials jobber than by a friendly and willing book jobber who offers to handle the serials list along with book orders. Many serials librarians find it best to use domestic dealers for domestic serials and either an international dealer or, if the number of titles from a country is large, a dealer in that country. Choosing a dealer that can effectively handle subscriptions from other countries can be a challenge. Libraries in the United States can turn to the American Library Association's *International Subscription Agents: An Annotated Directory* for help. The publication lists agents and provides information about countries and regions the agent handles, the types of material serviced, catalogs or listings provided to customers, notes about special services (standing orders for monographs, for example), and name and address. Part of the challenge for vendors handling international subscriptions is keeping up-to-date on currency exchange rates and providing accurate information about expected price increases. It is advisable to ask other librarians about their experience with the dealers one is considering. If the acquisitions staff cannot identify anyone using a dealer, they might start by placing one or two subscriptions with the dealer and increase the volume of business if service is satisfactory. Another option is to join and monitor an electronic discussion list such as SERIALST (http://www.uvm.edu/~bmaclenn/serialst.htm).

Service is what the library is looking for in a serials vendor just as it does for book vendors. To provide service, a company must make a profit. How does it do that? In the past, vendors offered discounts. Today, libraries generally pay a service charge based on a percentage of the total subscription price. Serial vendors have one minor and two major sources of income. One major source is the discount publishers offer vendors. (Publishers offer these discounts because it is more convenient for them to deal with one billing and ordering source rather than with subscriptions from many individual subscribers.) Recently, librarians have blamed publishers for rising subscription costs, but a few publishers claim that vendors share the blame because they are not passing on a share of the discount they receive from the publishers. Whatever the case may be, vendors depend on publishers' discounts to make a profit.

The second major revenue source for vendors is the service charge they add to their invoices to libraries. The service charge varies from library to library, depending on several factors. It often requires a good deal of work to determine just what the service charge is, in part because, when the subscription list contains thousands of titles, it is unlikely there will be only one invoice, if for no other reason than that prices change during the year and supplementary invoices arrive. Sales representatives may not know all the factors involved in calculating the charge and can give only an overview explanation. There may be various rates for various types of publications; in part, the service charge depends on the size of the discount the vendor receives.

Another variable in the calculation of a library's service charge is what services the library uses. Often, there is an extra charge for handling unusual serials, such as government publications. The types and number of management reports the library receives from the vendor also affect the service charge. Title mix is another factor, just as it is with book jobbers. For serial vendors, it is more a matter of knowing which titles generate additional work for the vendor rather than a bookseller's pricing concerns about popular titles (low price/high discount) versus scholarly titles (high price/low discount). If a library has a high percentage of problem titles, its service charge may be somewhat higher than that of another library with a similar number of subscriptions, costing about the same, but with fewer problem titles.

The setting of the service charge is an art, and the service charge is open to negotiation. A good book on the acquisition aspects of serial work is N. Bernard Basch and Judy McQueen's *Buying Serials*.[11] A growing source of income comes from a variety of extra services most agencies offer, such as automation packages, publishing and electronic services (CD-ROMs, for example), or custom lists.

What does the customer receive beyond the basic advantage of one order, one invoice, and one check for multiple subscriptions? Automatic renewal by a vendor saves library staff time, and when the invoice arrives, there is the opportunity to cancel titles no longer needed. Jobbers may offer multiple-year subscription rates that will save the library money. Notifying libraries about discontinuations, mergers, changes in frequency, and other publication alterations is a standard service provided by a serials jobber. The jobber is more likely to learn of changes before a library does, especially if the jobber has placed hundreds of subscriptions with the publisher.

Vendors also provide some assistance in the claiming process (missing issues, breaks in service, and damaged copies). Several of the larger U.S. subscription agents such as EBSCO and Readmore have fully automated serial systems that libraries use to handle their serials management programs, including online claiming. (Faxon supports a backfile service, *SerialsQuest*, that includes data from libraries and dealers.) For libraries with manual claiming systems, most vendors offer two forms of claims: one by which the library notifies the vendor, which in turn contacts the supplier; and one by which the vendor supplies forms for the library to use to contact the publisher. Assistance in claiming has become more important in the past ten to fifteen years as popular market publishers increasingly use fulfillment centers. These centers serve as a publishers' jobber, that is, a center handles a number of different publishers' titles by receiving, entering subscriptions, and sending copies to subscribers. (For such centers, the mailing label is the key to solving problems; until recently, few libraries worried about serials' mailing labels.) Often, the subscription vendor is more effective in resolving a problem with a fulfillment center than is a single library.

Management information is another service serial vendors offer. Their information regarding price changes can be most useful in preparing budget requests. (A sample of this type of data appears in Figure 14.1, page 303).

Other types of management information that may be available (at an extra cost) are reports that sort the subscription list by subject or classification category accompanied by the total amount spent for each group, or (if there are several groups) a record of how many titles and how much money was charged to each group.

A good place to learn about the variety of services available, and who offers which services, is at the national meetings of various library associations. For example, representatives of most national serial vendors, as well as a number of foreign vendors, attend the ALA annual conventions. They will supply more than enough promotional material to fill a suitcase. Collecting the information (including a formal request to quote), making comparisons, and talking with other librarians about their experiences with various vendors is the best way to go about selecting a vendor for a library.

ISSUES AND CONCERNS

Several major issues face libraries today in regard to their serials collections. Cost is perhaps the major concern (cost of subscriptions, processing, storing, changing value of currencies, and tight budgets). Another issue is the delivery of serial information to customers without subscribing to the title by using document delivery or, as some librarians phrase it, "just in time rather than just in case." Related to document delivery are questions about copyright and traditional ILL services; on a percentage basis, ILL does more work with serials than monographs.

Continued growth in the number of serials and their spiraling costs are two issues of grave concern, especially for scholarly journals. Areas of knowledge constantly are being divided into smaller and smaller segments; at the same time, these smaller audiences want more information about the narrower topic. The problem is illustrated by what happened at the journal department of Academic Press, which announced one new journal, *Applied Computational Harmonic Analysis*; one journal dividing into two parts: *Journal of Magnetic Resonance—Series A* and *Series B*; and seven titles increasing the number of issues per volume. All these changes carried with them price increases.

Costs of producing a special-interest journal will rise no matter how many or how few people are interested in reading about the subject. When a journal reaches a certain price level, the number of individual subscribers drops quickly. More often than not, any price increase to individual subscribers only makes the problem worse. Increasingly, journal publishers have adopted a "dual pricing system," one price for individuals and another, higher price (often double or triple the individual rate) for institutions (read: libraries). The publishers' premise is that an institutional subscription serves the needs of many readers, which justifies the higher price. An interesting ethical question for librarians in general, and acquisitions department personnel in particular, is: Is it ethical for a library to regularly accept an individual's gift of a journal that has a high dual-rate subscription? (Our view is that the library should not do that. If not for ethical reasons, there are practical concerns about the regularity with which the person delivers the issues as well as securing missing issues.)

If publishers take the dual-pricing concept to its logical conclusion, they will demand that libraries track the use of each serial and pay an annual service fee based on that number. Or, as one occasionally sees in the literature, publishers will make the title available only on a site-licensed basis. Before dismissing the idea as unrealistic, consider two things. First, for years libraries subscribing to H. W. Wilson's periodical indexes have been paying an annual service fee or subscription fee based on the number of journals indexed to which the library subscribes. Second, some countries, including Canada, now pay authors a lending fee for each copy of their books in a selected list of libraries.

There are two types of journal price studies with which acquisitions department staff should become familiar: *macro pricing* and *micro pricing*. Macro information deals with subscription prices, rates of increase, and projections of coming price increases. This type of data about the library's subscription list can be obtained from the library's serials vendor. Information about overall price changes appears in several sources for U.S. serials, including *Library Journal* and *American Libraries*. One problem for many libraries is that information about projected price changes appears at a time when it is of little help in preparing the budget request for the next fiscal year. The information may be useful, but it is about a year behind the budget. That is, the library uses 2001 projections for preparing the 2002–2003 budget request. (See Chapter 14 for more information about budgeting.) What was clear at the time we prepared this edition was that there is no relief in sight in terms of price increases. (One serials vendor issued an information sheet in late 2001 indicating that price escalation had not really slowed. The vendor projected the 2002 increases in prices to range from 7.5 percent to 9.5 percent; perhaps this drop to single digit inflation will continue even if it is at least double the general inflation rate. After almost twenty-five years of double digit increases, the announced changes seem almost modest.)

Libraries have been facing this pattern for years. Publishers don't understand why libraries cut their subscription lists, and libraries and users don't understand why the prices must rise by so much more than the CPI. Acquisitions department staff are caught in the middle and often must attempt to explain what is going on with journal prices, especially if the library must undertake a dreaded journal cancellation project.

Micro studies examine the cost of the information in the journal, number of articles per volume, number of pages, page size, and cost per 1,000 words or characters. Such studies are helpful in the retention and cancellation activities in which more and more libraries must engage on an annual basis. (Finding micro studies takes a little effort; one good article dealing with the subject and presenting some examples is by Barbara Meyers and Janice Fleming.)[12] Not all publishers are pleased to see micro studies published, but such studies do provide useful data for maintaining a cost-effective serials collection. The library must use these data in conjunction with other information, such as local use patterns.

For the most part, serials will continue to escalate in price, and budgets may or may not keep pace. Clearly, serials will continue to play a major role in meeting customer information needs, and likewise may command a growing share of a limited collection development budget. How far can a library or information center go in cutting back on the acquisition of other formats to maintain the subscription list? Will switching to electronic sources for on-demand material really help with the budget problem or just make matters worse? Answers to such questions vary from institution to institution.[13] Electronic services and document delivery may or may not be a viable answer. (There is more about e-serials/journals in Chapter 11.)

Robert Pikowsky has written a good article outlining the both the history of journal price problems and the potential for electronic journals solving the problem, at least for academic and special libraries.[14] Not surprisingly, he did not see how e-journals would change the picture, and at present it appears he was correct.

Many libraries and information centers face the problem of buying a journal twice, in paper and electronic formats. Even in a networked environment, it is likely that some potential users will not have network access. Does the library ignore these users and provide only the electronic version, or does it offer both versions? Libraries think twice about dropping the paper version because some publishers (*Biological Abstracts*, for example) charge a higher fee for the CD-ROM or online version if the library does not have a paper subscription as well. Often, the higher fee is equal to the price of both subscriptions. Networking the material also entails extra expenses, such as license fees, that can equal or surpass the basic subscription price. Libraries should not expect to save money by shifting from paper to electronic formats, unless they also shift some of the costs to the users.

Short of providing full text in electronic form, the library can provide document delivery services backed by indexing and abstracting and table of contents access in electronic form. (A summary of these services and their costs is an article by Ronald Leach and Judith Trible.[15] Although the specific information in this article is outdated, the issues and considerations they raise remain valid.) Commercial services, such as UMI's Article Clearinghouse and ISI's Genuine Article, provide documents based on their indexing and abstracting services. Newer services are based on the tables of contents of a large number of titles (11,000–12,000). Subject searching is generally limited with the table of contents approach; basically, searching is keyword in title. In essence, with table of contents services, the user gives up depth of subject access for broader scope in title coverage. Most table of contents services have also entered the document delivery field. CARL *UnCover 2* is the oldest such service, with OCLC's *ContentFirst* and *ArticleFirst*, and RLG's *CitaDel* also available to users. As with full text, there are a variety of charges to consider before the library can decide to drop a paper subscription.

As mentioned previously in this chapter, a significant part of controlling serials relates to the constant changes that serials undergo. Dozens of new serials titles appear each month, and the life span of many serials is very short. The so-called little magazines begin and cease publication with great frequency, and they often fail to notify subscribers of changes. Delays in publication—as long as four and five years between the appearances of consecutive numbers—occur occasionally.

The most frequent change is a change in title, which is a constant headache for everyone who deals with serials. Journals split into two or more separate titles, and separate titles merge to form new serials. One title may be absorbed into another; another serial may separate from yet another. A journal appears with one volume and issue number; the next issue continues the same volume number and the succeeding issue number, but the journal has a new title. Or the new title may start the numbering at volume 1 again.

One example of this type of title change is *The Gale Directory of Publications and Broadcast Media*, listed as a serials guide previously in this chapter and also discussed in Chapter 7. This publication started in 1869 as *Rowell's American Newspaper Directory*. In 1908 it was absorbed by *N. W. Ayer and Son's American Newspaper Annual*, which started publication in 1880. In 1910 the title changed to *N. W. Ayer and Son's American Newspaper Annual and Directory*, which in 1930 became *N. W. Ayer and Son's Directory of Newspapers and Periodicals*. In 1970 the title changed again to the *Ayer Directory, Newspapers, Magazines, and Trade Publications*, which became the *Ayer Directory of Publications* in 1972. In 1983 the title changed yet again to the *IMS Ayer Directory of Publications*, and in 1986 to the *IMS Directory of Publications*. A year later, it became the *Gale Directory of Publications* and in 1990 became the *Gale Directory of Publications and Broadcast Media;* it could change again before this textbook is published. Numerous examples of this type of change can be found in the *Union List of Serials*, *New Serials Titles*, and by searching on the bibliographic utilities.

If title change is the number one problem in serials control, the second most common problem is a change in the volume or numbering sequence without notification to the subscribers. For example, say the library subscribes to a bimonthly title (six issues per volume year). Suddenly, after four issues have been received, the fifth arrives with a new volume number. The library cannot be certain what the situation is without contacting the publisher; perhaps policy has changed with no notice to the subscriber; perhaps the library failed to receive issues; or perhaps, as sometimes happens, the printer made a mistake.

INVOICES

A careful recording of invoice information is important in controlling periodicals. When a publisher or vendor sends an invoice, it must be carefully examined both for the price and for the date on which the subscription is to begin (or to continue, if it is a renewal, to avoid a gap of one or two issues).

In the spring or at the beginning of a new fiscal year, the serials vendor often sends an extremely long invoice. This invoice must be carefully examined item by item to verify that every element is correct. It is very unusual for an invoice of several hundred titles to be error-free: unwanted titles, incorrect prices, inaccurate beginning or continuation dates, and so forth will appear on the list. Correction of these errors is vital even though it involves valuable staff time. Sometimes large libraries with many subscriptions arrange with the vendor to have these long invoices divided into smaller chunks, perhaps by fund or even with ceilings on the amount of money each invoice can total, for example, $5,000 or $10,000 per invoice. This makes the checking process easier for the library to handle and often means that the vendor will be paid fund by fund or in increments instead of having to wait until the entire list of subscriptions is verified. Some vendors send price quotes prior to sending the invoice; libraries can make their renewal and cancellation requests on these, thus spreading the work out over a longer period of time.

Some libraries have a policy of not approving payment of an invoice until all of the problems relating to it are cleared up. If the library is dealing with a vendor, who must in turn check with the publisher, that delay could jeopardize the receipt of issues of all titles on the invoice. Other libraries are able to pay the invoice if all appears to be correct and then receive a credit from the vendor later if problems are discovered. Regardless of how a library handles payments, the invoice must be checked and corrected as quickly and as accurately as possible, and errors must be noted and brought to the vendor's attention as early as possible.

BINDING AND REPAIRS

Binding library materials is usually the responsibility of some part of technical services. Because serials are the materials most often bound by the library, the serials department or the serials section of technical services often handles this function. Some large libraries do their own binding, but usually outside companies provide this service. Bindery work is a little like house painting: The preparation is more complicated and time-consuming than the work itself. Because binding itself is a complicated and fascinating operation, library staff should make an effort to visit a bindery to see the actual process.

Materials preservation is an important element in any library's overall service plan. A preservation program for a library encompasses many elements, from building design to teaching the proper handling of library materials to users and staff. The companion book to this one, *Introduction to Library Public Services* (Libraries Unlimited, 1999), covers many of the preservation issues because they are an integral part of public service areas and activities. This book focuses on binding and repair activities. The bindery unit usually handles book repairs and the shipping and receiving of materials to and from commercial binderies.

Almost every library engages in minor book repairs. A torn page or a ripped binding can be repaired by almost anyone. Improper repair methods can cause more harm than good; using the right materials and knowing the correct procedures are the first steps in a sound repair program. A good manual that explains and illustrates basic book repair procedures is Abraham Schechter's *Basic Book Repair Methods* (Englewood, CO: Libraries Unlimited, 1999).

Knowing when to repair an item in-house, when to send it to a commercial bindery, and when to buy a new copy takes training and experience. The amount of expected use, type of use and by whom, the value of the existing copy, and ease of obtaining a replacement copy all enter into the decision. In small libraries the repair and binding activities will probably be spread among the staff. Someone in the circulation department is likely to be responsible for minor repairs. Another person who works with serials will be responsible for sending periodicals to the commercial bindery. When a book in the collection becomes worn, a collection development officer may send it to a commercial bindery. Sometimes a book is only available in paperback. The selector may decide that because of expected use that the item must be hardbound before it goes into the collection. In that case, the acquisitions department may become involved if the decision is to acquire a "prebound" copy, that is, a copy from a company that specializes in binding paperbacks. (Public libraries and school media centers often use such companies because they are able to incorporate the paperback's colorful cover into the new binding.)

Usually large libraries have sufficient repair and bindery preparation work to have one or more full-time staff handle the work. Having a bindery unit allows the staff to develop greater skills and knowledge about binding procedures and methods.

Because of the variety of library materials that need preservation and conservation, most libraries use several types of binderies. Typical bindery operations handle large quantities of work—binding serials and rebinding books—using modern production techniques. Binderies of this type are often members of the Library Binding Institute, which gives a library some assurance that the work will meet the institute's standards. The standards are jointly formulated by librarians and binding company officials, who consider changes in technology as well as existing standards. At the other end of the spectrum are restoration binders. These are individuals who attempt to restore old or valuable volumes to their original condition, usually using hand-binding techniques. Such work is expensive and normally reserved for items of special value. No matter what type of bindery the library uses, binderies follow the library's instructions about what should be done to an item. Thus, it is important for the staff preparing bindery shipments to have some knowledge of what is possible and what the outcome will be if they select a given treatment.

Bindery preparation staff should know the differences between saddle-stitching (sewing through the fold of a signature), side-sewing (sewing in front of the fold; this produces a volume that does not lie flat when opened), and over-sewing (similar to side-sewing but slightly more flexible; often used in periodicals binding). A visit to a book bindery and regular reading of the *New Library Scene* (a publication of the Library Binding Institute) will help staff understand terms and appreciate the work involved.

The bindery usually needs the following information about books sent for rebinding: (1) the exact placement of the title on the spine; (2) the author's last name, also on the spine; (3) the call number for the spine; and (4) the desired color of binding. Each bindery has its own special requirements and ways of handling material. Figures 10.1 and 10.2 are the bindery forms that the LMU library employs. The form is typical of U.S. practice in terms of the type of information supplied to the bindery firm. The staff person supervising the preparation of bindery material definitely should become familiar with the routines of the bindery used by the library.

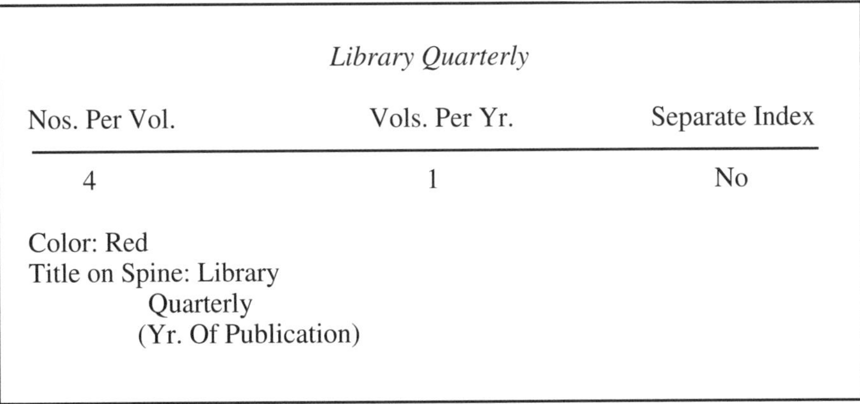

Library Quarterly

Nos. Per Vol.	Vols. Per Yr.	Separate Index
4	1	No

Color: Red
Title on Spine: Library
Quarterly
(Yr. Of Publication)

Figure 10.1. Bindery information card.

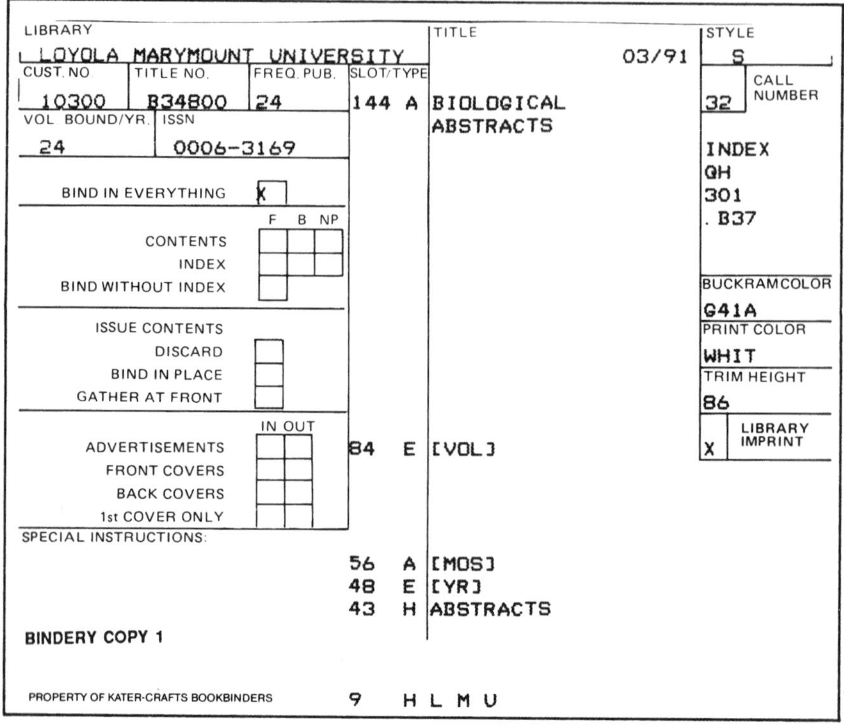

LIBRARY
LOYOLA MARYMOUNT UNIVERSITY
CUST. NO. 10300
TITLE NO. B34800
FREQ. PUB. 24
SLOT/TYPE 144 A
VOL. BOUND/YR. 24
ISSN 0006-3169

BIND IN EVERYTHING X

F B NP
CONTENTS
INDEX
BIND WITHOUT INDEX

ISSUE CONTENTS
DISCARD
BIND IN PLACE
GATHER AT FRONT

IN OUT
ADVERTISEMENTS
FRONT COVERS
BACK COVERS
1st COVER ONLY

SPECIAL INSTRUCTIONS:

BINDERY COPY 1

PROPERTY OF KATER-CRAFTS BOOKBINDERS

TITLE
03/91
144 A BIOLOGICAL ABSTRACTS
84 E [VOL]
56 A [MOS]
48 E [YR]
43 H ABSTRACTS
9 H L M U

STYLE S
32 CALL NUMBER
INDEX
QH
301
. B37
BUCKRAM COLOR G41A
PRINT COLOR WHIT
TRIM HEIGHT 86
X LIBRARY IMPRINT

Figure 10.2. Completed sample form for serials binding.

Serials, particularly periodicals, are a little more difficult to prepare for binding. The check-in file for serials usually contains the necessary binding information. Because serials are bound at regular intervals and over many years, libraries attempt to keep the binding uniform for each title, that is, the same color for the binding, the same placement of spine information, and the same typeface and color of ink.

A library should have the following information available for *each* serial title:

1. Frequency of binding and the number of issues to be bound in a volume (weekly, quarterly, monthly, annually, etc.).
2. Whether the serial has a separate index that must be included in the volume.
3. The exact form of the title and volume numbers as they should be printed on the spine.
4. The color of the binding.

Exactly where the library keeps this information varies, but once a procedure is established, checking to ensure that the binding was done correctly is a simple matter.

One policy question the library must decide is when to make shipments to the bindery. With books this is not an especially difficult question; they can and should go whenever the next shipment goes. However, with journals there are several questions to consider beyond waiting for a complete volume. One is how long to hold the complete volume if the journal issues a separate index or table of contents for the volume. Sometimes it takes as long as six to nine months for the index to arrive. During that waiting time, should the complete volume remain on the open shelves? The longer issues remain unbound, the greater the risk that an issue will disappear. As mentioned previously, locating replacement copies of missing issues is expensive.

A similar issue arises when deciding how many volumes should go into one bound volume. Here the library must balance one type of cost against another. There are three types of interacting costs. Most binderies have a basic price for a bound volume of serials up to a certain thickness (2 or 2½ inches or 5 or 6½ cm.), with additional charges as the thickness increases. They do not reduce the basic charge if a volume is thinner. In some cases, with newsletters and quarterlies, it is possible to bind two or even three title volumes in one physical volume at the basic price.

However, just as waiting for a separate index increases the risk of having to locate replacement issues, so does waiting for one or more additional volumes. Annual volumes could remain unbound for two years or more. Libraries sometimes attempt to reduce the risk of losing issues by keeping the complete but unbound volumes in the bindery preparation area. When a user needs an issue, a staff member retrieves it and signs it out. When the user returns the issue, a staff member takes it back to the bindery area and puts it in its proper place among the other unbound issues. This approach trades staff time and effort for money (the cost of replacing missing issues).

The library must also consider the costs to users when making the binding decision. Binding more than one much-used issue in a physical volume is a disservice to the users. It may also increase the risk of people cutting out the material they want rather than risking a wait while someone else is using a volume that contains several issues. Having unbound issues of complete volumes paged (retrieved by library staff from a nonpublic area) almost guarantees that the issue requested will be available. If someone else is using an issue, the library knows who has it and when it will be back, unlike materials kept on shelves open to public use.

How the library answers these questions depends on the local needs and situation. Having a closed stack (paged) section for all unbound serials can be effective. However, most users like to browse through many periodical issues, and filling out forms for each issue is a source of irritation. Realistically, few libraries have the staff to handle such a system.

Another decision the library must make is when to send the shipments. Most schools and academic institutions try to wait for slow periods during their educational cycle. Thus, binderies tend to receive many shipments during the summer and other times when there are long breaks at academic institutions. If public and special libraries can avoid these peak periods, their bindery turnaround time will be better. The bindery firm is always willing to identify periods when the work volume is low because they want to keep their work flow as even as possible.

Bindery preparation requires a significant amount of staff time, and the staff must understand something about binding operations. Careful record keeping is a key to keeping errors and costs to a minimum. A well-planned and smoothly functioning bindery unit is important to the library's overall purpose of providing access to materials by preserving the collections.

SUMMARY

Serials are a vital part of any information collection. They are complex and costly, regardless of their format. Cost is probably going to remain the primary concern for some time. For the past fifteen years, serial prices have had double-digit rate increases, higher than anything else a library adds to its collection. Thus, serials continually take a larger and larger share of the materials budget, unless the library begins to cancel titles and provide access to the information in some other manner. Technology is changing the way libraries handle serials and is making it possible to provide access to more titles. However, technology will not solve the economic concerns of either the publishers and producers or the consumers. How the two groups will solve the problem is impossible to predict. It is likely the serials price problem will be present for some time.

NOTES

1. The quotation is from a friend's letter. The poet is unknown.

2. Thomas Nisonger, *Management of Serials in Libraries* (Englewood, CO: Libraries Unlimited, 1998).

3. Heartsill Young, ed., *ALA Glossary of Library and Information Science* (Chicago: American Library Association, 1983).

4. *Webster's Third New International Dictionary* (Springfield, MA: G & C Merriam, 1976).

5. Fritz Machlup et al., *Information Through the Printed Word* (New York: New York University, 1978).

6. Judith Bernstein, "Corporate Annual Reports: The Commercial Vendors," *College & Research Libraries News* 47 (March 1986): 178-180.

7. Wallys Conhaim, "Linking Up to the Global Network," *LinkUp* 15 (January/February 1998): 5-11.

8. Carol Foggin, "Title Changes: Another View," *Serials Librarian* 23, nos. 1/2 (1992): 71-83.

9. Nancy Nelson, "Serials Title Changes: What's in a Name?" *Computers in Libraries* 13 (February 1993): 4.

10. William Katz and Linda Sternberg Katz, *Magazines for Libraries,* 9th ed. (New York: R. R. Bowker, 1997).

11. N. Bernard Basch and Judy McQueen, *Buying Serials* (New York: Neal-Schuman, 1990).

12. Barbara Meyers and Janice Fleming, "Price Analysis and the Serial Situation: Trying to Solve an Age-Old Problem," *Journal of Academic Librarianship* 17 (May 1991): 86-92.

13. Marifran Bustion, John Eltinge, and John Harer, "On the Merits of Direct Observation of Periodical Usage," *College & Research Libraries* 53 (November 1992):537-550; Anna Price and Kjestine Carey, "Serials Use Study Raises Questions About Cooperative Ventures," *Serials Review* 19 (Fall 1993):79-84; Christie Degener and Marjory Waite, "Using an Automated Serials System to Assist with Collection Review and Cancellations," *Serials Review* 17 (Spring 1991):13-20; Maiken Naylor, "A Comparison of Two Methodologies for Counting Current Periodical Use," *Serials Review* 19 (Spring 1993): 27-34, 62.

14. Robert Pikowsky, "Electronic Journals as a Potential Solution to Escalating Serials Costs," *Serials Librarian* 32, nos. 3/4 (1997): 31-55.

15. Ronald G. Leach and Judith E. Trible, "Electronic Document Delivery: New Options for Libraries," *Journal of Academic Librarianship* 18 (January 1993): 359-364.

SUGGESTED READING

Anderson, B. "CONSER on the Internet: Facilitating Access to Serials Information." *Serials Librarian* 31, nos. 1/2 (1997): 77-94.

Association for Library Collections & Technical Services, Serials Section of the American Library Association. *Serial Standards Bibliography*. Available: http://www.ala.org/alcts/publications/serials/serialsstds.html (Accessed 29 September 2001).

Baker, Tim. "A Maintenance Perspective." *New Library Scene* 18 (December 1999): 14-15.

Basilone, Mary. "Mergers and Acquisitions in the Serials Industry." *Serials Review* 26, no. 3 (2000): 75-77.

Herzog, Susan. "The Hardest Choices: Money & Space." *Against the Grain* 12 (September 2000): 30-36.

Kniffel, Leonard. "For Some Things, Paper Is Better." *American Libraries* 32 (August 2001): 36.

Kriner, Gretchen. "Establishing an In-house Repair Facility for a Small Academic Library." *Current Studies in Librarianship* 23 (Spring/Fall 1999): 35-49.

Marcinco, R. W. "Issues in Commercial Document Delivery." *Library Trends* 45, no. 3 (Winter 1997): 531-550.

Morris, Sally. "Archiving Electronic Publications: What Are the Problems and Who Should Solve Them?" *Serials Review* 26, no. 3 (2000): 64-66.

Nisonger, T. *Management of Serials in Libraries*. Englewood, CO: Libraries Unlimited, 1998.

Prabha, C., and E. C. Marsh. "Commercial Document Suppliers: How Many of the ILL/DD Periodical Article Requests Can They Fill?" *Library Trends* 45, no. 3 (Winter 1997): 551-558.

Tobia, Rajia, Jude A.Lynch, Thomas Raymond, and Bonnie O'Connor. "Electronic Journals: Experiences of an Academic Health Sciences Library." *Serials Review* 27, no. 1 (2001): 3-17.

REVIEW QUESTIONS

1. What is a serial?
2. List the serial categories developed by Machlup and their implications for the acquisitions department's workload.
3. In what ways do serials subscriptions differ from orders for other formats?
4. Cost/price is a recurring theme for serials. Discuss this issue and its impact on acquisitions departments.
5. Discuss the differences between serial and book vendors.
6. What are the basic steps in serials processing?
7. Discuss the steps in the serials binding process.

Electronic Serials

Almost all the issues related to print serials discussed in Chapter 10 apply to digital serials as well. One reason for having a separate chapter on electronic versions of serials is that they are becoming more and more important to libraries. There is no question about the popularity of such materials with library customers. They often prefer the electronic version, especially because of indexing and abstracting capabilities. One advantage of the electronic index is the capability to perform complex searches quickly, such as a Boolean search (that is, using combinations of search terms). Another advantage is the ease of printing or downloading the search results. Most of the serials that are currently digitized fall into one of five of Fritz Machlup's categories (discussed in Chapter 10): journals, magazines, newspapers, newsletters, and loose-leaf services.

DIGITAL SERIALS

Just as there are several terms used by individuals for paper-based serials, so there are for the digital format: *electronic journal*, *online journals*, *digital journal*, and the more all-embracing *electronic resources*. According to Thomas Nisonger, there is no standard accepted definition of an electronic journal or serial.[1] *E-journal* is a reasonably short term and one we will use here to save space. Producers take three broad approaches to e-journals: an electronic-only version of a new title, an electronic-only version of a title converted from a paper version, and both an electronic and a paper version.

In the past decade or so, libraries and producers have struggled with how to migrate from a print-only world to one that is a mix of paper and electronic resources. The electronic side is becoming more and more dominant and will continue to do so in the future, at least in some serial categories. One of the first forays into the digital world that is still widely used is the CD-ROM product. Those CDs first seen in libraries were primarily DOS-based; CDs have since evolved to a Windows environment. Starting principally with indexing and abstracting services, the CD-ROM products quickly became popular in reference departments. Proprietary software and differing search engines created and continue to create challenges for the library's public service staff. Stand-alone systems were satisfactory at first, but it was not long before there was significant pressure to "network" the stations and allow users to select from a number of products from any station. Making CD "jukeboxes," network software, servers, and user computers all work together was and continues to be a challenge for libraries and acquisitions departments.

When the producers moved into "full text" products, the issues of compatibility became even more complex. Naturally, more and more people wanted more and more access, and variations in computer platforms and equipment become increasingly complex. Full-text products were most often the result of scanning printed pages. Producers then converted the scanned data into bitmapped images and manufactured and distributed them on CD-ROM. Early scanners had fairly high error rates and there was a step between scanning and creating the bitmap images, where the scanned results were compared against the original. All these steps took time, resulting in products that might be electronic in character but were some weeks or even months behind their paper-based original format. (This problem still exists, at the beginning of the new millenium, with some Web-based products from e-journal aggregators.) Essentially the CD-ROM products complement traditional paper-based ones, even if end-users seem to have a misplaced faith that electronic products must be the most current and complete. What they are best at is solving the problems of misplaced, mis-shelved, and mutilated journals as well as "at the bindery" issues.

Today, the move to Internet/Web-based products has helped to bring a balance to access issues. Up to a point, any "authorized" user who has access to the Web will have the same access to a product regardless of the computer platform. This assumes that all users have equal computer systems, which is of course not the case except perhaps in a special library situation where all employees have the same equipment. In the rest of the world, libraries have a few users with the very latest high-end configurations, many with the current "average" setup, and a fairly large number with rather old "slow" machines. Nevertheless, Web-based e-journals and indexing and abstracting services do provide much more equal access for end-users. Where the next stage in the migration will come from and take us is impossible to predict with any degree of assurance. What we do know is that, despite the advantages of electronic resources, print is still with us and is likely to be so for some time to come.

Hazel Woodward and her colleagues outlined what they called fifteen myths about electronic journals.[2] Although they based their article on research they conducted in the United Kingdom, primarily at Loughborough University, the myths they discuss are universal in nature:

- Electronic journals will provide better access to journal articles.
- Academics and researchers read journals at their office desks.
- Readers want electronic journals.

- Electronic journals are quick and convenient to access.
- Readers know and care who publishes a journal.
- Readers want page integrity.
- Electronic journals will bypass libraries and make them redundant.
- Electronic journals will save libraries money.
- Storage and dissemination of electronic journals is inexpensive or free.
- Electronic journals will save paper.
- Publishers care about readers.
- Electronic journals will save publishers money.
- Electronic journals will make subscription agents redundant.
- Only recent issues of journals are required.
- All scholarly journals will be available electronically in a few years.

To this extensive list we add several more "myths":

- Electronic journals are always more current than their print counterpart.
- Electronic journals provide all the graphic materials of their print counterpart.
- Electronic journals are always accessible.
- All readers have equal access to required computers at any time.
- Electronic journals will save library staff time and effort in handling serials.

We point out these myths not to suggest that electronic serials are unimportant but rather to note that they are *not* the final answer to the issues of providing readers with access to the most current and accurate information in the most timely manner. They certainly are an important step in the process, but as they now exist, they are not the ultimate solution. Many of the myths exist because the popular press and somewhat over-enthusiastic technology people promote the concept far beyond its current actual capabilities.

Librarians have, all too often, encountered the chief financial officer who believes at least one of these myths, that electronic journals will save the library money. We have not found that e-journals save the library money; in fact, they add to the cost of operations, as they are almost always add-ons rather than replacements. Several years ago the LMU library tried to cover the cost of an aggregator's product that offers the full text of a large number of journals online by canceling the paper subscriptions to the titles that would be available electronically. After one year, the library reinstated all but five of the paper subscriptions because of the lack of full graphics as well as delays in coverage compared to paper-based titles.

There are a number of issues to ponder in the interplay between digitized and paper-based serials. One issue is how to provide access. Digital serials, in theory, are accessible anywhere, anytime as long as there is a connection between a computer and the database containing the desired material. Many customers and technology supporters believe this is the ideal future—anywhere at anytime. Library literature generally approaches this issue in terms of ownership versus access.

When a library subscribes to a paper journal, the library owns those copies of a title for which it paid the appropriate fee. Electronic formats are often a different matter. Producers of the electronic material usually include with it a license agreement that limits the library's ability to use the material, which normally states that the library has access rights only as long as the annual fee is current. In essence, the library only leases the data. If a library has any responsibility for long-term retention of information, leasing is a problematic policy even if the producer says it will archive the files and the library will always have the right to access them for the years for which it paid a lease fee.

Without a doubt, digitized serials are a mixed blessing. They are very popular, they provide more flexibility in searching than their paper-based counterparts, and remote access at any time is a possibility. Although they do not reduce library operating costs, they do present new challenges for the library's staff—both public and technical services. Electronic systems can fail, as do power supplies, which causes customer and staff frustration. Also, as anyone who has spent much time with Internet-based services knows, "electronic" does not always translate into "fast." Waiting for files to download, to have the server "accept" a query, or being abruptly cut off in mid-session are sources of frustration that do not exist with paper-based serials. On the other hand, torn out articles, mis-shelved or missing volumes, or finding the library closed for a holiday are not problems with electronic serials (provided off-site access to the required systems is available). Without question, e-serials are going to be increasingly important in any overall service plan for any type of library. Thus one must understand their benefits as well as their limitations.

ACQUIRING E-SERIALS

Is the process of acquiring e-serials different than that followed for print serials? The answer is no, not really; however, there are some additional steps. All the factors that apply to acquiring paper titles also apply to e-journals. One factor that differs is that often, at least in the case of journal aggregator services, the purchasing decision is made in terms of a package of titles rather than title by title. That in turn means the cost being considered is substantially higher than any single typical library paper subscription. Thus, factors of new costs, vendor support, and a "package" of titles are added.

Another factor complicating the decision is that electronic resources require more staff involvement than is typical for paper-based additions. If nothing more, there are questions about technology requirements and capabilities that systems staff must answer. Furthermore, the public service staff must be involved. Few users need assistance in opening a paper journal, but often need it when locating and using an electronic title. Packages from either producers or aggregators often employ different search engines, which in turn require staff to remember which database operates in which manner. Thus, public service staff often want a voice in deciding what, if any, new electronic products to add to the service program.

Mary Jean Pavelsek outlined a set of eleven "guidelines" for evaluating e-journals and their providers.[3]

Economics

Ease of use/user flexibility

Archival implications

Future accessibility

Access

Licensing, copyright, and distribution restrictions

Single or multiple publishers

Print versus electronic comparisons

User support

If a package, is it "all or nothing?"

Planned enhancements

To her list we add cost per user, technological issues, and aggregators.

The two typical methods for securing e-serials are direct from the publisher or producer or from so-called aggregators. An aggregator is an organization that develops "packages" of electronic serials. The aggregator enters into contracts with a number of publishers or producers to offer their titles as a package. Producers gain by not having to invest in as much marketing, programming, and technology. Then the aggregator adds value to the package by providing a consistent search engine for searching all the titles. Naturally, aggregators then add a charge for their services on top of what the cost was from the producers—often as much as 30 percent to 40 percent. Some of the large aggregators are OCLC, UMI, Lexis/Nexis, and EBSCO.

Using aggregator packages usually entails accepting a number, sometimes a substantial number, of titles the library would never subscribe to in print. Few of the aggregators allow a library to take only the titles of interest. Of course, that means the library pays for titles it does not want. Thus, one question to consider is whether the overall cost is really appropriate for the number of titles the library does want. In 1999 the California State University System issued a Request for Proposal (RFP) to aggregators to supply access to a list of 1,279 journals in what they called the "Journal Access Core Collection."[4] The titles on the list were those in highest demand in the system's twenty-two libraries. The project was not as successful they had hoped. Several aggregators declined to respond to the RFP, perhaps because of problems in being able to negotiate different prices or the challenge of negotiating with over 1,200 publishers was too great.

One system for evaluating aggregators as well as the publishers or producers of titles is the weighted system developed by the California State University Libraries for deciding on systemwide purchases. They have a committee of twelve members, representing the twenty-two campuses of the system, who serve for two years. Evaluations are made independently by each committee member, using the weighted system, during a two-week trial period. Results of their evaluations are available on the system's Web page (http://www.co.calstate.edu/irt/seir).

Canadian electronic serials can be accessed on the National Library of Canada's Web site at http://collection.nlc-bnc.ca/e-coll-e/index-e.htm.

Staff and customer "comfort level" with a chosen product is important. Outstanding content in a product that is complex or difficult to use, even if the cost is relatively modest, may not be the most cost-effective purchase. An unused resource is a waste of funds.

Technical issues of network capability, stability, and compliance with general standards are all key factors. Also, how much support is available from the vendor and during what hours? If required, how is authentication handled? Domain access—recognizing IP ranges—is a low-cost option for the library; however, remote users with private Internet service providers will not have access without special arrangements such as a proxy server. These are all new issues for the acquisitions department staff to become familiar with to carry out their purchasing activities.

Content concerns relate to the usual subject issues and also to how complete the material is, assuming there is a print counterpart. Another concern should be whether there are "additions" to the product and whether they are necessary or beneficial. Some vendors or producers will add some form of "multimedia"—sound or video clips—to their material. Often this is of the "gee whiz look what technology allows us to do" type rather than being a true added value. Such additions create hardware and software compatibility problems for both library-owned and remote users' machines.

HANDLING E-SERIALS

Handling e-serials? What does that mean? Unlike a print subscription, after the appropriate record keeping files are in place, e-serials require more set-up steps. Generally a new print subscription merely goes into its appropriate place with the other current issues of the print journals.

In the case of e-serials, someone must ensure that the technical issues are addressed before implementing the service. If the access is Web-based and domain-restricted in nature, providing IP ranges is fairly straightforward. However, password verification is still a requirement of some systems, and libraries must decide who will have access to these passwords. Will the library log in users or will certain users (such as faculty members) be given the password to use as needed? Testing to determine compatibility with other services needs to be done (e.g., changes in hardware or software configurations). Libraries must also consider what, if anything, will appear in the library's OPAC about the product. If a package of 1,000 full-text journals is purchased, will the library add a note to the holdings statements for titles the library also has in a print format? What about entries for the "new" titles, even those that may not be important to the library's customer base? Will the OPAC reflect just title, electronic address only, or both? Will there be a "hot link" in the OPAC or on the library Web site? (More work for the catalog department.) If images are included in the package, does the library need "helper" applications (such as Adobe Acrobat Reader) installed on its public machines?

Every library using electronic materials needs one person or office that handles and maintains a file of license agreements. Someone must review the agreement and notify staff of any new requirements. A good article outlining all the steps and issues in implementing a new e-serial is Cindy Stewart Kaag's "Collection Development for Online Serials."[5]

Janet Hughes and Catherine Lee published an article in 1998 that can serve as a case study of the process of selecting, acquiring, and implementing a full-text journal package. This case study addresses issues related to multiple service points. The authors describe the process used at Pennsylvania State University and its statewide, twenty-three-campus system. They conclude by stating: "Overall, although the experience of implementing the first networked full-text databases at Penn State was a positive one, its success depended upon careful planning and dedicated inter-departmental and campus cooperation. These qualities will be needed to make future forays into full-text equally successful."[6]

PRICING

As noted in the lists of myths, e-serials do not save either the producer or the library money. Perhaps at some point in the past there was a reasonable expectation for such savings. However, by the mid-1990s it was clear to both vendors and libraries that this would not be the case. For example, Robert Marks noted that the American Chemical Society estimated its CD-ROM journals cost 25 percent to 33 percent more to produce than their print versions. The reason for the higher cost was attributed to the need to provide and maintain a search engine.[7] Tom Abate has reported that the American Institute of Physics estimated that providing both a print and an electronic copy of a title cost between 10 and 15 percent more than just offering a print version of the same title.[8] Conversations with publishers of electronic-only serials indicate that they see no difference in costs—they claim it costs just as much for an e-only version as it does for print-only. Janet Fischer of MIT Press indicated that the reason producers of e-only serials see costs as equal was not so much a function of production costs as of an overall loss of revenue: no back issue sales, no renting of subscriber mailing lists, and perhaps most important, the loss of advertising income.[9]

The dual pricing found with many scholarly print serials (that is, one price for individuals and a higher price for institutions) continues in the electronic environment, if in a slightly different guise. Individuals do not face the same licensing issues as libraries and do not pay for more than one user, nor are they asked about number of potential users in the household or office. Libraries usually have to pay extra fees, rather substantial at times, for more than one simultaneous user license. Different producers use different increments, such as one to four users at one rate, five to nine at another rate, and so forth, up to a rate for unlimited access.

Another pricing mechanism is by size of the service population, frequently based on the number of full-time students or staff—full-time equivalent (FTE)—at an institution. This is probably one of the most costly approaches for libraries when it comes to specialized serials or other products. For example, say a fictitious university (ICU with 12,000 total students and faculty) has an anthropology department with 10 faculty, 68 graduate students, and 129 undergraduate majors, and its course offerings each year enroll a total of 1,400 different students. The library considers subscribing to an electronic version of a print product in the field of anthropology that has a record of modest use. The producer uses the FTE pricing model and indicates that its price is 50 cents per FTE. Unfortunately, typically the vendor calculates the cost on the basis of the institutional FTE, not that of the department, or even a realistic estimate of the potential users. Thus, if the institutional FTE (staff/faculty/students is the typical request) is 12,000, then the cost becomes $6,000 for a product that has had only modest use in the print format. Certainly there is the prospect that the electronic version will have greater use, assuming the product comes with a reasonably good search engine, but there is no reasonable expectation that every person at the institution will access the database at some point during the year.

Transaction-based fees are another pricing mechanism that can drive up the cost of electronic serials for a library (this is the model that OCLC was using for *FirstSearch* in 2002). In some ways, this approach is less costly than the FTE model, as actual usage determines the price. One drawback of this model is that the library is never certain what its costs will be until after the fact. With *FirstSearch,* OCLC, at least for consortia, sets an annual fee that includes a fixed number of searches. The fee is paid in advance, and at the end of the year there may be additional charges if the search limit was exceeded. The amount may be something of a shock for the library if it has not been carefully monitoring usage. (The LMU library belongs to a consortium that purchased access to *FirstSearch,* and members discuss what databases they can "turn off" to control the year-end charges. Somehow it seems strange to be buying access to databases, then begin to discuss which ones to restrict public access to in order to save money.) Part of the problem with the transaction-based approach is that every search *counts*—even those where the person has misspelled a word or does not understand how to search the database. It is difficult to know how much value for money expended is actually received from this model. At least with paper formats, user and staff mistakes do not cost the library additional money.

Some publishers and producers have not decided which model to follow. As a result, some offer free access to an electronic version of a title if the library has a subscription to the print format. Others offer such access for a modest fee (10 percent to 15 percent) above the print subscription cost as long as the library maintains the paper title.

Where pricing will go is difficult to predict beyond the fact that prices will continue to escalate. As Bill Robnett has stated, "The complexities of online serials pricing may increase as more publishers enter the electronic publishing market.... One consideration is that serials budgets will be redefined as libraries purchase access in units of articles, an open-ended concept quite different from the now prevalent subcription."[10]

One probable direction for acquiring electronic products is through a consortial process. The idea, which has worked for many consortia in the United States, is that if the pricing model is FTE based, the larger that number the lower the price will be. Certainly the group that LMU belongs to has allowed the library to acquire many more products than it could have on its own because of the lower group rate the consortium negotiated. The downside for the acquisitions department is that the process often is unpredictable in terms of products under consideration and how much they will cost, if and when a deal is struck. This makes for very difficult budget management and being unable to predict the amount of money that will be available to purchase materials—even the electronic ones.

SUMMARY

Electronic serials are probably the "wave of the future," but perhaps a more distant future than technology enthusiasts would have us believe. Despite the advantages realized from having materials available in such formats, it appears likely that there will be little prospect of either producers or libraries realizing any cost savings as a result of migrating to an all-electronic environment. How libraries will handle the ever-escalating costs of serials, regardless of format, is something to ponder seriously. Electronic serials certainly do not reduce the workload for technical services.

NOTES

1. Thomas Nisonger, "Electronic Journal Collection Development Issues," *Collection Building* 16, no. 2 (1997): 58.

2. Hazel Woodward et al. "Electronic Journals: Myths and Realties," *OCLC Systems & Services* 13, no. 4 (1997): 144-151.

3. Mary Jean Pavelsek, "Guidelines for Evaluating E-Journal Providers," *Advances in Librarianship* 22 (1998): 39-58.

4. Michael Rogers, "Cal State Proposes New E-Journal Buying Model," *Library Journal* 124 (February 15, 1999): 107.

5. Cindy Stewart Kaag, "Collection Development for Online Serials: Who Needs to Do What, and Why, and When," *Serials Librarian* 33, nos. 1/2 (1998): 107-122.

6. Janet Hughes and Catherine Lee, "Giving Patrons What They Want: The Promise, the Process, and the Pitfalls of Providing Full-Text Access to Journals," *Collection Building* 17, no. 4 (1998): 148-153.

7. Robert Marks, "The Economic Challenges of Publishing Electronic Journals," *Serials Review* 21 (Spring 1995): 85-88.

8. Tom Abate, "Publishing Scientific Journals Online" *Bioscience* 47 (March 1997): 175-179.

9. Janet Fischer, "True Costs of an Electronic Journal," *Serials Review* 21 (Spring 1995): 88-90.

10. Bill Robnett, "Online Journal Pricing," *Serials Librarian* 33, nos. 1/2 (1998): 68.

SELECTED WEB SITES

Back Issues and Exchange Services, http://www.uvm.edu/~bmaclenn/backexch.htm.
A source of missing issues and exchange of serials and other materials. Maintained by Birdie MacLennan; her main site (http://www.uvm.edu/~bmaclenn/) is "Serials in Cyberspace," a collection of resources and services of use to serials librarians.

CONSER Program Home Page, http://lcweb.loc.gov/acq/conser/.
The Library of Congress's Web site for information about the Cooperative Online Serials Program (CONSER).

Ejournal SiteGuide, http://www.library.ubc.ca/ejour.
Joseph Jones's Web site, with annotated links to sites for e-journals.

Electronic Journal Miner, http://www.coalliance.org/ejournal.
The Colorado Alliance of Research Libraries site that provides information on a wide variety of e-journals. Provides subject headings, producer information, contact data, ISSN, and other useful information.

enews.com, http://www.enews.com
A list of more that 1,000 commercial magazine resources available on the Web.

ICOLC Statement on Electronic Information, http://www.library.yale.edu/consortia/statement.html.
Site for information on the International Coalition of Library Consortia (ICOLC), which deals with consortial purchases of electronic resources.

The Journal of Electronic Publishing, http://www.press.umich.edu/jep/.
A good source of information about e-publishing of electronic resources.

Liblicense: Licensing Digital Information, http://www.library.yale.edu/~llicense/index.shtml.
Archive for LIBLICENSE-L discussion list.

NewJour, http://gort.ucsd.edu/newjour/.
List of archived networked e-journals.

North American Serials Interest Group, http://www.nasig.org.
NASIG is an important group in serials management programming and information. A site worth bookmarking.

Scholarly Electronic Publishing Bibliography, http://info.lib.uh.edu/sepb/sepb.html.
References on electronic publishing.

Scholarly Journals Distributed Via the World-Wide Web, http://info.lib.uh.edu/wj/webjour.html.
A University of Houston libraries Web site that lists more than 120 free Web-based academic journals.

Serials discussion list site, http://uvmvm.uvm.edu/~bmaclean/serialst.html.
Subscribe by e-mailing to LILSTSERV@uvmvm.uvm.edu. Type message SERIALST and then your name.

UK Serials Group WWW Page, http://www.uksg.org.
An excellent source of information about UK and European serial vendors and services.

Web Tools for Serialists, http://www.lib.utk.edu/~techserv/serials/sertools.htm.
Kathy Ellis's site listing Web sites related to serials work. Three major divisions: General Serials Resources, Serials Acquisitions, and Cataloging and Online Publications.

Welcome to JSTOR, http://www.jstor.org.
The home page of Journal Storage (JSTOR).

Welcome to United States Book Exchange, http://www.usbe.com/.
USBE has been a mainstay for serials librarians as a source of missing journal issues and exchange serials.

SUGGESTED READING

Abate, T. "Publishing Scientific Journals Online." *Bioscience* 47 (March 1997): 175-179.

American Library Association. "Directory of Union Lists of Serials." *Serials Review* 14, nos. 1/2 (1998): 115-159.

Barnes, J. H. "One Giant Leap, One Small Step: Continuing the Migration to Electronic Journals." *Library Trends* 45 (Winter 1997): 404-415.

Born, Kathleen. "Searching for Serials Utopia." *Library Journal* 126 (April 15, 2001): 53-58.

Cameron, R. D. "Not Just E-Journals: Providing and Maintaining Access to Serials and Serials Information Through the World-Wide Web." *Serials Libraries* 29, nos. 3/4 (1996): 209-222.

Duranceau, E. F. "Beyond Print: Revisioning Serials Acquisitions for the Digital Age." *Serials Librarian* 33, nos. 1/2 (1998): 83-105.

Fritseh, D. "A Capital Idea: Electronic Serials from Acquisition to Access." *Serials Review* 23 (Winter 1997): 83-88.

Geller, Marilyn. "Serials Pricing Update—The Real Cost and Price of Ejournals." *Against the Grain* 13 (June 2001): 82-84.

Gilbert, N. "Aggregators of Electronic Journals" (1997). Available via e-mail from LIBLICENSE-L@pantheon.yale.edu.

Gray, Sharon. "The Myth and Reality of Electronic Journals." *Serials Review* 26, no. 4 (2000): 58-64.

Guthrie, K. M., and W. P. Lougee. "The JSTOR Solution: Accessing and Preserving the Past." *Library Journal* 122, no. 2 (1998): 42-44.

Halliday, Leah. "Development in Digital Journals." *Journal of Documentation* 57 (March 2001): 261-283.

Harter, S. P., and H. K. Kin. "Accessing Electronic Journals and Other E-Publications." *College & Research Libraries* 57 (September 1996): 440-456.

Hawbaker, A. C., and C. K. Wagner. "Periodical Ownership Versus Fulltext Online Access: A Cost-Benefit Analysis." *Journal of Academic Librarianship* 22, no. 2 (1996): 105-109.

Hawkins, L. "Network Accessed Scholarly Serials." *Serials Librarian* 29, nos. 3/4 (1996): 19-31.

Ketcham, L., and K. Born. "Projecting Electronic Revolution While Budgeting for the Status Quo." *Library Journal* 121 (April 15, 1996): 45-53.

Knight, N. H. "Electronic Pubs Pricing in the Web Era." *Information Today* 15 (September 1998): 39-40.

Krumenaker, Lawrence. "A Tempest in a Librarians Teapot: EBSCO, ProQuest, Gale Exclusive, and Unique Titles." *Searcher* 9 (July/August 2001): 40-45.

Lewis, Marilyn. "Unwrapping the Serials Package." *Serials Review* 26, no. 3 (2000): 79-80.

Lynch, C.A. "Technology and Its Implications for Serials Acquisition." *Against the Grain* 9 (February 1997): 34, 36-37.

Machovec, G. S. "Pricing Models for Electronic Databases on the Internet." *Online Libraries and Microcomputers* 16 (March 1998): 1-4.

McGinnis, Suzan D. "Selling Our Collecting Souls: How License Agreement Are Controlling Collection Management." *Journal of Library Administration* 31, no. 2 (2000): 63-76.

Metz, P., et al. "A Standardized Form for Evaluation and Description of Electronic Resources Under Consideration by the Virginia Tech University Libraries." *Technicalities* 18, no. 10 (November/December 1998): 9-10.

Phelan, Daniel F. "Biz of Acq.—Canadian National Site Licensing Project." *Against the Grain* 13 (February 2001): 1, 18.

Pikowsky, R. A. "Electronic Journals as a Potential Solution to Escalating Serials Cost." *Serials Libraries* 32, nos. 3/4 (1997): 31-56.

Prior, Albert. "Acquiring and Accessing Serials Information—The Electronic Intermediary." *Interlending & Document Supply* 29, no. 2 (Spring 2001): 62-68.

Rowland, J. F. "Electronic Journals: Delivery, Use, and Access." *IFLA Journal* 22, no. 3 (1996): 226-228

Russell, Bill. "A Way Forward for E-journal Pricing." *Library Association Record* 103 (July 2001): 422-423.

Schottlaender, B. "Development of National Principles to Guide Licensing Electronic Resources." *Library Acquisition* 22, no. 1 (1998): 49-54.

Tenopir, C. "The Complexities of Electronic Journals." *Library Journal* 122 (February 1, 1997): 37-38.

Winter, Ken. "From Wood to Web: The Online Evolution." *American Libraries* 31 (May 2000): 70-74.

Woodward, H. "Electronic Journals: Issues of Access and Bibliographic Control." *Serials Review* 21 (Summer 1995): 71-78.

Wusteman, J. "Electronic Journal Formats." *Program* 30 (October 1996): 319-343.

Yocum, P. B. "Libraries and Electronic Journals in Science." *IFLA Journal* 22, no. 3 (1996): 181-247.

REVIEW QUESTIONS

1. Discuss the myths regarding e-serials.
2. Discuss the "guidelines" for evaluating e-serials.
3. How do aggregators differ from other vendors?
4. What are the special factors regarding the handling of e-serials that are different from other formats?
5. Discuss the issues relating to the pricing of electronic products.

Chapter 12 Government Information

Government information is available in a variety of formats, encompassing all the types that libraries collect such as print and electronic books, sound recordings, and maps. Government agencies (national to local) and quasi-governmental bodies (such as the United Nations and World Health Organization) are also the world's most prolific producers of information materials. These materials are the least expensive to acquire, at least in terms of money. However, they are often labor intensive for acquisitions and cataloging units.

All types of libraries acquire some kinds of government information. People who have access to accurate information make more informed, if not necessarily better, decisions. When it comes to understanding government actions and processes, having free access to information is essential, if people are to respond effectively. Further, as noted in Chapter 6, commercial publishers need to make a profit on the majority of their publications. There is a vast amount of information available that would not be commercially viable due to the cost of collecting and compiling it; it also has a relatively limited sales appeal. Government publications fill the gap between no profit and no information.

As James Madison wrote in 1832:

> A popular government without popular information, or the means of acquiring it, is but a prologue to a farce or a tragedy; or perhaps both. . . . And a people who mean to be their own governors, must arm themselves with the power that knowledge gives.[1]

As this statement shows, interest in and concern about society's access to government information has a long history in the United States. The issue of open access to government information is a worldwide concern, and libraries play a key role in the dissemination of such information.

Government documents and information form a mysterious and frequently misunderstood part of a library's collection. Because of their special nature, these materials can confuse and frustrate staff and user alike. Yet they also constitute an important, current, and vital part of any collection, and they can provide a surprising wealth of information on almost any topic. People use various labels for this type of material, such as *government publications, government information, official documents, federal documents, agency publications, legislative documents,* and *executive documents.* Libraries house the materials in several ways, ranging from a separate collection containing nothing but government material to complete integration into the general collection. How the library houses these materials affects their technical service processing, from fully to partially cataloged or uncataloged.

Documents may be classified using the system employed for the other collections or one designed by the national government for organizing its publications. In the United States, that usually means employing either the Library of Congress Classification System, Dewey Decimal System, or the Superintendent of Documents (SUDOCs) system. Libraries also handle access in several ways. The materials may be included or excluded from indexes, card catalogs, and online catalogs.

To add to the confusion created by their diverse management, the documents themselves have only one common trait: Many are all official publications of some government or international body. Thus, many have corporate rather than personal authors, which makes it more difficult for users to know how to search for desired material. If the material is included in an online catalog that has subject or keyword searching, end-users will identify and use more government information than they will if the material is cataloged in manual files. Government information comes in a variety of sizes, shapes, and media formats: books, technical reports, periodicals, pamphlets, microforms, posters, films, slides, photographs, CD-ROMs, online databases, audio recordings, and maps. They have no special subject focus, because they are the product of many diverse branches and agencies of government. They usually reflect the concerns of the agency that produced them. Predictably, a document produced by the U.S. Department of Agriculture (USDA) probably deals with a subject related to agriculture, such as livestock statistics, horticulture, or irrigation. The relationship may be less direct, because USDA also publishes information about nutrition, forestry, and home economics. As remote as the connection may seem, most government publications do have some connection to the issuing agencies' purpose and function.

Compounding the confusion about the nature of government information is the fact that any level of government may issue an official document. Although national government documents are frequently the only official publications easily identified or treated as government publications, all other levels of government—local, regional, state/provincial, national, and international—also produce official publications that are "government documents." Although national government documents are the most numerous and important in the library's collection, other levels of government publications are also valuable and useful. A library may choose to include only one type or level of document in its government documents section, or it may include several levels.

Defining what is government information is not always easy. Are reports prepared by nongovernmental agencies (also known as NGOs—nongovernmental organizations) but required by a government agency truly government publications? What about the publications produced by short- and long-term multijurisdictional groups? Usually discussions of government information include materials published by the United Nations, which is clearly not a government body in the usual meaning of the term. Rather, countries contribute funds to operate the UN, including their information and publications program. We take a broad view of this and, for our purposes, any information that has government involvement, with or without direct government funds, is included in this chapter.

The inherent diversity of government agencies and their publications combines with the diverse library management techniques concerning government documents to create bibliographic schizophrenia about government information. However, this immense body of information, available at a modest cost, makes government publications and services a worthwhile information resource, even if they are a major challenge for both acquisitions and cataloging departments.

The cost of government publications varies among the levels of government and according to purchase plans or depository agreements. However, most government publications cost very little. For example, U.S. law states that the federal government may not make a profit from selling documents. The price, by statute, may only recover publication and overhead costs. This can lead to remarkable bargains for libraries. Where else can a library purchase a major reference tool like the annual directory of the federal government, which includes names, addresses, organizational charts, and brief descriptions of the mission and activities of each agency, for U.S. $30?[2] Other levels of government follow a similar philosophy concerning pricing and distribution of documents.

Although price and subject coverage are attractive features, the variety of target audiences of documents within any subject area also offers many advantages for collection building. The USDA may publish information on nutrition, ranging from bilingual pamphlets to nutritional research studies. The National Aeronautics and Space Administration (NASA) likewise publishes a variety of documents, ranging from space science for school children to extremely technical studies of space flight and the possibilities of extraterrestrial life. Some CD-ROMs issued by federal agencies include the Department of Defense's *Hazardous Materials Information System*, the Department of Commerce's *U.S. Imports of Merchandise*, and the Central Intelligence Agency's *World Factbook*. Canadian federal and provincial governments and governments in other countries produce equally diverse materials and almost in the same volume as does the U.S. government. Information about most subjects related to government is available at a surprising number of reading and use levels that can serve the needs and interests of most age groups. Perhaps the most attractive feature of government documents is their timeliness. Frequently, they provide the most current information available about popular topics.

BACKGROUND

Some scholars suggest that society's right to government information, at least in the English-speaking world, has its origin in the English *Magna Carta* of 1215.[3] The U.S. Constitution contains the requirement that Congress "keep a journal of its proceedings, and from time to time publish same, excepting such parts as may in their judgment require secrecy; and the yeas and nays of the members of either house on any question shall, at the desire of one-fifth of those present, be entered on the journal."[4] By 1813, selected U.S. libraries were part of a depository program that covered congressional materials. In 1857 the program expanded to cover items produced by the executive branch. The "depository" program grew over the next 130 years both in types of material distributed and in the number of libraries receiving all or some of the available material. (The depository program is discussed later in this chapter.)

At some point, in small steps, the U.S. government decided that citizens not only needed easy access to information about government activities but also to information that would improve the economy or enhance daily living. How-to publications, such as those on gardening and carpentry, became part of the government's publication list. Thus, a second purpose of a government publication program is to help people improve the quality of their lives. As Bruce Morton noted, "The consumption of information, like the consumption of food, is vital to the nourishment of the pursuit of life, liberty and happiness in a democratic society."[5]

Some people question the role the government should play in producing such publications. Morton summarizes the situation as follows:

> The first information obligation of the government of the United States is to produce the information it needs to effectively govern, and in so doing provide accurate information about its activities for itself and so it can be held accountable to, and by, its constituents.
>
> To accomplish this, the government, libraries, and the press all must, and do, play important roles. The government, however, is neither obliged (nor should it feel so) to produce, let alone provide it, based on the needs of the researchers who occupy the nation's libraries. One neither disputes the needs of these researches nor their researches.
>
> Indeed, their needs are compelling, as is the need for government information in meeting those needs. However, it must be understood that what is called government information describes not necessarily a source of information, but rather the point of collection and data origination.[6]

By the beginning of the 1980s, there were more than 1,300 U.S. government document full and partial depository libraries. During President Ronald

Reagan's first term in office, the Office of Management and Budget (OMB) received authorization to develop a federal information policy as the result of the passage of the Paperwork Reduction Act of 1980 (Public Law No. 96-511). The OMB was given the responsibility to minimize the cost of "collecting, maintaining, using, and disseminating information."[7]

One of OMB's initiatives supported the concept of disseminating federal information as raw data in an electronic format, often without software for using or searching for the desired data.[8] Certainly OMB's role in shifting the emphasis from paper to electronic means of dissemination has been significant. In 1996, Congress began debating the Government Printing Reform Act of 1996; the core concept of which was to provide easy access to government information by electronic means.

A major problem was, and remains at the time we wrote this chapter, that the necessary national, much less local, technological infrastructure that would make the concept viable does not exist. Another significant issue was the lack of governmentwide standards for making information available electronically. Experience in the late 1980s and 1990s with the electronic dissemination of U.S. federal information demonstrated the necessity of a single governmentwide standard. Some departments employ two or more software programs with their various databases. Even the most experienced computer user has difficulty securing the desired information. Very few individuals who want such information have the skills to retrieve what they need without assistance. Realistically, until there is a single standard, most people will have to depend on either their place of employment or libraries to provide the needed assistance.

As for the Internet, the Government Information Locator Service (GILS) is a federal standard for describing information. However, even this "standard" does, and will continue to, contain complexities for public service staff as well as for end-users. The GILS consists of two basic elements. One is the centrally maintained "GILS Core," which is for "general" access to information. The second element is the fact that agencies can and do maintain a GILS designed to meet the special requirements of their primary constituency. Specialized GILSs are linked back to the Core GILS, but there are a host of variations within GILS.

The GILS provides for two search modes, intermediated and direct. It appears that the expectation, on the government's part, is that the intermediated use will be through libraries, schools, and places of employment, or information brokers. Direct users, according to the plan, "must have network access, and be literate in English to at least the secondary-school level, capable of using a personal computer, *and aware, if any, of limitations of their own hardware and software environment* (emphasis added)."[9] How many individuals are aware of what limitations may be relevant or even what exactly is meant by the last clause?

It is unlikely the founders of the depository system envisioned the federal government becoming the country's largest publisher, or really debated which documents should be available to the public. Today, there is a debate about what information should be available, and the debate can have and has had some impact on libraries.

From the library point of view, government publications still provide a means of inexpensively expanding a collection. Given the range and content of government information packages, all types of libraries can acquire useful, authoritative materials at minimal cost. The Smithsonian Institution, for example, is issuing a twenty-volume set, the *Handbook of North American Indians.* The published volumes range in length from 700 to 930 pages, have extensive illustrations (maps, line drawings, and photographs), and have text prepared by leading scholars. Prices for the volumes range between $23.00 and $78.00 (averaging $39.43). As a rough comparison, the average price for the seventy-eight Native American reference books listed in the 1997 and 2001 volumes of *American Reference Books Annual* ranged from $16.95 to $385.00, with an average price of $155.89. None of the commercial publications matched the length and overall quality of the Smithsonian volumes. Although the government did not create its publication program for the purpose of building library collections, this is a real, if unanticipated, benefit of the program.

Staff members who work regularly with government information also believe that better and more frequent use of government material would benefit most library customers. They believe that if individuals understood the broad range of information and subjects available, usage would increase. Two factors work against increased usage. First, in depository collections, the lack of full cataloging for all received items means users interested in accessing such items often cannot find them using the OPAC. The high volume of material received is a major factor in not fully cataloging depository items. Even though the items in the *Monthly Catalog* are now being listed in OCLC, the size of uncataloged older collections keeps the old uncataloged system in place. Second, if depository items are not fully cataloged, libraries normally establish a separate area to house the items. Frequently the government documents collections reside in a corner or basement of the library with the lowest volume of traffic. The old saying "out of sight, out of mind" is all too true about government documents. To some extent even the public service staff forgets to direct users to government information. The forgetfulness is not only due to the location of the material but also because of the difficulty in identifying appropriate material. This is true for both print and electronic information.

The National Library of Canada provides cataloging copy in its free AMICUS service for all items chosen for depository. This cataloging is completed by the time these items are distributed.

In nondepository libraries, government publications usually receive full cataloging because the material goes into the general or reference collection. This may be particularly true in special library collections, where government documents are fully integrated into the collection alongside their private counterparts. Undoubtedly many people in such libraries use government publications and never realize it. Thus, a government publication represents no unique problem for users, if government material receives the same treatment as other formats, that is, if it is housed in the general reference or circulating collection.

TYPES OF DOCUMENTS

U.S. Documents

The executive, judicial, and legislative branches, as well as executive cabinet-level agencies and independent agencies, all issue documents. However, it appears that presidential statements, reorganization plans, and executive orders are the publications most users want. Sources used to identify such publications are *Code of Federal Regulations—Title 2 (President) Weekly Compilation of Presidential Documents,* and *GPO Access* (http://www.access.gpo.gov/su_docs/). Presidential commission reports belong to this class of publications, as do the *Budget of the United States Government* and *Economic Report of the President Transmitted to the Congress.* Such documents are valuable for academic and general interest purposes, and most large and medium-sized public and academic libraries collect some or all of them. School media centers may collect a few publications that relate to curriculum concerns.

Cabinet-level departments (e.g., Department of Agriculture or Department of the Interior) include administrative units, such as agencies and bureaus. Most of these units issue reports, regulations, statistics, and monographs; many issue educational and public relations materials as well. Some sample titles are *Statistical Abstract of the United States, Yearbook of Agriculture, Handbook of Labor Statistics,* and *The Smokey the Bear Coloring Book.* All types of libraries will find publications of interest from the various units. Special libraries collect many of the technical publications. Most academic libraries collect heavily in this area, but media centers and public libraries are rather selective in their acquisition of such materials. In addition to cabinet-level agency publications, many independent agencies publish a similar range of items. The Tennessee Valley Authority, Federal Reserve Board, and Central Intelligence Agency are examples of independent agencies that publish documents.

Cabinet-level and independent agency publications constitute the core of the widely collected federal documents. Many departments publish general interest periodicals that are very popular with library users. Media centers also find these agencies a good source of inexpensive, high-quality visual materials.

Judicial documents (aside from case law reports) are not as numerous as those from the other two branches of government. The best known and most important title is the *Supreme Court Reports*, which contains Supreme Court opinions and decisions. (Note: Private commercial publishers issue the decisions of lower federal courts; these are not normally considered government documents.) Although large legal libraries must have a set of the *Supreme Court Reports,* other libraries may find them useful for patrons for historical, political, or personal reasons. As a result, many larger public and academic libraries acquire a set for the general collection, even when there is a good legal library nearby.

Congressional publications are second in number and popularity only to executive publications. In addition to the text of proposed and passed legislation, these publications include materials documenting House and Senate deliberations. Floor debates appear in the *Congressional Record;* assessments of the need for legislation are available in congressional committee reports; testimony before congressional committees appears in documents that bear the words *Hearings of* or *Hearings on;* and there are also several important reference books, such as *Official Congressional Directory*, *Senate Manual*, and *House Rules*.

The *Congressional Record* provides a semi-verbatim transcript of the proceedings on the floor of each house of Congress (semi-verbatim because it is possible for a congressperson to add or delete material in the *Congressional Record.* Thus, it is not a completely accurate record of what actually transpired on the floor of Congress). Many libraries, including large public libraries, find that there is a strong demand for the *Congressional Record.*

House and Senate committee hearings offer a surprising wealth of material for libraries, because most hearings address controversial issues. The reports become a source containing the pros and cons about the subject, as well as information about what groups support or oppose proposed legislation. Often, the hearings contain the first detailed reporting of topics under consideration in Congress. Such hearings may have immediate general interest for library clients, and they also are important for scholars of legislative history.

Reports that accompany bills out of committee form another important information resource for libraries. These reports document recommendations concerning the proposed legislation and background on the need for it. Often these reports are central in interpreting the law after the bill becomes law. Many of the current practices regarding copyright law are the result of interpreting such reports.

Laws of the United States first appear as "slip opinions." They next appear in the chronological list *Statutes at Large,* and they finally are published in codified form in the *United States Code.* For most nonlegal libraries, the *United States Code* is the more useful publication because it provides access by subject and popular name, in addition to placing a specific law in the broad context of other laws on the same subject.

The *Congressional Directory* provides biographical information and current addresses for members of Congress, plus useful information about the executive and judicial branches of government. It is a basic reference work, and many libraries acquire it. Any library with patrons having an interest in the federal government or doing business with the federal government should have a copy. Fewer libraries collect congressional procedure manuals, but these publications do help the public and scholars better understand how the federal legislative process works and assist them in following legislation of interest.

Some collection development officers think of the special congressional publication methods and formats in terms of "all or nothing." Certainly it is possible and appropriate for many libraries to acquire all the items mentioned in this discussion, plus many others. But it is also reasonable and possible to select one or two series, such as *Reports* or *Hearings.* It also is possible to collect by subject, for example, all congressional publications about the elderly or Native Americans. In many cases, especially in smaller libraries, it may be appropriate to acquire only a few items of high local interest.

Federal publications are an important source to consider for current information at a modest price. It is not a matter of all or nothing, any more than it is a matter of acquiring all or none of the books and serials on a given topic. Learning more about federal publications and their content will pay dividends in meeting the information needs of a library's community in a timely and cost-effective manner.

The Government Printing Office (GPO) home page (http://www.access.gpo.gov/su_docs) allows searching the *Monthly Catalog* (the online version has the shorthand title *MOCAT*) for recent publications as well as which depositories selected the item. It also provides access to *Pathfinder,* which identifies government Web sites as well as providing links to other federal agency home pages.

Previously we mentioned that end-users face the prospect of losing their favorite print publication as federal agencies move into electronic dissemination of their information. Joe Morehead is one of, if not *the*, leading scholar of U.S. government publications and their distribution. He wrote an article in 1997 about the migration of federal periodicals from print to an electronic format, labeling the electronic versions "govzines."[10] His baseline was the Congressional Information Services's *U.S. Government Periodical Index* and information taken from the University of Memphis Government Documents Department's Web site, in particular its database of "migrating government publications." In all, Morehead discussed fourteen govzines. When describing *The Third Branch* he noted, "with this govzine (and others, especially *FDA Consumer*, encountered in my cybersurfing expedition), the print version turned out to be considerably more current than the electronic version, a refutation of a guiding Internet principle, the rapid access to information."[11] (Some agencies, such as the General Accounting Office [GAO], no longer automatically send out printed reports. It is now up to the user to monitor the GAO's site at http://www.gao.gov, and either download documents in Adobe Acrobat form or request print copies. This adds yet another element to acquisitions departments' workload.)

An ongoing concern about electronic resources, both government and commercial, is how permanent is permanent? Who will archive and assure continued access to electronic information as operating systems, software, and hardware change repeatedly? In classic Moreheadian prose, Joe Morehead concluded his article by noting:

> It seems that while the GPO gets a grand makeover, the using public suffers a bad hair day. To change the metaphor, the migration to the Internet and the concomitant extirpation of print-equivalent sources will falter if it proceeds with the same frenetic exigency exhibited by the thundering herds of wildebeest across the Serengeti plains.[12]

State and Local Governments

Several differences exist between U.S. states' and federal information. One difference is that there is still a very strong print orientation at the state and local level. Certainly there is a movement to have more state information available through the Web; however, it was not until 1996 that all states had a presence there, and even then not all the sites were "official." Very few states produce audiovisual materials, which means *state* publication or information refers to textual material, whether printed, mimeographed, or occasionally in microformat or some type of electronic format. A second and often overlooked difference is that states can and frequently do copyright their publications. Some shared characteristics between state and federal information are diversity of subject matter, relatively low purchase price, and increasing difficulty in identifying what is an "official" publication.

Like the federal publishing program, most state programs now produce materials mandated by law; that is, they record government activities and release a variety of statistical data and general information about the state. Many of the federal statistical publications are compilations of state data, which means the most current information, by as much as two or three years, is in the state publications. The volume of general information and how-to publications from states is low compared to federal output.

Documents of state and local government agencies have limited availability in most libraries. In the past twenty years, most states established or passed legislation to establish depository programs that roughly parallel the federal depository program. Those depository programs are a mixed blessing for technical service units.

Access to, and identification of, state publications is often difficult, and the most comprehensive source is the *Monthly Checklist of State Publications,* printed by the U.S. Government Printing Office, based on material received by the Library of Congress.[13] No one claims the publication is a complete listing, but it is all that exists, and with the addition of a subject index starting in1987, it is a useful tool for both reference and acquisitions department staffs. Some states do publish lists of their new titles, for example *California State Publications*; however, not all states do so. Two Web resources that help locate state and local information are "State and Local Government on the Net" (http://www.piperinfo.com/state/index.cfm) and Yahoo!'s "Government: State Government" (http://dir.yahoo.com/Government/U_S__Government/State_Government/).

The Council of State Governments (http://www.statenews.org) has provided states with products that assist in governing. It also publishes items such as *The Book of the States* and *State Trends* (based on fifty state surveys as well as historical data). Most of their products are available in print, on disk, and online.

Depository practices and requirements differ from state to state. The statutes of any particular state will provide the frequency and the statutory framework of the depository program. The state library can provide more detailed information about its state depository program, including a list of depositories, sales and acquisition information, and information about which materials are available from a central source and which are available only from individual agencies.

Historically, the most effective method for acquisition of state and local documents has been through direct agency contact. Like the federal government, most state agencies produce and sell publications at or near cost. Often, complimentary copies are available to libraries. One problem in acquisition of state documents has been their short press runs, which results in state documents being out of print practically before they are off the press. Although state and local agencies are usually willing to provide copies of their available publications, they rarely accept standing orders, deposit accounts, and other convenient methods of library acquisitions. Usually, acquisition is possible only on a case-by-case basis, which is time-consuming and frustrating. Frequently, the only way a library learns about a timely document is through a newspaper article or a user request.

Privately published indexes provide some guidance. LEXIS-NEXIS (owner of CIS *Statistical Reference Index*) contains state government published statistics as well as national and international, and local or otherwise narrowly focused, data with research value beyond the limited areas of coverage. It is available in print and microfiche and as a CD-ROM titled *Statistical Masterfile*® and on the Web through CIS *Statistical Universe*. The *Index to Current Urban Documents (ICUD),* published by Greenwood Publishing Group, offers both bibliographic control of state and local documents and online access to PDF versions of the documents. Given the poor bibliographic control of state and local documents, these sets, although expensive, sometimes offer the most cost-effective option for acquiring such publications.

Local Government Publications

In general, local government publications offer even fewer selection and acquisition tools and less bibliographic control than do state publications. However, some major publications of special interest, such as long-range county plans, demographic studies, or almost anything with local impact, get local publicity. Often, inexpensive or free copies are available to local libraries. The problems of acquisition roughly parallel those for state documents; that is, no agency mailing lists or standing orders and no effective acquisitions options (such as deposit accounts) are available. Furthermore, there is the need to negotiate individually with agencies to acquire reports and short-run publications. The strategic problems are almost identical to those for state documents without the advantage of the state document depository programs. In many communities, the central public library becomes an unofficial local documents depository, and it may offer support to other libraries seeking local documents.

Collecting and retaining local, city, and perhaps county documents is reasonable for a central public library and perhaps one local academic library. Collecting from more than two or three local governments becomes expensive in terms of staff time. Very few libraries attempt to collect from more than twenty local governments, unless they are buying microforms through the Greenwood Press program, in which documents listed in *ICUD* documents are available on microfiche.[14]

Bibliographic control of these publications is almost nonexistent, except for *ICUD*. *ICUD* covers cities that are over 100,000 in population and does not cover county publications. Very few cities or counties set up depository programs, and most do not have a central publications office. Tracking down reports of various departments and programs is obviously time-consuming. Adding to the problem are various short- and long-term associations formed of several local governments. Where would you go to get a copy of the 1987 survey of visitors to the Monterey Peninsula produced by AMBAG (Association of Monterey Bay Area Governments)? For that matter, how would anyone learn about such a publication? We found our example in an article about the Monterey Peninsula published in the February 1990 issue of United Airlines' magazine *Vis à Vis*. Local area documents can be high-interest items. They also will represent the biggest challenge for the acquisitions staff to identify and secure.

CANADA

Types of government documents in Canada are similar to those in the United States. Canadian Government Publishing is the official publisher of federal documents (publications.pwgsc.gc.ca/pubindex-e.html). For many years annual, quarterly, and weekly listings of federal government publications appeared in book format. However, in the 1980s and early 1990s the annual and the quarterly lists disappeared, leaving the weekly lists, which now are found both in paper and on the government Web site (dsp-psd.pwgsc.gc.ca/search_form-e.html).

Provincial governments also list their publications on their Web sites. Many governments have bookstores where their publications can be purchased or designate independent bookstores to sell their publications. Some cities, such as Toronto, have arranged for the selective deposit of municipal documents.

DOCUMENTS FROM OTHER COUNTRIES

In many countries, the government publication program equals the U.S. program in volume and complexity. The good news is that these large-scale programs generally have an agency, like the U.S. GPO, that is the primary distributor of the publications. Although dated, Cherns's *Official Publications: An Overview* does provide a good starting place for information about the twenty countries with the largest publishing programs.[15] Very few countries offer a depository program to libraries in other countries. Only the large research libraries actively collect such documents because few users need the material.

International documents, especially UN publications, however, do have a wider appeal. The major source of international publications and information is IGOs (intergovernmental organizations). An IGO may be defined as a group of three or more member countries working together on one or more long-term, common interests. Without doubt the largest IGO is the United Nations. NGOs such as the World Health Organization also issue publications and information of interest to a fairly large number of library users.

The UN has an extensive publications program, and like other government bodies is beginning to issue material in electronic formats. The UN Web site provides a broad range of information about the organization, including the *UN Publications Catalogue* (http://www.un.org/Pubs/sales.html), which includes ordering information. The site also has a listing of all UN depository libraries worldwide. For most libraries that have some UN documents, the material is part of the regular collection, circulating or reference, rather than held in a separate document area, simply because they do not acquire very many titles.

Another interesting source that few librarians are aware of is the UNESCO Collection. This collection of representative works from various countries contains more than 900 titles, most in English and French, and is available online (http://upo.unesco.org). Each year, the UNESCO director and member countries select the best titles in all genres from each country. UNESCO then underwrites translation costs and selects a commercial publisher to issue the inexpensive edition. The following provides a sense of what the collection contains:

> [U]pcoming additions to the collection will include an anthology of Ukrainian contemporary poetry in Spanish, complete short stories of Gael Cortazar in French, an anthology of contemporary short stories from South Africa in English, 'memory poems' of America in Spanish, an anthology of contemporary short stories by Turkish women in French, and new Albanian poetry in English.[16]

This UNESCO series can be useful to smaller libraries seeking to expand their collections of international authors. Many of the authors included in the series are Nobel Prize winners. The series also saves the acquisitions department a great deal of time attempting to locate such material on its own.

In addition to the UNESCO collection, UNESCO also publishes some excellent reference titles, such as *Statistical Yearbook, World Education Report, World Science Report,* and *Study Abroad*. Some other titles published by agencies related to the UN are the International Labor Organization's (ILO) *Year Book of Labour Statistics*, the UNICEF *State of the World's Children Report,* the Food and Agriculture Organization's (FACE) *State of Food and Agriculture*, and the UN's *Yearbook of the United Nations.*

The international document acquisitions situation has benefited from the existence of UNIPUB, a private distributor that collects international documents, creates catalogs, and offers the documents for sale from a central facility (http://www.bernan.com). This vendor offers a unique opportunity to build an international documents collection from a variety of agencies; UNIPUB provides all the conveniences found in the trade book field, such as standing orders, sales catalogs and subject pamphlets, deposit accounts, and a central sales office. An important fact to keep in mind is that UNIPUB also handles many intergovernmental agency publications, such as the International Atomic Energy Agency, United Nations University Press, General Agreement on Tariffs and Trade (GATT), World Bank, and the International Monetary Fund.

Like state and federal documents, international documents profit from inclusion in computerized bibliographic databases. Privately published indexes, such as CIS's *Index to International Statistics* (*IIS*), are among the tools creating some degree of bibliographic control and acquisitions assistance. As does CIS's state and federal documents program, *IIS* offers companion fiche collections.

As is the case for U.S. federal materials, libraries can elect to collect legislative, judicial, or executive materials from other national governments. Generally, for legislative material, it is all or nothing for a particular series, for example, the British parliamentary papers or France's *Journal Official*. Frequently, a library can acquire, in microformat, sets of retrospective legislative material from commercial vendors or the originating government. Like that of the U.S. executive branch, foreign executive branch material can be a challenge to collect. More often than not, it requires title-by-title selection from each agency, office, bureau, or other entity. Standing order programs are few and far between.

Although very few countries offer depository arrangements for libraries in other countries, some do allow libraries to establish a deposit account. Variations in exchange rates often cause problems about how much money is still available. One method that works, if a library wishes to buy a substantial number of publications from a country, is to have a book dealer or vendor in the country purchase the documents. This approach may result in a higher volume of acquisition than the library can handle. There is a wide variation in bibliographic control, from almost total to nonexistent.

Each type of document has its own place in a library's service program, and each poses special acquisitions challenges. Depository programs offer free documents but may involve problems resulting from depository status requirements, such as being open to the public. Or a library may not wish to assume depository responsibilities just to acquire documents. This is especially true because there is a wide variety of items available to nondepository libraries.

U.S. DEPOSITORY LIBRARY PROGRAM

The Federal Depository Library Program (FDLP) has a long history. It has been successful in getting government information to the public. At the 1998 ALA convention in Washington, D.C., the GPO representative indicated that there were 1,365 depository libraries in the United States. (Note: The number has been declining over the past ten years because many libraries that were "selective" members dropped out of the program as collection space and staffing problems grew in magnitude and electronic resources multiplied.)

There are two types of depository libraries, full and selective. A full depository agrees to accept all items available to FDLP participants; selective institutions take only a portion of the material. The selective libraries are encouraged to take at least 15 percent of the items available—the depository program does *not* include all publications issued by federal agencies and organizations. All the items in MOCAT are part of the program, so locating an entry in that product means it should be available at the closest full member library and might be available at a selective member. (To locate the nearby members electronically, access http://www.access.gpo.gov/su_docs/findlibs/index.html). The GPO provides government information products at no cost (at least at present) to members of FDLP. Member institutions are, in turn, required to provide local, no-fee access in "an impartial environment" to the public, to provide professional assistance in using the material, and to retain the materials indefinitely.

The composition of FDLP is heavily weighted toward academic libraries (50 percent), with public libraries a distant second (20 percent). The breakdown of the balance of members is 11 percent academic law libraries, 5 percent community college libraries, 5 percent state and special libraries, 5 percent federal and state court libraries, and 4 percent federal agency libraries. The academic/legal libraries dominate the program in terms of numbers. Many people view academic libraries as intimidating, so increasing the number of public libraries in the program might well increase usage by the general public.

As the federal government moves toward increasing dependence on electronic dissemination of information, some people raise questions such as

- Is the FDLP still necessary?
- Is the FDLP a remnant of the nineteenth century?
- Is the FDLP really the best way to get information to people in the twenty-first century?
- Is there a way to change the system to make it more cost effective?

An article that explores the challenges facing FDLP is Patrick Wilkerson's "Beyond the Federal Depository Library Program," in which he concluded, "The traditional FDLP is dead. . . . The new entity will be created to fill the country's need for free and open access to government information in the twenty-first century."[17] However, Prudence Adler holds the alternative view, believing that the FDLP "has stood the test of time because of the role that it has played in promoting access to government information, and in support of teaching and learning and in stimulating economic development. That role continues and, indeed, should be strengthened and reaffirmed."[18] One means of doing so may be through the U.S. "Core Documents" program currently underway, in which selected documents are made available online (http://www.access.gpo.gov/su_docs/locators/coredocs/about.html).

As previously mentioned, all too often locations of separate government documents collections are in low-use areas of the library. The primary issue is not the physical location but rather integration versus separation of government information and the general collections. In essence, intellectual access is the primary concern.

One reason that integration of government material into general collections does not occur is that few libraries have enough catalogers to catalog all the books, journals, other media, and government publications, at least in those libraries on depository programs. Most of the depository collections use the Superintendent of Documents number (SUDOC number) to organize their U.S. document collection. A 1996 survey of private academic depository libraries showed that 88 percent employed SUCDOC numbers.[19] (The survey covered 285 libraries.) A service of OCLC called GOVDOC has helped to reduce this problem:

> The service was created to enable libraries, whether they are OCLC members or not, to rapidly but accurately catalog government documents without straining the budget or staff's time. Each month GOVDOC will generate OCLC-MARC tapes or catalog cards for everything distributed through the federal depository program, e.g., posters, charts, audiovisual materials,

> and machine readable files. Libraries will then use a customized order form to select the materials they want.[20]

The service makes integrating federal documents into the general collection less of a problem, at least in terms of cataloging and classification issues.

For the majority of libraries that do not actively collect government documents, the integrated approach is the only reasonable option and is the one most libraries employ. If the library is a partial depository taking 25 percent or less of the items available and there is no full-time public service documents staff, we believe the integrated approach is best. (Note: The GPO expects partial depository libraries to take 25 percent or more of available items, but many do not do so.) Without the experienced public service documents staff, the separate collection is too often forgotten and vastly under-used for the shelf space occupied. Undoubtedly, the large separate collection with a full-time staff will be more effective if the general reference staff *remembers* to direct users to it.

As governments move toward ever-greater dependence on electronic formats for the dissemination of information, the issue of how to handle print materials is less critical. Nevertheless, at least in the near term, FDLP members will continue to receive a substantial amount of print material. Even when, or if, all government information is available only in electronic format, there will be the question of what to do with over 185 years' worth of print publications. Thus, there will still be a few challenges for depository libraries that relate to traditional formats.

One obvious way to achieve greater utilization of government publications is through the online catalog, even when there is a separate collection that uses SUDOCS or some other system to organize its holdings. S. D. Zink has made a strong case for this approach, while acknowledging the technical service concerns.[21] Perhaps OCLC's GOVDOC service will help alleviate the problems of access to the content of government documents. With more libraries having online public catalogs that allow patrons to search a variety of files using the same search methods, patrons should begin to increase their use of government documents, if they remember to or can afford to add a documents database to the system. An article by Daniel Blazek indicated that the majority of private depositories had less than 25 percent of the depository titles in their OPACs.[22]

Another aspect of the depository program is mandated retention. Adequate collection space is a chronic problem in most libraries. One method for gaining space is deselecting material from the collection. A traditional "weeding" or deselection technique is to remove the lowest-use items and either store them in less-expensive space or discard them. Government publications more often than not fall into the low-use category, yet the depository may not be as quick to remove these items as they might be to delete low-use purchased materials. All depository libraries must retain items for at least five years after receipt. Regional (full) depositories *must* retain their collections, and selective depositories must offer items identified as discards to the regional library and local partial depositories before discarding them. On the plus side, periodic reviews of the documents collection may also encourage a review of the general collection low-use items that also occupy valuable shelf space.

This discussion provides an overview of access issues in a depository environment. A thoughtful reader may wonder about the costs associated with being a depository library. A 1993 study by Robert Duggan and Ellen Dodsworth indicated that the Georgetown University library expended $217,970 in direct, support, and overhead costs on its depository program.[23] One can only wonder what the costs would be in 2002, if such a study were done again. For smaller depository programs the dollar costs would be much smaller, but we suspect that the proportions of depository costs to total operating expenses would be very similar. There is no question that there are substantial dollar and staff costs associated with depository status. For at least some selective depositories in southern California, those costs and related issues caused libraries to rethink the value of being a selective depository, especially in terms of technical service staff time and steadily shrinking collection storage space.

CANADIAN DEPOSITORY PROGRAMS

There are forty-eight full depositories for Canadian federal government documents in Canada, and one each in England, Germany, Japan, and the United States. These libraries automatically receive all publications listed for distribution in the Depository Program in the *Weekly Checklist of Canadian Publications* for that week. Canadian public libraries and educational institutions that have libraries open to the general public at least twelve hours a week and one full-time staff member can become selective depositories. These libraries may choose designated items from the *Weekly Checklist*. The National Library of Canada provides cataloging records for all items in the depository collection.

Canadian provincial governments also provide depository programs. For example, Ontario only has selective depositories. Ontario used to publish a weekly checklist but now publishes its checklist on its Web site (www.gov.on.ca/MBS/english/publications) under the heading "New Releases." Depository libraries make their selections from this list electronically.

ACQUISITIONS

Libraries acquire government documents in a variety of ways. Some assume the responsibilities of depository collections if they can. Others purchase documents to match a collection profile. Some have standing orders through official or commercial vendors; others purchase documents individually or acquire most of their documents free of charge.

Even if a library is a full depository, it will still need to acquire a substantial number of documents in the traditional book manner, if it wants to have a reasonably comprehensive collection. Documents librarians have always known that the system did not provide complete coverage. However, few were probably aware of the magnitude of the problem. A 2001 report from the U.S. General Accounting Office (*Information Management: Electronic Dissemination of Government Publications*) found that 50 percent of all the federal documents published in 1996 were not indexed, cataloged, or disseminated to the depository libraries.[24]

Of course, many documents are available free of charge from issuing agencies and congressional representatives. They are also available as gifts or exchanges from libraries that have held them for the statutory period and wish to dispose of them or from other libraries with extra nondepository copies. Another common method of acquisition is purchase through the agency's official sales program. The agency may or may not offer a standing order program. Some commercial jobbers and bookstores do deal in documents, and some booksellers, especially used or rare booksellers, may stock some documents.

One large vendor of government documents is Bernan Associates of Maryland. Bernan Associates handles federal documents and offers several standing order programs. Through UNIPUB (mentioned previously), a library may acquire UNESCO, UN, and other international organization publications. One reason for using UNIPUB rather than the UN sales office in New York is that UNIPUB handles materials that the sales office does not, such as those published by FACE and the International Atomic Energy Agency. Bernan Associates offers several standing order programs.

In terms of federal documents, only publications chosen for the sales program are available from the GPO. These are documents that the GPO has screened and evaluated for sales potential and public interest. The GPO produces these documents in quantities sufficient for sale and adds them to the sales program. The GPO operates regional bookstores as well as a sales office in Washington, D.C. through which publications in the sales program are available for purchase. The bookstores exist in several cities, including Atlanta, Denver, Houston, and Los Angeles; a complete list is available online at http://bookstore.gpo.gov/locations/index.html.

Libraries can order publications listed in the GPO's *Sales Product Catalog* (*SPC*) from any sales office. GPO deposit accounts are available to minimize purchasing problems. These accounts also apply to NTIS purchases, and NTIS accounts also work for GPO purchases. In addition, the GPO accepts major credit cards for purchases of GPO publications from Washington, D.C., or regional bookstores. Items may also be ordered online at http://www.access.gpo.gov/su_docs/sale/index.html.

The GPO sales office offers a series of subject bibliographies based on the current *SPC*, which is republished regularly, adding new publications and deleting out-of-print items. The subject bibliographies are particularly useful as acquisition tools for libraries that have particular subject interests or strengths or for libraries with limited access to the *SPC*. The bibliographies provide patrons with ordering information and an idea of the availability of documents that they might wish to acquire. The GPO sales office also creates a series of sales brochures and catalogs. These range from catalogs to fliers and are available through the GPO sales office and bookstores.

Some congressional publications, such as hearings and committee prints, and a few agency publications, may be obtained by contacting the local or Washington, D.C., offices of congressional representatives. Obviously, this is not an appropriate acquisitions technique for large quantities or standing orders, but it can be quite effective for current issues or special subject publications. It is especially effective for acquisition of information about current legislation or information covering a wide range of subjects. School and media centers should take advantage of this source of free government documents. The best method for acquiring recently out-of-print or nonsales publications is to contact the issuing agency directly. The annual *United States Government Manual* provides a list of addresses and telephone numbers for the major and minor agencies of the federal government. Individual contact can produce copies of many federal documents, often free of charge.

SUMMARY

Government information is an important element in any library's service program. It is fundamentally important for society to have the information easily available, even if people do not use it heavily. All types of libraries can acquire useful information from government agencies at a reasonable cost. The idea that private, for-profit firms would provide the variety and depth of information and keep the costs reasonable seems naive. One only has to look at the cost of scholarly serials to see how privatization might affect the cost of government information. However, securing and processing the desired material can present significant challenges for technical services units.

NOTES

1. James Madison, Letter written in 1832.

2. *U.S. Government Manual* (Washington, DC: Government Printing Office, 1999).

3. Michael White, "The Federal Register: A Link to Democratic Values," *The Record* (January 1996): 7.

4. U.S. Constitution, art.1, sec. 5.

5. Bruce Morton, "The Depository Library System: A Costly Anachronism." *Library Journal* 112 (September 15, 1987): 54.

6. Ibid., 53

7. Charles McClure, A. Bishop, and P. Doty, "Federal Information Policy Development," in *United States Government Policies: Views and Perspectives,* edited by C. McClure, P. Hernon, and H. Relyea, 54 (Norwood, NJ: Ablex, 1989).

8. U.S. Congress, Office of Technology Assessment, *Informing the Nation* (Washington, DC: Government Printing Office, 1988), 9.

9. E. J. Christian, "Helping the Public Find Information: The U.S. Government Information Locator Service," *Journal of Government Information* 21, no. 4 (1994): 307.

10. Joe Morehead, "Govzines on the Web: A Preachment," *Serials Librarian* 23, nos. 3/4 (1997): 17-30.

11. Ibid., 25.

12. Ibid., 29.

13. *Monthly Checklist of State Publications,* vol. 1- (Washington, DC: Library of Congress, 1970-).

14. *Index to Current Urban Documents* (Westport, CT: Greenwood Press). Quarterly.

15. S. J. Cherns, *Official Publications: An Overview* (Oxford: Pergamon Press, 1979).

16. www.un.org/publications.

17. Patrick Wilkerson, "Beyond the Federal Depository Library Program," *Journal of Government Information* 23, no. 3 (1996): 417.

18. Prudence Adler, "Federal Information Dissemination Policies and Practice," *Journal of Government Information* 23, no. 4 (1996): 441.

19. Daniel Blazek, "Private Academic and Public Depositories," *Journal of Government Information* 24, no. 4 (1997): 288-289.

20. "OCLC Introduces New Service," *Library Journal* 115 (Feb. 1, 1990): 14.

21. S. D. Zink, "For Collection Development Offices: An Introduction to Government Publications," *Collection Building* 6, (Fall 1984): 4-8.

21. Blazek, "Private Academic and Public Depositories," 289.

22. Robert Duggan and Ellen Dodsworth, "Costing a Depository Library," *Government Information Quarterly* 11 (1994): 268.

23. "GAO Releases Report on GPO, Studies Electronic Format, LC," *Library Hotline* (April 6, 2001): 2-3.

SUGGESTED READING

Carpenter Brian B., and Margaret Carpenter. "Zeroing In On An Elusive Target: The Search for Government Documents." *Technical Services Quarterly* 17, no. 1 (1999): 23-29.

Gnassi, Bruno. "Accessing Canadian Federal Information." *Library Collections, Acquisitions, and Technical Services* 24 (Fall 2000): 403-404.

Jobe, Margaret M. "Government Information at a Crossroads." *Library Journal* 126 (May 15, 2001): 62-66.

——. "State Publications." *Journal of Government Information* 27 (November/December 2000): 733-768.

Meister, Marcia. "Technical Reports and Nondepository Documents." *Journal of Government Information* 27 (November/December 2000): 721-731.

Moen, William E. "The Metadata Approach to Accessing Government Information." *Government Information Quarterly* 18, no. 3 (2001): 155-165.

Oppenheim, Michael R., James Church, and Lorraine Kram. "Local Publications and Resources." *Journal of Government Information* 27 (November/December 2000): 769-782.

Picton, Howard. "Easier Access to UK Government Information." *Library Association Record* 103 (April 2001): 210.

Robinson, Judith S. *Tapping the Government Grapevine: A User-Friendly Guide to U.S. Government Information.* 3rd ed. Westport, CT: Greenwood Publishing, 1998.

Silver, Barbara Ceizler. "Preferred Access Is Still Paper." *Library Journal* 125 (May 15, 2000): 54-58.

Stierholtz, K. "U. S. Government Documents in the Electronic Era: Problems and Promise." *Collection Management* 21, no.1 (1996): 41-56.

"Technical Reports and Non-depository Publications." *Journal of Government Information* (November/December issue each year).

Van Fossen, Michael G., and Paula P. Hinton. "United Nations and Other International Organizations." *Journal of Government Information* 27 (November/December 2000): 857-882.

REVIEW QUESTIONS

1. What factors make government information useful and important for libraries to collect?
2. Discuss the types of government information materials.
3. What are the major challenges in securing such materials?
4. How can libraries improve the usage of such materials?
5. Discuss the advantages and disadvantages of depository programs for libraries.

Chapter

Nonbook Materials

As noted in Chapter 3, one of the issues contributing to the "more factor" for technical services has been the steady increase in audiovisual materials going into libraries' collections. Over the past thirty years, librarians and those who fund libraries have become more and more accepting of the idea that libraries should include nonbook materials in their collections. In fact, formats other than print have an important role to play in providing the level of service the community expects and wants. Certainly some libraries have had media collections for much longer than thirty years. However, the advent of cable television, home videocassette recorders (VCRs), cassette and CD players in motor vehicles, computers, and the Internet have created an environment in which almost every library has some type of nonbook collection. Although there are some individuals, both librarians and nonlibrarians, who agree with Will Manley's views about videos in libraries, their ranks are shrinking. (Will Manley wrote an opinion piece several years ago in which he suggested that videos were the "twinkies" of library collections, expensive, draining much-needed funding from the important materials, only attracting nonreaders, and creating more potential censorship issues, and that libraries' collections were unnecessary competition for video rental operations.)[1] Libraries have come to recognize that they are in the *information* rather than just the book and magazine business.

WHY NONBOOK COLLECTIONS?

Books are useful only to persons who are literate. Depending on where in the world one is, the percentage of persons who are literate ranges from 1 percent to 100 percent. Throughout a large portion of the world, less than 50 percent of the population is literate. Even in countries with apparently high literacy rates, such as the United States and Canada, there is a difference between the reported and the actual literacy rate. In North America, many people express concern about "functional illiteracy," which describes a condition in which persons may have gone through the required educational system (twelve years of schooling) but are unable to read beyond the level reached by the third or fourth year of schooling. (In addition, many colleges and universities worry about the inability of entering students to read and write effectively. There is a growing difference in the United States between young people's ability to use and understand the spoken, as opposed to the written, word.) Because of functional illiteracy and numerous immigrants entering the United States and Canada, many communities have established literacy programs outside the formal educational system. A number of these programs operate out of, and with the support of, the public library.

For many purposes, textual material is not the most effective or most reasonable method for conveying a particular message. For teaching, research, and recreation, collections of graphic and sound materials are increasingly being considered appropriate and useful. Some librarians still see these materials as less intellectually important than print, or as "toys," fit only for purely recreational purposes, and they resist adding such formats to a collection. However, as the number of people who have used multiple formats to learn about a subject increases, so does the pressure to have all appropriate formats in a collection. With each passing year, as multimedia computer systems combine text, graphics, sound, and video clips, the distinction between books and nonbook materials becomes less clear. Information that once was available only in printed formats is now available in several forms, including books, microfiches, CD-ROMs, and online. Book publishers, especially publishers of scholarly journals are, in increasing numbers, publishing their material electronically. Many publishers expect to, and are, using CD-ROM packages to distribute reference material. Almost all software mail-order catalogs include one or two CD-ROM packages or online services of reference material. The Library of Congress is experimenting with the use of laser discs (similar to DVDs) to store the contents of brittle books.

Primary school, secondary school, and community college libraries took the lead in incorporating all formats into their service programs. In these library settings existed an instructional aspect to media and the recognition that many ideas are best expressed using a form other than the printed word. Further, the media were integrated into the library's collection. Undoubtedly one reason for this, at least in the case of schools, was the relatively small size of the organization and the need to keep things simple. Why have two units, one for books and magazines, and one for media, when one unit could handle the workload for both? Unlike four-year colleges and universities, these institutions have a long-standing tradition of using media in classrooms.

In university settings, the pattern was to establish separate units to handle media needs. Academic institutions tended to view media, essentially films, as solely classroom material; even then there were doubts about their real instructional value. Some professors believed, and some still do today, that use of media in classroom was the lazy person's way of not "doing" the teaching directly. Art, film, music, and theater departments were exceptions, but they tended to create their own departmental collections for the use of staff and majors.

Today it is not uncommon for a student to have an assignment to review several scenes from *Hamlet*, requiring both reading the text and watching how different actors and directors portray the scenes. In fact, faculty now make frequent use of media both in and out of the classroom, and often assignments require the combined use of print and nonbook items. It is less costly for the institution, as well as less time-consuming for the student, to have a single service point. What has been happening is the integration of the two services, more often than not in, or administratively part of, the library. Continued integration of all formats will be what most people will demand and expect in the future.

Public libraries were early collectors of sound recordings, and a number developed large film collections. Sound recordings circulated and over time expanded from just classical music to all forms of music and the spoken word. Motion pictures attracted groups for in-house showings, and were also available for loan to groups such as scouts, churches, and occasionally schools. Today, few libraries collect films except in a video format, and the number of public libraries with video collections is growing.

Sally Mason, although specifically addressing public libraries, summed up the situation for all types of libraries when she wrote:

> Clearly, the visual media will only become more important to library service in the future. . . . It is not enough for librarians to 'capitulate' on the issue of visual media. We must become leaders and advocates . . . helping the public to learn what is available, to sort through multiple possibilities, and offering guidance in the use of media to obtain needed information.[2]

A 1998 *Library Journal* article on media services and collections in public libraries indicated that many are acting on Sally Mason's statement.[3] Between 1993 and 1998, media collection budgets grew by 53 percent, compared to just 36 percent for books (based on the 486 public libraries included in the survey). Audiobooks are a major factor in the escalation of both demand for and circulation of media resources. Like best-selling books, audiobooks can be leased by libraries. The major sources for leasing are Landmark and Brodart's McNaughton Service (which also leases books).

DIFFERENCES BETWEEN PRINT AND MEDIA

There are many differences between print and other media resources. However, six differences in particular have an impact on technical service activities. Perhaps the most significant is that some type of equipment is necessary to use most media covered in this chapter. One goal of media services is to make the use of the equipment so simple that it is "transparent." This means that users focus their attention on the information presented rather than on operating the equipment. In the past, using the equipment was so complex that some people refused to learn how. Now most of the equipment is easy to use, as long as all one wants to do is play back the information. However, there are many "flavors" of media equipment, which often means there are technical and equipment issues that need to be addressed before placing an order for an item.

The ideal OPAC should reflect the total holdings of the library regardless of format. Thus, a subject search for "Native American basketry" would produce a listing of books, journals, slides, videotapes, oral histories, and, perhaps, in a museum setting, even some indication of holdings of actual baskets. One reason for the separation of media and print formats in catalogs of the past was the result of administrative and work patterns. Having a book catalog, a serials catalog, a government documents catalog, a microform catalog, and, perhaps, a media catalog was common not too many years ago.

Another difference between print and media acquisitions is that there is less bibliographic control or access to a number of media formats. Formats that have a wide consumer base such as video and sound recordings have relatively good access and control; others require the department to maintain labor-intensive files of producer addresses and information about the firms' policies regarding discounts and order handling.

A fourth difference is that on average media formats may be more expensive than print materials. Media producers are also less willing to accept returns, other than for defective items. This means that order process must be even more precise than that for print items, especially in the area of technical elements.

For some formats library staff need to preview the items before making a final purchase decision. Although the process is somewhat similar to the approval plan for books, it differs in that it is usually a title-by-title process, or at best, producer by producer. This takes up additional staff time.

The fifth difference, related to the technical and cost issue, is that the field tends to change rapidly, and today's "in" format is often quickly superseded by some "newer, better" format. This leaves the library with a collection of items of historic interest, but in so-called legacy technology that may be difficult to maintain, much less replace. Anyone with more than ten years of media experience can easily name a few formats that have come and gone, such as the Beta video format.[4]

Finally, for some formats, especially videos, there are copyright concerns about how the library may use the material. These "performance rights" are discussed later in this chapter.

MEDIA FORMATS

Media formats, like print formats, exist in a variety of sizes and shapes. Unlike print, most media formats require special equipment or handling to gain access to their information. Thus, a decision to add sound recordings to a collection requires additional decisions about which type of recordings to acquire: CDs, tape, sound files from the Internet, or all of the above.

This chapter discusses only the most commonly collected media formats and their implications for technical services. It devotes more space to video and sound recordings because they are the formats that have had the greatest growth and impact on technical services. Today, videotapes are part of almost all library collections, and even special libraries are building such collections.

Any list of current media formats quickly becomes dated as new technologies and new combinations of older forms appear. Just when librarians think they have identified the latest developments and have decided to invest money in the equipment and software, a new, even more exciting, and potentially valuable format is likely to appear. With this in mind, the following list provides a snapshot of media formats of interest to libraries at this writing:

- Sound recordings (single and multiple track, CDs, and audiobooks)
- CD-ROM/DVD multimedia products
- Flat pictures (photographs, illustrations, original artwork, posters, and the like)
- Maps (including globes)
- Microforms (all types)
- Mixed-media packages (kits)
- Printed music (performance and study scores)
- Slides (all types)
- Video formats

Considering the range of material, and remembering the special aspects of the media trade, it is obvious why acquisition of media formats presents a number of challenges.

Once a library decides to develop a media collection, how does the staff select and acquire appropriate items? There are four sets of factors to consider—programming, content, technical aspects, and format—with criteria related to each factor. The following section highlights major selection criteria. These factors have implications for technical services.

Selection and Acquisitions Issues

Programming Factors

Programming (that is, use of material) is important in deciding what to acquire. Many articles and books about this topic are available (see the Selected Reading section at the end of this chapter). Programming questions include the following:

- Will the medium be used in formal instructional situations, or is it only for recreational use?
- Who is the primary audience: adults, children, or all ages?
- Will the item circulate, or will it be available only for in-house use? If used in-house, will it be available to individuals or only to groups? Will group use involve a library staff member or an expert in the field to guide group discussions before or after the item's use?
- Will the library be a member of a resource sharing network? If so, will the item become part of the shared material pool?

Answers to these questions will affect the types of media purchased and the price paid for them. For example, many videos for home use are less expensive than videos for instructional use, even when both packages are the same title. Anticipated usage will determine whether the library should purchase performance rights. Although it is always possible to purchase the performance rights after acquiring the item, it is not possible to get a refund of a performance rights fee if it turns out there was no need for it. Thus, having accurate information about what the programming expectations are at the time of purchase will either save money (no unnecessary performance fees) or staff time (no paperwork associated with follow-up payments for performance rights).

Content Factors

Content is a second acquisition consideration. When reel-to-reel films were the typical format, rather than today's videos, selection was a group process rather than the sole responsibility of a selector. Today, with the prices of videos dropping and increasing numbers of titles needed for the collection, the selection process is more like book selection, that is, an individual process. The reason for the group process was, and to an extent still is, that the cost of a "mistake" in the choice was more expensive for a library, and the cost was not always monetary in character. School media centers still emphasize the group process, in part because of limited funds, but also because the possibility of someone objecting to an item's presence in the collection is higher than in other types of libraries.

The "preview process" doubles the order work. First the library secures a preview copy, which it normally returns to the supplier, then it orders a "new copy" if the decision to purchase the title is made.

Whether selection is a group or individual process, using an evaluation form is useful. Keeping the forms for several years, for titles rejected as well as those purchased, can save both the selectors' and acquisitions department's time in the long run by not repeating the preview process. (Typically the acquisitions department maintains such files.)

Technical Factors

Technical issues vary in importance from format to format, but some general considerations apply to several formats. In most instances, judging technical matters is less subjective than judging many other selection criteria. On the other hand, it will take time and guidance from experienced selectors to develop a critical sense for these factors. Most individuals entering the field of library and information work are more attuned to good literature, well-manufactured books, and the various methods of literary review and criticism than is the average person. Although our exposure to television, film, and videorecordings may be greater than to books, few of us have the background for assessing the technical aspects of these formats. This fact is evident during film and television awards ceremonies—the public interest is in the best film or program and performance categories. It is the rare individual who can name the winners in the technical areas (direction, production, special effects, cinematography, and so forth).

Technical issues are a factor for acquisitions staff both at the time of purchase—being certain to specify critical components—as well as upon receipt in order to determine that the material matches the order. There is a surprising amount of "defective" media shipped compared to print materials.

Format Factors

Format issues also drive (or should influence) the acquisition decision. Questions to consider about format follow:

- Is the format the best one for the stated purposes of the producer?
- Is the format the least expensive of those that are appropriate for the content?
- Will the carrier medium (the base material that supports the image or sound layer) stand up to the amount and type of use that library patrons would give it?
- If damage occurs, can it be repaired (locally or by the producer), or must one buy a replacement copy? Does it require maintenance, and if so, what kind?
- What are the equipment requirements to use the medium? How portable is the equipment, and how heavy? What measures are needed to secure the equipment from theft or tampering?

These factors do not have much impact on technical services. However, it is useful for the staff to know what types of equipment the library owns so as to catch obvious mistakes in a request that would require equipment the library doesn't have.

Microforms

The question often arises, Where do microformats belong—with books or with nonbook materials? The answer is, probably in both places. Most of the guides to microform materials cover microfilms and microfiches that contain previously published information. It is rare for a microformat title to contain original (new) material. One major exception to this is technical reports, which may be available only in microform.

Microforms are also a means of access to primary research material or to items that are very rare and may only be available, in their original form, in one or two libraries in the world. Thus, while many librarians and most of the public view microforms with some degree, or a great deal, of displeasure, they do serve a useful function in providing access to materials that might not otherwise be available locally. These are often only available as expensive sets.

Another reason for using microformats is to save space, especially with low-use backfiles of serials. (As discussed in Chapter 10, a backfile or back run is a set of older volumes of a current serial subscription. For example, if a library's current issues of *Newsweek* begin with volume 92, then volumes 1 through 91 are the backfile for that library's *Newsweek* collection.) When a library has long runs of low-use material, it wastes valuable shelf space by keeping the physical volumes in the library. A serial that occupies several hundred feet of shelving may be reduced to less than a foot of space when converted to a microformat. Naturally, there is a trade-off in space; the more material there is in microformat, the more equipment the library needs to meet user demand. Some serial librarians use a microformat for backfiles of popular titles that have a high incidence of mutilation or a habit of disappearing. If the library has a reader-printer (a device that allows a person to read the microform and to push a button to receive a hard copy of the page on the screen), loss and mutilation rates tend to drop.

One major drawback to using microforms to any major degree is user resistance. Many persons claim that they cannot read anything in a microformat, that it gives them headaches and causes eyestrain and other problems. Occasionally, someone will complain that reading microformats causes nausea. However, many individuals are able to use the material without such problems. Admittedly, it takes time to get used to using microforms; it is more difficult in some formats, such as reels, to locate a specific portion of text than in the traditional book format. Without proper maintenance, the image quality will be poor, and that will cause eyestrain. Equipment breaks down and malfunctions at times, causing user and staff frustration.

Because individuals dislike reading material in microform, and to meet the need to have paper copies of sections of the material, libraries have provided "reader/printers." Unfortunately, the paper copy is often little better than what appears on the reader screen. Today, digital technology can resolve the print quality issue, if the library can afford the equipment. Several reader/printer manufacturers offer a digital system that combines the microform reader with a computer and printer. The result is almost laser quality prints that are especially welcome for photographs and other graphic images. LMU library was able to secure such a system—the result of the purchase of a substantial collection of journal backfiles—to save shelf space. Users now wait to use that machine rather than the older reader/printers. These systems can handle either positive or negative films.

Two guides to in-print microformats are *Guide to Microforms in Print* (K. G. Saur) and *National Register of Microform Masters* (Library of Congress). There is also the *Online National Register of Microforms Masters,* which is the largest file of microform masters in the United States. (This source saves time and unnecessary duplication when a library is thinking about converting some material to a microformat that it holds, or in searching for out-of-print items.) Both titles try to be international in scope, include both commercial and noncommercial sources of supply (for example, libraries and historical associations), and cover more than sixteen types of microformats. (The latter information clearly shows the variations within a single format as well as why "technical" issues become significant in the ordering process.) The *National Register* includes only U.S. suppliers, but the material available is international in scope. *Microform Market Place* (Microform Review) is an international directory of micropublishing, which includes microform jobbers. A major source of reviews of microform series, both current and retrospective, is *Microform & Imaging Review* (K. G. Saur). UMI publishes two very useful catalogs—*Newspapers in Microform* (covering more than 7,000 titles) and *Serials in Microform* (covering 20,000 titles)—and offers a useful back/missing issues service for many of the serial titles. Major producers offer extensive catalogs of what they have available. It is necessary to keep a file of their catalogs, because it is even less common for micropublishers than for book publishers to contribute information to the in-print guides.

The two most common microform formats in libraries are reels and fiche. Reel formats are the older of the two and are still widely used for newspapers and serials. Reel microfilms are long strips of film on the appropriate size reel and come in several sizes: 16, 35, and 70 mm. The film can be positive (clear with black text) or negative (dark with white text). Most libraries try to confine the microfilm collection to one or two sizes (35 mm and 70 mm) and one type (positive). With any large-scale collection, however, more variety is inevitable, because the information needed by the library is only available in a particular size and type of microfilm. The choice is often either not to get the information or to accept yet another variation in format.

Microfiches are sheets of film with the images of the original document arranged in columns and rows. Fiche is typically employed with materials that are likely to have many people needing access at the same time or with multiple means of access. The COM (computer output microfiche, a common format in the recent past) catalog is an example of both these qualities. Although it is possible to reduce a large card catalog of fifteen to twenty full reels of 70 mm microfilm, it would also mean that only fifteen to twenty people could consult the material at any one time. Fiche can be a great space-saving device while providing much greater access by breaking up the file into smaller units, somewhat like drawers in the card catalog. A microfiche with *headers* legible to the unassisted eye is particularly useful. Such legible titling helps individuals to quickly locate the desired material as well as helping the staff keep the fiches in order. The most useful headers are those with numbers and that use different colors to distinguish content (for example, a COM catalog with white headers for author entries, blue for title entries, and yellow for subject entries).

Like many other media, microfiche comes in a variety of sizes as well as reduction ratios. Common sizes are 3 by 5 inches (ca. 8 x 13 cm.), 3 by 6 inches (ca. 8 x 15 cm.), and 6 by 7 inches (ca. 15 x 18 cm.); reduction ratios range from 12 to over 200. The greater the reduction ratio, the more information the producer can fit on a single fiche. An item marked *10x* means the image is 1/10 the size of the original. Currently, producers use five categories of reduction: low (up to 15x), medium (16–30x), high (31–60x), very high (61–90x), and ultra high (greater than 90x). Reduction ratios are important to note because the user must, in most cases, change lenses in the reader when using microforms at various reduction ratios. Most microform collections contain materials produced using various reduction ratios.

Libraries also try to limit the variation in fiche size and reduction ratios but, as with microfilm, a variety of types is inevitable. Lacking an accepted standard, commercial vendors select the size and ratio most convenient for them, and perhaps increase their income if they produce enough material that libraries believe they must own.

Another concern is whether the film treatment is silver halide, diazo, or vesicular. The latter two are less expensive but have relatively short shelf lives, even with good storage and handling conditions. Silver halide, though more expensive, is the option to choose when there is a choice and long-term retention is an issue. A related issue is the polarity of the film (positive or negative). A negative film produces a black image on a white background (the traditional image people expect) in hard copy. Some of the more expensive reader/printers automatically produce the traditional image, regardless of polarity, and most require the user to select the film's polarity before printing. Ordering the correct treatment is often critical, as frequently microform sets are produced on demand rather than supplied from existing stock. In such cases, there is no returning a "mistake in the order." When the wrong treatment is ordered the library accepts the mistake rather than paying for another set done with the desired treatment. Naturally this does not apply to a mistake on the part of the vendor.

Videorecordings

One of the challenges for acquisitions departments ordering media is the fact many producers are small and only sell direct; there are few jobbers of media. In some cases a producer may let one vendor distribute its titles thus making it important to know all the distributors and the producers they handle. A good resource for identifying video producers is *Leonard Maltin's Movie and Video Guide* (New York: Plume/Penguin, annual).

A number of videorecording formats exist. Mika Iisakkila's *Video Recording Formats* Web site (http://www.hut.fi/~iisakkil/videoformats.html) lists fifteen. (This site will provide more than adequate technical information about each format, at least for library purposes.)

In addition to the physical format, there is a need to understand that different countries have different video standards. This means that a video produced in Europe, intended for that market, will not play in a standard U.S. or Canadian VCR. There are three major standards and four "minor" standards around the world.

- NTSC—Canada, Korea, Japan, Taiwan, and United States
- PAL—B/G—Germany, Spain, and Western Europe

  I—Hong Kong and United Kingdom

  /K—China
- SECAM—B/G—Egypt, Iran, and Saudi Arabia

  D/K—Eastern Europe

  L—France

There are also PAL—M in Brazil, Pal—N in Argentina, and NTSC4.43 and MESECAM, used in the Middle East.

Although it is unlikely that any library will be acquiring large quantities of such videos from around the world, this list does make it clear that ordering a format that will play on library-owned equipment is important. Now that an increasing number of academic libraries are building video collections, there are frequent requests for videorecordings from other countries. Unless the library has a "universal VCR"—one that can play any standard—it is very important when attempting to secure a video from another country to determine whether the library can purchase a tape produced to play on its VCRs.

Videorecordings, in the cassette format, reduce the equipment problems that were associated with motion picture collections. More and more people own videocassette player-recorders and therefore know something about how to operate the equipment, unlike the situation with motion picture projectors.

As of 2001, some libraries were purchasing laser discs or DVDs but few had circulating collections. Of the public libraries surveyed in 1998, 11 percent had DVD or laser disc collections.[5] In time, the DVD may replace the VHS cassette in library collections. What is happening with the home video is very similar to what has taken place with sounding recordings: a constant shift from one format to another. Essentially this forces libraries to repurchase content that is already in the collection in an older format. This is not always a bad thing, but as the speed of technology accelerates, the costs can exceed the library's ability to respond.

What can a library do with videocassettes? For example, can it use a video sold for home use in a classroom? What is meant by *public performance*? Public performances are any performances the public may attend, even when there is no fee. Library programs, including story hours and senior discussion groups, as well as programs by any formal group, such as scouts, churches, and service organizations, are public performances. The issue of performance rights is important for classroom use, and this is a growing area of use. According to Lillian Gerhardt, classroom use of videos in educational institutions, elementary through graduate school, is the steadiest-growing area of video use.[6]

Many special libraries also are facing a growing demand for videos. Publications like Ellen Miller and Timothy Hallahan's dated but still valuable *Media Guide for Lawyers*[7] and Bowker's *Law Books and Serials in Print*[8] and *Legal Video Review*[9] indicate a high level of interest in one profession. The same is true of the medical field, where, among other titles, there is *Media Profiles: The Health Sciences*.[10] In addition, the visual arts, such as architecture, interior design, fashion design, and commercial art, make extensive use of video materials.

Verifying videos is becoming easier and easier. *Bowker's Complete Video Directory*,[11] *Video Source Book*,[12] *Audio Video Market Place*,[13] and *Film and Video Finder*[14] all provide long lists of available video titles. Unfortunately, no one source is comprehensive, so the staff must consult several sources when placing orders.

Access to theatrical films is reasonably easy because of the number of retail video stores and their need to have bibliographic control. Documentary film access also is fairly good, in the sense that there are a number of guides available. However, independent filmmakers come and go with great speed; many never appear in a guide, and others remain in the guides long after they are out of business. Keeping current with changes in the independent filmmakers' field could become a full-time occupation, if serious collecting is a goal.

Slides

For most people the term *photographic slides* brings to mind the traditional family collection of 35 mm slides from various vacation trips and family events. The common 35 mm slide is a part of many library collections, but it is not just a matter of collecting the garden variety paper-mounted 2-by-2-inch (ca 5-by-5-cm.) 35 mm slide. As with all the other media formats, there are several variations on a common theme. Large slide collections are likely to consist of 2-by-2-inch (ca 5-by-5-cm.), $2\frac{1}{4}$-by-$2\frac{1}{4}$-inch (ca $5\frac{3}{4}$–by-$5\frac{3}{4}$-cm.), and 3-by-4-inch (ca 8-by-10-cm.) slides, perhaps with even a few old glass lantern slides. In a sense, slides are simply filmstrips cut into individual frames and mounted for projection onto a screen. The larger the size, the better the image will project for large audiences. There are combined sound and slide packages, primarily for the educational market.

Slide mountings vary from paper to plastic to metal to glass. Each type of mounting material results in a different thickness for the final slide, which may create some projection and projector problems. Many of the projectors are capable of handling the various thicknesses but are better with one or two types of mounts (paper and plastic). Common problems include jamming, with potential damage to the slide, and the need to adjust the focus for each type of mount is common. Thus, ordering slides with the appropriate mount becomes an issue for acquisitions staff.

While the 35 mm slide is satisfactory for most general purposes, high-definition slides require a larger film format. Such slides are commonly found in special libraries, especially those supporting scientific, medical, and art museum work. Historical picture collections may include stereo slides as well as a variety of still photographs and negatives. Stereo slides and photographs may also be part of a map collection. (Stereo slides or photographs are slightly overlapping images that, with special viewers, give the illusion of three dimensions.)

Only special and academic libraries collect extensively in the slide format. Special libraries (museums, medical, technical, art and architecture) will have working slide collections. It is rare for a public library to have a slide collection, even in the standard 35 mm format, despite the number of homes that have slide projectors. Some high school and most academic libraries will have instructional collections. Anyone teaching an art appreciation course will want slides for classroom use as well as for students to view independently. A constant problem for the staff members who are responsible for the slide collection is keeping track of thousands of small square and rectangular thin pieces of film and mounting material. Another problem is loss of color when slides are exposed to light, including the projector's lamp (there is more about this in the discussion of preservation later in this chapter). Efforts to "copy" slides into a digital database, via scanning, can result in a well-preserved collection but may violate copyright.

Perhaps the greatest problem in collecting slides is the large number of sources, which may produce packages of highly variable quality. A major issue with slides is color quality and the quality of lighting and exposure. Slow exposure using a fine-grained film produces the best-quality slides, assuming the photography (focus, composition, and so forth) and film processing were performed competently. Staff must check incoming slide orders to ensure that they are at least in focus and have no developing chemical residue visible; selectors will probably also wish to check the order before the library pays for the shipment to make certain other technical requirements are met.

Transparencies

Transparencies and opaque projector materials are used primarily in education. Of all the media choices available, this form is the most group-oriented, designed to aid in the presentation of graphic material to small and medium-sized groups. Although an individual can use the material, it has no advantage over flat pictures. A library could obtain materials in this format related to adult education classes, especially in the science fields. Because this format has limited value to the individual user, public libraries seldom collect it. One of the long-published guides to educational transparencies is *Elementary School Library Collection*, 22nd edition (Brodart, 2000; also available on CD-ROM).

School media centers may collect overhead transparencies. As with the picture files, the transparency collection focuses on the teaching units of the school district and normally supplements the teachers' personal collections. Commercial sources produce quantities of transparencies geared toward supplementing major text series. Textbook publishers often offer their own series of transparencies based on or using illustrations from their books. Generally the library must order the transparencies separately because few publishers automatically provide "supplementary teaching materials" with a textbook.

Flat Pictures

Flat pictures, such as paintings, posters, postcards, photographs, and other pictorial materials are often part of a library's collection. School libraries often have a collection of pictures from magazines and other sources that teachers use to supplement their personal collections. The collection focuses on the teaching units in the particular school district. Some public libraries have a circulating collection of art reproductions, both paintings and sculptures. Museums and academic libraries often have extensive collections of posters, usually housed in special collections in the case of academic libraries. Photographic archives, museums, and academic libraries often have collections of photographs and occasionally postcards. The archive normally focuses on historic photographs.

Aside from a few UNESCO publications, there is little bibliographic control in this field. Selectors and acquisition staff must learn about producers and maintain files of catalogs to secure these materials in a timely fashion. Once in a great while there are reviews of these formats in *LJ, Booklist,* and *SLJ* that provide the producer's name, which at least provides a starting point for tracking a purchasing source.

Maps

Maps are a form of pictorial material, and most libraries have at least a small collection, in addition to atlases in the reference collection. Small collections of local area maps pose no particular problem other than having them disappear into an individual's books or brief case. Large public libraries, academic libraries, and many business and industrial libraries have extensive map collections. Maps, as graphic representations of geological, physical, and natural features, take many forms and shapes, from folded road maps to raised relief globes. Any major map collection must determine its scope and define what to collect. Most would include aerial photographs, including satellite photographs, but should they also house the remote sensing data from satellites? Are raised relief maps worth including in a collection, or are they a commercial product of no real information value? Clearly the users' needs will determine the answers to these and many other questions about the collection.

Globes and maps, although different in form and requiring different handling, usually are available from the same sources. Most libraries have always had a small collection of local maps and atlases, along with a globe or two. Increased leisure time and increased interest in outdoor recreational activities have generated a demand for maps of recreational areas for boaters, campers, and hikers.

The control of map production is very uneven. One source that helps track down map producers is MapLink (http://www.maplink.com). This is a Web site for the International Map Trade Association that provides information about more than 800 map producers around the world. (Note: This is *not* an acquisitions site but rather a location to search for maps and identify a purchasing source.) The largest producers of maps are government agencies, and the tools discussed in Chapter 12 may be of some use in identifying potential sources of such materials. Although national agency maps are reasonably well controlled, state and local agencies have little central control. Acquisitions departments need to develop and maintain their own lists, if map collecting becomes a significant activity.

An interesting development is the growing use of computer-based (CD-ROM and tape) geographic and demographic data. The Geographic Information System (GIS) opens a new and challenging area of image collecting for many libraries. (GIS is a computer-based tool for analyzing and mapping features. It combines database operations, such as statistical analysis, with unique visualization and geographic analysis capability to create maps.) It does, however, require equipment that is capable of handling the images and color graphics these products contain.

Sound Recordings: Discs and Tapes

Returning to a widely held format, sound recordings, we again encounter great diversity and incompatibility. Sound recordings were among the first nonbook formats collected by libraries. In public libraries, the recordings are usually part of the circulating collection. For educational libraries, the purpose is usually instructional, with limited use outside the library. This is the media category that most clearly reflects the long-term influence of changing technology on a library collection.

Sound tapes and CDs are the most popular formats of today for sound recordings. With increased portability of radios and tape and CD players, the popular music industry dropped the 45 rpm recording in favor of cassette tapes and, later, CDs and CD "mini-discs." The life span of each new and better recording method (except possibly the CD) is getting shorter and shorter, and most are not compatible with other forms. An old sound recording collection *could* consist of cylinders, disks (16½, 45, 33⅓, 78 rpm, and CDS), tapes (reel-to-reel with both acetate and wire recordings recorded at a variety of speeds), and cassettes (both dual track and 8-track, and recorded on tapes with different characteristics that may or may cause equipment problems). Each format needs its own equipment or older, more flexible equipment, either of which requires special skills to maintain.

For public libraries the spoken word tapes, or "audiobooks," have become almost as important as the video collection. (*Audiobook* is the best term to use, as many of the other shorthand labels people use are in fact copyrighted names—e.g., Books on Tape, Talking Book, Recorded Book, BookCassette, and Talking Tape.) Automobile and portable handheld tape players have created a market for audio books. Even reading a small paperback book on a crowded subway or bus can be difficult. Popping a tape into a small player that fits in one's jacket pocket and has a small headset allows the listener to close out the noise, to some degree, and enjoy a favorite piece of music or listen to a current best-selling book. The same is true for those commuting in cars or just out for their "power walk."

The audiobook format has substantial sales to individuals as well as libraries. In a 1996 article in *Publishers Weekly*, one of the titles on tape passed the 1 million copy mark (*The Seven Habits of Highly Effective People* by Stephen R. Covey, S&S Audio).[15] The same article listed twenty-nine titles that had surpassed the 175,000 sales mark. An interesting feature of the list was that seventeen of the titles were nonfiction. The fact that *PW* has a regular section on audiobooks is an indication of their importance to the trade.

One of the drawbacks of sound cassettes, spoken word or music, is that they have a relatively short life span, five to six years, even under favorable usage conditions. They are also small objects that have few places upon which a library can attach a security strip or device, so their loss rate (*shrinkage* in retail terms) can be rather high. Replacing lost items can be costly.

Some of the same issues about tape length and so forth apply to music recordings as well. As noted previously, libraries have had music recording collections for a great many years. Some have also collected music scores; a question for the library is, should the scores and recordings be housed together? In the case of academic institutions the music department, if it does have a separate library, would like the two together. The reality for most libraries is that, if they do combine the two, scores probably will have to move to the media department, first, because that is where the equipment is that can play back the recordings and where the staff has the training to assist the public in the use of the equipment, and second, because few libraries have the resources to buy additional playback equipment and find space for it where the scores are located (usually in the main book collection stacks). Finally, the storage needs of the formats are very different. In the 1997 edition of *A Basic Music Library*, the editors made the following statement:

> [D]ifferences reflect inherent, practical distinctions between print and recordings: printed music is typically sought by players or students of a particular instrument (bassoon) or medium (choral), while recordings tend to be thought of in relation to a stylistic category (salsa) with less concern towards details of instrumentation.[16]

This view may or may not help those libraries attempting to provide both recordings and scores for their service population, at least in terms of deciding on integrating the two formats.

The commercial music and spoken-book trade is reasonably well controlled in a bibliographic sense; certainly there is more control than for any other nonbook format.

Other Media

Printed Music

One rather surprising void in public and academic libraries is sheet music. When both recorded music and books about music are available, why is it so difficult to secure the scores? Cost is one explanation, but most other media cost more than books. Difficulty in handling (storage and checking in the parts) may be another aspect of the problem, but other media are also difficult to handle in some ways. Libraries ought to reconsider this format; music publishers' catalogs are available, and there is frequently a community need.

Most academic music departments would like the library to collect full-sized scores (also called complete, open, or performance scores) and miniature scores (pocket or study scores). Music accreditation groups expect to find scores on campus, and because of the problems in maintaining them and controlling their use, the library is the location of choice. One of the biggest factors limiting the growth of score collections, other than cost, is that scores are unbound and need special handling. Because they are and must remain unbound, pages easily get lost and damaged, usually requiring the purchase of another full score. Information about scores appears in the Music Library Association's *A Basic Music Library* guide,[17] and there are reviews in Notes, Music Review, Music and Letters, and other journals.

Models

Models have had a long history of use in education, especially in the sciences. Libraries have not been active collectors, in part because instructors frequently want to keep the models in the laboratories and classrooms for regular use. Students need access to these items for study at times when the labs and classrooms are unavailable. Perhaps computer-generated virtual reality models providing a satisfactory three-dimensional alternative, such as *A.D.A.M.*, will be more widely used in the future. For the present, libraries should consider physical models.

One factor limiting the acquisition of models is their cost. Good models are expensive, and small institutions may be able to afford only one model for classroom use. Storage of models is another limiting factor because most are bulky and vary in size, making it difficult to store them on standard library shelving.

Reviews of these materials are few and far between. *Booklist* occasionally reviews models. Three curriculum journals, *Curator*, *Instructor*, and *Curriculum Review,* also publish model reviews. Libraries usually purchase models from educational supply houses.

PREVIEWING

To some degree, the cost of the material under consideration, rather than the usual collection development factors, drives the question of whether the purchase decision is an individual or group process. Making a mistake about a twenty-minute sound, color, educational video has more serious economic consequences for the library budget than most single mistakes about a book, transparency, or sound recording. Educational videos are very expensive, especially for multiple cassette packages. Having multiple opinions about a prospective purchase helps prevent costly mistakes. In public libraries and school media centers, a nonbook selection committee is the typical mechanism employed for securing multiple points of view. In academic libraries, often a single faculty member makes the recommendation, assuming the purchase will use departmental funds, or the head of the library's media program selects titles on the basis of reviews and a knowledge of instructional needs.

Previewing as a group means the acquisitions staff must know the date or date range that will meet the scheduling needs of those doing the previewing. (This may be a rather lengthy process if the supplier cannot ship the item(s) at the desired time; that usually results in several interactions, with the acquisitions staff serving as the go-between to find an acceptable date.) The typical approach is for the acquisitions department to request the preview items. The staff must be careful to keep the preview material from becoming intermingled with purchased materials and retain the shipping material for returning the previewed items.

Keep in mind several other factors for previewing as well. A preview copy may have had some prior use; therefore, the quality may not be as high as that of a new copy. If the library can determine from the supplier how often the item went out for previewing, it is possible to gain insight into the durability of the product. In assessing this information (assuming one can get it), the librarian must remember that the preview copy's use was by individuals who know how to properly handle the material (unlike many library users).

ACQUISITIONS TOOLS

At this time, there is no comprehensive source for nonbook materials similar to *Books in Print.* This makes identifying potentially useful nonbook materials something of a challenge. The National Information Center for Educational Media (NICEM) focuses on educational materials; however, because NICEM employs a rather broad definition of education, the publications are useful to all types of libraries and its resources come the closest to being a media *BIP* for the United States. NICEM Net (http://www.nicem.com) allows searching the entire database by subject, age level, and media type. The 2001 subscription was $895 for a single user license for a year. (Online access to the database is available through *SilverPlatter* and *EBSCOHost*. There are CD-ROM, tape load, and print versions available.) The database contains almost 465,000 records in English and sixty other languages. Its primary strengths lie in the video, sound recording, and CD-ROM formats, although there are records for almost every format discussed in this chapter. The database also has a 300-page thesaurus of terms used to index it, which is a great help in formulating accurate searches.

Some of the most active nonbook discussion lists are MEDIA-L@BINGVMB.CC.BINGHAMTON.EDU, from the ALA Video Round Table videolib@library.berkeley.edu, and VIDEONEWS@library.berkeley.edu. These provide information on how to handle various media issues as well as information about sources.

Canadian sources for nonbook materials are mentioned on page 288. Additional guides are listed in the Suggested Reading section at the end of this chapter.

ORDERING MEDIA

For all practical purposes, the process of ordering materials in the formats discussed in this chapter is the same for ordering books and serials, with a few exceptions. One difference is that libraries place most of these orders directly with the producer, because there are no general audiovisual jobbers as there are for books and serials. Some book jobbers, such as Baker & Taylor and National Book Service, handle some of the most widely collected formats, for example, videos and sound tapes, but they do not handle the full range of nonbook materials. Another difference is the need to obtain preview copies.

There is a major difference between review copies of books and preview copies of other media. With books, if the purchaser likes what he or she sees, the library keeps it, pays the invoice, and perhaps orders multiple copies at the same time. With nonbook materials, for a number of reasons (risk of loss, damage, and so forth), the library requests preview copies from the supplier, views the copy, and then generally returns the item. (Some producers now send a new copy—especially for videos—and expect the library to keep the copy if it decides to buy the item. These producers generally impose a previewing fee, but deduct the charge from the purchase price. The library must request the preview copy well in advance of the preview date. Normally, a librarian writes to the producer or supplier, asking for preview copies of certain titles and listing a number of alternative dates. This becomes an issue when previewing with a group, which may cause scheduling problems. The librarian also must know when specific items will be available for previewing. A preview file thus becomes a very important aid in the selection process; it contains a listing of each title requested, the dates requested, scheduled preview dates, and the result of the preview.

Upon receiving the purchased copy, a staff member should view the item to be certain it is (1) a new print, (2) the item the library ordered, and (3) technically sound (checking for breaks, sound quality, and quality of processing). Checking for technical soundness upon receipt should be standard procedure for all nonbook items, not just for previewed items. Generally, other media are not mass produced in the same manner as are books. Many are produced on demand, that is, in response to orders. The producer has several preview copies and a master copy; when an order arrives, the producer uses the master copy to produce a new print.

One issue to decide before ordering is that of performance rights. Does the library pay an additional fee for public performance rights, or are they part of the quoted price? (This is a typical issue for videos.) There may be some justification for paying a somewhat higher price for performance rights in an educational setting, but not when the videos are for circulating home use. The classic example of the confusion between "the home market" and "the library market" was Public Broadcasting System's release of its series *The Civil War* in 1990. Initially it was available to libraries for $450; in only a few months PBS released it to the "home market" for just under $200. Another example, from 1995, was *Malcolm X: Make It Plain*—$99.95 from PBS Video (with public performance rights) and $29.95 from MPI Home Video (with home video rights).[18] Failing to obtain public performance rights and using a video in a "public performance" setting could lead to a very costly lawsuit. Knowing how the item is most likely to be used, acquiring the appropriate rights, and maintaining a record of what was purchased can be important in building media collections.

Not many jobbers handle a wide variety of media formats; most handle only one or two. Baker & Taylor handles a wide range of sound, video, and more recently DVD titles. The firm also offers a standing order service for the sound and VHS formats as well as cataloging and processing. National Book Service in Canada provides videos, CD-ROMs, puppets, posters, and banners, as well as books, library supplies, and cataloging and processing.

SUMMARY

Acquiring media is a labor intensive and time-consuming undertaking, but it is important and worthwhile for both the library and its service population. Each new format is capable of doing certain things that no other format can do, but each also has its limitations, and as a result, they supplement rather than replace each other. It is clear that there are various preferences among those seeking and enjoying information. If the library is to be responsive to the community, it must build a collection of materials that reflects that community's various interests and tastes. That in turn will mean technical services will have to be equal to the challenge.

NOTES

1. Will Manley, "Facing the Public," *Wilson Library Bulletin* 65 (June 1991): 89-90.

2. Sally Mason, "Libraries, Literacy and the Visual Media," in *Video Collection Development in Multitype Libraries,* edited by G. P. Handman, 12 (Westport, CT: Greenwood Press, 1994).

3. Norman Oder, "AV Rising: Demand, Budgets, and Circulation Are All Up," *Library Journal* 123 (November15, 1998): 30-33.

4. See Jean Weihs' series in *Technicalities* titled "Forgotten Media," in the following issues: "Part 1: Filmstrips," v. 21 #2 (Mar/Apr 2001): 1, 12-13; "Part 2: Motion on Film," v. 21, #3 (May/Jun 2001): 5-7; "Part 3: Microforms . . .," v. 21, #6 (Nov/Dec 2001): 7-9; "Part 4: Videorecordings," v. 22, #1 (Jan/Feb 2002): 1, 10-11.

5. Oder, 32.

6. Lillian Gerhardt, "Sharpening the AV Focus," *School Library Journal* 37 (April 1991): 4.

7. Ellen Miller and Timothy Hallahan, eds. *Media Guide for Lawyers* (Owings Mills, MD: National Law Publishing, 1982).

8. *Law Books and Serials in Print 1999* (New York: R. R. Bowker, 1999).

9. *Legal Video Review* (Boston: Lawrence R. Cohen Media Library, 1985-).

10. *Media Profiles: The Health Sciences* (Hoboken, NJ: Olympic Media Information, 1983-).

11. *Bowker's Complete Video Directory* (New York: R. R. Bowker, 2001).

12. *Video Source Book* (Syosset, NY: National Video Clearinghouse, 1979-).

13. *Audio Video Market Place* (New York: R. R. Bowker, 1984)

14. *Film and Video Finder,* 5th ed. (Medford, NJ: Plexus Publishing, 1997).

15. "*Seven Habits* Reaches Million-Selling Milestone for S&S," *Publishers Weekly* 243 (September 2, 1996): 43.

16. The Music Library Association, comp., *A Basic Music Library: Essential Scores and Sound Recordings*, 3rd ed. (Chicago: American Library Association, 1997), xii.

17. Ibid.

18. Randy Pitman, "The Outer Limits of Video Pricing," *Library Journal* 120 (May 15, 1995): 34.

SUGGESTED READING

General

Ach, William. "Micrographics: A Quarter-Century Perspective." *Microform & Imaging Review* 29 (Fall 2000): 118-121.

Breland, June Meadows. "Acquiring Minds Want to Know: The Acquisitions Process and Collection Development of Videos and CD-ROMs." *Library Collections, Acquisitions, and Technical Services* 24 (Summer 2000): 296-299.

Hudson, A. "Spoken Word: The Book of the Future?" *Assistant Librarian* 89 (March, 1996): 44-46.

Luchs, K. *Developing and Managing Audio Collections in Libraries: A How-to-Do-It Manual*. New York: Neal-Schuman, 1995.

Mason-Robinson, Sally. *Developing and Managing Video Collections*. New York: Neal-Schuman, 1996.

Rosenblum, Trudi. "Audiobooks: Soaring Upward." *Publishers Weekly* 248 (June 11, 2001): 38-41.

Scholtz, James C. *Video Acquisitions and Cataloging: A Handbook.* Westport, CT: Greenwood Press, 1995.

Treadway, Gary, Barbara Stein, and Lauralee Ingram. *Finding and Using Educational Videos.* New York: Neal-Schuman, 1998.

Video Collection Development in Multi-type Libraries: A Handbook. 2nd ed. Edited by G. P. Handman. Westport, CT: Greenwood Press, 2002.

West, Amy E. "DVD Basics." *DttP* 28 (Fall 2000): 7-8.

Academic

Video Collections and Multimedia in ARL Libraries: Changing Technologies. Edited by K. Brancolini. Washington, DC: Association of Research Libraries, 1997.

Public

Rankin, K. L., and M. L. Larsgaard. "Helpful hints for small library collections. (Basic information to start and maintain a map collection)." *Public Libraries* 25 (May/June 1996): 173-179.

REVIEW QUESTIONS

1. Discuss the factors that make media both essential and a challenge for libraries and technical services.
2. What are the typical media formats that libraries acquire?
3. What are the three overarching factors in selecting and acquiring media formats?
4. What are the two most typical microformats found in libraries?
5. Discuss the technical issues that must be addressed prior to ordering films, videos, and sound recordings.
6. Discuss the issue of performance rights.

Chapter 14 Fiscal Management

As is true for most individuals, libraries never seem to have enough money to do everything they would like accomplish. Ultimately, the sole purpose of a library is to provide information to the end-user and its collections are the key element in that service. Acquisitions departments play an essential role in the effective use of the funds that are available. Library fiscal management is a joint activity involving everyone who participates in the process: selectors, acquisitions staff, and senior management. Controlling expenditures and securing adequate funding are two key activities. Monies spent on materials for the collection constitute the second largest expense category for the majority of libraries and information centers. Traditionally, in U.S. and Canadian libraries, salaries represent the largest percentage of the total budget, followed by the materials ("book") budget, and finally, all other operating expenses. That order applies today, but the percentage spent on materials has decreased as salaries have risen and the overall budget has increased slowly, if at all. Although percentages vary, the order also remains the same in any type of information environment or any size collection. Most of the literature on the topic of collection budgeting reflects a large research library orientation. However, the same issues exist in other libraries. Similarly, most of the ideas and suggestions contained in such articles apply equally well to other information settings.

In the recent past there has been a constant pressure on the materials budget of most libraries. This pressure has resulted in a decline in the percentage of the total budget spent on acquiring items for the collection. The almost yearly double-digit inflation of serials prices has further skewed the traditional balance in collection fund allocations. In many libraries in the United States, serials expenditures exceed monographic purchases, even in institutions that have traditionally emphasized book collections.

Comparing the total amount of money expended on materials thirty years ago with the current funding levels, today's total is considerably higher. Unfortunately, the total expenditures do not tell the entire story. Looking at the number of items acquired for the money reveals that the increase in acquisitions is not proportional to the funding increases. Libraries are spending more and acquiring less. Since the 1970s, many libraries, along with many other organizations, have dealt with budgets that some call "steady state," others call "zero growth," and still others call "static." At best, budgeting of this type uses the previous year's inflation rate as the base for the next fiscal year's increase. An average inflation rate, like all averages, contains elements that increase at both above and below the average rate. For libraries this is a problem, because the inflation rate for information materials has been running well ahead of the overall inflation rate.

PROBLEMS IN FISCAL MANAGEMENT

Over the years, collection development staffs in the United States and Canada have faced several problems. Book and journal prices have generally increased, and continue to increase, at rates well above the U.S. average inflation rate as measured by the Consumer Price Index (CPI). As a result, most libraries have experienced some decline in acquisition rates. Serials prices increased even more rapidly than did monographic prices. To maintain serial subscriptions, libraries took monies from book funds, thus further reducing the number of monographs acquired. Eventually, libraries started canceling subscriptions. Thus, differential inflation rates and the use of national average rates as the basis for calculating budgets have contributed to declining acquisition rates for many libraries.

A second problem was, and still is, that the materials budget is vulnerable in periods of tight budgets. Expenditures on materials are somewhat discretionary in that (in theory) a library could wait to buy an item until the next fiscal year. Institutions set staff salaries on an annual basis, and staff reductions are rare during the middle of a fiscal year, unless the organization faces a major financial crisis. Salaries are the last item organizations cut when attempting to save money. Without heat, light, and water (utility bills), the organization cannot remain open, so those expenditures generally are not cut during a fiscal year. There are some operating expenses that are discretionary: pens, pencils, paper, printer cartridges, and so forth (i.e., office supplies). Professional development and travel reimbursements may be frozen in an attempt to save funds. Institutions may achieve small savings, in terms of percentage of the total budget, by cutting back in such areas. Institutions with relatively large library collections view the materials budget as one of the largest available pools of funds that could be cut in an emergency. (Even a medium-sized library, such as the Von der Ahe Library at Loyola Marymount University, has a materials budget of well over U.S. $2.3 million. This amount is large enough to make the financial officers look at it as a source of significant funds if needed.) Further, the reality is that the monograph materials budget is the only place where significant cuts are easy to make because the material is not purchased on an ongoing basis. All too often, the long-term impact of such decisions does not receive enough consideration, and the other choices appear, at least in the short run, to be even less acceptable. These issues are institutional and apply to corporate and special libraries as much as to publicly funded libraries.

During the 1970s and 1980s libraries shifted collecting emphasis from monographs to maintaining periodicals collections. Today, that shift is slowly reversing, and through careful library budget preparation and presentation, funding authorities appear to be more willing to accept differential budget increases that more closely reflect the actual expense experience. If nothing else, the problems of the past thirty years have caused collection development officers to become better planners and to develop more accurate methods for calculating budgetary needs. As a result, they have more credibility with funding authorities.

LIBRARY FUND ACCOUNTING

The vast majority of libraries and information centers are part of not-for-profit (NFP) organizations. Being not-for-profit affects how the library maintains its financial records, particularly when contrasted with for-profit organizations. For libraries that are part of a government jurisdiction, most revenues are received through an annual budget. The funding authorities review the budget requests and authorize certain levels of funding for various activities. The three most common forms of income for libraries are appropriations (monies distributed by the governing body to its agencies to carry out specific purposes), revenue generated by the library as a result of service fees and fines, and endowments and donations.

Because of the nature of the financial activities, certain accounting terms and concepts are different for NFP organizations than for for-profit organizations. However, some general accounting rules and practices do apply. One special term for NFP accounting is *fund accounting.* (Fund accounting has been defined as a set of self-balancing account groups.) Another difference is that whereas the profit-oriented bookkeeping system equation uses *assets*, *liabilities*, and *equity,* NFP accounting uses assets, liabilities, and *fund balance*. One of the equations for NFP bookkeeping is that assets must equal liabilities plus the fund balance; another is that the fund balance is the difference between assets and liabilities. Substituting "equity" for "fund balance" would make the equation apply to for-profit organizations. (A difference between these equations is that an increase in fund balance carries with it no special meaning, whereas an increase in equity is a positive signal in a for-profit organization.) Other terms, such as *debit, credit, journalizing, posting,* and *trial balance,* have the same meaning regardless of the organization's profit orientation. Balance sheets are discussed in greater detail later in this chapter.

Accounting is "the process of identifying, measuring, and communicating economic information to permit informed judgments and decisions by users of the information."[1] Several groups or individuals in the library use accounting information (the term *accounting* includes bookkeeping activities). Selectors need to know how much money they have to spend. The head librarian needs data to maintain control over the library's operation. The business office must have the information to ensure that the library handles its funds properly. It is the acquisitions department that provides this information, at least about that portion of the library's budget used for building the collections. Usually there is a support staff member who handles the accounting activities. This person needs to have training and experience in accounting and bookkeeping. Anyone interested in a career as a support staff member in acquisitions might consider taking coursework in accounting, because such work expands employment opportunities (in seeking both a position and promotions).

The bookkeeping unit usually handles all of a library's accounting work (payroll records, accounts payable/receivable, purchasing, inventory control, and some cost accounting). Frequently, this unit is part of the acquisitions department. When this is not the case, the unit must work very closely with the acquisitions department because a large percentage of the work involves both units. Consequently, everyone in acquisitions must have some basic understanding of accounting and bookkeeping, even those not directly involved in those activities.

Although library bookkeeping requires some variations from the standard practice, it is important for the library staff handling the internal books to understand standard accounting procedures. The library bookkeeper, for example, must reconcile library records with those of the business office. Because the results concern many people, it is important to understand the business office's records and what they represent.

ACCOUNTING

The term *accounting* covers several activities that many people view as separate fields:

1. *General accounting* deals with the process of recording fiscal data (includes bookkeeping).
2. *Cost accounting* determines business costs (most frequently, unit costs).
3. *Tax accounting* determines liability for taxes, especially income and Social Security taxes.
4. *Auditing* is the process of verifying the accuracy of financial records.
5. *Budgetary accounting* is the preparation of systematic forecasts of operations in fiscal terms.
6. *System building* is the development and installation of the appropriate financial records in an organization.
7. *Governmental accounting* deals with maintaining financial records for governmental units.

Library accounting takes in the first four fields and the last; the fifth and sixth fields seldom apply to library situations.

The difference between accounting and bookkeeping is that accounting emphasizes theory and bookkeeping emphasizes technique. Accounting is comprehensive in scope, whereas bookkeeping focuses on the methods by which the bookkeeper records fiscal transactions.

The Balance Sheet

One important element in accounting and bookkeeping is the balance sheet, which indicates the institution's financial condition at any given time. Although the library may not always have a balance sheet, its parent/funding body will have one, and the library's expenditures must fit into that larger fiscal picture. Thus, having some basic knowledge of the balance sheet assists the staff in understanding some of the requirements of the funding authorities. The funding authorities are also usually accountable to other agencies that frequently require audits of the "books." (There is more about audits later in this chapter.)

A balance sheet shows the amounts and nature of assets, liabilities, and proprietorship of an organization. As noted previously, the balance sheet is the statement of the basic equation of accounting: assets = liabilities + proprietorship. Assets are anything of value owned; liabilities are obligations to pay (money or other assets) or to render service to persons or organizations now or in the future; proprietorship is the difference between assets and liabilities. A library has proprietorship only when it derives a portion of its funds from endowments. (Normally there is an annual distribution of endowment income. Otherwise, the term "fund balance" may be substituted for "proprietorship.")

No uniform format exists for the balance sheet. However, two very common methods of presenting a statement of financial condition are the account form (horizontal form) and the report form (vertical form). Account forms list assets on the left-hand side of a page and liabilities and proprietorship on the right-hand side. The final totals of the columns are equal. The report form lists all assets, then all liabilities, and finally the proprietorship. A great many variations exist on these basic forms, but the important point to remember is that the assets must equal the liabilities and proprietorship.

Regardless of the format employed on a balance sheet, assets can never be greater than the total of liabilities and proprietorship (fund balance). If the assets are greater, a mistake exists in the recording or the assignment of the data. Liabilities and proprietorship can be greater than the assets, but this is an indication that the organization or individual is or may soon be in financial difficulty.

Accounts and Ledgers

Every business transaction has dual elements (a part of the "dual entry" system described later). Every financial entry in the journals and ledgers in the acquisitions department is a business transaction of some type. The dual elements arise because each transaction is an exchange of values: Something of value is given up for something else, presumably of equal value. The bookkeeper must record both elements. As these factors change, they change the value of the assets, liabilities, and proprietorship. Thus, it is important to have a recording system that will show the changes with a minimum of space, effort, and error. A poor system can create a tremendous amount of extra work.

Most automated systems provide a short, accurate method for recording transactions, separating the increases from the decreases for each amount. This means balancing assets against liabilities and proprietorship. An account records the effects of a transaction. An acquisitions department uses as many accounts as necessary to provide adequate detailed information. Usually, there is one account for each fund in the department, and once a month the bookkeeper assembles the data in these accounts into a balance sheet. The conventional method of handling accounts places additions to assets on the left side of the account and additions to liabilities and proprietorship on the right.

Two terms used in recording changes in value are *debit* (Dr.) and *credit* (Cr.). Debit refers to the left side of an account (assets). Credit refers to the right side (liabilities). Thus, a debit is an entry on the left, and a credit an entry on the right. The idea of debits tied to assets and credits to liabilities can be very confusing to beginners and to anyone not acquainted with accounting terminology. Perhaps the best way to keep the relationships in mind and to remember how the terms affect the balance is to use a chart like the following:

"Debit" indicates that	**"Credit" indicates that**
Assets increase	Assets decrease
Liabilities decrease	Liabilities increase
Proprietorship decreases	Proprietorship increases
Income decreases	Income increases
Expenses increase	Expenses decrease

A basic rule of accounting is that for every debit there must be a credit. This does not mean that the number of debit and credit entries must be equal, but rather that the debit and credit amounts must be equal.

The name for a group of accounts is the *ledger*. This is a derived record presenting in an analytical form the total effect of all transactions. Data are taken from the books in which the bookkeeper made the original entries (called journals, discussed shortly). Normally, there is only one account on a "page" of the ledger. In the past, a loose-leaf ledger was very common because it was flexible. Today's automated systems have made the paper-based ledger a thing of the past, although some acquisitions departments maintain a paper-based "shadow system" in case the computer system goes down. Accounts can be arranged and rearranged in whatever order works for the department.

Once a month the bookkeeper prepares a *trial balance*. This is a listing of ledger accounts showing debit and credit balances. The object is to determine whether the debits and credits are equal, or in "balance." A trial balance serves several purposes:

1. It provides a partial check on the accuracy of bookkeeping by proving the equality of total debits and credits.

2. It provides a way to more quickly detect errors and their sources.
3. It provides a condensed picture of each account as well as a summary of all accounts.
4. It is often the basis for preparing financial statements.

Trial balancing uses three columns. One column is for the account total, and the other two are for the account debits and credits. Bookkeepers use two techniques to show the amounts for each account on the trial balance. One technique is to list only the balance of each account; this approach reduces the initial amount of work. The other method is to list the amounts in the debit and credit columns for each account, which provides more detailed information.

The trial balance is an essential accounting tool, but it does not reveal some kinds of errors. It indicates whether debits and credits are equal, but not whether compensating errors have occurred on both sides of the account. An item may be properly posted—that is, the right amounts on the debit and credit sides—but to the wrong account. A trial balance does not reveal a mistake in classifying information in the journal. Of course, an unrecorded ledger transaction will also go undetected during a trial balance. Therefore, even if the trial balance appears to be correct, there may be a number of errors in the system. This is one of the reasons that it is necessary to have the books audited.

The Journal

As indicated, the ledger is not a complete record of transactions. For a number of reasons, it is desirable to have a preliminary record in which one records transactions in chronological order with an explanation of the nature of each entry. In an acquisitions department, sequential order numbers constitute, in part, such a primary record. The order file used to be a part of what accountants called the daybook, an informal record of the day's activity. Today, most organizations do not use a daybook but make entries directly into the electronic *journal*. The journal is the book of original entry, with transactions recorded in chronological order. Entries to the journal come from whatever records now substitute for the daybook (e.g., invoices, orders, sales slips, cash register tapes). A journal may be more than just a book with account numbers, debits, credits, and a brief explanation about the transaction. Often associated with it are files of documents, punched cards, tapes, or other media (backup material explaining the transaction). Following are the important features of the journal:

1. It is a day-to-day record of each transaction.
2. It is the point at which the debit and credit aspects of all transactions can be analyzed. This very important activity can cause a great many problems if done improperly.
3. It is the point at which a transaction becomes a series of numbers. The explanation of the transaction may not be extensive. However, it must

be adequate to direct someone from the journal entry to the proper backup file to find a full explanation.

The term used to indicate recording entries in a journal is *journalizing*. Many libraries now employ one of several computer-based spreadsheet programs to handle this task.

Journals and ledgers are the basic items in what accountants call the *double-entry* accounting system. Double-entry simply means recording each transaction both in the journal and in the ledger. The journal is the original chronological record; the ledger is a secondary analytical record. Perhaps the most important difference between the journal and the ledger is that because the journal contains the first entries, it usually carries greater weight as legal evidence.

In most libraries, the major fund is the operating fund. Other funds may be endowment and physical plant funds. The operating funds are the group of accounts used to handle the day-to-day activities of the library for a given time, usually twelve months, covering such items as salaries, materials purchases, and utility bills. Within the operating fund there may be two categories of accounts: restricted and unrestricted.

Restricted accounts require using the monies only for specific purposes. Collection development and acquisition staffs often work with such accounts (frequently referred to as *funds* in the monetary rather than the accounting meaning of the term). More often than not, these accounts are the result of donations by individuals who have expressed definite ideas about how the library may spend the money.

Some libraries have endowments that are a combination of individual and corporate or foundation gifts; an example is endowments developed under the National Endowment for the Humanities' Challenge Grant program. Sometimes gifts are for current use, and sometimes they are for an endowment. Endowments should generate income for the library indefinitely. The normal procedure for endowments is to make available some percentage of the interest earned. The balance of the interest is returned to the endowment to increase its capital base. Private libraries, and an increasing number of publicly funded libraries, have one or more endowments. Often, the donor's restrictions are narrow. When the restrictions are too narrow, it is difficult to make effective use of the available monies. Most collection development officers prefer *unrestricted* accounts (used for any appropriate item for the collection) or broad-based restricted accounts.

The purpose of the accounting system is to ensure the proper use of monies provided and to make it possible to track expenditures. That is, one must record (charge) every financial transaction to some account, and a record exists of what the transaction involved. With a properly functioning fund accounting system, it is possible to tie every item acquired to a specific account and to verify when the transaction took place. With a good accounting system, one can easily provide accurate reports about all financial aspects of collection development activities. Furthermore, it is a great planning aid. It takes time to understand accounting systems, but librarians must understand them if they wish to be effective and efficient collection development officers.

A good book to consult for accounting information is G. Stevenson Smith's *Managerial Accounting for Libraries and Other Not-for-Profit Organizations.*[2] For budgeting, two titles to consult are Richard S. Rounds's *Basic Budgeting Practices for Librarians*[3] and Alice Sizer Warner's *Budgeting: A How-to-Do-It Manual for Librarians.*[4]

ESTIMATING COSTS

Several factors influence the funding needs for collection development and thus the amount of money the acquisitions department must handle. Changes in the composition of the service community may have an important impact in either a positive or negative manner. Another factor is changes in collecting activities, such as the scope or depth desired in a subject area. These factors do not arise very often. The two cost factors that do come up year in and year out are the price of materials and inflation.

From time to time, libraries encounter problems establishing the credibility of collection building funding requirements. Although a good accounting system will assist in justifying budget requests, additional data about material expenditures is often necessary. One example of the problems caused by inflation, stable budgets, and rapidly rising prices for materials (and perhaps limited credibility) is what has happened to the expenditures and acquisition rates for U.S. academic libraries. Between 1993 and 1998, monograph prices rose just over 25 percent. For serials, the data were almost shocking: between 1986 and 1996 prices rose 169 percent. Although the total amount of money expended was higher in 1998 than in 1993, the number of monographs purchased fell by 14 percent.[5] Libraries of every type and size experienced similar problems during this time. *Library Journal* periodically publishes surveys of spending and other activities of various types of libraries. Although the surveys are issued irregularly, when they become available they provide useful national data to determine where one's library falls.

Data about price increases have been available for some time. During the 1970s, U.S. librarians made an all-out effort to create useful library price indexes that measure rates of change. A subcommittee of the American National Standards Institute, the Z39 Committee, was able to develop guidelines for price indexes.[6] By the early 1980s, it was necessary to revise the guidelines. Another group effort was that of the Library Materials Price Index Committee (Association for Library Collections & Technical Services of ALA). The committee has produced a price index for U.S. materials and some international publications. These efforts provide consistent data on price changes over a long period, which, when averaged, is as close as anyone can come to predicting future price changes.

The most recent U.S. data are in journals; historical data appear in *The Bowker Annual.* Using *The Bowker Annual* may be adequate for some purposes, but the librarian needs to be aware that the information that appears in the "current" volume is almost two years old. Preliminary data for books published during a calendar year appear in *Publishers Weekly* (often in late February or early March). Final data appear some months later (September or October). The major problem with the published indexes is that when preparing a budget request, up-to-date information may not be readily available. Vendors can sometimes provide more current data. Some vendors will provide custom pricing information, and others may provide a general set of data based on their experience, such as the Yankee Book Peddler material illustrated in Figures 14.1, page 303, and 14.2, page 304. These information sheets contain price data about books handled in the firm.

It is also possible to obtain information about serials subscriptions from a vendor. Figure 14.3, page 305, reproduced from EBSCO's *Serial Price Projections— 2001*, and Figures 14.4, page 306, 14.5, page 307, and 14.6, page 308, reproduced from EBSCO's *Serials Price Projections—1999*, illustrate the differences among types of libraries as well as the relationship between subscription prices and exchange rates.

Just as libraries prepare budget requests at different times of the year, pricing data appear at various times during the year in a variety of sources. The challenge is to find the most current data, which may determine whether the library receives requested funding.

Libraries that purchase a significant number of foreign publications need to estimate the impact of exchange rates. Volatile exchange rates affect buying power almost as much as inflation. For example, in January 1985, the pound sterling was at $1.2963 (U.S.); in January 1988 it was up to $1.7813 (U.S.); in 1992 it was $1.7653 (U.S.); by January 1994 it was down to $1.4872 (U.S.), and in March 1999 had moved up to $1.6064 (U.S.). During the same period, the Canadian dollar went from $0.6345 to $0.7693 (U.S.), then to $0.7913 (U.S.), down to $0.736 (U.S.), and then to $0.5199 (U.S.). Although it is impossible to accurately forecast the direction and amount of fluctuation in the exchange rates for the next twelve months, some effort should go into studying the previous twelve months and attempting to predict future trends. (One source for historic data is the Federal Reserve Board, at http://www.federalreserve.gov/release/G/A.) The librarian must have good data about the amounts spent in various countries during the previous year. The country of publication may be less important than the country in which the vendor is located. For example, if the library uses the vendor Harrassowitz, prices will be in deutsche marks, regardless of the country of origin of the items purchased. After collecting the data, the budgeter can use them as factors in estimating the cost of continuing the current acquisition levels from the countries from which the library normally buys.

(Text continunes on page 309.)

Annual Roundup of Publisher Title Output: 1997 vs. 1998

The next six pages are YBP's traditional examination of the publishing harvest, in statistical terms and as captured in our U.S. Approval Plan coverage. The numbers usefully mirror some of the market forces that cause output and prices to go up and down. Note, however, that variations can occasionally be the result of mergers or distribution changes. Unusually expensive titles or sets can skew the average price per title for the year.

SELECTED UNIVERSITY PRESSES

	JAN 1997 - DEC 1997		JAN 1998 - DEC 1998		
	TITLES	*AVG. LIST*	*TITLES*	*AVG. LIST*	*PRICE VARIANCE*
Alabama	44	$32.38	40	$33.75	4.23%
Alaska	6	$23.66	4	$30.46	28.74%
Arizona	26	$32.63	80	$38.82	18.97%
Arkansas	23	$34.13	26	$26.42	-22.59%
Associated Univ. Presses	120	$40.55	138	$43.15	6.41%
Bowling Green	16	$45.58	11	$45.50	-0.18%
British Columbia	40	$55.70	34	$52.11	-6.45%
Brookings Institution	102	$24.79	156	$25.27	1.94%
California	212	$43.52	220	$38.27	-12.06%
Cambridge	1,078	$64.44	996	$64.79	0.54%
Carleton	16	$18.48	16	$27.33	47.89%
Carnegie-Mellon	11	$15.50	19	$16.53	6.65%
Catholic	20	$43.65	26	$44.45	1.83%
Chicago	196	$45.05	210	$42.99	-4.57%
Colorado	36	$36.31	30	$30.41	-16.25%
Columbia	219	$55.99	192	$49.74	-11.16%
Cornell	134	$38.26	185	$39.86	4.18%
Dist. de Livres (see note #1)	38	$27.22	75	$24.45	-10.18%
Duke	105	$47.12	103	$46.47	-1.38%
Florida	67	$40.34	77	$41.76	3.52%
Fordham	39	$28.33	39	$27.34	-3.49%
Georgetown	24	$45.05	22	$52.76	17.11%
Georgia	93	$35.55	80	$31.61	-11.08%
Harvard	145	$34.88	200	$35.82	2.69%
Hawaii	106	$38.30	147	$43.24	12.90%
Hoover	25	$9.31	3	$19.28	107.09%
Idaho	10	$33.46	8	$31.21	-6.72%
Illinois	103	$34.18	90	$37.66	10.18%
Indiana	147	$32.55	144	$34.16	4.95%
Iowa	38	$25.66	29	$29.81	16.17%
Iowa State	49	$49.26	57	$51.04	3.61%
Johns Hopkins	194	$33.75	192	$36.50	8.15%
Kansas	40	$33.08	46	$34.93	5.59%
Kent State	27	$31.74	27	$38.57	21.52%
Kentucky	56	$30.83	56	$28.53	-7.46%
Louisiana State	85	$26.14	69	$26.46	1.22%
Loyola	25	$29.34	22	$21.75	-25.87%
McGill-Queens	78	$49.60	34	$48.51	-2.20%
Manchester Univ. Press	59	$57.95	63	$64.79	11.80%
Massachusetts	41	$39.01	31	$37.12	-4.84%
Medieval Institute	6	$19.83	15	$38.60	94.65%
Mercer	40	$28.42	38	$27.97	-1.58%
Michigan	171	$40.69	147	$45.38	11.53%
Michigan State	26	$31.91	18	$30.46	-4.54%

(continued on next page)

Figure 14.1. Annual roundup of publisher title output: 1997 versus 1998.

SELECTED SCHOLARLY TRADE AND PROFESSIONAL PRESSES

	JAN 1997 - DEC 1997		JAN 1998 - DEC 1998		
	TITLES	*AVG. LIST*	*TITLES*	*AVG. LIST*	*PRICE VARIANCE*
A.H.A. Press (Amer. Hosp. Assoc.)	28	$86.06	39	$97.60	13.41%
Abbeville	69	$48.66	72	$46.01	-5.45%
ABC-CLIO	67	$67.94	47	$83.29	22.59%
Abingdon Press	115	$18.92	90	$18.93	0.05%
Ablex	32	$73.64	45	$76.02	3.23%
Abrams	147	$47.87	161	$45.88	-4.16%
Academic	351	$105.23	344	$102.34	-2.75%
Addison Wesley Longman	499	$38.90	598	$42.41	9.02%
Africa World	40	$55.76	51	$63.83	14.47%
AMACOM	66	$37.40	71	$38.20	2.14%
Amer. Ceramic Society	25	$86.20	15	$103.93	20.57%
Amer. Chemical Society	103	$125.92	46	$105.22	-16.44%
Amer. Enterprise Institute (AEI Press)	19	$17.32	20	$21.25	22.69%
Amer. Institute of Aeronautics (AIAA)	17	$73.52	35	$74.13	0.83%
Amer. Institute of Architects	15	$33.32	3	$25.63	-23.08%
Amer. Library Association	26	$50.46	61	$38.66	-23.38%
Amer. Psychiatric Press	43	$38.26	42	$44.17	15.45%
Amer. Psychological Assoc.	55	$34.47	54	$40.60	17.78%
Amer. Soc. of Civil Engineers	79	$46.94	59	$68.14	45.16%
Amnesty International USA	27	$6.11	34	$6.20	1.47%
Anthroposophic Press	21	$18.66	43	$21.30	14.15%
Antique Collectors Club	139	$64.20	182	$53.07	-17.34%
Applause Theatre Book	30	$21.12	18	$15.06	-28.69%
Appleton & Lange	41	$58.98	56	$66.59	12.90%
Ariadne Press	13	$23.02	13	$25.56	11.03%
Jason Aronson	179	$33.22	124	$39.13	17.79%
Arte Publico	20	$13.95	20	$14.00	0.36%
Artech	58	$76.95	50	$79.26	3.00%
Ashgate (ex-Gower)	594	$77.57	531	$79.40	2.36%
ASM International	19	$123.32	17	$137.58	11.56%
Asme Publications	5	$186.99	66	$150.01	-19.78%
Aspen Pub.	88	$65.56	78	$61.50	-6.19%
ASQC (Amer. Soc. Quality Control)	27	$28.77	15	$31.17	8.34%
Augsburg Fortress	70	$19.75	39	$23.74	20.20%
Avon Books	49	$22.24	61	$21.69	-2.47%
Baker Book House	125	$19.33	73	$22.73	17.59%
A.A. Balkema	76	$108.82	105	$97.43	-10.47%
Ballantine/Fawcett/Del Rey	125	$17.50	258	$19.52	11.54%
Bantam Doubleday Dell	394	$21.09	409	$20.82	-1.28%
Barron's Educational	163	$12.28	148	$13.00	5.86%
John Benjamins	71	$81.22	81	$74.43	-8.36%
Berghahn Books	23	$54.10	24	$48.60	-10.17%
Bernan Associates	106	$40.82	52	$49.29	20.75%
Black Sparrow	12	$28.33	9	$27.50	-2.93%
Blackwell	227	$60.28	205	$63.69	5.66%
Blackwell Science	201	$84.56	155	$101.01	19.45%
BNA Books	22	$138.64	11	$102.27	-26.23%
Books Nippan	59	$64.77	18	$69.69	7.60%
Boydell & Brewer	113	$75.35	83	$73.91	-1.91%
Brassey's	70	$45.56	50	$30.48	-33.10%
George Braziller	15	$28.31	21	$28.37	0.21%
Brill Academic Publishers	169	$123.45	189	$112.40	-8.95%
Broadview Press	26	$18.07	6	$16.78	-7.14%
Brookes	28	$38.26	31	$37.60	-1.73%
David Brown Book Co.	43	$46.31	33	$46.37	0.13%
Butterworth-Heinemann	392	$52.78	413	$51.29	-2.82%
Camden House	27	$48.99	33	$55.96	14.23%
Carol Publishing	91	$18.71	85	$16.42	-12.24%
Carolina Academic Press	21	$42.30	41	$36.32	-14.14%
Frank Cass	71	$41.43	82	$45.26	9.24%

(continued on next page)

Figure 14.2. Selected scholarly trade and professional presses.

SERIALS PRICES 1997-2001
WITH PROJECTIONS FOR 2002

Other Library Cost History

	Average # Titles	1997 Average Cost Per Title	1998 Average Cost Per Title	Change from 1997-1998	1999 Average Cost Per Title	Change from 1998-1999	2000 Average Cost Per Title	Change from 1999-2000	2001 Average Cost Per Title	Change from 2000-2001	Change from 1997-2001
OTHER LIBRARY											
U.S. TITLES	190	$128.33	$134.92	5.14%	$143.75	6.54%	$152.84	6.32%	$161.41	5.61%	25.78%
NON-U.S. TITLES	42	$360.20	$387.55	7.59%	$424.98	9.66%	$453.85	6.79%	$483.13	6.45%	34.13%
ALL TITLES	232	$170.31	$180.66	6.08%	$194.66	7.75%	$207.33	6.51%	$219.65	5.94%	28.97%

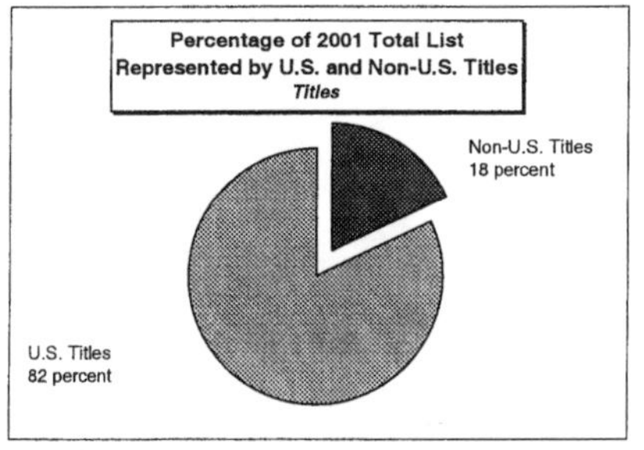

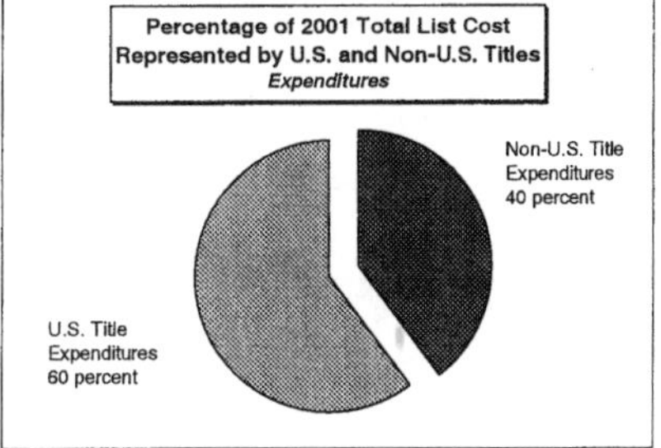

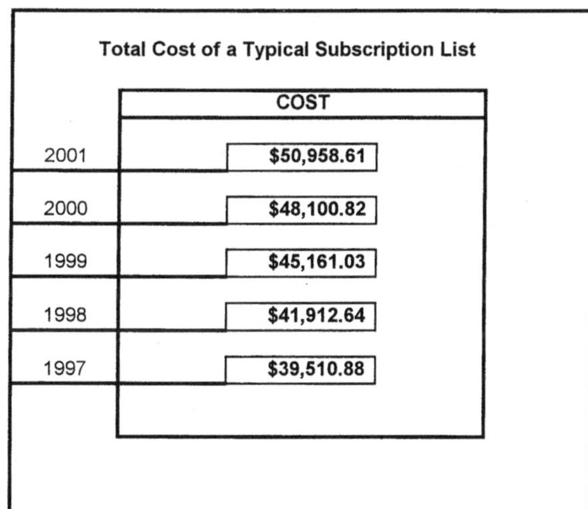

Figure 14.3. Serials prices 1997–2001 (with projections for 2002): Other library cost history. Reprinted by permission of EBSCO.

SERIALS PRICES 1995-1999
WITH PROJECTIONS FOR 2000

University Research Library Cost History

	Average # Titles	1995 Average Cost Per Title	1996 Average Cost Per Title	Change from 1995-1996	1997 Average Cost Per Title	Change from 1996-1997	1998 Average Cost Per Title	Change from 1997-1998	1999 Average Cost Per Title	Change from 1998-1999	Change from 1995-1999
UNIVERSITY RESEARCH LIBRARY											
U.S. TITLES	3,367	$195.67	$214.28	9.51%	$233.86	9.14%	$255.19	9.12%	$280.10	9.76%	43.15%
NON-U.S. TITLES	1,537	$472.78	$567.99	20.14%	$634.28	11.67%	$675.89	6.56%	$724.04	7.12%	53.15%
ALL TITLES	4,904	$282.51	$325.12	15.08%	$359.34	10.53%	$387.03	7.71%	$419.22	8.32%	48.39%

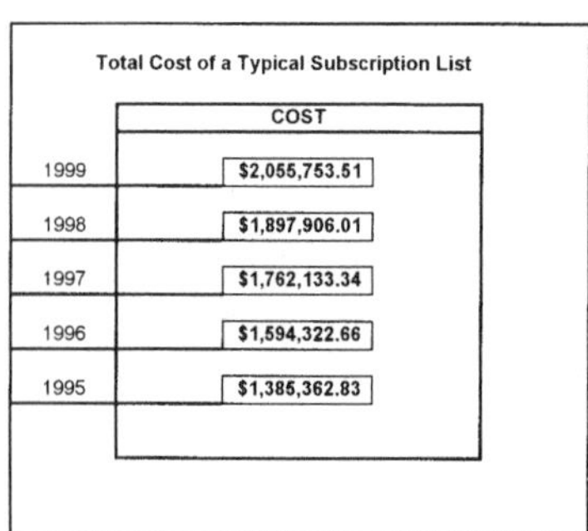

Total Cost of a Typical Subscription List

	COST
1999	$2,055,753.51
1998	$1,897,906.01
1997	$1,762,133.34
1996	$1,594,322.66
1995	$1,385,362.83

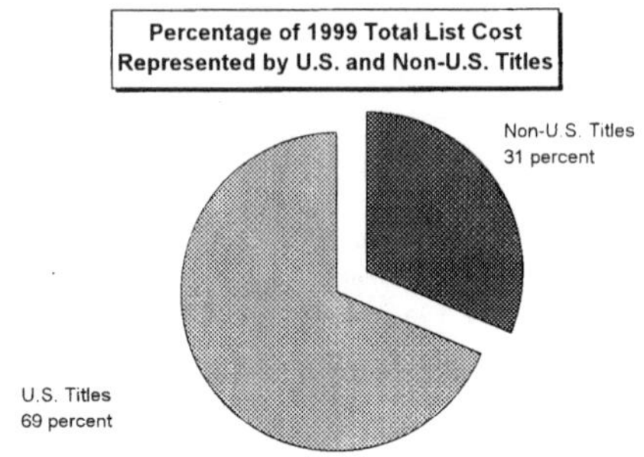

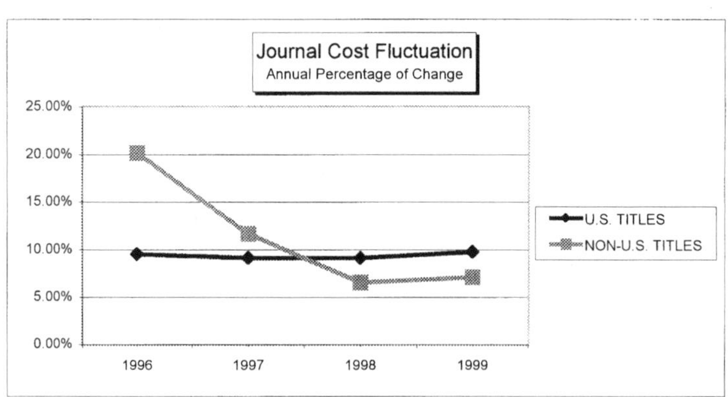

Figure 14.4. Serials prices 1995–1999 (with projections for 2000): University research library cost history. ***Source:*** **EBSCO,** ***Serials Price Projections—1999.*** Reprinted by permission of EBSCO.

SERIALS PRICES 1997-2001
WITH PROJECTIONS FOR 2002

Public Library Cost History

	Average # Titles	1997 Average Cost Per Title	1998 Average Cost Per Title	Change from 1997-1998	1999 Average Cost Per Title	Change from 1998-1999	2000 Average Cost Per Title	Change from 1999-2000	2001 Average Cost Per Title	Change from 2000-2001	Change from 1997-2001
PUBLIC LIBRARY											
U.S. TITLES	2,524	$52.76	$54.79	3.85%	$56.94	3.92%	$58.90	3.44%	$60.61	2.90%	14.88%
NON-U.S. TITLES	113	$164.46	$174.05	5.83%	$185.97	6.85%	$196.37	5.59%	$207.49	5.66%	26.16%
ALL TITLES	2,637	$57.55	$59.90	4.08%	$62.47	4.29%	$64.79	3.71%	$66.91	3.27%	16.26%

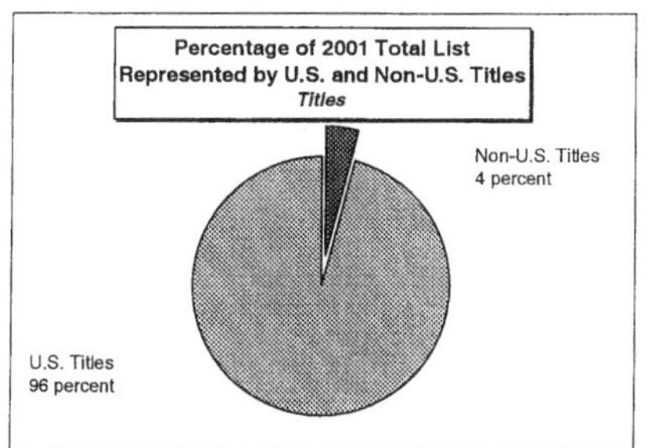

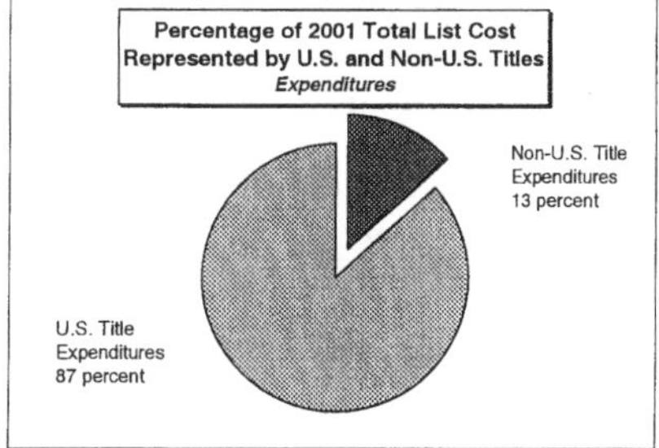

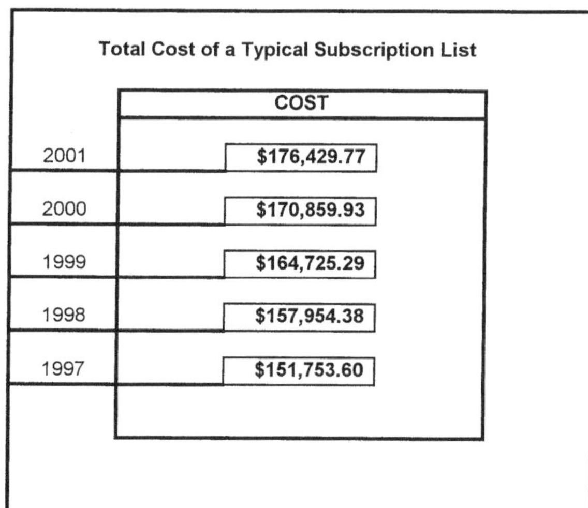

Total Cost of a Typical Subscription List

	COST
2001	$176,429.77
2000	$170,859.93
1999	$164,725.29
1998	$157,954.38
1997	$151,753.60

Figure 14.5. Serials prices 1997–2001 (with projections for 2002): Public library cost history. ***Source:*** **EBSCO,** ***Serials Price Projections—1999.*** Reprinted by permission of EBSCO.

SERIALS PRICES 1997-2001
WITH PROJECTIONS FOR 2002

Academic Research Library Cost History

	Average # Titles	1997 Average Cost Per Title	1998 Average Cost Per Title	Change from 1997-1998	1999 Average Cost Per Title	Change from 1998-1999	2000 Average Cost Per Title	Change from 1999-2000	2001 Average Cost Per Title	Change from 2000-2001	Change from 1997-2001
ACADEMIC RESEARCH LIBRARY											
U.S. TITLES	3,284	$216.80	$236.16	8.93%	$258.52	9.47%	$282.37	9.23%	$307.78	9.00%	41.96%
NON-U.S. TITLES	1,457	$600.18	$640.60	6.73%	$685.03	6.94%	$736.48	7.51%	$785.41	6.64%	30.86%
ALL TITLES	4,741	$334.62	$360.45	7.72%	$389.60	8.09%	$421.93	8.30%	$454.56	7.73%	35.84%

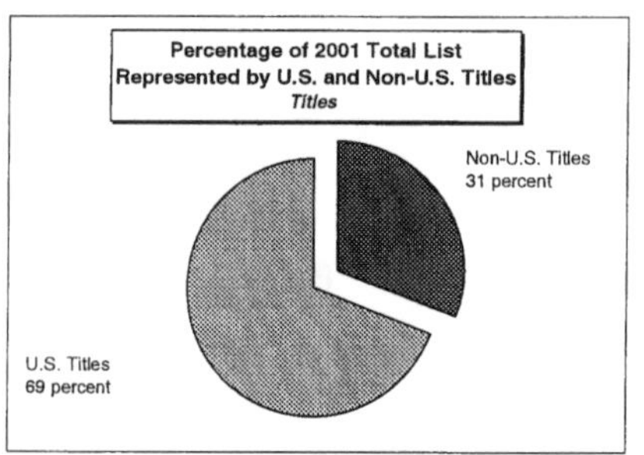

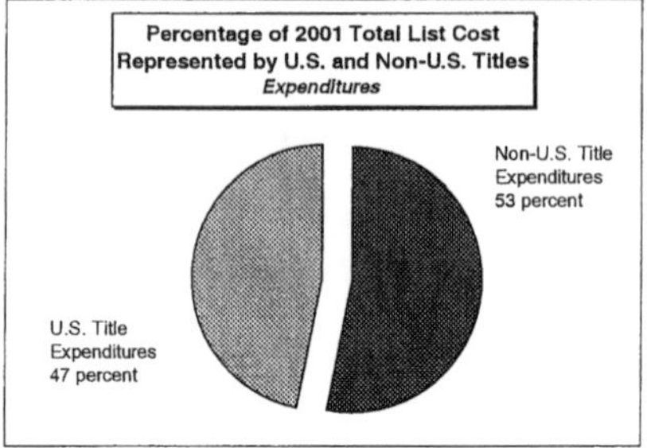

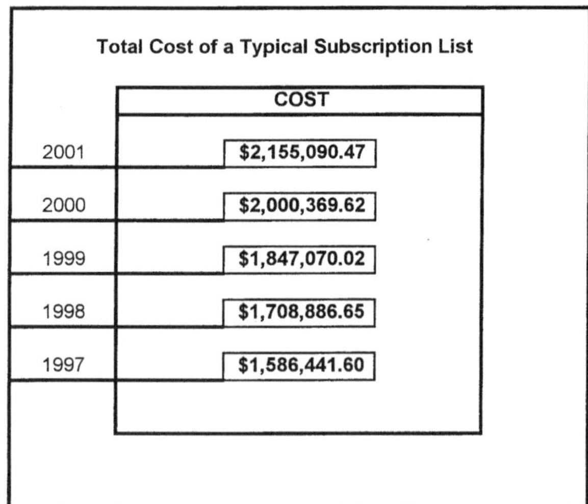

Total Cost of a Typical Subscription List

	COST
2001	$2,155,090.47
2000	$2,000,369.62
1999	$1,847,070.02
1998	$1,708,886.65
1997	$1,586,441.60

Figure 14.6. Serials prices 1997–2001 (with projections for 2002): Academic research library cost history. ***Source:*** **EBSCO,** ***Serials Price Projections—1999.*** Reprinted by permission of EBSCO.

ALLOCATION OF MONIES

As mentioned previously, collection development funds may be restricted or unrestricted. For most libraries, the unrestricted allocation represents the majority of monies available for collection development. Libraries employ internal allocation systems in an attempt to match monies available with needs and to ensure that all collecting areas have some funding for the year. These systems provide guidelines for selection personnel; the allocation sets limits on, and expectations for, purchases in subject areas or for certain types of material.

Ordinarily, the method selected reflects the library's collection development policy statement priorities. If the library employs a collecting intensity ranking system in the collection development policy, it is reasonable to expect to find those levels reflected in the amount of money allocated to the subject or format. Almost all allocation methods are complex, and matching the needs and monies available requires that the library consider several factors.

Among those factors are past practices, differential publication, unit cost and inflation rates, level of demand, and actual usage. Implementing a formal allocation system takes time and effort. Some professionals question whether it is worthwhile allocating the monies. Opponents to allocation claim it is difficult to develop a fair allocation model, and it is time-consuming to calculate the amounts needed. Certainly allocations add to the workload in the acquisitions department. Those opposed to the process also claim that, because the models are difficult to develop, libraries tend to leave the allocations in place too long and simply add in the next year's percentage increase rather than recalculating the figures annually. They suggest that selectors may not spend accounts effectively because there is too much or too little money available. Finally, they argue that it is difficult to effect transfers from one account to another during the year. Proponents claim that allocations provide better control of collection development and are a more effective way to monitor expenditures.

A good allocation process provides at least four outcomes. Its overall purpose is to match available funds with needs. Second, it provides selectors with guidelines for how they should allocate their time. That is, if someone is responsible for three selection areas with funding allocations of U.S. $15,000, $5,000, and $500, it is clear which area requires the most attention. (In some cases, it is more difficult to spend the smaller amount, because one must be careful to spend it wisely.) Third, the allocation process provides a means of assessing the selector's work at the end of the fiscal year. Finally, it provides clients with a sense of collecting priorities, assuming the allocation information is made available to them. The library can communicate the information in terms of percentages rather than specific monetary amounts if there is a concern about divulging budgetary data.

The allocation process should be collaborative, with input from all interested parties. Two things are certain, regardless of whether the library uses a formal or informal approach to gaining input: the process has political overtones, and the outcome will invariably disappoint an individual or group. This is particularly true when introducing a revised allocation when the budget is static. Those who receive more money will be happy, but those who lose funds will object to the method used to reallocate the funds. Unfortunately, sometimes the objectors are influential enough to get the allocations changed, which defeats the purpose of the process—matching funds to needs.

Which allocation method the library selects is influenced, in part, by internal library practices, institutional needs, and extra-institutional requirements (such as those of accreditation agencies). Internal factors include operational practices that determine what type of information is readily available to those making the allocation decisions (e.g., vendor's country of origin, number of approval titles versus firm orders, format and subject data, and use). How the library organizes its services—centralized or decentralized—also plays a role. Other internal factors affecting which allocation method is used include past practices for allocation and the purpose of allocation (that is, its use as a control mechanism or guideline). Institutional factors, in addition to the obvious importance of the institution's mission and goals, include the type of budget control it employs, its organization, and its overall financial condition. Extra-institutional factors are the political atmosphere (for example, the degree of accountability), economic conditions, social expectations and values regarding information services (such as equal access and literacy levels), and outside agencies (such as accreditation bodies or governmental bodies) that monitor or control the institution.

Allocation methods can be regarded as a continuum, with "impulse" at one end of the scale and "formula" at the opposite end. Between the two extremes are several more-or-less structured methods. *Impulse allocation* can take the form of allowing active selectors to have greatest access to available funds or, a slightly more structured approach, to allocate on the basis of perceptions of need. History of past use and some annual percentage increase for each allocation area is a little more formal; it is probably one of the most widely employed methods. Allocating on the basis of organizational structure (main and branch units) is still more formal (often, the allocation is a fixed percentage of the fund pool). Adding to that method some incremental funding based on workload (such as circulation data), moves the library closer to the formula end of the continuum. Also, somewhere in the middle of the continuum is the *format allocation method* (such as funds for books, serials, audiovisual, electronic resources, and reference).

Format allocation may be as simple as dividing monies between monographic and serials purchase accounts. Even this "easy" division is no longer so, because serials prices increase more rapidly than other materials costs. How long can a library shift monies from other accounts to maintain serials subscription levels without damaging the overall collection? Libraries employ several category allocation methods in addition to format, such as subject, unit, users, language, and formula. Most libraries that use a format allocation system use several approaches. Many small libraries, including most school media centers, employ the format system, with monographs, serials, and audiovisuals being the broad groupings. The library divides these funds by subject (e.g., language arts), grade level (e.g., fifth grade), or user group (e.g., professional reading). Occasionally, libraries divide monograph funds into current, retrospective, and replacement categories. In libraries using approval, blanket order, or standing order plans, it is normal practice to set aside monies for each program before making any other allocations. A typical approach would be to set aside an amount equal to the prior year's expenditure for the category with an additional amount to cover expected inflation. The reason for setting aside these funds first is that they are ongoing commitments.

Formula allocations have become more and more popular, especially in large libraries. Librarians have proposed many formulas over the years, but no one formula has become standard. Each library must decide which, if any, formula is most appropriate for its special circumstances. A 1992 article by Ian R. Young described a project that compared seven formulas.[7] His results showed that, although each formula employed one or more unique variables, there were no statistically significant differences among the formula results in terms of a single institution. He concluded that there was a high degree of similarity among the seven formulas, at least when applied to his institutional setting. Based on our experience with formulas and the selection of a formula in several institutional settings, we would say that the library selects the formula that contains all the variables necessary to satisfy all the interested parties. (Thus, political rather than practical considerations dictate which formula is used.) Only quantifiable factors (for example, average price, number of titles published, and use data) can be used as variables in formulas. This does not mean that subjective judgments do not play a role, but the allocation process as a whole depends on weightings, circulation data, production figures, inflation and exchange rates, number of users, and so forth. Figure 14.7, page 312, shows the allocation formula used at Loyola Marymount University.

Department	Use	Average Cost	Cost-Use	Percent Cost-Use	Formula Allocation	Present Allocation
Psychology (BF& RC 435-577)	4,674	$38.55	180,183	0.07	$12,693	$15,033
Sociology (HM-HX)	5,311	$37.85	201,021	0.09	$14,542	$6,587
Theater Arts (PN 1600-1989, 2000-3310)	144	$38.14	5,492	0.003	$361	$3,908
Theology (BL-BX)	6,503	$36.49	237,294	0.1	$16,258	$7,409
Totals			2,491,436		$181,342	$180,652

Use = Circulated use of the class numbers associated with the department
Average Cost = Price listed as average for that discipline in *Choice*
Cost-Use = Average cost times use for the field
Percent Cost-Use = Percentage of library's total cost-use for the field
Formula Allocation = Amount of new allocation under new formula
Present Allocation = Amount of current allocation

Figure 14.7. Loyola Marymount University library book allocation formula.

ALA's *Guide to Budget Allocation for Information Resources* indicates that there are six broad allocation methods: historical, zero-based (no consideration of past practice), formulas, ranking (a variation of formulas), percentages, and other modeling techniques.[8] The book also outlines some of the variations in formulas by type of library. For example, academic libraries might consider enrollment by major or degrees granted in a field (the factors used in Figure 14.7 are widely used in academic libraries as well). Public libraries might factor in differences in the service communities being served, the ratio of copies per title of bestsellers to general titles, or the demand (in terms of use or requests) in popular subject fields. Special libraries employ factors such as delivery time expectations of the clients, service chargebacks, and the number of clients or departments served. Many school media centers use factors like changes in curriculum, number and ability of students by grade level, and loss and aging rates of various subject areas in the collection. The guide provides a starting point for librarians thinking about changing the allocation process their library uses.

Allocating funds is an involved process, and changing an existing method is almost more difficult than establishing a new one. Often, past practices and political issues keep the process from moving forward or evolving. Serials inflation rates (almost 700 percent since 1970)[9] make it difficult to provide both ongoing subscriptions and a reasonable level of monographic acquisitions. How much to allocate to current materials and how much to allocate to retrospective purchases is related, in part, to the serials inflation rate. If the decision is to maintain serials at the expense of monographs, in time there will be a significant need for retrospective buying funds to fill in gaps in the monograph collection. Subject variations also complicate the picture. Science materials are very expensive; social science materials are substantially less costly but are more numerous. Electronic access, rather than local ownership, also clouds the picture, especially because electronic access often involves cost at the individual level, something with which allocation models have not dealt. Although allocation work frequently involves political issues and occasionally involves upset individuals, in the long run careful attention to this process will produce a better collection for the organization the library or information center serves.

ENCUMBERING

One aspect of accounting and financial management in collection development that differs from typical accounting practice is the process of *encumbering*. This is a process that allows the library to set aside monies to pay for ordered items. When the library waits 60, 90, or 120 days or more for orders, there is some chance that the monies available will be over- or underspent if there is no system that allows for setting aside monies.

The following chart shows how the process works. Day 1, the first day of the fiscal year, shows the library with an annual allocation of $1,000 for a particular subject area. On day 2, the library orders an item with a list price of $24.95. Although there may be shipping and handling charges, there probably will be a discount. Because none of the costs and credits are known at the time, the list price is the amount a staff member records as encumbered. The unexpended column reflects the $24.95 deduction, although there is still nothing in the expended category. Sixty-two days later, the item and invoice arrive; the invoice reflects a 15 percent discount ($3.74) and no shipping or handling charges. The bookkeeper records the actual cost ($21.21) under expended and adds the $3.74 to the unexpended amount. The amount encumbered now is zero.

	Unexpended	**Encumbered**	**Expended**
Day 1	$1000.00	0	0
Day 2	$975.05	$24.95	0
Day 62	$978.79	0	$21.21

This system is much more complex than the example suggests, because libraries place and receive multiple orders every day. With each transaction the amounts in each column change. *The library seldom knows the precise balance, except on the first and last day of the fiscal year.* If the funding body takes back all unexpended funds at the end of the fiscal year (a *cash accounting* system), the acquisitions department staff must know the fund(s) balances as they enter the final quarter of the year.

Several factors make it difficult to learn the exact status of the funds, even with the use of encumbrance. One factor is delivery of orders. Vendors may assure customers they will deliver before the end of the fiscal year but fail to do so. Such a failure can result in the encumbered money being lost. With a cash system, the acquisitions department staff must make some choices at the end of the fiscal year if there are funds in the encumbered category. The main issue is determining if the items still on order are important enough to leave on order. An affirmative answer has substantial implications for collection development. Using the foregoing example and assuming that day 62 comes after the start of a new fiscal year and the new allocation is $1,000, on day 1 of the new fiscal year, the amount unexpended would be $975.05 ($1,000 minus $24.95), encumbered $24.95, and expended zero. In essence, there is a reduction in the amount available for new orders and the library lost $24.95 from the prior year's allocation. (One of the authors once took over as head of a library on June 25, and the system financial officer reported the entire acquisitions allocation was encumbered for the coming fiscal year, starting July 1. To have some funds for collection development over the next twelve months, it was necessary to cancel 347 orders.)

With an *accrual system*, the unexpended funds carry forward into the next fiscal year. Under such a system, using the previous example, the day 1 figures would be unexpended $1,000, encumbered $24.95, and expended zero.

The staff also needs to consider how reliable the vendor or producer is, because occasionally an item never arrives. How long should the library wait? The answer varies from producer to producer and country to country. If the library buys substantial amounts from developing countries, waiting several years is not unreasonable. Because print runs tend to be very close to the number of copies on order, the chance of never being able to acquire the item makes it dangerous to cancel the order.

There is a problem in leaving funds encumbered for long periods under either system, especially when there is rapid inflation or exchange rates are unfavorable. The latter are two reasons why a firm but reasonable date for automatic cancellation of unfilled orders is important.

Other factors making it difficult to know the precise fund balance during the year are pricing and discounts. Prices are subject to change without notice on most library materials, particularly online resources, which means the price may be higher on delivery than when ordered. In addition, discounts are unpredictable. Because of the uncertainty, most libraries encumber the list price without freight charges and hope the amount will be adequate. Exchange rates enter the picture for international acquisitions, and the question of when the rate is set can be a critical issue. Certainly, the rate is not firm on the date the order is placed, but is it firm at the time of shipment, the date of the invoice, the date the library receives the invoice and items, the date the financial office makes out the check, or even the date the supplier deposits the check? With international orders, libraries can expect four months or more to elapse between order placement and delivery. In periods of rapid rate changes, even a four-month difference can significantly affect the amount of money available for purchases.

Shipping and handling rates and taxes on items purchased have taken a toll on the funds available for additions to the collection. Vendors that in the past paid for shipping now pass the cost to customers. The U.S. Postal Service has reduced the difference between postal rates such as the book rate and parcel post. In 1970 it cost $0.18 to ship a two-pound book; in 1980 it cost $0.80; by 1999 the rate was $1.54; and in 2001 the cost had risen to $2.38. All the charges on the invoice (postage, handling, shipping, taxes, and so forth) must come from the acquisitions budget. As these charges mount there is less money for the items the library wishes to add.

The point of all this work is to allow the library to spend all the materials funds available in a timely manner without over-ordering. Remember that an order is a legal contract between the library and the supplier. Certainly most suppliers who have a long-standing relationship with libraries will be understanding of an occasional over-commitment of funds, but they have a legal right to full, prompt payment for all orders placed. One way they allow libraries to handle the problem is to ship the order on time but hold the invoice until the start of the next fiscal year.

A major problem confronting a bookkeeper in the acquisitions department is the number of accounts with allocations. In some libraries the number may run over 200. Restricted funds are especially problematic because the library may charge only certain types of materials to the account. Although the bookkeeper's job may be to assign charges to the various accounts, that person also must know approximately how much money remains as free balance, as encumbered, and as expended. As the number of accounts goes up, so does the bookkeeper's workload.

Moving monies back and forth, especially in a manual system, can lead to errors, so the acquisitions department must have a good bookkeeper. Automated accounting systems speed the recording activities and provide greater accuracy, as long as the data entry is correct. Despite the uncertainty that exists with the encumbering system, it is still better than just having unexpended and expended categories, because without it libraries would not know how much of the unexpended balance was actually needed for items on order.

VOUCHERS

Most government accounting methods, as well as the methods used by many other organizations, use a voucher system. A *voucher* provides verification of all transactions involving expenditures and the authorization for such expenditures. It is a form that both summarizes an expenditure and carries the signatures vouching for its correctness. Further, it authorizes entry into the books and approves payment of charges. Libraries do not usually issue vouchers as such; however, the requirement of the librarian's signature on a purchase order and on invoices is part of the voucher system of the library's parent organization (city, university, school district, etc.).

Without a voucher, there will be no payment to a vendor. Because it takes a long time for a voucher to make its way through a government system, a substantial amount of correspondence can occur between the library and vendors regarding when payments will take place. This points to the need for accurate bookkeeping records and close cooperation between bookkeepers in the acquisitions department and the authority that finally issues the checks or voucher.

ORDER-INVOICE CONTROL

Bookkeepers control the vendor's compliance with the library's governing agency's fiscal regulations. For example, they are responsible for checking invoices for all the required information: signature, purchase order number, and so forth. If materials on prepaid orders do not arrive by the end of the fiscal year, the library will request a refund because the vendor may want to hold the money as a credit for future orders. As noted previously, it is very convenient to work with the same vendors, because they become familiar with the library's payment procedures. Whenever a library selects a new vendor, it is wise to send a letter explaining the library's financial arrangements and why it may take up to three months to receive payment.

RECONCILIATION OF ACCOUNTS

One difficulty facing the bookkeeper is knowing precisely where the library stands financially. The encumbered amount is always greater than the amount expended because some items have discounts but not others. Some monthly routines are part of the acquisitions department's bookkeeper workload. One such routine is the reconciliation of the library's estimate of its financial status with that of the supervising agency. The agency that oversees the library's expenditure of funds will probably not list all of the separate funds used internally. Rather, it will show only the amount allocated to the library to buy library materials. How the library distributes the funds is of no interest to the agency, as long as the monies actually go for materials for the collection. The agency's concern is with two categories of funds: expended and unexpended.

The library has a third category of money—encumbered funds—that makes reconciliation complex. As part of the reconciliation process, the bookkeeper normally creates for each library fund a statement of its unencumbered balance, encumbered funds, and liquidated or expended funds. When selectors have budgetary responsibility, monthly statements go to them so that they know their available balance. The final reconciliation sheet shows when the library received an invoice, the dealer's invoice number, the amount of money encumbered, and the discount received. The next column (net) indicates the amount actually paid to the dealer for the items; the tax column represents the tax on the monies expended.

The library must also carry out a number of end-of-fiscal-year routines, and the bookkeeper is responsible for many of these. The library is normally on a one-year fiscal cycle. That is, any money remaining in the library's budget at the end of the fiscal year reverts to the funding agency. Libraries seldom are able to carry forward into the next fiscal year any unexpended funds, including encumbered funds. Therefore, several months prior to the end of the fiscal year, it is necessary to check with the vendors on outstanding orders to determine whether they will make delivery in time. If they are unable to deliver the items before the fiscal year ends, libraries usually cancel the order and place one for something that is available or will be before the end of the fiscal year. This year-end exercise can create bookkeeping nightmares.

The bookkeeper's primary duty is to ensure that the library neither overspends nor underspends its budget. Because discounts and cancellations are unknown quantities up until the moment the invoice arrives, it becomes a challenge for the bookkeeper to estimate accurately just where the library stands financially.

AUDITS

Are audits really necessary in libraries? Must we remember how, where, when, and on what we spent every cent? Unfortunately, the answer is *yes*. Not many years ago, Herbert Synder and Julia Hersberger published an article outlining embezzlement in public libraries.[10]

One aspect of having the power to manage and expend substantial amounts of money is fiscal accountability. The amount of money does not need to be "substantial" if it involves public or private funds. The process of establishing how well libraries have handled the monies they are responsible for expending is the audit.

A legalistic definition of an *audit* is the process of "accumulation and evaluation of evidence about quantifiable information of an economic entity to determine and report on the degree of correspondence between the information and established criteria."[11] More simply put, it is the process of ensuring that the financial records are accurate and that the information is presented correctly using accepted accounting practices, and of making recommendations for improvements in how the process is carried out. The basic questions and required records relate to whether the purchase was made with proper authorization, was received, and was paid for in an appropriate manner, and whether the item is still available. (If the item is not still available, there should be appropriate records regarding its disposal.) With automated acquisitions systems, undergoing an audit is less time-consuming than in the past, where the "paper trail" was in fact a number of different paper records that had to be gathered up and compared. At least now the system can pull up the necessary information fairly quickly.

SUMMARY

Fiscal management, bookkeeping, and a basic understanding of how trained bookkeepers do their work is important in an acquisitions department. Libraries are accountable for the funds they receive, and the acquisitions department is one of the few places in the library where library funds are committed to obligations. For most libraries, the two largest segments of the budget are staff salaries and monies to build the collections. Only the collection development funds are actually available for the staff to expend. It is important for the staff to understand and use proper bookkeeping methods. This chapter covers only the most elementary aspects of accounting. The concepts and terms that technical services staff should be familiar with include *account, balance sheet, credit, daybook, debit, double-entry accounting, journalizing, ledger, posting, encumbering, trail balance, voucher, account reconciliation,* and *audit*. Additional resources are listed in the Suggested Reading section.

Libraries must constantly be aware of changes in prices and in invoicing practices to gain the maximum number of additions to the collection. Watch for changes, and demand explanations of freight and handling charges, inappropriate dual-pricing systems, or other costs that may place additional strain on the budget. By understanding basic accounting principles and using the reports and records generated by the library's accounting system, the library will be better able to monitor the use of available monies and use them effectively to meet the needs of the public.

NOTES

1. *A Statement of Basic Accounting Theory* (Evanston, IL: American Accounting Association), 1.

2. G. Stevenson Smith, *Managerial Accounting for Libraries and Other Not-for-Profit Organizations* (Chicago: American Library Association, 1991).

3. Richard S. Rounds, *Basic Budgeting Practices for Librarians,* 2nd ed. (Chicago: American Library Association, 1994).

4. Alice Sizer Warner, *Budgeting: A How-to-Do-It Manual for Librarians* (New York: Neal-Schuman, 1998).

5. Barbara Hoffert, "Book Report, Part 2: What Academic Libraries Buy and How Much They Spend," *Library Journal* 123 (September 1, 1998): 144-146.

6. American National Standards Institute, Z39 Committee, *Criteria for Price Indexes for Library Materials* (New York: American National Standards Institute, 1974). ANSI Z39.20.

7. Ian R. Young, "A Quantitative Comparison of Acquisitions Budget Allocation Formulas Using a Single Institutional Setting," *Library Acquisitions* 16, no. 3 (1992): 229-242.

8. *Guide to Budget Allocation for Information Resources,* edited by Edward Shreeves. Collection Management and Development Guides, no. 4 (Chicago: American Library Association, 1991).

9. Frank W. Goudy, "Academic Libraries and the Six Percent Solution: A Twenty-Year Financial Overview," *Journal of Academic Librarianship* 19 (September 1993): 212-215.

10. Herbert Synder and Julia Hersberger, "Public Libraries and Embezzlement: An Examination of Internal Control and Financial Misconduct," *Library Quarterly* 67 (January 1997): 1-23.

11. Alvin Arens and James Loebbecke, *Auditing: An Integrated Approach* (Englewood Cliffs, NJ: Prentice-Hall, 1994), 1.

SUGGESTED READING

General

Barnes, Marilyn, "Managing with Technology: Automating Budgeting from Acquisitions." *Bottom Line* 10, no. 2 (1997): 65-73.

Granskog, K. "Basic Acquisitions Accounting and Business Practice." In *Understanding the Business of Library Acquisitions,* 2nd ed., edited by K. Schmidt, 285-320. Chicago: American Library Association, 1999.

Johnson, P. "Preparing Materials Budget Requests." *Technicalities* 15 (April 1995): 6-10.

Lynden, F. C. "Impact of Foreign Exchange on Library Materials Budgets." *Bottom Line* 9, no. 3 (1996): 14-19.

Martin, M. S., and M. T. Wolf. *Budgeting for Information Access: Managing the Resource Budget for Absolute Success.* Chicago: American Library Association, 1998.

Snyder, Herbert W. "It's Accrual World, Or How Did My Variance Report Get to Be So High If I Didn't Do Anything Different?" *Library Administration & Management* 15 (Spring 2001): 107-109.

———. "Staying Balanced: How Financial Statements Are Constructed." *Library Administration & Management* 15 (Winter 2001): 44-46.

Academic

Allen, F. R. "Materials Budgets in the Electronic Age: A Survey of Academic Libraries." *College & Research Libraries* 57 (March 1996): 133-143.

Public

Smith, M. I. "Using Statistics to Increase Public Library Budgets," *Bottom Line* 9, no. 3 (1996): 4-13.

Waznis, Betty, "Materials Budget Allocation Methods at San Diego County Library." *Acquisitions Librarian* 20 (1998): 25-32.

School

Miller, M. L., and M. L. Schontz. "Small Change: Expenditures for Resources in School Library Media Centers," *School Library Journal* (October 1997): 28-37. (These authors compile biennial reviews of acquisitions and price data.)

REVIEW QUESTIONS

1. Who in the library needs accounting information, and why?
2. What is the primary function of the bookkeeping section in a library, and what are the three basic steps in bookkeeping?
3. Define *accounts, balance sheet, credit, debit, journal, ledger, posting, trial balance,* and *voucher.*
4. Define *encumber.*
5. Name one monthly routine the bookkeeper performs, and one yearly routine.
6. Describe the purpose of an audit.

Part Three

Cataloging and Processing

Chapter 15 Cataloging—Overview

WHY CATALOG?

Materials acquired for library collections must be made accessible to the library users who want them. Most libraries—even small ones—have many thousands of materials stored on-site and available electronically. As a result, materials cannot be offered at random to library users. Materials should be organized well so users can find what they want quickly and easily. Providing access involves organizing large numbers of materials for efficient retrieval of any single item from the entire collection.

Access generally takes two forms: direct and indirect. Direct access to materials themselves is accomplished through organized shelving or, in the electronic world, through the ability to call up the full text of a document. Direct access sometimes is called "physical access," because large numbers of library materials are objects such as books, videos, and so forth, stored physically on the shelves. Library users can go directly to the shelves and find what they want or browse until they do. Indirect access, also known as "bibliographic access," "intellectual access," "catalog access," and, for electronic materials, "metadata," means supplying information about the materials that will lead library users to the materials themselves. Indirect access is accomplished by putting detailed information about the materials into a searchable catalog. Cataloging and classifying the materials are the ways libraries create both types of access.

WHAT'S THE PROCESS?

When a title is acquired, technical services staff members keep records that document the transactions involved, such as placing the order for the title, receiving it, and paying for it. Cataloging operations often start with basic information from the acquisition record, and edit or add to it to produce a complete and accurate record for the material called a bibliographic record—"bib" record for short. The record includes a full description of the material and its contents. Part of the cataloging process is the assignment of a call number or shelf address where the material will be placed if it is stored in-house, or directions about how to obtain it if it is not.

Bib records for each title acquired are put in the public catalog in several places library users expect to find them, such as under their titles, the name(s) of the author(s), and words indicating their subjects. Searchable titles, names, and subject words are called headings, and there are rules that govern their selection and formatting. These are not the only possible headings. Some catalogs can also be searched by call numbers, languages, publication dates, academic course numbers, and other elements.

Bib records are the basis for inventory control files kept by a library for every item in its stock of materials (shelflist) and for borrowing by library users (circulation). The catalog is thus simultaneously a valuable tool for library users and reference librarians to use in finding materials they need and an internal tool for keeping track of library collections.

BIBLIOGRAPHIC CONTROL

Cataloging is said to produce "bibliographic control." What does this mean? The first word refers to materials ("bibliographic" = relating to books, articles, or other documents) and the second to managing or manipulating them ("control"). "Bibliographic" once referred solely to books, but now it includes materials in all physical formats. The goal of bibliographic control in libraries is to identify the materials the library has to offer its users and, at the same time, to manage them all effectively.

How can bibliographic control be created? The method librarians have employed for hundreds of years is to create records that substitute a small amount of data for each item collected and file them all in a catalog, which can be searched in place of physically examining the entire collection when something is wanted. If cataloging is the process by which libraries produce the records that enable them to provide bibliographic control, the catalog is the principal end product of the process. Catalogs are the tools by which libraries identify the materials they have and through which they manage them.

FUNCTIONS OF THE CATALOG

In 1876, Charles A. Cutter first published his cataloging manual, *Rules for a Dictionary Catalog*. It opened with what has become the most famous expression of the functions of the catalog, which he called its "objects":

1. To enable a person to find a book when one of the following is known:
    a) The author
    b) The title
    c) The subject

2. To show what the library has
   d) By a given author
   e) On a given subject
   f) In a given kind of literature

3. To assist in the choice of a book
   g) As to the edition (bibliographically)
   h) As to its character (literary or topical).[1]

Despite much research and analysis on cataloging questions since Cutter's time, his objects remain the definitive statement of what catalogs try to accomplish. They sound simple, but Cutter's ideals have never been completely realized. They remain goals toward which to strive, achievable only in theory.

The reason Cutter's objects are difficult to attain is that the kinds of actions that promote finding a book when the author, title, or subject is known (the identity function) work against gathering related works to show all works by a given author, in a given subject, or to assist readers in choosing editions or genres (the managing function), and vice versa. For example, if one copy of Beethoven's last symphony uses the title *Symphony No. 9* and gives the author's name as Luigi van Beethoven (as he occasionally signed himself) and another uses the title *Ninth Symphony* and gives the author's name as Ludwig van Beethoven, the following problems occur:

1. If the titles and names are used exactly as they appear on each of these scores, which promotes their identification, neither the names nor the titles will file together.
2. If one form of the title and one form of the author's name is used for both scores, which promotes proper management by keeping them together, the headings will file neatly in the same place, but the library will have used names and titles that cannot be found on the scores themselves.

Current cataloging and classification rules come close to achieving both functions of the catalog. The rules for headings for names, subjects, and series titles generally permit only one form to be used for all occurrences of each name, subject, or series title. This brings together all the works by an author, all works on a particular topic, and all works in the same series, regardless of discrepancies in vocabulary, spelling, language, and other elements that could occur. A special heading called a "uniform title" is created for works whose own titles vary on different versions (as in the example of the Beethoven symphony). The uniform title brings together all editions and versions of a title, just as the one permissible name, subject, and series title headings do.

The rules that pertain to the identification of a work, called its "bibliographic description" often require the exact transcription of data from the item being cataloged. This ensures that someone who uses the catalog record can match it exactly against a copy of the item it represents, confirming that the correct item has been found. Transcribed edition information in the bibliographic description enables different editions of the same work to be identified and organized. Title headings consisting of the exact title transcribed in the bibliographic description also facilitate successful matching. When one work is published in many versions with varying titles, two title headings are made for each version cataloged: one that exactly matches the title on the item, thus helping searchers match it, and one authorized uniform title that gathers the variations in one place in the catalog.

Even in their imperfect state, catalogs accomplish a great deal. They are the keys to library collections everywhere, helping people find the materials they seek in any particular place. Catalogs help form links between collections, enabling one institution to share information and materials with others. Shelf arrangements also contribute to access by physically collocating materials that are related, first by subject, then within a subject by author, and finally by the titles of an author's work in a subject.

Good cataloging and classification accomplish two things. First, they do a better job as reference tools for the materials in the library, and second, they enable a library to link more effectively with partners in local, county, regional, state, provincial, and national bibliographic networks. The ultimate goal of these networks is to make any title owned anywhere available to a person with a need for that material.

CATALOG DISPLAYS

Catalog information may be presented to library users in one of the following types of displays: books, cards, microfilms or microfiches, or computer screens. Typically, catalogs in twenty-first-century libraries are electronic databases mounted on computers, called online public access catalogs (OPACs) or public access catalogs (PACs). Card catalogs still are used in libraries that have not computerized their operations, but each type has enjoyed a measure of popularity at different times. Book catalogs were popular until the latter part of the nineteenth century, after which they were replaced by card catalogs. Microfilm and microfiche catalogs were an interim stage between card catalogs and computerized catalogs in the 1970s and early 1980s, but few examples remain in use. Some libraries choose to create microform or printed book catalogs from their electronic databases, but most prefer to utilize the database directly via computers.

Examples of book catalogs—either printed or handwritten listings—going back to medieval times have been documented by library historians and were generally used by libraries in North America until the end of the nineteenth century.[2] Printed books were easy to duplicate and distribute; they could even be sold, if a market existed. However, book catalogs could not be kept up to date except by printing new editions, which was a great deal of work and could be very costly. When cards were introduced, their ability to facilitate updating the catalog easily by interfiling new cards among the existing ones far outweighed the disadvantages that it was hard to duplicate and distribute them to multiple locations. For that reason, libraries rapidly adopted cards.

By the middle of the twentieth century, "card catalog" was a synonym for "library catalog." Early on, when new materials were added to the collection, cards for them could be prepared and filed immediately or within days; similarly, when older materials were withdrawn from the collection or deemed lost by library users, the cards could be removed quickly. Later, significant time lags between receipt of new materials and cataloging began to occur, the result of an "information explosion" in which greatly increased acquisitions outstripped catalogers' ability to deal with them. Materials awaiting cataloging accumulated, and in some institutions it could take months—even years—before cards for a new title were prepared and filed. Similarly, removing the cards for older titles that were withdrawn or lost could take as long or longer, depending on the priority attached to this type of catalog maintenance. Huge backlogs of uncataloged materials and unfiled cards were a constant reminder that card catalogs were failing to function well, especially in large libraries.

Research into using computers for library catalogs began to produce results in the 1960s. Bibliographic data vary a great deal, and individual records contain large numbers of elements and characters. These were obstacles that had to be addressed by developers. Software had to accommodate numerous elements and subelements in catalog records—everything from complex call numbers, bibliographic descriptions, and multiple headings, to publishers' numbers and order numbers assigned by the Library of Congress to the card sets it sold. Hardware had to have enough storage space for the data, indexes, and retrieval software. Fortunately, within a few years computer capacity expanded, costs dropped, and programming became ever more sophisticated. Newer, better, smaller computers continued to be built in the 1970s and 1980s, while costs continued to drop and search software to improve. By the middle of the 1980s, computerized catalogs mounted on minicomputers and microcomputers began replacing the old card files, which had ruled for nearly a century.

The way catalog records look in book catalogs, on cards, or on computer screens may be very much alike or differ considerably. Whereas books and cards benefited from minimizing the size of each record as well as the total number of records in the catalog,[3] computerized catalogs currently offer far greater capacities for both longer records and more of them, filing, matching, and retrieving records automatically. Early OPAC screens imitated the look of data on cards, one interface even enclosing the data in an outline of a card, complete with a hole at the bottom (used in card catalogs for a rod that kept the cards anchored in their trays). Newer OPACs are experimenting with entirely different displays, some adding prefixes that identify each element in a line-by-line listing, and offering brief records at first and fuller records on request, and so forth. A selection of OPAC screen styles is shown in Figures 15.1, 15.2, and 15.3, pages 330–32.

Catalog records for an individual library's public catalog can be prepared within the library technical services unit in a cataloging department or purchased from external sources. Both types of catalog preparation have long traditions, although until the advent of computers, the final steps of incorporating records from external sources into local catalog files generally involved several operations for which each individual library was responsible.

```
BAQ-6940         Entered: 05/28/1999       Modified: 08/23/2001
Type: a Bib l: m Enc l:   Desc: a Ctry: enk Lang: eng Mod:   Srce:
 Ill:       Audience:   Form:   Cont: b    Gvt:    Cnf: 0 Fst: 0 Ind: 1
 Fic: 0 Bio:    Dat tp: s Dates: 1999      Control:

   005;     ;a 19980709094858.4 $
   010;     ;a     98035617  $
   020;     ;a 0415169097 $
   020;     ;a 0415169100 (PB) $
   035;   00;i LCMARC/AWT-9124/BISWAS $
   039;     ;f //ht $
   040;     ;a DLC $c DLC $d CaOTU $
   043;     ;a n-us--- $
   050;   00;a HQ1064.U5 $b G35 1999 $
   082;   00;a 305.26 $2 21 $
   090;    8;a HQ 1064 .U5G35 1999 $b SCAR $
   090;    8;a HQ 1064 .U5G35 1999 $b ERIN $
   090;    8;a HQ 1064 .U5G35 1999 $b NEWC $
   090;   08;a HQ 1064 .U5G35 1999 $b ROBA $c 1 $
   100;   1 ;a Gannon, Linda. $
   245;   10;a Women and aging : $b transcending the myth / $c Linda R.
               Gannon. $
   260;     ;a London ; $a New York : $b Routledge, $c 1999. $
   300;     ;a xii, 228 p. $
   440;    0;a Women and psychology $
   504;     ;a Includes bibliographical references and indexes. $
   650;    0;a Aged women $z United States $x Psychology. $
   650;    0;a Aged women $z United States $x Physiology. $
   650;    0;a Sexism $z United States. $
   650;    0;a Ageism $z United States. $
---------------------------- End of Record ------------------------
```

Figure 15.1. Sample screen for DRA record.

In the twenty-first century, purchased catalog records may be further edited by the staff of the library, or simply used as purchased in the library OPAC. Thus, in-house library cataloging operations are divided into two subunits: (1) original cataloging, which creates catalog records for items "from scratch"; and (2) copy cataloging (also called "derived" cataloging), which takes purchased bibliographic data from outside sources and processes it for the local catalog. Some small libraries have no cataloging department at all, using whatever data is purchased without further processing.

Much of the information covered in Part Three describes the steps of original cataloging. By understanding how catalog records are created, librarians are empowered to do more than prepare new records, though it does that. They should also be able to do a better job of selecting external sources for local cataloging and ensuring that the local catalog provides searchers with good bibliographic service, even if they do not prepare the records themselves.

```
+LD     Recor  n     Type   a     Bibli  m
        Type   _     Encod  _     Descr  a
        Linke  _
001     AEP-3544
005     19990806171833
008     Date   980629        Type s       Date 1999
        Date   ____  Place  nyu   Illus  ____
        Targe  g     Form   _     Natur  b___
        Gover  _     Confe  0     Fests  0
        Index  1     Undef  _     Liter  0
        Biogr  _     Langu  eng   Modif  _
        Catal  _
010 _ _ $a    98035617
020 _ _ $a 0415169100 (PB) : $c $31.99
020 _ _ $a 0415169097
040 _ _ $a DLC $c DLC
043 _ _ $a n-us---
050 0 0 $a HQ1064.U5 $b G35 1999
082 0 0 $a 305.26 $2 21
090 1 _ $a 305.26 GAN
100 1 _ $a Gannon, Linda.
245 1 0 $a Women and aging : $b transcending the myths / $c Linda Gannon.
260 _ _ $a New York : $b Routledge, $c 1999.
300 _ _ $a xii, 228 p.
440 _ 0 $a Women and psychology
504 _ _ $a Includes bibliographical references and index.
650 _ 0 $a Aged women $z United States $x Psychology.
650 _ 0 $a Aged women $z United States $x Physiology.
650 _ 0 $a Sexism $z United States.
650 _ 0 $a Ageism $z United States.
901 _ _ $b AEP-3544
```

Figure 15.2. Sample screen for DYNIX record.

A Word About the Examples. Examples in Part Three have been provided to illustrate different standard cataloging styles. In their descriptive cataloging, some examples contain smaller amounts of information, called "Level 1" description, whereas others have more information, called "Level 2" description. These "Levels" are defined in Chapter 16 and identified in the examples. To match the varying choices of subject tools used in practice, wherever first level description is done, the subject headings are taken from *Sears List of Subject Headings* and classification numbers from the abridged Dewey Decimal Classification; wherever second level description is done, subject headings come from *Library of Congress Subject Headings* and classification numbers from the unabridged Dewey Decimal Classification. Examples that use Library of Congress

Classification numbers have been added to several figures. Individual libraries should make their own decisions about the level of subject analysis specificity needed for their collections as well as which subject tools to adopt.

```
001      39464706
003      OCoLC
005      20010130145803.0
008      980629s1999     enka      b     001 0 eng  cam4a
010      98035617
019      41465250
020      0415169097
020      0415169100 (PB)
040      DLC|cDLC|dIAC|dC#P|dNLM|dUKM
042      pcc
043      n-us---
049      LMLM
050 00 HQ1064.U5|bG35 1999
100 1  Gannon, Linda
245 10 Women and aging :|btranscending the myths /|cLinda Gannon
260      London ;|aNew York :|bRoutledge,|c1999
300      xii, 228 p. :|bill. ;|c24 cm
440  0 Women and psychology
504      Includes bibliographical references (p. 179-216) and
         indexes
650  0 Aged women|zUnited States|xPsychology
650  0 Aged women|zUnited States|xPhysiology
650  0 Sexism|zUnited States
650  0 Ageism|zUnited States
949  1 |i35069008152930|llmlm|t00
```

Figure 15.3. Sample screen for INNOVATIVE record.

NOTES

1. Charles A. Cutter, *Rules for a Dictionary Catalog,* 4th ed. (Washington, DC: Government Printing Office, 1904), 12.

2. See, for example, Edward Edwards, *Memoirs of Libraries, Including a Handbook of Library Economy* (New York: B. Franklin, 1964) [reprint]; and James Ranz, "The History of the Printed Book Catalogue in the United States," Ph.D. dissertation, University of Illinois, 1960.

3. Emphasis was put on abridging and abbreviating data to fit small, standard-sized cards and excluding the catalog records for some materials, such as serials and nonbook materials, from the main catalog to keep it from growing too large. These practices caused search problems for library users and librarians alike, and caused them to miss materials they may have wanted to use.

REVIEW QUESTIONS

1. Why do libraries need to catalog the materials they acquire?
2. How does the library provide direct access to materials?
3. What is a "bib" record?
4. What is "bibliographic control," and how is it accomplished?
5. Name two functions that library catalogs perform.
6. Why was it difficult to computerize library catalogs?
7. Name three types of catalog displays and explain one advantage and one disadvantage of each type.

Decisions

Many decisions are made before cataloging can begin, but the one to adopt standard cataloging practices is the most important. As a result, the *Anglo-American Cataloguing Rules,* second edition, 1998 revision (AACR2-98) automatically becomes the tool for creating bibliographic descriptions and selecting headings associated with the description.[1] Other decisions—for example, how to provide subject access and what classification to use for arranging materials on the shelves—are also discussed in this chapter.

HOW MUCH DATA?—LEVELS OF DESCRIPTION

Unlike previous codes, which offered a single standard style of description, AACR2-98 prescribes three different styles, one of which must be selected for an institution's original cataloging. The styles are called "levels of description" and differ in the amount of data each one contains. Level 1 description is the simplest and contains the least information. Level 3 is the most complex. Level 2 contains more information than Level 1, but less than Level 3. Level 2 is the style recommended by bibliographic networks and used for derived (or "copy") cataloging.

Level 1 descriptions may be adequate for small general purpose collections used by young people and adult nonspecialists. Level 2 (and 3) descriptions can include more information than these searchers require as well as being more time-consuming and costly to produce. However, although they satisfy AACR2-98's standards, Level 1 records are not considered full records by national bibliographic networks. A decision to adopt Level 1 should be made carefully, considering a library's future as well as immediate needs. If the library is likely to grow rapidly, Level 2 should be considered, even if it is not necessary at the moment.

AACR2-98 Level 1 descriptions and less-than-full-level cataloging accepted by computerized networks are not defined in quite the same way. In fact, every library that uses any form of less-than-full cataloging—called *minimal level cataloging*—seems to have its own idea of what the records should contain. Some include one subject heading or two descriptive headings. Others do not permit either of these "luxuries."

Research libraries do minimal level cataloging for some of their materials, because otherwise their cataloging backlogs would become unmanageable. Together with a group of cooperating libraries known as the Program for Cooperative Cataloging (PCC), the Library of Congress has helped develop a standard for less-than-second-level cataloging known as the "core" record. Core records include access points that are expected to conform to current standards for each heading type and include the associated authority work. The PCC aims for good catalog records containing enough strictly accurate data for searchers to be able to locate and identify the materials represented. The PCC has formulated a set of values to guide its work and a training program to ensure that its members' contributed cataloging is of the same high quality as if it were full-level cataloging. PCC member libraries include some of the U.S. and Canada's most prestigious institutions.

Level 2 bibliographic descriptions require that more rules be applied and more details included in the records. It is the level usually chosen by large and medium-sized general libraries whose catalogs are used for research purposes. It also is required by bibliographic networks to meet full-level input standards (although simpler cataloging is acceptable also as long as it is appropriately identified).

Level 3 is the fullest form of description, requiring that every applicable rule and all available information from an item being cataloged be included in catalog records. Few libraries follow it for routine materials, not even the Library of Congress or university research libraries, which do second-level descriptive cataloging. One appropriate use of Level 3 is for materials in special collections, where researchers might need the detailed information provided by this level of treatment. It should not be adopted unless decision-makers are certain it serves clearly defined purposes, because the work of adding extra information to catalog records is time-consuming and costly, and wasteful if searchers routinely ignore it.

The information contained in bibliographic descriptions will determine the headings that can be chosen as retrieval points (see Chapter 18). Higher level cataloging maximizes the number of possible headings, while lower level cataloging limits them.

In this book, it is assumed that libraries will choose Level 2 as the appropriate style for original cataloging. Examples are done at Level 2 unless a different style is indicated. Figure 16.1, page 336, illustrates some of the differences between Level 1 and Level 2 cataloging, including the headings made as a result of the choice of bibliographic level.

This example is an illustration of:

- work emanating from a corporate body entered under personal author
- three joint authors
- optional addition of fuller form of personal name
- other title information
- publication date not listed, copyright date given
- descriptive illustration statement
- quoted note
- edition and history note
- two levels of cataloging

1st level cataloging

Gillespie, D.I.
  Wetlands for the world / D.I. Gillespie, H. Boyd, and P. Logan. -- Canadian Wildlife Service, c1991.
  40 p.

  ISBN 0-662-18517-X.

  1. Wetlands conservation -- Canada. 2. Wildlife conservation -- Canada. 4. Nature conservation -- Canada. I. Boyd, H. II. Logan, Patricia. III. Canadian Wildlife Service. IV. Title.

2nd level cataloging

Gillespie, D.I. (Douglas I.)
  Wetlands for the world : Canada's Ramsar sites / D.I. Gillespie, H. Boyd, and P. Logan. -- Ottawa : Canadian Wildlife Service, c1991.
  40 p. : ill., maps ; 28 cm.

  "The Convention on Wetlands of International Importance Especially as Waterfowl Habitat (The Ramsar Convention)."
  ISBN 0-662-18517-X.

  1. Wetland conservation -- Canada. 2. Estuarine area conservation -- Canada. 3. Wildlife conservation -- Canada. 4. Nature conservation -- Canada. I. Boyd, H. II. Logan, Patricia. III. Canadian Wildlife Service. IV. Title. V. Title: Canada's Ramsar sites. VI. Title: Ramsar sites.

Recommended DDC for both levels: 577.68
Recommended LCC: QH77.C32G44 1991

Figure 16.1. Sample Level 1 and Level 2 cataloging of book.

CHIEF SOURCE OF INFORMATION

Title Page

Wetlands for the World: Canada's Ramsar Sites

The Convention on Wetlands of International Importance Especially as Waterfowl Habitat (The Ramsar Convention)

D.I. Gillespie, H. Boyd, and P. Logan

Également disponible en français sous
Le titre *Des zones humides pour la Planète : sites Ramsar du Canada*

A member of the Conservation and Protection family

Information on Verso

Published by Authority of the Minister of Environment
Canadian Wildlife Service
© Minister of Supply and Services Canada, 1991
Catalogue number CW66-115/1991E
ISBN: 0-662-18517-X

Design: Ove Design Group

The Canadian Wildlife Service

The Canadian Wildlife Service of Environment Canada handles wildlife matters that are the responsibility of the Canadian government. These include protection and management of migratory birds as well as nationally significant wildlife habitat. Other responsibilities are endangerted species, control of international trade in endangered species, and research on wildlife issues of national Parks Service, and other federal agencies in wildlife research and management.

For more information about the Candian Wildlife Service or its other publications, please write to:

Publications
Canadian Wildlife Service
Ottawa, Ontario
K1A 0H3

Figure 16.1—*Continued*

SUBJECT AUTHORITIES

This chapter has been discussing the objective aspects of items being cataloged. The subject matter or content of each item being cataloged also must be identified and represented in the catalog. Indexing, also known as subject cataloging, is the process of identifying an item's subject matter and selecting words to represent those contents in the catalog. The words chosen for this purpose are called *subject headings* or *subject descriptors*.

Subject headings can and should be standardized by selecting them from a published list of authorized terms known as a *subject authority*. Some subject authorities cover all subject matter, whereas others cover limited topical areas, such as science or law. In cataloging, subject authorities that are limited in scope are referred to as *thesauri*. Thesauri tend to be used by special libraries and information centers whose collections, while small, contain many highly specialized materials. Libraries with general collections, which include most academic, public, and school libraries, use general subject authorities. Two general subject authorities that have attained international recognition as standards and are used by the majority of libraries in the United States and Canada are *Sears List of Subject Headings* (Sears)[2] and the *Library of Congress Subject Headings* (LCSH).[3] These lists also have Canadian counterparts.[4]

Sears is a small list, used primarily in small schools and public libraries. Its broader, simpler headings are sufficient for the number and types of materials they collect. LCSH, used by most large and medium-sized academic and public libraries, may be a better choice if a small public library or school has large numbers of materials on some topics; is part of a larger group sharing cataloging data that use LCSH, or hopes to join such a group in the future; or if it wishes to obtain cataloging from outside sources likely to use LCSH. The initial decision to adopt one of the two subject authorities, and any subsequent decision to change from one to the other, should be made very carefully.

The aim of the subject index is to bring together enough works in a topical area to satisfy the needs of searchers looking for material in the area, but not to overload them with retrieved works whose focus may be only marginally related to their interests. Given their relative sizes and numbers of available headings, if Sears and LCSH were used for the same collection, one could expect that the Sears index would bring together many more items under fewer, broader terms than the LCSH index.

The decision over which subject list to use can be made by asking which one brings together a better number of works—with "better" defined as not too many and not too few. The answer will vary depending on the cataloger's subjective view of the ideal number of retrievals per heading. Knowing that some topics, such as U.S. or Canadian history, will be heavily represented in any library collection, the cataloger can make the choice based on how well such heavily collected subject areas are treated or might exclude heavily collected subject areas and make a choice based on how well the other subject areas are treated.

Not only is LCSH a much larger compilation of terms than Sears, it tends to use the scientific or technical terms for topics. This may or may not be appropriate for the searchers who will use the catalog. An elementary school might wish to avoid technical terms, but a secondary school or public library serving adults might find them acceptable. If the group of searchers is heterogeneous, neither choice will be perfect for everyone, but it should be geared to the needs of most searchers. Librarians can assist the rest.

Despite its size, LCSH does not have all the terms needed to index large specialized collections in some subjects. Specialized subject authorities called thesauri can be used in addition to, or in place of, LCSH. Thesauri often are sponsored by professional associations or leading special libraries such as the National Library of Medicine in Bethesda, Maryland, which sponsors the *Medical Subject Headings* (MeSH),[5] or the Getty Art History Project in Santa Monica, California, which sponsors the *Art & Architecture Thesaurus* (AAT).[6] Specialized thesauri are not discussed in this book, but more information about them can be found in *Special Libraries: A Cataloging Guide.*[7]

Catalogers also can decide to supply subject headings for all materials or only some of them. Traditional practices have long included subject headings for all nonfiction, nonbook materials, and children's fiction, but excluded most adult literary works from subject cataloging. In recent years, this exclusion has evolved into a freer system of choice. The Library of Congress (LC) and other professional leaders now encourage catalogers to assign subject headings to such works using specially created genre headings as well as ordinary terms found in topical and name authorities.

CLASSIFICATIONS

Another important decision concerns the classification scheme selected to arrange materials on the shelves. Like published subject authorities, which control the words used for subject headings, published classification schemes list "authorized" subject categories and give codes for them, thus serving as classification "authorities." Catalogers call these published lists of categories and codes *classification schemes, classification systems,* or, simply, *classifications.* The codes themselves may consist of numbers, letters, symbols, or combinations of numbers, letters, and/or symbols. The codes are referred to as *classification numbers*, regardless of the types of characters they contain.

Classification numbers represent subject matter, very much like subject headings. However, because an item can stand in only one place on the shelf, it can bear only one classification number. Thus, the subject expression of classification numbers is less precise than that of the combined group of subject headings assigned to an item, because it must summarize the entire content with only one number.

Two standard general classification schemes dominate in the United States and Canada: Dewey Decimal and Library of Congress.[8] In both countries, Dewey is the heavy favorite of school and public libraries regardless of their size. In Canada, the United Kingdom, and many other Commonwealth countries, it is used also by the national libraries for shelving their collections and arranging their national bibliographies. In the United States, however, the Library of Congress, which serves as the de facto national library, uses its own classification scheme. When computer networks began distributing LC's cataloging records in the 1960s and 1970s, many colleges and universities adopted the LC classification in order to copy them. Copying officially assigned LC numbers seemed more economical and easier for their large collections than having to classify each item "from scratch" in the Dewey classification scheme.

Before long, however, LC began assigning Dewey numbers as well in its cataloging, and members of shared cataloging networks could choose to copy either scheme. Dewey still is used by some large libraries in which research is a primary function. An important disadvantage of switching classifications is that all the previously acquired material has to be converted to the new scheme, which is a costly project. Otherwise, the library's collection is divided between two schemes, forcing librarians and users alike to deal with them both, searching two places for every subject, fragmenting materials on the same subjects, and destroying the collection's browsability.

Local policy determines the classification scheme adopted by individual libraries. The classification numbers that result form the basis for *call numbers*, the shelf addresses for materials in library collections. In addition, local policies govern other marks, called *shelf marks,* added to classification numbers to complete the call numbers. Shelf marks may include branch and/or collection designations, coded versions of main entries called cutter numbers, author letters, dates, volume numbers, and so forth.

OTHER DECISIONS

Two decisions about how to deploy cataloging products will affect the efficiency and effectiveness of a library's catalog and shelf arrangement. One is whether to interfile all catalog records, and the other is whether to intershelve all materials. Integrating the catalog accomplishes its objectives more fully than keeping several separate catalogs and minimizes the steps a searcher must take to locate materials of interest. The authors recommend putting cataloging for all materials into one integrated catalog. This is also the method of choice for computerized networks.

Before the advent of OPACs, some librarians believed that searching was more efficient in small files and divided their card catalogs into two files: author/title and subject files. A user could fail to retrieve desired material because of searching in the wrong file, e.g., "Shakespeare" and "Hamlet" as subjects were in the author/title file with "Shakespeare" as an author's name and "Hamlet" as a title, while the subject file was limited to topical subject headings (that is, nonname, nontitle). Something similar has happened with OPACs, although the OPAC database might seem to be automatically integrated. In reality, the degree of integration or division within an OPAC file is governed by the software used for searching and retrieval operations. If the software requires the searcher to select a file (author, title, subject, keyword, call number) before entering a search statement, this automatically divides the file. Searchers must be able to browse all the headings together without specifying a file—names and titles as descriptive headings, names and titles as subject headings, and topical subject headings—to achieve integrated searching and retrieval in an OPAC.

Some libraries routinely apply core level standards to specialized monographs likely to be wanted by very few users (e.g., foreign-language books, primary research materials, and dissertations) and to ongoing publications such as journals. Internal institutional publications are sometimes treated differently than externally published materials, especially if access to them is limited to a small number of users.

The intershelving of all materials has had its proponents and detractors. Studies show that all materials circulate better when they are intershelved, so this is our recommendation.[9] Many librarians believe that the best information on some topics is contained in nonbook materials, but this information will be difficult to find and use if nonbook materials are kept out of sight in corners or locked cabinets, while books are shelved on open stacks in full view.[10]

On the other hand, libraries are free to choose different options for specific types of materials and may have good reasons for doing so. Libraries acquire materials that come in distinctly different packages: books, maps, slides, cassettes, tapes, discs, and so forth. It can be difficult to place items in all the packages together on the same shelves, and some types require repackaging if they are to be housed comfortably with others. The difficulty of shelving different packages together and the cost of repackaging some items are reasons often given for failing to intershelve.

Regular classification and shelving routines can be suspended for reasons other than the accommodation of materials in different physical forms. Some libraries classify journals and shelve them in ordinary call number order. Others prefer not to classify their journals, but arrange them alphabetically by title in a separate location. Some libraries exclude fiction or biographies from classification, shelving these, also, in separate locations in alphabetical order by the names of the authors or biographees. (Students in Sheila Intner's cataloging classes assigned to identify all the different locations for literary works in their local public libraries have found them in up to twenty different places in a single library, including regular nonfiction call number ranges such as the Dewey 800s or the LC Ps.) Some libraries maintain separate shelves for newly acquired materials, identifying them with special spine labels. Special spine labels are also employed to identify types of genre fiction (science fiction, mysteries, westerns, etc.), sometimes in an integrated arrangement with ordinary fiction and sometimes in separate blocks of shelves. Some Canadian libraries add maple leaf spine labels on works by Canadian authors. Nor are these the only possibilities. Any variation can be "right" or "wrong" for a particular library. Whenever some materials are shelved out of call number order, signs that explain the anomalies are essential.

Monographs issued in series[11] require a special set of policy decisions. The basic choice is whether to catalog the entire series as an ongoing collection or to catalog each part individually when it is acquired. (Treatment of series data is discussed in greater detail in Chapter 17.) If the choice is to treat the series as a collection, only one catalog record will be made under the series title, encompassing all the parts, even though each part also has its own title and could stand alone. If librarians want to provide information about the parts, their titles and other pertinent data can be given in contents notes and headings made for them as "analytic" (that is, "part") title headings. The alternative is to treat each part as a separate item with its own catalog record. To bring all the parts together in one place in the catalog, the series title is given in each catalog record and a series title heading made for it.

Two issues can help guide the decision about how to treat monographic series: (1) whether users seek individual parts more often than the collection and (2) whether the subject matter of the parts is similar enough to merit being put in just one classification number. If users are likely to want only one part, not the whole collection, and if the subject of each part differs enough to warrant separate classification numbers, cataloging each part individually seems the best course. If users are likely to want the entire collection and the subjects are similar enough to warrant shelving them together, treating all the parts as one collection seems sensible. When a monographic series is cataloged as a collection, individual parts might not be listed in the catalog at all unless a contents note is made. If the contents note is made, each part can be given a title heading in the catalog. However, if a library chooses Level 1 cataloging, it is allowed to omit giving series titles and might choose not to provide contents notes. Then, no headings for the individual parts can be made.

Some catalogers establish one policy for all series, whereas others divide them into two groups: those that will be treated collectively and those that will be treated individually. The policy gives the criteria by which a new series is placed in one group or the other. Some libraries try to recognize scholarly series but ignore those that seem aimed primarily at mass marketing.

Decisions on options such as these should be written down so staff and users can consult them. However, no decision can serve all users equally well, and what works well at one time may not succeed forever, so cataloging decisions bear periodic review and evaluation. Monitoring reference queries can help to confirm whether the library's current practices seem to help most users succeed in their searches or prevent users from finding the materials they want.

SUMMARY

Cataloging decisions relate to objective and subjective aspects of materials. Procedures identifying objective aspects of materials (called *manifestations* of cataloged works) fall under the rubric of descriptive cataloging. Descriptive cataloging decisions include adopting AACR2-98 as a cataloging code, choosing an appropriate amount of data to be included in bibliographic descriptions (the bibliographic level), and deciding whether to treat monographs issued in series individually or collectively. Procedures identifying subjective aspects of materials, which refer to their contents, fall under the twin rubrics of subject cataloging and classification. Subjective decisions include selecting a subject authority as a source for subject headings and a classification scheme as a source for classification numbers. Both subject headings and classification numbers represent the contents of cataloged materials, but the latter tend to be less precise, because catalogers limit themselves to one classification number per cataloged item, whereas they assign multiple subject headings.

Descriptive cataloging, subject cataloging, and classification each operate to provide access, although in different ways. Descriptive cataloging provides headings for the identifying features of materials, such as the names of authors and titles. This is known as *bibliographic* access, because authors and titles are bibliographic features. Subject cataloging indexes the contents of items, resulting in the assignment of subject headings that furnish searchers with *intellectual* access. Classification assigns numbers used in placing materials on the shelves according to their contents, resulting in *physical* access to items in library collections (the shelf addresses where materials are located). It also provides somewhat less precise intellectual access than subject cataloging.

Chapter 17 looks more closely at descriptive cataloging.

NOTES

1. *Anglo-American Cataloguing Rules,* 2nd ed., 1998 revision, prepared under the direction of The Joint Steering Committee for Revision of AACR (Ottawa: Canadian Library Association; London: Library Association Publishing; Chicago: American Library Association, 1998).

2. *Sears List of Subject Headings,* 17th ed., edited by Joseph Miller (New York: H. W. Wilson, 2000).

3. Library of Congress, Subject Cataloging Division, *Library of Congress Subject Headings,* 24th ed. (Washington, DC: Library of Congress, 2001).

4. *Sears List of Subject Headings: Canadian Companion,* 6th ed., revised by Lynne Lighthall with the assistance of Shana Bystrom and others (New York: H. W. Wilson, 2001); *Canadian Subject Headings,* 3rd ed., edited by Alina Schweitzer (Ottawa: National Library of Canada, 1992).

5. National Library of Medicine, *Medical Subject Headings* (Bethesda, MD: NLM, 1996).

6. *Art & Architecture Thesaurus,* 2nd ed. (New York: Oxford University Press, 1994).

7. Sheila S. Intner and Jean Weihs, *Special Libraries: A Cataloging Guide* (Englewood, CO: Libraries Unlimited, 1997).

8. *Dewey Decimal Classification and Relative Index,* 21st ed., edited by Joan S. Mitchell et al. (Albany, NY: OCLC Forest Press, 1996); Library of Congress, Subject Cataloging Division, *Classification* (Washington, DC: Library of Congress, 1901-).

9. See, for example, Jean Weihs, *The Integrated Library: Encouraging Access to Multimedia Materials,* 2nd ed. (Phoenix, AZ: Oryx Press, 1991).

10. Sheila S. Intner, *Access to Media: A Guide to Integrating and Computerizing Catalogs* (New York: Neal-Schuman, 1984), 77, 136-138.

11. A series is defined as a group of monographs having, in addition to their own titles, a common series title.

SUGGESTED READING

Hoffman, Herbert. *Small Library Cataloging*. 3rd ed. Lanham, MD: Scarecrow Press, 2002.

REVIEW QUESTIONS

1. What is the most important decision about cataloging that must be made?
2. Define "levels of cataloging" and explain what factors determine an appropriate level for a library.
3. Name two popularly used subject authorities and explain how they differ.
4. Define "thesaurus" and explain why a library might use one.
5. When did the Library of Congress classification become popular among U.S. academic libraries, and why?
6. What is the basic policy decision to be made in the cataloging of monographic series?
7. Why would a library wish to catalog a series as a collection, putting all the parts on one catalog record?
8. Name and define three types of access.

Chapter

Description and Access

A standard cataloging record begins by describing an item according to an accepted set of rules—currently, the *Anglo-American Cataloguing Rules,* second edition, 1998 revision.[1] This chapter describes how bibliographic descriptions are built and headings relating to them are derived.

AACR2-98, the current standard, is available as a clothbound or paperback book, on a CD-ROM disc, called *AACR2-e*; and in unbound, prepunched pages that an owner of the loose-leaf binder edition can put in the old binder (new ones are unavailable). *AACR2-e* can be licensed for use by one individual or, with a site license, by several catalogers. It is also part of the Library of Congress's *Cataloger's Desktop* product.[2] AACR2-e employs FolioBound Views software for access to the text, which is completely indexed, enabling catalogers to search by any word in the text or by rule numbers. Search words can be truncated and combined using AND, OR, and NOT. *AACR2-e* users can "bookmark" and highlight items and annotate the text. Links help users move through the text quickly, and multiple windows can display different pages of text simultaneously.

AACR: PAST, PRESENT, FUTURE

In 1908, the first set of international cataloging rules was devised by a group of British librarians working with a visiting party of American colleagues. The meeting of minds from opposite sides of the Atlantic Ocean was disrupted for a period during and after World War II, and the American Library Association unilaterally published a new code in 1949. But joint efforts were to resume before very long. In 1961, due in large part to the efforts of American theorist Seymour Lubetzky, an International Conference on Cataloguing Principles was convened in Paris. The meeting resulted in a statement of principles on which cataloging rules should be based, known afterward as the Paris Principles.[3]

Efforts following the Paris conference to forge an Anglo-American cataloging code resulted in the publication of the *Anglo-American Cataloging Rules* (AACR1) in 1967. Differences between British and North American librarians could not be resolved, so AACR1 was published in one version for the British and another for North Americans. Even the titles differed: the British used the "u" in *cataloguing*; the North Americans dropped it.

In 1974, AACR1's publishers formed the Joint Steering Committee for Revision of AACR (JSC) to be the final authority on the rules. The result of their efforts was a second edition that used British spellings, known as AACR2, published in 1978 simultaneously by the American Library Association, Canadian Library Association, and Library Association (United Kingdom). AACR2 has since been reissued twice, in 1988 (AACR2R) and 1998 (AACR2-98), to incorporate subsequent revisions into one text.

AACR2 was an integrated code for all materials. It followed the rules of International Standard Bibliographic Description (ISBD), which provided a uniform outline consisting of eight bibliographic elements and a system for punctuating them. The elements of description were already familiar to catalogers and bibliographers (title, author, edition, publisher, etc.). The order in which they should appear in catalog entries was formalized into ISBD by authority of the International Federation of Library Associations and Institutions (IFLA) for use all over the world. The punctuation—called confusing and superfluous by critics—made catalog records from different countries understandable and interchangeable for computer entry or for use by catalogers who did not know the language in which the entry was written.

The presence of a single order of elements of description for all materials regardless of their physical form was a revolutionary concept in the early 1970s. AACR2's developers also believed that headings chosen for items cataloged using the rules for description could be done in exactly the same way for any type of material. Materials such as legal, religious, art, and musical works, and a few others, were singled out for unique treatment, but not because of their physical format. Generally, catalogers simply choose the best headings for an item based on the information given in its description.

In October 1997, a conference was convened in Toronto to assist JSC in determining whether fundamental rule revision was needed and, if so, what its nature and direction should be.[4] Delegates, who came from ten nations, recommended adding a statement of principles and functions of a catalog, changing the rule stating that physical format is primary over content, revising the rules for cataloging serials, and considering greater internationalization of AACR. Work proceeds on these and other matters.[5]

Rule revision is a slow process, and new formats sometimes appear in libraries before rules for them are developed. Figure 17.1, pages 347–48, shows a compact disc that is both sound recording and electronic resource, depending on the hardware used. The item is cataloged with existing rules as a sound recording because music is its focus. A note is made about its alternate use.

This example is an illustration of:

- sound disc with a CD-ROM component
- entry under performing group
- general material designation
- phonogram date
- optional omission of "sound" in extent of item (in 1st level example)
- accompanying material ephemeral and not given
- publisher's number given in proper place in 2nd level example and in optional placement as first note in 1st level example
- contents note
- physical description note for CD-ROM aspect
- system requirements note given after notes about sound disc
- two levels of cataloging

2nd level cataloging

Squirrel Nut Zippers (Musical group)
  Hot [sound recording] / Squirrel Nut Zippers. -- Carrboro, NC : Mammoth, p1996.
  1 sound disc : digital ; 4¾ in.

  Contents: Got my own thing now -- Put a lid on it -- Memphis exorcism -- Twilight -- It ain't you -- Prince Nez -- Hell -- Meant to be -- Bad businessman -- Flight of the passing fancy -- Blue angel -- The interlocutor.
  May be used in a computer CD-ROM drive. System requirements: minimum 8MB RAM; Macintosh system 7 or Microsoft Windows 3.1 or greater; color monitor; double speed CD-ROM player.
  Mammoth: MR0137-2.

  1. Swing (music). 2. Jazz. I. Title.

Recommended DDC: 781.654

1st level cataloging

Squirrel Nut Zippers (Musical group)
  Hot [sound recording]. -- Mammoth, p1996.
  1 disc : digital ; 4¾ in.

  Mammoth: MR0137-2.
  May be used in a computer CD-ROM drive. System requirements: minimum 8MB RAM; Macintosh system 7 or Microsoft Windows 3.1 or greater; color monitor; double speed CD-ROM player.

  1. Jazz music. 2. Swing music. I. Title.

Recommended DDC: 781.65

Figure 17.1.

Figure 17.1—*Continued*

INFORMATION ON CONTAINER

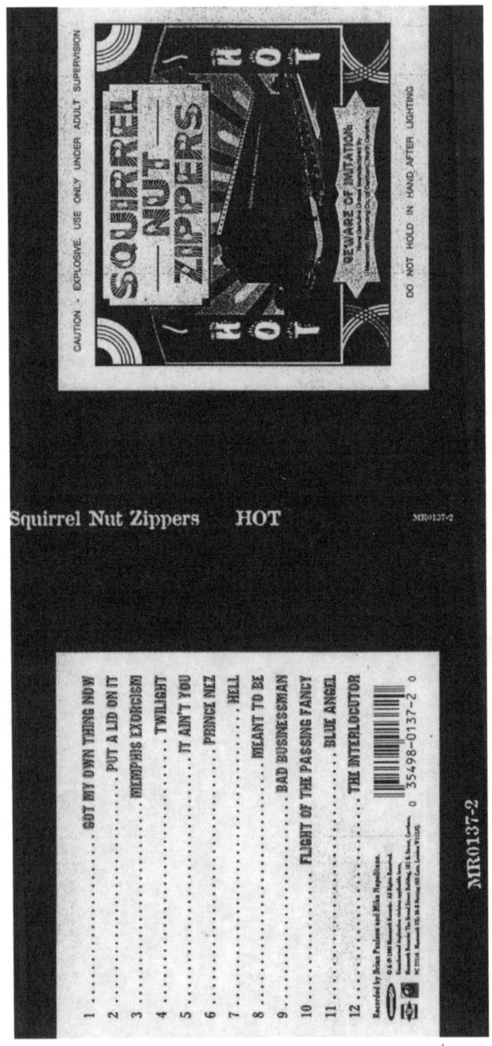

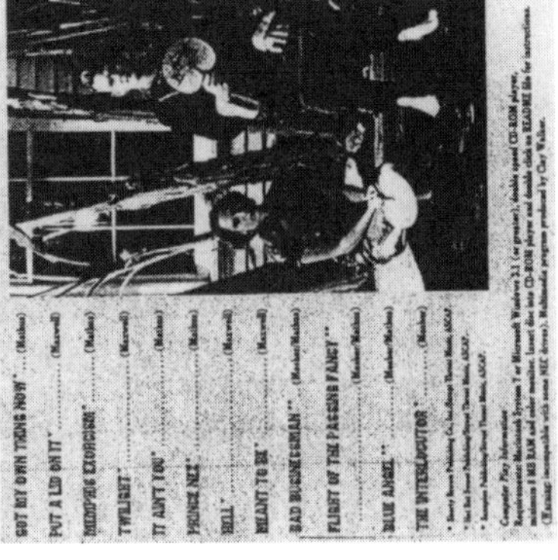

ORGANIZATION OF AACR2-98

AACR2-98 is divided into two main sections. The first section covers description of materials; the second covers their retrieval. Rules for retrieval involve the choice and form of headings, called access points, based on the description. The chapters in the first section are numbered in the ordinary way, from 1 to 13. The chapters in the second section begin with Chapter 20 and are then numbered consecutively, 21–26.

Chapter 1 contains rules applying to all materials, to supplements, to items made up of several types of materials, and to reproductions. Chapters 2 to 13 each cover a group of media. AACR2-98 rule numbers are mnemonic: The first digit stands for the chapter and the second stands for the element of description. After that, letters of the alphabet stand for subelements and roman numerals for subdivisions of subelements. Rules relating to the title (first element of description) are numbered x.1, where x is the chapter (e.g., maps are covered in Chapter 3 and videorecordings in Chapter 7, so rules for map titles are numbered 3.1, while rules for video titles are 7.1). This serves as a shorthand for specific rules.

The first step in cataloging is to decide what the item is and select the appropriate rules to apply. Ask: "Is this item made up of one part or more than one?" If there is just one part, next ask to which group it belongs, according to the following choices:

Chapter 2: Books, pamphlets, and printed sheets

Chapter 3: Cartographic materials (maps, globes, etc.)

Chapter 4: Manuscripts (including typescripts)

Chapter 5: Music

Chapter 6: Sound recordings

Chapter 7: Motion pictures and videorecordings

Chapter 8: Graphic materials (includes visual images of all kinds)

Chapter 9: Electronic resources

Chapter 10: Three-dimensional artefacts and realia (including toys, games, and "found" objects)

Chapter 11: Microforms

Chapter 12: Serials (items issued in parts intended to continue indefinitely)

Chapter 13: Analysis (items that are part of a larger item)

The corresponding chapter, with Chapter 1, is used to describe the item. To catalog a serial, Chapter 12 and Chapter 1 are all that are needed for print-on-paper items, but if it is in any other format (e.g., a serially issued sound recording, videorecording, or electronic resource), three chapters are used: Chapter 1, the chapter for the physical format, plus Chapter 12.

If the item consists of more than one piece (except serials), ask: "Are all the pieces in one format?" Examples are multidisc sound recordings and CD-ROMs, and multivolume books. If the answer is "yes," proceed in the same way as above. Choose the appropriate chapter and begin. If the answer is "no," ask: "Is one of the pieces more important than the rest?" If so, the item is cataloged by the chapter for that piece, called the *predominant* piece. All the other pieces are considered accompanying material. If the answer is "no," or if at least two pieces in different formats are equal in importance, the item is cataloged as a kit (or, if using the British interpretation of the rules, multimedia), using rule 1.10 (from Chapter 1) and the chapters appropriate to the formats involved.

Importance is subjective. A useful rule of thumb to judge importance is to consider how the content of the item is conveyed. If each piece conveys the whole content, none is most important and the item is a kit. If none conveys the whole content and the pieces must be used together, there is no predominant piece and the item still is a kit. But if one piece conveys the whole content and the others do not, that piece is most important and the catalog record should be made for it alone, with the other pieces treated as accompaniments. Figures 17.2 and 17.3 illustrate these choices. Figure 17.2, pages 351–52, shows a filmstrip and sound recording set in which the sound recording is considered predominant because it is intended to be played with or without the filmstrip, which only has pictures that add minimally to the enjoyment of the music. This item is cataloged as a sound recording with an accompanying filmstrip.

Figure 17.3, pages 353–54, shows a sound cassette, response sheets, a post test, and a teacher's guide set. None of the parts conveys the whole content. There are references in the sound cassette to the response sheet and vice versa; the post test needs both to be understood; and the teacher's guide contains more information on the topic. This set is cataloged as a kit.

For practical reasons, Library of Congress catalogers follow a policy that directs them to select one piece of a multipiece item as predominant and catalog the other pieces as accompanying material; but others can decide what an item is according to AACR2-98's definitions.

Games (including handheld games with computer chips), puzzles, and dioramas are exceptions to the definition of kits. Although usually comprising many pieces in different media, they are considered single units for cataloging purposes and follow Chapter 10's rules. However, an item in several media that is not designed to be manipulated according to a set of rules is not a game and must be judged by the other possibilities outlined previously.

AACR2-98 operates on the assumption that, when in doubt, the cataloger's judgment is the ultimate authority. For that reason, do not be afraid to exercise it. Catalogers have more training and experience in making these judgments than anyone else in the library. It is better to make a judgment promptly that one decides, later, was not correct than to hold an item indefinitely until one gets help with it. A catalog record can be changed to reflect the change of mind, but patrons will have been able to use the material in the meantime.

This example is an illustration of:

- two-media set in which one medium is predominant
- bilingual item in which the title is in one language only so a parallel title is not given
- uniform title
- optional placement of the general material designation at end of title proper
- phonogram date
- accompanying material given in the physical description area
- physical description note
- contents note
- publisher's number note given in proper place in 1st example and in optional placement as first note in 2nd example
- 2nd level cataloging

Champagne, Claude.
  [Symphonie gaspésienne]
  Symphonie gaspésienne [sound recording] / Claude Champagne. -- Toronto : Mead, p1979.
  1 sound disc (19 min., 10 sec.) : analog, 33 1/3 rpm ; 12 in. + 1 filmstrip.

  May be played on mono or stereophonic equipment.
  Contents: Side 1. Study version -- Side 2. Listening version.
  Mead: SSC 1002.

Any of the following options can be used:

- the general material designation may be listed after the uniform title
- "sound" may be omitted from "1 sound disc"
- a statement of physical description may be added to accompanying material
- publisher's number may be listed as the first note

Champagne, Claude.
  [Symphonie gaspésienne. Sound recording]
  Symphonie gaspésienne / Claude Champagne. -- Toronto : Mead, p1979.
  1 disc (19 min., 10 sec.) : analog, 33 1/3 rpm ; 12 in. + 1 filmstrip (100 fr. : col. ; 35 mm.)

  Mead: SSC 1002.
  May be played on mono or stereophonic equipment.
  Contents: Side 1. Study version -- Side 2. Listening version.

  1. Symphonies. I. Title.

Recommended DDC: 784.2
Recommended LCC: M1001.C425 1979

Figure 17.2.

Figure 17.2—*Continued*

CHIEF SOURCE OF INFORMATION (DISC LABEL)

INFORMATION ON SLIPCASE

SYMPHONIE GASPÉSIENNE

claude champagne

This set consists of a record and a correlated filmstrip. The record offers two versions of the same music.

Side 1. Study Version — This side is designed to be played with the filmstrip. It presents a performance of the music with a distinctive electronic signal superimposed on the music to indicate when filmstrip frames are to be changed.

Side 2. Listening Version — This side presents the same performance without any electronic signals. It is designed solely for listening.

Instructions for record 1002 correlated with filmstrip SF1002.

1. Load the filmstrip projector and advance to the frame that indicates when to start the accompanying record.
2. Using the record side marked "audible signals"; start at the indicated filmstrip frame.
3. Advance one frame at each electronic signal on the record.

The filmstrip
The photography in this filmstrip portrays the vitality of the life and land of the Gaspé region.

This example is an illustration of:

- kit
- publication and copyright dates unknown
- summary
- two levels of cataloging

2nd level cataloging

George, Miriam H.
Reference books [kit] / author, Miriam H. George. -- Baltimore : Media Materials, [19--]
1 sound cassette, 30 identical response sheets, 1 post test, 1 teacher's guide ; in container 29 x 23 x 4 cm.

Summary: The difference between abridged and unabridged dictionaries and the use of cross references in information searches are explained and specialized reference books introduced.

1st level cataloging

George, Miriam H.
Reference books [kit]. -- Media Materials, [19--]
1 sound cassette, 30 identical response sheets, 1 post test, 1 teacher's guide.

Tracing for both levels
1. Reference books. I. Title.

Recommended DDC for both levels: 028.7

Figure 17.3.

Figure 17.3—*Continued*

INFORMATION ON TEACHER'S GUIDE (THE UNIFYING PIECE)

The container is a standard box used for all Media Materials, Inc. Packages of this size. All contents have title: Reference Books.

TITLE REFERENCE BOOKS

AUTHOR Miriam H. George, B.S.Ed.

APPROXIMATE LESSON TIME

40-45 minutes

PERFORMANCE OBJECTIVES

-Show students that dictionaries and encyclopedias have many uses.

-Practice in using guide words and cross references.

-Introduce students to the wealth of information found in atlases, Readers' Guide, World Almanac, Dictionary of American History, Dictionary of American Biography, Current Biography, Who's Who in America, Twentieth Century Authors, and Familiar Quotations.

SUMMARY

The difference between the abridged and unabridged dictionary is shown. The use of guide words in dictionaries and encyclopedias is stressed. The use of cross references in the card catalog, the Readers' Guide, and in encyclopedias is explained. Specialized reference books are introduced.

DESCRIPTIVE STRUCTURE AND SOURCES

The ISBD structure for description, which is the generally accepted international standard mandated by the IFLA, has eight elements called *areas of description*:

Area 1: Title and statement of responsibility

Area 2: Edition

Area 3: Material specific details

Area 4: Publication, distribution, etc.

Area 5: Physical description

Area 6: Series

Area 7: Notes

Area 8: Standard number and terms of availability

All areas of description do not apply to every item cataloged; for example, many items do not have information about the edition and, where it does not appear, edition information is left out of the description. This also is true of series information and notes, most of which are optional. Material specific details are used for only a few of the formats: serials in any physical form, electronic resources, maps, and music. Not all materials have standard numbers.

Descriptive cataloging is like a puzzle with eight blank spaces, some or all of which are filled in according to the information appearing on the item being cataloged. There may be more information than needed or several competing sources of information on an item. Rules in AACR2-98 help different catalogers choose the same sources of information for cataloging purposes, if more than one source is likely to be present. These rules are numbered with a zero (.0) because they precede determining any of the areas of description, which are numbered one through eight (.1 - .8). Rule 5.0B covers information sources for music, rule 9.0B covers information sources for electronic resources, and so forth.

At the start of each chapter, all the sources for cataloging information for that format are discussed. One is designated the *chief* source for that format; the rest are considered *prescribed* sources. Area 1 data must come from the chief source. It is the most important piece of information, and people using the catalog record should be able to assume it came from the chief source. If, for some reason, it does not—for example, because there is no information at all on the item, which is the case with realia (see Figure 17.4, page 356)—catalogers alert the user to that fact by putting the information supplied from elsewhere into square brackets and listing the source of the information in the notes (area 7). This note is especially important for serials. The first issue is designated as chief source, but if it is unavailable and another issue (the earliest available) is used instead, that must be noted.

```
This item is a mineral found in Payne Mine.  When it arrived at
the library, it was placed in a transparent container.


This example is an illustration of:
      •  realia
      •  naturally occurring object
      •  title main entry with supplied title
      •  source of title note
      •  edition and history note
      •  2nd level cataloging


[Uraninite] [realia].
  1 sample ; 5 x 7 x 6 cm. in container 8 x 8 x 8 cm.

  Title supplied by cataloger.
  From Payne Mine, Gatineau Park, Que.

  1. Uraninite.  I. Title.

Recommended DDC: 549.528
```

Figure 17.4.

Each area of description has specific sources prescribed for it. Only area 1 is limited to the chief source. Data for all the other areas may come from any of several sources listed. Areas 5, 7, and 8 may come from *any* source, including personal knowledge. When information is taken from sources outside those prescribed, square brackets are put around it to identify it. When appropriate, notes explain the sources of bracketed data.

The general principle followed by AACR2-98 about information sources is to *prefer information from the item itself over information from other locations.* If a chapter covers a format that requires hardware to see or view the item itself, alternatives are provided for catalogers who have no equipment. Some formats have multipart chief sources, such as a videorecording with opening and closing credits screens or a set of sound discs with labels pasted permanently on each disc. Practical guidelines for choosing among them are given. If an alternative to the preferred chief source for the format is chosen, it becomes chief source, and information from it does not have to be bracketed, but it should be explained in a note.

ISBD PUNCTUATION

IFLA's experts devised a system of punctuation that distinguishes each part of a catalog record and helps a cataloger unfamiliar with the language of a record to understand and use it. Unfortunately, when punctuation rules are read together at the beginning of each section, they seem terribly complicated. It is easier to put in the punctuation after the descriptive elements are assembled. Practice also helps do this mechanical part of preparing catalog records faster. Figure 17.5, below and page 358, illustrates the punctuation for a typical Level 2 description. It can be imitated provided all the same data elements are present, but if any element or subelement is missing, the punctuation changes. Basic punctuations used are described below. Others may be found in AACR2-98, which gives all the correct marks.

This example is an illustration of:

- other title information
- distributor
- publishing date not listed, copyright date given
- contents note
- Canadian CIP
- 2nd level cataloging

```
Reeves, Janet.
  One potato, two potato : a cookbook and more! / Janet Reeves.
-- Charlottetown, P.E.I. : Ragwood Press ; Distributed by
General Distribution Services, c1987.
  244 p. : ill. ; 23 cm.

  Includes index.
  ISBN 0-920304-70-2.

  1. Cookery (Potatoes).  2. Potatoes.  I. Title.
```

Recommended DDC: 641.6521

Figure 17.5.

Figure 17.5—*Continued*

CHIEF SOURCE OF INFORMATION
(Title Page)

ONE POTATO
TWO POTATO

A Cookbook and More!

Janet Reeves

(Information on Verso)

Eighth Printing 1997

Illustrations: Brenda Whiteway
Cover Photographs: John Sylvester
Printed and Bound in Canada by: Webcom

Published with the kind assistance of the Department of Communications and the Prince Edward Island Cultural Product Development Fund

PUBLISHED BY:
Ragweed Press
P.O. Box 2023
Charlottetown, Prince Edward Island
Canada C1A 7N7

DISTRIBUTED BY:
Canada: General Distribution Services

Canadian Cataloguing in Publication Data

Reeves, Janet, 1942 —

One potato, two potato

Includes index.
ISBN 0-920304-70-2

1. Cookery (Potatoes). I. Title

TX803.P8R44 1987 641.6'521 C87-093694-8

Unless an area of description begins a paragraph, it is preceded by a period-space-dash-space (. —). In North America, it is customary to combine areas 1–4 in one paragraph, areas 5 and 6 in a second, and each note in its own paragraph. Area 8 also is given a separate paragraph. In some countries, all elements of description appear in one paragraph, so it is useful to have the period-space-dash-space define them.

Colons (:), semicolons (;), slashes (/), and commas (,) are used for several kinds of identification, an equals sign (=) denotes the same data in another language, and a plus sign (+) identifies accompanying materials (area 5). In area 1, colons separate title proper from the rest of the title; in area 4, they separate the place of publication from the name of the publisher; and in area 5, they separate the extent from other physical details. Slashes identify statements of responsibility in areas 1, 2, 6, and 7. Within statements of responsibility, semicolons separate names when responsibilities differ, but commas are used when the responsibilities are the same, but are shared by more than one person. Examples follow:

1. A book written by one person, illustrated by another, and edited by a third party:

   / by Sheila S. Intner ; illustrated by Jean Weihs ; edited by John Robert Jones.

   (All the words given above appear on the title page as shown.)

2. A book written by all three:

   / by Sheila S. Intner, Jean Weihs, John Robert Jones.

   (The word "by" appears on the title page, with the names listed underneath.)

3. A book written by two people and edited by a third:

   / by Sheila S. Intner, Jean Weihs ; [edited by] John Robert Jones.

   (The words "edited by" do not appear on the title page and are supplied by the cataloger to explain Jones's contribution to the book.)

Whenever colons, semicolons, and slashes are used in ISBD punctuation, a space is put both before and after the mark. Commas and periods (called "full stops") only have spaces after the mark, none before it. Catalogers need not worry much about punctuation errors, since most patrons do not notice them and they rarely affect retrieval.

ISBD punctuation marks precede the elements they identify just as statements in a computer program tell the computer what kind of data it is going to receive before sending it (for example, many OPACs instruct searchers to enter statements such as "title=hamlet" or "au=shakespeare"). When a descriptive element or subelement is missing, the punctuation that precedes it is omitted, not the punctuation that follows it.

BIBLIOGRAPHIC DESCRIPTION—CREATING THE RECORD

Area 1—Title and Statement of Responsibility

The first information in any description is the main title, called *title proper*. It is chosen from the chief source and transcribed *exactly as it appears* on the item as to the order and spelling of the words, even if they are wrong. The reasoning behind precise transcription is to ensure that a catalog record can be matched to the item it represents, especially when several versions of a title or similar-sounding titles exist.

The layout and typography of the words on the chief source of information are used to determine where a title proper begins and ends. AACR2-98's rules aid in determining titles proper in some special cases that are encountered frequently; for example, if two separate versions of Charles Darwin's voyage appear in the two ways shown in Figures 17.6 and 17.7, pages 360–63, rules in Chapter 1 direct the cataloger to transcribe them as given. When there is no rule to determine what should be done, follow your instincts and decide.

```
This example is an illustration of:
     •  edition statement taken from outside prescribed sources
        (many libraries place such an edition statement in the
        note area, sometimes as a quoted note)
     •  publication date not listed, copyright date given
     •  numbered series statement
     •  index note
     •  2nd level cataloging


Darwin, Charles.
  The voyage of the Beagle / by Charles Darwin with introduction
and notes. -- [2nd ed.]. -- New York : Collier, c1909.
  547 p. : ill. ; 20 cm. -- (The Harvard classics ; v. 29)

  Includes index.

  1. Beagle Expedition (1831-1836).  2. Natural history.
3. Geology.  4. Voyages around the world.  5. South America --
Description and travel.  I. Title.  II. Series.


Recommended DDC: 578.09
```

Figure 17.6.

Figure 17.6—*Continued*

CHIEF SOURCE OF INFORMATION
(Title Page)

THE HARVARD CLASSICS

EDITED BY CHARLES W. ELIOT LL D

THE VOYAGE OF THE BEAGLE

BY CHARLES DARWIN

WITH INTRODUCTION AND NOTES

VOLUME 29

P F COLLIER & SON COMPANY

NEW YORK

(Information on verso)

Copyright, 1909
By P. F. Collier & Son

Manufacturered in U. S. A.

This example is an illustration of:

- edition statement taken from outside prescribed sources (many libraries place such an edition statement in the note area, sometimes as a quoted note)
- multiple places of publication
- publication date not listed, century uncertain
- 2nd level cataloging

2nd level cataloging for a Canadian library

Darwin, Charles.
  Journal of researches during the voyage of H.M.S. "Beagle" / by Charles Darwin. -- [2nd ed. rev.] -- London ; Toronto : T. Nelson, [19--?]
  543 p. ; 16 cm.

  1. Beagle Expedition (1831-1836). 2. Natural history. 3. Geology. 4. Voyages around the world. 5. South America -- Description and travel. I. Title.

2nd level cataloging for a U.S. library

Darwin, Charles.
  Journal of researches during the voyage of H.M.S. "Beagle" / by Charles Darwin. -- [2nd ed. rev.] -- London ; New York : T. Nelson, [19--?].
  543 p. ; 16 cm.

  1. Beagle Expedition (1831-1836). 2. Natural history. 3. Geology. 4. Voyages around the world. 5. South America -- Description and travel. I. Title.

Recommended DDC: 578.09
Recommended LCC: QH11.D2 1900z or QH31.D2 1990z

Figure 17.7.

Figure 17.7—*Continued*

CHIEF SOURCE OF INFORMATION
(Title Page)

JOURNAL OF
RESEARCHES

DURING THE

VOYAGE OF H.M.S. "BEAGLE"

BY

CHARLES DARWIN

Thomas Nelson and Sons Ltd.
London Edinburgh New York
Toronto and Paris

(The verso is blank)

Capitalization and punctuation of the title proper are not transcribed exactly as they appear on the chief source. Capitalization of all parts of the description follows standard rules contained in AACR2-98's Appendix A. In English-language titles, usually only the first word and proper nouns are capitalized. Different rules govern capitalization for other languages. Punctuation is not transcribed as it appears, particularly when it might be confused with ISBD punctuation.

Sometimes an item is published in two (or more) languages and has titles in both of them. Both are considered part of the title proper. A bilingual title does not always mean the material is a bilingual work. In Figure 17.8, page 364, despite the presence of a bilingual title on the title page, the book is not written in two languages. (ᓄᓇᕗᑦ pronounced "Nunavut" and translates as "Our land.") Most cataloging departments do not have the syllabic typeface to list the Inuktitut title as required for second level cataloging, so first level enriched cataloging—defined as more data than required by Level 1, but not as much as required by Level 2—may be a simple, practical solution for titles with nonroman alphabets.

This example is an illustration of:

- bilingual title in a nonroman script
- publication date not listed, copyright date given
- unnumbered series statement
- series other title information
- contents note
- 1st level cataloging enriched

Weihs, Jean
 Nunavut : our land. -- M.O.D. Publishing, c1999.
 32 p. -- (Our country : provinces & territories)

 Glossary of English and equivalent Inuktitut words in roman alphabet and in syllabics with pronunciation guide: p. 29.
 ISBN 1-89446109-6.

 1. Nunavut. I. Title. II. Series.

Recommended DDC: 917.19

CHIEF SOURCE OF INFORMATION
(Title Page)

NUNAVUT: OUR LAND

ᓄᓇᕗᑦ

Jean Weihs
Illustrated by Cameron Riddle

M.O.D. Publishing
Mississauga, Ontario

(Information on Verso)

© 1999 Jean Weihs

ISBN: 1-89446109-6

(Information on Cover)

OUR COUNTRY:
PROVINCES & TERRITORIES

NUNAVUT

Figure 17.8.

After the title proper, the rules suggest that a *general material designation* be given, to alert the catalog user to the item's physical format. AACR2-98 has two lists of permissible general material designations (gmds), one for use by British catalogers, one for catalogers in Australia, Canada, and the United States.

Gmds are optional. In libraries consisting mostly of books, the gmd for books, *text,* usually is omitted and only gmds for other formats are used. If books are not the library's primary material, the cataloger may decide to use *text* along with all the others. If using gmds, put them immediately after the title proper, except for uniform titles.

Following the gmd (or title proper if gmd is not used) the rest of the title appears, called *other title information* by AACR2-98. (This part of area 1 is not required for Level 1 descriptions.) Figure 17.9, below and page 366, presents an example of other title information.

This example is an illustration of:

- main entry under corporate body
- other title information
- responsibility not attributed in chief source of information
- edition statement taken from outside prescribed sources (Many libraries place such an edition statement in the note area, sometimes as a quoted note)
- publication date not listed, copyright date given
- work consisting mostly of illustrations
- credits note
- edition and history note
- added entry for designer
- added entry for author of a part of the work
- optional addition of full form of given names
- additional title added entry
- 2nd level cataloging

```
McMichael Canadian Collection.
  A heritage of Canadian art : the McMichael collection. --
[Rev. and enl. ed.]. -- Toronto : Clarke, Irwin, c1976.
  198 p. : chiefly ill. ; 27 cm.

  Designed by A.J. Casson; biographies by Paul Duval.
  Previous ed. published in 1973 under title: A vision of
Canada.
  ISBN 0-7720-1209-1.

  1. McMichael Canadian Collection -- Catalogs.
2. Painting, Canadian -- Ontario -- Kleinburg -- Catalogs.
3. Art, Canadian -- Ontario -- Kleinburg -- Catalogs.
4. Artists -- Canada -- Biography.  I. Casson, A.J. (Alfred
Joseph).  II. Duval, Paul.  III. Title.  IV. Title: A vision of
Canada.
```

Recommended DDC: 759.11074
Recommended LCC: N910.K5712 A56 1979

Figure 17.9.

Figure 17-9—*Continued*

CHIEF SOURCE OF INFORMATION
(Title Page)

A HERITAGE OF CANADIAN ART

The McMichael Collection

Clarke, Irwin & Company Limited, Toronto, Vancouver

(Information on Verso)

Designed by A. J. Casson, LL.D., R.C.A.
Photography Hugh W. Thompson
Portraits of Artists by Joachim Gauthier, A.R.C.A., O.S.A.
Produced by Sampson Matthews Limited, Toronto

(Information on page 16)

ACKNOWLEDGEMENTS

Paul Duval, well-known author of many books on Canadian art, contributed to the text for the introduction and is the author of each of the biographies. His assistance in the preparation of this book has been invaluable.

We are indebted to Bernhard Cinader F.R.S.C., an eminent Canadian scientist who prepared the text, *Woodland Indian Art*. He was among the first to recognize the aesthetic value of the contemporary art of the Woodland Indian, and to organize two of the first exhibitions of their work.

After eight trips to the Arctic to expand her special

© 1976 McMichael Canadian Collection
ISBN 0 7720 1060 X
Printed in Canada

16

(Information on Book Jacket)

A Heritage of Canadian Art

an enlarged and revised study of
The McMichael Canadian Collection

Design by A. J. Casson

This new book about the famous McMichael Canadian Collection in Kleinburg carries all the impact of its highly acclaimed predecessor, *A Vision of Canada*. A completely new chapter on the Woodland Indians has been added, and sections on other indigenous Canadian cultures have been considerably expanded. A new introduction covers more fully the philosophy and history of the collection, and the works of art contained in it.

Vital Indian and Eskimo creations are presented alongside the work of the Group of Seven and their contemporaries. Masks and totems from the West Coast, stone carvings from the Arctic, magnificent landscapes of the Canadian wilderness, all combine to provide a rich record of our artistic heritage.

The book contains 1076 reproductions in black and white and 126 in full colour. Each facet of the collection is described by an expert, and sixteen individual biographies with full colour portraits of each artist by Joachim Gauthier supplement the text. *(continued on back flap)*

Very long other title information can be given in the notes (as shown in Figure 17.28 on pages 402–3), where LC has chosen to do this in its CIP record. The Library of Congress also opts to omit other title information for serials.

The last part of area 1 is the *statement of responsibility*. Here, the name(s) of the author(s), composer(s), artist(s), programmer(s), or other people or groups responsible for the overall content of the item are given, *provided* they appear "prominently" on the item being cataloged. Some catalogers interpret prominence as just appearing on the chief source or outer covering, but others choose to include only the names that appear in large print, or that are identified as being important contributors to the work. Some never give the names of writers of forewords, no matter how they are displayed. If no names appear on the item, this element is omitted.

Names that are important to the library but are not prominently displayed on the item being cataloged can be given in area 7 (the note area) to form the basis for headings. Any name used as an access point must be given somewhere in the catalog record. If the name has not appeared in areas 1 through 6, a note provides the basis for the access point. Some computerized catalogs have the capacity to search all fields of the record, so putting a name in the note field provides access without having to make a separate access point. For example, in Figure 17.9, A. J. Casson, an important Canadian painter, is the book's designer. Usually book designers are not given in the catalog record, but an art school might want to provide access to all Casson's work in its collection.

If more than one name is given for the same kind of contribution to the creation of the work—for example, joint authors or joint producers—they are separated by commas. If more than one name is given but each is for a different contribution to the creation of the work—for example, an author and an illustrator or a producer and a director—they are separated by different punctuation to indicate that they did not have the same kind of responsibility. (Level 1 descriptions give only the first statement of responsibility if it differs from the item's main heading, or if there is no personal name main entry heading.)

Area 2—Edition

If an edition is named on the prescribed sources of information for this area, it is transcribed as it appears in the second area of description. It should be abbreviated if abbreviations for one or more of the words being transcribed are listed in AACR2-98's Appendix B or C. Figure 17.10, page 368, uses many abbreviations, but transcribes the words in the order in which they appear.

1st ed.	(appears in item as: First Edition) (Note that if the item is a first edition, but is not labeled as such, no edition statement would be listed.)
2nd ed.	(appears in item as: Second Edition or as 2nd Edition)
Colorized version	(appears in item as: Colorized version, Avanti Studios)
Rev. ed.	(appears in item as: Revised Edition)
2nd ed., rev. & enl.	(appears in item as: Second Edition, Revised & Enlarged)
2nd rev. and enl. ed.	(appears in item as: Second Revised and Enlarged Edition)
Release 3.1	(appears in item as: Release 3.1, 1999)
Large print ed.	(appears in item as: LARGE PRINT EDITION)
American ed.	(appears in item as: American Edition)
Book Club ed.	(appears in item as: Book Club Edition)

Figure 17.10.

Area 3—Material Specific Details

Four kinds of materials require use of area 3: cartographic materials, printed music, electronic resources, and serials in all formats. Each type of material has its own information for this area, hence the name *material specific*. For cartographic items, the scale and, when found on the item, the projection and, optionally, a statement of coordinates and equinox are given; for music, the musical presentation; for electronic resources, when such information is readily available, the type of file and information relating to the number and size of files; and for serials, the numbering of the first volume. Serials in one of the nonbook formats also requiring area 3 may have two different types of data for this area.

Serials employ area 3 to record numbering and dating of issues. These data are followed by a hyphen and spaces to indicate that the area is unfinished. If the publisher stops issuing the title, data for the final issue will be added in the spaces. Examples follow:

The first issue of a magazine says "Issue number 1"

Area 3: Issue no. 1- .

The last issue of the same magazine says "Issue number 101"

Area 3: Issue no. 1-101.

The first screen of an electronic periodical says "Volume 1, number 1, 1999"

Area 3: Vol. 1, no. 1 (1999)- .

The first screen of an electronic periodical says "Volume 1, number 1, January 1999"

Area 3: Vol. 1, no. 1 (Jan. 1999)- .

The rules assume the original numbering style will not change over the life of a serial, but occasionally it does. Sometimes a publisher begins by numbering issues sequentially, but finds, later on, that it wants to supply volume and issue numbers. This happened with *Library Hi-Tech,* which displays both its old and new numbering systems (see Figure 17.11, page 370).

Figures 17.12 through 17.14 (pages 371–74) illustrate area 3 for nonbook materials that require it. (Area 3 is required for Level 1 cataloging, but not every subelement must be included.)

Area 4—Publication, Distribution, Etc.

Area 4 gives the locations and names of publishers or distributors of published items being cataloged and the dates they were issued. (For cataloging purposes, all remote access electronic resources, which includes all those on the Internet, are considered published.)

For serial items, the date on the issue used as the basis of cataloging is given, but it is left open by adding a hyphen and spaces following the date. For unpublished materials, locations and names are omitted; but, based on the rationale that dates are too important to omit, the date of an item's creation is given in this area. Naturally occurring objects that have not been packaged for commercial distribution are the only exception; no date is given for them (see Figure 17.4). (Level 1 records require only the first publisher's name and the date, and also leave the date open for serials.)

ISSN 0737-8831

Consecutive Issue 5; Vol. 2, No. 1/1984

LIBRARY HI TECH

PUBLISHER
C. Edward Wall

EDITOR-IN-CHIEF
Nancy Jean Melin

ASSOCIATE EDITORIAL DIRECTOR
Thomas Schultheiss

MANAGING EDITOR
Linda Mark

EDITORIAL ASSISTANTS
Karen Bell
Susan Gooding
Jon Hertzig

ADVERTISING
Eileen Parker, *Advertising Manager*
Mary Beth Bimber, *Advertising Assistant*

PRODUCTION
Peggy Cabot, *Production Supervisor*
Bronwyn Beeler, *Production/Layout*
Rebecca McDermott, *Production Assistant*

DESIGN
Bronwyn Beeler
Eileen Parker

Library Hi Tech © Copyright 1984 by the Pierian Press, Inc.

Published quarterly: Spring (published April); Summer (published July); Fall (published October); Winter (published January).

Subscriptions are $39.50 per year; $36.00 per year for each additional subscription, same customer; Foreign subscriptions (including Canada and P.U.A.) are $46.50 per year. Single issues, $12.50; individuals may subscribe for $19.50 per year.* Combined subscriptions to **Library Hi Tech Journal** and **Library Hi Tech News** (11 issues per year) are $90.00 per year. Individuals may purchase a combined subscription for $54.00 per year.* Send all subscription orders, changes of address, and claims to Pierian Press, P.O. Box 1808, Ann Arbor, MI 48106: (313) 434--5530.

*(Individual subscriptions must be paid by personal check or money order and deliverable to home address only.)

LHT accepts advertising for products or services applicable to libraries/information centers or of interest to those involved with information management. LHT reserves the right to reject any advertisement which is deemed inappropriate to the advertising profile of the periodical or which, in view of the Editors, features misinformation, distortion of facts, or exaggerated claims. Direct advertising correspondence to Eileen Parker, P.O. Box 1808, Ann Arbor, MI 48106. Rates upon request. (313) 434--6409.

Reader letters and queries may be forwarded directly to the Editor at 42 Grandview, Mt. Kisco, NY 10549, or call 914/666-4099. Editorial specialists are identified at the back of the journal and should be consulted for matters relating to potential and submitted manuscripts as appropriate.

Library Hi Tech is unique as a current guide to all available and forthcoming technologies applicable to libraries and information centers; as a single source reviewing related literature in periodicals, books, reports, studies and conference proceedings; as a major journal of practical articles related to all available and forthcoming technologies. LHT evaluates, describes, and reports on the selection, installation, maintenance, and integration of systems and hardware. Library Hi Tech is indexed in *Current Index to Journals in Education*.

FEATURES

DEPARTMENTS

Figure 17.11.

This example is an illustration of:

- map
- main entry under corporate body
- general material designation
- other title information
- joint responsibility
- statement of scale and projection with optional addition of projection statement
- place, publisher, and date not listed on item; decade of publication known
- language note
- contents note
- 2nd level cataloging

Tungavik Federation of Nunavut.
  Inuit owned lands [cartographic material] : Nunavut / prepared by the Tungavik Federation of Nunavut (TFN) and JLC Repro Graphic. -- Scale 1:3,000,000 ; Lambert conformal conic proj., standard parallels at 49°N and 77°N central meridian of origin, longitude 95°W and latitude 77°N. -- [S.l. : s.n., 199-]
  1 map : col. ; 109 x 100 cm.

  Legend in English, Inuktitut (both eastern and western orthography), and French.
  Inset: Sanikiluao.

  1. Nunavut -- Maps, I. Title.

Recommended DDC: 917.195

INFORMATION ON THE FACE OF THE MAP

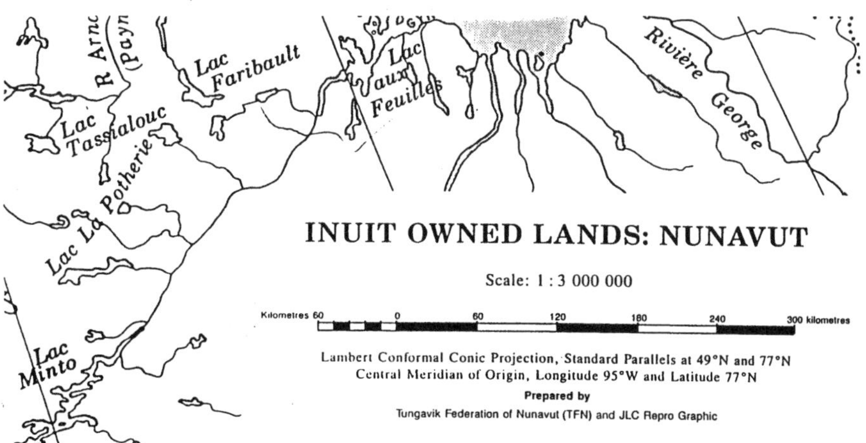

Figure 17.12.

Figure 17.12—*Continued*

THIS LEGEND IS REPEATED IN EASTERN-ORTHOGRAPHY INUKTITUT, WESTERN-ORTHOGRAPHY INUKTITUT, AND FRENCH

NUNAVUT LEGEND

NUNAVUT SETTLEMENT AREA .... ———

See Article 3 and Schedule 3 1 of the Agreement for full description

HIGH ARCTIC AREA EXEMPT FROM INUIT LAND OWNERSHIP... • • • •

See Section 19 2 6 and Schedule 19 1 of the Agreement for full description.

INUIT LAND QUANTUM

Regions	Surface only excluding minerals Article 19.2.1b	Surface and Subsurface including minerals Article 19.2.1a
North Baffin	31 026 sq miles	2.372 sq miles
South Baffin	23.941 sq miles	1,771 sq miles
Sanikiluaq	0 sq miles	1,001 sq miles
Keewatin	32 092 sq miles	5.040 sq miles
Kitikmeot East	13.790 sq miles	592 sq miles
Kitikmeot West	21.973 sq miles	3.852 sq miles
Nunavut Totals	**122,822 sq miles**	**14.628 sq miles**

1 sq mile - 2 5898 sq kilometers

*(Regional totals above are larger than the negotiated quantum totals listed in Schedule 19 2 to 19 7 of the Agreement and the above are the actual amounts of land Inuit will own)

FORM OF TITLE

See Article 19 of the Agreement for details, especially see Sub-section 19.2.1(a) and 19.2.1(b).

EXISTING MINERAL INTERESTS ON INUIT LAND

See Section 19.2.2 to 19.2.4 of the Agreement for details.

INUIT OWNED LANDS WITHIN MUNICIPALITIES

Not shown on this map. The following communities contain Inuit Owned Lands within their municipalities:

Iqaluit	Pond Inlet	Coppermine
Cape Dorset	Rankin Inlet	Cambridge Bay
Pangnirtung	Whale Cove	Taloyoak
Lake Harbour	Broughton Island	

The Hamlet offices of the above communities have copies of maps showing Inuit Owned Lands within their municipality.

CROWN (PUBLIC) LANDS

All other lands are Crown lands. Inuit have the right to hunt, trap, fish and participate in the management of all these lands. Please see the Agreement for more details.

TOTAL INUIT OWNED LANDS: 137,450 Square Miles

```
This work does not have a title page.
- - - - - - - - - - - - - - - - - - - - - - - - - - - - - -
The caption states:
     Symphony No. 4
     for Orchestra
     Jean Sibelius, Op. 63.
- - - - - - - - - - - - - - - - - - - - - - - - - - - - - -
The cover states:
     Miniature Score Edition
     JEAN SIBELIUS
     SYMPHONY No. 4
     in A minor
     Op. 63
     British & Continental Music Agencies Ltd.
     125 Shaftesbury Avenue, London, W.C.2
     Printed In England
- - - - - - - - - - - - - - - - - - - - - - - - - - - - - -
```

This example is an illustration of:

- musical score
- uniform title
- optional placement of general material designation at end of title proper
- musical presentation statement (optional area 3)
- publication and copyright dates unknown
- 2nd level cataloging

```
Sibelius, Jean.
  [Symphonies, no. 4, op. 63, A minor]
  Symphony no. 4 in A minor, op. 63 [music] / Jean Sibelius. -
Miniature score. -- London : British & Continental Music
Agencies, [19--]
  1 miniature score (68 p.) ; 18 cm.

  1. Symphonies.
```

Recommended DDC: 784.2
Recommended LCC: M1001.S52 1900z

Figure 17.13.

```
Chief source of information (the title screen) has:
- - - - - - - - - - - - - - - - - - - - - - - - - - - - - - - -
Nutrition and Agriculture in Eighteenth-Century Europe
Compiled by Virginia S. Hanson.
Update 5.1         00/02/01
- - - - - - - - - - - - - - - - - - - - - - - - - - - - - - - -
```

This example is an illustration of:

- electronic resource (remote access from central database)
- optional addition of fuller form of given names
- general material designation
- edition statement
- file characteristics statement
- nature and scope note
- mode of access note
- source of title note
- item described note
- 2nd level cataloging

```
Hanson, Virginia S. (Virginia Susan).
  Nutrition and agriculture in eighteenth-century Europe
[electronic resource] / compiled by Virginia S. Hanson. --
Update 5.1. -- Electronic data (1 file : 650 records). -- 2000.

  Bibliography.
  Mode of access: METRONET.
  Title from title screen.
  Description based on contents viewed Mar. 31,2000.

  1. Agriculture -- Europe -- History -- Bibliography.
2. Europe -- Social life and customs -- Eighteenth century --
Bibliography.  3. Nutrition -- Europe -- History --
Bibliography.  I. Title.
```

Figure 17.14.

If one publisher is listed, the city in which it is located, its name, and the date the item was published or distributed are given. If the publisher has several locations, the first-named city always is given, but, if another is listed more prominently, it also is given. In addition, if neither the first-named city nor a more prominently named city is located in the cataloger's home country, a city in the home country, if one is listed, also is given.

Catalogers should not equate production of nonbook items with publication. For films and videos, production means creation, and belongs in area 1. Many nonbook items are said to be "released." The releasing agent and/or distributor is named in area 4, and is equivalent to the publisher of a book.

In Figure 17.15, below and page 376, four places of publication are listed on the title page. The first of these—Melbourne—must be given in the catalog record. The second—Oakland—is given in a catalog record for U.S. libraries because it is the first-named place in the home country; "Oakland" is not given in a Canadian record.

If the item lists more than one publisher or distributor, the first-named always is given. When another is listed more prominently than the first and/or when the first is located in a country foreign to the cataloger but a subsequently named publisher or distributor is located in the home country, two or three are given. If the item being cataloged does not list places or names of any publishers or distributors, the cataloger can supply the abbreviations [s.l.] and/or [s.n.] in square brackets, meaning *sine loco* (without a place) and *sine nomine* (without a name), as substitutes.

This example is an illustration of:

- multiple places of publication
- work containing only one type of illustration
- series statement
- contents note
- National Library of Australia CIP
- 2nd level cataloging

2nd level cataloging for a U.S. library

```
Kerr, Alex.
  Lost Japan / Alex Kerr. -- Melbourne, Victoria ; Oakland,
Calif. : Lonely Planet, 1996.
  269 p. : map ; 20 cm. -- (Lonely Planet journeys)

  Glossary: p. 264-269.
  ISBN 0-86442-370-5.
```

2nd level cataloging for a Canadian library

```
Kerr, Alex.
  Lost Japan / Alex Kerr. -- Melbourne, Victoria : Lonely
Planet, 1996.
  269 p. : map ; 20 cm. -- (Lonely Planet journeys)

  Glossary: p. 264-269.
  ISBN 0-86442-370-5.
```

Tracing for both

```
  1. Japan -- Civilization, 1945-.  2. Japan -- Description and
travel.  I. Title.  II. Series.
```

Recommended DDC: 952.04

Figure 17.15.

Figure 17.15—*Continued*

CHIEF SOURCE OF INFORMATION
(Title Page)

LOST JAPAN

ALEX KERR

LONELY PLANET PUBLICATIONS
Melbourne • Oakland • London • Paris

(Information on Cover)

(Information on Verso)

Lost Japan

Published by Lonely Planet Publications
Head Office: PO Box 617, Hawthorn, Vic 3122, Australia
Branches: 155 Filbert St, Suite 251, Oakland, CA 94607, USA
10 Barley Mow Passage, Chiswick, London W4 4PH, UK
71 bis rue du Cardinal Lemoine, 75005 Paris, France

Published 1996

Printed by SNP Printing Pte Ltd, Singapore

Translated and adapted from *Utsukushiki Nippon no Zanzo* (Shincho-sha, Tokyo, 1993), © Alex Kerr 1993

Author photograph by Philip Gostelow
Map by Trudi Canavan
Calligraphy by Alex Kerr

National Library of Australia Cataloguing in Publication Data

Kerr, Alex, 1952-
Lost Japan

ISBN 0 86442 370 5.

1. Kerr, Alex, 1952-
2. Japan – Civilization – 1945-
3. Japan – Description and travel.
I. Kerr, Alex, 1952 – Utsukushiki Nihon no zanzo
II. Title. III. Title: Utsukushiki Nihon no zanzo.

952.04

Text © Alex Kerr 1996
Map © Lonely Planet 1996

The date of publication or distribution—the third element of information included in this area—must always be given, even if the item bears no dates of any kind. There is only one exception to this rule—dates are not given to naturally occurring objects (see figure 17.4). Various kinds of dates are found on materials, including publication (or distribution) dates, copyright dates, printing dates, production dates, manufacture dates, and so forth. The preferred date for area 4 is *publication* or *distribution,* not copyright, printing, production, or manufacture. If there are several dates, all publication or distribution dates, choose the one that matches the edition statement in area 2. If there still is a choice among publication or distribution dates applying to that edition, choose the latest date.

When there is no publication or distribution date given on the item, the next best choice for area 4 is the copyright date. Nonbook materials may be copyrighted long before they are released, so some care should be exercised in selecting old copyright dates for new distributions, e.g., a 1990s video production of a 1940s film. It is better to make an educated guess than to use a copyright date from the 1940s for a video that could not possibly have been made and distributed during that decade. The guessed date may be given in one of the following ways, depending on the degree of certainty that it is correct:

[1999]—the year is not in doubt, but the source is not one of those prescribed

[1999?]—the year is in doubt; the cataloger guesses it is 1999

[199-]—the exact year is in doubt, but the cataloger knows it is in the 1990s

[199-?]—the exact year is in doubt; the cataloger guesses it is in the 1990s, but is not certain of it

A copyright date is identified by preceding it with a "c" or, in the case of some recordings, a "p" ("phonogram"). If copyright and publication dates differ, both may be given in this area, publication date first, or, the copyright date may be given in a note.

In the absence of either a publication/distribution date or a copyright date, the date of manufacture may be given in area 4, but it must be identified as such. When no dates appear on the item, the cataloger must guess, based on whatever information is available. The cataloger may look up the item in a reference work, consider the technology, or glean clues from the item itself. As shown above, AACR2-98 suggests many ways to express an approximate date, depending on the cataloger's degree of certainty and the time span.[6]

Figure 17.16, pages 378–79, illustrates how research and common sense help approximate a date of publication. The preface is dated 1932 and the book's verso says it is a wartime book. To what war does it refer? World War II is a logical assumption. Reference sources reveal that C.H. Best, a well-known scientist who helped discover insulin, was active then. The book was printed in the United States, which entered the war in 1941, making 1942–1945 the likely range of years in which it was published.

This example is an illustration of:

- joint responsibility
- other title information
- edition statement taken from outside prescribed sources (many libraries place such an edition statement in the note area, sometimes as a quoted note)
- estimated date of publication
- both black and white and colored illustrations
- publication note
- index note
- 2nd level cataloging

Best, C.H.
  The human body and its functions : an elementary text-book of physiology / by C.H. Best and N.B. Taylor. -- [Special ed.]. -- New York : H. Holt, [1942-1945]
  371 p. : ill. (some col.) ; 20 cm.

  "A wartime book". Pref. dated 1932.
  Includes index.

  1. Physiology. 2. Human anatomy. I. Taylor, N.B. II. Title.

Recommended DDC: 612
Recommended LCC: QP34.B47

CHIEF SOURCE OF INFORMATION
(Title Page)

THE HUMAN BODY
AND ITS FUNCTIONS

AN ELEMENTARY TEXT-BOOK OF PHYSIOLOGY

BY

C. H. BEST, M.A., M.D., D.Sc. (Lond.), F.R.S. (Canada),
F.R.C.P. (Canada)

Professor of Physiology and Director of the Department, Associate
Director of the Connaught Laboratories, Research Associate
in the Banting-Best Department of Medical Research,
University of Toronto

AND

N. B. TAYLOR, M.D., M.R.C.S. (Eng.), L.R.C.P. (Lond.),
F.R.C.S. (Edin.), F.R.C.P. (Canada)

Professor of Physiology, University of Toronto

NEW YORK
HENRY HOLT AND COMPANY

Figure 17.16.

Figure 3-16—*Continued*

(Information on Spine)

Title Proper

Author's Surnames

Special Edition

(Information on Verso)

A WARTIME BOOK

THIS COMPLETE EDITION IS PRODUCTS IN FULL COMPLIANCE WITH THE GOVERNMENT'S REGULATIONS FOR CONSERVING PAPER AND OTHER ESSENTIAL MATERIALS

PRINTED IN THE
UNITED STATES OF AMERICA

Area 5—Physical Description

Physical description includes the number and kind of pieces, called the *extent of item,* which includes the specific material designation (smd) and, for some media, duration; other physical details; dimensions; and accompanying materials, if any. (Only extent is required for Level 1 records.) Extent, physical details, and dimensions vary by medium, but accompanying materials—added pieces physically separate from the item being cataloged—are treated the same way for all materials.

For books, extent is given as the number of pages, leaves (pages with text on only one side), or volumes. A special case is books issued with loose-leaf pages. For them, only the number of volumes is given, with the word "loose-leaf" following in parentheses. Plates in a book are another special case. By definition, plates are separate pages bound in with a text after it is prepared. They are considered a separate part of the extent and are counted and listed after the regular pagination.

Electronic resources, sound recordings, and videos are described in terms of the number of discs, cartridges, cassettes, reels, or other carrier types. Motion pictures usually are described in terms of the number of reels, although carriers other than reels may be encountered. Microforms, like motion pictures, may be described as reels of film, but they also can be fiches, opaques, and so forth. It is not always possible to anticipate development of media formats, so rules in AACR2-98 Chapters 7 through 10 allow catalogers to create an appropriate smd for an item.

The abbreviation "ill." is given for illustrations in printed materials and their reproductions, for example, microforms. Tables, illustrated title pages, and minor illustrations are not considered "ill." Optionally, specific types of illustrations may be given.[7] This option has been adopted for demonstration purposes in the figures and examples in this book.

Examples of typical physical descriptions for materials covered by individual chapters of AACR2-98 are listed in Figure 17.17. Notice that the spelling of disc/disk varies for electronic resources: magnetic disks are spelled with a "k"; optical discs are spelled with a "c." Sound and videodiscs are spelled with the "c."

Books

[132] leaves ; 20 cm. (all unpaged leaves with no illustrations)

3 v. (124 p., 243 p., 222 p.) : ill., maps ; 28 cm. (multivolume set with pagination for each volume, an AACR2-98 option)

xvi, 245 p. ; 23 cm. (includes numbering of preliminary pages)

x, 245 p., [10] p. of plates : ill. ; 23 cm. (includes numbering of preliminary pages and total number of unpaged plates)

1 v. (loose-leaf) : ill., maps (some col.) ; 29 cm.

84 p. : all ill. ; 29 cm. (contains no text except captions)

84 p. : chiefly ill. ; 29 cm. (contains some text)

Nonbook Materials

1 map : col. ; 60 x 80 cm.

10 leaves : parchment ; 30 cm. (for a manuscript)

1 score (27 p.) ; 32 cm. + 5 parts

1 sound disc (60 min.) : digital, stereo. ; 4 3/4 in.

4 videocassettes (60 min. each) : sd., col. ; 1/2 in.

1 art original : oil on canvas; 45 x 60 cm.

1 art print : engraving, col. ; 31 x 42 cm.

1 electronic disk : sd., col. ; 3 1/2 in. + 1 user manual.

1 quilt : cotton, blue and yellow ; 120 x 100 cm.

3 microfiches (100 fr. each) ; ill. (standard dimensions omitted)

   v. : ill. ; 28 cm. (open serial record, with no extent; note that three spaces are left for future entry of the number of volumes)

Figure 17.17.

Area 6—Series

If an item belongs to a series, the name of the series is given in this area. (Level 1 records omit this area entirely.) The main title of a series is transcribed exactly as it appears on the item, even if the cataloger wishes to make a heading for it that is slightly different. When they are important for identification, statements of responsibility associated with a series may be given, also. If an ISSN has been assigned to the series or a number within the series has been given to the item, these are included. Some items regularly bear both ISBNs and ISSNs, so catalogers can treat them either serially or monographically (see Figure 17.18), below and pages 382–83).

```
This example is an illustration of:
     •  named conference
     •  entry under corporate body
     •  joint editors
     •  place of publication supplied
     •  bibliography and index note
     •  serial
     •  marks of omission
     •  open entry
     •  frequency note
     •  source of title note
     •  title information note
     •  relationship with other serials note
     •  added entries for editors
     •  added entry for corporate body
     •  ISBN and ISSN
```

2nd level cataloging as a monograph

```
Clinic on Library Applications of Data Processing(34th : 1997 :
    University of Illinois at Urbana-Champaign)
  Visualizing subject access for 21st century information
resources / edited by Pauline Atherton Cochrane, Eric H. Johnson
with the editorial assistance of Sandra Roe. -- [Urbana, Ill.] :
Graduate School of Library and Information Science, University
of Illinois at Urbana-Champaign, 1998.
  176 p. : ill. ; 24 cm.

  Includes bibliographical references and index.
  ISBN 0-87845-103-X.

  1. Libraries -- United States -- Data processing --
Congresses.  2. Information storage and retrieval systems --
Congresses.  3. Computer graphics -- Congresses.  4. Image
processing -- Digital techniques -- Congresses.  I. Cochrane,
Pauline A.  II. Johnson, Eric. H.  III. University of Illinois.
Graduate School of Library and Information Science.
```

Figure 17.18.

Figure 17.18—*Continued*

2nd level cataloging as a serial

Clinic on Library Applications of Data Processing(University of Illinois at Urbana-Champaign)
Papers presented at the ... Clinic on Library Applications of Data Processing. -- 1980- . -- [Urbana, Ill.] : Graduate School of Library and Information Science, University of Illinois at Urbana-Champaign, c1981- .
v. : ill. ; 24 cm.

Annual.
Title from half-title page.
Each issue has a distinctive title.
Continues: Proceedings of the Clinic on Library Applications of Data Processing.
ISSN 0069-4789.

1. Libraries -- Automation -- Congresses. I. University of Illinois. Graduate School of Library and Information Science.

Recommended DDC for both: 025.078

CHIEF SOURCE OF INFORMATION
(Title Page)

VISUALIZING SUBJECT ACCESS FOR 21ST CENTURY INFORMATION RESOURCES

Edited by
PAULINE ATHERTON COCHRANE
ERIC H. JOHNSON

with the editorial assistance
of Sandra Roe

GRADUATE SCHOOL OF LIBRARY AND INFORMATION SCIENCE
UNIVERSITY OF ILLINOIS AT URBANA-CHAMPAIGN
1998

(Information on Page Opposite Title Page

VISUALIZING SUBJECT ACCESS FOR 21ST CENTURY INFORMATION RESOURCES

PAPERS PRESENTED AT THE
1997 CLINIC ON LIBRARY APPLICATIONS OF DATA PROCESSING
MARCH 2-4, 1997
GRADUATE SCHOOL OF LIBRARY AND INFORMATION SCIENCE
UNIVERSITY OF ILLINOIS AT URBANA-CHAMPAIGN

Figure 17.18—*Continued*

(Information on Page Preceeding Title Page)	(Information on Verso)
CLINIC ON LIBRARY APPLICATIONS OF DATA PROCESSING: 1997	© 1998 The Board of Trustees of The University of Illinois Manufactured in the United States of America Printed on acid-free paper ISBN 0-87845-103-X ISSN 0069-4789

Area 7—Notes

With some exceptions, notes are optional at all bibliographic levels; however, in rules for other areas of description catalogers are directed to make specific notes, for example, noting the source of title proper if it does not come from the chief source. "Title supplied by cataloger" and "Title from cover" are seen in catalog records explaining bracketed titles proper. For electronic resources, notes explaining the source of title proper and of an edition statement if different from the source of title proper, as well as the systems requirements, are mandated at all levels.

AACR2-98 prescribes the order in which notes should appear. They follow the order of descriptive elements, with notes relating to titles given before notes relating to editions, notes relating to editions before notes relating to publication, distribution, and so forth. AACR2-98 allows an important note to be put first. Such a decision is made on a medium-by-medium basis; for example, the publisher's or producer's number is given first for all sound recordings. Changes must be approved by the appropriate national bodies before becoming part of standard practice for that nation. Other nations may choose not to follow suit.

Optional notes that are important to make include the following:

1. *Physical description:* For videorecordings and electronic resources, this is the only place to include information about needed hardware. Books and other formats also benefit; for example, in Figure 17.19, pages 384–85, it informs users the book is chiefly photographs.

This example is an illustration of:

- title main entry with no statement of responsibility listed on the item
- other title information
- descriptive illustration statement
- all illustrations are in color
- illustration note
- index note
- also issued note (used for information about items not part of the collection)
- colophon as source of information
- prime mark in Dewey decimal classification
- 2nd level cataloging

The chateaux of the Loire : 66 locations, 291 photos. -- Blois, France : Valoire, 1997.
127 p. : col.ill., geneal. table, map, ports. ; 27 cm.

Consists chiefly of photographs.
Includes index.
Also issued in Dutch, French, German, Spanish, Swedish, and other languages.

1. Castles -- France -- Loire River Valley. 2. Loire River Valley (France) -- Guidebooks.

Recommended DDC: 728.81'0445 or 914.45

CHIEF SOURCE OF INFORMATION
(Title Page)

THE CHATEAUX
OF THE LOIRE

66 locations - 291 photos

VALOIRE publications
PRINTED BY LECONTE
BLOIS 41260 LA CHAUSSEE-ST-VICTOR

Figure 17.19.

Figure 17.19—*Continued*

(Information in Colophon)

Photographs by Editions Valoire
with the collaboration of P. Viard
and the assistance of Messrs. Berneron (p. 44 c) and Velut (p. 120 b, p. 97);
© Conseil Général du Loiret - Photos Dominique Chauveau (p. 12 a/b);
Photélico-Berger (pp. 14 b, 77 a); Héliflash (p. 19 b).
All rights reserved. Reproduction prohibited.
Printed in the EU. Legal deposit: 3rd quarter 1997.
ISBN 2-909575-03-9

2. *System requirements*: Figure 17.20 shows two different kinds of notes for electronic resources. These notes are mandatory. Electronic resources physically held in a library are given a systems requirements note. Electronic resources accessed from remote sources need a note to describe how to gain access, called a "mode of access" note, which should include the electronic address or Uniform Resource Locator (URL). The date the item was viewed for cataloging purposes should be added to the record as the final note.

For an electronic resource in a remote location:

System requirements: Requires Adobe Acrobat reader, 3.0 or higher

For an electronic resource stored in the library or media center:

System requirements: Intel Pentium processor or equivalent; Windows 95, 98, or NT Workstation 4.0; 16 MB RAM (32 recommended), 57 MB free hard disk space; VGA video (296-color minimum); CD-ROM drive.

For an Internet resource:

Mode of access: Metronet

Figure 17.20.

3. *Contents notes*: These should be made when an item contains more than one *work,* such as a CD-ROM containing two or more titles (see Figure 17.21, below and page 387). Limits on the number of titles to include in a contents note are hard to set. Between the extremes of very few and too many, catalogers must use judgment. The decision should rest on an estimate of how often people want only one work and whether they can find it another way. This also facilitates making added entries for each work, which cannot be done unless their titles appear somewhere in the catalog record.

This example is an illustration of:

- electronic resource (CD-ROM)
- title main entry
- general material designation
- no statement of responsibility
- edition statement
- publication date not listed, copyright date given
- accompanying material
- systems requirements note
- source of title note
- contents note
- additional title added entries
- two levels of cataloging

2nd level cataloging

The 1999 Canadian encyclopedia [electronic resource]. -- Version 5, World ed. -- Toronto : McClelland & Stewart, c1998.
2 CD-ROMs : sd., col. ; 4¾ in. + 1 user guide.

Systems requirements: Windows 3.1 or Windows 95 or Macintosh 68040 and Power PC or higher; double speed CD-ROM drive.
Title from title screen.
Contents: Disc 1. The Canadian encyclopedia, The Columbia encyclopedia (5th ed.), The Gage Canadian dictionary (recently rev.), over 700 articles from Maclean's magazine, French-English and English-French dictionary, Thesaurus, Timeline of Canadian and world events, Canadiana quiz, CanuckletHead interactive quiz -- Disc 2. The prime ministers.

1. Encyclopedias and dictionaries. 2. Thesauri. 3. Prime ministers -- Canada. 4. Canada -- Encyclopedias. I. Title: Canadian encyclopedia. II. Columbia encyclopedia. III. Title: Gage Canadian dictionary.

1st level cataloging

The 1999 Canadian encyclopedia [electronic resource]. -- Version 5, World ed. -- McClelland & Stewart, c1998.
2 CD-ROMs.

Systems requirements: Windows 3.1 or Windows 95 or Macintosh 68040 and Power PC or higher; double speed CD-ROM drive.
Title from title screen.

1. Encyclopedias and dictionaries. 2. Thesauri. 3. Prime ministers -- Canada. 4. Canada -- Encyclopedias. I. Title: Canadian encyclopedia.

Recommended DDC for both: 030

Figure 17.21.

Figure 17.21—*Continued*

Title screen on disc 1 states:

The 1999 Canadian Encyclopedia: World Edition

Title screen on disc 2 states:

The Prime Ministers

(Information on Disc)

(Information on Insert)

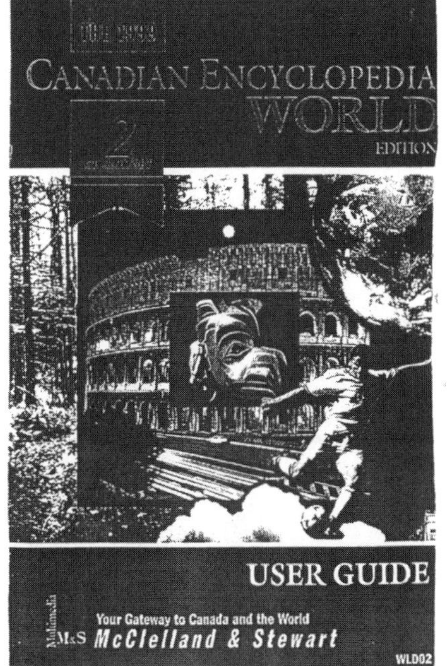

User Guide advertises other versions of the Canadian Encylopedia

4. *Summaries*: These should always be made for items that are not available for browsing or having very little eye-readable information for the browser to use, unless the rest of the catalog record describes them clearly. If searchers must rely on the catalog record to decide if an item is what they want, they should find enough information to make that decision. Summaries help a great deal (see Figure 17.22).

```
Chief source of information (the item itself) has:
     • the title on a label affixed to the mount
     • no other information is given


This example is an illustration of:
     • transparency
     • unpublished, unique item with a stated title and no
       indication of responsibility
     • title main entry
     • general material designation
     • probable date
     • audience level
     • summary
     • 2nd level cataloging


The Internal-combustion automobile engine [transparency]. --
  [1989?]
  1 transparency (7 overlays) : col. ; 26 x 20 cm.

  Intended audience: Grade 8 and up.
  Summary: Shows the fundamental structure and parts of a
typical six-cylinder, overhead-valve, internal combustion
gasoline automobile engine.

  1. Internal combustion engine, Spark ignition.
2. Automobiles -- Motors (Two-stroke cycle).


Recommended DDC: 629.2504
Recommended LCC: TL213.I57 1989
```

Figure 17.22.

5. *Details of the library's copy*: This is where to note torn pages, autographs, or other details present only in the cataloging library's copy of an item (see Figure 17.23, below and page 390).

```
This example is an illustration of:
     •  main entry indicated by typeface
     •  statement of subsidiary responsibility
     •  publishing date not listed, copyright date given
     •  all illustrations are in color
     •  unnumbered series statement
     •  audience level
     •  contents note
     •  copy being described note
     •  2nd level cataloging
```

2nd level cataloging for a Canadian library

```
Blum, Mark.
  Coral reef / photographs by Mark Blum ; text by Andrea Holden-
Boone. -- Toronto : Somerville House, c1998.
  32 p. : col. ill. ; 21 cm. -- (Eye to eye books)

  Audience level: ages 8-12.
  Includes Glossary (p. 31) and index.
  Library's copy has the 24 stereograph cards and viewer
detached and placed in back pocket.
  ISBN 1-894042-06-9.

  1. Coral reefs and islands.  I. Holden-Boone, Andrea.
I. Title.
```

Recommended DDC: 578.7789

N.B. If a U.S. library wishes to indicate that this book has also been published in the United States, a cataloger would add the place of publication in square brackets, if known. If the place of publication cannot be ascertained, the publication, distribution, etc., statement would read: Toronto ; United States : Somerville House, c1998.

Figure 17.23.

Figure 17.23—*Continued*

CHIEF SOURCE OF INFORMATION (Title Page)

Photographs By
Mark Blum

Text By
Andrea Holden-Boone

Somerville House Publishing
Toronto

(Information on Verso)

Copyright © 1998 by Somerville House Books Limited
Photographs © 1998 by Mark Blum

All rights reserved. This publication may not be reproduced or transmitted in whole or in part in any form or by any means — electronic or mechanical, including photocopy, recording or any information storage and retrieval system — without written permission from the Publisher, except by a reviewer who wishes to quote brief passages.

ISBN: 1-894042-06-9

Illustrated by Julian Mulock
Art Director: Neil Stuart
Design: FiWired.com
Printed in Hong Kong

Published simultaneously in the United States by
Somerville House, USA

Published in Canada by
Somerville House Publishing
a division of Somerville House Books Limited
3080 Yonge Street, Suite 5000
Toronto, Ontario M4N 3N1

(Information on Back Cover

This book includes:
- 3-D StereoFocus™ viewer
- 24 full-color sterogrpahic cards and a handy storage pocket
- 32 pages of facts, photos, and illustrations

For Ages 8-12
$13.95
Book printed in CHINA
Lenses manufactured in U.S.A.
Copyright©1998 Somerville House Books Limited

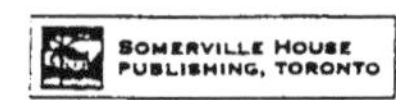

6. *Numbers on the item*: This is where to give numbers *other than* the ISBN or ISSN that appear on an item, such as Library of Congress Control Numbers.

Notes for serials include the frequency of issue, which AACR2-98 mandates should be given as the first note. Another specifies relationships with other serials, where catalogers can record earlier and later titles, mergers and splits, absorptions, supplements, and so forth.

Area 8—Standard Numbers and Terms of Availability

The final area of description is optional and is used for the ISBN or ISSN and the purchase price, rental fee, or other terms of availability for the item. No other numbers are given in area 8. When there is no standard number, area 8 may be left blank or only the terms of availability recorded, if desired.[8]

For serials, the key-title, an identifier of the International Serials Data System (ISDS), can be entered here. ISDS is an international program of serials identification similar to ISSN sponsored by UNESCO; ISSN is sponsored by IFLA. Data describing book bindings and paper, if the paper was treated to reduce acidity, also may be added in parentheses following the number; for example, ISBN 0-8389-7809-6 (pbk.) or ISBN 0-8389-0624-9 (alk. paper).

RULE INTERPRETATIONS

The experience of LC's and NLC's catalogers in applying the rules can be helpful for others, if they wish to adopt them. The Library of Congress's official policies are available in its *Cataloging Service* bulletin, an inexpensive periodical, and NLC's are available via the Internet.[9] The LC and NLC rule interpretations (LCRIs and NLCRIs) are not as authoritative as rules of AACR2-98, but they carry the weight of the largest and most important originators of catalog records in the United States and Canada, respectively, and the major computerized bibliographic networks follow them.

ACCESS POINTS—RETRIEVING THE RECORD

The next step in the cataloging process is creating headings for the description. Rules for headings appear in part 2 of AACR2-98. Chapter 21 covers choosing which elements from the description should be selected as headings. When searched in the catalog, the selected names, titles, or combinations of names and titles will result in retrieving the record.

All but one of AACR2-98's remaining chapters have rules for putting the chosen headings into the proper form. They explain how to construct headings for personal names (Chapter 22); geographic names (Chapter 23); names for entities made up of groups of people acting together, known as *corporate bodies* (Chapter 24); and conventional titles assigned to works that may appear with varying titles even though the work is the same, called *uniform titles* (Chapter 25). (Dates and control numbers are not mentioned, because searching under numeric elements is a feature of computerized systems, not a result of applying the rules.)

Chapter 26 describes references made to assist catalog users—see, see also, name-title, and explanatory references—and how to make them for names of persons, places, corporate bodies, and uniform titles. The chapter also discusses references to added entries for series and serials, and the use of references in place of added entries.

Headings are divided into two kinds: main and added entries. The only difference between them is that the first and most important heading chosen is designated the main entry; all the others are added entries. Main and added entries are distinguished for several reasons. In catalogs providing only one heading per item represented, main entry usually is the one chosen. The most important reason today for retaining the main entry concept is that shelf marks, additions to the classification number that form shelf addresses, are derived from the main entry. Without main entries, rules for creating shelf marks would be needed.

The Anglo-American cataloging tradition assumes a work's creator is its primary identifying feature. Therefore, AACR2-98 usually, although not always, assigns main entry to the creator of a work. Two other possibilities for main entry are a corporate body creator or a title. Only a single person, corporate body, or title can be the main entry. There are no "joint" main entries, even if an item being cataloged has two co-equal authors.

When one person is responsible for the content of an item, he or she usually is chosen as main entry, although there are exceptions. If the item comes from a corporate body (called *emanating* by AACR2-98), the person might *not* be chosen as main entry, although he or she would be named as an added entry. Figure 17.24, pages 393–94, shows a work of this type, for which a title main entry is selected. Another exception applies to compiled or edited works, in which the true creators are the authors of the various pieces, such as *The Ark in the Garden,* collected by Albert Manguel (Figure 17.25, pages 395–96). Editors and compilers are not considered creators, and AACR2-98 avoids selecting either of them for main entry.

Special rules about items created by more than one person or corporate body, where all share the same creative function, such as writing a book or composing a musical piece, are called rules for *shared responsibility* in AACR2-98. If one person or body is determined as having most responsibility, catalogers choose that one as main entry. If not, the one named first on the chief source of information is chosen, unless more than three are listed.

The chief way to decide whether one person has the most responsibility is to look at the wording of the statement of responsibility. If the chief source says, "Programmed by Bill Atkinson, with the assistance of members of the Macintosh staff," the cataloger can conclude that the contribution by the Macintosh staff is less important than Atkinson's. The predominant person's name can be given in larger type than the others (see Figure 17.20), set apart from other names, or appear out of alphabetical order. These devices indicate predominance among a group of creators. If no such devices are present, then all parties probably are equally responsible.

If there are two or three co-equal creators, main entry is assigned to the first named. If there are four or more, the title is selected instead. This *Rule of Three* (a library-wide rule of thumb) assumes people will not know any one creator when a work has many co-creators; thus the title is a better choice.

This example is an illustration of:

- edited work
- title main entry
- edition statement more accurately stated on the verso
- multiple places of publication
- detailed pagination
- contents note

2nd level cataloging for a Canadian library

The Oxford companion to English literature / edited by Margaret Drabble. -- 5th ed. rev.-- Oxford : Oxford University Press, 1998.
viii, 1154 p. ; 24 cm.

Includes a chronology, a list of the Poets Laureate, and a list of the winners of literary awards.

2nd level cataloging for a U.S. library

The Oxford companion to English literature / edited by Margaret Drabble. -- 5th ed. rev.-- Oxford ; New York : Oxford University Press, 1998.
viii, 1154 p. ; 24 cm.

Includes a chronology, a list of the Poets Laureate, and a list of the winners of literary awards.

Tracing for both

1.American literature -- Dictionaries. 2. English literature -- Dictionaries. 3. American literature -- Bio-bibliographies. 4. English literature -- Bio-bibliographies. I. Drabble, Margaret.

Recommended DDC: 820.3

Figure 17.24.

Figure 17.24—*Continued*

CHIEF SOURCE OF INFORMATION
(Title Page)

THE OXFORD
COMPANION TO
ENGLISH
LITERATURE

REVISED EDITION

EDITED BY
MARGARET DRABBLE

Oxford New York
OXFORD UNIVERSITY PRESS
1998

(Information on Verso)

Oxford University Press, Great Clarendon Street, Oxford OX2 6DP
Oxford New York
Athens Auckland Bangkok Bogota Buenos Aires Calcutta
Cape Town Chennai Dar es Salaam Delhi Florence Hong Kong Istanbul
Karachi Kuala Lumpur Madrid Melbourne Mexico City Mumbai
Nairobi Paris Sao Pàolo Singapore Taipei Tokyo Toronto Warsaw
and associated companies in Berlin Ibadan

Oxford is a registered trade mark of Oxford University Press

Published in the United States
by Oxford University Press, Inc., New York

© Margaret Drabble and Oxford University Press 1985, 1995

First edition 1932
Second edition 1937
Third edition 1946
Fourth edition 1967
Fifth edition 1985
First revision 1995
Second revision 1998

All rights reserved. No part of this publication may be reproduced, stored in a retrieval system, or transmitted, in any form or by any means, without the prior permission in writing of Oxford University Press. Within the UK, exceptions are allowed in respect of any fair dealing for the purpose of research or private study, or criticism or review, as permitted under the Copyright, Designs and Patents Act, 1988, or in the case of reprographic reproduction in accordance with the terms of licences issued by the Copyright Licensing Agency. Enquiries concerning reproduction outside these terms and in other countries should be sent to the Rights Department, Oxford University Press, at the address above

British Library Cataloguing in Publication Data
Data available

Library of Congress Cataloging in Publication Data
Data available

ISBN 0-19-866233-5

This example is an illustration of:

- compiled work
- item with many separately titled parts, different authors for these parts, and a collective title for the item as a whole
- title main entry
- other title information listed at head of title proper
- date inferred from the copyright date of the individual parts
- contents note
- Canadian CIP
- 2nd level cataloging

The ark in the garden : fables for our times / collected by Alberto Manguel. -- Toronto : Macfarlane Walter & Ross, [1998?].
63 p. : ill. ; 19 cm.

Contents: A Christmas lorac / Margaret Atwood -- The ark in the garden / Timothy Findley -- Come, said the eagle / Neil Bissoondath -- The axe and the trees / Jane Urquhart -- From plus-fours to minus-fours/ Rohinton Mistry -- The banana wars / Yves Beauchemin.
ISBN 1-55199-030-X.

1. Political satire, Canadian (English). 2. Canadian fiction -- 20th century. 3. Canada -- Politics and government -- 1993- -- Humor. I. Manguel, Alberto.

Recommended DDC: 819.7208

Figure 17.25.

Figure 17.25—*Continued*

CHIEF SOURCE OF INFORMATION
(Title Page)

Fables for Our Times

The Ark in the Garden

Collected by

Alberto Manguel

Macfarlane Walter & Ross
Toronto

(Information on Verso)

"A Christmas Lorac" copyright © 1996 O. W. Toad Ltd.

"The Ark in the Garden" copyright © 1998 Pebble Productions Inc.

"Come, Said the Eagle" copyright © 1998 Neil Bissoondath.

"The Axe and the Trees" copyright © 1998 Jane Urquhart.

"From Plus-Fours to Minus-Fours" copyright © Rohinton Mistry 1996. Reprinted with permission of the author.

"The Banana Wars" copyright © 1998 Yves Beauchemin. Translation copyright © 1998 Alberto Manguel.

Macfarlane Walter & Ross
37A Hazeelton Avenue
Toronto, Canada MSR 2E3

Canadian Cataloguing in Publication Data

Main entry under title:
The ark in the garden: fables for our times

ISBN 1-55199-030-X

1. Political satire, Canadian (English).* 2. Canadian fiction (English) - 20th century.* 3. Canada - Politics and government - 1993- - Humor.* I. Manguel, Alberto, 1948-

PS8375.A74 1998 C813'.5408'0358 C98-932031-6
PR9197.8.A74 1998

Macfarlane Walter & Ross gratefully acknowledges financial support for its publishing program from the Canada Council for the Arts, the Ontario Arts Council, and the Government of Canada through the Book Publishing Industry Development Program.

Printed and bound in Canada

(Table of Contents)

A Christmas Lorac
Margaret Atwood 7

The Ark in the Garden
Timothy Findley 15

Come, Said the Eagle
Neil Bissoondath 25

The Axe and the Trees
Jane Urquhart 35

From Plus-Fours to Minus-Fours
Rohinton Mistry 41

The Banana Wars
Yves Beauchemin 53

More special rules, called rules for *mixed responsibility,* explain how to choose when people or bodies perform different creative functions for an item being cataloged, such as drawing and coloring a cartoon. The rules lean toward writers of text over illustrators, composers of music over arrangers or librettists, and artists over other contributors when works of art are considered. Some items, such as films and videos, usually are the product of many different kinds of creative effort—producing, directing, acting, costuming, music, and so forth—not three or fewer. In these cases, none is chosen and the item receives a title main entry.

If an item emanates from a corporate body or a corporate body is named "author" on the chief source of information, that corporate body is not automatically named main entry. Rule 21.1B2 limits the use of a corporate body as main entry to six specific instances:

1. When the item is an internal document of the corporate body, such as the catalog of one's library or information center, or the membership directory of an association.
2. When the item is an administrative document, such as the budget of the organization or an annual report. Even though these documents are prepared for external distribution, they are, nonetheless, a reflection of the body itself.
3. When the item represents the collective thought of the body, such as the minutes of a meeting or reports of a committee. Figure 17.26, pages 398–99, illustrates such a report.
4. When the item represents the collective effort of a voyage, expedition, or a conference meeting the definition of a corporate body, and the event is named in the item. If, however, the event has no official name, it does not meet the full definition of a corporate body, which is "an organization or a group of persons that is identified by a particular name and that acts, or may act, as an entity."[10] Figures 17.27 and 17.28, pages 400–404, show examples of named and unnamed conferences (more likely to be encountered these days than voyages or expeditions).
5. If the item is a sound recording, film, or video, *and* the responsible corporate body does more than just perform it. This involves judging when a performing group does something that qualifies as *more than mere performance,* i.e., something we would call *creation.* The cataloger asks to what extent new notes, words, or movements are being created, typical of improvisation. In classical music, improvisation is unusual; in popular or jazz music, the opposite is true. Thus, popular performing groups often earn main entries. This also is true of some videos and films. The rule is applicable to performers who act together as a group and have a name, such as the rock group Kiss. It would not apply to individuals who happened to be on the same program for a recording date or a concert.

6. When the item is a cartographic representation and the corporate body is responsible for more than publication. An example is the National Geographic Society, which may finance expeditions to explore the territories it maps, hire and direct staff who do the cartographic work, and perform other functions as well.

When an item emanates from a corporate body but does not fit into these categories, it is not given a corporate body main entry. The emanation is excluded and either a creator or a title would be selected as main entry. According to AACR2-98, the cataloger should name as main entry "the personal author, the principal personal author, or the probable personal author."[11]

This example is an illustration of:

- main entry under corporate body
- two statements of other title information
- marks of omission to shorten lengthy other title information
- same organization responsible for intellectual content and publication
- detailed pagination statement
- bibliography note
- two levels of cataloging

2nd level cataloging

```
Kansas Library Network Board. Preservation Committee.
  Saving the past to enrich the future : a plan for preserving
information resources in Kansas : report ... to the citizens of
Kansas. -- Topeka, Kan. : The Board, 1993.
  vi, 52 p. : ill. ; 28 cm.

  Includes bibliography: (p. 39-45).
```

1st level cataloging

```
Kansas Library Network Board. Preservation Committee.
  Saving the past to enrich the future. -- The Board, 1993.
  vi, 52 p.
```

Tracing for both levels

```
  1. Library resources -- Kansas -- Conservation and
restoration.  I. Title.
```

Recommended unabridged DDC: 025.84
Recommended abridged DDC: 025.8

Figure 17.26.

Figure 17.26—*Continued*

CHIEF SOURCE OF INFORMATION
(Title Page)

Saving the Past to Enrich the Future

A Plan for Preserving Information Resources in Kansas

Report of the Kansas Library Network Board's
Preservation Committee to
the citizens of Kansas

Published with support from the
National Endowment for the Humanities,
Division of Preservation and Access

Published by the Kansas Library Network Board
March 1993

(Information on Verso)

Published with support from the National
Endowment for the Humanities

Kansas Library Network Board
300 SW 10th Street, Room 343
Topeka, KS 66612-1593
(913) 296-3296

This book includes a bibliography on pages
39 to 45

Size: 28 cm.

Paging: vi preliminary and 52 pages of text

Illustrations: general in black and white

This example is an illustration of:

- bilingual item
- unnamed conference
- title main entry
- edited work
- two other title information statements
- extensive other title information optionally given in the note area
- detailed pagination
- title information note
- language note
- statement of responsibility note
- Library of Congress CIP
- Prime mark in Dewey classification number
- two methods of cataloging

2nd level cataloging in a unilingual catalog

Dewey decimal classification : francophone perspectives : papers
from a workshop presented at the General Conference of the
International Federation of Library Associations and
Institutions (IFLA) Amsterdam, Netherlands, August 20, 1998 /
edited by Julianne Beall and Raymonde Couture-Lafleur. --
Albany : Forest Press, 1999.
vii, 58, 60, vii p. ; 23 cm.

Added title page title: Classification décimale Dewey : perspectives francophones.
English and French.
Sponsored by the IFLA Section on Classification and Indexing.
ISBN 0-910608-67-9.

1. Classification, Dewey decimal -- Congresses. 2. Library science -- French-speaking countries -- Congresses. I. Beal, Julianne. II. Couture-Lafleur, Raymonde. III. International Federation of Library Associations and Institutions. Section on Classification and Indexing. IV. IFLA General Conference (64th : 1998 : Amsterdam, Netherlands)

Recommended DDC: 025.4'31

Figure 17.27.

Figure 17.27 —*Continued*

```
2nd level cataloging in a bilingual catalog

Dewey decimal classification : francophone perspectives /
  edited by Julianne Beall and Raymonde Couture-Lafleur =
  Classification décimale Dewey : perspectives francophones /
  préparées par Julianne Beall et Raymonde Couture-Lafleur. --
  Albany : Forest Press, 1999.
  vii, 58, 60, vii p. ; 23 cm.

  Papers from a workshop presented at the General Conference of
the International Federation of Library Associations and
Institutions (IFLA) Amsterdam, Netherlands, August 20, 1998.
  Sponsored by the IFLA Section on Classification and Indexing.
  ISBN 0-910608-67-9.
```

CHIEF SOURCE OF INFORMATION
(Title Pages)

Dewey Decimal Classification
Francophone Perspectives

Papers from a Workshop
Presented at the General Conference
of the International Federation of
Library Associations and Institutions (IFLA)
Amsterdam, Netherlands
August 20, 1998

**Edited by Julianne Beall
and Raymonde Couture-Lafleur**

Sponsored by the
IFLA Section on Classification and Indexing

FOREST PRESS
A Division of
OCLC Online Computer Library Center, Inc.
Albany, New York
1999

Classification décimale Dewey
Perspectives francophones

Communications d'un Atelier
présentées à la Conférence générale
de la Fédération Internationale des
Associations de Bibliothécaires
et des Bibliothèques (IFLA)
Amsterdam, Pays-Bas
20 août 1998

**Préparées par Julianne Beall et
Raymonde Couture-Lafleur**

Atelier organisé par la
Section de classification et indexation de l'IFLA

FOREST PRESS
A Division of
OCLC Online Computer Library Center, Inc.
Albany, New York
1999

Figure 17.27—*Continued*

Information on Verso

Library of Congress Cataloging-in-Publication Data

Dewey decimal classification--francophone perspectives : papers from a workshop presented at the General Conference of the International Federation of Library Associations and Institutions (IFLA) Amsterdam, Netherlands, August 20, 1998 / edited by Julianne Beall and Raymonde Couture-Lafleur .
Forest Press, 1999.
p. cm.
Added title page title : Classification décimale Dewey--perspectives francophones
"Sponsored by the IFLA Section on Classification and Indexing."
English and French.
ISBN 0-910608-67-9
1. Classification, Dewey decimal--Congresses. 2. Library science--French-speaking countries--Congresses. I. Beall, Julianne, 1946- . II. Couture-Lafleur, Raymonde, 1934- . III. International Federation of Library Associations and Institutions. Section on Classification and Indexing. IV. IFLA General Conference (64th : 1998 : Amsterdam, Netherlands)
Z696.D7D495 1999 99-35669
025.4'31--dc21 CIP

This example is an illustration of:

- named conference
- main entry under corporate body
- other title information
- multiple places of publication and publishers
- detailed pagination
- publishing note
- contents note
- Library of Congress and Canadian CIPs

2nd level cataloging for a Canadian library

International Conference on the Principles and Future of AACR (1997 : Toronto, Ont.)
The principles and future of AACR : proceedings of the International Conference on the Principles and Future of AACR, Toronto, Ontario, Canada, October 23-25, 1997 / Jean Weihs, editor. -- Ottawa : Canadian Library Association, 1997.
xi, 272 p. ; 28 cm.

Co-published by American Library Association and Library Association.
Includes bibliographies and index.
ISBN 0-88802-287-5.

Figure 17.28.

Figure 17.28—*Continued*

2nd level cataloging for a U.S. library

International Conference on the Principles and Future of AACR
(1997 : Toronto, Ont.)
The principles and future of AACR : proceedings of the International Conference on the Principles and Future of AACR, Toronto, Ontario, Canada, October 23-25, 1997 / Jean Weihs, editor. -- Ottawa : Canadian Library Association ; Chicago : American Library Association, 1997.
xi, 272 p. ; 28 cm.

Includes bibliographies and index.
ISBN 0-8389-3493-5.

Tracing for both

1. Anglo-American cataloging rules -- Congresses.
2. Descriptive cataloging -- Congresses. I. Weihs, Jean.
II. Title. III. Title: Principles and future of Anglo-American cataloging rules.

Recommended DDC: 025.32

The Principles and Future of AACR

Proceedings of the
International Conference
on the Principles
and Future Development
of AACR

Toronto, Ontario, Canada
October 23–25, 1997

JEAN WEIHS
Editor

CANADIAN LIBRARY ASSOCIATION / Ottawa
LIBRARY ASSOCIATION PUBLISHING / London
AMERICAN LIBRARY ASSOCIATION / Chicago
1998

CHIEF SOURCE OF
INFORMATION
(Title Page)

Figure 17.28—*Continued*

(Information on Verso)

Published by

AMERICAN LIBRARY ASSOCIATION
50 East Huron Street, Chicago, Illinois 60611
CANADIAN LIBRARY ASSOCIATION
200 Elgin Street, Ottawa, Ontario K2P 1L5
LIBRARY ASSOCIATION PUBLISHING
7 Ridgmount Street, London WC1E 7AE

Library Assocation Publishing is wholly owned
by The Library Association

Library of Congress Cataloging-in-Publication Data
International Conference on the Principles and Future Development of
AACR (1997 : Toronto, Ontario, Canada)
The principles and future of AACR / Jean Weihs, editor
p. cm.
"Proceedings of the International Conference in the Principles and
Future Development of AACR, Toronto, Ontario, October 23-25, 1997
American Library Association, Chicago and London, 1999."
Includes bibliographical references (p.) and index.
ISBN 0-8389-3493-5
1. Anglo-American cataloguing rules—Congresses. 2. Descriptive
cataloging—United States—Rules—Congresses. 3. Descriptive
cataloging—Great Britain—Rules—Congresses. 4. Descriptive
cataloging—Canada—Rules—Congresses. 5. Descriptive cataloging —
Australia—Rules—Congresses. I. Weihs, Jean Riddle. II. Title.
III. Title: Principles and future of Anglo-American cataloguing rules.
Z694.15.A5155 1997
025.3'2—dc21 98-34562

Canadian Cataloguing in Publication Data
International Conference on the Principles and Future Development of
AACR (1997 : Toronto, Ont.)
The principles and future of AACR : proceedings of the International
Conference on the Principles and Future Development of AACR.
Toronto. Ontario. Canada. October 23-25, 1997
Co-published by American Library Association and Library Association
Includes bibliographical references.
ISBN 0-88802-287-5
1. Anglo-American cataloguing rules—Congresses. 2. Descriptive
cataloging—United States—Rules—Congresses. 3. Descriptive
cataloging—Great Britain—Rules—Congresses. 4. Descriptive
cataloging—Canada—Rules—Congresses. 5. Descriptive cataloging—
Australia—Rules—Congresses. I. Weihs, Jean, 1930- II. American
Library Assocation. III. Library Association. IV. Title. V. Title:
Principles and future of Anglo-American cataloguing rules.
Z694.15.A5158 1997 025.3'2 C98-901015.5

British Library Cataloguing-in-Publication Data
A catalogue record for this book is available from the British Library
ISBN 1-85604-303-7

Copyright © 1998. American Library Association.
Canadian Library Association, and The Library Association

The third option, title main entry, is applied when there is no known creator; when there are more than three creators sharing equal amounts of the same responsibility for the item, if their contributions are the same (see Figure 17.29, pages 405–6); when the item emanates from a corporate body but is not eligible for corporate body main entry and has no personal author (see Figure 17.30, pages 407–8); or when the work is produced under editorial direction (see Figure 17.24).

This example is an illustration of:

- item with more than three authors
- title main entry
- other title information
- marks of omission
- statement of subsidiary responsibility
- publication date not listed, copyright date given
- detailed pagination statement
- all illustrations are in color
- width of book greater than height
- index note
- Library of Congress CIP
- two levels of cataloging

2nd level cataloging

Melloni's illustrated review of human anatomy : by structures--arteries, bones, muscles, nerves, veins / June L. Melloni ... [et al.] ; illustrated by the authors. -- Philadelphia : Lippincott, c1988.
vii, 268 p. : col. ill. ; 23 x 31 cm.

Includes index.
ISBN 0-397-50956-1.

1. Human anatomy -- Outlines, syllabi, etc. 2. Human anatomy -- Atlases. I. Melloni, June L. II. Title: Illustrated review of human anatomy.

Recommended DDC: 611.00222

1st level cataloging

Melloni's illustrated review of human anatomy / June L. Melloni ... [et al.]. -- Lippincott, c1988.
vii, 268 p.

ISBN 0-397-50956-1.

1. Human anatomy 2. Human anatomy -- Atlases. I. Melloni, June L.

Recommended DDC: 611.0022

Figure 17.29.

Figure 17.29—*Continued*

CHIEF SOURCE OF INFORMATION
(Title Page)

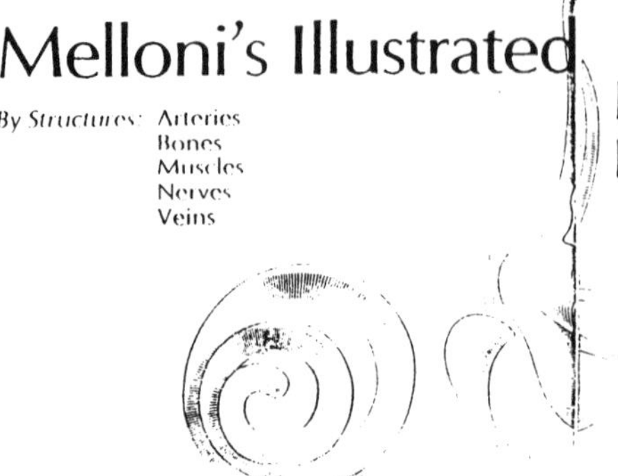

Melloni's Illustrated
REVIEW OF
HUMAN ANATOMY

By Structures: Arteries
Bones
Muscles
Nerves
Veins

June L. Melloni, Ph.D.
Ida Dox
H. Paul Melloni
B. John Melloni, Ph.D.
Illustrated by the authors

J.B. Lippincott Company Philadelphia
London Mexico City New York
St. Louis São Paulo Sydney

(Information on Verso)

Acquisitions Editor: Lisa A. Biello
Developmental Editor: Delois Patterson
Design Coordinator: Michelle Gerdes
Cover Designer: Stephen Cymerman
Production Manager: Carol A. Florence
Production Editor: Rosanne Hallowell
Production Coordinator: Barney Fernandes
Compositor: McFarland Graphics
Text Printer/Binder: Kingsport Press
Cover Printer: The Lehigh Press, Inc.

Copyright © 1988 by Biagio John Melloni, Ph.D.
Copyright under the International Copyright Union

All rights reserved. No part of this book may be used or reproduced in any manner whatsoever without written permission from Biagio John Melloni, Ph.D., 9308 Renshaw Drive, Bethesda, Maryland 20817. Printed in the United States of America. For information write J.B. Lippincott Company, East Washington Square, Philadelphia, Pennsylvania 19105.

1 3 5 6 4 2

LIBRARY OF CONGRESS
Library of Congress Cataloging-in-Publication Data

Melloni's illustrated review of human anatomy : by structures—arteries, bones, muscles, nerves, veins / June L. Melloni . . . [et al.] ; illustrated by the authors.
p. cm.
Includes index.
ISBN 0-397-50956-1
1. Anatomy, Human—Atlases. 2. Anatomy, Human—Outlines, syllabi, etc. I. Melloni, June L. II. Title: Illustrated review of human anatomy.
QM25.M45 1988
611'.0022'2—dc19 88-722
CIP

This example is an illustration of:

- electronic resource accessed through Internet
- work emanating from a corporate body entered under title
- general material designation
- type and extent of resource area
- place of publication not stated in sources of information, but known
- mode of access note
- source of title note
- other formats note
- item described note
- 2nd level cataloging

ISBD(ER) [electronic resource] : international standard bibliographic description for electronic resources : revised from the ISBD(CF), international standard bibliographic description for computer files / recommended by the ISBD(CF) Review Group. -- Electronic data. -- [London] : International Federation of Library Associations and Institutions, 1999.

Mode of access: World Wide Web. URL: http://www.ifla.org/VII/s13/pubs/isbd.htm.
Title from title screen.
Also issued in printed form (Muenchen : K.G. Saur, 1997).
Description based on contents viewed on Nov. 16, 2001.

N.B. According to the rules for assigning subject headings (see page xx), the appropriate subject heading would be ``International standard bibliographic description for electronic resources.'' However, the authors suggest the following tracing may be more useful.

1. Descriptive cataloging -- Standards. 2. Cataloging of electronic resources. I. ISBD(CF) Review Group. II. International Federation of Library Associations and Institutions.

Figure 17.30.

Figure 17.30—*Continued*

CHIEF SOURCE OF INFORMATION
(Title Screen)

ISBD(ER): International Standard Bibliographic Description for Electronic Resources

Revised from the ISBD(CF):
International Standard Bibliographic Description
for Computer Files

Recommended by the ISBD(CF) Review Group

(Originally issued by K. G. Saur, Muenchen, 1997
as Vol. 17 in the UBCIM Publications, New Series)

CONTENTS

The following questions and caveats form a useful decision-tree for determining main entry:

1. Does the item emanate from a corporate body? No? Proceed to question 8. Yes? Go to question 2. (If in doubt, assume the answer is no and proceed to question 8.)
2. Is the item an administrative work dealing with the body itself? Yes? Assign a corporate body main entry. (If more than one corporate body is involved, follow the rules for multiple personal authors, below.) No? Go to question 3.
3. Is the item one of the designated types of works in rule 21.1B2b? Yes? Assign a corporate body main entry. (If more than one corporate body is involved, follow the rules for multiple personal authors, below.) No? Go to question 4.
4. Does the item record the collective thought of the body? Yes? Assign a corporate body main entry. (If more than one corporate body is involved, follow the rules for multiple personal authors, below.) No? Go to question 5.
5. Does the item record the collective activity of an event? Yes? Assign a corporate body main entry. (If more than one corporate body is involved, follow the rules for multiple personal authors, below.) No? Go to question 6.
6. Does the item result from the collective activity of a performing group as a whole that goes beyond mere performance? Yes? Assign a corporate body main entry. (If more than one corporate body is involved in the performing group, follow the rules for multiple personal authors, below.) No? Go to question 7.
7. Is the item cartographic, and does the responsibility of the corporate body go beyond publication/distribution? Yes? Assign a corporate body main entry. (If more than one corporate body is involved, follow the rules for multiple personal authors, below.) No? Go to question 8.
8. Is the work by one or more persons? No? Assign a title main entry. Yes? Go to question 9.
9. Is one person the sole creator or principal creator of the work? Yes? Assign that person as main entry. No? Go to question 10.
10. Are two or three persons equally responsible for the creation of the work? Yes? Assign the first-named as main entry and give added entries for the rest. No? Go to question 11.
11. Are more than three persons responsible for the creation of the work? Assign a title main entry.

CAVEAT #1: Questions 10 and 11 assume shared responsibility. Consult the special rules for mixed responsibility when there are different types of contributions. Apply the Rule of Three both to the types of contributions and number of persons or bodies sharing a single type. If either of those elements exceeds three and none are predominant, assign title main entry.

CAVEAT #2: Editors are not creators of the works they edit. An edited work having contributions by one or more authors is considered the collective work of those authors, whether persons, corporate bodies, or both. BUT, bibliography compilers are creators, even if the term applied to the compiler on the title page is "editor."

Once main entry is chosen, it is time to consider choosing other access points, called added entries. Some added entries are mandated by the rules for main entry. A rule will say, "Choose A as the main entry and make an added entry for B." Any added entries may be made if a cataloger thinks they are needed by users of the catalog, so long as they are mentioned in the bibliographic description. Notes are made about variant titles, titles of parts, or secondary statements of responsibility, in order that they may be selected as headings. This is not true of main entries. A name or title may be chosen main entry of an item even if it never appears in the bibliographic description. Uniform titles are constructed by catalogers and cannot be transcribed. When an item is erroneously attributed on the chief source, but the cataloger knows who truly created it, the rules prescribe giving the main entry to its true creator (or its probable creator, if there is doubt).

Added entries made routinely include joint creators; people or bodies making other creative contributions if they are named prominently on the item and do more than distribute it; titles proper or uniform titles not chosen as main entry; title variations found on the item; analytical titles; and series titles. A new type of added entry is an electronic resource's URL. Many guidelines for cataloging Internet resources recommend making it, preferably as a direct link.

FORM OF HEADINGS—NAME AND TITLE AUTHORITIES

Once headings are chosen, AACR2-98 provides numerous rules for putting them into authorized form (called "establishing" them) for use in the catalog.

Personal Names

Two principles underlie the rules in AACR2-98 for the form into which a personal name heading is put: The heading form should be the one most familiar to searchers, and in most instances, only one heading should be used for a single individual, ensuring that all his or her works are collocated in the catalog.

The first principle seems logical, but is the reverse of the AACR1 principle. AACR1 required that catalogers determine and use the fullest form of a person's real name. AACR2-98 follows Charles Cutter's idea that catalog headings should match what searchers expect to find. It instructs catalogers to use the most commonly known name form and sometimes permits more than one to be used simultaneously. AACR2-98 also permits pseudonyms, initials, and appellations to be used as headings if they are how an individual is most commonly known.

To determine the most common form of name, catalogers count the number of times each form appears on published works and use the one that appears most often. Some contemporary creators change the names on their works often. In this case, AACR2-98 allows catalogers to use whatever form appears on the item being cataloged, and suggests references to link the various forms. If a creator has different name forms, cross-references should be made for forms that are not used as well as multiple name forms that are used.

Fortunately for catalogers, most creators do not use multiple name forms. The form established when an individual's first work is cataloged often is the only authoritative heading needed. National libraries prepare files of the name forms they establish and catalogers can choose to adopt them. They do not always select the same form for a person (see the CIPs in Figure 17.28 for Jean Weihs). LC and NLC have a formal policy for the establishment of the names of corporate bodies, but this agreement does not cover personal names.[12]

Corporate Bodies

The same principles apply to corporate bodies. One heading generally is used for a corporate body. When a corporate body changes its name, however, it may also become a new body. Changes are more likely to be substantive, resulting in the presence of more than one heading for a corporate body that has evolved over time.

Using the most commonly known form of name as the authoritative form holds for corporate bodies as well as for people's names, but the application differs. The name used by the group on its stationery, official documents, and publications is selected. Problems occur when a body updates its image by changing its logo. Rules define substantive changes to a corporate body name to eliminate multiple headings for a body undergoing a change of this kind. Sometimes corporate bodies announce an intention to change names, e.g., Trenton State College to College of New Jersey. Multiple names are appropriate in that case.

If a corporate body is part of a larger body, catalogers must decide how to formulate its name: alone (called "direct" entry) or as a unit under the larger body (called "subordinate" entry). It is even more difficult when multiple layers of bureaucracy separate the parent body and the subordinate unit; for example, the Committee on Cataloging: Description and Access (CC:DA)—the committee that governs AACR2-98 in the United States—has two intervening layers of hierarchy between its parent entity, the American Library Association (ALA), and the unit itself:

1. American Library Association (parent body)
    2. Association for Library Collections and Technical Services (sub-unit of the parent body, one of its divisions)
        3. Cataloging and Classification Section (sub-unit of the division)
            4. Committee on Cataloging: Description and Access (sub-unit of the section)

When the name of a corporate body implies that it is a subordinate unit—clearly the case with a "committee," "division," or "section"—the name of the higher body is included. AACR2-98 instructs catalogers to include the name of the lowest unit of hierarchy that can stand alone, provided it is a unique identification. For CC:DA, the only higher body that needs to be added is Association for Library Collections and Technical Services (ALCTS). The authoritative name form for CC:DA is, thus, *Association for Library Collections and Technical Services. Committee on Cataloging: Description and Access.* "Cataloging and Classification Section" is not used, because it is subordinate and no other section of ALCTS has a committee by this name.

The Cataloging and Classification Section of ALCTS has a Policy and Research Committee, but its authoritative heading would not be *Association for Library Collections and Technical Services. Policy and Research Committee,* because another section within ALCTS, the Serials Section, also has a committee by that name. Each one must be identified uniquely. The authoritative form of the Cataloging and Classification Section's Policy and Research Committee is, therefore, *Association for Library Collections and Technical Services. Cataloging and Classification Section. Policy and Research Committee.*

For searchers, the best aid is making cross-references to any potential search term and programming OPACs to match any combination of words in corporate body headings and retrieve all sets that include the requested terms. Thousands of corporate bodies are listed in LC's *Name Authority File* and NLC's *Canadiana Authorities,* which can help catalogers.

Geographic Names

Geographic names also are used in headings for the catalog. One can imagine the confusion that would result if different forms of name were used for the same geographic entity. Should we use Britain, Great Britain, or United Kingdom as the authoritative heading for the territory inhabited by our colleagues across the Atlantic? For places located in non-English-speaking countries, do we use the English name form or the vernacular name form (e.g., Florence/Firenze)? What about nonroman languages, such as Chinese or Russian?

Chapter 23 instructs catalogers to use English forms for place names if there are such forms in general use; if not, the vernacular form in the official language of the country is preferred.[13] When place names change, catalogers are instructed to use as many names as are required by the rules in Chapter 24 for government names, additions to corporate and conference names, or other corporate body name headings.

Sometimes one name is used for more than one place (e.g., Cairo, Egypt and Cairo, Illinois). Rules about additions serve to distinguish them. Additions differ for various countries, with one group comprising Australia, Canada, Malaysia, and the United States. Localities within these places are augmented by the addition of the name of the state, province, territory, and so forth. The countries of the British Isles—England, the Republic of Ireland, Northern Ireland, Scotland, and Wales as well as the Isle of Man and the Channel Islands—form a second group, for which local place names are augmented by the addition of the appropriate country or island name. This practice applies to other countries of the world.

Special rules cover places that require more specific identification or special kinds of identification, for example, localities with identical headings even after the appropriate additions are made (Saint Anthony, Hennepin County, Minnesota and Saint Anthony, Stearns County, Minnesota), communities within cities (Hyde Park, London, England and Hyde Park, Chicago, Illinois), or names of political jurisdictions. These rules and their interpretations in LCRIs and NLCRIs can be consulted if an item being cataloged requires establishing that kind of heading. Place names are included in LC's and NLC's name authorities.

Uniform Titles

Most works appear in one edition with one title. The title proper transcription is its title heading. A few works are issued many times over the years and the same title proper is not always used, for example, *The Holy Bible, The Douay Bible*, *The Anchor Bible*. Works appearing in different forms depending on the issuer's whim are given a single title by catalogers called a *uniform title,* so they all file together in the catalog. Uniform titles also are employed to distinguish identical titles, such as musical works called "Symphony," or serials called "Journal."

The most widely used uniform titles are found in AACR2-98's Chapter 25, along with rules for creating and assigning uniform titles to works catalogers think should have one. Uniform titles are common among six types of works: classics, music, religious works, laws, works issued complete or in parts, and works appearing in several physical formats. Translations also may call for uniform titles, if a library owns multiple versions.

Uniform titles need not be made for every work that exists in multiple versions unless several are represented in the catalog or are likely to be added to it. Some, however, such as the Bible, may require the addition of a uniform title to meet the requirements of cataloging networks, even though a library owns only one version.

Records of established headings, cross-references, and sources of information used to establish them are called *authority files.* Large libraries doing much original cataloging often keep such files, but they are costly and time-consuming to maintain. As mentioned previously, when faced with a new name, catalogers can consult LC's *Name Authority File* or the NLC's *Canadiana Authorities* for an already established heading for the person, corporate body, place name, series title, or uniform title in question (see Figures 17.31 and 17.32). These tools are available directly from the two libraries, or indirectly as part of services offered to customers of bibliographic networks, commercial cataloging services, on LC's *Cataloging Desktop*, and in other sources.

```
Library of Congress authority record for a personal name

ARN:     1131636
Rec stat: c         Entered:        19840524
Type:       z       Upd status:    a      Enc lvl:     n       Source:
Roman:              Ref status:    n      Mod rec:             Name use:  a
Govt agn:           Auth status:   a      Subj:        a       Subj use:  a
Series:     n       Auth/ref:      a      Geo subd:    n       Ser use:   b
Ser num:    n       Name:          a      Subdiv tp:           Rules:     c
  1  010         n  84048778
  2  040         DLC   c DLC   d DLC
  3  005         19860703135455.4
  4  100 10      Intner, Sheila S.
  5  670         Her Access to nonprint materials, 1984:   b CIP t.p. (Sheila S.
ntner)
  6  670         Her Circulation policy in academic, public, and school
ibraries, c1986:  b CIP t.p. (Sheila S. Intner) data sheet (b. 1935)
```

Figure 17.31.

```
Leader              nz    22      n  4500

005            19990714104132.0
008            980122nneacnnnaabn            a ana

016       a    $a1003-K-9881E
110 2     a    $aCanadian Council for Health and Active Living at Work

040            $aCaOONL$beng$cCaOONL$dCaOONL
042            $anlc

410  2         $aCCHALW

670            $aWalk and roll, c1998:$bp. 2 (CCHALW)

710 25         $aConseil canadien de la santé et de la vie active au
                travail$0(CaOONL)1003-K-9881F
```

Figure 17.32.

NOTES

1. Full citations for this standard rule book for description in the United States and Canada and major earlier editions include *Anglo-American Cataloguing Rules,* 2nd ed., 1998 revision, prepared under the direction of The Joint Steering Committee for Revision of AACR (Ottawa: Canadian Library Association; London: Library Association Publishing; Chicago: American Library Association, 1998) [hereinafter AACR2-98]; *Anglo-American Cataloguing Rules,* 1988 revision, edited by Michael Gorman and Paul W. Winkler (Ottawa: Canadian Library Association; Chicago: American Library Association, 1988) [hereinafter AACR2R]; *Anglo-American Cataloguing Rules,* 2nd ed., edited by Michael Gorman and Paul W. Winkler (Chicago: American Library Association; Ottawa: Canadian Library Association, 1978) [hereinafter AACR2]; *Anglo-American Cataloging Rules, North American Text,* edited by Sumner Spalding (Chicago: American Library Association, 1967) [hereinafter AACR1]. It also includes the update, *Amendments 2001* (The Associations, 2001).

2. *Cataloger's Desktop* [CD-ROM subscription, issued quarterly] (Washington, DC: Library of Congress, Cataloging Distribution Service, 1997-).

3. For a brief report of the Conference and the Principles, see the *Reader in Classification and Descriptive Cataloging,* edited by Ann F. Painter (Washington, DC: NCR-Microcard Editions, 1972).

4. Jean Weihs, ed. *The Principles and Future of AACR: Proceedings of the International Conference on the Principles and Future of AACR, Toronto, Ontario, Canada, October 23–25, 1997* (Ottawa: Canadian Library Association, 1998).

5. Documents on work emanating from the conference can be found at http://www.nlc-bnc.ca/jsc/index.htm.

6. AACR2-98, 41.

7. Ibid., 77

8. If the policy is to record prices in the catalog record, bear in mind that prices change over time and become obsolete rapidly, should an item have to be replaced. Also, the list price, not the discounted price, should be recorded.

9. NLCRIs may be found at http://www.nlc-bnc.ca/catalog/aacr/econtent.htm.

10. AACR2-98, 312.

11. Ibid.

12. Correspondence with Margaret Stewart, Chief, Standards and Support, Acquisitions and Bibliographic Services, National Library of Canada, September 21, 1999.

13. AACR2-98, 434.

SUGGESTED READING

AACR

"The Anglo-American Cataloguing Rules." *National Library of Canada Bulletin* 2, nos. 7/8 (July/Aug. 2000): 11-12.

IFLA Study Group on the Functional Requirements for Bibliographic Records. *Functional Requirements for Bibliographic Records: Final Report.* München: K. G. Saur, 1998.

Maxwell, Robert L., with Margaret F. Maxwell. *Maxwell's Handbook for AACR2R, Explaining and Illustrating the Anglo-American Cataloguing Rules and 1993 Amendments.* Chicago: American Library Association, 1997.

Schottlaender, Brian E. C., ed. *The Future of the Descriptive Cataloging Rules.* Chicago: American Library Association, 1998.

Weihs, Jean. "Interfaces: Cardinal Rule Change and the OPAC." *Technicalities* 19, no. 4 (January 1998): 1, 11-13.

———. "Interfaces: The Joint Steering Committee Plots the Future of AACR2." *Technicalities* 18, no. 1 (January 1998): 1, 6-8.

———. "Interfaces: Will the Toronto Tenets Replace the Paris Principles?" *Technicalities* 17, no. 5 (May 1997): 1, 6-7.

Bibliographic Descriptions

Association for Library Collections & Technical Services, Committee on Cataloging: Description and Access. *Guidelines for Bibliographic Description of Reproductions.* Chicago: American Library Association, 1995.

Catskill, version 2.0. [Interactive CD-ROM]. Englewood, CO: Libraries Unlimited, 1998- . (Available for individual or site use licenses.)

Ferguson, Bobby. *Blitz Cataloging Workbooks.* Englewood, CO: Libraries Unlimited, 1999–2000. (See volumes on nonbook materials and AACR2/MARC.)

Geer-Butler, Beverley, and Beatrice L. Caraway. *Notes for Serials Cataloging.* 2nd ed. Englewood, CO: Libraries Unlimited, 1998.

Smiraglia, Richard P. *Describing Music Materials.* 3rd ed. Lake Crystal, MN: Soldier Creek Press, 1997.

Access Points

Authority Control in the 21st Century: An Invitational Conference, March 31–April, 1996. Dublin, OH: OCLC Inc., 1996. (Available online at http://www.oclc.org /oclc/man/authconf/confhome.htm.)

Carlyle, Alyson. "Fulfilling the Second Objective in the Online Catalog: Schemes for Organizing Author and Work Records into Usable Displays." *Library Resources & Technical Services* 41, no. 2 (April 1997): 79-100.

The Future Is Now: Reconciling Change and Continuity in Authority Control: Proceedings of the OCLC Symposium, ALA Annual Conference, June 23, 1995. Dublin, OH: OCLC, 1995.

Talmacs, Kerrie. "Authority Control." In *Technical Services Today and Tomorrow,* 2nd ed., edited by Michael Gorman, 129-139. Englewood, CO: Libraries Unlimited, 1998.

Taylor, Arlene G. *The Organization of Information.* Englewood, CO: Libraries Unlimited, 1999.

REVIEW QUESTIONS

1. Explain the mnemonic numbering of the rules in AACR2-98.
2. What chapters of AACR2-98 would be used to catalog a map serial?
3. When does a cataloger give a statement of responsibility?
4. What should a cataloger do when there is no date on an item?
5. What are "Rule Interpretations," and how are they used?
6. Explain the difference between shared and mixed responsibility.
7. What two principles underlie AACR2-98's rules for establishing personal name forms?
8. What rule of thumb is followed in establishing geographic name forms?
9. Name three kinds of corporate body names that must be entered subordinately.
10. What is a name authority record, and what three kinds of information does it contain?

Chapter 18 Subject Analysis

Completing the descriptive cataloging is half the cataloging process—the half dealing with works as physical entities and identifying them in terms appropriate to the formats in which they are manifested. Next, the contents of the materials are considered. Contents are defined, identified, and represented in terms of their subject matter in two ways: through the assignment of subject headings and by means of classification.

No single code of rules governs *subject cataloging,* the term for assigning subject headings to an item, or *classification*, the term for assigning category codes that form the basis for call numbers. Instead, the primary decisions catalogers make are to adopt one of several available standard tools for these purposes and then to follow accepted practices in applying them.

Subject cataloging and classification are very similar in that both processes require as their first step determining the subject content of the works being cataloged. Once this determination is made, the subject content can be represented in two ways: in words (subject headings) and in codes that stand for categories of knowledge (classifications). These processes of representing subject content of materials are sometimes referred to as providing *intellectual access* to materials. General principles of subject analysis—both subject cataloging (assignment of subject headings to materials being cataloged) and classification (assignment of category codes)—are discussed in this chapter. Specific tools—subject lists and classification systems—are discussed in Chapters 19 and 20.

DETERMINING SUBJECT MATTER

The first step in representing the content of materials being cataloged is deciding what the subject matter is. However, putting the process by which one makes such a decision into words is difficult. Each cataloger brings his or her personal background, knowledge, and experience to the task of deciding what something is about and whether the approach taken to the material also is relevant. Depending on how much a cataloger knows about a subject area, he or she might recognize different aspects of content in a particular item. This will affect the determination of subject matter made for that item.

Typically, catalogers glean clues directly from the items being cataloged that reveal their contents, whether or not the catalogers have special knowledge of those subject areas. Sometimes the cataloger must conduct sufficient research into an unfamiliar subject area to be able to handle items on that subject, but in most libraries and for most materials, catalogers are expected only to be generally conversant with subjects, not experts. Where can the subject clues be found?

Four places are likely sources for clues to the contents of items being cataloged: (1) titles, including alternative titles and subtitles; (2) tables of contents and their equivalents such as menus and site maps; (3) indexes; and (4) introductions and prefaces. Catalogers are not supposed to read every word of a book or Web site or view every inch of a videotape to ascertain its subject. Instead, the item should be read or viewed "technically," which is to say, a few key sources should be examined carefully and subject matter, scope, and coverage determined from them. Often, subtitles are more revealing of subject content than titles proper; chapter or segment titles can suggest scope and coverage; and introductions or prefaces can include the author's intended audience, important inclusions or exclusions, and other subject-related information. Back of the book indexes, Web site index terms, and similar devices also offer evidence of the range of subtopics covered in an item. A quick scan of the rest of the item can answer any questions that remain after the cataloger has concluded the technical examination.

Other places catalogers can find information about the content of an item are in publishers' or producers' descriptions of the item and in published reviews of the item. These can augment information gleaned from the item itself when technical reading or viewing fails to reveal the subject matter clearly or completely. Information from book jackets and similar promotional blurbs on nonbook material is unreliable and should be used with great caution. These sales devices are designed well before an item is published or released and are aimed at enticing buyers, not providing accurate and complete descriptions.

An item's content also can be affected by the approach taken to the material. An item that gives an overview of the whole field of chemistry and an item that is solely a dictionary of terminology used in the field of chemistry both are "about" chemistry, but the dictionary approach merits recognition. It is different from an introductory overview of the subject. General coverage of the subject is assumed when catalogers say a book is about chemistry or a video is about exercise. If the approach is not general, catalogers usually identify it by specifying its form. A chemistry dictionary is about chemistry, but its form is that of a dictionary. An exercise video is about exercise, but its approach may be that of a lecture on the subject (general coverage) or an activity session in which the viewer is expected to participate (directed exercise itself), and the physical form of the item is an audiovisual presentation recorded on videotape. Thus, catalogers speak of subject and form, where form may be defined as a genre (dictionaries, biographies, bibliographies, essays, etc.), a medium, or a specific type of approach to the subject.

Subject matter may be limited to one location or time period, and geographical and chronological specifications often are added to reflect those limitations. If a Web site about divorce is limited to Canada, catalogers want to express that explicitly, so that a searcher seeking information about divorce in Mexico or the United States would not think the item answers their need. Both subject headings and classification sources provide for geographic and chronological approaches to subjects.

ENUMERATION VERSUS FACETING OR SYNTHESIS

Subject headings and classification categories share other features, among them the way the headings or categories are formulated and displayed. The source of the headings or categories may list all or most of the terms or numbers that can be assigned, and be deemed "enumerative." To make an assignment, the cataloger browses the listings and selects the subject heading or classification category that corresponds to the contents of the item being cataloged. The other option is for the source to list only parts or building blocks, called *facets*, from which complete subject headings and classification categories can be assembled (or synthesized). This is called being "faceted" or "synthetic." To make an assignment, the cataloger selects and combines the appropriate facets and synthesizes the subject heading or classification category corresponding to the content of the item being cataloged. Although it is possible to list all the combinations that could be synthesized from the facets of a faceted classification and create an enumeration, the number of combinations would be so large that such a project would not be viable.

Another way of looking at enumeration versus faceting is to ask whether a subject source provides prebuilt combinations of complex headings or categories or expects catalogers (and searchers) to do the work of building them. When the combinations are prebuilt or prepared in advance before use, the source is called "precoordinated"; when they are not, the source is called "postcoordinated," because the work is done at the point of use. Enumerative sources are precoordinated, and examples include all the subject heading lists and classification schemes popular in the United States and Canada (described in Chapters 19 and 20). Faceted or synthetic sources are postcoordinated, and examples include the keywords used in searching computer databases or the Internet. A keyword, although it might be used as a subject by itself, is likely to be combined with other keywords to represent complex subjects, thus behaving like a facet (or part) of the whole.

Searching a keyword such as "food" on a huge database such as the Internet could retrieve tens of thousands of "hits," but combining "food" and "Boston" and "reviews" could whittle them down to a group of reviews for Boston's restaurants (where food is likely to be served and reviewed), if that was what was wanted. Postcoordination permits the parts—location (Boston), the approach (reviews), and the topic (food)—to be entered in any order to retrieve the items that contain all three. A precoordinated subject source might have a subject heading or classification category for reviews of food served in Boston, but the parts would have to be combined and expressed only one way and no other, for example, BOSTON—RESTAURANTS—REVIEWS or RESTAURANTS—BOSTON—REVIEWS, or, perhaps, REVIEWS, RESTAURANT—BOSTON. The precoordinated classification scheme could subordinate location and approach under the topic, food, or it could subordinate reviews of food services under the location, Boston, but it would not do both.

To succeed in searching the precoordinated index or classification, the cataloger needs to know what the source considers its principal focus or where the topic is located. For example, the Dewey Decimal Classification appends an index it calls its "Relative Index," in which subject terms such as "computers," "water," or "children," which, as part of different disciplines, would be classified in very different locations are brought together for consultative purposes. In this way, a classifier can easily see that children's diseases are classified with topics in medicine, but children's educational programs such as kindergartens and nursery schools are classified with topics in education.

SUBJECT AUTHORITIES: VOCABULARIES FOR SUBJECT CATALOGING

Words used to represent the subject of an item in the catalog can be taken from different sources, depending on individual library policy. Standard terms come from published lists accepted by the cataloging community for use as subject headings in the catalog, called *subject authorities*. Subject authorities are much like the name authorities discussed in Chapter 17. Because the lists control which words can and cannot be used as subject headings, they are called *controlled vocabularies*. All catalogers do not use the same list.

Catalogers also can use the terminology found in the items being cataloged by compiling lists of terms from the important title words. (Articles and other words that do not reflect subject matter are ignored.) The cataloger cannot control the words an author will choose; therefore, title words used as subject headings are referred to as uncontrolled terms or *uncontrolled vocabularies*. Computer-based catalogs frequently are programmed to search title words as well as authorized subject headings. To maximize the possibility of finding desired materials, both types of subject terms should be used.

Subject cataloging is a type of indexing done by catalogers for the materials they catalog. Specialists known as indexers sometimes do similar work on the text of a single book, for which they prepare an extensive index that is part of that book. Indexers also work on journal articles, for which they prepare ongoing periodical indexes, such as the *Readers' Guide to Periodical Literature,* and similar reference tools. Periodical indexes are used by people searching for information in articles published in magazines and journals. Like library catalogs, periodical indexes also list authors' names and article titles. The same principles apply to all types of indexing, including subject cataloging, and the same search skills are needed to retrieve indexed material from catalogs and reference works. The main difference among the types of indexing is the nature of the material being indexed and the depth of the indexing. Back of the book indexers work on individual items and prepare very deep indexes consisting of hundreds of terms for one item. Periodical indexers work on ongoing sets of articles appearing in specific journals (or article equivalents, such as book chapters), and do broader indexing, consisting of several terms per article. Subject catalogers work on the items they catalog, generally monographs or whole title runs, and the indexing is very broad, assigning a few terms to describe the contents of the item at a summary level.

SUBJECT AUTHORITIES: NUMBERS FOR CLASSIFICATION

Another type of subject authority is the source from which numbers for classification are taken. The Dewey Decimal Classification (DDC) and the Library of Congress Classification (LCC), two popular classification systems, are discussed in Chapter 20. Both of these consist mainly of lists of numbers, each paired with a term for the subject matter the number represents. Other helpful information may be added to the list of numbers, such as introductions giving history and background of the system, instructions on how to assign the numbers, and indexes (that is, lists of verbal terms) to the numbers. A library generally chooses only one of the classifications to assign to its materials, although no rule says more than one cannot be used simultaneously. In the United States and Canada, the numbers form the basis of shelf addresses that group together materials covering the same topics; in other parts of the world, classification is used to organize bibliographies as well.

Classifications, like subject vocabularies, may be precoordinated or postcoordinated, enumerative or faceted/synthetic. In fact, elements of both kinds of listings appear in DDC and LCC to different degrees. The latter is overwhelmingly precoordinated, enumerating hundreds of thousands of numbers or categories from which to choose the appropriate number for an item. Nevertheless, it also has tables listing specific aspects of topics to be added to the numbers from the main list if the classifier wants that topic to be limited in one particular aspect. In contrast, DDC has many fewer numbers in its enumeration and a great many more tables listing aspects of topics as well as numerous instructions in one part of the list to apply its subdivision to similar topical areas. Although the lists of numbers are precoordinated and enumerated, the tables and instructions add a limited amount of synthesis to the systems. Facets provide a way of economizing on the total number of classification numbers that must be listed in a source. Over the years, DDC has grown from fewer than 50 pages to more than 3,000, and LCC now consists of more than forty volumes, so such economies are valuable from a practical, as well as a theoretical, point of view.

Fully faceted classifications are not used very much in North America, but they have enjoyed greater popularity elsewhere in the world. Among the better-known faceted classifications are the Colon Classification, the Universal Decimal Classification, and the Bliss Classification. Colon Classification was devised in the early part of the twentieth century by S. R. Ranganathan, an Indian theorist, and was adopted by a number of Indian libraries, although their number has dwindled in recent years. It divides the universe of knowledge into forty-one main classes to which numbers for five types of facets are added to build the complete number. Ranganathan called his five facet types Personality, Matter, Energy, Space, and Time. A complex system of letters from multiple alphabets, numbers, and symbols was used for the numbers. The Universal Decimal Classification, a transformation of DDC devised by Belgians Henri Otlet and Henri La Fontaine, internationalized DDC by translating it into French. It was also intended to be more accommodating to automatic manipulation. Universal Decimal Classification, which uses Arabic numbers and a few symbols, was adopted and updated in the latter part of the twentieth century by UNESCO and has been used in Europe for organizing bibliographies. The Bliss Classification, devised by Henry Evelyn Bliss, librarian at the City College of New York, was used for many years in that library and a few libraries in England, but it did not develop much more of a following. It uses capital letters and a few symbols. After Bliss's death, practical considerations in keeping the system up-to-date and teaching classifiers how to assign the numbers led the City College of New York library to switch to LCC. John Mills continues to update the Bliss system,[1] but its users remain a very small group of libraries.

The discussion of faceted classifications raises the question of the choice of characters used to represent the categories. Known as the *notation*, classifications may use only one type or more than one; for example, letters only or letters and numbers. Single-character notation is called *pure notation,* and multiple-character notation is called *mixed notation.* The DDC uses pure notation (Arabic numbers, punctuated once with a dot or point, hence the name "decimal"), whereas LCC uses a mixed notation consisting of capital letters and Arabic numbers, sometimes punctuated by a dot or point. The type of notation used creates a kind of limitation on how specific the subject categories tend to be by resulting in longer or shorter combinations for topics at narrower levels of specificity. The more specific a category is, the longer the number representing it will be in a pure notation system; a mixed notation system has more flexibility to vary the types and positions of the characters as needed to keep numbers short.

Call Numbers

Classification numbers, as mentioned, are the basis for placing materials on library shelves. Numbers or alphabetic codes representing elements such as main entries, particular collections, dates of publication, volume or copy numbers, and so forth, known collectively as shelf marks, usually are added to the classification number to complete the "addresses" for materials. The entire combination, consisting of the classification number plus the shelf marks, is known as a *call number.* Catalogs arranged by call number are common in libraries. They are known as *shelflists* because they arrange the catalog records by each item's placement on the shelf.

Librarians are not unanimous about assigning a different call number to each title in a library's collection. Larger agencies often choose to assign a unique call number to each title; smaller ones may not have more than a few items with the same classification number and shelf marks, and, thus, choose to ignore the fact that several different titles can be shelved at the "same" address. The word "same" is enclosed in quotations because two physical entities cannot occupy the same space; rather, this means all the titles that share the same call number may be randomly shelved at the designated location.

The first shelf mark assigned after an item is classified usually is, by an unofficial agreement, an alphanumeric code representing the main entry of the item called a *cutter number*. The name comes from the fact that Charles A. Cutter was the first to publish a list of these codes, later revised by a librarian named Margaret Sanborn, into tables called Cutter tables or Cutter-Sanborn tables.[2] Today the name is spelled with a small "c" in the phrase cutter number and is also a verb—librarians refer to assigning these numbers as "cuttering" them.

Small agencies sometimes add call letters (one or several) rather than cutter numbers to their classification numbers to form call numbers, because call letters are easier to apply. The first letter, first two letters, or first three letters of the main entry are used as call letters. If the main entry is a title, the call letters are not taken from initial articles but from the word following them. Call letters for a book by Jane Austen could be A, AU/Au, or AUS/Aus, depending on the size of the collection and type of lettering preferred. Call numbers resulting from this system often are not unique for each item, because items with the same classification number and call letters will have the same call number, for example, books on the same subject by authors named Rose, Rosen, and/or Ross. In a small collection this does not hinder retrieval and saves money in the classifier's time and the purchase of special tools for cuttering.

Other elements in a call number include a symbol, usually a letter of the alphabet, for the particular collection to which an item belongs, such as "R" for reference materials or "J" for children's materials. Such symbols often precede classification numbers and identify the location of an item. Alphabetic designations for biography (B), fiction (F/FIC/Fic), oversized items (O), and audiovisual materials (AV) are popular, also. Within a collection, subcategories may be distinguished, also, by the use of spine labels depicting icons for science fiction (an atom), mystery (a gun), westerns (a rearing horse), or Canadian items (a maple leaf). These labels describe content rather than location but can be used for location as well.

A popular addition to a cutter number symbolizing an author main entry for an author who wrote more than one title is a letter or two from the first significant word in each title. This addition results in arranging the author's works on the shelf in alphabetical order by title without having to look beyond the call number to read the entire title. This is an ingenious method, but it tends to lengthen call numbers and make them complicated to assign as well as to use in retrieving desired items from the shelves.

Other call number elements frequently encountered in libraries are dates, used particularly to distinguish two or more editions of the same title. Thus a copy of the 21st edition of DDC shelved in the reference collection might have the complex LCC call number R/Z696/.D519/1999, in which the meaning is as follows:

R	=	Reference collection
Z696	=	LCC classification number for classifications
.D519	=	The cutter number for Dewey, the author main entry
1999	=	Date of the edition

Because the DDC is a four-volume work, each volume would also be identified by its number, following the date. Complex call numbers such as this may be useful for staff in large libraries who shelve many items with similar or identical classification numbers, cutters, and other shelf marks, but they are hard for members of the public to remember when they go from the catalog to the shelf, and difficult to write down without making mistakes.

PRINCIPLES OF SUBJECT CATALOGING

Two kinds of principles apply to subject cataloging—those that apply to the way words and phrases are chosen to be used as subject headings and those that apply to the way those words and phrases are assigned to materials. According to Cutter, the catalog should show what the library has on a subject and bring together all items on a single subject. Both objectives—identifying and gathering—apply to subject headings and subject catalogs as well as to authors, titles, and editions. Subject headings, which consist of words, raise issues arising from the nature of language and, also, the use of words to represent subject concepts.

Subject catalogs can be arranged alphabetically or in classified order. North Americans are familiar with alphabetical subject indexes because this is how their library catalogs usually are arranged. Classified catalogs may contain the same terms, but arranged in *subject* order, with the broadest topics given first, followed by related but narrower topics in a logical organization for each major subject division. The library shelflist is a good example of a classified catalog. However, the rest of this section focuses on subject catalogs consisting of catalog records filed by their subject headings.

In a classified catalog, the entire catalog might be divided into a few sections or main classes, for example, HUMANITIES, NATURAL SCIENCES, and SOCIAL SCIENCES. NATURAL SCIENCES would be the broadest term in that section, followed by individual scientific disciplines: ASTRONOMY, MATHEMATICS, PHYSICS, CHEMISTRY, BIOLOGY, GEOLOGY, and so forth. In turn, CHEMISTRY would be followed by still smaller topics, such as ORGANIC CHEMISTRY and INORGANIC CHEMISTRY. It is easy to see the contrast with an alphabetical, or dictionary, catalog such as those in most media centers and public libraries. There, the same topics would be arranged as follows: ASTRONOMY, BIOLOGY, CHEMISTRY, GEOLOGY, HUMANITIES, INORGANIC CHEMISTRY, MATHEMATICS, NATURAL SCIENCES,

ORGANIC CHEMISTRY, PHYSICS, and SOCIAL SCIENCES. HUMANITIES seems oddly placed, sandwiched in between GEOLOGY and INORGANIC CHEMISTRY, and five of the natural science disciplines and one subdiscipline appear before the heading for natural sciences as a whole. To users of a classified catalog, this would seem peculiar. Classified catalogs often employ classification numbers—coded representations of topics and subtopics.

A hybrid catalog, partly classified and partly alphabetical, also has been devised, called an *alphabetico-classified* catalog. In this catalog, principal headings are in classified order, but within each level of hierarchy, subheadings are arranged alphabetically (see Figure 18.1)

HUMANITIES
- ART
- LITERATURE
- MUSIC
  - DYNAMICS (MUSIC)
  - HARMONY
  - MELODY
  - RHYTHM
  - TEMPO
- RELIGION

NATURAL SCIENCES

ASTRONOMY
- COMETS
- PLANETS
- STARS

CHEMISTRY

PHYSICS
- MECHANICS
- OPTICS
- THERMODYNAMICS

SOCIAL SCIENCES

Figure 18.1. Sample alphabetico-classified listing.

In Figure 18.1, levels of hierarchy are distinguished by indentations, but other devices, such as thumbtabs or guidecards, and color coding, can be used when indentations are inconvenient to display, and the hierarchical levels need not be identified at all. A knowledgeable searcher knows that ASTRONOMY falls under NATURAL SCIENCES and that STARS follows COMETS and PLANETS under the broader heading ASTRONOMY.

The arrangement of terms can vary, but the choice of terms and their assignment flow from one set of principles:

1. Synonyms cannot be used simultaneously as headings in a single catalog. Librarians rely on subject authorities to avoid using two headings that mean the same thing, e.g., AUTOMOBILES versus CARS. If both terms are likely to be searched, both may be listed, but only one is authorized for use; the other will refer to the term actually used.
2. Words used for subject headings should have one clear and precise meaning. Subject authorities avoid words with more than one meaning, or, when they must use such a word, they add something that indicates the intended meaning, for example, BARS (ENGINEERING), BARS (FURNITURE), BARS (GEOMORPHOLOGY), and BARS (DRINKING ESTABLISHMENTS).
3. The meaning of terms assigned as subject headings must be defined precisely and must match the topics they represent. The terms should not be broader or more specific than the topics they represent; for example, if CALCULATORS is a heading, it should be defined to exclude computers, which, although they manipulate numbers, are a different type of machine. In *Sears List of Subject Headings*, the scope note at CALCULATORS says: "Use for materials on present-day calculators or on calculators and mechanical computers made before 1945. Materials on modern electronic computers developed after 1945 are entered under Computers."[3]
4. Each subject heading term should be discrete with respect to all others at the same topical level. Problems occur when overlaps in meaning occur between subject headings at the same level of hierarchy, such as BIOLOGY, BIOCHEMISTRY, and CHEMISTRY. Where does BIOLOGY end and BIOCHEMISTRY begin? Where does BIOCHEMISTRY end and CHEMISTRY begin? If all are used in the same catalog, each must cover discrete territory.

David Judson Haykin, a respected head of LC's subject division in the 1950s, codified the principles that should apply to subject heading assignment at LC. They are based, for the most part, on Cutter's ideas, and remain to this day the definitive expression of our basic assumptions about subject heading practice:

1. *The Reader as the Focus.* The primary consideration in choosing a word as a subject heading is that it is the one searchers are most likely to seek in the catalog.

2. *Unity.* A subject catalog must gather under one heading all the materials that deal with the subject, whatever terms are applied to it by authors, and whatever changing terms are used at different times. The cataloger must choose the term with care and apply it uniformly to all materials on the subject.
3. *Usage.* The heading chosen should be in common usage.
4. *English versus Foreign Terms.* English-language terms are preferred unless a concept is foreign to Anglo-American experience, or when a foreign term is precise while its English counterpart is not.
5. *Specificity.* When assigned, headings should be as specific as the topics they cover, not broader. Rather than apply a broader heading, catalogers should use two specific headings that will approximately cover the topic.[4]

PRINCIPLES OF CLASSIFICATION

Classification systems use language to identify the categories into which they divide knowledge, but words do not appear in the codes ultimately assigned to materials. These codes are called "numbers," even when they consist of characters other than digits. It is the notation that appears, which frees classifications from many of the linguistic issues that affect subject headings and subject catalogs. Still, the principles on which classifications are based raise other issues and generate problems of their own.

An issue of importance is the underlying philosophy of the classification, which dictates the method chosen to distinguish subjects from one another. A series of main classes is selected as the first analysis of knowledge into smaller components. Then, subsequent subdivisions may follow the same pattern or different patterns, and all subject areas may be treated alike or each subject area may be treated differently, according to ideas associated solely with that area. One might begin by dividing the universe of knowledge into animal, vegetable, and mineral. Or one might divide it into humanities, social sciences, and sciences. Some might divide it into earth, sky, fire, and water. Library classifications usually divide knowledge into disciplines familiar to academia. The DDC begins with ten main classes; LCC with twenty-one; Colon Classification with forty-one. None of these systems is "good" or "bad," "better" or worse"; none is "right" or "wrong." They simply start from different perspectives and draw their boundaries differently.

A classification must cover all the knowledge areas needed for the materials in the collection, which, for general libraries, means all of them. A medical library might not need a classification that deals in detail with music and religion, but some subtopics related to these disciplines need to be covered. For example, music therapy and medical problems unique to musicians, and faith healing and religious tenets pertaining to medicine and medical practice, would have to be included, subsumed under rubrics other than "music" or "religion."

To function over time, a classification must be open to the inclusion of new subjects not known when the classification was first devised, called "hospitality." It is difficult to predict where new topics and subtopics will emerge or whether changes will occur in the relationships among topics, but since knowledge does not stand still, the classification must be able to handle the changes.

To be easily used, the system must follow logical, recognizable patterns, both for the people using its numbers to find materials and for those assigning its numbers to materials. Easily memorized notation is a feature that contributes to ease of use. Short numbers also are more convenient than long ones, although in hierarchical classifications in which the whole hierarchy preceding a very specific topic must be represented, the numbers can be quite long.

The DDC and LCC both employ the principle of relative location, which means that materials are shifted as new ones are acquired in order to incorporate the new items with others on the same subjects. Both also operate on the principle of classification by discipline, although their definitions of the word differ. The DDC has fewer main classes than LCC, even though both cover the entire range of subject matter. The following examples reveal some (although not all) of the differences between the two systems:

- DDC has one main class for all social sciences (300), LCC has four: H, J, K, and L.
- DDC makes medicine a subdivision of technology and applied science (612), while LCC makes it a main class R.
- DDC divides language and literature into two separate main classes (400 and 800, respectively), whereas LCC combines them into one huge main class (P).

The philosophies underlying DDC and LCC differ considerably. The former is a "natural" classification of all knowledge, whereas LCC is intended merely to shelve LC's materials in a logical kind of subject order. The DDC follows one set of rules for all parts of the classification; LCC only requires that the same rules be used within a main class, but permits different rules to apply between classes.

Library classifications use different methods of subdividing subjects within the classification. The DDC usually employs hierarchy, breaking subject matter down from the broadest to the narrowest category according to the nature of the subject. Numbers are given to the broadest category (e.g., science = 500), then to the subcategories into which that subject can be broken down (e.g., astronomy = 520, physics = 530, chemistry = 540, etc.), then to the sub-subcategories into which the subcategories can be divided (e.g., inorganic chemistry = 546 and organic chemistry = 547), and so on until the smallest identifiable category receives a number. The LCC uses more than one strategy for subdividing topics, including hierarchy, geography, chronology, and simple alphabetization, often provided by means of cuttering.

Some classification systems choose not to reflect the subject content of materials and primarily provide shelf location, not subject access. One such system assigns numbers to materials sequentially as each item is added to a collection; for example, book 1 is the first book acquired, book 2 is the second, and so forth. This is called an "accession number" system and reflects the order of acquisition. In an accession number system, materials are not shifted when new items arrive. Once classified, materials can be expected to remain in the same place for as long as they are held. A similar system alphabetizes materials, shelving them by a chosen element, usually authors' names or title words. These systems are logical, follow recognizable patterns, and provide shelf addresses for materials, but they fail to reveal subject matter or group materials on a subject in one place on the shelves. Caution should be used before adopting these systems, because they do not promote browsing and are costly to change.

Canadian and U.S. library classifications, because they are used primarily for shelving, tend to be two dimensional or linear. The numbers start at the first one and proceed one after the other to the last one, for example, 001-999 for DDC or A-Z for LCC. Knowledge does not behave in a linear fashion. It moves in many directions simultaneously. Think of the topics mentioned previously: medicine, music, and religion. These are disciplines in their own right, but they also have cross-disciplinary meetings, such as music therapy or faith healing. Music therapy is also related to religious music and aroma therapy, and faith healing is related to faith-based charities and meditational chants, both of which can be involved in medical treatment. Topics do not proceed one after the other in linear fashion, but branch out helter-skelter in all directions. All the relationships cannot be maintained simultaneously, except in a faceted system in which the related parts can be moved about to stand together, on request. When a faceted classification is used for shelving, only some of the numbers can be used. In a catalog or a bibliography, however, all the numbers can be displayed, as appropriate, in different places in the number sequence to show each of the facets to a searcher, as shown in Figure 18.2. (Note the similarity to keyword searching.)

In the DDC, Music = 780; Medicine = 610; and Religion = 200. If DDC were faceted, the topics discussed above could be expressed as follows:

Music therapy	= 780 + 610 (music plus medical treatment)
Faith healing	= 200 + 610 (religion plus medical treatment)
Religious music	= 200 + 780 (religion plus music)

A catalog or a bibliography could list them as follows:

200 + 610	= Faith healing
200 + 780	= Religious music
610 + 200	= Healing by faith
610 + 780	= Healing by music
780 + 200	= Music in religion
780 + 610	= Music therapy

Rules for shelving can permit only one sequence, however, such as listing the facets from lower to higher numbers only. Each topic is shelved in one place, based on the six assigned numbers. The result is:

200610	= Faith healing
200780	= Religious music
610780	= Music therapy

Figure 18.2. DDC as a Faceted Scheme.

EVALUATING SUBJECT CATALOGS

Subject catalogs can be evaluated using at least six criteria: recall, relevance, precision, exhaustivity, ease of use, and cost. They are described in detail in this section.

Recall

Recall refers to the amount of material retrieved when a heading is used in a search. To be "good," the catalog should provide "enough" material, but not overwhelm. If every movie in a very large collection of videorecordings of made-for-television movies had a different subject heading, the recall would be one item per subject heading. If all the items were assigned TELEVISION MOVIES, the searcher would retrieve all of them with that heading. Between these extremes, a balance is sought. Someone using a subject heading should recall all items related to the subject but exclude unrelated items.

Relevance

Relevance refers to how well materials retrieved using a subject heading match the searcher's needs. A "good" subject catalog earns high marks here. The more specific a search is, the more likely what is found will be relevant. If a searcher wants something about computer programming and uses the subject heading PROGRAMMING (ELECTRONIC COMPUTERS), he or she should recall every item in the collection about the subject. However, that heading is assigned only to items entirely about the topic, not to items with just a chapter about it. If the broader subject heading COMPUTERS were added to the original search, the searcher could retrieve items having a chapter or two about programming, but this larger batch of material would also contain material about hardware, computer architecture, network design, and other irrelevant subjects. The quality of relevance tends to decrease as the amount of recall increases. These two qualities are said to have an *inverse relationship.*

Precision

Precision is the ability to specify exactly what is wanted, without using broader subject headings representing other things as well. Imagine that the searcher in our previous example was really interested only in items about programming in BASIC, one programming language. PROGRAMMING (ELECTRONIC COMPUTERS) would retrieve material on all programming languages, including BASIC. If, however, the searcher used the subject heading BASIC (COMPUTER PROGRAM LANGUAGE), that would allow for much more precision than if COMPUTERS and PROGRAMMING (ELECTRONIC

COMPUTERS) were the only terms available. Precision varies with term specificity as well as with definition and application. Precision is also affected by the presence of overlapping and ambiguous terms.

Exhaustivity

Exhaustivity refers to the amount (or depth) of subject cataloging. Some catalogers give each item only one subject heading. Others may give up to three or five headings, both common practices, to cover the overall subject matter of each item. Some catalogers might wish to furnish subject headings for each chapter of a book or each part of an electronic resource. This is a deeper level, furnishing greater exhaustivity. The highest marks for exhaustivity go to the catalog furnishing subject headings for every idea contained within an item.

Ease of Use

Two kinds of people use the subject catalog: staff members who assign subject headings to materials or search the catalog to answer questions, and library users who search the catalog themselves. The subject heading system should be easy for both kinds of people to use.

Cost

A "good" subject catalog should maximize value by providing the most service possible for the money spent on it. It also must be affordable. Evaluating the cost is done by considering the impact. If searchers need to ask for help less often, freeing the reference staff for other duties, costly subject cataloging is justified. If searchers have to ask for help just as frequently, the expense is not worth it. A subject system that enabled a computer or clerical staff to do the work would be less costly than one that only librarians could apply. Cost is relative, and no standard measures for high- and low-cost cataloging exist. However, variations in cost and resulting service can be measured, if objective definitions of service are devised (e.g., "better" service = fewer requests for assistance with searches, or "better" service = an increase in use of materials with no more than a 2 percent increase in requests for assistance with searches). Then, experiments for balancing cost and service can be done.

There are tradeoffs in producing and using subject catalogs. One criterion cannot measure a catalog's worth, and all must be put into a reasonable balance to achieve good service at bearable cost. No magic formulas dictate how deeply to index or how many cross-references to make, but problems demand the attention of concerned practitioners.

PROBLEMS OF THE SUBJECT CATALOG

Problems occur when different terms are used to express a topic (often due to changes in the meaning and usage of words over time or between the works of different authors); when topics overlap; when the number of records recalled in an average search is too great or too small; and, perhaps most critical of all, when authorized headings and searchers' vocabularies do not match. A person using a term that is not present in the catalog either as a subject heading or a cross-reference will find nothing. To promote the identification feature of the subject catalog, all words used by searchers and authors should be present as headings. But if that were done, how would works on a single subject be brought together? To promote the collocating feature, synonymous and quasi-synonymous terms must be combined in a few carefully defined terms, whose specificity results in reasonable numbers of relevant retrieved items.

These conflicts have no single resolution, but computers offer new possibilities. Computers enable catalog users to search terms found in titles, summaries, or other areas in bibliographic descriptions containing information about the content of works in "natural language" in addition to the designated subject headings. Computers permit searching any word of a subject heading, called a subject "keyword," even if it is not the first word of a heading, which was not possible with card catalogs, in which only the word in the filing position (called the "lead term") could be searched. Additional retrieval capabilities made possible when subject catalogs are computerized include the following:

- Searches with partial data (e.g., if an asterisk stands for any letters, COMPUT* can retrieve both COMPUTERS and COMPUTING, while *COMPUT* can retrieve both of those plus MICROCOMPUTERS and MINICOMPUTERS);
- Saving search requests and using them in more than one database or catalog;
- Combining more than one subject heading into complex requests, e.g., COMPUTERS **AND** ART, or MUSIC **AND** POPULAR **NOT** JAZZ, or combining a subject heading with other bibliographic elements in a single search, e.g., SU=SYMPHONIES **AND** AU=MOZART;
- Accessing the catalog from outside the library via networks; and
- Accessing local acquisition and circulation data as well as catalog records, so a searcher can determine an item's availability.

This list is not exhaustive. The boundaries between search capabilities that require use of a particular kind of subject vocabulary and those that only need a properly programmed computer system are blurring The use of computers did not make controlled vocabularies obsolete, as some predicted in the 1980s; rather, it led to intensified efforts to improve controlled vocabularies and develop new ways to search data elements likely to express subject content.

EVALUATING CLASSIFICATIONS

Criteria similar to those used in evaluating subject catalogs can be applied to classifications. They include the level of specificity afforded by the system; the browsability it produces; its ease of use, including understandable notation, mnemonics, indexing, and simple rules for the assignment of numbers; its hospitality to new subjects; regular updating; and its cost.

The level of specificity should be appropriate to the size and distribution of the library's collections. If it has only a few broad numbers, many items on diverse aspects of a topic will be classified in the same number. If it has a great many narrow numbers, very few items will be classified in the same number even if their content is closely related. A balance appropriate to the collection being classified should be sought, although accommodations must be made by individual libraries to classification systems intended for large numbers of users.

Browsability as a feature of classifications depends to a large degree on the subject relationships it presents. In most instances, progression from broader to narrower topics in a subject area enhances browsing. The logic of subject relationships should be clear to a searcher, making it possible to anticipate where to look for a desired subject or subdivision. The juxtaposition of subjects is also a concern relating to browsability. Folklore and cannibalism are only a few numbers apart in the DDC, whereas English language and English literature are several hundreds of numbers apart. Similarly, dance and drama are quite far apart in the LCC even though many people think of these as closely related performing arts.

The ease of use depends on many factors, including an easily remembered, easily understood type of notation. The flexibility of the notation to handle numerous narrow categories while still being economical also affects the ease of use, as does mnemonic numbering (using the same number for a topic or subtopic wherever it appears). The presence of good indexes to the numbers is essential, both for classifiers and ordinary searchers. An asset for classifiers is the existence of relatively uncomplicated rules for assigning the numbers.

No classification system can boast that it covers subjects as yet unknown, but how these are handled when they emerge is a matter of concern. Ideally, a hospitable system will be able to incorporate them into the list of numbers in a way that retains appropriate relations with related subjects. Practically speaking, this can also mean having to revise many related areas, as was the case when the subject of computers emerged. Thus, classifications must be updated regularly to add or alter categories as our knowledge of subjects and perceptions of their relationships change over the years.

Finally, the cost of using a classification is an important aspect of its total value. If a cataloger adopts the same classification as his or her peers and can share the burden of assigning numbers to commonly held materials, it is likely to be less costly than using a unique classification and doing all the work alone. Cost was a major factor in the decision of many college and university libraries to change from previously used classifications to the LCC after OCLC's shared cataloging database was established. Because LC's cataloging constituted the lion's share of the records in OCLC in its early days, it was less costly for other

OCLC member libraries to copy its numbers and avoid the burden of classifying the same materials differently. Other cost factors include the relative ease or difficulty for classifiers of assigning the numbers—the longer it takes to classify a title, the more it costs—and the cost of the tool itself, along with whatever accompanying manuals, supplements, and so forth are needed to use it.

It may be difficult to quantify some of these features, such as browsability or ease of use, but it is worth making a serious effort to do so whenever changes in a library's classification practices are contemplated. It may be that savings will be achieved in some areas, while new costs are incurred in others. Sometimes the savings is only to the library, and the searchers must do more work to find what they want. Thus, the value of a classification should be figured as a total package.

MAINTAINING SUBJECT CATALOGS AND CLASSIFICATIONS

Policy decisions about maintenance of subject catalogs should be made and publicized to those who use them. An important decision is whether to interfile subject headings with headings for authors and titles. When card catalogs were the rule, the choice usually was a function of the size of the file and the ease with which people could search it. Since the advent of OPACs, even large catalogs are interfiled, because the computer does the legwork. If, however, searchers must select an index (subject, title, keyword, or name) when they enter a search term, as is common in OPACs, it is the same as dividing the file. The user must remember to search other files if the first attempt does not bring desired results.

Another policy issue concerns cross-references. It may be difficult keeping track of cross-references and changing them when necessary. They tend to proliferate rapidly—one heading can have several cross-references, each of which has more of its own. Decisions must be made about how extensively these will be made.

One thing searchers dislike are cross-references that lead to terms having no materials listed under them, called a *blind reference*. Policies for maintaining the cross-reference structure can prevent this from happening. Some librarians believe cross-references teach users about related subjects and that all references given in the subject heading list should be present in the catalog whether or not they lead to any entries. (If such a policy is followed, catalogers can add notations to recordless headings explaining that the library has no holdings on those topics.) Others believe the cost of creating and maintaining a living cross-reference structure (called a *syndetic* structure) is unwarranted when it doesn't lead to use of materials.

Each library must weigh the various alternatives—to include all, some, or no cross-references—and arrive at a viable policy for its searchers and its catalog. Some may find it necessary to decide about cross-references on a case-by-case basis, but it is more efficient to systematize the policy so that individual decisions are unnecessary.

Finally, there are implications for maintenance in the way subject headings are filed. Two different arrangements of subject headings are furnished by the rules used at LC and those published by ALA.[5] The Library of Congress's filing rules distinguish between different subject heading forms and types of subdivisions, whereas ALA's do not. Figure 18.3 illustrates how the use of each method would cause an identical group of headings to be arranged. (The headings in the two lists are fictitious.)

Filed by the LC (1980) Filing Rules	Filed by the ALA (1980) Filing Rules
Art—16th century	Art—16th century
Art—Adaptations	Art—Adaptations
Art—Themes, motives	Art, Aegean
Art—Australia	Art, American
Art, Aegean	Art, Ancient
Art, American	Art and anthropology
Art, Ancient	Art and industry
Art, Comparative	Art—Australia
Art, Modern—17th-18th centuries—History	Art, Comparative
Art and anthropology	Art, Modern—17th-18th centuries—History
Art and industry	Art—Themes, motives
Art treasures in war	Art treasures in war

Figure 18.3 Impact of Filing Rules.

Maintenance of the library's classification system also involves policy decisions. Foremost among these is how to incorporate updates to the system. Ideally, all changes to the numbers should be adopted, which means the affected materials and their catalog records are reprocessed with new numbers first, after which the materials are shelved in their new locations. In a less-than-ideal world in which staff time is at a premium, this might mean allowing new materials to go untreated while staff revise materials that have already been treated once. Librarians view such developments with displeasure and tend to resist adopting changes in classification numbers. The authors recommend adopting changes judiciously, over time, thus allowing the library to benefit from the results without committing all its resources to the change at once. (This is discussed in greater detail in Chapter 22.)

A second matter of importance, especially for large collections, is the physical organization of the shelves. Choices include starting with the first number and following through to the last, all in one sequence; or, alternatively, grouping parts of the collection out of sequence in specially designated locations. For those who make the latter choice, music and art are two subjects often chosen to be shelved out of sequence. Science and technology numbers are also frequently grouped apart from the rest of the collection, sometimes in buildings of their own. Reference works are often deployed out of sequence to provide equipment or work space for users of these materials. Age can play a role, with older materials stored in less accessible locations and new materials shelved in highly visible locations. Every exception to the expected shelving system is likely to add some extra time to a browser's task as well as to staff workload, but doing so is justified if it can be shown that the majority of people focus solely on specific out-of-sequence materials. Few studies have been done to demonstrate whether this is the case, but lack of data has not dissuaded those who like the nonsequential arrangements.

SUBJECT ANALYSIS FOR LITERARY WORKS

Assigning subject headings and classification numbers to literary works—novels, plays, stories, poetry, and so forth—also called works of imagination, should be considered carefully. Regarding subject headings, policies at LC, NLC, and other large libraries have limited the assignment of subject headings to nonfiction works unless they are collections of texts by more than one author, texts augmented by literary criticism, or historical or biographical works. People are thought to seek literary works in the catalog by their authors or titles, not by their subjects. Children and youth, however, often choose (or are guided to choose by parents, teachers, media specialists, and librarians) to learn about something by reading about it in stories. In the 1960s, in response to many requests from librarians and media specialists, LC established new policies for children's fiction providing both subject headings and summary notes (see Figure 18.4).

Searchers have come to expect subject headings for children's fiction. More recently, practitioners have argued for the assignment of headings for literary genres to adult fiction, for which ALA's Subject Analysis Committee published guidelines and terminology.[6] The Library of Congress experimented with the new genre headings, found them helpful, and encourages others to do the same. Libraries need to establish policies for subject access to literary works based on estimates of searchers' need for them and the library's ability do the added work.

Similarly, many public libraries choose not to classify fiction and biography, preferring to assign them all one code such as F or Fic, B or Bio, or variations on those themes, and shelve the materials in alphabetical order by the author's or biographee's surname. This assumes people will either browse the shelves in person or search such materials in library catalogs by elements other

```
This example is an illustration of:
     • edition statement
     • publishing date not listed, copyright date given
     • edition and history note
     • summary
     • Library of Congress annotated card subject headings
     • fiction subject headings
     • Library of Congress annotated card program CIP
     • 2nd level cataloging


Calvert, Patricia.
  Sooner / Patricia Calvert. -- 1st ed. -- New York : Atheneum,
c1998.
  166 p. ; 22 cm.

  Sequel to: Bigger.
  Summary: With the realization that his father may not return
now that the Civil War is over, thirteen-year-old Tyler finds
himself the man of their Missouri farm and the master of a new
dog, the strikingly colored Sooner.
  ISBN 0-689-81114-4.

  1. Farm life -- Missouri -- Fiction.  2. Missouri -- Fiction.
3. Dogs -- Fiction.  4. Reconstruction -- Fiction.  5. United
States -- History -- 1865-1898 -- Fiction.  I. Title.
```

CHIEF SOURCE OF INFORMATION
(Title Page)

PATRICIA CALVERT

SOONER

ATHENEUM BOOKS FOR YOUNG READERS

(Information on Verso)

Atheneum Books for Young Readers
An imprint of Simon & Schuster Children's Publishing Division
1230 Avenue of the Americas
New York, New York 10020

Copyright © 1998 by Patricia Calvert

Library of Congress Cataloging-in-Publication Data
Calvert, Patricia
Sooner / Patricia Calvert.—1st ed.
p. cm.
Sequel to: Bigger.
Summary: With the realization that his father may not return now that the Civil War is over, thirteen-year-old Tyler finds himself the man of their Missouri farm and the master of a new dog, the strikingly-colored Sooner.
ISBN 0-689-81114-4
[1. Farm life—Missouri—Fiction. 2. Missouri—Fiction. 3. Dogs—Fiction. 4. Reconstruction—Fiction. 5. United States—History—1865–1898—Fiction.] I. Title.
PZ7.C139So 1998
[Fic]—dc21
97-28007
CIP AC

Figure 18.4. LC Subject heading and summary note.

than call number. Both assumptions may not be true, making the materials more difficult to find. Academic libraries tend to classify everything, including works of imagination, keeping them in the order prescribed by the classification scheme. This aids catalog searchers and should not hinder browsers at the shelf.

WHY USE STANDARD SYSTEMS?

A library might be tempted to dispense with standard subject headings and standard classification numbers. It might seem easier to make up appropriate headings and numbers than to buy expensive tools like Sears, LCSH, DDC, or LCC, and be bound by the terms they offer. Why invest time and money in them? First, making up local subject headings and classification numbers puts the burden of keeping track of selected terms entirely on the cataloger's shoulders. The cataloger must also decide how to define terms and numbers and how they should be applied. In the case of subject headings, the cataloger must decide what cross-references should be made for each term; in the case of classification, a consistent notation must be constructed. It is time consuming to create and maintain subject and classification authorities, both in terms of other work one hasn't time to do as well as the dollars paid. If other personnel help do subject cataloging and classification, the list of headings and numbers must be made available to them in a usable form. Even if all the work is done alone, a properly written list is needed for searchers to consult.

Second, a cataloger cannot use subject headings or classification numbers assigned by other catalogers or benefit from the work he or she does. If the library enters a network environment, the terms can be accommodated as locally defined headings and classification numbers, but no one else can use them. Also, the cataloger cannot gain from copying the work of other network partners, because nearly all use standard subject and classification authorities.

Third, the catalog is an ongoing tool, not the individual expression of one collection at one point in time, managed by one librarian. Complete, explicit instructions on how headings or classification numbers have been chosen, used, and managed, and a complete list of terms, cross-references, or numbers must be provided to the cataloger's successors. Another librarian might not wish to continue the system or decide that it is not cost effective and opt to change to a standard system. Then the entire collection would require conversion. Establishing unique subject headings or classification numbers should be undertaken only after the library has assessed the alternatives and rejected them for good reasons. A nonstandard subject or classification authority could result in less effective service, overall.

The next two chapters examine the subject heading lists and classification systems used by most libraries in North America: Sears, LCSH, DDC, and LCC.

NOTES

1, *Bliss Bibliographic Classification,* 2nd ed., edited by J. Mills and Vanda Broughton (London: Butterworths, 1977-).

2. Charles Ammi Cutter, *Two-Figure Author Table* (Chicopee Falls, MA: H. R. Huntting; distr. Littleton, CO: Libraries Unlimited, 1969-); Charles Ammi Cutter, *Three-Figure Author Table* (Chicopee Falls, MA: H. R. Huntting; distr. Littleton, CO: Libraries Unlimited, 1969-); *Cutter-Sanborn Three-Figure Author Table,* Swanson-Swift revision (Littleton, CO: Libraries Unlimited, 1969). These tools are available also, if preferred, on CD-ROM from Libraries Unlimited.

3. Joseph Miller, ed., *Sears List of Subject Headings,* 17th ed. (New York: H. W. Wilson, 2000), 105.

4. David Judson Haykin, *Subject Headings: A Practical Guide* (Washington, DC: Government Printing Office, 1951), 7-9.

5. John C. Rather, *Library of Congress Filing Rules* (Washington, DC: Library of Congress, 1980); *ALA Filing Rules* (Chicago: American Library Association, 1980). An earlier set of rules issued by ALA is followed in libraries that still have card catalogs: *ALA Rules for Filing Catalog Cards,* 2nd ed. (Chicago: American Library Association, 1968).

6. Association for Library Collections & Technical Services, Subject Analysis Committee, *Guidelines on Subject Access to Individual Works of Fiction, Drama, Etc.,* 2nd ed. (Chicago: American Library Association, 2000).

SUGGESTED READING

Subject Headings

Cleveland, Donald B., and Ana D. Cleveland. *Introduction to Indexing and Abstracting.* 3rd ed. Englewood, CO: Libraries Unlimited, 2000.

Cochrane, Pauline Atherton, and Eric H. Johnson, eds. *Visualizing Subject Access for 21st Century Information Resources.* Urbana-Champaign: Graduate School of Library and Information Science, University of Illinois at Urbana-Champaign, 1998.

Ferguson, Bobby. *Blitz Cataloging Workbook: Subject Analysis.* Englewood, CO: Libraries Unlimited, 1998.

Foskett, A. C. *The Subject Approach to Information.* 5th ed. London: Library Association Publishing, 1996.

Guidelines on Subject Access to Individual Works of Fiction, Drama, Etc. 2nd ed. Chicago: American Library Association, 2000.

Hjørland, Birger. *Information Seeking and Subject Representation: An Activity-Theoretical Approach to Information Science.* Westport, CT: Greenwood Press, 1997.

Olson, Hope A. and John J. Boll. *Subject Analysis in Online Catalogs.* 2nd ed. Englewood, CO: Libraries Unlimited, 2001.

Classification

"Classification: Options and Opportunities." *Cataloging & Classification Quarterly* 19, nos. 3 and 4 (1995).

Olson, Hope A., and John J. Boll. *Subject Analysis in Online Catalogs*. 2nd ed. Englewood, CO: Libraries Unlimited, 2001.

Sauperl, Alenka. *Subject Determination During the Cataloging Process*. Lanham, MD: Scarecrow Press, 2002.

Schwartz, Candy. *Sorting Out the Web: Approaches to Subject Access*. Westport, CT: Ablex, 2001.

Scott, Mona L. *Conversion Tables: LC-Dewey; Dewey-LC; Subject Headings—LC and Dewey*. 2nd ed. Englewood, CO: Libraries Unlimited, 1999. (Available on disk.)

Taylor, Arlene G. *The Organization of Information*. Englewood, CO: Libraries Unlimited, 1999.

REVIEW QUESTIONS

1. Where can catalogers find information about the subject content of materials?
2. Describe two ways subject content is represented in catalog records.
3. What is the difference between topic and form? Give an example.
4. Define "enumerative" and "faceted" and discuss their differences.
5. What linguistic problems do controlled vocabularies help to address and eliminate?
6. How do classification systems employ word-based expressions of subject matter?
7. Describe the difference between pure and mixed notation.
8. Name and describe the parts of a call number.
9. What are the two ways a subject catalog can be organized?
10. Explain the meaning of the statement that relevance and recall in subject catalogs have an inverse relationship.

Chapter 19

Subject Headings Lists

In this chapter, two lists used as the sources for subject headings, *Library of Congress Subject Headings* and *Sears List of Subject Headings,* are described. Together they are the most popular subject heading authorities used by libraries in North America.

LIBRARY OF CONGRESS SUBJECT HEADINGS (LCSH)

Library of Congress Subject Headings (LCSH) began publication in 1909, based on a list of subject headings compiled and issued by the American Library Association (ALA) called *The List of Subject Headings for Use in Dictionary Catalogs*. The Library of Congress's subject catalogers adopted many headings as they appeared in the ALA list, modified others, and created new ones when they did not find what they needed. New editions appeared about once every ten years until 1988, when conversion to a computerized database was completed. Then, printed editions began to be issued annually. Versions in other forms have also been made available.

LCSH's wide appeal is attributable to three factors: (1) that LC collects many more books in nearly all subjects than other general libraries, (2) that it does a fine job of maintaining and distributing the ever-growing list of authorized subject headings and cross-references, and (3) that it charges very little for the work.

Because LCSH's vocabulary grew, and continues to grow, based on the contents of items in LC's collection, it lacks headings for topics not included in that collection. Moreover, LCSH has lacked a consistent set of rules for creating new headings during nearly a century of growth. Subject headings were created according to the theories and ideas of many catalogers and heads of subject cataloging.

Detailed instructions for applying LCSH are provided separately in *Subject Cataloging Manual: Subject Headings*, available on the *Cataloger's Desktop* CD-ROM.[1] The manual cumulates decisions and interpretations originally used by LC's subject catalogers and later published in response to requests for guidelines that everyone who uses LCSH could follow. The manual covers general issues first, followed by sections on the treatment of selected types of topics, and, last, the use of each of the general subdivisions known as *free-floating* subdivisions (see below), arranged alphabetically.

Cataloging networks and some individual libraries have access to the online subject authority file maintained at LC, but most libraries buy it in offline form. It is available in annually issued books or more frequent issues in microfiche and CD-ROM. The CD-ROM version is titled *Classification Plus*.[2]

The printed LCSH contains approximately 750,000 authorized terms and cross-references on more than 5,000 pages bound in five massive volumes with distinctive red covers. They are not a complete system, however, because they lack the list of free-floating subdivisions that can be added to topical descriptors to give them greater specificity. Free-floating subdivisions are found in *Subject Cataloging Manual: Subject Headings* and in a separate publication, *Free-Floating Subdivisions: An Alphabetic Index,* issued annually.[3] Rules for their use are found in both publications. Updates to the printed LCSH are available in electronic form on the World Wide Web at http://lcweb.loc.gov/catdir/cpso/wls.html, and in printed form in weekly lists[4] and quarterly *Cataloging Service* bulletins (CSB).[5] Together, the books, the manual, the subdivision guide, and the updates constitute a complete LCSH subject heading authority system.

Authorized headings are listed in bold print; unauthorized headings and cross-references in plain print. LCSH prints headings three columns to a page (see Figure 19.1).

Most headings and cross-references are topical terms. Although some names appear in the list (see Figure 19.1), LCSH does not control them; instead, names of people, geographic locations, and corporate bodies, and all titles used as subject headings in the catalog, are controlled by a name authority file separate from the subject authority file. (LC's name authority file can be used for this purpose by any institution.) Catalogers are directed to add name and title headings as needed, using the form prescribed by AACR2-98. With a few exceptions, catalogers may not add topical headings; instead, they must use the most appropriate authorized heading *already present* in the list, and hope that LC will add the desired headings before long.

Coded instructions (UF, BT, RT, SA, and NT, explained below) for making cross-references appear with their subject headings. Cross-references are given in that order and, within each category, in alphabetical order. If a subject heading's meaning might be in question, instructions are given about how to use it, beginning with the words "Here are entered . . ." The instructions usually are framed in positive language, but occasionally will add what should *not* be entered under a particular heading as well.

College and school drama, Philippine (English) *(May Subd Geog)*
UF College and school drama, English—Philippines
Philippine college and school drama (English)
BT Philippine drama (English)
College and school drama, Polish *(May Subd Geog)*
UF Polish college and school drama
BT Polish drama
College and school drama, Puerto Rican *(May Subd Geog)*
UF Puerto Rican college and school drama
BT Puerto Rican drama
College and school drama, Russian *(May Subd Geog)*
UF Russian college and school drama
BT Russian drama
College and school drama, Swahili *(May Subd Geog)*
UF Swahili college and school drama
BT Swahili drama
College and school drama, Ukrainian *(May Subd Geog)*
UF Ukrainian college and school drama
BT Ukrainian drama
College and school drama, West Indian (English) *(Not Subd Geog)*
UF College and school drama, English—West Indies
West Indian college and school drama (English)
BT West Indian drama (English)
College and school journalism
USE College student newspapers and periodicals
Journalism, College
Journalism, Elementary school
Journalism, High school
Journalism, Junior high school
Journalism, School
College and school periodicals
USE College publications
College student newspapers and periodicals
Student newspapers and periodicals
Student publications
College annuals
USE College yearbooks
College applications *(May Subd Geog)*
[LB2351.5-LB2351.52]
UF Applications for college
Universities and colleges—Applications
RT Universities and colleges—Admission
College art museums *(May Subd Geog)*
UF Art museums, University and college *[Former heading]*
Campus art museums
University art museums
BT Art museums
College museums
College athletes *(May Subd Geog)*
UF Student-athletes
BT Athletes
— **Recruiting** *(May Subd Geog)*
[GV350.5]
UF Recruiting of college athletes
— **Selection and appointment** *(May Subd Geog)*
NT College sports—Scouting
College athletics
USE College sports
College attendance *(May Subd Geog)*
[LC148]
UF Academic probation
Attendance, College
College enrollment
Probation, Academic
School attendance—College
University attendance

College autonomy
USE University autonomy
College BASE (Test)
USE College Basic Academic Subjects Examination
College Basic Academic Subjects Examination
[LB2367.25]
UF College BASE (Test)
BT Universities and colleges—Examinations
College boards (Examinations)
USE Universities and colleges—Entrance examinations
College boards of trustees
USE College trustees
College bookstores
USE College stores
College buildings *(May Subd Geog)*
[NA6600-NA6605 (Architecture)]
UF Universities and colleges—Buildings *[Former heading]*
University buildings
BT College facilities
School buildings
SA *subdivision* Buildings *under names of individual educational institutions, e.g.* Harvard University—Buildings
— **Access for the physically handicapped** *(May Subd Geog)*
BT Architecture and the physically handicapped
— **Energy conservation** *(May Subd Geog)*
[TJ163.5.U5]
— **Arizona**
NT Grady Gammage Memorial Auditorium (Tempe, Ariz.)
— **California**
UF Technical institutes—California—Buildings *[Former heading]*
NT Herbert Hoover Memorial Building (Stanford, Calif.)
Throop Hall (Pasadena, Calif.)
— **Connecticut**
NT Dwight Hall (New Haven, Conn.)
Sterling Law Buildings (New Haven, Conn.)
Yale Art and Architecture Building (New Haven, Conn.)
Yale University Hall of Graduate Studies (New Haven, Conn.)
— **Florida**
NT Bailey Center (Pensacola, Fla.)
— **France**
NT Hôtel de Mortemart (Paris, France)
— **Germany**
NT Gottesaue (Karlsruhe, Germany)
— **Idaho**
NT William H. Kibbie-ASUI Activity Center Dome (Warsaw, Idaho)
— **Illinois**
UF Universities and colleges—Illinois—Buildings *[Former heading]*
NT Assembly Hall (Urbana, Ill.)
Crown Hall (Chicago, Ill.)
Social Science Research Building (Chicago, Ill.)
University Hall (Urbana, Ill.)
— **Indiana**
NT Bess Meshulam Simon Music Library and Recital Center (Bloomington, Ind.)
IUPUI University Library (Indianapolis, Ind. : Building)
Woodburn Hall (Bloomington, Ind.)
— **Italy**
NT Villa La Quiete (Florence, Italy)
— **Mexico**
NT La Colostitla (Tlalpan, Mexico)

— **Michigan**
UF Community colleges—Michigan—Buildings *[Former heading]*
NT Roll Building (Battle Creek, Micl
— **New Jersey**
NT Brown Hall (Princeton, N.J.)
Graduate College (Princeton, N.J
— **New York (State)**
NT Willard Straight Hall (Ithaca, N.`
— **Ohio**
NT University Hall (Cleveland, Ohio
— **Oregon**
NT Collier House (Eugene, Or.)
— **Pennsylvania**
UF State universities and colleges—Pennsylvania—Buildings *[Former heading]*
Universities and colleges—Pennsylvania—Buildings *[Former heading]*
NT Biemesderfer Executive Center (Millersville, Pa.)
Cathedral of Learning (Pittsburgh Pa.)
Walton Hall (Saint Davids, Pa.)
— **Scotland**
UF Universities and colleges—Scotlar—Buildings *[Former heading]*
NT Old College (Edinburgh, Scotland
— **Washington (State)**
NT Baker Faculty Center (Walla Walla, Wash.)
Kenneth S. Allen Library (Seattle Wash.)
Suzzallo Library (Seattle, Wash.)
College campus violence
USE Campus violence
College catalogs
USE Catalogs, College
College chaplains *(May Subd Geog)*
[BV4376]
UF Campus clergy
Campus ministers
Chaplains, University and college *[Former heading]*
University chaplains
BT Chaplains
College characteristics index
UF CCI
College cheers
USE Cheers
College choice *(May Subd Geog)*
[LB2350.5]
UF Choice of college
College, Choice of *[Former heading]*
Universities and colleges—Selection
BT School choice
College colors
USE School colors
College communities
USE University towns
College community centers
USE Student unions
College cooperation
USE University cooperation
College costs *(May Subd Geog)*
[LB2342-LB2342.2]
UF College education costs
Student expenditures
Tuition
BT Education—Finance
Universities and colleges—Finance
NT Tuition tax credits
— **Law and legislation** *(May Subd Geog)*
College counseling
USE Counseling in higher education
College credits *(May Subd Geog)*
[LB2359.5]
BT School credits

1290

Figure 19.1. Library of Congress subject headings sample page.

Library of Congress classification numbers are listed for many headings and some of the subdivisions as well. These are just suggestions and should not be assigned without consulting the full classification schedules. They are a useful shortcut alternative to consulting page after page of numbers in crowded portions of the schedules or as a guide in unfamiliar territory.

LCSH uses several grammatical constructions, from one-word headings to complex multiword headings. One-word headings usually are nouns or verb forms used as nouns, such as, BLEACHING. Different meanings can depend on whether the noun is singular or plural, for example, BONE is used for the generic skeletal material, while BONES is used for skeletal structures in humans and animals.

A noun modified by an adjective or a second noun used as an adjective is another grammatical type, for example, CABLE TELEVISION. LCSH sometimes reverses the order in which the words appear to bring the more important word to the filing position, for example, CARBOHYDRATES, REFINED. With computer-based keyword searching, the order of words is not critical, but in card files where only the initial word is searchable, it is important. Two-word headings also are formulated as nouns with explanatory qualifiers to ensure their correct interpretation, such as EQUILIBRIUM (ECONOMICS) and EQUILIBRIUM (PHYSIOLOGY).

Another heading type is two nouns connected by a conjunction, such as "AND," for example, CARRIAGES AND CARTS or ART AND SCIENCE. The nouns can represent similar things or opposites. Complex headings in this category may include modified nouns, such as LANDSCAPE ARCHITECTURE AND ENERGY CONSERVATION. Prepositions also can link two nouns or modified nouns in another type of heading, for example, HISTORY IN ART, TITLES OF BOOKS, COOKERY FOR THE SICK, and BIBLE AS LITERATURE.

More complex headings can involve both multiword concepts and combinations of concepts, such as DO-IT-YOURSELF PRODUCTS INDUSTRY. Sometimes these are simplified; for example, ERRATA (IN BOOKS) was changed to ERRATA, and CONVENTS AND NUNNERIES, BUDDHIST to BUDDHIST CONVENTS. In other cases, revisions add to headings to clarify them or expand their scope; for example, some years ago PETER'S DENIAL IN ART became JESUS CHRIST—DENIAL BY PETER—ART, and the one-word heading CLARET was changed to WINE AND WINE MAKING—FRANCE—BORDELAIS.

LCSH headings and subject heading strings are filed according to a set of rules that facilitates computerized filing, devised by John C. Rather.[6] The system files word by word with digits preceding alphabetic characters, and treats letter combinations as they appear (for example, Dr. files as "D-r-period," not "Doctor"). LC's filing rules distinguish between different kinds of subject heading forms and subdivisions, unlike the rules used to file Sears headings (see below). Recognition of headings and heading-subdivision forms occurs automatically, based on their computer coding. (Coding is discussed in Chapter 21.) The result is that headings consisting of one word and this word plus subdivisions all appear before multiword headings beginning with the same word. In filing, the order of the subdivisions is chronological subdivisions first, followed by topical subdivisions, then geographical subdivisions. In LCSH and in large catalogs in which many entries appear under a term and its subdivisions, searchers need to realize that ART AND INDUSTRY, which is a multiword heading, can be many pages or screens beyond ART—THEMES, MOTIVES, which is a subdivided heading, because the rules give filing preference to subdivided headings.

Cross-References in LCSH

Cross-references in LCSH are identified by a set of standard mnemonic abbreviations mandated by the National Information Standards Organization: BT (Broader Term), RT (Related Term), NT (Narrower Term), UF (Use For), SA (See Also), and USE. LCSH does not specify the highest term in a subject hierarchy, identified as TT (Top Term), nor does it show the entire range of steps in a subject area from the broadest to the narrowest term such as those found in the National Library of Medicine's *Medical Subject Headings* (MeSH).[7] Cross-references in LCSH lead a searcher one level of hierarchy broader (BT) or narrower (NT), but the practical application policy is to make only NT references in the catalog display. BT references are given in the list for consultation only. RTs at the same level of hierarchy have reciprocal cross-references, and both appear in the catalog display.

As the name implies, BTs lead from the heading at which they appear to broader headings in the same subject. This is called leading "upward." Similarly, NTs lead to narrower terms in the same subject, called leading "downward." RTs lead to headings at the same level of hierarchy in a related area, which might be in the same subject or another subject associated with it. The relationships of these three types of cross-references to the heading at which they appear are clear from their names. The other three types—SA, UF, and USE—bear more explanation.

SAs are references from the heading at which they appear to groups of headings, rather than individual headings. They also can instruct catalogers to consult other headings or add headings and subdivisions that do not appear in the list. For example, at BOOKS, it says: "SA *headings beginning with the word book* " and at COMMERCIAL PRODUCTS, it says, "SA *names of individual products.*" Occasionally, catalogers are told to use the heading at which the SA appears as a subdivision under specific types of other headings; for example, at ART it says, "SA subdivision ART under names of individual persons who lived before 1400, under names of deities or legendary figures, and under headings of the type [TOPIC]—[SUBDIVISION] . . . ." In most instances, terms used as subject headings may not be used as subdivisions, and vice versa.

UF and USE are reciprocal, that is, wherever a UF is given leading to another heading, a USE heading will appear at the target heading leading back to the original one. UFs appear at authorized headings and are intended mainly for catalogers, telling them to make cross-references from unauthorized headings for a subject that searchers are likely to try to the authorized headings for that subject. The reciprocal USE headings appear under the unauthorized headings and reveal which authorized headings to use instead for the subject. The two headings ACCELERATED EROSION (unauthorized) and SOIL EROSION (authorized) illustrate the point. ACCELERATED EROSION has a USE reference to SOIL EROSION; SOIL EROSION has a reciprocal UF for ACCELERATED EROSION. In practice, this means that when the heading SOIL EROSION is first assigned, catalogers should also make a cross-reference for the UF heading ACCELERATED EROSION. Then, when a searcher looks up ACCELERATED EROSION, which is a common term for the subject not authorized by LCSH, he or she will find the cross-reference to the authorized heading, "USE SOIL EROSION." The reference should look like this:

ACCELERATED EROSION. *Use* SOIL EROSION

The USE reference remains in the catalog until the last item on the subject SOIL EROSION is removed from the collection and that heading is removed. Accompanying the removal of SOIL EROSION, the cross-reference ACCELERATED EROSION, which would then be obsolete, also is removed. Otherwise, the cross-reference leads to a heading with no materials under it, known as a *blind reference*. Blind references frustrate searchers because they fail to retrieve relevant materials, although some believe that just learning the proper subject heading to use for future searches is a sufficiently productive result.

Instructions direct that cross-references are made for the public catalog display only from a given heading to the narrower and related headings listed with it, and not to the broader headings, which are provided mainly for the cataloger's use. For example, at BOAT LIVING an NT reference leads to SAILBOAT LIVING and at SAILBOAT LIVING a BT reference leads to BOAT LIVING. When the first item is cataloged under the narrower heading, SAILBOAT LIVING, no cross-reference is made to the broader heading, BOAT LIVING; but when the first item is cataloged under the broader heading, BOAT LIVING, a cross-reference should be made to the narrower heading, SAILBOAT LIVING (provided materials are listed under it). It will look like the following:

BOAT LIVING. *See also* SAILBOAT LIVING

RTs are reciprocal and both are displayed. For example, at CONCERTS an RT reference leads to MUSIC FESTIVALS; at MUSIC FESTIVALS an RT reference leads to CONCERTS. Each refers to the other. They look like this:

CONCERTS. *See also* MUSIC FESTIVALS

MUSIC FESTIVALS. *See also* CONCERTS

RT references assume that someone interested in items about concerts is likely to be interested also in items about music festivals, and vice versa.

Cross-references can appear on computer screens if the library has an OPAC, or on cards, if the library has a card catalog. Catalog format does not affect the display of cross-references.

Subdivisions in LCSH

LCSH is full of subdivisions. One level of subdivision is sufficient to represent most topics in detail, but some headings require two, three, or even four subdivision levels.

Subdivisions are listed following the cross-references for a heading, each with the scope notes, classification numbers, and cross-references that pertain to that particular subdivision. Each subdivision is indented and printed with a long dash preceding it to indicate that it is not to be used alone, but only as a subdivision of the heading under which it appears. Subdivisions of a subdivision, necessary for very large topics that have several kinds of subdivisions (e.g., topical, chronological, and geographic) are indented further and are given additional dashes, depending on their level in the hierarchy. For example, a topic such as the history of Chinese calligraphy in the twentieth century would be expressed by the LCSH heading CALLIGRAPHY, CHINESE—HISTORY—20TH CENTURY, which is a two level hierarchy; and a topic such as the attribution of Chinese calligraphy from the Sui dynasty would be expressed as CALLIGRAPHY, CHINESE—HISTORY—THREE KINGDOMS-SUI DYNASTY, 220-618—ATTRIBUTION, which is a three level hierarchy. Figure 19.2, page 450, shows how these hierarchies appear in the list.

Broad topics such as art, music, and science are likely to have numerous cross-references and subdivisions, some of which have their own subdivisions as well. This makes for confusion in locating a particular one, because it can be pages away from the main heading. LCSH has all these subdivisions because it is used to organize large files for topics about which much has been and still is being written.

Three types of subdivisions predominate in LCSH: topical, chronological, and geographical. A fourth variety, form subdivision, also is present in the list, but these terms can be construed as a special type of topical subdivision. Subdivisions are indicated in the list in several ways, so catalogers must be alert to all the possibilities. Individual subdivisions should be assigned according to LC policies, given in *Subject Cataloging Manual: Subject Headings*. In particular, beginning catalogers should be aware that two main headings cannot be combined in a heading-subdivision relationship, unless one is listed specifically as a subdivision under the other, or unless one heading functions both as a main heading and a subdivision and is permitted as a subdivision under the second heading. The cataloger should avoid assuming that the absence of an instruction *not* to subdivide is permission to go ahead. Quite the contrary—if there is no clear indication of permission to subdivide a heading, it should not be subdivided. An important exception to the rule is the group of pattern headings listed in the preface to LCSH, discussed below.[8]

LCSH headings can be subdivided four ways: (1) The subdivision may appear in the list under the heading, (2) an instruction to subdivide may be given with the heading in the list, (3) the heading may be one of the designated pattern headings to which subdivisions may be added, and (4) the heading may be a term to which particular free-floating subdivisions can be added.

Calligraphy, Chinese

Calligraphy, Chinese *(May Subd Geog)*
UF Chinese calligraphy
— Sung-Yüan dynasties, 960-1368
USE Calligraphy, Chinese—History—Sung-Yüan dynasties, 960-1368
— Appreciation *(May Subd Geog)*
UF Appreciation of Chinese calligraphy
BT Art appreciation
— Attribution
UF Attribution of Chinese calligraphy
Calligraphy, Chinese—Reattribution
BT Calligraphy, Chinese—Expertising
— Expertising *(May Subd Geog)*
NT Calligraphy, Chinese—Attribution
— History
— — To 221 B.C.
— — Three kingdoms-Sui dynasty, 220-618
UF Calligraphy, Chinese—History—Three kingdoms, six dynasties-Sui dynasty, 220-618 [*Former heading*]
— — Three kingdoms, six dynasties-Sui dynasty, 220-618
USE Calligraphy, Chinese—History—Three kingdoms-Sui dynasty, 220-618
— — Three kingdoms-Sui dynasty, 220-618
— — — Attribution
UF Attribution of Three kingdoms-Sui dynasty Chinese calligraphy
Calligraphy, Chinese—History—Three kingdoms-Sui dynasty, 220-618—Reattribution
BT Calligraphy, Chinese—History—Three kingdoms-Sui dynasty, 220-618—Expertising
— — — Expertising *(May Subd Geog)*
NT Calligraphy, Chinese—History—Three kingdoms-Sui dynasty, 220-618—Attribution
— — — Reattribution
USE Calligraphy, Chinese—History—Three kingdoms-Sui dynasty, 220-618—Attribution
— — Ch'in-Han dynasties, 221 B.C.-220 A.D.
— — T'ang-Five dynasties, 618-960
— — Sung-Yüan dynasties, 960-1368
UF Calligraphy, Chinese—Sung-Yüan dynasties, 960-1368 [*Former heading*]
NT Yün-chien school of calligraphy
— — Ming-Ch'ing dynasties, 1368-1912
NT Yün-chien school of calligraphy
— — 20th century
— Inscriptions
[*ND1457.C53*]
UF Inscriptions on Chinese calligraphy
BT Inscriptions
— Reattribution
USE Calligraphy, Chinese—Attribution

Figure 19.2. Hierarchy of subject headings.

The easiest and most straightforward method of providing for subdivisions is listing them under the headings to which they can be assigned, but doing so for all possible subdivisions would cause LCSH to expand far beyond its current size. Thus, although this method is used, alternatives also are employed for reasons of economy and flexibility.

Geographic Subdivision Instructions

The fact that a heading can be subdivided geographically usually is noted by the parenthetic instruction *(May Subd Geog)* after a primary heading or after a subdivision. The preferred method of subdividing geographically is to put the name of a country after the heading being subdivided. Geographic entities larger than countries, such as continents or other multicountry regions, may be given the same way, but entities wholly within a country are preceded by the name of the country in which they are located. This practice is called *indirect geographic subdivision.* For example, headings and their geographic subdivisions assigned to books about agriculture in North and South America, the Amazon Region, the Andes Mountains, Argentina, Brazil, Ecuador, the Andes mountains of Venezuela, and the cities of Buenos Aires and Rio de Janeiro would create the following file:

AGRICULTURE—AMAZON RIVER REGION

AGRICULTURE—ANDES REGION

AGRICULTURE—ARGENTINA

AGRICULTURE—ARGENTINA—BUENOS AIRES

AGRICULTURE—BRAZIL

AGRICULTURE—BRAZIL—RIO DE JANEIRO

AGRICULTURE—ECUADOR

AGRICULTURE—NORTH AMERICA

AGRICULTURE—SOUTH AMERICA

AGRICULTURE—VENEZUELA—ANDES REGION (VENEZUELA)

The resulting file intermingles geographic entities at different hierarchical levels by interfiling countries and continents with regions that span more than one country, but it places cities and localities within the files for their countries. This makes it possible to search localities either by browsing their country files or by requesting the desired locality in a keyword search.[9]

Three countries—the United States, Canada, and Great Britain—have special rules for indirect subdivision. (Although *United Kingdom* is the proper name of the country and should be used in place of Great Britain, LCSH uses Great Britain because of the difficulty of making the change.) For them, the names of states, provinces, and constituent countries, respectively, are used. Thus, materials on agriculture in Iowa City, education in London, and advertising in Toronto are assigned the following subject descriptors:

AGRICULTURE—IOWA—IOWA CITY
not AGRICULTURE—UNITED STATES—IOWA CITY

EDUCATION—ENGLAND—LONDON
not EDUCATION—GREAT BRITAIN—LONDON

ADVERTISING—ONTARIO—TORONTO
not ADVERTISING—CANADA—TORONTO

Policies for geographic subdivision have changed over the years, sometimes favoring direct subdivision, sometimes indirect, and sometimes accepting both depending on the country. The current policy favoring indirect subdivision results in a file gathered first at the country level, then at the local level. Even the three exceptions gather records first at the state, province, or constituent country level before grouping them at the local level. Because much geographically distinctive material in libraries is about these countries, this strategy avoids gathering them at the country level, preferring the state or province level instead.

Current LC policy is to subdivide indirectly, but older headings that were subdivided directly remain. LCSH is not governed solely by one policy but is an amalgam of many policies implemented throughout its existence. New direct geographic subdivisions will not be established under the current policy.

Other Subdivision Instructions

Instructions to use a particular nongeographic heading as a subdivision under other descriptors may be given with the heading in the list; for example, under BASEBALL, it says: "SA *subdivision* Baseball *under names of individual schools, e.g.,* Harvard University—Baseball."[10]

Pattern Headings

LCSH's creators identify twenty-three groups of headings as *pattern headings.* Each member of a pattern heading group can be expected to need the same set of subdivisions; but instead of repeating the whole set under each, one heading is fully subdivided in the list and catalogers are instructed to use this pattern for all the others. For example, all plants and crops can be subdivided with the same terms as those given under CORN and all sacred works can be subdivided exactly like BIBLE. Some heading groups are provided with more than one pattern; for example, subdivision of diseases may follow the pattern under CANCER or the one under TUBERCULOSIS. Pattern headings are listed in LCSH.

Free-Floating Subdivisions

Some subdivisions—all topical terms, including many representing literary forms—are designated as *free-floating.* Some have such widespread potential for use as subdivisions that it is difficult to anticipate and list them all. Instead, they can be assigned under a broad range of headings. Specific guidance on how to assign free-floating subdivision terms is given in *Subject Cataloging Manual: Subject Headings.*

Form Subdivisions

Form subdivisions, mentioned previously in connection with the list of free-floating terms, include terms that describe the format in which a work appears, such as —CATALOGS. This group of terms also includes literary genres, such as —DICTIONARIES and —BIOGRAPHIES. Most form subdivisions are free-floating.

Chronological Subdivisions

Chronological subdivisions, most of which are not free-floating, are almost always given in the list of terms for those subject headings and subdivisions that may be subdivided by period. History is frequently subdivided by time period, and historical topics often are specific to particular places. The introductory explanations warn catalogers not to use the historical periods developed for one place under other places. This is to be expected because each country, state, or province will have its own chronological landmarks. Chronological periods that can apply to many topics, such as the names of the centuries, e.g., —EIGHTEENTH CENTURY, appear both as primary headings and as subdivisions under other headings.

Topical Subdivisions

Topical subdivision is exactly what the name implies: a subdivision representing a topic,such as BUILDINGS—MAINTENANCE. MAINTENANCE, the subdivision, does not represent a geographical, chronological, or form subdivision. It is a topical subdivision, but it cannot be used just anywhere, as the free-floating subdivisions can. If it was not given in the list under BUILDINGS, catalogers cannot "make it up." They have to use BUILDINGS alone or use two headings to embody the concept.

Because subdivision is done only as LC directs, uniform strings of headings and subdivisions are created that can be combined in only one way. ARCHITECTURE—ARID REGIONS and ARID REGIONS—ARCHITECTURE mean the same thing, but LCSH only permits the former. Catalogers examining both terms will find —ARID REGIONS listed as a subdivision under ARCHITECTURE, but no listing for —ARCHITECTURE as a subdivision under ARID REGIONS. This happens because LCSH is *precoordinated.*

LCSH's Canadian Complement

Canadian Subject Headings, third edition (CSH3) is a one-volume work with 550 pages containing about 6,000 headings and many supporting references.[11] It is neither a comprehensive list nor a substitute for LCSH. It is to be used for items containing Canadian subject matter; whereas LCSH is to be applied to all other materials. CSH3's headings and references expand and adapt LCSH where Canadian topics are not adequately covered or where LCSH headings are not acceptable in a Canadian context. The differences in the sociopolitical structure between Canada and the United States is an obvious area where subject headings suitable to a Canadian topic are needed, for example, GOODS AND SERVICES TAX—CANADA. Figures 19.3 and 19.4 both illustrate the application of CSH3. Although the subject headings in Figure 19.3 could be built from LCSH, it is easier to use CSH3, where they are found fully constructed. Furthermore, for works dealing with specific aspects of prime ministers' activities, CSH3 provides many more subdivisions for prime ministers than LCSH does and, therefore, a greater depth of analysis in this subject area. Figure 19.4 is an example of the difference in approach and terminology between CSH and LCSH.

CSH3 provides more user guidance in its text than does LCSH (which has a separate manual), with fifty-three preliminary pages of introductory explanation and many more scope notes. The headings conform to LCSH patterns and directives, but the cross-reference structure (x = see from, xx = see also from, sa = see also) once also used by LC has been retained. CSH3 is available free of charge on NLC's Web site (www.nlc-bnc.ca/cshweb/index-e.htm). *CSH on the Web* is updated monthly and provides full authority records displayed in both MARC 21 and thesaurus formats. Subject authority records for *Canadian Subject Headings* also are available on AMICUS, NLC's bibliographic and authorities database, a free service, available at www.nlc-bnc.ca/cshweb/index-e.htm.

Although the subject heading list itself is composed of English-language terminology, the introduction to CSH3 is in English and French, and there are four indexes: English to French and French to English for both the main headings and subdivisions. The indexes link CSH3 to French-language headings found in *Répertoire de vedettes-matière*.[12]

NLC has been contributing new subject concepts identified in Canadian publications to LCSH since 1994. LC also uses CSH3 as a basic source when considering new headings.

This example is an illustration of:

- edition statement taken from outside prescribed sources (many libraries place such an edition statement in the note area, sometimes as a quoted note)
- publishing date not listed, copyright date given
- detailed paging
- edition and history note
- bibliography and index note
- Canadian subject headings
- author/title added entries
- additional title added entries
- comparison between Library of Congress and National Library of Canada classification
- Canadian CIP data
- 2nd level cataloging

Donaldson, Gordon.
  The Prime Ministers of Canada / Gordon Donaldson. -- [4th ed.]. -- Toronto : Doubleday, c1994.
  x, 380 p. ; 22 cm.

  Previous eds. published as: Fifteen men (1969), Sixteen men (1975), Eighteen men (1985).
  Includes bibliography (p. 370-373) and index.
  ISBN 0-385-25454-7.

  1. Prime ministers -- Canada -- Biography. 2. Canada -- Politics and government. I. Donaldson, Gordon. Fifteen men. II. Donaldson, Gordon. Sixteen men. III. Donaldson, Gordon. Eighteen men. IV. Title. V. Title: Fifteen men. VI. Title: Sixteen men. VII. Title: Eighteen men.

Recommended DDC: 971.00922
Recommended LCC: F1005.D65 1994
Recommended NLC classification: FC26.P7D65 1994

Figure 19.3.

Figure 19.3—*Continued*

CHIEF SOURCE OF INFORMATION
(Title Page)

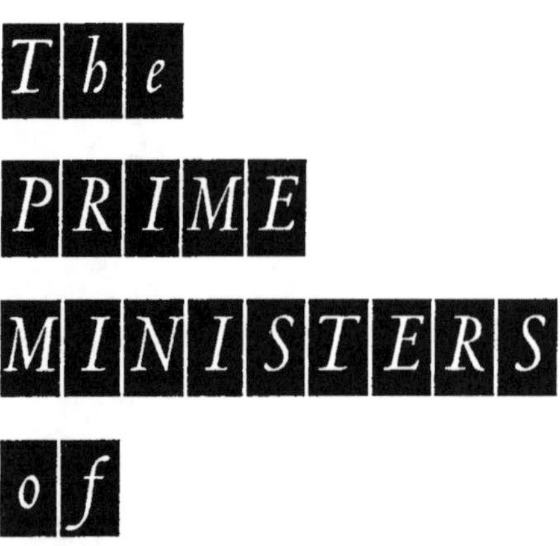

GORDON DONALDSON

Doubleday Canada Limited

Preface

This is a revised and extended version of *Fifteen Men*, which first appeared in 1969, was updated in 1975, and became *Sixteen Men*, and then *Eighteen Men*. *Twenty Persons* didn't have the same ring to it, hence the new genderless title.

(Information on Verso)

Canadian Cataloguing in Publication Data

Donaldson, Gordon, 1926-
The Prime Ministers of Canada

Includes index.
ISBN 0-385-25454-7

1. Prime ministers — Canada — Biography.
2. Canada — Politics and government. I. Title

FC26.P7D65 1994 971'.009' C93-095409-2
F1005.D65 1994

Cover design by John Terauds
Printed and bound in the USA

Published in Canada by
Doubleday Canada Limited
105 Bond Street
Toronto, Ontario
M5B 1Y3

```
The Government of Canada certification card received with the
item provides the only information:

SIMANUK KILABUK
BIRDS ON BASE (walrus tooth)


This example is an illustration of:
     •  art original
     •  general material designation
     •  date not listed on it em
     •  source of title note
     •  difference in Library of Congress Subject Headings and
        Canadian Subject Headings
     •  2nd level cataloging


Kilabuk, Simanuk.
  Birds on a base [art original] / Simanuk Kilabuk. --
[19--]
  1 sculpture : walrus tooth ; 6 x 13 x 3 cm.

  Title from certification card.
```

Tracing with Library of Congress Subject Heading:

```
  1. Inuit sculpture -- Canada.  I. Title.
```

Tracing with Canadian Subject Heading:

```
  1. Inuit -- Canada -- Sculpture.  I. Title.
```

Recommended DDC: 730.9719

Figure 19.4.

Problems with LCSH

Until recently, LCSH evolved very slowly, and critics claimed that the Library of Congress resisted needed changes in spelling and terminology. In theory, LCSH is constantly under revision, with catalogers able to propose new or altered headings at any time. A slow pace of change in any list this large is understandable. LC has a great many more items cataloged under any one heading than smaller libraries do; therefore, the number of operations needed to update LC records whenever there is a change to an existing heading is considerable, running into the tens or hundreds of thousands for some headings used also as subdivisions. Thus, subject catalogers at LC resisted for many years changing the now-obsolete heading NEGROES to AFRO-AMERICANS and BLACKS (the former referring to black people in the United States and the latter to black people outside the United States), even though they acknowledged that the word *Negroes* had negative connotations. (*Canadian Subject Headings* does not have a heading for "Afro-Canadians," using instead BLACK CANADIANS.) Similarly, LC resisted changing MOVING PICTURES to MOTION PICTURES until 1989, which necessitated the change of many derivative headings. In the 1990s, however, the transfer of LC's catalog records and authority files to an online file was completed and speeded up the process of change. New printed editions appear every year, and greater flexibility in revising old headings and introducing new ones is an encouraging trend.

Selected problems of LCSH have been or are being addressed by the Subject Analysis Committee, a standing committee of the Cataloging and Classification Section of the Association for Library Collections & Technical Services. It appoints and maintains many subcommittees and task forces, each devoted to a particular problem or issue. Members are appointed on the basis of their interest and expertise, and their reports often are instrumental in adding new headings to LCSH, changing older ones, or modifying its application policies. A subcommittee of the Subject Analysis Committee succeeded in ridding the list of sexist headings that intimated it was unusual for women to be doctors, authors, or other kinds of professionals. The offensive "WOMEN AS" headings were deleted from the list and, instead, headings for such topics are constructed on the model WOMEN AUTHORS, WOMEN PHYSICIANS, and so forth. The subcommittee prepared a list of nonsexist subject headings demonstrating how to represent topics without prejudice.[13] Since then, other nonsexist thesauri have been published.[14] Catalogers sensitive to gender issues also saw the presence of heading pairs that singled out only the female sex (such as "authors" and "women authors") as unequal treatment of women in subject headings. They lobbied to have gender-specific headings for both sexes, and LC has complied; for example, LCSH now has MALE AUTHORS and WOMEN AUTHORS.

Other groups also have lobbied LC successfully to create needed headings (e.g., the Music Library Association) or, alternatively, created their own thesauri to augment or supplement LCSH (e.g., the film archivists who jointly sponsored the publication of *Moving Image Materials: Genre Terms*). These terms also have been accommodated by special fields in LC's computer encoding system.

The National Library of Canada presents changes proposed for CSH3 to the Canadian Committee on Cataloguing for discussion. From time to time, the National Library forms ad hoc committees with membership drawn from the cataloging community to advise on special aspects of subject analysis.

LCSH has informative scope notes and instructions for the application of some of its descriptors, but there are not nearly enough of them. With so many headings appearing over such a long period of time, overlaps are inevitable, e.g., CONFORMITY and COMPLIANCE; COMPUTERS, ELECTRONIC DIGITAL COMPUTERS, MINICOMPUTERS, and MICROCOMPUTERS (but no heading appears for "mainframes," not even as a cross-reference). The distinctions LC makes between similar headings can easily be missed by searchers unfamiliar with the terminology; for example, AFRO-AMERICANS and BLACKS differ only in whether the specified people live within or outside of the United States. Subject cataloging specialists who work with LCSH are aware of the distinction, but users searching the catalog often are not.

LC's Annotated Card Program

In 1965, LC responded to an expressed need on the part of librarians working with children and youth for modifications in subject headings for children's materials by initiating its "Annotated Card" (AC) program. Four modifications were made to the materials treated under the program: (1) subdivisions referring to age level, such as —JUVENILE LITERATURE, were dropped; (2) selected terms were added, revised, or simplified; (3) subdivision practice was altered; and (4) summaries were added in the descriptive cataloging to inform searchers about the content of the materials (hence the term "annotated").

Examples of AC headings that differ slightly from LCSH are ALPINE ANIMALS, used instead of LCSH's ALPINE FAUNA, and BEDWETTING, used instead of LCSH's ENURESIS. Clearly, "animals" and "bedwetting" are recognized and understood by youngsters more easily than "fauna" and "enuresis," respectively. In other instances, the modification is subtler; for example, ROBOTS is used in the AC program for materials about androids as well as other kinds of robots, while ANDROIDS is used for adult materials specifically about that type of robot. Two important modifications in subdivision practice are the use of —BIOGRAPHY for individual biographies in subject fields where LCSH lacks terms for persons in the field, and —FICTION, which can be added to all topical headings.

The list of Annotated Card Program headings (or "AC" headings) immediately precedes the regular list of headings, and is similar to the regular list, three columns to a page, with scope notes, cross-references, subdivisions, but no classification numbers. AC headings are assigned in addition to LCSH headings. They appear in square brackets following the regular LCSH headings; the summaries appear in the note area of the descriptive cataloging.

SEARS LIST OF SUBJECT HEADINGS

Sears List of Subject Headings (Sears) was initiated by its original compiler, Minnie Earl Sears, in response to requests from librarians for subject headings that were simpler to understand and use than those in LCSH. Publisher H. W. Wilson adopted Sears subject headings on the catalog cards it produced for its commercial card distribution service, which catered mainly to small public and school libraries.

Sears recognized the value of maintaining a uniform structure between LCSH and her list. It was convenient and made it possible to coordinate terms from both lists. If a cataloger wanted to use a heading that Sears did not have but LCSH did, the heading could be added without fear of conflicting with the structure of existing headings. If a small library grew large enough that Sears headings were no longer effective, it could "graduate" to LCSH. The LCSH structure was not unacceptable by itself, but the terms chosen for the headings were sometimes too technical for unsophisticated searchers, and the breakdown of subjects into categories was too specific for smaller institutions with limited collections of materials. Sears's small size and simple terminology also appealed to those who felt LCSH was difficult to learn to use. Figure 19.5 demonstrates both the similarity between Sears and LCSH and LCSH's greater range of specificity.

Sears

Education (May subdiv. geog.) **370**
Subdivisions listed under this heading may be used under other education headings where applicable.
UF Instruction
Pedagogy
Study and teaching
SA types of education [to be added as needed], e.g. **Vocational education;** classes of persons and social and ethnic groups with the subdivision *Education,* e.g. **Deaf—Education; African Americans—Education;** etc.; and subjects with the subdivision *Study and teaching,* e.g. **Science—Study and teaching** [to be added as needed]

Education—Aims and objectives 370.11

Education and church
USE **Church and education**

Education and radio
USE **Radio in education**

Education—Curricula 375
UF Core curriculum
Courses of study
Curricula
Schools—Curricula
SA types of education and schools with the subdivision *Curricula,* e.g. **Library education—Curricula** [to be added as needed]
NT **Articulation (Education)**
Colleges and universities—Curricula
Curriculum planning
Library education—Curricula

Education—Data processing
USE **Computer-assisted instruction**

Education—Developing countries 370.9172
UF Developing countries—Education

Education, Elementary
USE **Elementary education**

Education—Experimental methods 371.3
UF Activity schools
Experimental methods in education
Progressive education
Teaching—Experimental methods
SA types of experimental methods, e.g. **Nongraded schools; Open plan schools;** etc. [to be added as needed]
NT **Experimental schools**
Nongraded schools
Open plan schools
Whole language

LCSH

Education *(May Subd Geog)*
[L]
UF Children—Education
Education, Primitive
[Former heading]
Education of children
[Former heading]
Human resource development
Instruction
Pedagogy
Youth—Education
SA *subdivision* Education *under names of denominations, sects, orders, etc., e.g.* Jesuits—Education; *and under special classes of people and various social groups, e.g.* Blind—Education; Mentally handicapped children—Education; Children of migrant laborers—Education; *also subdivision* Study and teaching *under special subjects, e.g.* Science—Study and teaching; *and headings beginning with the word* Educational

— Aims and objectives *(May Subd Geog)*
[LB41 (Essays)]
UF Aims and objectives of education
Educational aims and objectives
Educational goals
Educational objectives
Educational purposes
Goals, Educational
Instructional objectives
Objectives, Educational
Purposes, Educational

— Curricula
[LB1570-LB1571 (Elementary schools)]
UF Core curriculum
Courses of study
Curricula (Courses of study)
Schools—Curricula
Study, Courses of
BT Instructional systems
SA *subdivision* Curricula *under names of individual educational institutions, and under types of education and educational institutions, for listings of courses offered, or discussions about them, e.g.* Harvard University—Curricula; Technical education—Curricula; Universities and colleges—Curricula
NT Articulation (Education)
Combination of grades
Curriculum change
Curriculum enrichment
Curriculum planning
Disability studies
Gay and lesbian studies
Lesson planning
Men's studies
Schedules, School
Student evaluation of curriculum
Teacher participation in curriculum planning
Women's studies

— — Law and legislation
(May Subd Geog)
BT Educational law and legislation

— Data processing
[LB1028.43]
UF Computer uses in education
Computers in education
Educational computing
Microcomputer uses in education
Microcomputers in education

Figure 19.5. Comparison of Sears and LCSH (excerpts). [*Sears List of Subject Headings* © Copyright 2000 The H. W. Wilson Company. All rights reserved. Permission to reproduce granted by The H. W. Wilson Company.]

H. W. Wilson updates Sears for its customers. New editions of Sears were issued about every five to seven years when new editions of LCSH were appearing only about once a decade. This changed in 1988, when LCSH began issuing new editions annually. The most recent edition of Sears followed its predecessor by just three years. At this writing, Sears is in its seventeenth edition.[15] Joseph Miller, its current editor, is only the fifth in the series of editors who followed Sears. *Sears List of Subject Headings: Canadian Companion* (SearsCC), which provides headings for items containing Canadian subject matter, is in its sixth edition. Lynne Lighthall is its editor.[16]

Sears is contained in one volume of nearly 800 pages. The headings are listed in two columns to a page; thus the list contains between 15,000 and 16,000 authorized subject headings and cross-references. The book has an extensive introductory chapter giving Sears's history, the principles on which the list is based, instructions for applying it, and a bibliography of basic sources for more information. A list of headings from the previous edition that have been changed immediately precedes the first page of subject headings. Some changes are minor, such as the replacement of ART FORGERIES with ART—FORGERIES; others are more far-reaching, such as the replacement of BUYING with PURCHASING. The former change involved only adding a dash between the two parts of the term which, although primarily cosmetic, also changes the way the term is filed. The latter change alters the word used for the concept and shifts the file for it from the "Bs" to the "Ps." Some changes are even more extensive, such as the change from GRANDPARENT AND CHILD to GRANDPARENT-GRANDCHILD RELATIONSHIP. The list of changed headings expedites identifying the revisions that should be made in the catalog when adopting the new edition. Changed headings also are identified in the list as "Former headings."

Authorized headings are always printed in boldface type, whether they are found in the main filing order or as cross-references under other headings. Roman print is used for terms unauthorized for use as headings but used as cross-references. For example, CARNIVOROUS PLANTS appears in boldface print as a main heading in the "Cs", while INSECT-EATING PLANTS appears in roman print under it. In the "I"s, INSECT-EATING PLANTS appears in roman print as a main heading with the cross-reference "USE CARNIVOROUS PLANTS" following it in boldface.

In addition to the subject headings and cross-references, many of the headings have suggested classification numbers, taken from the thirteenth edition of *Abridged Dewey Decimal Classification and Relative Index* (DDC-Abridged).[17] When a subject has more than one viewpoint, more than one classification number may be suggested for a particular topic, depending on which one is represented in an item.[18] For example, COMPUTER BULLETIN BOARDS is followed by two numbers, 004.693 and 384.3, depending on whether the focus is computer science or commerce. The editor explains that Dewey numbers are not assigned to very general topics and are deliberately kept short, but can be extended if desired by the addition of subdivision numbers in DDC tables.[19]

Some headings are followed by instructions on how to apply or subdivide them. For instance, under the heading MAGNET SCHOOLS, the instruction states: "Use for materials on schools offering special courses not available in the regular school curriculum and designed to attract students without reference to the usual attendance zone rules, often as an aid to voluntary school desegregation";[20] and under DIRECTORIES, the instruction states: "Use for materials about directories and for bibliographies of directories. S[ee]A[lso] subjects and names of countries, cities, etc., with the subdivision Directories, for lists of persons, organizations, objects, etc., together with addresses or other identifying data [to be added as needed]."[21] The instructions may include information about when *not* to use a heading and furnish alternatives for similar works with different emphases. For example, under DINNERS, the instruction states: "Use for materials on menus and recipes for dinners. Materials on dining customs and gastronomic travel are entered under Dining."[22]

Sears does not list personal names and other proper nouns or the names of particular animals, plants, or diseases, and so forth that would be difficult to anticipate and add to the list. An example of such an addition is the heading shown in Figure 19.6, below and page 463. Instructions allow catalogers to add these headings as needed.[23]

```
This example is an illustration of:
      • other title information
      • publishing date not listed, copyright date given
      • detailed pagination statement
      • descriptive illustration statement
      • bibliography and index note
      • Library of Congress subject headings
      • Sears subject headings
      • abridged and unabridged Dewey classification numbers.
        (See page xx for a discussion of other possible
        classification numbers)
      • Canadian CIP
      • two levels of cataloging
```

2nd level cataloging

```
Ayre, John.
  Northrup Frye : a biography / John Ayre. -- Toronto : Random
House, c1989.
  472 p., [8] p. of plates : ill., ports. ; 24 cm.

  Includes bibliographical references (p. 453-458) and index.
  ISBN 0-394-22113-3.

  1. Frye, Northrop -- Biography.  2. Scholars -- Canada --
Biography.  3. Critics -- Canada -- Biography.  4. College
teachers -- Canada -- Biography.  5. Victoria College (Toronto,
Ont.) -- Faculty -- Biography.  I. Title.
```

Recommended unabridged DDC: 801.95092

```
  801 (philosophy and theory of literature)
     .95 (criticism)
        092 (treatment of persons)
```

Figure 19.6.

Figure 19.6—*Continued*

```
1st level cataloging

Ayre, John.
  Northrup Frye. -- Random House, c1989.
  472 p., [8] p. of plates.

  ISBN 0-394-22113-3.

  1. Frye, Northrup. 2. Colleges and universities -- Canada --
Faculty -- Biography.  3. Victoria College (Toronto, Ont.) --
Faculty -- Biography.  I. Title.

Recommended abridged DDC: 801.92
```

CHIEF SOURCE OF INFORMATION
(Title Page)

NORTHROP
FRYE

A
Biography

JOHN AYRE

Random House
Toronto

(Information on Verso)

Published in Canada by Random House of Canada Limited, Toronto.

Canadian Cataloguing in Publication Data
Ayre, John
Northrop Frye: a biography
ISBN 0-394-22113-3

1. Frye, Northrop, 1912- – Biography.
2. Scholars – Canada – Biography. 3. Critics – Canada – Biography. 4. College teachers – Canada – Biography. 5. Victoria College (Toronto, Ont.). – Faculty – Biography. I. Title.
PN75.F7A9 1989 801'.95'0924 C89-094447-4

The headings in Sears are arranged according to a 1980 edition of filing rules sponsored by the American Library Association.[24] These rules, based on the principle of filing subject headings as they appear and without taking account of punctuation, were simplified from a more complicated version published earlier, and they facilitate automated filing in computerized catalogs. Subject headings are now filed word by word with digits preceding letters, and punctuation is ignored. Figure 19.7, shows a list of hypothetical subject headings filed by these rules.

Children

Children, Adopted

Children and strangers

Children—Books and readings

Children in literature

Children—Research

Children (Roman law)

Children—United States

Children, Vagrant

Figure 19.7. Example of alphabetization according to the 1980 *ALA Filing Rules.*

Inverted terms requiring commas, such as CHILDREN, VAGRANT, have been eliminated from Sears, as the editor says, "on the theory that most library users search for multiple-word terms in the order in which they occur naturally in the language."[25] Ignoring punctuation in filing disperses some headings more closely related to one another than to those filed next to them; however, it is a boon to patrons who do not know different types of punctuation have special meanings.

SUMMARY

Despite its problems and idiosyncrasies, LCSH remains the subject heading list in widest use among U.S. and Canadian libraries. In small libraries and media centers, Sears often is used. However, network records almost always contain LCSH subject headings. The need to exploit the power of cataloging networks is causing many librarians and media specialists to rethink their adherence to systems that are little used in computerized databases.

There is no requirement that narrow headings be used when broader ones will do an acceptable job. If a library has only a few books on a subject, a cataloger could decide not to distinguish them and put them all under one broad heading. These decisions should be based on a clear idea of how the collection will grow in the future. If a library has small collections that are unlikely to grow much larger, Sears headings might be applied instead of LCSH, because they are broader.

Subject headings must bring together enough material so that someone looking under a particular heading will find all the materials relevant to that topic collocated there. At the same time, they must not bring together too many items, or the file will be rendered useless to all but the most persistent searchers. If an agency uses a cataloging network as its source for cataloging data, decisions also must weigh the cost of changing headings on derived cataloging against putting up with more or less collocation than would be optimal. Maintaining a local subject authority file that describes the library's unique practices has its costs.

The delicate balance between gathering and distinguishing materials by subject shifts according to the needs of individual groups of materials and individual searchers. The best the cataloger can do is to try to please *most* of the searchers *most* of the time, while working toward an ideal subject catalog in which all users find exactly what they need under whatever headings they choose to use.

NOTES

1. Library of Congress, Subject Cataloging Division, *Subject Cataloging Manual: Subject Headings,* 5th ed. (Washington, DC: Library of Congress, Cataloging Distribution Service, 1996-); *Cataloger's Desktop: Library of Congress Rule Interpretations, Subject Cataloging Manual: Subject Headings, Subject Cataloging Manual: Classification, USMARC Format for Bibliographic Data, USMARC Format for Authority Data, and Other Cataloging Tools* (Washington, DC: Cataloging Distribution Service, 1999-). (Whenever Subject Cataloging Manual; Subject Headings is cited, the entire title must be given, because LC publishes companion volumes titled *Subject Cataloging Manual: Shelflisting* and *Subject Cataloging Manual: Classification,* with which it would otherwise be confused.)

2. Library of Congress, Subject Cataloging Division, *Classification Plus* (Washington, DC: Cataloging Distribution Service, 1999-).

3. Library of Congress, Subject Cataloging Division, *Free-Floating Subdivisions: An Alphabetic Index,* 11th ed. (Washington, DC: Library of Congress, Cataloging Distribution Service, 1999). This tool is a compilation of and index to the free-floating subdivisions found in *Subject Cataloging Manual: Subject Headings* pages H1095 to H1200.

4. *Library of Congress Subject Headings Weekly Lists* (Washington, DC: Library of Congress, Cataloging Distribution Service, 1984-).

5. *Cataloging Service Bulletin* (Washington, DC: Library of Congress, Cataloging Distribution Service, 1978-).

6. John C. Rather, *Library of Congress Filing Rules* (Washington, DC: Library of Congress, 1980).

7. National Library of Medicine, *Medical Subject Headings: An Annotated Alphabetic List* (Bethesda, MD: National Library of Medicine, 1975-); National Library of Medicine, *Medical Subject Headings: Tree Structures* (Bethesda, MD: National Library of Medicine, 1975-).

8. Library of Congress, Subject Cataloging Division, *Library of Congress Subject Headings,* 24th ed. [hereinafter LCSH] (Washington, DC: Library of Congress, Cataloging Distribution Service, 2001), vol. 1, xiii-xv.

9. The alternative—*direct* subdivision—would take Buenos Aires away from Argentina and place it between Brazil and Ecuador, move Rio de Janeiro to a spot between North America and South America, and put the Andes Region of Venezuela between the whole Andes range and Argentina. Venezuela would disappear as a subdivision altogether. The directly subdivided file would look like this:

AGRICULTURE—AMAZON RIVER REGION
AGRICULTURE—ANDES REGION
AGRICULTURE—ANDES REGION (VENEZUELA)
AGRICULTURE—ARGENTINA
AGRICULTURE—BRAZIL
AGRICULTURE—BUENOS AIRES
AGRICULTURE—ECUADOR
AGRICULTURE—NORTH AMERICA
AGRICULTURE—RIO DE JANIERO
AGRICULTURE—SOUTH AMERICA

10. LCSH, vol. 1, 515.

11. National Library of Canada, *Canadian Subject Headings,* 3rd ed., edited by Alina Schweitzer (Ottawa: Canada Communication Group Publishing, 1992).

12. *Répertoire de vedettes-matière* (Quebec: Université Laval, 1989-). *RVM* is cumulative and published twice a year on microfiche and on CD-ROM. It also is updated each month on the National Library of Canada's Web site. For information in English, see www.nlc-bnc.ca/wapp/rvm/introe.htm. For information in French, see www.bibl.ulaval.ca/info/rvm.htm.

13. Joan K. Marshall, comp., *On Equal Terms: A Thesaurus for Nonsexist Indexing and Cataloging* (Santa Barbara, CA: ABC-CLIO, 1977).

14. Mary Ellen S. Capek, ed., *A Women's Thesaurus: An Index of Language Used to Describe and Locate Information by and about Women* (New York: Harper & Row, 1987); Ruth Dickstein, Victoria A. Mills, and Ellen J. Waite, *Women in LC's Terms: A Thesaurus of Library of Congress Subject Headings Relating to Women* (Phoenix, AZ: Oryx Press, 1988).

15. *Sears List of Subject Headings,* 17th ed., [hereinafter Sears], edited by Joseph Miller (New York: H. W. Wilson, 2000).

16. *Sears List of Subject Headings: Canadian Companion,* 6th ed., [hereinafter Sears CC], revised by Lynne Lighthall with the assistance of Shana Bystrom and others (New York: H. W. Wilson, 2001).

17. Dewey, Melvil, *Abridged Dewey Decimal Classification and Relative Index,* 13th ed., edited by Joan S. Mitchell et al. (Albany, NY: OCLC-Forest Press, 1997). (Author's note: In 1999, Forest Press moved its operations to Dublin, Ohio, headquarters of its parent firm, OCLC, Inc.)

18. Sears, xi.

19. Ibid.

20. Ibid., 423.

21. Ibid., 208.

22. Ibid., 207.

23. Ibid., xxxviii.

24. *ALA Filing Rules* (Chicago: American Library Association, 1980).

25. Sears, x.

SUGGESTED READING

Chan, Lois Mai. *Library of Congress Subject Headings: Principles and Application.* 4th ed. Englewood, CO: Libraries Unlimited, 1999.

DeZelar-Tiedman, Christine. "Subject Access to Fiction: An Application of the Guidelines." *Library Resources & Technical Services* 40, no. 3 (July 1996): 203-210.

OCLC CatCD for Windows: LC Subject Authorities. Dublin, OH: OCLC, 1996- .

Stone, Alva T. "The LCSH Century: A Brief History of the Library of Congress Subject Headings, and Introduction to the Centennial Essays." *Cataloging & Classification Quarterly* 29, nos. 1/2 (2000). (Theme issue about LCSH.)

REVIEW QUESTIONS

1. How did LCSH and Sears originate, and how often do new printed editions appear?
2. What additional publications are needed to assign LCSH subject headings?
3. Describe four ways main headings in LCSH and Sears are subdivided.
4. LCSH and Sears differ in the number of headings, their specificity, and the way they are alphabetized. Explain the impact of these differences on subject catalogers and on searchers.

Classifications

In this chapter the Dewey Decimal Classification (DDC) and the Library of Congress Classification (LCC) are described. Both are widely used by libraries in the United States and Canada to shelve books and other materials in an organized manner. Classification numbers are the element in shelf addresses (or call numbers) that reflects the subject content of the materials. By assigning similar classification numbers to material on similar topics, browsers find them gathered together for easy access.

DEWEY DECIMAL CLASSIFICATION

The DDC is a universal, enumerative, hierarchical classification system. It employs the system of decimal division; that is, all knowledge is divided into ten main classes, each of which is subsequently subdivided into ten more subclasses and so on, theoretically, *ad infinitum.* Forest Press, its publisher, claims it is the most popular classification system in the world.[1] The DDC is used widely in the United States and Canada and more than 100 other countries. The National Library of Canada uses DDC to classify its collection, and it is the basis for arrangement of the *British National Bibliography* and other national bibliographic agencies in the Commonwealth and elsewhere.

Principles Underlying DDC

Seven principles underlie the organization and structure of DDC:

1. *Decimal division.* This is the primary method of division used by DDC. It merits notice because it is a familiar and useful method of dividing—division by tens is something most people think of as "round" numbers—and because it is at the root of some of DDC's most troubling limitations.

2. *Classification by discipline.* The primary attribute applied in dividing knowledge is discipline, represented by the ten main classes. That may seem natural to readers of this book, because it is so familiar to most librarians, but it is not the only possibility. Knowledge could be divided first by a different element, such as time period or geographic location, and only after that, by discipline, genre, or form, and other attributes.

3. *Hierarchy.* Although the principle of moving from the broadest categories to narrower ones and from these to still narrower ones until the narrowest possible category is reached is encountered frequently in classification, DDC emphasizes it and uses it obviously in complex numbers. Ideally, the hierarchy built into DDC numbers identifies topics at the same level and clarifies which are broader and narrower, merely by noting the number and character of the digits in the class. In practice, this works out only part of the time, because not all topical areas divide neatly into ten elements. In areas such as literature, a number with three digits (e.g., 813, American fiction) might be at the same level as a number with five or more (e.g., Russian fiction, 891.43).

4. *Mnemonics.* Dewey liked time-saving devices and incorporated them into his classification. Specific groups of numbers may represent the same topic in many places in the classification. An example is the number "-73," which stands for United States in geography (917.3), cookery (641.5973), political parties (324.273), and so forth. However, it doesn't always work; for example, the number 730 does not mean anything related to United States. It stands for sculpture.

5. *Literary warrant.* This principle dictates that classes are created only after materials exist that require them. The DDC purports to be a classification of all knowledge, and it does an outstanding job of including topics. However, no classification of limited size can anticipate or list all topics, and DDC is no exception. "Computers" is a good example of a topic that was added when the need for it became clear. In the nineteenth and earlier editions of DDC, computers occupy a tiny category (001.64) under the larger topic of "Research" (001). In the twentieth edition, computers expanded to occupy three newly established sections of their own (004–006).

6. *Enumeration.* This principle dictates the listing of potential class numbers in contrast to the principle of faceting or synthesis, that is, providing topical elements and allowing classifiers to put them together to build complex topics. Although this principle still generally guides DDC, recent editions incorporate more instances of number building because it is more economical of page space. Expansion of many subject areas in recent years would require huge increases in enumerated numbers to represent them, while instructions to use existing expansion techniques without enumerating each of them do not.

7. *Relative location.* At one time in the United States, Canada, and elsewhere, library books were shelved in fixed locations. Once an item was given its place on the shelves, for example, the second book on the third shelf of the fourth stack, it would never be moved, no matter what new materials were added to the collection. The DDC assumes that as new books are added and shelved, existing items will be moved to maintain their subject relationships. The DDC number merely identifies a place relative to other items in the collection.

None of these principles operates perfectly throughout DDC. They are observed as far as possible when they do not conflict, create unwanted juxtapositions of subjects, or interfere with practical considerations. Enumeration is abandoned to save space, mnemonics are superseded, and other principles may be modified when it is important to do so. Nevertheless, the principles govern many of the decisions made by DDC's editors with regard to class numbers and relationships.

An eighth principle—integrity of numbers—was promised by Melvil Dewey to DDC users in the classification's early days. This meant numbers assigned to represent a particular topic would not be changed. Changed numbers create a lot of work in a library trying to keep all its materials shelved in a consistent, up-to-date manner. At the least, call number labels and markings in or on materials must be changed, catalog records must be altered to display new call numbers, and materials must be moved to their new locations. Sometimes, entire spans of numbers were changed to reflect profound changes in a subject area, called "phoenixing." A phoenixed schedule was entirely discarded and rebuilt (risen from its ashes, like the mythical bird). At several points in DDC's history, users rebelled at having to absorb too many changes. In recent years, phoenixing has been replaced by the milder term "complete revision" and the practice modified, although not entirely abandoned.

Format of DDC

The DDC may be purchased in book or CD-ROM form. The book version of DDC is in four volumes totaling more than 4,000 pages. The first volume contains introductory matter and seven auxiliary tables used to expand class numbers derived from the main schedules. Part of the introductory matter is a manual explaining generally how to use the classification, which is augmented by a very detailed manual in the final volume.[2] The brief manual has many helpful instructions on accepted methods of building numbers using all the resources at hand: the schedules, tables, instructions, and conventions. The schedules themselves are contained in the second and third volumes. The Relative Index, the detailed manual on the use of specific numbers, and the policies and procedures of LC's Decimal Classification Division are found in the fourth volume. At this writing, DDC is in its twenty-first edition.

"Electronic Dewey" or *Dewey for Windows*™ was in version 2.00 at this writing. It contains the Schedules, Tables, Manual, and Relative Index, as well as a User Guide explaining how to use program functions to assist in operations. The software offers flexible, efficient computerized retrieval using words or phrases, numbers, index terms, and Boolean combinations. This edition has an automatic cuttering function. Individual libraries can annotate their discs with local notes.

The principal advantages of the electronic version over the book version, aside from computerized retrieval, are the inclusion of frequently used LCSH subject headings associated with a class number, taken from LC records in OCLC's database; the ability to verify a classification number application by sampling a catalog record that uses the number, also drawn from OCLC's database; a popular, easy-to-use "windowed" user interface; cut-and-paste functions that help minimize keying; and online help screens. All published updates to DDC appear on updated CD-ROM discs, issued annually every January. Updates also appear on the DDC Web site, available to any user with Internet access.

The DDC's Relative Index was Melvil Dewey's original contribution to classification. Its great value lies in bringing together all the various aspects of a topic under the term used to represent it, no matter where they would be classified. For example, under COMPUTER in the Relative Index the user will find 144 references to classes as far apart as musical composition employing computers (781.34) and computer science (004) or computer-assisted printing (686.22544) and computer sorting for library catalogs (025.3177).[3] Under HEALTH are dozens of references, including health care facilities (362.1) and their architecture (725.51), health foods (641.302), and health services in the United States during the Civil War (973.775).[4] The Relative Index does more than just list topics in alphabetical order with their associated class numbers. It also collocates the different contexts in which a single term might be used, or the different classes or disciplines in which a single topic might be found.

The DDC is available in an abridged edition suitable for general collections totaling up to 20,000 volumes.[5] Over the years, the abridged version has contained about one-tenth as many classification numbers as the unabridged. At this writing, the abridged version is in its thirteenth edition, published in one volume of just over 1,000 pages. Numbers in the abridged edition, while broader in meaning and shorter in total numbers than the full edition, are intended to be compatible with those in the full edition.

The DDC's main classes, based to some degree on an inversion of Sir Francis Bacon's classification of knowledge, include the following:

000	=	Generalities	500	=	Natural Sciences & Mathematics
100	=	Philosophy & Psychology	600	=	Technology (Applied Sciences)
200	=	Religion	700	=	The Arts
300	=	Social Sciences	800	=	Literature & Rhetoric
400	=	Language	900	=	Geography & History

By covering knowledge in only ten main classes, DDC forces some odd companions into a single class. For example, in the 100s, philosophy, psychology, and the occult are found grouped together. Statistics, etiquette, commerce, and war share the 300s with sociology, economics, political science, law, and education. The 700s, primarily covering the arts, also include sports and games. Geography and history are grouped together in the 900s in one huge main class, even though they are quite different topics. One might expect to find library science with the social sciences or education, but instead it is located in the 000s (read this as *zero hundreds*) along with research, publishing, and other generalities.

At the start of the second volume are three summaries of numbers: the ten main classes, the one hundred divisions, and the thousand sections. (These summaries are also available as a separate pamphlet.)[6] This is a good place to begin when trying to assign a Dewey number for an unfamiliar topic. The first and most important decision made in the process (after deciding about the topic itself, of course) is the choice of an appropriate main class.[7] It would be much easier to have only one place to put a book on computers, for example. But if the book emphasizes the machinery, it is classified with other books on machinery, in the 600s, applied science and technology. If it emphasizes the mathematics of programming, it is more logically classed with other books on mathematics, in the 500s. If it emphasizes the programs and applications, it is classed nearer to research in the 000s. A video about trucks might emphasize the truck as a machine or a type of vehicle (600s) or it might emphasize transportation via truck (300s).

In some cases, a classification number will be chosen to reflect the interests of a library's users. For example, the book in Figure 20.1, page 474, concerns the Canada/United States free trade agreement. Depending on the library, either 382.971073, stressing Canada's agreements with the United States, or 382.973071, stressing U.S. agreements with Canada, are equally correct. In both cases, assigning the full nine-digit number enables the classification to reflect an item involving both countries, no matter which comes first.

The DDC allows options in classification for some topics. Biography is one of these. The DDC states that the preferred method is to place a biography with the topic for which the person is well known. The biography of Conrad Black in Figure 20.2, page 475, has been classified in economic production.

However, DDC provides an alternate series of numbers in the 920s for libraries that wish to shelve all biographies together. The DDC suggests the following options:

a) use the 920-928 schedule, e.g., 923.871 (biography of Canadian persons in commerce, communication, transportation)

b) use 92 for individual biographies

c) use B (indicating Biography) for individual biographies

d) use 920.71 for biographies of men, 920.72 for biographies of women

In addition, the following practice is found in many libraries:

e) use 920 for collected biographies, 921 for individual biographies.

```
This example is an illustration of:
      •  joint authors
      •  other title information listed on title page before title
         proper
      •  detailed pagination
      •  bibliography and index note
      •  Library of Congress subject headings
      •  joint author added entry
      •  difference in Dewey decimal classification number according to
         emphasis desired
      •  2nd level cataloging

Doern, G. Bruce.
  Faith & fear : the free trade story / G. Bruce Doern & Brian W.
Tomlin. -- Toronto : Stoddart, 1991.
  xi, 340 p. ; 24 cm.

  Includes references (p.319-333) and index.
  ISBN 0-7737-2534-2.

  1. Free trade -- Canada.  2. Free trade -- United States.  3. Canada
-- Commercial policy.  4. United States -- Commercial policy.  5. Canada
-- Commerce -- United States.  6. United States -- Commerce -- Canada.
I. Tomlin, Brian W.  II. Title.

Recommended DDC: 382.971073 (for Canadian emphasis)
                 or
                 382.973071 (for U.S. emphasis)
```

CHIEF SOURCE OF INFORMATION
(Title Page)

THE FREE TRADE STORY

FAITH & FEAR

G. BRUCE DOERN & BRIAN W. TOMLIN

Stoddart

(Information on Verso)

Copyright © 1991 by G. Bruce Doern and Brian W. Tomlin

All rights reserved. No part of this publication may be reproduced or transmitted in any form or by any means, electronic or mechanical, including photocopy, recording, or any information storage and retrieval system, without permission in writing from the publisher.

First published in 1991 by
Stoddart Publishing Co. Limited
34 Lesmill Road
Toronto, Canada
M3B 2T6

ISBN 0-7737-2534-2

Cover Design: Leslie Styles
Typesetting: Tony Gordon Ltd.

Printed and bound in the United States of America

Figure 20.1. Catalog record showing DDC classification for Doern's book on the Canada/United States free trade agreement.

```
This example is an illustration of:
      •  other title information
      •  publication date not listed, copyright date given
      •  work containing illustrations of specific types
      •  index note
      •  two ISBNs (one that applies to item in hand given)
      •  ISBN qualified
      •  DDC explained
      •  DDC prime mark
      •  2nd level cataloging


Newman, Peter C.
  The establishment man : a portrait of power / by Peter C. Newman.
Toronto : McClelland and Stewart, c1982.
  349 p. : genealogical table, port. ; 25 cm.

  Includes index.
  ISBN 0-7710-6785-2 (trade).

  1. Black, Conrad.  2. Businessmen -- Canada -- Biography.
3. Capitalists and financiers -- Canada -- Biography.  I. Title.


Recommended DDC: 338'.092
                 338 (production)
                     092 (biography)
```

CHIEF SOURCE OF INFORMATION
(Title Page)

The Establishment Man

A Portrait of Power

BY

Peter C. Newman

McClelland and Stewart

(Information on Verso)

© 1982, Power Reporting Limited

All rights reserved. The use of any part of this publication reproduced, transmitted in any form or by any means, electronic, mechanical, photocopying, recording, or otherwise, or stored in a retrieval system, without the prior consent of the publisher is an infringement of the copyright law.

The Canadian Publishers
McClelland and Stewart Limited
25 Hollinger Road
Toronto, Ontario M4B 3G2

Figure 20.2. Catalog record showing DDC classification of Newman's book on the biography of Conrad Black.

A good rule of thumb to remember about classification is that it aims to bring related works together. To do this, a cataloger can look in the shelflist or on the shelves to see what kinds of subjects were assigned to any particular number under consideration. If they do not appear to be related to the work in hand, one should look elsewhere for the classification number.

Throughout the schedules, selected numbers are left blank (or "unoccupied") to allow for future expansion without disturbing the existing classes. In the 000s, for example, 007-009, 024, 029, and 040-049 are unoccupied. Although many areas of the 500s and 600s are very crowded, having classes with seven or more digits, 517, 518, 524, 626, 654-656, and 699 are unoccupied. Each of the main classes has two or more unoccupied sections; the 000s and 200s have entire divisions that are not assigned.

A Closer Look at the DDC Schedules

In this section, DDC's main classes are explored in greater detail, noting the subjects each typically includes; however, no attempt is made here to list all the subjects included in the main classes. Familiarity with the schedules is best acquired by using them, together with the library's shelflist and common sense.

000s: Generalities includes works about knowledge in general; research; communication in general; computers; controversial knowledge such as UFOs, the Loch Ness monster, and the Bermuda Triangle; reference materials such as bibliographies and catalogs; library and information science, including reading in general; encyclopedias and other encyclopedic works; organizations; publishing; and collections that cover many topics.

100s: Philosophy, Paranormal Phenomena, and Psychology includes concepts and schools of thought in detail, as well as the occult, the entire field of psychology, logic, and ethics (subtitled *moral philosophy*).

200s: Religion is one of the most straightforward classes, dealing entirely with this one subject area. Two changes were made to the twenty-first edition in an effort to address long-standing criticism that the great majority of numbers represent topics in Christianity, leaving few sections for all topics relating to all the other religions of the world. The bias is traceable to literary warrant in nineteenth-century U.S. college libraries, where collecting was largely confined to books about the Christian religion, and it has persisted for more than a century. First, the most general numbers, 201-209, which were devoted to generalities of Christianity only, were relocated to 230-270 with other topics in Christianity. Second, 296 and 297, covering Judaism and Islam respectively, were revised and expanded.

300s: Social Sciences, in keeping with its label, covers sociology, political science, economics, law, public administration, and social problems. It also includes statistics (but in this case referring to demographic statistics, not probability theory, which is found in mathematics); military science; education;

commerce; and an odd group of topics headed "Customs, Etiquette, and Folklore," under which subtopics such as marriage, death, war, holidays, chivalry, suicide, and cannibalism are subsumed. A major revision was made in public administration (351-354) in the 1996 twenty-first unabridged edition, followed by a similar update in 1997 in the thirteenth abridged edition.

400s: Language is a perfectly straightforward class. Language in general (i.e., linguistics) is covered first, followed by individual languages beginning with English and other Western European languages. Preferential positioning of English and European languages probably is due to literary warrant and the fact that this is an American scheme, but the schedules include an instruction explaining how classifiers can give local emphasis to any other language of their choice.

500s: Natural Sciences and Mathematics includes mathematics, astronomy, chemistry, physics, geology, the sciences of the ancient world, paleontology and paleozoology, and the life sciences, first in general and then the separate subjects of botany (called "Plants" in the 1996 edition) and zoology (called "Animals" in the 1996 edition). The life sciences (560-590) underwent a major revision in the 1996 unabridged and 1997 abridged editions. As mentioned previously, computer programming is found at 519.7, immediately after probability theory and statistical mathematics. Examining the subdivisions of computer programming, however, shows that materials classed here really are concerned with the mathematical process of programming, not the applications themselves, that is, *computer programs,* which are found in the 000s.

600s: Technology (Applied Sciences) includes medicine, engineering, agriculture (both raising plant crops and animal husbandry), management, manufacturing, and buildings (but not architecture, which is found in the next main class, fine arts) as well as home economics and family living. Popular topics found here include parenting, pets, cookbooks, gardening, and automobiles. Many very fine distinctions must be made between pure and applied sciences, necessitating careful examination of other works in the collection to bring together related items, for example, between botany (580) and horticulture (630), or between immunity in animals (591.29) and immunity in human beings (616.079).

700s: The Arts, Fine and Decorative Arts, as previously mentioned, combines the familiar topics of art in general, architecture, painting, sculpture, crafts, and music, with performing and recreational arts. Thus, one finds circuses, movies, and television at 791, titled generically "Public performances"; theater, vaudeville, and ballet, called "Stage presentations" are at 792; and other kinds of dancing are grouped at 793 as "Indoor games and amusements," together with puzzles, riddles, magic, and so forth. The characterization of television as a "public performance" and folk dancing as an "indoor amusement" may be leftover nineteenth-century perceptions. We might be more inclined to think of television as an indoor amusement, while in some small towns folk dances are held outdoors as public events even if they are not professional public performances. Games of skill, including computer games and chess, are classed in 794, whereas games of chance (where some might prefer putting computer games) are in 795. Bowling is classed as an "indoor game of skill," in 794, while baseball and football are at 796 with other "Athletic and outdoor sports and games." The distinctions are, perhaps, transparent to those who watch all three sports and more on their television sets. "Aquatic and air sports" are at 797, and outdoor sports that bring people closer to nature—horseback riding, animal racing, hunting, and fishing—are found at 798 and 799. An interesting placement in the 700s is photography. One might expect that photographic art and techniques would be found under different main classes, in much the same way computer software and hardware are separated, but the entire section 770-779 is devoted to the art of photography, its techniques, and its processes. Specialists who see film and television art as a subset of photographic arts in general might be critical of the separation of these topics. The music schedule (780-789), although it resembles all the other schedules in outward appearance, was revised completely in the twentieth edition, and is, in actuality, a faceted scheme based on the British Classification for Music.

800s: Literature (Belle-Lettres) and Rhetoric in general is followed in this class by the individual literature of different countries, beginning, as one might expect, with American literature in English. An instruction here similar to the one for languages enables a different national/language's literature to be assigned the preferential position, if desired. English and Anglo-Saxon literature is followed by European literature, including Latin and Greek, both ancient and modern, consuming all but the final ten sections, 890-899. Into these last few numbers are squeezed all of Asian, Middle Eastern, and African literature as well as Russian, Polish, and other languages less familiar to North Americans. Shakespeare is the only author with his own number, 822.33. The citation order in the 800s is strictly observed: country/language first, followed by genre and chronological period, but only the most popular literatures have defined periods. Three tables for literature (see A Closer Look at DDC's Tables section in this chapter) augment what can be represented.

900s: Geography, History,, and Auxiliary Disciplines, the final class, begins with three divisions for general works on both geography and history (900-909), general works on geography alone, including travel books (910-919), and biography (920-929). Regarding biography, however, application policies given in the manual and used at LC's Decimal Classification Office recommend using the 920s solely for collective biographies, and classing the life stories of individuals in the subjects with which each is associated. Thus, biographies of mathematicians Gauss and Lobachevski, who pioneered non-Euclidian geometry, would be in 516.9 with that subject, and a biography of Sigmund Freud would be in 150, with other works on psychology. The other seven divisions (930-999) are devoted to history alone, beginning with a division for the ancient world and followed by one each for the continents of Europe, Asia, Africa, North America, and South America. All other countries and regions are grouped into the final division, including the final section, 999, for extraterrestrial worlds.

A Closer Look at the DDC Tables

Because many instructions require use of the tables, a closer look at them may be helpful. Each number in the tables is preceded by a dash to show that it may not be used alone, but must be attached to a number from the schedules.

Table 1: "Standard Subdivisions" is the table most frequently used, because applying it does not require an explicit instruction in the schedules. There are frequent instructions in the schedules, however, to apply the standard subdivisions in special ways. These instructions must be heeded and supersede the unfettered application of numbers from Table 1. The entire list is preceded by a table of precedence directing classifiers how to handle items having several applicable subdivisions.

The DDC's mnemonics are recognizable to a great degree in the standard subdivisions. The philosophy of a subject is designated -01, just as the 100s represent that field; -06 standard for organizations and management, just as the 650s stand for management; -09 stands for historical and geographic treatment, just as the 900s stand for those fields. The analogies are not complete, however; -05 stands for serial publications, not scientific aspects, -08 stands for history and description of a subject among groups of persons, not literary treatments, and so forth.

Table 2: "Geographic Areas, Historical Periods, Persons" and all other tables that follow may only be used when an explicit instruction in the schedules directs classifiers to do so. Table 2 gives numbers for geographic areas, beginning with general areas such as frigid zones at -11 (-113 if they are north of the equator and -116 if they are south of it), or land and land forms at -14. Locations in the ancient world are identified by -3 in this table, while those in the modern world are assigned numbers between -4 and -9. Some locales, particularly in the United States, have their own specific numbers; for example, the borough of Manhattan in New York City is -7471. Other much larger areas do not. The entire continent of Antarctica is represented by -989 and the whole universe of worlds outside of Earth has just one class, -99. Table 2 has another major use. When standard subdivision -09 is added to a number to show that a topic is limited to a particular place, the cataloger is instructed to go to Table 2 for a number to represent the area, and add it to the -09. For example, if an item is about forest lands in France, the number is 333.75'09'44. (The meaning of the prime marks appearing after the 5 and 9 in this number is explained below.) The first five digits represent forest lands in general, and the addition of -09 from Table 1 represents geographical treatment, and, following the instruction there, the addition of -44 from Table 2 represents France. Major changes to this table in the twenty-first edition and subsequent updates, some available at the DDC Web site or on *Dewey for Windows*™, address the breakup of the Soviet Union (-47) and other political changes affecting jurisdictions and boundaries.[8]

Table 3: "Subdivisions for the Arts, for Individual Literatures, for Specific Literary Forms," contains numbers designed to be used with 810-890 from the main schedules, namely, the numbers for various individual literatures. Table 3 is made up of three subordinate tables: Table 3-A, "Subdivisions for Works by or about Individual Authors"; Table 3-B, "Subdivisions for Works by or about More than One Author"; and Table 3-C, "Notation to Be Added Where Instructed in Table 3-B, 700.4, 791.4, and 808-809." In Tables 3-A and 3-B, the general categories of genre and criticism are subdivided finely for arranging very large collections of literary materials about authors. In Table 3-C, different categories with their subdivisions are found, such as literary qualities or themes, to be used for arranging very large collections of general literary criticism.

Table 4: "Subdivisions of Individual Languages and Language Families" contains numbers used, according to instructions, with numbers 420-490 from the main schedules. Among the most frequently used numbers from this table are -3, which represents dictionaries, and -86, which stands for readers. The numbers in this table do not all represent publication forms, however, but various other characteristics of language materials; for example, -5 is "Grammar of the standard form of the language."

Table 5: "Racial, Ethnic, National Groups" contains numbers for racial, ethnic, and national groups, organized more or less by geographic origins; for example, -1 stands for North Americans, -2 for people of the British Isles, -3 for Nordics, and so forth. There are some interesting divisions in this table; for example, Modern Latins (-4) does not include Italians, Romanians, and related groups, who have their own numbers beginning -5, or Spanish and Portuguese peoples, whose numbers begin with -6. The -6s do, however, include all Spanish-Americans at (-68) as well as Brazilians, subsumed under Portuguese-speaking peoples at -69. The number for groups not previously given their own numbers, -9, includes Semites, North Africans, Asians, Africans, and all native peoples (this is DDC's terminology, not the authors') of America and Australia. Individual peoples within this large grouping are given their own numbers, also; for example, Sri Lankans are at -91413 and Romany are at -91497. There is an option in Table 5 to class a group other than North Americans at -1 if a library wishes to give local emphasis to that group.

Table 6: "Languages" contains numbers for languages of the world, but is not intended to be used with the 400 class. Instead, it provides for representing the language characteristics of materials classed in other schedules. If, for example, one is classifying a translation of the Bible into Dutch, the notation for Dutch language, -3931, is added to the number for the Bible, 220.5, to form the precise class for Dutch-language Bibles, 220.53931. Here, as in the 400s, 800s, and elsewhere, there is an option to class a particular language first, at -1. English (-2) and European languages (-3 to -8) are given preference, and all the African, Asian, and other, languages are found in -9. Table 6, similar to several of the others, is a tiny encyclopedia of the world's languages, enumerated in just twenty-five pages.

Table 7: "Groups of Persons" identifies types of persons, with each section of the table representing a particular characteristic such as age, sex, race, ethnicity, or nationality. The category for young adults, interestingly, covers persons from twelve to twenty years of age, not the teenage years from thirteen to nineteen as one might expect. Children are divided into three groupings: infants, birth to two years of age; preschool, three to five years of age; and school ages, six to eleven. This is a curious division, since it cuts off sixth graders from other elementary school-aged children and promotes them to young adulthood. (Because most schools group children into grades kindergarten (K) through 4 or K through 6, or, occasionally, K through 8, but rarely K through 5, one wonders how DDC arrived at this decision. And if age is the primary distinguishing feature, why are the terms *preschool* and *school children* used at all?) The specificity in this table is quite deep, with numbers assigned to subgroups such as Black Muslims at -2977 and insurance agents at -368.

New classifiers are reminded to use Tables 2 through 7 solely when instructions for a number from the main schedules tells them to do so. Only the numbers from Table 1 (standard subdivisions) may be used without explicit directions in the main schedules. At the same time, classifiers must be alert to instructions limiting or changing the normal pattern for standard subdivisions. They may be directed to use -001 to -009 in place of the usual -01 to -09; they may be instructed to use -03 to -09, which means the first two standard subdivisions (-01 and -02) cannot be used for the particular number or number span to which the instruction applies. Although situations sometimes arise for which there are no instructions in either the schedule or the manual, the editors try hard to give needed guidance about the way table numbers should be assigned.

LIBRARY OF CONGRESS CLASSIFICATION (LCC)

The Library of Congress Classification (LCC) is the result of applying very practical solutions to practical problems. When the library's collections were destroyed by fire during the War of 1812, Thomas Jefferson sold Congress his personal library, then numbering about 7,000 volumes, as the basis for establishing a new collection. Along with the materials came Jefferson's own classification system, which remained in place until the turn of the twentieth century. Herbert Putnam, then the new Librarian of Congress, implemented many changes at LC, including the launching of a new classification. The choice was not an easy one. The DDC was in its fifth edition at the time, and Cutter's Expansive Classification, a popular rival, was in its sixth. However, after consideration of these and other alternatives, Putnam and Charles Martel, LC's chief cataloger, decided to devise a new and different scheme having as its primary objective solely the orderly arrangement of LC's current and future holdings. They wanted to avoid adopting an existing scheme into which LC's holdings had to be fitted.

One result of the main objective—organizing LC's holdings for effective retrieval—was to release LC from any obligation to a higher authority, such as the DDC's editors. (The Library of Congress has total control over the classification.) Another was to permit literary warrant to govern the scheme, which evolved into a loose federation of schedules, each fitting a particular subject area according to what LC owned and expected to add in the years to come. Although several overarching principles are found throughout LCC, each schedule is an individual entity in which the breakdown and organization of the subjects need not relate to any other schedule. Thus, some schedules are in their fourth or fifth editions, while others may be in a third, and the most recently developed schedules (for the law of particular countries) are still in their first editions (for example, KDZ, KG, KH, Law of the Americas, Latin America, and the West Indies, was first published in 1984; KE, and KJ-KKZ, Law of Europe, was first published in 1989). Toward the end of the twentieth century, LC abandoned numbered editions in favor of dated editions.

The LCC is updated on a continuous basis. The latest decisions on new or revised classification numbers are disseminated between editions through publication in *Additions and Changes* (A&C), a quarterly newsletter from LC's Subject Cataloging Division; via LC's Web site; and in the classification's computer-based version, *Classification Plus*. Printed cumulations of newly established, dropped, and altered numbers are published irregularly by Gale Research.

Other aids to using LCC for original classifying include LCSH (for general guidance only; numbers listed there should never be used without consulting the schedules themselves) and the *Library of Congress Shelflist in Microform,* a listing of LC's holdings by call number, including official cutter numbers and other shelf marks (available from University Microfilms International or the United States Historical Documents Institute). Several indexes to the scheme as a whole have been marketed commercially,[9] but none has been kept current. The most complete guide to LCC is *Immroth's A Guide to the Library of Congress Classification* by Lois Mai Chan.[10]

Principles Underlying LCC

Eight principles underlie the organization and structure of LCC:

1. *Classification by discipline.* Like DDC, LCC divides knowledge first into disciplines, but there are twenty-one rather than ten, and the concept of what constitutes a "discipline" differs considerably from Dewey (see Figure 20.3, page 486).
2. *Literary warrant.* This principle, which dictates that classes be created only when materials exist that require them, operates much more prominently in LCC than it does in DDC. In DDC, literary warrant acts more as a priority check, because DDC attempts to classify all knowledge, not just the knowledge covered by existing documents. (Even DDC does not include all potential subjects, because to do so would require an infinite number of classes.) The LCC aims only to classify all of LC's holdings, not all knowledge, as already explained. As a result, it is relieved of the need to anticipate and accommodate topics outside LC's collecting interests. The experts who devised the original schedule created numbers for existing holdings and for those

topical areas in which they believed publication would flourish *and* LC would continue collecting.

3. *Geographical arrangement.* In the course of legislative research, inquiries often involve particular places. As a result, subarrangement by geographical location often is preferred over subarrangement by other characteristics geared to a subject's "natural" hierarchy.

4. *Alphabetical arrangement.* A second subarrangement technique employed by LCC is cutter numbers, which alphabetize when they are applied. The LCC cutters many elements throughout the schedules, including geographic names, topical terms, and personal names. Although cutters are thought of as mnemonic devices, they do not assist memory very much in LCC, because they are applied differently in different parts of the schedules; that is, there is no guarantee the same term will be cuttered identically if it appears in different places, or, conversely, that the same cutter will represent the same word or name in different places in the classification.

5. *Economy of notation.* The LCC uses mixed notation, employing both alphabetic and numeric characters. It can represent extremely narrow topics with a smaller number of characters than DDC uses for topics at the same level of specificity.

6. *Close classification.* The LCC originated at a time when LC's collection contained more than 1 million books and was devised to handle not only this many items but an ever-growing total. Thus, it assumes a deep specificity that DDC does not, even though DDC can be extended to accommodate equally deep levels of specificity. Classifiers are more likely to find in LCC a number that matches the topic of an item being classified than they are if they use DDC—provided, of course, that LC collects in this subject area.

7. *Enumeration.* Similar to DDC, LCC enumerates a very large proportion of the classes it provides and minimizes the use of number-building devices that allow classifiers to synthesize their own classes. The enormous size of LCC is evidence of its heavy reliance on enumeration.

8. *Relative location.* Like DDC, LCC employs the principle of relative location, although its use of geographic and alphabetic subarrangements tends to fragment materials related to one another in a topical hierarchy.

Like DDC, none of LCC's principles operate perfectly throughout the entire classification, but they are observed as long as they do not conflict, create unwanted juxtapositions of subjects, or interfere with practical considerations. Enumeration sometimes is abandoned to save space; choices between geographic, alphabetic, and topical subarrangements may be forced; and other principles may be modified as LC's managers desire. Nevertheless, the operation of the principles can be observed throughout the schedules.

In addition to the eight principles, the following seven-point intellectual structure devised by Charles Martel may be seen in the arrangement of materials within classes and subclasses. However, current policies have abandoned it, so it will not be visible in newly created numbers.

1. *Form.* The first few numbers of classes and subclasses are allocated to general form subdivisions, including periodicals, often linked with society publications, yearbooks, congresses, documents, exhibitions and museums, and directories.
2. *Theory and philosophy.*
3. *History and biography.*
4. *Treatises and general works.*
5. *Law.* Until the K classes were completed, legal materials focused on a subject were classed with the subject; for example, building codes were classed in TH219 with building construction, TH9500 with fire prevention, and so forth. Since the publication of separate law classes, these numbers have been deleted and the materials relocated within K.
6. *Education.* Materials dealing with study, teaching, and research on a subject as well as textbooks on that subject are included in this section.
7. *Specific subjects and subdivisions.* These numbers were likely to be the bulk of the schedules. Martel's seven-point structure also was applied to topics at each level of hierarchy. For example, TH1 is "Periodicals and societies" for building construction as a whole; TH1061 is "Periodicals, societies, etc." for systems of building construction; and TH2430 is "Periodicals, societies, congresses, etc." for roofing. Not every topic has a number for periodicals; for example, floors and flooring, the topic following roofing, does not. The existence of a special number for periodicals depended not only on the logical structure but on the likelihood that periodicals would be developed for particular subjects and that LC would collect and classify them. Note that the phrase used differs in each of the three instances in the example, combining different types of materials.

Format of LCC

More than forty separate volumes of schedules make up LCC at this writing, and it is also available on the *Classification Plus* CD-ROM. Although each volume represents a different subject area, some disciplines are divided among several volumes; for example, Class P, literature, is contained in eleven volumes plus a separate volume of tables. Each volume contains many, if not all, of the following parts:

1. *Preface.* Provides a brief history of the schedule and its editions.

2. *Synopsis.* Lists the primary divisions of the class (or subclass) of the volume.
3. *Outline.* Summarizes the main subdivisions of the class. From time to time, a cumulation of all of the outlines is published, which is very helpful for both classifiers and searchers.
4. *Schedule.* Enumerates all the numbers in the class (or subclass).
5. *Tables.* Gives selected tables intended for use throughout the schedule. The LCC has three interschedule or auxiliary tables: cutter numbers for countries of the world, U.S. states and Canadian provinces, and cities. The auxiliary tables are not printed in all volumes, but appear in H, T, and Z. Other tables, such as those used with the P schedules, are published separately from the schedules.
6. *Index.* Provides access to terms used in the volume.

The lack of a combined index to LCC is a serious drawback. Equally troublesome for classifiers is the lack of coordination between LCSH and LCC. Terminology for a topic may differ between the two tools, and the LCC numbers provided in LCSH are not prescribed, merely suggested. Scope notes and helpful instructions are rare in LCC schedules, although there are a few cryptic aids; for example, at S414 (Calendars. Yearbooks. Almanacs) it says: "Popular farmers' almanacs in AY, e.g. AY81.F3."[11]

Originally, volumes of LCC were typeset, printed, and sturdily bound in heavy-duty library bindings. Currently, computer processing of newly issued volumes results in neat, attractive pages, although they are bound in paper covers. Libraries often rebind them to ensure they remain in good condition despite heavy use. The CD-ROM version is more convenient to store, search, and use, but it is costly. The CD-ROM version also is more up-to-date and does not require a shelf of supplements listing new, changed, and deleted numbers between editions.

Main Classes of LCC

The main classes in LCC are designated by letters of the alphabet. Depending on how one counts, one or two letters may define a main class. For example, if a cataloger takes the broad view, P stands for languages and literatures, while PR is English literature, and PS is American and Canadian literature. The same idea is applicable to B (Philosophy and religion), H (Social science), and K (Law), which may be seen broadly as three individual classes or narrowly as several classes each. The other classes all are given one letter, with the exception of history, which encompasses four single letters (C, D, E, and F). A complete outline of LCC appears in Figure 20.3, page 486.

A	= General works	M	= Music
B	= Philosophy and Religion	N	= Fine arts
C	= Auxiliary sciences of history	P	= Literature
D	= Old World history	Q	= Science
E/F	= New World history	R	= Medicine
G	= Geography	S	= Agriculture
H	= Social sciences	T	= Technology
J	= Political science	U	= Military science
K	= Law	V	= Naval science
L	= Education	Z	= Bibliography

Figure 20.3. Outline of Library of Congress Classification.

A quick perusal of the outline reveals several differences between LCC's and DDC's overall structures. First, several subjects grouped together in DDC are given their own schedules in LCC: agriculture and medicine are not part of technology; education, political science, law, and military and naval science are not part of social science; and generalities and bibliography are distinguished into two separate classes, A and Z, respectively, that are as far apart in the alphabet as possible. Second, the wide divergence between languages and literature found in DDC is not present in LCC. Both are combined in P. Third, in LCC, music and fine arts each has its own schedule, separated from recreation, which is located at the end of the G schedule. Finally, history and geography, separated into several different schedules, are located toward the beginning of the scheme, immediately after religion, instead of at the end as they are in DDC. History and law are among LC's largest groups of holdings, so it is understandable that between them these two subject areas cover fifteen of the volumes, or nearly one-third of the scheme.

The Library of Congress does not use the two schedules developed by the National Library of Canada (NLC) for materials relating to Canadian history and literature: FC (Canadian history) and PS8000 (Canadian literature). Canadian libraries trying to assign more specific classification numbers to Canadian topics may prefer to use derived records from NLC rather than LC for those subject areas. Figure 19.3 in Chapter 19 demonstrates the difference in classification schedules for Canadian history.

Subdivision in LCC

The use of geographical location to subdivide a topic is frequently encountered in LCC. Geographic subdivisions may be arranged alphabetically or by area, and the latter arrangements often give preference to the United States and/or the countries of Europe and the Western Hemisphere. An example of this arrangement can be found at "Exploitation of timber trees" (S434-534). After a number for general works, the topic is further subdivided by country, beginning with the United States and followed by the rest of the Americas, Europe, Africa, Australia, New Zealand, Atlantic Islands, and, finally, Pacific Islands. Elsewhere, the countries are listed in alphabetical order, as can be seen in the next part of the schedule at "Plant culture: study and teaching" (SB51-52). In this case, SB51 is used for general works and SB52 is used to further subdivide the topic geographically with the instruction to add a cutter number "by region or country, A-Z." This means that every country is assigned a cutter number using the initial letter of its name and one or more digits to represent a subsequent letter or letters, thus producing an alphabetical subarrangement.

Topical subdivisions under each geographic locality sometimes are represented by special number spans for different countries and sometimes by a different letter-and-number device resembling a cutter number. To subdivide the topic "Regulation, inspection, etc. of seeds" (SB114), the cataloger uses .A1 for the publications of societies, .A3 for general works, and .A4-Z for specific regions or countries. Although the first two subdivisions resemble cutter numbers, they do not represent words or names as ordinary cutters do. The United States has a special cutter number under the .A4-Z portion: .U6-7, where .U6 represents general works and .U7 is further subdivided by state, A-W. According to this instruction, a work about the inspection of seeds in the state of Georgia would be SB114.U7G+. (An additional level of subdivision allows the classifier to add a third cutter number to represent a specific locality within each state.)

Topical subdivisions of a subject unrelated to geographic locations also can be arranged alphabetically by means of the cuttering device. The S schedule is particularly rich in lists of cuttered subtopics such as different types of crops, ornamental plants, plant diseases, and trees. In the list of trees, some of the cuttering goes to five digits beyond the initial letter. Topical subdivisions often are represented by numbers in a sequence of whole numbers. For example, in the HV schedule (Social pathology):

HV6085 = general works on the language of criminals;
HV6089 = prison psychology;
HV6093 = general works on intellectual and aesthetic characteristics of criminals;
HV6097 = prison literature, wall inscriptions;
HV6098 = tattooing;
HV6099 = other forms of intellectual and aesthetic expression among criminals.

The lack of consistent treatments for similar subarrangements makes for an extremely complicated scheme. In addition, the lack of any major aids to its application makes LCC difficult to implement for original classification outside the Library of Congress. Libraries that adopt LCC do so under the impression they will find all or nearly all of the materials they buy already classified; they expect to do little, if any, original classification.

Use of cutter numbers as part of the classification is one of the disadvantages of LCC for libraries other than LC; no one but LC can assign an official cutter number for anything—a location, a topic, or a book mark. Other libraries must wait until LC classifies an item requiring the appropriate cutter number before it is officially established. A cataloger might encounter a book on a particular type of tree that is not in the list given under SD397. If it is to be classified, the cataloger must guess at which numbers LC will use in the numeric portion of the cutter, and if there is any doubt about the proper name of the tree, the initial letter as well. (Take the following hypothetical example: Suppose a cataloger was assigning cutters for the different types of people who receive discount fares on public transit. Would that cataloger call student recipients "students" or "educational recipients," or would they be identified by their grade levels, "elementary" and "secondary?" Would older people be identified as "seniors," "aged," or "elderly"? Would civil servants be lumped into one group or divided into "police," "transit workers," "fire fighters," etc.?)

The Library of Congress establishes new cutter numbers after consulting its shelflist to see what already has been assigned. In doing so, its classifiers may decide that they should depart from their usual pattern, a simple formula with just a few rules (see Figure 20.4, page 489), because of some unique problem, or because of their expectation about future assignments likely to affect few libraries outside of LC. The first element in an LC cutter number consists of the initial letter of the word to be represented, combined with one or more Arabic numerals chosen according to the rules shown in Figure 20.4.

Subject Cataloging Manual: Shelflisting and *Subject Cataloging Manual: Classification,* the companion policy manuals to *Subject Cataloging Manual: Subject Headings,* are helpful for local classifiers in deciding on original cutters.[12] Another useful tool is LC's shelflist, which can be purchased on microfiche from University Films International.[13]

1. After initial vowels

for the 2nd letter:	b	d	l,m	n	p	r	s,t	u,y
use number:	2	3	4	5	6	7	8	9

2. After the initial letter S

for the 2nd letter:	a	ch	e	h,i	m-p	t	u
use number:	2	3	4	5	6	7-8	9

3. After the initial letters Qu

for the 2nd letter:	a	e	i	o	r	y
use number:	3	4	5	6	7	9

for names beginning Qa-Qt

use: 2-29

4. After other initial consonants

for the 2nd letter:	a	e	i	o	r	u	y
use number:	3	4	5	6	7	8	9

5. When an additional number is preferred

for the 3rd letter:	a-d	e-h	i-l	m	n-q	r-t	u-w	x-z
use number:	2*	3	4	5	6	7	8	9

(*optional for 3rd letter a or b)

Figure 20.4. LC rules for creating Cutter numbers.

COMPARISON OF DDC AND LCC

The LCC has many more numbers and many more specific classes than DDC in which to place very narrowly defined topics. For instance, LCC has individual numbers for most nineteenth-century English and American authors, and often individual numbers for each of their works. Contemporary U.S. authors are assigned numbers according to the first letter of their surnames. The difference is made clear by an example: In DDC, Kurt Vonnegut would join most of his contemporaries at 813.54 (U.S. writers of fiction working after 1945) and in LCC, he would join only those U.S. writers working after 1961 whose surnames begin with "V" at PS3572. That is a large difference in specificity. The desire for specificity is one reason large libraries such as the Boston Public Library and many university libraries turned to LCC.

Smaller libraries that made the change to LCC did so not to achieve greater specificity but to take advantage of the much larger proportion of titles classified in LCC than in DDC by the Library of Congress and other major originators of cataloging copy, freeing them from having to do as much original classification. Small or medium-sized college libraries using OCLC felt they would save a great deal of time (and, therefore, money) by copying the LCC numbers found online instead of doing original classification.

Another contrast is the nature of the classification number produced by each scheme. LCC numbers usually are shorter for topics of the same specificity, but their combination of alphabetic characters and numbers is not necessarily easier to remember or use. Some people may find the alphanumerics more understandable and logical, but others prefer the purely numerical system of DDC, particularly when libraries add cutter numbers as book marks and other marks in various alphanumerical sequences to the classification number to give each item a unique shelf location. This can result in very complicated combinations of all sorts of characters, including upper- and lowercase letters, whole and decimal numbers, and punctuation. To accommodate all of this information on books with narrow spines, libraries often break up the arrangement of the classification number into several lines. It may be hard to tell where the class numbers end and the book marks begin, or what follows what; for example, should JX1977.8.C53q1984 come before or after JX1977.D5b1987? (In the Simmons College library, it would come after.)

The general use of cutter numbers in all libraries as book marks or shelf marks becomes confusing when they also are part of the classification numbers. It is especially confusing when an item has several cutter numbers, perhaps with one denoting geographic location, another denoting a topic subdivision, and a third for the shelf mark.

The LCC's methods of subdividing are quite different from DDC's. One of LCC's favorites, shown in the examples above, is to add cutter numbers for subtopics or geographical subdivisions (or, sometimes, for both). The LCC also uses numerical expansions to subdivide topics, but they are added differently. When DDC instructs classifiers to add to a number, it means that some other number from a table or another section of the schedule will be tacked on to a base number from the schedules. For example, to expand the number for cooking, 641.5, to French cooking, one adds 9, representing geographic focus and 44 for France, to obtain 641.5944. In LCC, the instruction to add a number from a table to a base number in the schedules may mean to add the two numbers arithmetically. For example, to expand the number for classical art in countries other than Greece and Italy (N5801-5896), one adds a number from a designated table to the base number N5800. Using the number 13 for Canada, one adds it to 5800 to get N5813, representing classical art in Canada. Sometimes, when whole numbers are lacking to subdivide a topic as desired, LCC employs decimal numbers. In the previous example, to subdivide classical art in the United States for the colonial period, one adds 03.5 to 5800, to arrive at N5803.5.

The LCC occasionally contains instructions to subdivide (or subarrange) a topic like some other in the schedule, but this is done far less frequently than in DDC. Rather, LCC simply lists various subarrangements in the schedules, and most differ from one another.

The degree of browsability that results from using LCC or DDC also is an important consideration. Because of its principle of hierarchy, DDC produces arrangements that tend to be more satisfying to browse from a subject searcher's point of view. Use of alphabetical instead of hierarchical subarrangements, which LCC does by means of cuttering, tends to scatter materials on related topics and bring together topics at different levels of hierarchy. Even geographical subarrangement may be less browseable, despite its logic, for subject searchers who are more interested in topical issues than in locational ones.

Finally, the difference in cost of the two tools is a practical matter that bears mention. The DDC's four printed volumes (or the CD-ROM) are a great deal less expensive than LCC's forty-plus volumes, even though individual LC schedules are good value for their price.

"COPY" CLASSIFICATION

Many catalogers use the DDC and LCC numbers provided by LC in the CIP information located on the verso of the title pages of books, or they find classification numbers in computer network records, such as OCLC. If so, conventions followed by larger institutions should be understood. For DDC numbers, the most important of these is the method used to show where numbers have been expanded. An apostrophe (also called a *prime* or *hash* mark) is placed at the end of the basic number and again after each complete expansion of a number (see Figure 20.2 for an example of a prime mark.)

Some agencies using DDC prefer that numbers not become too long and institute policies to limit them. Such policies should involve the addition or omission of expansions, for example, to limit a classification number to the basic number, or to one or more expansions beyond the basic number. They should not dictate a stated number of digits, such as no more than four digits after the decimal point, because for some numbers, the meaning of the categories that digits in an expansion represent would be lost. For example, the correct DDC number for slavery in ancient Athens is 306.3620385. This is a very long number that would only be necessary if a library has (or expects to have) many items about slavery in the ancient world in its collection. The length assigned to the number can be limited in the following ways according to the needs of the collection:

306	culture and institutions
306.3	economic institutions
306.36	systems of labor
306.362	slavery
306.36203	slavery in the ancient world
306.362038	slavery in ancient Greece
306.3620385	slavery in ancient Athens

Some libraries, including LC, furnish more than the class number, adding shelf marks such as cutters, call letters, and so forth, to it. When using another library's catalog records, shelf marks should be ignored unless it is a local policy to follow these practices, also. If so, then the cataloger must be careful about *whose* practices are followed. In some places, the initial letter of the main entry is used in place of a cutter number. In others, two- or three-digit cutters are used. It might be confusing to adopt all of these practices simultaneously.

SUMMARY

The DDC is widely used all over the world. It is the basis for the Universal Decimal Classification and some national classifications as well (for example, in Korea and Japan). Its popularity in the United Kingdom is assured by its use in the *British National Bibliography* and all the British Library's authoritative online cataloging. Its flexibility is sufficient to serve many purposes, and its ease of use is enhanced by the mnemonics, the Relative Index, and its easily grasped overall logic.

The LCC is widely used among academic libraries in the United States and, because of the likelihood that LC numbers are used in bibliographic network records, by some libraries outside of the United States as well. The LCC is much larger and more complex than DDC. Its overall arrangement of subjects is, perhaps, more logical and better organized for contemporary use than DDC is, particularly in the fields of science and history. Using it to classify materials "from scratch," however, is difficult for librarians outside of LC, because it is controlled entirely by LC and devoted to the arrangement of LC's own collections.

The LCC requires less number building than DDC does and provides shorter classification numbers than does DDC (although they are made up of letters and numbers) for subjects of the same specificity. The LCC seems more hospitable to new topics and allows for far greater subdivision of topics. In addition, it avoids trying to force differing disciplines into a single mold and allows every subject area to have the arrangement most "natural" to its literature.

The bias of LCC toward the United States, its neighbors, and traditional allies is, perhaps, even more pervasive than DDC's, but more understandable. The LCC does not try to be a universal classification of knowledge, but only an orderly arrangement of LC's books. The difficulty of applying LCC to nonbook materials probably is no greater than applying DDC to them. Both schemes were developed to arrange books, not other forms of materials. In LCC's favor is the fact that there are more opportunities for close classification, a useful attribute because nonbook items often have very narrowly defined topics.

The Library of Congress and other libraries using LCC are unlikely to change to DDC. The LCC is equally unlikely to become ubiquitous in the United States or anywhere else. Rather, the dichotomy in the classification of library materials between DDC and LCC is likely to continue, with the choice depending on an agency's traditions, size, and orientation toward a particular source of cataloging and classification data. Heightened awareness of the workings of each system and an understanding of their differences and implications for use are valuable both for librarians and patrons.

Before going on, readers may want to try assigning DDC and/or LCC numbers to the examples on page 493. The answers are on page 497 at the end of this chapter.

1. TITLE: *Distance learning : a list*
SUMMARY: Correspondence schools operating in Ontario, Canada, are listed and described with details of their degree programs and curricula.

2. TITLE: *Birds of a feather*
SUMMARY: Interesting facts about birds are revealed in the letters of famous ornithologists.

3. TITLE: *Mythology and the Conquistadors*
SUMMARY: An examination of Spanish-language mythology in Spain, Mexico, and Peru.

4. TITLE: *Food from the sea*
SUMMARY: A description of the life cycle of crabs and oysters.

5. TITLE: *New England's small-town treasures*
SUMMARY: Text and pictures about museums in small towns of New England.

6. TITLE: *How to fill out your Michigan income tax forms*
SUMMARY: A guide to filling out Michigan state income tax forms.

7. TITLE: *The way things work*
SUMMARY: Descriptions of simple and complex mechanical devices from the inclined plane to microcomputers and flight simulators.

8. TITLE: *Lifetime encyclopedia of letters*
SUMMARY: Compilation of 850 model letters for business and personal occasions with general instructions on how to formulate selected types of letters.

9. TITLE: Cookwise: the hows and whys of successful cooking
SUMMARY: Explanation of the chemical reactions caused by a selection of cooking procedures as well as more than 200 recipes.

10. TITLE: *Sourcebook of ophthalmology*
SUMMARY: Illustrated bibliography of rare books on the subject of ophthalmology.

NOTES

1. Lois Mai Chan, et al., *Dewey Decimal Classification, A Practical Guide* (Albany, NY: Forest Press/OCLC, 1996), 8.

2. The manual for the nineteenth edition of DDC was published as a separate title: *Manual on the Use of the Dewey Decimal Classification,* edited by John P. Comaromi et al. (Albany, NY: Forest Press, 1982). Its incorporation into the classification proper was made with the twentieth edition, also edited by Comaromi.

3. *Dewey Decimal Classification and Relative Index,* 21st ed., [Hereinafter DDC21], edited by Joan S. Mitchell et al. (Albany, NY: Forest Press/OCLC, 1996), vol. 4, 172-174.

4. Ibid., 352-353.

5. *Abridged Dewey Classification and Relative Index,* 13th ed. (Dublin, OH: Forest Press/OCLC, 1997).

6. *DDC 21 Summaries* (Dublin, OH: OCLC-Forest Press, 1999).

7. "The guiding principle of the DDC is that a work is classed in the discipline for which it is intended rather than in the discipline from which the work derives." DDC21, vol. 1, xxx.

8. The DDC issued the following update to Table 2: *Table 2. Geographic Areas: Great Britain and Republic of South Africa* (Dublin, OH: OCLC-Forest Press, 1999).

9. These indexes include James G. Williams et al., *Classified Library of Congress Subject Headings,* 2nd ed. (New York: Marcel Dekker, 1982); J. McRee Elrod et al., *An Index to the Library of Congress Classification; with Entries for Special Expansions in Medicine, Law, Canadiana, and Nonbook Materials,* preliminary ed. (Ottawa: Canadian Library Association, 1974); and Nancy B. Olson, *Combined Indexes to the Library of Congress Classification Schedules* (Washington, DC: U.S. Historical Documents Institute, 1974). A newer tool of value in this area is Mona L. Scott, *Conversion Tables: LC-Dewey, Dewey-LC* (Englewood, CO: Libraries Unlimited, 1993). *Conversion Tables* is available in print and on CD-ROM.

10. Lois Mai Chan, *Immroth's A Guide to the Library of Congress Classification,* 5th ed. (Englewood, CO: Libraries Unlimited, 1999).

11. Library of Congress, Subject Cataloging Division, Processing Services, *Classification: Class S: Agriculture,* 4th ed. (Washington, DC: Library of Congress, 1982), p. 8.

12. Library of Congress, Subject Cataloging Division, *Subject Cataloging Manual: Shelflisting* (Washington, DC: Library of Congress, 1987); Library of Congress, Office for Subject Cataloging Policy, *Subject Cataloging Manual: Classification,* 1st ed. (Washington, DC: Cataloging Distribution Service, Library of Congress, 1992). A third tool with similar application is LC's Geography and Map Division's publication of geographic cutters, *Geographic Cutters,* 2nd ed. (Washington, DC: Library of Congress, 1989). These tools are also available on CD-ROM.

13. Library of Congress, *The Library of Congress Shelflist in Microform,* microfiche ed. (Ann Arbor, MI: University Microfilms International, n.d.).

SUGGESTED READING

DDC

Chan, Lois Mai, John P. Comaromi, Joan S. Mitchell, and Mohinder P. Satija. *Dewey Decimal Classification: A Practical Guide.* Dublin, OH: Forest Press, 1996.

Davis, Sydney W., and Gregory R. New. *Abridged 13 Workbook for Small Libraries Using Dewey Decimal Classification Abridged Edition 13.* Dublin, OH: OCLC-Forest Press, 1997.

Dewey Decimal Classification. Available: http://www.purl.org/oclc/fp.

Mitchell, Joan S. "Options in the Dewey Decimal Classification System: The Current Perspective." *Cataloging & Classification Quarterly* 19, nos. 3/4 (1995): 89-103.

Mitchell, Joan S., and Mark A. Crook. "A Study of Libraries Using the Dewey Decimal Classification in the OCLC Online Union Catalog: Preliminary Findings." In *Annual Review of OCLC Research 1994*, 47-50. Dublin, OH: OCLC, 1995.

Mortimer, Mary. *Learn Dewey Decimal Classification (Edition 21).* Lanham, MD: Scarecrow Press, 2000.

O'Neill, Edward T., and Patrick McClain. "Copy Cataloging Practices: Use of the Call Number by Dewey Libraries." In *Annual Review of OCLC Research 1995*, 11-15. Dublin, OH: OCLC, 1996.

Sifton, Pat, et al. *Workbook for DDC 21: Dewey Decimal Classification Edition 21.* Ottawa: Canadian Library Association, 1998.

Winkel, Lois. *Subject Headings for Children: A List of Subject Headings Used by the Library of Congress with Abridged Dewey Numbers Added.* 2nd ed. 2 vols. Dublin, OH: OCLC-Forest Press, 1998.

LCC

C. A. Cutter's Three-Figure Author Tables [on CD-ROM]. Englewood, CO: Libraries Unlimited, 1995.

C. A. Cutter's Two-Figure Author Tables [on CD-ROM]. Englewood, CO: Libraries Unlimited, 1995.

Chan, Lois Mai. *Immroth's A Guide to the Library of Congress Classification.* 5th ed. Englewood, CO: Libraries Unlimited, 1999.

Cutter-Sanborn Three-Figure Author Tables [on CD-ROM]. Englewood, CO: Libraries Unlimited, 1995.

Dittmann, Helena, and Jane Hardy. *Learn Library of Congress Classification.* Lanham, MD: Scarecrow Press, 2000.

FC: A Classification for Canadian Literature. 2nd ed. Available: http://www.nlc-bnc.ca/pubs/abs/eclassfc.htm.

Library of Congress. Subject Cataloging Division. Processing Services. *LC Classification Outline.* Washington, DC: Library of Congress, 1995- ; also available: http://www.loc.gov/catdir/cpso/cpso.html.

REVIEW QUESTIONS

1. Name five of the seven principles on which the Dewey Decimal Classification is based and describe each briefly.
2. What is a mnemonic device? Name one such device in the Dewey Decimal Classification.
3. What kind of notation does the Dewey Decimal Classification employ, and why do people like it?
4. Name one drawback to the type of notation used by the Dewey Decimal Classification.
5. How are updated numbers for the Dewey Decimal Classification communicated to its users between editions?
6. Name five of the eight principles on which the Library of Congress Classification is based and describe each briefly.
7. What kind of notation does the Library of Congress Classification employ?
8. Name an advantage to the type of notation used by the Library of Congress Classification.
9. What is a cutter number, and how are cutter numbers used in the Library of Congress Classification?
10. Describe two advantages of using the Dewey Decimal Classification and two advantages of using the Library of Congress Classification. If you had to choose between the two, which would you select for a new library, and why?

ANSWERS TO EXAMPLES ON PAGE 493

1. DDC: [374.4'713]
2. DDC: [598.'0922]
3. DDC: [398.204'61]
4. DDC: [594.4]
5. DDC: [069,09'74]
6. LCC: [HD4186]
7. LCC: [T47]
8. LCC: [PE1483]
9. LCC [TX714]
10. LCC: [Z6669]

Chapter

The MARC Formats

INTRODUCTION

The MARC formats are a set of markup protocols for bibliographic, authority, classification, holdings, and community information data. Adding these protocols to the data puts them into a form that can be understood and used by properly programmed computers. MARC is similar in principle to SGML, HTML, and other markup languages used for transmitting electronic resources. It is intended to be used for library data.

The MARC formats are called *communications* formats, which means that once in this form, one computer can transmit the data to another computer. The term *bibliographic data* applies to all of the elements of a bibliographic record that have been described in this book so far: descriptions, access points, subject headings, and call numbers. *Authority data* covers all of the elements of an authority record for names, titles, or subject descriptors, including the authorized form of the name or topic, cross-references to other name forms or topical terms, and references to the source material used in creating the authority record. *Holdings data* are the specific data relating to any item in a library's collection, including its copy number, cost, acquisition source, holding unit (such as a main library or branch library) or collection within a library or information center, and so forth. A fourth MARC format was developed for *classification data* and used to automate the Library of Congress classification. The fifth format is for *community information*, such as local officials and agencies or lists of events.

Institutions outside LC, including the National Library of Canada, were consulted during the development of the MARC formats and still contribute to their ongoing evolution, but they were initiated and devised primarily by LC, and they reflect the needs of its cataloging products and processes. This chapter concentrates on the format for bibliographic data.

HISTORY AND BACKGROUND

The first MARC format was devised for the bibliographic data of books in the 1960s. It went through several versions before being published as a national standard in the 1970s by the National Information Standards Organization (NISO). Before long, a MARC format for serials was devised, followed by MARC formats for other types of materials for which LC produced bibliographies. After many years during which the number of separate MARC formats continued to grow, an integrated MARC format was implemented during the 1990s in which all fields were made uniform across all the physical forms of materials collected by libraries. All fields and codes still are not applicable to every type of material, but if they do apply, their meanings are the same, thereby simplifying the processes of learning and using the system of MARC protocols.

Individual bibliographic networks have issued manuals containing versions of MARC intended for use by their participants. Selected fields have been defined in unique ways by an individual network; for example, the coded version of the basic features of a document are known in the Online Computer Library Center (OCLC) and Research Libraries Information Network (RLIN) as *fixed fields* and in MARC 21 as field 008, shown in Figures 21.2 through 21.4 (see pages 504–6).

Between 1994 and 1997, LC and NLC worked with their user communities through their MARC committees to reconcile the differences between the official Canadian and U.S. formats, known as CAN/MARC and USMARC, respectively. The result is MARC 21. MARC 21 is not a new format; it is the new name for the harmonized CAN/MARC and USMARC. MARC 21 consists of the five communications formats described previously: bibliographic data; authority data; holdings data; classification data; and community information. There also are concise formats for each of these.

Individual countries employing the MARC formats have their own official versions, including the United Kingdom's UKMARC; a generalized or universal version also exists, called UNIMARC. Minor differences appear among the versions of MARC formats, but their fundamental structure is identical and the same principles apply to them all.[1]

It is important to know what the MARC formats are *not*. They are not a set of cataloging rules or a cataloging code. Instead, they are designed for use with data created by applying the standard cataloging rules, subject heading systems, and classification schemes discussed in previous chapters of this book. Some accommodations are made for local data, but there are limits to how far the formats can be stretched. For example, the bibliographic format is geared to AACR, so the library that does not follow these rules will find itself having to create AACR-compatible records anyway to code them successfully.

The MARC formats are not computer systems, either. They are intended to be used *in* computer systems as templates for database structures, but by themselves they are not designed as information storage and retrieval systems. Additional programming is required to utilize the MARC protocols for information storage and retrieval systems.

Although ultimate authority over the MARC 21 formats rests with LC and NLC, other groups in the two countries play consultative roles. In the United States, a major influence is MARBI, the Committee on Representation in Machine Readable Form of Bibliographic Information. MARBI is an interdivisional committee of three American Library Association divisions: the Association for Library Collections & Technical Services (ALCTS), the Library and Information Technology Association (LITA), and the Reference and User Services Association (RUSA). MARBI's counterpart in Canada is the Canadian Committee on MARC (CCM), a committee with representatives from the English- and French-speaking national library associations, the Canadian Library Association and l'Association pour l'avancement des sciences et des techniques de la documentation, respectively. Major bibliographic networks, such as OCLC and RLIN in the United States and A-G Canada (described later in this chapter), also contribute important advice. The MARC Editorial Office at LC and MARC Office at NLC make and publish the final decisions.

The MARC formats look very complicated because they must include everything needed to identify every detail of a record to a machine that cannot understand any part of it by itself.

ELEMENTS OF A MARC RECORD

Fields

Computer data generally are divided into parts called *fields,* and each field is further subdivided into *subfields.* Each catalog record (or bibliographic record, as it is called in the computer system) is made up of fields that correspond to each area of the catalog record (title, edition, publication information, physical description, series statement, notes, etc.). The subfields in each field, in turn, correspond to particular elements of the area; for example, subfields in the physical description field include one each for the extent, other physical details, dimensions, and accompanying materials; and the subfields in the Dewey Decimal call number field correspond to the classification number, the shelf marks, and the edition of the classification used.

Every MARC record has two kinds of information in it, contained in two kinds of fields: fixed and variable. The kind of information discussed in the paragraph above is variable in nature. The names of personal authors are an example. A person's name may consist of a forename alone (Homer); a forename and a surname (William Shakespeare); a forename and a compound surname (Walter de la Mare or Sir Alec Frederick Douglas-Home); or a family name (Adams family). Or it may be another variant, such as initials or descriptive phrases. The name may have seven, seventeen, or twenty-seven letters. It could require the inclusion of numbers, frequently encountered for royalty (Elizabeth II or Louis XVI). Titles, too, may be short or long; contain letters, numbers, and/or symbols; and have one word or many. These data must be contained in fields that are flexible enough to admit all these possibilities. Such fields have variable lengths and are called, appropriately, *variable fields.* Variable fields contain almost all of the data we have studied.

Some information in entries does not vary but is always entered the same way, either because the data are naturally invariant or because they are intentionally coded to eliminate variation. An example of naturally occurring invariable bibliographic data is the ISBN. It always appears in the same form and sequence (ten characters, all digits or with a final "X"). An example of information deliberately coded in an invariant form is the geographic focus of a title. Geographic locations are reduced to seven characters representing the applicable continent, country, and locale. These kinds of information are contained in invariable or *fixed fields.*

Information from the variable fields may be coded and duplicated in the fixed fields to facilitate manipulation by the computer system. One such type of information relates to the physical description of materials. The physical description for nonbook materials is a good example. Each type of nonbook medium has its own kind of physical details. Films, videos, photographs, and electronic resources may have color or be in black and white. Sound recordings may be stereophonic or not. Microforms may be reduced to any one of several possible reduction ratios. In each instance, however, the number of possibilities is limited, so it is easy to use a few letters or numbers to reduce them to a short and invariable code and add it to the computerized record. It is useful to include the language of the item, its country of origin, the presence or absence of multiple parts, and a host of other important aspects of an item, some of which might not be given in the eye-readable portions of catalog records. All of these data, in fixed and unchanging form, are given in fixed fields.

The order of elements in the MARC format (see Figure 21.1) is very similar to the order of elements in a catalog record. The main exception is that the call numbers, standard numbers, and other coded elements, called *control fields,* appear first. Many would be missing on catalog entries in most libraries or, on LC printed cards, they would appear at the bottom of the card below the tracings. They are put first in the computerized record because they generally identify the record or item and, as such, are more efficiently utilized if they are read first; they generally are in coded form, such as a single character or a short string of characters in fixed order, and are not understandable until they are translated. Therefore, it is better to have these identifying or controlling fields at the start of the record and not in the middle, where they would interrupt the bibliographic fields, or at the end, where a processing unit would have to scan through the first part of the record to reach them.

0xx	Includes fixed fields and control numbers.
1xx	Main entries, including personal author, corporate body author, conference names, and uniform title main entries.
2xx	Transcribed titles, editions, material specific details, and publication/distribution information.
3xx	Physical descriptions.
4xx	Transcribed series statements.
5xx	Descriptive notes.
6xx	Subject descriptors.
7xx	Added entries for names of contributors and titles other than main entry titles and titles proper (the latter are coded by different means, described below).
8xx	Series added entries traced differently than transcribed.
9xx	Intended for local data.

Figure 21.1. Summary of MARC bibliographic field tags.

Subfields

Subfields are parts of fields. The title area in a bibliographic description generally is made up of four elements: title proper, general material designation, other title information, and statement of responsibility. The title field corresponds to the title area as a whole, and each of the four elements corresponds to a specific subfield within the title field. The title proper subfield is the first subfield in the title field, while the date subfield usually is the third subfield in the publication/distribution field, following two subfields for the place and name of the publisher and/or distributor.

Content Designators

Each field and subfield must be identified by a name, known as a *content designator*. In the MARC format, the fields are identified by three-digit codes called *tags,* and subfields are identified by a single letter, number, or, occasionally, a symbol, all called *subfield codes.* Subfield codes always are preceded by a symbol called a *delimiter* that identifies the next character as a subfield code. In the OCLC network, the delimiter appears as a double dagger, whereas in the A-G Canada system it appears as a dollar sign. The function of the delimiter is the same—to identify subfields—even when various keyboards and printers interpret its symbol in different ways.

The application of appropriate tags and subfield codes to cataloging data frequently is called *tagging and coding* a record, or sometimes just *tagging* or just *coding* it. All of these terms, as well as *encoding a record* or doing *content designation,* mean the same thing: that the protocols of the MARC format are being applied to cataloging data for entry into a computer system programmed to utilize it.

Fixed fields, usually the first fields in the record, are given a tag beginning with 0 (zero). Access points generally have tags beginning with 1 (main entries), 6 (subject descriptors), 7 (added entries), or 8 (series added entries). Title proper added entries are the main exception here. They are identified as access points in the 245 field by the use of a special character called an indicator, described below. Fields relating to the descriptive elements have tags beginning with 2, 3, 4, and 5. Few MARC fields beginning with 9 are defined for use.

Indicators

Between the tags and the start of the data in the field itself are two numerical characters known as *indicators.* One or both of the indicators may be defined for a field, or neither may be defined. When only one indicator is defined it may be in either the first or the second position. For the most part, indicators are values that instruct the computer system to treat the data within the field to which they are assigned in particular ways, such as how to index the character string, whether to print or not to print the data in the field on a catalog card or a screen produced from the computerized record, or whether to create or not to create an access point for the data in the field. In the fields in which personal or corporate body names are entered, the indicator informs the computer of the type of name being entered, that is, whether it is in the form of a surname followed by a forename (e.g., Einstein, Albert), a forename first (e.g., Leonardo, da Vinci), or the name of a whole family (e.g., Kennedy family). A computer system needs this information to file these names properly in its name indexes.

The most important thing to remember about indicators is that their meaning differs for each field in which they are used. Originally, they were a vital element in printing catalog cards from computerized data, and they are equally useful to computer programmers working with online systems, who can use them to specify desired procedures having nothing to do with cards or printing.

MARC DISPLAYS

Figures 21.2, 21.3, and 21.4, pages 504–6, show bibliographic records for titles as they appear in three national bibliographic networks, with their tags, indicators, delimiters, and subfield codes. All are MARC formatted records even though there are recognizable differences in the way they look. Some of the differences occur because of the differing capabilities of various printers to print data from visual displays. Some occur because of the differing procedures followed by each network. Close inspection will reveal new MARC 21 data in the A-G Canada record.

```
#A3           59168708 07/10/00 12:47 cam a
001           59168708
003           CaOEAGC
005           20000626135547.0
008           000121s2000····mbc···········000·d·eng··
016    --     a 009001719
020    --     a 1896239633 : c$25.95
035    --     a (CaAEU)ANT-6968
040    --     a (CaOONL b eng c CaOONL d CaOONL d AEU
043    --     a n-cn-mb
055    -3     a PS8315.5.M35 b M36 2000
082    0-     a C812.54/08/097127 2 21
245    02     a A map of the senses : b [twenty years of Manitoba
              plays] / c edited by Rory Runnells ; with an
              introduction by Doug Arrell.
260    --     a [Winnipeg] : b Scirocco Drama, c 2000.
300    --     a 519 p. ; c 23 cm.
650    -5     a Canadian drama (English) z Manitoba.
650    -5     a Canadian drama (English) y 20th century.
650    -0     a Canadian drama z Manitoba.
650    -0     a Canadian drama y 20th century.
700    1-     a Runnells, Rory.
Owner: 9 ALBa PS 8315.5 M3 M36 2000b AEU
```

Figure 21.2. A-G Canada MARC record.

```
                                    ¶  CAT                    SID: 09401       OL
Beginning of record displayed.

OLUC  ti "STANDARD CATALOGING FOR SCHOOL AND PUBLIC LI...   Record 2 of 2
 NO HOLDINGS IN OCL - 232 OTHER HOLDINGS
  OCLC:  33983358            Rec stat:    c
  Entered:     19951221      Replaced:    19970729      Used:    20000701
▶ Type:  a     ELvl:         Srce:        Audn:         Ctrl:         Lang:  eng
  BLvl:  m     Form:         Conf:  0     Biog:         MRec:         Ctry:  cou
               Cont:  b      GPub:        LitF:  0      Indx:  1
  Desc:  a     Ills:  a      Fest:  0     DtSt:  s      Dates: 1996,      ¶
▶   1  010       95-53186 ¶
▶   2  040       DLC ‡c DLC ‡d NLC ¶
▶   3  015       C97-10475-8 ¶
▶   4  020       1563083493 ¶
▶   5  043       n-us--- ¶
▶   6  050 00    Z693 ‡b .I56 1996 ¶
▶   7  055 02    Z693.3* ¶
▶   8  082 00    025.3 ‡2 20 ¶
▶   9  090       ‡b  ¶
▶  10  049       OCLC ¶
▶  11  100 1     Intner, Sheila S. ¶
▶  12  245 10    Standard cataloging for school and public libraries / ‡c Sheila
S. Intner and Jean Weihs. ¶
▶  13  250       2nd ed. ¶
▶  14  260       Englewood, Colo. : ‡b Libraries Unlimited, ‡c 1996. ¶
▶  15  300       viii, 278 p. : ‡b ill. ; ‡c 27 cm. ¶
▶  16  504       Includes bibliographical references (p. 211-213) and indexes. ¶
▶  17  650  0    Cataloging ‡z United States. ¶
▶  18  650  0    Public libraries ‡z United States. ¶
▶  19  650  0    School libraries ‡z United States. ¶
▶  20  650  6    Catalogage ‡x Normes ‡z ´Etats-Unis. ¶
▶  21  650  6    Biblioth`eques publiques ‡x Normes ‡z ´Etats-Unis. ¶
▶  22  650  6    Biblioth`eques scolaires ‡x Normes ‡z ´Etats-Unis. ¶
▶  23  650  6    Catalogage ‡x Litt´erature de jeunesse ‡x Normes ‡z ´Etats-
Unis. ¶
▶  24  700 1    Weihs, Jean Riddle. ¶
```

Figure 21.3. OCLC MARC record.

```
MC/PROD  Archival    FUL/BIB   DCLV00-A2572              Catalog           CRLG-EEG
IN ID DCLV00-A2572 - Record 1 of 1 - SAVE record

 ID:DCLV00-A2572               RTYP:d     ST:s     MS:          EL:5         AD:07-19-00
 CC:9554  BLT:pc       DCF:a   CSC:d    MOD:     PROC:                      UD:07-19-00
 CP:mtu      L:eng      PC:i     PD:1879/1881    REP:                       TOC:a
 010       00520290
 040       MtHi‡cDLC‡dDLC‡eappm
 100 1     Rose, John Baker,‡d1853-1884.
 245 00    John Baker Rose diary,‡f1879-1881.
 300       1 item.
 545       Helena, Montana, area rancher.‡bJohn Baker Rose was born in Hampstead
         Cedar Grove, Virginia, in 1853.  He left St. Louis, Missouri, with two f
         riends to set up a cattle business in Montana.  He settled near Helena,
         Montana, and remained there until 1881. He drowned in the Mississippi Ri
         ver near St.Louis, Missouri, on July 11, 1884.
 520 8     Diary of John Baker Rose.‡bCollection consists of a diary (July 1879-S
         ept. 1881) describing Rose's relocating to Montana, and his experiences
         operating a cattle business near Helena.
 555 8     Finding aid in the repository.
 650  0    Frontier and pioneer life‡zMontana.
 650  0    Overland journeys to the Pacific.
 650  0    Ranches‡zMontana‡zLewis and Clark County.
 651  0    Lewis and Clark County (Mont.)‡xHistory.
 797 2     NUCMC/Montana Historical Society
 797 2     NUCMC/MULP
 852       Montana Historical Society,‡bLibrary and Archives Dept.‡e(Helena)‡z(SC
         13).
```

Figure 21.4. RLIN® MARC record.

Figures 21.5, 21.6, 21.7, and 21.8, below and pages 506–8, show authority records from the LC Name Authority File and Subject Authorities for a personal name, corporate body name, geographic name, and an LCSH subject descriptor, respectively. Differences in the meanings of tags and subfield codes are obvious in these records when they are compared with the bibliographic records.

```
ARN:    86904
Rec stat: c       Entered:       19800903
Type:       z     Upd status:   a       Enc lvl:    n      Source:
Roman:            Ref status:   a       Mod rec:           Name use:  a
Govt agn:         Auth status:  a       Subj:       a      Subj use:  a
Series:    n      Auth/ref:     a       Geo subd:   n      Ser use:   b
Ser num:   n      Name:         a       Subdiv tp:         Rules:     c
  1  010       n  50051972
  2  040       DLC  c DLC
  3  005       19840407101817.5
  4  100 10    Weihs, Jean Riddle.
  5  400 10    Riddle, Jean
  6  400 10    Weihs, Jean
  7  670       Her Non-book materials ... 1970.
  8  670       Her Accessible storage of nonbook materials, 1984:  b CIP t.p.
(Jean Weihs)
  9  678       Course Director, Library Techniques, Seneca College of Applied
Arts and Technology;  a b. 1930
```

Figure 21.5. Library of Congress personal name authority record.

```
ARN:    348749
Rec stat: n       Entered:      19791029
Type:     z       Upd status:   a       Enc lvl:    n       Source:
Roman:            Ref status:   a       Mod rec:            Name use: a
Govt agn:         Auth status:  a       Subj:       a       Subj use: a
Series:   n       Auth/ref:     a       Geo subd:   n       Ser use:  b
Ser num:  n       Name:         n       Subdiv tp:          Rules:    c
   1  010       n  79117036
   2  040       DLC  c DLC
   3  005       19840322000000.0
   4  110 20    Boston Public Library.
   5  410 10    Boston (Mass.).  b Public Library
   6  410 20    Public Library of the City of Boston
   7  410 10    Boston (Mass.).  b Boston Public Library
   8  410 10    Boston.  b Public Library.  w nnaa
   9  510 20    Mercantile Library Association (Boston, Mass.)
  10  667       AACR 1 form: Boston Public Library
  11  670       Its Monthly bulletin, 1896-
  12  670       Lectures for inventors, 1983:  b CIP t.p. (Boston Public
Library; Public Library of the City of Boston
  13  678       Opened to the public in 1854.
```

Figure 21.6. Library of Congress corporate body authority record.

```
ARN:    2029822
Rec stat: n       Entered:      19860211
Type:     z       Upd status:   a       Enc lvl:    n       Source:
Roman:            Ref status:   n       Mod rec:            Name use: b
Govt agn:         Auth status:  a       Subj:       a       Subj use: a
Series:   n       Auth/ref:     a       Geo subd:           Ser use:  b
Ser num:  n       Name:         n       Subdiv tp:          Rules:    n
  1  010       sh 85136126
  2  040       DLC  c DLC
  3  005       19860211000000.0
  4  151  0    Toronto (Ont.)
```

Figure 21.7. Library of Congress geographic name authority record.

```
ARN:    2659069
Rec stat: c        Entered:        19891026
Type:     z        Upd status:   a        Enc lvl:     n        Source:
Roman:             Ref status:   a        Mod rec:                Name use:  b
Govt agn:          Auth status:  a        Subj:        a          Subj use:  a
Series:    n       Auth/ref:     a        Geo subd:               Ser use:   b
Ser num:   n       Name:         n        Subdiv tp:              Rules:     n
  1  010         sh 89006162
  2  040         DLC  c DLC  d DLC
  3  005         19940422110444.5
  4  150   0     IBM-compatible computers
  5  450   0     Clones of IBM computers
  6  450   0     Compatible computers, IBM-
  7  450   0     IBM clones
  8  450   0     IBM compatibles (Computers)
  9  550   0     Microcomputers   w g
 10  670         Work cat.: Pilgrim, A. Upgrade your IBM compatible and save a
bundle, c1990.
```

Figure 21.8. Library of Congress subject authority record.

BIBLIOGRAPHIC NETWORKS AND ONLINE CATALOGING

Efforts to share the planning, development, costs, and products of computerized data began in the 1960s and led to the formation of bibliographic networks, although some groups of libraries had banded together earlier in noncomputerized network cooperatives to share tasks among their members. The history, background, and basic services of OCLC and RLIN, based in the United States, and A-G Canada, based in Canada, are described in Chapter 4. In this section, online cataloging issues are described in greater detail.

An important feature common to all the bibliographic networks is their use of the MARC format to enter and transmit their data. This acceptance of the MARC format by the networks helped make it an international standard. On the other hand, each network adapts MARC in ways that aid its users. Some have altered the appearance and entry style of the 008 control field to make it easier to code; for example, OCLC provides mnemonic prefixes in place of delimiters and subfield codes. Local fields unique to a network have been defined that are not present in the official format. Generally, however, MARC records are interchangeable and easily recognized.

All the networks incorporate national library cataloging. The Library of Congress's MARC records formed the nucleus and lion's share of all network databases when they started and continued to constitute a majority of records for a number of years. The relative balance between LC and member-contributed original cataloging shifted during the 1980s and, since that time, the proportion of LC and national library records has been shrinking. In the 1990s, LC began using the original cataloging of network member libraries as the basis for its own cataloging. The project proceeded smoothly, with appropriate caution and attention to quality. This change put real meaning into the phrase "cooperative cataloging," which formerly was defined as everybody else copying LC's original cataloging (hence the phrase *copy cataloging*).

As mentioned in Chapter 4, all network records are not alike in quality and fullness, which has put limits on the acceptability of catalog records from libraries other than the national libraries. Some libraries single out selected member library records for more editing and revision. Others are not as concerned about the quality of individual records as they are about getting cataloging done rapidly, preventing backlogs, and minimizing costs. Either way, a choice usually must be made between maximizing the use of the network (greatest speed and least cost) and maximizing the quality of the cataloging (greatest accuracy and appropriateness for the individual library). Such choices never are simple and are likely to differ from one library to another as well as from one cataloger to another.

Joining a network will not mean that original cataloging no longer has to be done in a local library. That depends on whether the materials being acquired and cataloged are held widely enough to be found already cataloged by one of the network members.[2] In general, the materials most likely to have cataloging available online are English-language trade books from publishers who participate in the CIP and ISBN programs. Materials least likely to have cataloging available online are nonbook and non-English-language items, and the publications of small presses and government agencies, especially at state, provincial, or local levels.

Similarities and differences among the networks may be seen in their database design and system architecture, searching and retrieval capabilities, and the presence (or absence) of automatic authority control and other quality control processes.

Networks are employed directly by thousands of libraries and indirectly by many more to minimize the load of original cataloging that would otherwise burden them all. For many libraries, catalog records for virtually all the materials they purchase are available from the network, and nothing needs to be done "from scratch." For those with collections of unusual materials, catalog records for numerous titles are not available, and original cataloging still is necessary for those items.

Maximizing use of the network keeps the amount of costly, time-consuming original cataloging as low as possible for any individual library, but it may involve incorporating records that contain errors or that include more or less information than is preferred. Network records contain some proportion of subject headings and classification numbers based on standards that are not used in a particular place. Catalogers are faced with many decisions about how best to use the network: Should all network records be accepted, or only those from designated libraries? How much time should be spent searching for existing cataloging before inputting an original record? (To minimize unwanted duplicates, networks expect a diligent search to be done before a new record is added to the database.) How much editing should be done to existing records to make them acceptable?

Care must be exercised in weighing the needs of the local library against the potential savings of using imperfect cataloging from a network database. Cataloging that is so undesirable that it is better to have nothing at all should be identified.

Each individual library that joins a network or anticipates using one should clarify what it wishes to accomplish and develop a policy governing the use of network records that ensures its objectives will be met. If the idea is to save money or speed processing, a higher level of error and some differences from ideal cataloging will have to be borne. It would be wise to experiment using the network to do copy cataloging (that is, using network records as the cataloging source) with a representative sample of materials to anticipate problems *before* making these decisions.

In addition, benefits of joining a network other than cataloging must be considered, such as gaining access to enormous amounts of bibliographic data for reference and resource sharing, as well as electronic communications with other agencies. For some, these benefits may have a higher priority than the suitability of the cataloging. Networks themselves share information, and some libraries might find it advantageous to join more than one network.

Individual libraries should understand the responsibilities they shoulder upon joining a network. Any original cataloging contributed to the shared database must be consistent with the network's input standards. The old adage "garbage in, garbage out" is highly relevant here. If catalogers wish to take good cataloging out of online systems, they must put good cataloging into them. In the network environment, "good" cataloging means agreeing to follow network standards and to minimize the types of local deviations that might save time or effort in the local database but may not be appropriate or beneficial in a shared system.

SUMMARY

The MARC format and its adoption by bibliographic networks, and subsequent use by designers of individual library computer systems for cataloging, circulation, acquisitions, serials control, and other technical services functions, has created a library-wide standard for computerized bibliographic data. Criticized by some as too complicated or too idiosyncratic, MARC has exhibited a remarkable ability to change with the times and accommodate many different kinds of data. Although newer markup systems, such as the Dublin Core, are attractive because they have few rules and require very little memorizing, they lack the sophistication and precision of MARC. At this writing, no trend toward abandoning MARC appears to be present. Time will tell whether simpler systems can be adapted to do as good a job as MARC does of identifying and relating individual items in large databases such as OCLC's.

Bibliographic networks are transforming themselves into global information networks, with services that go far beyond their originators' initial vision of shared cataloging and shared resources, with other functions based on the same core bibliographic files thrown in for good measure. OCLC, for instance, supports reference services with bibliographic and full-text databases, multilingual offerings, and collection development services derived from the purchasing track records of its members. RLIN has wide-ranging document delivery services and is a leader in preservation management. The dependence of individual libraries on network services seems likely to increase, even as these nonprofit networks compete with profit-making firms offering the same or similar types of service. At this writing, the electronic marketplace is characterized by constant change in almost every aspect of its existence—hardware, software, products, services, marketing, distribution, and cost—but observers believe it will continue to grow unabated for some time to come.

NOTES

1. Advantages for the British of harmonizing UKMARC with MARC 21 would be to broaden access to bibliographic records from North American sources, including a great deal of data for nonbook media. On the negative side, it could hinder cooperation with European neighbors based on compatibility with UNIMARC, which would not be possible with MARC 21. For discussion of this issue, see James Elliot, "MARC Harmonisation Moves to Major Consultation," *Select* 28 (Summer 2000): 1-2.

2. For a discussion of the problems of maximizing network benefits, see Sheila S. Intner's "Interfaces" columns: "Bibliographic Triage" and "Bibliographic Triage Revisited," *Technicalities* 7 (December 1987): 10-12 and 8 (October 1988): 3-4.

SUGGESTED READING

Byrne, Deborah J. *MARC Manual: Understanding and Using MARC Records.* 2nd ed. Englewood, CO: Libraries Unlimited, 1998.

Ferguson, Bobby. *MARC/AACR2/Authority Control Tagging: A Blitz Cataloging Workbook.* Englewood, CO: Libraries Unlimited, 1998.

Fritz, Deborah A. *Cataloging with AACR2R and USMARC for Books, Computer Files, Serials, Sound Recordings, and Videorecordings.* Chicago: American Library Association, 2000.

Furrie, Betty. *Understanding MARC: Bibliographic: Machine-Readable Cataloging.* 6th ed. Washington, DC: Cataloging Distribution Service, Library of Congress, 2000. (Also available on the LC Web site at http://www.loc.gov/marc/umb.)

Hagler, Ronald. *The Bibliographic Record and Information Technology.* 3rd ed. Chicago: American Library Association, 1997.

InfoTrain: Catskill; Format Integration Made Easy; USMARC Made Easy. [Interactive multimedia CD-ROMs]. Englewood, CO: Libraries Unlimited, 1999- .

Jones, Wayne, et al. *Cataloging the Web: METADATA, AACR, and MARC 21.* Lanham, MD: Scarecrow Press, 2002.

Library of Congress. *MARC Homepage.* Washington, DC: The Library, 2000- . (Available at http://www.loc.gov/marc/marc.html.)

Library of Congress. Network Development and MARC Standards Office, in cooperation with Standards and Support, National Library of Canada. *MARC 21 Format for Bibliographic Data Including Guidelines for Content Designation.* 1999 ed. Washington, DC: Library of Congress Cataloging Distribution Service; Ottawa: National Library of Canada, 1999. (The concise format for bibliographic data is available online at http://lcweb.loc.gov/marc/bibliographic/. Formats for authorities, holdings, classification, and community information data are available from LC and NLC; concise versions are available on their Web sites.)

Millsap, Larry, and Terry Ellen Ferl. *Descriptive Cataloging for the AACR2R and the Integrated MARC Format: A How-to-Do-it Workbook.* Revised ed. New York: Neal-Schuman, 1997.

Schultz, Lois Massengale. *A Beginner's Guide to Copy Cataloging on OCLC/PRISM.* Englewood, CO: Libraries Unlimited, 1995.

Warwick, Robert T., and Kenneth Carlborg. *Using OCLC under PRISM: A How-to-Do-It Manual for Libraries.* New York: Neal-Schuman, 1997.

Weitz, Jay. *Music Coding and Tagging: MARC 21 Content Designation for Scores and Sound Recordings.* 2nd ed. Lake Crystal, MN: Soldier Creek Press, 2001.

REVIEW QUESTIONS

1. What is the MARC format, and how is it applied to cataloging data?
2. Name the five types of MARC formats and explain briefly what they cover.
3. Who is responsible for the MARC format, and who governs it?
4. Name three types of content designators and describe how each is used to encode data.
5. Explain the division of catalog records into fields and subfields.
6. Name three types of fields and describe the kind of data each contains.
7. Give two reasons a library would want to join a network.
8. What obligations does a library undertake on joining a network?

Chapter 22 Managing the Cataloging Department

Responsibility must be taken for setting policies and managing the library's cataloging and classification operations. In small institutions, this role may be assumed by the same person responsible for reader's services, collection development, and all other information-related operations. In larger ones, it can be assumed by one person as his or her primary job or it can be handled by a group that makes important decisions as a team. The ultimate aim is the same: to ensure that someone sees to it that cataloging and classification operations are performed properly, in a timely manner, and according to established policies.

MANAGEMENT TASKS

The title "department head" or "department manager" carries with it the responsibility to perform a variety of tasks having less to do with cataloging and classification than with managing the library as a whole, or, for that matter, managing operations of any kind. These tasks are connected with any or all of the following activities:

1. *Staffing*—recruiting personnel, training and integrating them into the staff, supervising their work, and evaluating both the work and each staff member's overall performance (such as reliability, promptness, adaptability) for the purposes of salary determination, promotion, and so forth.
2. *Budgeting*—preparing budgets periodically, monitoring expenditures, and supplying the library or media center director with a financial report at the end of the budget period (usually a year).
3. *Planning*—proposing departmental goals and objectives and how departmental operations should proceed; devising workflow routines and all procedures for accomplishing the work of the department; and, when necessary, thinking up and trying new methods for getting the work done.

4. *Decision making*—taking the risk of choosing among alternative goals and objectives, potential plans or proposals, policies, strategies, procedures, suppliers, staff members and staff assignments, budgets, and so forth for the department, and ensuring that all decisions made are consistent with the policies set by those who govern the media center or library.
5. *Directing*—taking charge, assigning tasks, arranging for things to be done properly, ensuring that people are functioning effectively, and providing leadership for the department.

NEEDED SKILLS

Knowledge of how bibliographic data are created and used is essential for a cataloging department manager to perform the tasks listed above. The manager must, however, have other skills as well, which do not involve bibliographic information at all. These include communication skills, political skills, financial skills, and leadership skills.

Communication skills—both speaking and writing—are important to convey one's ideas to the people with whom one comes into contact. Those who work in the cataloging department initially need training to do their work. Even if they are skilled at cataloging and classification, the local situation must be explained and any special rules and procedures described. This will be particularly important if the person has come from a different type of library. Workers at all levels need to know what is expected of them, the meaning of policies, and how local procedures are to be followed.

When new staff are recruited and interviewed, the department manager may be expected to write or edit the job description. When selected candidates are brought to the institution for onsite interviews, the department manager should be a major participant, and usually is expected to ask questions of each candidate and describe the work of the department.

The department manager must be able discuss the department with other staff, with administrators, and with peers at other libraries. Often the manager must speak or write to suppliers, computer system vendors, and a variety of outsiders who are involved in that department's operations from time to time. The department manager is responsible for writing periodic reports, evaluations of staff and operations, proposals for new equipment, new policies, and new procedures, and keeping up correspondence for the department within and outside of the organization.

Political skills—defined as the skills needed to get things done with people—are important to the cataloging department manager to have the department's needs recognized and its programs and budgets approved. Political skills encompass being persuasive, putting forth ideas in ways that will appeal to decision makers, and being able to build support for new proposals. Political skills also aid the department manager in building consensus within the department, establishing and maintaining an *esprit de corps* that gives everyone in the department a sense of satisfaction and helps the department run smoothly.

Financial skills are necessary for planning the department's budget, defending it successfully before higher authorities within the organization, monitoring expenditures, and evaluating the results at the end of the budget cycle. Computer software is available to assist with the statistical work involved, but even the best software cannot substitute for an understanding of basic financial management processes and techniques. The cataloging department manager should be able to determine the true costs and evaluate the total value of alternative expenditures, not just to learn the price of things.

Leadership skills combine envisioning goals and objectives for the department, imbuing others with the vision, and risking the decisions that make progress possible toward those goals and objectives. Any decision could prove to be right or wrong, and the department manager who makes decisions risks failure as well as success. If the cataloging department is to grow and change, develop and achieve, it must have leadership willing to take on the risks of making decisions because of the importance of achieving the goals.

DEPARTMENTAL POLICIES AND PROCEDURES

The cornerstone of a library's cataloging and classification operations should be a manual containing a record of all of the decisions governing the cataloging and classification of materials and provision of bibliographic services to patrons. Developing such a manual takes time and effort, but the result is a document that can be helpful to all staff members, whether they perform cataloging and classification tasks or merely use these organizing systems to help patrons find what they want. A policy and procedures manual also can help to highlight the way the mission of the library is served by its cataloging services.

A bibliographic policy manual should begin with a brief description of the library's community, school, or organization being served; an official mission statement; and a summary of its facilities, staff, collections, and patrons. Putting the description of these elements at the beginning of the policy clarifies the setting and context in which these policies must operate. Also, any obvious discrepancies between the setting, its mission, and the policies contained in the document might be made explicit at this point.

Next, a section for each part of the bibliographic system, arranged in any order that seems logical to the staff, should include the decisions pertaining to that part along with a brief explanation of why they were made. There is no one right way to organize policy documents, although the most frequently encountered order is chronological, beginning with the first step in the process and concluding with the final steps of shelving, usage, and deacquisition. But it might be just as useful to divide the manual into decisions concerning descriptive cataloging, the assignment of subject descriptors, classification, shelflisting, and processing. Or it might be organized by medium, with decisions about books, videos, databases, and so forth, in separate sections or chapters.

Assuming a manual is organized by the various aspects of bibliographic control, it can begin with a section on derived cataloging, if it is done by that library. Methods of searching, matching, capturing, and editing existing records from the source database should be outlined. Knowing that every change made to a derived record is an added cost, policy-makers will try to use bibliographic records "as is" to the greatest extent possible. Any mandated changes written into the policy should be scrutinized to ensure that the benefits they produce exceed their costs.

The section on original cataloging might begin with descriptive cataloging, specifying the level of description for various types of materials, the authority control system, the way items that are part of a series will be treated (that is, cataloged and classified separately or as a collection at the series level), whether some or all series titles will be traced, if or when multipart items will be analyzed (that is, provided with separate catalog records for each part), and how uniform titles will be adopted. Catalogers might decide to furnish analytic records for electronic resources in which the individual files may be used singly, but only one overall record for electronic resources in which the files are used in concert. Different descriptive treatments for different types of materials might be specified; for example, collections of tests or college catalogs might be given first-level descriptions, while reference collections and research materials might be given second-level descriptions. Decisions about the inclusion or exclusion of identifying data, the addition or deletion of descriptive access points, and so forth should be documented in the manual in this section.

The next section might deal with subject headings, explaining the source for descriptors, numbers of descriptors typically assigned, the desired depth of indexing, and any special treatments accorded to particular materials. For example, if broad headings are desired for a small collection, *Library of Congress Subject Headings* might be adopted as the source list for descriptors, but subdivisions (that is, subheadings) might be omitted for all but a few subject areas in which holdings are relatively abundant. Some materials might be indexed analytically, with descriptors assigned for each part of a multipart item, each chapter of a book, or each cut on a sound recording. For example, a collection of Shakespeare's plays, which usually are wanted one at a time, is a candidate for such treatment.

The section on classification might indicate the chosen system used, the level of complexity within the system, and how hard-to-classify materials such as periodicals or databases are treated. The method of assigning cutter letters or numbers and methods of adding them and other shelf marks to the classification number to complete the call number should be described. The choice between creating unique call numbers for each item or allowing more than one item to share the same call number should be documented here. Any designated anomalies in the shelving arrangement should be noted, such as keeping new acquisitions in a prominent display for a month or two; housing oversized books on special shelves; or dividing materials by instructor, grade level, class, and so forth.

Explanations for the decisions recorded in the policy document will enable one's successors to understand the reasoning behind them and, as conditions change, to recognize when there is a need to make changes.

A wise addition to any statement of policies or procedures is the establishment of regular review and amendment processes. Annual or biennial policy reviews might seem unnecessary at the time new policies are instituted, but they are a good idea. Frequent reviews head off crises caused by the continuation of outmoded policies. If reviewers take the responsibility seriously and are careful to examine every part of the document thoroughly—from the prefatory descriptions, through each section of the main text, to the closing amendment process—they might anticipate the need for change before a crisis occurs.

The manual can also have separate sections in which procedures are spelled out for accomplishing the tasks required to carry out each part of the bibliographic control system. These explanations of procedures, often comprising a separate manual or several separate manuals, should not be substituted for the policy manual. A procedures manual is different and need not document either the decisions that the designated procedures are intended to support or the reasons why those decisions were made.

Procedures seem best when they follow the chronological order of steps involved, but there is no reason why separate processes can't be arranged in any other order. One way to arrange the procedures manual is by physical medium, another is by bibliographic function, and a third is simply to put the procedures in alphabetical order according to their names. No matter what the arrangement of the procedures manual, it should be possible to locate an individual procedure very easily. Thus, if the manual is arranged by function, it should have an alphabetic index by title; and if it is arranged alphabetically by the names of the procedures or by physical medium, there should be a functionally organized list of contents provided as well.

RESPONSES TO CHANGES IN CATALOGING STANDARDS

An important set of decisions that should be included in the policy manual is the response to major changes in cataloging standards. When new versions of the descriptive cataloging code and the chosen subject and classification authorities appear, how will they be adopted and implemented? Such changes occur regularly, because their governing bodies all follow policies of continuous revision, so they need to be acknowledged and strategies for their implementation developed.

Among several possible responses are the following:

1. *Make all required changes for all holdings immediately.* This is the most desirable option for keeping the entire collection together in one style of organization and completely up-to-date, but it is the most costly alternative, both in terms of dollars and cents and the amount of staff time it will consume in the short run.

2. *Make no changes in existing holdings, but implement changes for new materials immediately.* This is the strategy followed by many librarians, because it seems the best that can be done with limited resources. The problem with this is that over time, even just a few years, the organization of the library starts to break down. What emerges is not one unified collection, but several fragmented collections, each following different rules. This was the strategy of choice for many libraries when they automated; when it finally became necessary to incorporate the older holdings into the automated system, it was a huge job costing more than anticipated.

3. *Make all changes over a limited period of time.* This strategy seems to be the most reasonable when circumstances don't permit the first approach, because all the materials remain in one unified organizational structure, even though the structure will take on different aspects as various changes are implemented. It probably has the best payoff in the long run, because it will ultimately result in the same organizational effectiveness as the first option but will not require as large an investment at one time.

4. *Make changes selectively.* This strategy also is popular with practitioners and can be the best overall strategy when changes in cataloging rules, subject descriptors, and classification schemes do not affect holdings to any great extent. If a library does not buy many items about music and its collection consists solely of a few works about music appreciation, the library might choose not to implement the changes in DDC's music schedules that appear in the twentieth edition. This strategy can lead to future problems, however, if the discrepancies become more significant over time.

5. *Make no changes and continue using older editions.* This strategy is deceptively simple, easy, and cheap. Eventually, however, it breaks down because it doesn't have the capacity to keep up with changes in materials, subject matter, and user needs. When the moment arrives that "something must be done" to improve it, it will cost a great deal more to address the changes than it would have when they first occurred.

Each of these alternatives—and they are not the only ones possible—has advantages and disadvantages, and each will have a different result both in the short term and over the long run. Although the first option might be an ideal response, it also is the most costly; and although the last option is the least costly, it probably will result in the least effective service to patrons, even though the problems might not become apparent for some time. The other options fall somewhere between these extremes, and libraries must weigh the alternatives in terms of their individual situations and the impact on budgets, staff, and patron services.

WRITING THE POLICY MANUAL

One person should be charged with writing the manual. This minimizes the possibility that individual differences in style and language will produce sections using different words for the same concepts and other potentially confusing linguistic problems. Over time, more than one person may write sections of the manual, but at any one time, one person should be assigned this responsibility.

A good way to begin preparing the policy manual is to draw up a table of contents, then circulate it among staff for suggestions about additions or changes to be made. It might be wise to indicate that just because suggestions are solicited does not mean they automatically will be followed. If major differences arise, negotiation can produce an acceptable solution so that the manual is a source of agreement, not contention. The table of contents, once defined, establishes the scope of the manual and identifies the way that the whole bibliographic system will be divided.

Writing the manual might then begin by listing all the decisions and operations that should be covered within each section; for example, decisions and operations relating to materials issued in series could be listed under "Descriptive Cataloging," "Tracing Practice," "Indexing," and "Classification," if the manual is divided into types of operations, or under "Series," if it is divided into types of material. Either way, all the decisions and practices relating to the handling of series must be covered somewhere in the manual. For the user's convenience, an index can bring together related information that falls into different sections or chapters (that is, to bring together all the descriptive cataloging decisions when the division is by material type, or all the decisions relating to series when the division is by operation). Word processing software enables indexes to be created automatically, making this a relatively easy task.

When the decisions and operations to be covered are listed, but before actual writing begins, questions about the style of the presentation should be answered. Some of them are as simple as whether one or both sides of a page should be used; whether sources will be cited at the bottom of pages or as endnotes; and whether illustrative examples, flowcharts, tables, and so forth will be given within text or as separate pages or sections. These decisions might sound trivial, but they affect the ease with which the manual can be updated; the size of the document ("document" is used as a generic term here; the manual need not be a book—it could be a database); the ease with which it can be consulted, excerpted, or duplicated; its applicability to the task of training new staff; and similar capabilities. Other decisions include the approach to describing operations, as step-by-step procedures or straight narratives; the amount and types of illustration; the inclusion or exclusion of supporting material (such as quoting Library of Congress rule interpretations in full or citing the page in a different document on which the interpretation appears); and so forth.

At this point, with the content, approach, and style clearly defined, writing can begin. If the person designated as the writer is knowledgeable in all the areas covered by the manual, he or she should begin writing each part, section, and chapter, completing them according to an agreed-upon schedule. If the manual includes procedures that the writer does not know well enough to describe them completely, these should be done jointly with a knowledgeable guide, or another person should submit a draft to the writer, who will put it into final format. Either way, as each portion is written, it is wise to circulate it among the staff who will be expected to implement the decisions, or who actually perform the tasks, to be certain the information given is clear and usable. The writer should expect to edit the work not only to account for solicited feedback from staff members, but also to enhance, clarify, sharpen, and polish the text, based on his or her own rereadings.

When enough of the manual is completed to warrant its distribution, the first few months (or longer) of its use should be considered a "test run" to see how well it functions. It might be issued in chapters or sections, or upon completion of the whole. With actual use, however, unanticipated problems can arise, which usually must be resolved by revising the language, examples and illustrations, finding aids, and so forth. Occasionally, enough difficulty is encountered to prompt reconsidering the basic organization, format, or style, and to suggest doing a major overhaul. In this event, it is best to weigh the true need for a total revision versus continuing to try making the existing manual "work." The first version of a manual need not be the last, but the difficulties should be evaluated carefully and estimates made that changes in style or approach can achieve the desired improvement before discarding an existing document. It is realistic to expect several months of revision to follow issuing any new manual to discover and work out all its "bugs." The problems are not anyone's fault. Revision is inherent in the process of obtaining an effective manual.

ADOPTING THE POLICY MANUAL

As a final step before a policy manual is adopted, it is essential for administrators to affirm whatever policies it presents. It will do little good to decide to put some bibliographic policy in place if those responsible for the library are unwilling to support its ideas, fund its implementation, and appreciate its value to the organization being served.

In connection with seeking administrative approval for policies, librarians must be prepared to document the needs served by particular policies, know their costs, and defend the expenditures. Whether or not a costly change is being contemplated, it is fair for an administrator to expect cataloging department managers to answer questions about the costs and benefits of bibliographic policies, to argue persuasively on behalf of proposed policies, and to negotiate compromise positions, when necessary.

PROCESSING MATERIALS FOR USE

After incoming materials have been cataloged and classified and their data entered into the library's catalog and shelflist, they should be processed for use. Physical processing aims to identify and protect library materials. It can include all or some of the following steps: (1) establishing library ownership, (2) labeling materials with call numbers and other location marks, (3) adding whatever is required by the library's circulation system, (4) inserting security devices, and (5) putting on protective covers, and so forth. A number of different methods are possible for accomplishing each step.

Commonly encountered ownership identification methods are stamping the library's name in indelible ink on pages, covers, or other parts of paper-based items, or, in the case of books, on the edges of the textblock (called edge-stamping); gluing or placing self-adhesive bookplates, decals, or labels bearing the library's name or logo in or on items; embossing a page of a book or other paper-based item with the library's name or logo; and engraving the name or logo on metal, plastic, and so forth. Tiny preprinted decals can be purchased to be applied to blank areas of optical or magnetic disks. Few of these methods are reversible, although some self-adhesive labels can be removed without leaving a noticeable residue. In practice, some methods are extremely obtrusive. Care should be taken that the glues, inks, and other substances used in establishing the library's ownership are not, themselves, destructive to the materials, and that they do not obscure information patrons want to see.

When library collections consisted mainly of clothbound books, call numbers were engraved or stamped into their spines, and they were likely to be decorated with gold- or silver-colored metals, or ink that contrasted with the colors of the covers. Labeling machines that permanently affixed call number labels with strong glue or tape were common in mid-twentieth century. Currently, library materials of many different types are stored in plastic, cardboard, or metal containers as well as traditional cloth boards, and self-adhesive labels that adhere to any surface can be applied to all of them. With use and frequent handling, however, these labels have a tendency to curl up and fall off, making it necessary for processors to add strips of clear tape to hold them on. The tape thus used should be harmless to the surfaces of the materials.

Library circulation systems used today usually require bar-coding the materials to provide each item with a unique computer-readable identifier. Bar codes have replaced copy numbers and supply a great deal more information embedded in the codes. In addition, libraries may wish to insert date due slips or cards in pockets in each item being circulated. Reserve materials and reference materials may receive different processing, depending on the particular loan-tracking system for the hourly loans these materials generally have. A different and less obtrusive date due system employed for new books at the Mount Holyoke College Library requires no permanent devices other than the bar codes. Instead, a small, easily removed self-adhesive label stamped with the due date is slipped on the part of the inside cover that lies behind the dust jacket and is removed when the book is returned.

Protective plastic sleeves are marketed in many sizes for books and selected types of discs. Paper sleeves are also made, but plastic has advantages, such as being able to see through to the information on the book or disc; resistance to ordinary tears; an absence of acid, which is inherent in some paper; and low cost. Clear plastic jewel cases are available for optical discs and cassettes of various sizes. Self-adhesive clear plastic sheeting can add sturdiness to paperback book covers and help them resist wear and tear; exposure to rain or spills; and the marks of pens, pencils, and so forth. All such coverings help keep materials clean and attractive. Similarly, clear plastic bags with handles or hooks at the top for hanging are listed in library supply catalogs to store book-record sets, small kits, and other nonbook materials that do not stand easily on bookshelves. Codex-style holders made of sturdy plastic or plasticized cardboard are designed to hold several cassettes or discs for circulation. Their "covers" are large enough to hold book-style card-and-pockets and, by using them, a library can retain and file the item's jewel case with its identifying labels. A 1995 book by Karen Dreissen and Sheila Smyth describes physical processing options for various nonbook formats in greater detail.[1] Perusal of the pages of library supply catalogs reveals processing options for nonbook materials as well as books.

None of the aforementioned methods, however useful they may be, can be thought of as having permanent preservative power. Library binding, routinely done to issues of printed journals to make them easy and convenient to store on bookshelves, is the preservation method of choice for paper-based materials in many libraries, but it is not the only possibility. Damaged books can be photocopied, provided the proper permissions are obtained. They may also be converted to microfilm or digital formats, again, with proper permission. Although these conversions will then require equipment to use the books (microreaders or computers), they preserve their content, which might otherwise be lost. Encapsulating fragile paper—pages of documents, maps, photographs, and so forth—between sheets of mylar from which the air has been removed can facilitate use while providing a higher degree of protection. Similarly, enclosing fragile books or films in boxes constructed of acid-free Bristol board can increase their useful life span.

When a decision is made to purchase materials in a new format, investigation into the appropriate packaging and housing for that format is needed; for example, magnetic fields that emanate from many sources can erase magnetic tapes, slides can be affected by fumes from many products, and variations in heat and humidity are the cause of many problems. The physical characteristics of each type of library material dictate different methods of storage and protection to maximize their shelf lives, and the choice of containers in which to store nonbook materials also depends on whether they are to be intershelved with the rest of the collection. The Northeast Document Conservation Center in Andover, Massachusetts, offers a wealth of information on preserving library materials at its Web site, free of charge (www.nedcc.org).

MANAGEMENT ISSUES

For several decades, the greatest challenge facing cataloging department managers was introducing computers into their operations and upgrading them as new hardware and software were made available. Far from being a better producer of catalog cards, automation eventually required reorganizing the workflow, retraining the staff, and incorporating all previous bibliographic data into the new computer-based systems being implemented. Among the profound changes that resulted are new patron services made possible by linking catalogs electronically. If a library or media center catalog is linked to the worldwide network called the Internet, searchers can go beyond the local library's holdings to seemingly limitless resources located all around the world. Even without external links, a local computer catalog can be linked to other internal information files within the organization, such as order files and circulation files, enabling searchers to determine the exact status of a desired title or when it is due to be returned when it isn't on the shelf.

As electronic resources become more sophisticated, the challenge to make wise use of them has not diminished but increased, putting pressure on library managers to continue making changes in the way locally owned holdings are cataloged, indexed, classified, and processed. The demand for high quality standard cataloging is increasing. One of the newest topics for consideration is the cataloging of "virtual" resources, that is, materials accessible via electronic networks, to alert searchers to their availability. OCLC used the Internet itself to distribute its publication, *Cataloging Internet Resources,* edited by Nancy B. Olson.[2]

Although computer-related issues continue to occupy a large proportion of cataloging department managers' attention, they aren't the only ones to be addressed. Another important issue is whether maintaining an in-house cataloging operation is as effective as contracting with an outside service to provide the library with cataloging for new acquisitions and to maintain the catalog system. Known as *outsourcing,* outside contracting has attracted much attention and prompted intense debate. Deciding whether to contract with a cataloging source outside the library or do one's own cataloging requires careful consideration of many factors, including the cost, speed, and quality of available products, as well as the loss of control over local operations and in-house expertise.

Other issues of note are opportunities to use several subject authorities in the catalog of a single library, made possible by the multiple subject fields in the MARC format; difficulties of recruiting well-trained catalogers, caused in part by the closing of a number of professional schools; development of standards for minimal level catalog records called *core records;* and the continuing struggle to make limited budgets stretch to cover everything cataloging departments are called upon or would like to do.

It may be just a matter of time until expert systems utilizing computerized cataloging tools are developed that create full standard records faster and more accurately than human catalogers can. Publishers could employ such expert systems to add full cataloging to every item they issue as part of the publishing process, much like Cataloging-in-Publication, but with greater control and accuracy. However, although the technological know-how for creating expert cataloging programs has been available for some time, the complexity of bibliographic variation has yet to be conquered. With the advent of this kind of automatic cataloging, department managers could turn their attention to assisting searchers in taking full advantage of it to find what they want more quickly and efficiently than ever before. Patron service is, after all, the object of cataloging. In the meantime, cataloging department managers must endeavor to employ computing and electronic access to accomplish the work that catalogers have performed in different ways since Callimachus classified texts in ancient times for the great library at Alexandria.

TEN HINTS FOR GOOD MANAGEMENT

1. Make basic decisions about bibliographic control policies, then write them down and stick to them until they are changed. When considering alternatives, keep in mind the needs of users, obligations to the network, and available budget and staffing.
2. Remember the tradeoffs between quality and quantity, trying to balance doing the best possible job with doing the whole job. In particular, beware of allowing uncataloged backlogs to grow while the department's resources are invested in doing more complex or sophisticated work than absolutely necessary.
3. Have the tools to do a good job of cataloging. An expensive reference tool will pay off in the long run in the form of higher quality cataloging with less anxiety.
4. When deciding on a local rule interpretation or subject application, write it down and use it for all other cases of the same kind.
5. Try to utilize the cataloging information that others have prepared. Examine what is being cataloged "from scratch" and determine how to expedite the work. If given the opportunity to outsource some or all of the cataloging to a reliable vendor, be objective in analyzing the costs and benefits of doing so.
6. Examine problems and experiment with solutions. Own up to mistakes quickly and honestly, then move on to more successful options. Try not to promise output that perhaps cannot be delivered.
7. Develop a support system, and work at both using it and contributing to it. Join the cataloging group in the state, provincial, regional, or national professional association, and be active in it. Befriend colleagues in the library, in peer libraries, and in nearby libraries of all types; network partners and network representatives; and cataloging experts. Write for help to us and other authors of cataloging texts, user group and association leaders, cataloging educators, and so forth.
8. Keep informed. Cataloging rules and tools are dynamic and are constantly accommodating new decisions. Read the literature, keep up with revisions, and take advantage of continuing education opportunities.
9. Inform those who use the library and public service staff members of decisions and procedures, and seek their input before making them.
10. *Trust yourself!* Undoubtedly, no one in the organization knows more about bibliographic issues than you do.

SUMMARY: PATRON SERVICE FIRST AND FOREMOST

Service to patrons is the ultimate object of all bibliographic policies and procedures, and should be the goal of department managers and all their operations. Standard tools and processes are recommended in this book because the authors believe they furnish good service and benefit patrons.

The fact that they change over time, however, indicates that standard tools are not perfect and that the changes made to them contribute positively to their utility. Librarians can benefit also by developing a positive attitude toward change in bibliographic services that will allow the combination of creative ideas, increasing knowledge, and dynamic systems to come together in providing better patron services. Ultimately, cataloging is a public service.

NOTES

1. Karen C. Dreissen and Sheila A. Smyth, *A Library Manager's Guide to Physical Processing of Nonprint Materials* (Westport, CT: Greenwood Press, 1995).

2. Nancy B. Olson, *Cataloging Internet Resources: A Manual and Practical Guide,* 2nd ed. (Dublin, OH: OCLC Inc., 1997). (Available on the OCLC Web site at http://www.oclc.org).

SUGGESTED READING

Belcastro, Patricia. *Evaluating Library Staff: A Performance Appraisal System.* Chicago: American Library Association, 1998.

Dale, Robin, et al. *Audio Preservation: A Selective Annotated Bibliography and Brief Summary of Current Practices.* Chicago: American Library Association, 1998.

Evans, G. Edward, et al. *Management Basics for Information Professionals.* New York: Neal-Schuman, 2000.

Gorman, Michael, and associates. *Technical Services Today and Tomorrow.* 2nd ed. Englewood, CO: Libraries Unlimited, 1998.

Hirshon, Arnold, and Barbara Winters. *Outsourcing Library Technical Services: A How-to-Do-It Manual for Librarians.* New York: Neal-Schuman, 1996.

Kascus, Marie A., and Dawn Hale, eds. *Outsourcing Cataloging, Authority Work, and Physical Processing: A Checklist of Considerations.* Chicago: American Library Association, 1995.

Larson, Jeanette, and Herman L. Totten. *Model Policies for Small and Medium Public Libraries.* New York: Neal-Schuman, 1998.

Ross, Catherine, and Patricia Dewdney. *Communicating Professionally: A How-to-Do-It Manual for Library Applications.* 2nd ed. New York: Neal-Schuman, 1998.

Sutton, Dave. *So You're Going to Run a Library: A Library Management Primer.* Englewood, CO: Libraries Unlimited, 1995.

Trotta, Marcia. *Successful Staff Development: A How-to-Do-It Manual.* New York: Neal-Schuman, 1995.

Warner, Alice Sizer. *Budgeting: A How-to-Do-It Manual for Librarians.* New York: Neal-Schuman, 1998.

Wilson, Karen A., and Marylou Colver, eds. *Outsourcing Library Technical Services Operations: Practices in Academic, Public, and Special Libraries.* Chicago: American Library Association, 1997.

Wilson, Lucile. *People Skills for Library Managers.* Englewood, CO: Libraries Unlimited, 1996.

Indexes

The three indexes that follow provide a detailed guide to the contents of the book. The first index is a topical guide to the text followed by an index of both personal and corporate names. The third index accommodates those who want to study the figures and examples more systematically, and is divided into four subsections: Type of Media, Access Points, Description, and Classification. Problems encountered in normal cataloging and rule interpretations can be checked across figures and examples using these indexes. This should provide valuable additional practice in learning the rules.

TOPICAL INDEX TO THE TEXT

INDEX TO NAMES

INDEX TO FIGURES AND EXAMPLES

Type of Media

Access Points

Author/Creator Main Entry

Title Main Entry

Added Entry

Subject Headings

Description

Title and Statement of Responsibility Area (Area 1)

Title and Statement of Responsibility Area (Area 1) (continued)

Edition Area (Area 2)

Material Specific Details Area (Area 3)

Publication, Distribution, Etc., Area (Area 4)

Physical Description Area (Area 5)

Series Area (Area 6)

Note Area (Area 7)

Standard Number and Terms of Availability Area (Area 8)

CLASSIFICATION